"Invaluable! To have a handbook that is this ministry-friendly and up-to-date is truly a gift to those who desire to lead church education programs that honor God. Many textbooks disappear when the class ends, but this one will become a dog-eared part of the practitioner's library. Along with the expected topics, subjects like pornography, celibacy, infertility, and reductional stereotypes are covered. Additional resources are suggested. A unique extra: As students study the chapters by leaders in their fields, they become acquainted with these authors through glimpses into their lives and ministries. These stories help bring this textbook to life."

—Marlene LeFever,
Author of *Creative Teaching Methods*

"If you want to be increasingly effective in teaching the Scriptures, then this book is for you. Dr. Hillman and Dr. Edwards have assembled a dream team of great teachers, mentors, and coaches. If this doesn't light your fire to improve as a teacher, then your wood is wet! This is a compelling invitation to become the teacher God created you to be."

—Dr. Dennis Rainey,
Cofounder of FamilyLife

"Nicely done! This introductory text on the church's teaching ministry is written by scholar-practitioners who are passionate about helping others grow spiritually. Their love for people, and for helping them learn and apply Scripture to their lives, shines through in what they share. I love the scope of the book, including chapters on ministry with people of all ages and stages of life, those with disabilities, and seekers. The book addresses a range of ministry models and approaches, helping readers think more creatively about a variety of ways available to help people learn and grow. This book will stretch your vision. The discussion questions at the end of each chapter are a helpful addition both for teaching and reflecting on together with colleagues in ministry."

—Dr. Kevin E. Lawson,
Professor of Educational Studies,
Talbot School of Theology of Biola University

"What a delight to recommend this fresh look at the educational ministry of the church. Using this book as a guide guarantees that biblical education will no longer be just about the transfer of information or an exercise in increasing biblical literacy. This book will empower teachers to honor the goal of Scripture as a resource for life transformation! A big thanks to Dr. Edwards and Dr. Hillman for putting into writing the exciting principles that they have taught to students in the classroom. 'Go to school' on this book and enjoy the rich reward of watching those you teach accelerate their journey of faith."

—Dr. Joe Stowell,
President of Cornerstone University

"Having a broad—even thorough—knowledge of the Bible is not that big of a deal. The second chapter of James reminds us that even the demons have that. They're still demons! What matters is when the Bible becomes the tool God uses to grab hold of a person's heart and transform it into one that's much more like his. This is more likely to happen when the person teaching the Bible is not only passionate about its content, but also compassionate towards the people on the receiving end of their teaching. *Invitation to Educational Ministry* is all about the what, who, and how of this passionate/compassionate kind of Bible teaching—teaching that truly transforms."

—Dr. Tim Kimmel,
Author of *Grace-Based Parenting* and *Grace Filled Marriage*

"As a young man, my heart was lit ablaze with a passion for Jesus through teachers who had a firm grip on the Word of God and a finger on the pulse of modern times. Truly transformational ministers must have both. I chose to attend Dallas Theological Seminary because it produced leaders like this. I am thrilled that Dr. Hillman and Dr. Edwards have taken insights from this great institution and locked them away in a resource for us all!"

—Ben Stuart,
Pastor of Passion City Church, Washington D.C.
and Author of *Single, Dating, Engaged, Married*

"While we are watching a staggering decline in basic biblical knowledge, Dr. Edwards and Dr. Hillman choose to joust the dragon. For us who aspire to teach or lead, education is an ongoing exercise; we will never be out of work unless we quit. In honor of our beloved "Prof," now more than in previous decades, we need a re-calibration of how to teach, how to train, and how to reproduce lifelong learners. Don't add this book to your shelf; keep it on your desk, close at hand. Refer to it often and become the tireless trainer of a generation that needs to know God and his word."

—Michael Easley,
President Emeritus,
Moody Bible Institute

"Finally, an up-to-date comprehensive book that covers every aspect of Christian education! This book is for every church, large or small. Written by experienced educators, it covers every topic from children to camps. Especially strong chapters are the first one on philosophy, also the ones on family ministry and singles. Writers have purposely based their topics on Scripture yet provide illustrations from current churches. A much needed book for every Christian educator!"

—Raye Zacharias,
former Senior Christian Education Consultant with David C. Cook Publishing

INVITATION TO EDUCATIONAL MINISTRY

Foundations of Transformative Christian Education

GEORGE M. HILLMAN JR.

SUE G. EDWARDS

EDITORS

Kregel
Academic

In dedication to Dr. Howard Hendricks,
affectionately known for decades on the DTS campus as "Prof"
for his investment in a generation of Christian educators
and for his personal belief in each of us.
We could all recount endless stories of how Prof
gave us a chance in our young careers
as professors in the department he started
and made the "outsider" feel welcome.
Your legacy lives on.

CONTENTS

CONTRIBUTORS

Dr. Joye Baker
Women's Advisor and Adjunct Professor of Educational Ministries and Leadership
Dallas Theological Seminary
DMin from Dallas Theological Seminary

Dr. Dan Bolin
International Director of Christian Camping International
Adjunct Professor of Educational Ministries and Leadership
Dallas Theological Seminary
DMin from Denver Seminary

John Dyer
Dean of Enrollment Services and Educational Technology
Adjunct Professor of Media Arts and Worship
Dallas Theological Seminary
PhD candidate from University of Durham in England

Dr. Sue Edwards
Associate Professor of Educational Ministries and Leadership
Dallas Theological Seminary
DMin from Gordon Conwell Theological Seminary

Dr. Karen Giesen
Adjunct Professor of Educational Ministries and Leadership
Dallas Theological Seminary
DMin from Dallas Theological Seminary

Dr. Mark Heinemann
Professor of Educational Ministries and Leadership
Assistant to the Academic Dean for Teaching and Learning
Dallas Theological Seminary
PhD from Trinity Evangelical Divinity School

Bill Hendricks
Executive Director of the Hendricks Center for Christian Leadership and Cultural Engagement
Dallas Theological Seminary
MS Mass Communication from Boston University
MA Biblical Studies from Dallas Theological Seminary

Dr. George M. Hillman, Jr.
Vice President of Student Life, Dean of Students
Professor of Educational Ministries and Leadership
Dallas Theological Seminary
PhD from Southwestern Baptist Theological Seminary

Dr. Sabrina Hopson
Associate Registrar
Adjunct Professor of Educational Ministries and Leadership
Dallas Theological Seminary
PhD from University of North Texas

Mike Justice
Educational Consultant for Educational Ministry and Leadership
Dallas Theological Seminary
ThM from Dallas Theological Seminary

Dr. Jerry Lawrence
Alumni and Placement Coordinator for Women
Adjunct Professor of Educational Ministries and Leadership
Dallas Theological Seminary
DMin from Dallas Theological Seminary

Dr. Michael S. Lawson
Senior Professor of Educational Ministries and Leadership
Coordinator of the Doctoral of Educational Ministry Degree
Dallas Theological Seminary
PhD from University of Oklahoma

Dr. Lin McLaughlin
Professor of Educational Ministries and Leadership
Assistant to the Dean of Academic Assessment
Dallas Theological Seminary
PhD from University of North Texas

Dr. Barbara Neumann
Adjunct Professor of Educational Ministries and Leadership
Dallas Theological Seminary
DMin from Dallas Theological Seminary

Dr. Paul Pettit
Director of Career Services
Adjunct Professor of Educational Ministries and Leadership
Adjunct Professor of Pastoral Ministries
Dallas Theological Seminary
DMin from Dallas Theological Seminary

A.J. Rinaldi
Minister of Adult Discipleship
Frisco Bible Church in Frisco, Texas
MA Christian Education from Dallas Theological Seminary

Dr. Jay Sedwick
Department Chair and Professor of Educational Ministries and Leadership
Dallas Theological Seminary
PhD from Southwestern Baptist Theological Seminary

Dr. Jim Thames
Dean of Academic Administration
Associate Professor of Educational Ministries and Leadership
Dallas Theological Seminary
PhD from University of North Texas

FOREWORD

IT'S HARD TO IMAGINE a more highly gifted and capable team of Christian educators than those who have assembled at Dallas Theological Seminary. For decades, this illustrious group of men and women have shaped the field of Christian education. In one way or another, the faculty at Dallas Theological Seminary have addressed how church educational ministries should be conducted.

Now, at long last, they have assembled together to create the quintessential primer on educational ministries for the local church. Taking on the challenge of preparing an introductory text in any academic discipline is not for the faint of heart. It requires the assemblage of a respectable team of educators who know both theory and practice. *Invitation to Educational Ministry* will become the desired text for those who aspire to disciple the nations through the local church. This text is exhaustive and comprehensive. There is something here for every reader. Whether a Sunday school teacher, first-year undergraduate student, or seasoned ministry professional, this book will help advance your understanding of both educational theories and praxis. I highly recommend this for every dedicated believer who desires to make disciples of all the nations.

DR. MICHAEL J. ANTHONY served as Professor of Christian Education at Talbot School of Theology for twenty-seven years, and is the author/editor of thirteen books in the field of Christian education. He currently serves as the COO & CFO at Dream Centers in Colorado Springs. In addition, he is a guest lecturer at several institutions around the world including Dallas Theological Seminary.

INTRODUCTIONS

WHY I LOVE TO TEACH

Sue Edwards

I DISTINCTLY REMEMBER THE first time I stood before a group to teach God's Word. I'd only been a Christian for four years. Being completely ill-equipped and knowing it, I spent several months preparing. I bathed the process in prayer. I studied the text like a detective. I read every commentary I could find. I used my Journalism degree to tighten up my word choice. I scoured good books for related illustrations.

When the day came for me to stand before the Bible study leader's group and teach the assigned passage, my voice trembled throughout the introduction. Thankfully, I'd practically memorized it, fearful I would forget otherwise, so I was able to get the words out. Regardless of the shaky start, the women put down what they were doing and our eyes locked. We opened the Bible and dissected its beauty. That moment remains etched in my mind.

Suddenly I forgot myself and my nervousness and the Holy Spirit took over. They listened intently. They learned. Their eyes sparkled with understanding and conviction. Heads nodded. Their faces beamed a desire to live out God's direction and the pictures painted. God's truth that had transformed me as I prepared was now transforming them. My spirit soared to be part of God's work in them, and I was hooked. Today, I tell my students it was like "Christian cocaine"—not that I've ever experienced cocaine, but the comparison seems to work.

I've taught the Bible hundreds of times since, and now I teach seminary students to teach it. Whether I'm in front of a group of church women or a mixed classroom at the seminary where I initially trained, the thrill continues. I love to find creative ways to introduce a topic or explain a deep and difficult idea clearly. I love to ask provocative questions that jump start a thoughtful, challenging discussion. I love to watch students tackle a related activity, another approach that helps learning stick. I love watching uncertain students forget what others think and dive into the issues, eager to understand or to share what God has taught them. I love when a learning community emerges from a group of former strangers who find they have much in common and much to learn from one another. I love to see discovery in their eyes. I love when they surprise themselves with serendipitous answers or comments. I love to encourage and witness their spiritual awakenings. I simply love to teach. God wired me that way, but I've learned that it's really not about me. I'm the conduit—and my gracious heavenly Father, in his kindness, allows me great joy in his work.

As much as I love to teach, I've come to deeply enjoy passing on this love of teaching to others just as much—maybe more. I surmise that since you have chosen to read this book that the "love of teaching" bug may have bitten you too. Or you've had a taste and you're seeking to discover whether God wants to use you in his teaching ministry too. If that's you, keep reading.

We've gathered a group of stellar teachers and ministers to guide you. We are a seasoned team of men and women; most have served students at Dallas Theological Seminary for many years. We've created curriculum together, brainstormed ways to improve our courses and our teaching, and often teamed up or taught in one another's classrooms.

We worship in different denominations. We specialize in teaching different demographics. Many of us write in those disciplines and lead or participate in professional organizations related to our fields. We rub shoulders with colleagues from other seminaries. We all serve or teach in the trenches, bringing practical expertise to our classrooms. Despite our varied gifts, backgrounds, and areas of expertise, we share a love of teaching and equipping men and women

for ministry. And we've come together to create a resource for you that is deep and wide, biblical and practical, whether you volunteer in a ministry in the local church or parachurch, you are on a teaching ministry staff, or you desire to serve in a school or the academy. Teaching is teaching and most of this book will apply in all these contexts.

You'll also find specialized chapters by experts in those fields that I encourage you to read even if you don't see yourself serving there. We end up where God wants us to be, often to our bewildered surprise and delight. And we support and lead our teams better when we understand their assignments and passions. Keep your mind and heart open as you digest these chapters.

We earnestly pray and hope that our words will help you discover God's place for you in his teaching ministry or strengthen your insight and skills if you are already there. May this project serve to pass on our love of teaching for your joy and God's glory.

IT'S ALL EDUCATION

George Hillman

MY JOURNEY TO CHRIST began in a preschool classroom in a local Baptist church one block from my house. While I do not have memories today of anything specific from preschool, that humble preschool ministry had eternal significance in my life and the life of my family. It was in that preschool classroom where a teacher introduced me to Jesus Christ at a level I could understand. Some of the friends I made in that preschool class became lifelong friends as we grew up in church together. Plus my parents (who were not attending church at the time) became active members of that church as a result of the connections from that preschool ministry.

While I may not remember much from preschool, I have vivid memories of children's Sunday school, children's choir, vacation Bible school, and summer day camp at that same church as a child. I still have the children's illustrated Living Bible I carried to church each week. I still have the church hymnal with my attendance stickers in it from choir. Furthermore I can still recite the King James Version of 1 John 4:7–8 because of a song I learned at church as a child ("Beloved, let us love one another: for love is of God; and every one that loveth is born of God, and knoweth God. He that loveth not knoweth not God; for God is love."). My faith grew through the Bible stories I heard, the crafts projects I made, the silly songs with the hand motions I learned, and the fun games I played.

As I became a teenager at that same church, I dearly recall summer youth camps and Monday night Bible studies at my youth minister's house. I remember an early Wednesday morning discipleship group that met before school each week, marking up my Bible as we studied the book of Daniel and the Pastoral Epistles. I remember mission trips to Mexico where I served through using my spiritual gifts. Plus I remember preaching my first sermon during a Youth Sunday at my church (where the youth of the church "took over" the various roles of the church for a Sunday) as a senior in high school.

There is a point in my trip down memory lane. All of these things I just described are educational ministries in a local church—a weekday preschool ministry, vacation Bible school, summer day camps, outdoor retreat centers, Sunday school classes, home Bible studies, and mission trips. I am a huge believer in educational ministry because I have personally benefited from it. I came to Christ and was matured in the faith through the various expressions of educational ministry.

More than the educational programs though, it was the people at the church who impacted my life. Programs don't just lead themselves. The vast majority of the individuals who had the biggest impact on my life were ordinary people with ordinary jobs who volunteered at the church—a local realtor, a clerk at the old downtown hardware store, an owner of the toy store at the mall, a traveling salesman, and a college student. These were ordinary people who had an eternal impact on my life.

We wrote this book to help ordinary people have an eternal impact on the lives of others. Through educational ministries, these ordinary people teach the Christian story and help others to live their faith out in daily life. We want this to be a book that anyone can pick up and immediately apply as you serve in any of the various expressions of educational ministry. We had both the professional minister and the lay leader in mind as we wrote.

We are very excited about the book you have in your hands. May God richly bless the reading of this book and its application. As you embark on this journey, may I offer a prayer from *The Book of Common Prayer*:

Almighty God, the fountain of all wisdom: Enlighten by your Holy Spirit those who teach and those who learn, that, rejoicing in the knowledge of your truth, they may worship you and serve you from generation to generation; through Jesus Christ our Lord, who lives and reigns with you and the Holy Spirit, one God, for ever and ever. Amen.

Prayer for Education from
The Book of Common Prayer

WHAT:
THE FOUNDATION

Chapter 1
WHAT MAKES A GREAT TEACHER?

Bill Hendricks

The student is not above the teacher,
but everyone who is fully trained
will be like their teacher.

—Luke 6:40

Dr. Howard G. Hendricks taught at Dallas Theological Seminary from 1951 through 2011. He founded the Department of Christian Education (now called Educational Ministries and Leadership), as well as The Howard G. Hendricks Center for Christian Leadership (today known as The Hendricks Center for Christian Leadership and Cultural Engagement). During his later years at the school, he was named distinguished professor emeritus of Christian Education and Leadership. More than thirty thousand students sat under his teaching, and millions of people throughout the world heard him speak, or read one of his many books. Drawing on testimonials from scores of his former students and others, his younger son Bill Hendricks here describes what was behind the mystique of the man affectionately known as "Prof."

Meet the "Prof"

PLAYWRIGHT AND POLEMICIST GEORGE Bernard Shaw derisively scoffed that "he who can, does; he who cannot, teaches."[1] A pity Shaw never met Howard Hendricks! If he had, his entirely low and skeptical view of pedagogy might have been thoroughly transformed. That's how powerful Hendricks was as a teacher. Give the man virtually any theme or subject, and not only could he give you a first-class education on the matter, he could provoke you into reconsidering your entire conception of the nature and practice of education itself.

Former students recall his style using such hyperbolic terms as "thrilling," "electric," "hypnotic," and "mesmerizing." One claims that Hendricks was so compelling that even when he contradicted himself, he proved to be equally persuasive both times. In a similar vein, he is said to have convinced one student that the lecture method is no longer effective—using the lecture method!

Nor did Dr. Hendricks require a classroom to work his magic. He was a master of the impromptu teachable moment, whether at a table in the seminary's snack shop, on walks to and from chapel services, or on a bench outside the campus library (perhaps his favorite venue for holding court). He didn't just invite questions from students; he insisted on them. He was perennially on the prowl to find out, "What do you guys want to know about? What are the real issues?"

The net effect of his dynamic was that he quickly became a magnet, drawing students to Dallas Theological Seminary (DTS) from across the country and, before long, around the world. Countless alumni articulate the same theme when asked why they chose DTS: "Two reasons: I wanted to learn the Bible, and I wanted to major in Prof."[2] By the time he retired (after sixty years in the classroom), an estimated thirty thousand students had sat under his teaching.

How does someone do that? How does a man compel thousands of young adults to decide to devote several years of their lives to learning as much as they can from him?

The Gift

Let's start with the fact that Howard Hendricks was unique. Of course, every human is unique. But to appropriate a famous line: "Some are more unique than others."[3]

"A man like Howie Hendricks only comes along once in a generation, if that," observed Fort Worth attorney and former DTS board member Bill Garrison, Hendricks' lifelong friend.

Chuck Swindoll, one of Dr. Hendricks' preeminent protégés and a former president and now chancellor of Dallas Theological Seminary, has pointed out that Hendricks was so unique that he gained the status of being recognized by a one-word name, like Solomon or Churchill. In his case, the name was Prof.

Another said that Prof was to teaching what legendary coach John Wooden was to basketball.

In truth, Hendricks was only a minor celebrity in the relatively small subculture of the evangelical church during the latter half of the twentieth century. But given other circumstances, he easily could have made a name for himself as world-renowned as Socrates or Michelangelo or Napoleon or Einstein or Bono or LeBron. Prof was genuinely world class in that he was among the best in the world at what he did.

There's little doubt that had he pursued a more lucrative field than teaching, he could have become a millionaire many times over.

Except that Prof was infinitely more interested in students than in money. "I love to teach!" he frequently exclaimed. "I *live* to teach! Why, I'd teach whether or not they paid me to teach!" At that point he always thrust an index finger in the air as he quietly joked, "Don't tell the seminary that!"

What makes someone a great teacher like Prof Hendricks? There's no way around the fact that it starts with a gift. A God-given gift. Some people have the gift of teaching. Most don't. Make no mistake, *everyone* has a gift of some sort (though sadly, most don't know what their gift is).[4] But only a finite number of people in the world are truly gifted to the task of teaching.

By "gifted" I mean both *able* and *motivated*. To do what? To cause learning to take place, of course. "Teaching is *causing*" Prof wrote. "Causing what? Causing people to learn. That's the simplest definition I know.... If the learner has not learned, we have not taught."[5]

> "*Giftedness* is a set of God-given core strengths and natural motivation that a person instinctively and consistently uses to do things that they find satisfying and productive. Giftedness is not just what someone *can* do, but what they are *born* to do, enjoy doing, and tend to do well."[6]
> —Bill Hendricks

Likewise, "The ultimate test of teaching is not what you [as the teacher] do or how well you do it, but what and how well the learner does.... Good teachers can't be focused on what *they* do, but on what their students are doing."[7]

That insight begins to crack the code on what the gift of teaching is all about. At the heart of the gift is a deep desire to see someone else "get" it, whatever *it* happens to be. Some of Prof's chosen *its* were educational ministry, leadership, discipleship and mentoring, the Christian home, and creativity. But the same principle applies to all education, whether teaching someone math or history or how to read a balance sheet or how to shoe a horse. True teachers—that is, gifted teachers—are driven by desire. They *want* to see others learn.

But in addition to desire, true teachers also have *ability*. Their desire translates into words and actions that have effect. Learning actually does take place.

Again, the proof of that learning is the change evidenced by the learner. The learner does something differently and more effectively after his or her encounter with the teacher.

Prof's Bible Study Methods course is a classic example of effective pedagogy.[8] To this day it remains mandatory for all incoming seminarians. Literally thousands of Dallas Theological Seminary alumni point to that class as a watershed experience in their ability to do inductive Bible study—a skill they regard as critically vital to their professional effectiveness.

So are we to conclude that the secret to great teaching is simply the presence of a certain gift? And that if you have that gift, you will be a great teacher, but if not, you shouldn't teach? Prof would be the first to answer with a resounding "No!" Because that's not how it works.

All effective teachers have a teaching gift, but not everyone who has a teaching gift becomes an effective teacher. Think of the gift as a core requirement, a foundation. The root of that foundation is a desire to cause others to learn. If someone doesn't have that, they may function in the role of a teacher, but they can never become a great teacher.

And no one can manufacture that desire. That is something sovereignly endowed by God. One either has it or one does not. If not, then as the crusty old running coach Sam Mussabini says in *Chariots of Fire*, "I can't put in what God left out."[9]

But desire, or motivation, is only half the equation. A gift also includes ability. And here is where we can start talking about the making of a *great* teacher. Ability (if present) not only can be developed, *it must be developed*. No one who desires to teach teaches well at first. Not even Prof. As with every other gift, the gift of teaching must be cultivated. The person who desires to cause learning to take place has to *learn* how to cause learning to take place, and then get better and better at causing it.

Learning to teach takes time and effort. To be precise, Malcolm Gladwell claims it takes ten thousand hours for someone to develop a skill to a world-class level.[10] That sounds about right, and that was certainly the case for Prof Hendricks. But what keeps someone on task for ten thousand hours to develop his or her teaching gift? Quite simply, the teacher's desire to see someone else "get" it. If someone doesn't have that desire, that teacher will drop out of the process long before he or she arrives at greatness. That's how important the desire is. It's the fuel that sustains the arduous and protracted (and mostly unheralded and unglamorous) process of learning to teach well.

So what are the elements in the journey toward becoming a great teacher? We can answer that by pointing out that Prof was a big believer

in fundamentals. He knew that the mastery of any skill—whether teaching or studying the Bible or playing a musical instrument or doing open-heart surgery—requires the mastery of a set of fundamental principles and techniques. That mastery is gained by practicing those principles and techniques over and over and over again. Ten thousand hours' worth, at least!

> "Excellence is not an act but a habit. The things you do the most are the things you will do best."
> —Marva Collins

So here are seven basic building blocks that Prof Hendricks never stopped working on throughout his entire career.

1. Showing Up Prepared

Prof was an absolute stickler for punctuality. He claimed his father used to threaten him, "Son, if you show up late, I'll send flowers to your funeral." Not surprisingly, a favorite motto became, "If you cannot show up on time, show up early."

But much of his penchant for punctuality flowed out of his intense conviction that a class or an appointment or a phone call was not just an item on the calendar, it was an *event*, a golden moment of opportunity that would be a crime to waste.

For that reason, he was obsessed about showing up prepared. Pam Cole served as his assistant longer than anyone else, and she came on board late in his tenure at the seminary. By then he had taught Bible Study Methods so many times that most of his handwritten class notes had faded. Yet she remembers how he pored over those notes for hours—oftentimes marking and amending them, sometimes even writing over the faded ink—before *each and every* class period. Just to be sure.

The same could be said for Prof's brilliant presentations, which were like handcrafted works of art. That's because they *were* handcrafted works of art. Students loved the countless alliterations and mnemonic devices he wove into his lectures: observation, interpretation, application, divergent thinking, deliberate thinking, defined thinking. Elijah in confrontation, Elijah in conflict, Elijah in crisis. On and on.

Likewise, they loved his humor (often self-directed) and his uncanny ability to provoke boisterous laughter just before plunging in a hypodermic of convicting truth. Much of his entertainment value derived from his nonverbal communication: his facial expressions, his tone, his imitation voices, his pauses, and especially his signature gestures, such as the sniffling nose wipe, the slouching simpleton, or the mock violinist.

In short, Prof was the consummate performer. But only because he spent inordinate amounts of time polishing his stuff until he could deliver it on command, with precisely the right effect. He literally lay awake at night working on the wording, the phrasing, the pacing, the timing of his presentations—all in the service of causing learning to take place.

For in the end, he regarded the causation of learning as his true calling: "My aim is not to entertain you, but to educate you," he often reminded his students. "My job as a teacher is not to impress you, but to impact your life."

Prof had a bedrock conviction that if someone is supposed to teach, that person had better pursue a mastery of his or her subject. That's why,

when he realized God was calling him into vocational ministry rather than medicine, he enrolled in Wheaton College as a Bible major.

Prior to college, Hendricks had never been a particularly good student. Indeed, by the end of his first semester he was failing in several subjects. But thanks to the wise tutelage of a couple of faculty members, along with Mortimer J. Adler's classic guide *How to Read a Book*, Hendricks slowly began to develop some basic study habits—habits he continued to use the rest of his life.[11]

After Wheaton, he came to Dallas Seminary, where he majored in theology. While he knew he was not destined to become a scholar, he nevertheless applied his perfectionist temperament to his studies, aware that educational ministry is all about the communication of theology in a relevant, practical way. He never wanted to be caught pitching theological principles that were half-baked, or worse, erroneous.

After seminary, Hendricks pursued further preparation for his career by doing additional graduate work at Wheaton. And in fact he was contemplating going on for doctoral studies at Yale when Dallas Theological Seminary President John E. Walvoord called to ask if he would immediately come back to the school and launch a Department of Christian Education (now called Educational Ministries and Leadership).

Teacher that he was, the invitation was a pitch he could not lay off. And so into the classroom he went.

But always, always prepared—right down to his dress. Following the fashion of the times, he invariably wore a dark suit with a stiffly starched, white dress shirt whose detachable paper collar bolted a perfectly tied bow tie (or, later, a long tie) to his neck, always matched by a silk handkerchief in the breast pocket of his coat. The effect of such a look was unmistakable. It said what no words could say: *I am here. I am ready. I am taking this seriously. I have shown up for the express purpose of having an encounter with you. So let's learn together, you and me!*

2. Striving to Communicate

A basic Hendricks maxim was, "The teacher has not taught until the student has learned." He meant that a teacher bears responsibility for providing everything possible to foster the likelihood that learning will take place. Surely students bear responsibility to do their part. But Prof's ideal was to communicate in such a way that a student could not *not* learn.

> "The mediocre teacher tells. The good teacher explains. The superior teacher demonstrates. The great teacher inspires."
> —William Arthur Ward

One student remembers how he would sit at the very back of Prof's classroom and arrange his books such that he could work on other subjects. "I was an Old Testament major, so I was only taking his class as an elective. And I'd try to tune him out. But invariably he would say or do something that caught my attention. And then it was over! I *had* to keep listening. I couldn't help it."

Then later at home: "I'd find myself spending hours on his assignments. I'd get completely engrossed in them. And it would end up being 9:30 or 10:00 at night when I'd finish—and I still had all this Hebrew and theology and Bible homework left to do!"

Many a student fell under Prof's spell. But the seeming magic at work was simply that Prof possessed a passion to communicate. Indeed, an obsession to communicate!

For him, communication began with a relentless effort to know everything he could about his audience. To that end, he spent as much time hanging out with students as he did teaching them and preparing for his classes. In part that was because students sought him out (how could they not, when he was so effective at inducing a response?). But it was also because he sought them out. They thought they were studying under him—and they were. But even as they were, he was studying them.

He had an intense curiosity to know: What was on their minds? What made them tick? Why were they in seminary? What were their dreams? What were their challenges—or, as he liked to put it, "What are the things kicking the slats out from under your life?"

On the surface, the answers to such questions had nothing to do with Bible study methods or leadership or creativity or the other courses Prof was teaching. But from his perspective, the answers had *everything* to do with what he was teaching. Because he understood that teachers do not teach subjects, they teach people.

As a student, Dale Burke heard Prof speak in chapel in the mid-1970s. As he looked up at the podium, he noticed the seminary's motto "Preach the Word" emblazoned on the wall over Prof's shoulder. Just at that moment, Prof fired off the emphatic declaration, "Men and women, God never called you to teach the Bible!"

He paused, letting the words sink in. And all the air went out of the room as the attendees sat there wondering: "Not called to teach the

Bible? Seriously? Is that going to get him fired? Has he become a heretic?"

Then, in classic Hendricks fashion, he nimbly vaulted off the pause to deliver the punch line: "He calls you to teach *people* (slight pause) the Bible. Therefore, you must study your Bible—but you must also study your people."

Prof believed that communication was all about building bridges of understanding: bridges between the world of the subject to be learned and the world of the student, as well as bridges between the teacher and the student.

3. Rigorously Evaluating Performance

One of the most powerful categories of ammo in Dr. Hendricks' arsenal of apprenticeship was the memorable maxim, a brief, pithy saying that would lodge itself like a burr in the mind (and imagination) of the hearer. Over time, these witty, thought-provoking one-liners became so numerous, so popular, and so expected that students started referring to them as "profisms."

One frequently repeated profism held that "experience is not the best teacher; *evaluated* experience is." Prof realized early on that while practice does indeed make perfect, practicing the wrong thing only makes one perfect at doing the wrong thing.

That's one reason why he had such an affinity for his admired friend Tom Landry, the first head coach of the Dallas Cowboys. For a period of time during Tom's tenure, Prof was the chaplain of the team, and Tom frequently invited him to attend their practice sessions.

On one occasion, after the players had ended their drills and headed off to the locker room, Prof lingered to have a conversation with Coach Landry. With dusk rapidly falling, he

noticed one of the wide receivers still running routes and catching balls from a trainer.

"Man, that's some dedication!" he remarked to Landry.

"Oh, he's always like that," the coach replied. "Sometimes I have to tell him to knock it off. But he's just determined to be the best in the league at his position. He'll run a route like that over and over until he can run it in his sleep. He keeps running it until he can run it right. Then he keeps running it until he can run it right without having to think about running it right. That's why he's consistently All Pro."

In truth, Prof had that same kind of relentless dedication to improving his own game. Several students remember team-teaching courses with him. After each and every class, he would sit down in their office (not his) and walk through his written list of observations about their methodology in the classroom—the good, the bad, and the ugly (but invariably with fair and constructive insights). Needless to say, that usually proved to be a daunting review!

But what always stunned the students was that after his appraisal of them, he would turn around and ask, "So what could I have done better?" At first the novice teachers drew a complete blank. How could they answer such a question? How do you tell Rembrandt how to do a better job of painting?

"A coach is someone who tells you what you don't want to hear, who has you see what you don't want to see, so you can be who you have always known you could be."
—Tom Landry

But then Prof began taking them through a series of questions he had developed over the years to evaluate his own performance: Had he shown up prepared? Was the classroom properly set up? Had he achieved the objectives the class was designed to achieve? Where had he been most clear, and where was he confusing? Did his presentation make sense? Was it logical? Were his illustrations relevant and "grabbing"? Did he maintain interest? Did he engage the students? Had he asked good questions? Was he faithful to Scripture? Was his theology correct? Were his audiovisuals interesting and instructive? What evidence could he show that the students were "getting" it? In short, every element of the class experience was open for consideration.

Prof submitted almost every class, sermon, lecture, seminar, chapel talk, devotional, or any other presentation he ever gave to that same method of self-examination. He regarded it as a non-negotiable discipline for anyone serious about pursuing excellence in teaching.

4. Constantly Learning

Prof's devotion to continuous improvement also included a lifelong devotion to learning. Another favorite "profism" was, "Leaders are readers." And in that regard, Prof definitely practiced what he preached.

For some people, reading is a pleasant pastime. For Prof, it bordered on a religious discipline. When not in a classroom, or engaged with a student, or otherwise practicing his craft, he could invariably be found buried in a book, pen in hand (preferably a blue, felt-tip Flair), mentally engrossed in a conversation with the author. Sometimes he spent hours in that activity. But frequently just five minutes between appointments.

And if one selects virtually any title from what remains of Prof's library, one finds no end of notes, markings, and underlinings denoting his active engagement with the material. In his characteristically crisp, elegant penmanship are reactions such as, "Good!" or "Great illus," or "Impt insight," or simply an exclamation point: "!"

One of the most important technologies to come along in Prof's lifetime was the cassette tape. That opened up a whole new avenue by which he could access great minds. He quickly turned into a "tapeworm" who listened to vast numbers of lectures, sermons, and other presentations during his commute to and from the seminary. (In no time at all, Prof himself became popular on the cassette tape market, especially after his student John Nieder set him up in the early 1980s with his own nationally syndicated radio program *The Art of Family Living*.)

Prof's appetite for learning was both insatiable and instinctive. He believed that the mind must be properly nourished every bit as much as the body. Indeed, as soon as computers were invented, he adopted the popular phrase of "garbage in, garbage out" to describe the significance of feeding one's brain quality material.

And he harvested such brain-food from any source he could find, whether at a church service, a graduation speech, the dedication of a building, or even a funeral. He habitually carried his felt-tip pen with him, and as soon as he heard anything that grabbed his attention, he began taking notes on whatever scrap of paper he could find: bulletins, napkins, flyers, a three-by-five card (if he had remembered to put one in his pocket).

Frequently in conversation in his office or over a meal, he would stop the other person and say, "Wait a sec! That's good. Hold on. Let me write that down." Out the pen would come, and he'd begin scribbling furiously.

One of his former students recalls the Sunday he got up to preach and realized that Dr. Hendricks was sitting in his congregation that morning. Shocked and thoroughly intimidated, he pressed on—as he had no other choice. Then, halfway through his sermon he glanced at Dr. Hendricks, and to his utter amazement, found him taking notes. "I could hardly believe it!" he said later. "Taking notes! From *me!*"

But that was Prof Hendricks' way. He collected illustrations the way some people collect rare coins. And he was unrepentant when it came to stealing great quotes (although he was always fond of citing his sources).

He also believed that the best learning comes by learning from the best. So he thrived on putting himself in the path of great teachers. He especially liked people who had distinguished themselves as surgeons, generals, pilots, historians, musicians, and craftsmen. And he loved to pick the brains of leaders in the business and professional worlds.

> "The illiterate of the 21st century will not be those who cannot read and write, but those who cannot learn, unlearn, and relearn."
> —Alvin Toffler

He had an uncanny way of tying his learnings back to his own specialization of educational ministry. In fact, despite what many might assume, an analysis of his content shows that a great deal of it was borrowed rather than original. He was a quintessential example of Steve Jobs'

observation that "good artists copy; great artists steal" (as Steve Jobs knew better than anyone!).[12] Prof had a genius for adaptation. He could spot a great idea—often imbedded in material that did not manage to communicate it with particular greatness—and re-package it so brilliantly that learners assumed the idea began with him (again, to his credit, he usually gave the source).

His Bible Study Methods course is a perfect case-in-point. In 1952, Robert A. Traina, a Methodist professor of biblical studies, published a book entitled *Methodical Bible Study*.[13] The book's table of contents reads as follows:

Observation, Interpretation, Application. That triad originated with Traina, not Hendricks. (In point of fact, Hendricks' syllabus for his Bible Study Methods class listed Traina as a key text.) But Hendricks popularized Observation, Interpretation, Application so well—so engagingly, so practically, so unforgettably—that today many automatically associate the formula with the name Hendricks (or Prof).[14]

Another example involved a celebration of Dr. Hendricks' sixtieth birthday in 1984, held at the Westin Galleria Hotel in Dallas. Organizers pulled out all the stops and secretly assembled several hundred well-wishers for the occasion. By some miracle, his wife, Jeanne, managed to get him to the ballroom without his guessing that something was afoot. When he walked in and was greeted by a spirited, "Happy birthday, Prof!" he genuinely was surprised for one of the few times in his life.

And the surprises kept coming. Tom Landry turned out to be the emcee. A who's who of Christian leaders had sent birthday greetings. A proclamation from Dallas Mayor Starke Taylor was read, proclaiming April 5, 1984 as Howard G. Hendricks Day. Longtime friends Ray Stedman and Walt Henrichsen (among others) showed up to offer personal greetings. Howard and Jeanne were provided a couch on stage, and a series of cherished friends were called forward to join them and express their appreciation for Howie's life and work. Then his family were brought to the dais—all four children and their spouses. Then his mother, Celia, who had been quietly flown in from Philadelphia, was introduced. Former Dallas Cowboys quarterback Roger Staubach took the podium to give a very moving tribute. And finally an original portrait of Howard and Jeanne was unveiled, followed by an extended standing ovation. Truly, Dr. Hendricks was an admired man!

Then the applause died down and everyone retook their seats. A quiet settled over the room, and Prof was left standing at the podium, all eyes fixed on him, all ears waiting for what he would say.

But what could he possibly say? How could he ever adequately express his gratitude for the beautiful sentiments that so many people had expressed to him that night? A simple thank you would be too trite—especially from the man who earned his living by saying amazing words in amazing ways. How could he possibly deflect so much glory that had been heaped upon him? It was not a moment for humor. Nor was it a moment for a sermon.

For an instant, the consummate communicator appeared to be speechless. Then he quietly began to tell a story. He recalled that as a boy he occasionally spent time out in the rural areas of Pennsylvania, walking along the country roads. On one such walk, he said, he came across a fencepost, and on the top of that fencepost sat a turtle, slowly and futilely flailing its legs. "When you see a turtle on a fencepost," he noted, "you know one thing for sure: it didn't get there by itself." Brief pause. "Ladies and gentleman, I'm just a turtle on a fencepost." And from there he launched into some very gracious words of appreciation to the many mentors who had encouraged him over the years, to all those who had come that night, to those who had sent tributes, to the mayor, to Tom and Roger, to his family, to Jeanne, to his mother, and most of all to God. In short, with absolutely no advance notice, he concocted on the spot an expression of gratitude that was at once simple, sincere, memorable, and fitting. It was a classic moment of HGH brilliance.

Yet the turtle story, genius as it was—and told as only Hendricks could tell such a tale—was by no means original with Hendricks. In truth, only four years before, one of his friends, a businessman in Massachusetts named Allen Emery, had written a little book entitled *A Turtle on a Fencepost*, which Prof had thoroughly enjoyed.[15] There can be no doubt that as he listened to all the praise being heaped upon him that evening, his recent exposure to Emery's grabbing image leaped to his mind, because Prof was never one for basking in the limelight.[16] One can easily imagine that as he sat there listening to all those kind words, a sort of internal warning system was going off in his head, blaring out the reminder,

"Hendricks, it's just like Allen Emery said: You're nothing but a turtle on a fencepost!"

Prof never viewed the use of someone else's idea as unethical, let alone any form of plagiarism. If anything, he saw it as a form of esteem: The concept had so impacted him that it would not be right to keep it to himself; he *had* to let others in on the treasure. But of course, he always had to present it through his own, unique persona. It was that gift for packaging his material that enabled him to elevate so many good ideas to greatness.

Thanks to his insatiable curiosity and commitment to lifelong learning, his teaching throughout his sixty-year career remained remarkably interesting, insightful, and relevant to everyday life.[17] His material consistently exhibited fresh thinking because in many cases he was sharing insights he had gained only days before.

Earlier it was pointed out that Prof lived to teach. By the same token, it could be said that Prof learned in order to live. In fact, he had a favorite saying to the effect that "the day you stop learning is the day you start dying." He knew that the only way he could become and remain a great teacher was to become an even greater student—for life.

5. Believing in the Student

Teaching is largely a "by faith" effort. A teacher invests time and energy in a student, hoping to induce change, growth, and development, but the return on that investment may not be seen until years later. Certainly that was the case for the students Dr. Hendricks taught.

Yet he seemed to possess boundless confidence that his efforts would pay off and those students would go out and make a difference in the world. And they have!

> "Fifth grade was probably the worst year of my life. [When] I graduated, I left with Miss Simon's words ringing in my ears: 'Howard, you are the worst behaved child in this school!'"
>
> "You can imagine what my expectations were upon entering the sixth grade. The first day of class, my teacher, Miss Noe, went down the roll call, and it wasn't long before she came to my name. 'Howard Hendricks,' she called out, glancing from her list to where I was sitting with my arms folded, just waiting to go into action. She looked me over for a moment and then said, 'I've heard a lot about you.' She smiled and added, 'But I don't believe a word of it!'"
>
> "I tell you, that moment was a fundamental turning point, not only in my education, but in my life. Suddenly, unexpectedly, someone believed in me. For the first time in my life, someone saw potential in me. Miss Noe put me on special assignments. She gave me little jobs to do. She invited me to come in after school to work on my reading and arithmetic. She challenged me with higher standards."
>
> —Howard G. Hendricks

But in most cases, not because *they* ever thought they would. Indeed, many of them came to seminary with fairly low expectations, and some with terribly low self-esteem. Many perceived themselves to be poor students (in truth, a few actually were) with little potential. And seminary had a way of magnifying those doubts: after the first few classes of Greek, for instance, many wondered whether they'd even make it through the first year.

But then they met Prof. And they'd hear him tell them, over and over again, "I believe in you more than you believe in yourselves!"

He absolutely did. He had an amazing gift for spotting the gifts, talents, and strengths of others. Oftentimes that treasure was entombed in a shroud of self-doubt, shame, timidity, or perhaps in the insidious coffin of a father wound. But he would recognize it nonetheless, then name it out loud. By that means, countless former students report that he essentially cast a vision for their life and life's work by simply affirming their gift and imploring them to unleash it.

That point cannot be overstated. Consider: He only spent one year pastoring a small church (ever after claiming he hadn't been a very good pastor), yet he deployed thousands of pastors into pulpits across the country. Likewise, he never served as an overseas missionary, yet hundreds of his students fanned out across the world as pastors, teachers, and mission leaders. He never started a seminary, yet today a number of seminary founders credit him with inspiring them to birth their institutions. He never formed a parachurch ministry, but a laundry list of such ministries could be devised that Prof either envisioned or significantly helped to launch. He never was a chaplain in a hospital or the military, but dozens of chaplains came through his tutelage. He never owned or ran a business, yet countless executives and workplace Christians looked to him as their guide for living out their faith in the marketplace. And of course,

he never played football, yet in 2008 a reunion of some fifty or so former Dallas Cowboys honored him at a dinner, and man after man—many with tears in their eyes—rose to give testimony to the powerful impact Professor Hendricks had made on their lives, not only while he was chaplain of the Cowboys, but even in the later years when they remembered things he had told them.

In short, Prof's legacy turns Bernard Shaw's sardonic saying on its head. It could be said of Prof: "Those who can do; those who can't prepare those who do." In other words, they teach (assuming they are gifted to the task of causing learning to take place).

Another way to say it is that only mighty rockets have what it takes to get into outer space, but no rocket achieves orbit without blasting off from a stable launching pad. Prof proved to be the launching pad for countless amazing rockets, thanks to his profound gift for believing that God truly had gifted the students who came his way.

"I was once asked in a television interview what I had learned in thirty-five years of teaching at a seminary," he wrote. "I said I had learned that my primary task is to convincingly tell the student, 'I believe in you! You're going to make it!'"[18]

In many ways, that gift for encouragement may have been the most valuable tool he possessed. It is certainly the gift cited most often by his former students as having made the biggest difference for them.

6. Staying Focused

Years ago, a marketing genius named Al Ries wrote a best-selling book entitled *Focus*. In his introduction he pointed out that the rays of the sun, for all their power, are easily defeated by a simple hat and some sunscreen. By contrast, a laser beam, which can be generated by just a few watts of energy, so concentrates light that it can drill a hole in a diamond or vaporize cancer cells.[19]

Such is the power of focus. And whether by insight or by innate bent, Howard Hendricks was about as focused a man as there ever was. Predictably so; some would say even boringly so. He had no hobbies, no "outside interests," no distractions. He lived simply and frugally (a relatively easy thing to do on a seminary professor's salary), so that there was not much by way of material possessions he needed to take care of.

He was also a creature of habit and set-your-clock-by-it routine, which minimized the amount of effort he had to spend on secondary and/or menial tasks. (Make no mistake, however: he had no trouble whatsoever summoning effort for primary tasks. Indeed, to say he was a hard worker would be a gross understatement. Early in his relationship to Jeanne, for example, she took him to visit her uncles and cousins in the farm country. They thought they would take the measure of the city boy by loading him down with enormous bales of hay. To their astonishment, he threw himself into the work with gusto—and, characteristically, with winning humor—and by the end of the day it was they, rather than him, who were winded.)

Howard Hendricks was committed to one basic purpose in life: to prepare students to go out and change the world for Christ. That was the great organizing principle of his time, his attention, his energy, his finances, and his relationships.

That single-minded focus enabled Prof to do the thing that separates the good from the great: to say no. That may be hard to believe, given that Prof had an irresistible impulse to say yes to almost any opportunity that might allow him to

make an impact from the front. Especially in the early going, he literally wore himself out between teaching classes at the seminary and then catching a plane on Friday afternoon for a weekend of speaking at a church, conference center, or other venue (in part, that habit was also driven by the urgency of providing for a wife and four growing children).

Not surprisingly, he had no end of requests to speak. As quickly as he dispatched students throughout the country and, eventually, around the world, those students would send a letter to Dallas requesting their admired Prof to come and visit the group they were now leading. He was only too eager to go and "see this thing which has come to pass." As a result, it didn't take long before his assistants were scheduling him a year out, two years out, sometimes three years out.

And it wasn't just former students asking for his time. He found himself increasingly in demand locally. For example, he taught students at Southern Bible Institute in South Dallas for many years—which meant an evening of classes after he'd already spent all day in classes at Dallas Theological Seminary.[20]

Along the same lines, when he realized that the wives of the seminary students were largely missing out on the rich material being offered in the curriculum, he asked the powers that be whether he could spend an hour or so teaching at Wives Fellowship. He was told, "Well, sure—but only if there's enough interest." Needless to say, it didn't take long for the women to start packing out the venue.[21]

As his reputation spread, he was asked to participate in no end of national venues: at Cru (formerly Campus Crusade for Christ) training events at Arrowhead Springs; at The Navigators' headquarters at Glen Eyrie; at countless conference centers like Mount Hermon, Hume Lake, Forest Home, Word of Life, Keswick, and The Cove; at Promise Keepers; at staff Bible studies at The White House; and on numerous boards: The Navigators, Ron Blue & Company, Search Ministries, Walk Thru the Bible, and Pine Cove, among others. As was mentioned, he was the chaplain of the Cowboys for eight years during the late 1970s and '80s. And throughout his life he was very committed to Christian leaders in the workplace who wanted to integrate their faith and their work.[22]

Given such a vast amount of time and energy spent outside the seminary, how could one argue that Prof had a single-minded focus on his students? Because the evidence shows that he always regarded them as his most important work. For example, if one listens to recordings of his presentations throughout the country—and especially any question-and-answer sessions following a talk—one finds that they often end with Prof firing off a parting shot to the crowd along the lines of, "Well, it's been a delight to be with all of you. I would love to stay and spend more time. But I've got a delicious room of students I can't wait to get back to in Dallas." And with that he would bow out.

Always, always, always he would come back to the classroom. He had an epic gift for communication, and he had no end of places where he could use it. But he always saved the best for his students.

Why? Because early on he discovered the principle that teaching teachers and leaders can expand one's impact logarithmically beyond what one can have in a single, one-shot presentation. He soon packaged that insight into what he called a "ministry of multiplication." That was ultimately the internal logic of his obsession with his students. Given the lengthy list

mentioned above for the kinds of ministries those students ended up leading, it proved to be his formula for effectiveness.

In fact, an analysis of Prof's travel and speaking schedule over the course of his career shows an increasingly refined emphasis on "ministries of multiplication." In the early days, he leaped at almost any opportunity that came along (at one point in the late 1960s, he woke up to the realization that he had booked out-of-town engagements for eight straight weekends, back to back; such a load began to compromise his health—to say nothing of the wear and tear it placed on his home life—and he contracted with Jeanne and with his assistant to never let him do that again).

But in the late 1980s, when he was seemingly at the height of his popularity and impact, he actually began to dial back many of those commitments. He began doing the math, and he realized that at a conference center or a church he might touch a few hundred people's lives for a week or a weekend (which was certainly good and worthwhile). But if he could spend that same time and energy devoted to arming leaders who would impact many lives over many years, the ripple impact of his efforts would be vastly greater.[23]

> "A teacher affects eternity; he can never tell where his influence stops."
> —Henry Adams

And so he always identified himself as a professor, and he always viewed his seminary students as his primary audience. There may have been some platforms outside the seminary where he knew that perhaps he was not as prepared or as focused or as "into it" as he should have been. But never, ever in the seminary classroom! When the bell rang and a class began, the Prof could *always* be found all ready, all focus, all in. The students *always* got his best.

In large part, that was because Hendricks stayed focused on what he could do well, and made peace with accepting his limitations. Satisfied that his core gift was teaching, he essentially outsourced everything that he wasn't very good at: writing, administration, investments and finances, legal matters, business affairs, marketing, car and home repairs, clothing, even leisure activities. He relied on friends like Dr. Trevor Mabry to fetch him for weekend trips to hunt, fish, and get away from the city.

Howard Hendricks personified the dictum of his contemporary Peter Drucker (a man he frequently quoted): "If there is any one 'secret' to effectiveness, it is concentration." Hendricks only appeared to do many things. In reality, he concentrated on doing one thing over and over (albeit in a vast variety of venues): He used his gift for teaching to prepare leaders who would go out and change the world for Christ.

7. Paying Attention to Character

One of most frequently cited "profisms" by former students is, "You cannot impart what you do not possess." In part, the saying meant that you can't teach what you don't really know about. But there was a deeper insight involved than mere head knowledge. Prof believed that teaching is ultimately a matter of the heart. He wanted students to not just know truth, but to *commit* to truth, to possess it and be possessed by it as a transforming act of the will.

The only way that happens is through trust. Students not only must trust the material to be learned; far more importantly, they must trust the teacher. For Prof, teaching was a matter of credibility. No one ever had more conviction about the idea that in teaching, more is caught than taught. "Nothing will create more doubt in your lives than trafficking in unlived truth," he constantly warned his students.

And so he took both proactive steps and protective steps to guard his own integrity. It sounds simple to say, but he was religious in practicing a daily routine of time in the Word and time in prayer. Not infrequently he devoted entire days and more to personal time with the Lord. When he was not out of town, he was relentlessly faithful in showing up at Northwest Bible Church with his family (Sunday mornings, Sunday nights, Wednesday nights, sometimes more). He cultivated a number of close male friends, and invited them to speak into his life. He and Jeanne met annually with an accountability group of five couples who were lifelong, trusted friends.

> "Ability may get you to the top, but you need character to keep you there."
>
> —Coach John Wooden

On the defensive side, he made a conscious commitment to submit himself and his department to the leadership of Dr. Walvoord, and after him to the other presidents of Dallas Seminary and their administrations. He turned over his finances to Ronald Blue & Company. He placed himself under a board of directors for his radio program *The Art of Family Living* and left it to Executive Director John Nieder to work out the various syndication and marketing deals. He stayed away from alcohol and took pains to stay in good health (helped in no small measure by his ability to laugh). And he remained utterly resolute in staying faithful to his marriage vows to Jeanne.

For all that, Dr. Hendricks was the first to confess that he was not perfect. Indeed, his perfectionistic tendencies periodically and predictably created crises of conscience for him, as he became painfully aware of the gap between the man he aspired to be and the man he was. But in that regard, he learned firsthand about the reality of God's grace. And so when he talked about grace with his students (which he frequently did), his authenticity and honesty about his own sins and struggles left no question whether he knew what he was talking about. Everyone came to the same conclusion: He was the real deal.

In the end, grace is the heart of the story when it comes to Prof Hendricks. From a human point of view, there is not a single reason in the world why this man should have existed. He was just a boy on the streets of Depression-era Philadelphia, playing ball with his buddies, peeking through the knotholes in the outfield fence at Shibe Park, prowling the taverns at night to find his grandfather and sneak the paycheck out of his back pocket before he drank up all the money.

For no other reason than grace, God plucked that boy out of insignificance and set him on a path to greatness. He was indeed a turtle on a fencepost. His path was paved with an amazing gift for connecting with people—a

capacity Howard discovered even as a small child, when his mother and aunt took him on the trolley cars and people would light up with delight when he engaged them. That felt like a mysterious power to him. He was almost afraid of it. But it was the one thing he had going for him. His five loaves and two fishes, as it were. So he gave those gifts over to the Gift-giver. And the fragments of the resulting miracle will be decades, if not more, in the gathering.

Conclusion

Dr. Howard Hendricks offers an excellent illustration of a great teacher. Greatness in teaching begins with a God-given gift for causing learning to take place. That gift is a combination of an inherent motivation to see others learn and a set of core strengths that one naturally and consistently uses to help others learn. The gift itself does not produce greatness. But when, as Dr. Hendricks did, one cultivates such a gift through the lifelong practice of several fundamental habits, the result is increasing skill, effectiveness, and excellence at teaching that eventually rises to the level of greatness.

Seven fundamentals that Prof Hendricks habitually practiced were:

1. Showing up prepared
2. Striving to communicate
3. Rigorously evaluating performance
4. Constantly learning
5. Believing in the student
6. Staying focused
7. Paying attention to character

Discussion Questions

1. Giftedness for teaching involves both motivation and ability. How can you assess whether you are "gifted" and motivated to teach others?

2. Dr. Hendricks believed that "the teacher has not taught until the student has learned." How many ways can you think of to assess whether students have learned from you, apart from giving them a written test? (Prof never gave exams!)

3. Today our world is full of multi-tasking, constant stimulation, and countless demands. Do you think it's possible to focus on one primary purpose like Dr. Hendricks? If so, what are the challenges and how might you overcome them?

4. Dr. Hendricks specialized in educational ministry, but he also read widely, listened to experts in other disciplines, and otherwise engaged in lifelong learning outside his field. What are some ways you could gather new knowledge, insights, skills, and advice in areas that are not your primary focus?

5. To be an effective teacher, your students must trust you. When you think of a trusted teacher, who comes to mind? Why? As you contemplate becoming a teacher, how will you earn your students' trust?

Resources for Further Study

Books

Baldwin, Ethel May and David B. Benson. *Henrietta Mears and How She Did It*. Ventura, CA: Regal Books, 1980.

Gangel, Kenneth O. and Howard G. Hendricks. *The Christian Educator's Handbook on Teaching: A Comprehensive Resource on the Distinctiveness of True Christian Teaching*. Grand Rapids: Baker Academic, 1998.

Hendricks, Howard G. *Teaching to Change Lives: Seven Laws of the Teacher*. Portland, OR: Multnomah Press, 1987.

Hendricks, Howard G. and William D. Hendricks. *As Iron Sharpens Iron: Building Character in a Mentoring Relationship*. Chicago: Moody Publishers, 1995.

Hendricks, Howard G. and William D. Hendricks. *Living by the Book: The Art and Science of Reading the Bible.* Chicago: Moody Press, 1991.

Palmer, Earl, Roberta Hestenes, and Howard G. Hendricks. *Mastering Teaching.* Portland, OR: Multnomah Press, 1991.

Videos

Hendricks, Howard G. *Living by the Book Video Series.* Dallas: Living By The Book, 2012.

Hendricks, Howard G. *The 7 Laws of the Teacher DVD: Curriculum.* Atlanta: Walk Thru the Bible, 2010.

Author Bio

Bill Hendricks is the younger son of the late Howard G. Hendricks, and is President of The Giftedness Center, a Dallas-based consulting firm that helps individuals think through their strategic life and career directions. He is also the Executive Director for Christian Leadership at The Hendricks Center at Dallas Theological Seminary. Bill has authored or coauthored twenty-two books—several of them with his father—and his latest title is *The Person Called YOU: Why You're Here, Why You Matter & What You Should Do With Your Life.* He holds an undergraduate degree in English from Harvard University, a master of science in mass communications from Boston University, and a master of arts in biblical studies from Dallas Theological Seminary. He is a member of SIMA® International, a board member for Pine Cove Christian Camps, and sits on the Steering Committee for The Theology of Work Project. He is married to Lynn Turpin Hendricks, and is the proud father of three accomplished daughters. You can learn more about Bill and his work at www.thegiftednesscenter.com.

Endnotes

1. George Bernard Shaw, "Maxims for Revolutionaries" in *Man and Superman* (1903).

2. The nickname, "Prof," came into use among Dr. Hendricks' students quite early in his career at Dallas Seminary. No one knows who first used it. For that matter, no one really remembers when he wasn't referred to as Prof. The name and the man quickly became indistinguishable.

3. The original line is, "All animals are equal but some animals are more equal than others." From George Orwell, *Animal Farm* (London: Secker and Warburg, 1945).

4. For more on this point, as well as more on the subject of giftedness, see Bill Hendricks, *The Person Called YOU: Why You're Here, Why You Matter & What You Should Do With Your Life* (Chicago: Moody Press, 2014).

5. Howard G. Hendricks, *Teaching to Change Lives* (Portland, OR: Multnomah Press, 1987), 122.

6. Bill Hendricks, *The Person Called YOU*.

7. Hendricks, *Teaching to Change Lives*, 56.

8. The essential content of that course remains available both in print and in video format. The book is by Howard G. Hendricks and William D. Hendricks, *Living by the Book: The Art and Science of Reading the Bible* (Chicago: Moody Press, 1991). The video is by Howard G. Hendricks, *Living by the Book Video Series* (Dallas: Living by the Book), available in twenty-part (extended) or seven-part (condensed) series, with companion workbooks.

9. *Chariots of Fire*, directed by Hugh Hudson, screenplay by Collin Welland, (20th Century Fox, 1981).

10. Malcolm Gladwell, *Outliers: The Story of Success* (New York: Little Brown and Company, 2008), 35–68.

11. Mortimer J. Adler and Charles Van Doren, *How to Read a Book: The Art of Getting a Liberal Education* (New York: Simon & Schuster, 1940).

12. Steve Jobs made the comment—which he attributed to Picasso—in a 1996 PBS documentary series entitled *Triumph of the Nerds*. Available at: https://www.youtube.com/watch?v=CW0DUg63lqU.

13. Robert A. Traina, *Methodical Bible Study* (Grand Rapids: Eerdmans, 1952).

14. It's worth pointing out that Traina himself borrowed much of his material in *Methodical Bible Study* from his own mentor Dr. Caroline Palmer. So much so that he inserted an author's note at the beginning of the book to that effect, admitting that "it would be ideal if individual credit could be given at every point where it is due, but for obvious reasons this cannot be accomplished" (Traina, *Methodical Bible Study*, vii).

15. Allen C. Emery, *A Turtle on a Fencepost: Little Lessons of Large Importance* (Houston: Worldwide Publishing Group, 1980), Introduction by Billy Graham. To be fair, Elton Trueblood himself had borrowed the turtle on a fencepost image from a longstanding joke about "post turtles" used in political discussions throughout North America. Again, so many of the best illustrations and ideas are borrowed and adapted, rather than conceived from scratch. The technique has doubtless been in use for as long as humans have been communicating.

16. For example, he frequently described the custom of parishioners greeting a preacher with fawning praise after his sermon as "the glorification of the worm ceremony."

17. One caveat that must be made on this point is that the older Prof got, the more he fell woefully behind in his understanding of technology (in the mid-2000s, he was telling students that "some of you have tapes running inside your heads that need to be reprogrammed"; many of the Millennials had no idea what he was talking about). He also had a hard time letting go of a useful illustration, even when it had become dated.

18. Hendricks, *Teaching to Change Lives*, 72.

19. Al Reis, *Focus: The Future of Your Company Depends on It* (New York: Harper Business, 1996).

20.   Dallas Theological Seminary was founded in 1924 to teach the Bible and theology to men. Reflecting the cultural realities then current in Dallas (and indeed throughout the South), African Americans were not eligible for enrollment. But in 1927, despite racial turmoil in the city, a DTS student named Edmund H. Ironside collaborated with Rev. L.G. Foster, an African-American preacher, to begin training African-American men at his home. The initial class of three students was the beginning of the Southern Bible Institute, which today continues to "equip men and women to be competent servant-leaders with a Bible-centered worldview." Like Dr. Ironside before him, Dr. Hendricks felt a deep conviction that Dallas' African-American churches should be led by men with the best possible training in exegeting Scripture and communicating its truths to their congregations. To that end, he gladly volunteered as a guest teacher at Southern, and always considered his time there among the happiest experiences of his career. (Today, all DTS programs are open to African-Americans and other minority students.)

21.   As referenced in the previous endnote, Dallas Theological Seminary was founded in 1924 as a school for men. Its student body remained exclusively male until 1975. Wives Fellowship was formed to offer the wives of men in seminary a place for fellowship, support, and community-building. However, there was no thought of making any of the courses or their subject matter directly available to wives. Any exposure a wife would get would be indirectly through her husband (or his textbooks). Dr. Hendricks pioneered in breaking down that wall by offering to teach at Wives Fellowship, and also by insisting that wives be allowed to sit in on his Christian Home course. In the summer of 1975, the seminary opened the new Master of Arts in Biblical Studies program to women (it was only offered in the summer at that time). Today, all DTS degree programs are open to women, and women comprise nearly 38 percent of the student body. The Wives Fellowship has been replaced by Seminary Wives in Ministry (SWIM), which exists "to equip wives to be competent servants alongside their husbands in ministry."

22.   In Prof's day, such folks were called "laymen" (and later the more inclusive "laypeople"). A fairly traditional distinction between "clergy" and "laity" still existed (something Dr. Hendricks was never particularly fond of).

23.   This is, of course, the principle of discipleship. Dr. Hendricks hammered home the observation that while Jesus taught enormous crowds, he devoted most of his time to the Seventy, and the most important times to the Twelve. Those apprentices would be the ones who would "go and make disciples of all nations" (Matt. 28:19).

Chapter 2
A PHILOSOPHY OF CHRISTIAN EDUCATION

Michael S. Lawson

...be transformed by the renewing of your mind.
—Romans 12:2

"I KNOW WE CAN'T do Christian education because we don't have slide projectors and overhead projectors," said the lovely lady in Mexico City. Her words stung me deeply. "That's correct!" seemed to jump out of my mouth. "I'm so sorry that all you have to work with here in Mexico is the inerrant word of God and the omnipotent Holy Spirit." The same God who works with slide projectors, overhead projectors, and now computer generated graphics from data projectors has successfully educated Christians for two thousand years without them.

Frequently, the casual observer associates the term Christian education with children's work, Christian schools, or fancy tools somehow attached to an otherwise drab presentation. Those who see Christian education as primarily children's work see little value other than keeping children entertained and amused while adults conduct more serious educational endeavors.[1] The casual Christian school observer views Christian education something like a cupcake. To them, the school merely offers a general education with a little Christianity smeared on top.[2] Others see Christian education as mostly window dressing with fancy gimmicks.[3] The dear lady in Mexico was so focused on my visual tools that she believed represented the essence of Christian education. Of course none of these do justice to the term or the responsibility entrusted to the Savior's church.

The Church's Strategic Role in Christian Education

While this chapter focuses on the church's role, the chapter on family ministry will examine the Christian home as another formative agent of Christian education. Yet, the church has a strategic role since families who come to faith in later seasons of life often need remedial help to assume their responsibilities. In addition, not all individuals have the advantage of growing up in Christian families.

While many wonderful parachurch agencies contribute to a global Christian education picture they are not as pervasive and certainly not the church Jesus promised to build (Matt. 16:18). After two thousand years, countless martyrs, heresy within, deniers without, and relentless attacks on her central document, the evidence overwhelmingly testifies to the continuing fulfillment of his promise.

> "...the church has not yet awakened to its responsibilities and potential in adult education."[4]
> —Kenneth Gangel and Jim Wilhoit

Just in case anyone wonders what Jesus thinks about churches in various conditions of obedience, they may read his personal letters in The Revelation but should be ready for his no-nonsense approach (Rev. 2–3). Jesus was and is very concerned about some bad teaching in those churches. Whether rich or poor, lazy or exhausted, free or persecuted, the church represent Christ's "boots on the ground" around the world. Make no mistake, Jesus is still building his church and as far as I can determine expects her to fulfill her disciple-making educational mission. Although the bride of Christ has had a wobbly educational journey to say the least, Christ has been and continues as her head;

cleansing her, admonishing her, encouraging her, and always present with her.

Jesus's teaching provides both substance and example of his expectations. The church's foundation lays on "apostles and prophets, with Christ Jesus himself as the chief cornerstone" (Eph. 2:20). The apostles followed Christ's pattern so the first church in Jerusalem "continued in the apostles teaching" (Acts 2). Because those original Jewish members had deep grounding in the Old Testament, I suspect the teaching centered on connecting Old Testament messianic predictions with Jesus's life and ministry. Perhaps Jesus himself set the pattern with his first lesson after the resurrection (Luke 24).

When the church transitioned into the Gentile world, she needed slightly different—or should we say—remedial teaching. The Gentiles lacked an adequate base in the Old Testament which provided the only documents at the time. So, Barnabas and Saul taught a "great number" of people for a year in Antioch (Acts 6).

High Christology characterizes much of Paul's writing and surely formed the foundation for his teaching as he planted churches westward. His letter to Philippi, written from his confinement in Rome, lovingly says, "It is no trouble for me to write *the same things* to you again, and it is a safeguard for you." Chapter two of that epistle contains rich summaries reflecting on the person and work of Jesus Christ.

Even though Paul's visit in Thessalonica ended prematurely after about three weeks, he had managed to teach that church about the Day of the Lord and the return of Christ (1 Thess. 4–5 and 2 Thess. 2). I suspect many church members today could not outline even the major events of that day. Yet Paul taught The

Day of the Lord as beginner's material when he founded that church.

The apostles do not represent the last teachers in the church. The teaching ministry of Christ's church continues one generation after another as the Holy Spirit provides gifted teachers. Each generation of church leaders faces the same question, "How do we fulfill the teaching responsibility in our church?" The church I grew up in offered a formal liturgy but not any serious teaching. The church my colleague grew up in focused on ecstatic experiences but again failed to provide substantive teaching. Anemic Christians result from neglected teaching ministry.

In 1969 I assumed the responsibility for staffing a large and active Christian education ministry with volunteer teachers. We offered the full age range of classes at Sunday school with multiple classes at certain levels; three levels of children's church to sixth grade for both morning services; and a full range of classes on Sunday evening training hour. One of the things I noticed involved the old saying, "I always learn more when I teach." I learned to embrace that wholeheartedly. If my church really wanted Christians to learn more, she would need to turn more of them into teachers. Anyone wanting to teach must first study the material, giving more time and energy to the process than simple attendance. We just turned a convert into a student. How easily we listen to a careful presentation then garble the message when we try to share it. We often conclude, "You just should have been there." And yes, it is true for me too, "I always learn more when I teach."

Jesus founded his church on teaching and he expects his followers to become students totally identified with him. The apostolic foundation received specific instructions about their teaching responsibilities.

Our task remains the same as theirs: Turn converts into obedient students. The Holy Spirit raises up teachers within the church in our generation to assume the responsibility handed down to us. In the apostles' generation the text says, "The *disciples* were called *Christians* first in Antioch" (emphasis mine). Mission accomplished. While we can look with pride on what the apostles accomplished, we carry the responsibility for teaching to our generation.

Shaping the Church's Philosophy

In educational jargon, we call this responsibility a "philosophy" or "love of wisdom." In reality, our Christian "love of wisdom" embraces a comprehensive approach to educating Christians in their faith. As much as possible, our design, construction, and implementation of education should ooze Christian values. This chapter on a philosophy of Christian education represents an attempt to construct that genuinely Christian approach to education.

A true philosophy of Christian education draws its lifeblood from the Bible. There, two general approaches to theological education appear. In essence, Old Testament education builds on a "come and see" approach. God intended Israel to serve as his living visual aid (Deut. 4:6 and Acts 7). Deuteronomy 6 captures the goal of the Old Testament approach with its central focus on a love for God. Imagine a whole nation devoting themselves to loving God and reminding each other constantly through their personal wardrobes, home decorations, eating habits, and daily conversations. That would certainly be something worth seeing. Other nations were to observe the hand of God blessing Israel as she followed his divine law. Although God worked patiently with Israel for generations, she never managed to follow him completely.[5]

In stark contrast, Jesus's commission to his New Testament followers involves a "go and tell" approach. Interestingly enough, the very same nations who failed to "come and see" would now become the target of Jesus's disciple-making mandate. Jesus introduces his new divine strategy with one word in Matthew 28, "Go."[6] At that moment, the Godhead alone fully understood the implications of the educational force Jesus unleashed. His educational imperative to the apostles has been handed down from generation to generation. We inherit his educational commission for our generation.

Our responses to God's calling should involve a *careful appraisal of the assigned task and understanding how "Christian" affects everything in education.* The remainder of this chapter examines how these two responses to Jesus's mandate undergird our philosophy of Christian education in the church.

Our Assigned Task: Mission Impossible

Many Bible verses enjoy popular appeal but I know of only one with its own name. Bible students have labeled verses 19 and 20 of Matthew 28, "The Great Commission." Jesus wraps this extraordinary mandate in his unlimited power and authority (v. 18) and punctuates the unprecedented imperative with his continuing personal presence (v. 20). His power, his authority, his presence, his mandate come woven together creating an irresistible educational force until he returns. The world had no

idea what was about to happen. Words fail to communicate the explosive educational consequences of "The Great Commission." Here is the verse: "Therefore, *go* and *make disciples* of *all nations, baptizing* them in the name of the *Father* and of the *Son* and of the *Holy Spirit,* and *teaching* them to *obey everything* I have *commanded* you" (emphasis mine).

> "The size and the significance of the educational task facing the church should cause it to think and act more aggressively in developing the Christian education program."[7]
> —Michael Lawson and Robert Choun

Based on the highlighted words, I suggest Jesus envisioned Christian education in this way:

1. Transportable
2. Educational
3. International
4. Incarnational
5. Doctrinal
6. Transformational
7. Universal
8. Commanded

Each and every word deserves attention and reflection in order to grasp the significance of our task.

Transportable

Jesus's first word in Matthew 28:19 created a limitless horizon for his educational endeavor.[8] Rather than "come and see," the apostles were to "go and tell." Normally, educational institutions expect students to relocate; Jesus's envisions education on wheels (or donkey back?) that comes to you. Not only is Christian education coming to a neighborhood near you, his followers actively seek you out. Even a quick read through the book of Acts reveals they did exactly that.

While the Gospels record a number of Gentiles interacting with Jesus from time to time, the Holy Spirit's push into the Gentile world caught the apostles by surprise. The murder of Stephen initiated a persecution that scattered believers in every direction. Philip ends up in Samaria (north of Jerusalem) and then with an Ethiopian on the road to Gaza (south of Jerusalem). God sends Peter to Cornelius in Caesarea (west of Jerusalem). Then, almost by accident—you do believe in accidents, don't you?—some Jews began to tell their Gentile friends in Antioch about Jesus and many came to faith. While the Jewish believers could build on their Old Testament heritage, Gentile believers needed a remedial educational design to catch up. Barnabas recruited the finest Old Testament scholar of his day, the soon-to-be apostle Paul, and the rest, as they say, is history. In less than one generation, Christianity would penetrate not just the Roman capital but the very household of Caesar (Phil. 4).

For roughly two thousand years, Christianity has been education on the move. God compelled the apostle Paul to turn west, and the Roman Empire came under the influence of Christianity. Thomas went east into India where he was martyred, but "Thomas Christians" remain to this day. Nestorians took the message through Persia and into China. They ultimately arrived in the very palace of Genghis Khan through his wife.[9] When told correctly, the relentless push of Christianity dominates world history.

Everywhere Christians went they took the scriptures as their basis for teaching. Today, the Wycliffe Bible Translators indicate that 97 percent of the world has the Bible translated into their language.[10] Having said that, they also note that 1,800 languages still need a translation project to begin. The followers of Jesus Christ have been and are making his words accessible to the last 3 percent of the world's population. One estimate suggests that through computers, satellite uplinks, and desktop publishing, the translations could be complete by 2025.[11] Now that is what I call a transportable educational juggernaut.

> I personally talked with an Iraqi diver who found a copy of the Bible on the floor of the ocean and converted after reading it.

Educational

First-century teachers normally found themselves surrounded by a small band of "disciples." Jesus set an unusual precedent when he chose his disciples rather than them choosing him. The apostles followed a similar pattern—shaping converts into Jesus's students. The seemingly simple task actually represents a formidable challenge. Getting someone to pray the sinner's prayer is one thing, turning them into conscientious students calls for a completely different process.

Although I have spent over twenty years in educational institutions as a student, most of that time I tolerated dull, tedious routine. With few glaring exceptions, my experience required more endurance than intellect.[12] Nothing in the classroom or homework sparked any internal energy to learn more. I became relatively skilled at passing tests and completing assignments. In a few cases, professors created enough fear that I pushed hard enough to avoid embarrassment. I have asked hundreds of adults how many would like to become students in high school once again. No one has yet volunteered although many would like to be that young and enjoy the freedom of those years.

> "One may well wonder why it is that, though books have been written about education since the Republic of Plato and about Jesus since the gospel of Mark, it is only the present generation that has seen books written about Jesus as educator."[13]
> —Herman Harrell Horne

When I suggest that Jesus wants us to turn someone into a student, many grimace from the same memories buried in me. I firmly believe Jesus had something much different in mind. The education Jesus squeezed into his disciples came at them from every direction. No one would ever forget the first time they ever saw Jesus:

- Touch a leper covered with oozing sores.
- Hush a life-threatening thunderstorm.
- Heal a man born blind.
- Raise a corpse to life.

Nor could we forget such laser-sharp words as:

- Your sins are forgiven.
- Let the little children come unto me.
- Before Abraham was, I am.

- If you have seen me, you have seen the Father.

Nothing about Jesus's education of his disciples smacked of dull or tedious. Instead, words like "mind-bending" or "excruciatingly convicting" come to mind. To be made into a student of Jesus ought to be the most exciting life-changing adventure ever envisioned. In my opinion, if we, as representatives of Jesus Christ, turn someone's sacred journey into a mind-numbing endurance test, we have profaned the mandate entrusted to the apostles and through them to us.

International

Jesus did not stutter when he said, make disciples of all nations," though we find the apostles struggling to assimilate that concept through the first eleven chapters of Acts. God's intentions become clearer as he invades the Samaritans through Philip, the Roman military through Peter, and the Gentile Antioch through conversations with Jerusalem refugees. As the small band of Jewish leaders huddled in Jerusalem to sort things out, they agreed there was no mistaking the work of the Holy Spirit in every case.

As an American, I cannot tell you how many years I misread Jesus's words. Individualism so permeated my thinking that I assumed Jesus meant "individuals within nations," but of course that is not what he says here in Matthew.[14] Perhaps many initial conversions were somewhat nominal, nevertheless whole nations opened their doors to a previously despised and persecuted sect beginning with Armenia followed by the Roman Empire under Constantine.[15] Later, Persia would welcome the

Nestorian brand of Christianity (nontraditional Christology) simply because they were declared anathema by Rome (always their mortal enemy). And, they would carry Christianity through Persia into China. The Arians (defective Christology) would carry their message to the Germanic tribes way ahead of the Roman church.[16] Ultimately, the merger of church and state became so strong that even today whole countries are often associated with a particular brand of Christianity:

- Anglicanism in England
- Orthodoxy in Greece
- Lutheranism in Germany
- Roman Catholicism in Spain
- Presbyterianism in Scotland[17]

Many nations have such large population segments adhering to one form of Christianity or another that they too would be thought of as Christian in the broad sense of the word. Russia, though officially atheistic, has a large Orthodox population. In addition, whole regions like Latin America are largely known for Roman Catholic constituents. As with the seven churches in the Revelation, these church states have varying levels of commitment to Christ's original teaching and the Bible as a whole.

The unfortunate outcome of these church-state alliances historically meant other forms of Christianity were persecuted. For that reason, the founders of the United States specifically planned to separate church from state and forge a government that allowed for a freedom of Christian expression. No founder was Muslim, Buddhist, or Hindu, though some certainly were Deists or casual about their faith.

Of course everyone recognizes the transgenerational essence of Christianity. When one generation fails to transmit a viral faith to the next, both individuals and nations drift away from Christianity. The work of disciple-making must reach horizontally to adult individuals and vertically to the next generation in every nation.[18]

Incarnational

Students become like their teacher. Jesus employs teaching rather than preaching as the essence of disciple making. In fact he says, "Everyone who is fully trained will be like his teacher" (Luke 6:40). Of course, he and the apostles did both (Matt. 11:1). But here, in Matthew's record of Jesus's educational mandate, teaching takes center stage.

Commentators rightly place a great deal of emphasis on "make disciples." After all, "make disciples" is the only true imperative in these verses. One interesting but often overlooked feature in this passage involves Jesus giving the mandate to make disciples to those who were already disciples (v. 16). In other words, those who would MAKE disciples must BE disciples first. The disciples animated the term for anyone wishing to become a follower of Christ. In reality, every disciple of Jesus Christ should say, as Paul did say, "follow my example as I follow the example of Christ" (1 Cor. 11:1). Disciple-making involves so much more than proper instruction. Imagine yourself as Jesus's living visual for others. That thought still gives me the shivers.

If I truly embrace the Christian faith, then I use the cognitive information about God's values to make choices and decisions. That kind of faith characterized the early followers of Christ and made them attractive to their neighbors. I currently have two former oil-field workers in a Tuesday morning Bible study. Men in that occupation do not typically exude the Christian virtues of patience, kindness, compassion, or tenderheartedness … do I need to paint you a picture? One frankly admitted he had not read a book since high school. Charles had worked for Jack so these two knew each other's hard side. When Charles came to faith, the change stunned Jack and caused him to turn his life toward Christ as well. In essence, Charles became the lesson for Jack. Truth can and is genuinely transferred from life to life once we have absorbed and begun to obey Jesus's teaching. Jack and Charles are older now. From their gentle words, you would not guess their hard backgrounds. Christian education is incarnational.

Jesus did not send his disciples into all the world to make converts who give mere verbal assent to correct doctrine. He intended the good news to jump start a life-long maturing process gathered up in the term "disciple or discipleship." Christ intends to change our entire value system. Gratitude, generosity, hospitality, compassion, patience, peacemaking, and so many more Christian virtues develop in us under the Holy Spirit's influence.

Doctrinal

The baptismal formula alludes to a critical feature of our Christian education mission. Jesus sends the apostles out to baptize in the name of the Father, and of the Son, and of the Holy Spirit. He expects his followers to identify themselves with that intentionally triune marker. We have no authority to create an idea of God that we find more comfortable. The

apostles, and we as their heirs, work inside a truth-based system. We teach others about the God who revealed himself through his Son and now resides in us through the Holy Spirit. We acknowledge a truth that comes to us and binds us, and we are not free to change it to please us.

I have had numerous conversations admitting how much easier it would be if Jesus had not presented himself as the only way to God. Some people would like me better if I could tell them they could come to God any way they want to … but that would be a lie straight from Hell.

Jesus intends his teaching to set the standard for truth. Not only is his educational system truth based, its tentacles reach out and touch everything. We are free to teach about the physical order as long as we recognize its creator. We are free to teach about history as long as we honor the one who holds time in his hands and distinguishes the end from the beginning. We are free to celebrate all human accomplishments as long as we also affirm every good and perfect gift comes from the God of heaven. We are not free to declare the inherent goodness of man when the Bible declares " … all have sinned and fall short of the glory of God" (Rom. 3:23). We are not free to teach a universal acceptance into the presence of God when Jesus says to some, "I never knew you. Away from me, you evil doers" (Matt. 7:23).

Truth, by definition, is not internal and personal though that notion prevails in this generation. Truth is external and universal even if uncomfortable. When we obey the truth, it becomes internal and personal. Anyone who takes up Jesus's mandate must abide by his terms. Jesus warned there would be false teachers who would represent themselves as his disciples too (Matt. 7:13). Jesus's followers acknowledge that truth ultimately resides in his person and abide by his words.

> "One of the continuing needs of our time is the reassertion of the fact that all truth is of God, that Christ is the incarnate Word of truth, that the Holy Spirit is the Spirit of truth, and that Scripture is the written Word of truth. Along with this reassertion there should come a fuller realization that both the natural creation and the creative endeavors of man in all fields are in all their aspects related to God's truth. For a dichotomy between sacred and secular truth has no place in a consistently Christian philosophy of education."[19]
> —Frank Gaebelein

Transformational

"The Way," as we were known early on, changed due to believers' powerful association with Jesus. "Christians" or "Christ ones," intended as a "catcall," so captured their reputation that the church embraced the name. In my heart of hearts, I honestly wish those who claim his name today were so closely associated with Jesus that they displayed his teachings clearly to the world. Instead, many wear his name but make Jesus's teaching indiscernible. "Those who turned the world upside down" was not an overstatement. Our failure to distinguish ourselves

in our generation does not dull history or Jesus's expectation of us.

While teaching students everything Jesus said offers a significant challenge, teaching students to obey what Jesus said moves the educational goal posts. The usual two-dimensional transfer of information now becomes three-dimensional life transformation. Christian education in all its forms has too often focused on correct answers rather than better life decisions based on those correct answers. If we do not take students on an educational journey toward obeying everything Jesus taught, then we fail to implement Jesus's most significant educational distinction. Obedience sets our philosophy of Christian education apart from every other educational endeavor.

As the Christian leaders of this generation, we must examine the results of our work. When our teaching concludes, have we turned people into obedient active learners or merely passive listeners? Jesus commission involves a dangerously difficult educational process. If we fail to give careful attention to that educational process, we may immunize rather than activate those who would become Jesus's students. If those we teach turn into something other than Jesus's obedient students, we should change what we are doing. Those of us who take up this mandate will never persuade anyone to obey more than we ourselves obey. The mandate of the Great Commission begins with our own transformation.

Universal

The creator of every nation now sends his messengers into "all" nations with the good news that their sins are forgiven and access to God has been restored. We welcome men and women, boys and girls to become Jesus's students. He imposes no age, gender, or ethnic restrictions on anyone who would become his student. The gender restrictions of the temple, the popular disdain for children, and the ethnic preference for the nation of Israel vanish in Jesus's commission. This is truly a universal educational mandate.

Nothing before or since approaches the scope of Jesus's vision. He proudly lays this on the shoulders of his largely volunteer task force, equips them with his eternal words, empowers them with the Holy Spirit and sends them wave after wave and generation after generation into his world.

Commanded

Have you been counting how many times I have used "command," "imperative," and "mandate"? Need I say more? Jesus is not making a suggestion for the apostles to take under consideration and submit to a committee for a recommendation after considerable research. I am fascinated by the fact that Jesus entrusted this central command to ordinary people rather than those professionally trained in education. Jesus calls followers from every walk of life into his international educational transformational mission. Welcome home.

In summary, then, the brief verses representing the Great Commission introduce but do not exhaust our philosophy of Christian education. The Holy Spirit jam-packs the rest of the New Testament with implications for our responsibility. As we might expect from an omniscient God, when "Christian" touches "education" a fascinating transformation of all the variables emerges.

"Christian" Affects Everything in Education

All philosophical systems of education have common elements. Tamper with any one of these variables and you change the philosophy significantly. For example, what is the goal of general education in any given society? Is it to produce loyal citizens, solve social problems, or train better scientists than other countries? Perhaps the philosophy involves a delicate combination of these or others. If so, what percentage blend of these purposes is appropriate and even more importantly, who says so? Perhaps this explains why a philosophy of education—any kind of education—becomes so difficult to define precisely.

As mentioned earlier, this is why so many of us have viewed Christian education something like a cupcake—general education with a little Christianity smeared on top. But, comparing our experiences in public education with the Bible's expectation in Christian education is like comparing a pedal car with a stealth bomber. Yes, they both have steering mechanisms and a means of propulsion but beyond that the comparison breaks down. When Christian touches the variable of education, the pedal car morphs into a stealth bomber of educational strategies. Or, in the words of my personal hero who saved the universe week after week, Captain James T. Kirk of the Starship Enterprise, true Christian education offers "to boldly go where no man has ever been." Now that is an educational philosophy worth exploring.

Although our philosophy of Christian education has common elements with general education, one feature of the Christian system transforms all the rest, namely, The Holy Spirit.[20] As the personal and permanent representative of Jesus Christ until he comes back, the Holy Spirit transforms each and every element we share in common with general education. While some elements lie in seed form in the Great Commission, the remainder of the New Testament expands their educational implications. These elements in turn form an outline for the remainder of this section. The following list represents some of the more important common elements. I invite you to join me in looking at these common variables under the uncommon influence of the Holy Spirit:

- Goals and Measurements
- Methods and Curriculum
- Students and Teachers

Goals and Measurements

The stated educational goal of the great commission involves, "teaching them to obey everything I have commanded you." One goal unites two interlocking features. The content of Jesus's teaching must become the sieve through which daily choices flow. Truth becomes the basis for better decisions. Not only is the Holy Spirit the author of that truth, he provides both the will and the action in the process of obedience (Phil. 2:13).

Beyond the transfer of information, Christian education involves the transference of faith both within our generation and on to the next generation. The transfer of information is common to every system. But the transfer

of confidence in that truth to make different choices rests with the Holy Spirit. The goal of Christian education could not be clearer. Jesus's answer to the young Pharisee trying to prioritize the commandments cuts to the heart of the matter:

> Love the Lord your God with all your heart and with all your soul and with all your mind. This is the first and greatest commandment. And the second is like it: Love your neighbor as yourself. All the Law and the Prophets hang on these two commandments (Matt. 22:37–40).

Jesus emphasizes loving one another over and over again in John's upper room discourse. Of course the apostle Paul echoes Jesus words when he says, "The goal of this command is love, which comes from a pure heart and a good conscience and a sincere faith" (1 Tim. 1:5).

Paul and other New Testament authors connect love with maturity (Eph. 4:11–14). In other words, a genuinely maturing Christian always reflects a growing love for God and others, while an immature one does neither. The apostle John says it a bit more colorfully when he states, "Whoever claims to love God yet hates a brother or sister is a liar" (1 John 4:20). Genuine maturity bears fruit in flourishing loving relationships impossible without the Holy Spirit.

In Ephesians 4, maturity has several additional features. First, the teaching that brings about maturity manifests works of service. Second, that same teaching increases knowledge of and unshakable trust in Christ. Third, correct teaching creates a unifying rather than a divisive force among believers. Fourth, sound teaching stabilizes Christian faith and protects against error.

The author of Hebrews adds a significant but little discussed feature to maturity. In Hebrews 5:14 we read, "But solid food is for the mature, who by constant use have trained themselves to distinguish good from evil." This passage is similar to Ephesians 4 and 1 John 4 where knowledge of Christ, serving others, and healing relationships intersect. Nor should solid food be mistaken for sophisticated discussions using complicated jargon. I have endured more than my share through doctoral seminars. Instead, the solid food (clear truthful teaching about Christ) helps Christians exercise good judgment while making better decisions about daily life choices. Do not fail to note the choice between good or evil. Mature Christians know the difference and practice making good decisions consistent with solid teaching. Quality Christian education offers students opportunities to practice making those decisions—decisions based on the truth of Jesus teaching.

The love required in obedience to Christ's command grows within us as fruit of the Holy Spirit. Every Christian educator at every level must use loving God and loving others as the benchmark for measuring success or failure in their endeavor. In other words, "As a result of my teaching, do you love God more or less? Can you show me by your love for another?" No preacher or teacher has ever asked me to answer that question. However, periodically, I look back to see what changes I have made in my pursuit of God and service to others. I urge people to reflect specifically on changes they can see in those two categories. Progress in the Christian life can and should be evident and somewhat measurable to us and others.

Curriculum and Methods

Churches in different settings answer this question differently. When Christians enter remote settings, reducing the language to written form and translating the Bible often becomes a prerequisite to teaching the people to read the words of God in their own language. The Russian language was reduced to writing by two such missionaries who borrowed from the Greek language to form the Cyrillic alphabet.[21] The Christian curriculum must be built from the ground up. If they don't have a written language, create a written language. If they don't have the Bible in their language, translate the Bible. If they don't read their written language, teach them to read. If they can read, teach them to study. The whole counsel of God wrapped in the teaching of Jesus is the curriculum.

The Bible brings a distinct wrinkle to curriculum because the book lives. As a friend of mine once told me, "One morning as I was reading my Bible, I was surprised to learn that it was also reading me!" My friend experienced the intersection of the Holy Spirit indwelling him with the Holy Spirit's own words in print. The Bible's information always carries the implicit expectation of an obedient response. In fact, mere knowledge of the Bible without obedience carries the warning label: "puffs up." When we look at the student in the next section, we will notice how the curriculum requires a properly prepared recipient.

First Corinthians 2 and Hebrews 5 alert us to distinctions in Bible content. Some teachings are suitable for beginners while other material really belongs to those who have grown more.

In general, I would recommend the following guidelines for the various age groups:

Adults: Some ought to be in settings designed for those who have not yet started to think deeply about the scripture. Others, willing to give energy, study, and reflection should have sturdier fare linked to service. In both cases, every effort should be made to leave adults wanting more.

Youth: Here the curriculum design ought to reflect better decision-making processes based on attitudes and values consistent with God's desires. Ultimately, we want those growing up in the faith to embrace God's values and Christian attitudes.

Children: While the gospel ought to be frequently, carefully, and appropriately explained, the core for children ought to be the Bible stories.[22] These form the foundation for understanding the New Testament and formulating a biblical theology. Believe me on this one, I began my training at DTS without them. I eventually learned them while reading to my children. Count the number of times the stories in Genesis are referenced later on in the Old Testament and then the New Testament.

The Bible represents itself as truth, meaning its assertions are valid. They are valid whether anyone believes them or not. Many things have been said about Christ down through the centuries. The New Testament acknowledges that some of those things are absolute nonsense. The teaching of Christ and about Christ has a truth base, truth authored by the Holy Spirit. According to Ephesians 4, some deceitful schemers spread false information about Christ. That same statement, although two thousand years old, could be said of some pastors, teachers, and scholars today.

The church universal agrees on sixty-six books as the written portion of God's revelation.[23] However, many who read the scriptures overlook the numerous creative ways God revealed himself to the Bible authors. Talking animals, handwriting on walls, visions, stories, naked prophets, architecture, rituals, food, clothing, and miracles just begin a list of tools God used to impress his words on people's minds. Jesus himself used parables, object lessons, bread, wine, fish, baptism, open-ended questions, and paradoxes to stimulate the disciples and those who came to hear his teaching. Of course, he himself was the most complete revelation of God the Father.

Given the large, diverse, and creative communication of God's revelation, why are Christian teachers so glued to the lecture method? Wherever I go, the lecture seems to be the only approved "Christian" method. I am embarrassed by teachers' lack of creativity and innovation in the teaching of the most significant material ever written. Advertisers give more thought to selling products than Christian teachers do to opening God's revelation to the minds and hearts of their students. I fear many people conclude God must be really boring just because their teachers were boring. I think we would be justified in doing so much more with our teaching. Wouldn't a better option look something like this?

Figure 2.1 Creative Delivery

If the Bible was creatively delivered in the beginning, doesn't it make sense to creatively deliver it now?

- God creatively reveals himself to the Bible authors
- Bible authors reduce God's revelation to writing
- Bible teachers creatively deliver the writing to students

Our philosophy and delivery of Christian education ought to reflect the very God who stretches our imagination in every direction. Here are two passages worth considering for your philosophy of Christian education:

> What no eye has seen,
> what no ear has heard,
> and what no human mind has conceived
> the things God has prepared for those
> who love him
>   —1 Corinthians 2:9

> I have become all things to all men, that
> I may by all means save some.
>   —1 Corinthians 9:22

If our curriculum reveals an amazing God in both his written documents and created order, shouldn't our methods match the message?

Students and Teachers

In one sense, Christian education through the church offers a "Y'all come" as we say in Texas. There is no age, gender, or ethnic boundary. Jesus clearly welcomed women in his educational experiences; he specifically invited little children to be in his presence; and his mandate envisions all nations. In essence, everyone receives an invitation to become a student of Jesus. The church, unlike schools, accepts people in their "come as you are" condition. It is quite obvious how this multiplies the educational challenges.

At 6:30 on Tuesdays, I meet with a group of men in our church. When we started, one said he had not read a book since high school. Another said he did not know "Ezekiel" was a book in the Bible. We are learning to read a passage more than once, answer the six basic questions (who, what, where, when, why, and wherefore), and even find the verb in each sentence. Now, finding verbs was a real "hoot." "How long has it been since you looked for a verb?" I asked. Blank stares confronted me. Maybe in high school? Maybe never? Well, you get my point. Christian education begins where students are.

In addition to students' wide range of readiness, we face the variety of spiritual conditions mentioned in 1 Corinthians 2: the natural man, the "baby" man, the spiritual man, and the carnal man.[24] The carnal man operates from the same perspective as the natural man, ignoring the prompting of the Holy Spirit. The "baby" man is just learning how to respond to the basics of the faith and the prompts of the Spirit. I personally have "been there, done that" as I came to faith at the University of North Texas reading the "Van Dusen letter" alone in my room.[25] Of course the spiritual man welcomes the full operation of the Holy Spirit to activate his spiritual gift to serve others, convict his defective conscience, provide a moral guide for decisions, and produce lovely fruit within that blesses others without.

The Holy Spirit truly represents the "X" factor in our philosophy of Christian education. He continues to operate within students long after lessons have concluded. Given the common meeting times of once or twice a week, Christian education in churches represents a "slow drip" approach. When compared to six or seven hours a day, five days a week in primary or secondary education, the time invested seems like a pittance. But for students whose hearts are tender, the educational force of the Holy Spirit brings a persistent urge to change. The public sector has nothing comparable to offer their students.

As teachers, the original apostles represented non-professionals. Their wide-ranging occupational backgrounds enabled them to relate well with the masses that followed Jesus. (I have often said, "Jesus loved fishermen more because 1/3 of his original choices were fishermen! That helped me justify my lifelong passion to fish.) By modern standards, these men were woefully (or perhaps wonderfully) unprepared for the educational task confronting them in the Great Commission.

Historically, the Sunday school (the largest single Christian education program) started on similar footing, only with mothers teaching children in their kitchens. The Sunday school movement grew from ninety students to 250,000 in just three years. By comparison, it took the Methodist denomination fifty years to grow to 50,000.[26] Of course we must remember that the lady teachers were paid approximately twenty-five cents per day of teaching. I am sure that explains why the Sunday school movement succeeded so quickly.

Whether we examine the birth of the church in the early years or her expansion in recent times, the Holy Spirit continues to raise up teachers to strengthen the church. Four passages in the New Testament mention the gifts of the Holy Spirit (Rom. 12, 1 Cor. 12, Eph. 4, and 1 Peter 4). Not everyone who ends up in a teaching position has the spiritual gift. In my opinion, that gift has three markers: a love for study, a clarity of presentation, and a love for students. My counsel to you? Let others tell you whether you have the gift or not.

Lest someone should inadvertently assume that only the few and the gifted should engage in this task, Paul invites older women and older men to assume rightful places of teaching those younger than themselves. Hebrews 5 calls out laggards who should all be teachers by now but must enter a remedial form of Christian education beginning with the elementary milk of the Word. Notice how these passages assume an eerie silence on the spiritual gift of teaching. Those who assume the office of teacher without the gift may be like those of us who are called upon to give to the Lord's work without the gift of giving. The Holy Spirit works with those teachers too, just not in the same way. Anyone entering the office with or without the gift ought to heed James's warning: "Let not many *of you* become teachers, my brethren, knowing that as such we shall incur a stricter judgment" (James 3:1, NASB).

Rest assured, the Holy Spirit still raises up gifted teachers. I have met some of the young ones in various parts of the world. I have watched their eyes flash with an eagerness to learn the words of God. I have listened as their hearts ache to reach friends and neighbors with God's teaching. Their spirit-emboldened eagerness to express clearly the truth of God blesses me every single time.

> "As such, education is seen as an integrated part of the congregation's life, occurring through participation with the community's life and as a distinct ministry, providing intentional instruction in the faith."[27]
> —James Estep, Greg Allison, and Michael Anthony

Conclusion

The church provides the operational side of our philosophy of Christian education. Philosophies per se offer nothing more than words on paper without the means to activate them. The Church is God's consistently central means of Christian education.

If we embrace Christ's educational mandate, then we take people from where they are to where they need to be: Student followers of Jesus Christ who love God and serve others fervently. Christian education is no more and no less than Jesus's transportable, educational, international, incarnational, doctrinal, transformational, universal, command.

When "Christian" touches anything in education everything changes primarily because the Holy Spirit is now involved. Anyone who seriously represents him or herself as involved in Christian education must carefully discover how the Spirit affects every aspect of their endeavor. Christian education is not just fancy tools, children's entertainment, or a cupcake. Christian education is the King's business. We best think carefully about how everything fulfills his expectations and represent him accurately.

Discussion Questions

1. What comes to mind when you hear the term "Christian education"?

2. How important is "the teaching ministry of the church" where you worship now or where you have worshipped in the past?

3. What do you think constitutes a true comprehensive approach to educating Christians?

4. What do you learn from Matthew 28:19–20 about Christ's approach to educating Christians? How does his timeless command change your view of teaching and learning in the church?

5. Why is teaching as Jesus commanded impossible in our human strength? How can you become the kind of teaching minister who pleases Jesus?

Resources for Further Study

Anthony, Michael and Warren S. Benson. *Exploring the History and Philosophy of Christian Education*. Eugene, OR: Wipf and Stock, 2011.

Gaebelein, Frank. *The Pattern of God's Truth: The Integration of Faith and Learning*. Winona Lake, IN: BMH, 1985.

Knight, George. *Philosophy and Education: An Introduction in Christian Perspective*, 4th ed. Berrien Springs, MI: Andrews University Press, 2006.

Lawson, Michael and Robert J. Choun. *Directing Christian Education*. Chicago: Moody Press, 1992.

LeBar, Lois. *Education That Is Christian*. New ed. Colorado Springs: David C. Cook, 1998.

Lockerbie, Bruce. *A Passion for Learning*. 2nd ed. Colorado Springs: Powerful Design, 2007.

Author Bio

Dr. Michael S. Lawson is Senior Professor of Educational Ministries and Leadership at Dallas Theological Seminary and Coordinator of the Doctor of Educational Ministries Degree. At Dallas Seminary, he teaches doctoral cohorts in Family Ministry and Academic Ministry. For more than thirty years, he has conducted faculty development seminars and taught courses for Christian Colleges and Seminaries in North America, Europe, Africa, Central America, Eastern Europe, Asia, and the Middle East.

Endnotes

1.   Gordon Clark, *A Christian Philosophy of Education* (Jefferson, MD: The Trinity Foundation 1988), 176.

2.   The apparent view of a seminary academic dean who interviewed me for a teaching position in his school. For an excellent treatment of a philosophy of Christian education for schools see D. Bruce Lockerbie, *A Passion for Learning* (Chicago: Moody Press, 1994), 13–19.

3.   A conversation between Dr. Howard G. Hendricks and a colleague at Dallas Theological Seminary who "wanted a few tricks to spice up his lectures."

4.   Kenneth Gangel and Jim Wilhoit, eds, *The Christian Educator's Handbook on Adult Education* (Grand Rapids: Baker Book House, 1993).

5.   See Acts 7 as a summary of Israel's failure.

6.   See my reference for this participle in the next section.

7.   Michael Lawson and Robert Choun, *Directing Christian Education: The Changing Role of the Christian Education Specialist* (Chicago: Moody Press, 1992).

8.   In the NIV, "Go" is an imperative. However, "go" in the Greek text is a participle properly translated "going." For an explanation about why "go" is an acceptable translation, see Ron Blue, "Go, Missions," *Bibliotheca Sacra* 141 (Oct-Dec 1984): 341–53.

9.   United Bible Societies, "Christianity in the land of Genghis Khan," https://www.unitedbiblesocieties.org/christianity-land-genghis-khan/.

10. Wycliffe, "Why Bible Translation," https://www.wycliffe.org/about/why.

11. Electa Draper, "Bible Translators Hope to Have Every Language Covered in 15 Years," *The Denver Post*, June 21, 2010, http://www.denverpost.com/headlines/ci_15346948.

12. Perhaps the most glaring exception came while a student of and colleague with Dr. Howard G. Hendricks. He planned and delivered each and every lesson with energy and passion. I have known many wonderful people but none like him as an educator. See the chapter "What Makes a Great Teacher?" by Bill Hendricks for more on the life of Howard Hendricks. Also see http://www.talbot.edu/ce20/educators/protestant/ howard_hendricks.

13. Herman Harrell Horne, *Jesus the Master Teacher* (New York: Association Press, 1920).

14. I feel a tiny bit vindicated when Mark says "every creature" but am still embarrassed that I did not take "nation" seriously.

15. Kenneth Scott Latourette, *A History of Christianity Volume 1* (San Francisco: Harper, 1953), 79, 91.

16. Andrew Walls takes a very thoughtful approach to Christian expansion in his work *The Missionary Movement through Christian History: Studies in the Transmission of Faith* (New York: Orbis Books, 1996), 37–40. His whole volume is highly recommended reading.

17. Of course, many individuals in these countries do not follow the faith that is officially recognized by the state. But a Christian presence permeates the society. Walls identifies that as the first step toward discipling nations.

18. What if by November 1, 33 AD, the disciples had reached every man, woman, and child with the gospel? By November 2, a whole group of pagans would have been born needing both the gospel and the disciple-making process Jesus commissioned.

19. Frank Gaebelein, *The Pattern of God's Truth: The Integration of Faith and Learning* (Winona Lake, IN: BMH, 1985).

20.   Roy Zuck offers a comprehensive review of all the Holy Spirit's work as it relates to teaching in his book *The Holy Spirit in Your Teaching* (Wheaton, IL: Scripture Press, 1984).

21.   Latourette, *A History of Christianity Volume 1*, 307.

22.   The *Serendipity Bible* records ninety-six major stories. Lyman Coleman, ed., *The Serendipity Bible for Groups* (Littleton, CO: Serendipity House Publishers, 1988).

23.   The created order forms the other portion of God's revelation of himself. For a discussion of how theology emphasizes the written portion while ignoring the created portion see Carisa Ash, *A Critical Examination of the Doctrine of Revelation in Evangelical Theology* (Eugene, OR: Pickwick Publications, 2015).

24.   By using "man" here, it is intended for all people, male and female. For a full discussion of these categories of people see Lewis Sperry Chafer, *He That Is Spiritual* (Grand Rapids: Zondervan, 1967).

25.   The "Van Dusen letter" was the precursor to the "Four Spiritual Laws" booklet published by Cru (Campus Crusade for Christ). I still hand them out. This letter is now published as *The Great Adventure* by Bill Bright (Peachtree City, GA: New Life Publications, 1993).

26.   Wes Willis, *200+ Years and Still Counting: Past, Present and Future of the Sunday School* (Wheaton, IL: Victor Books, 1979).

27.   James Estep, Greg Allison, and Michael Anthony, *Theology for Christian Education* (Nashville, TN: B&H Publishing, 2008).

Chapter 3
THE HEART OF MAKING DISCIPLES

Mark Heinemann

When they had preached the gospel to that city and had made many disciples, they returned to Lystra and to Iconium and to Antioch, strengthening the souls of the disciples, encouraging them to continue in the faith, and saying that through many tribulations we must enter the kingdom of God.

—Acts 14:21–22, ESV

I REMEMBER THE EMPTY days and years prior to putting my trust in Jesus as my Savior. Life was busy but meaningless. While taking summer school I met a group of Christians. We joked around a lot and I spent more and more time with them. We ate together several times a week. I secretly wished for the contentment and peace I saw in them.

One of the people I got to know in their group was a small guy I'll call Mickey. He had severe heart problems that limited his growth and projected life span. But he didn't seem to be worried. Mickey's sense of humor was amazing and he kept us laughing. I wondered how he did it. With time I learned he and the others (including a young woman who would later become my wife) were disciples who knew how to make disciples. Their priorities put Jesus first in very practical ways. I sensed they cared about me and we discussed important life issues—including the gospel. I read the New Testament in a modern translation. After a few weeks, I put my trust in Jesus. God has since changed my life in many ways.

Fast forward many years and now I teach classes on making disciples at a Christian seminary. On the first day of my first class I discovered that many of the students had previous exposure to something they called *discipleship*—in a church youth group, at a retreat, during a Christian summer camp, on an overseas ministry trip, as part of a parachurch group in college, in an intensive ministry internship, and so on. But the discussion at our first meeting revealed that their understanding of the concept, based on their past experience, varied greatly from student to student.

Those for whom a given "discipleship" approach had been somehow transformative intensely and loyally argued for the methods, structure, books, goals, etc. of the process they had experienced. Some promoted their particular understanding of doing "discipleship" like avid sports fans. "Have you heard Dr. A in person? She's amazing! You haven't read Dr. B's book? Listen, he knocked it out of the park!" On the other hand, some were openly critical about other "inferior" ways of making disciples.

> "Keep in mind, discipling among gospel-believers doesn't mean you as the discipler always play the wise one, or that you must be a fount of Socrates-like wisdom with all the answers. Discipling in the gospel means that sometimes you lead the way in confessing weakness or sin. By doing so, you demonstrate what it looks like not to find your justification in yourself, but in Christ. "[1]
> —Mark Dever

I confess I have occasionally been sinfully proud of "my" discipleship approach and disdainful of other groups. This chapter is meant to help us abandon comparison games and get back to the biblical basics. I'll use the following well-known set of six one-word questions to give some structure to the concept of disciple-making: who, what, where, when, why, and how? Readers should see these questions as generally aiding understanding, not as constructing immovable divisions within the concept of disciple-making.[2]

The Who of Disciple-Making

The Master

In Christian disciple-making, everything begins and ends with the Master, Jesus Christ. His "Great Commission" (Matt. 28:18–20) made this clear: "Then Jesus came to them and said, 'All authority in heaven and on earth has been given to me. Therefore go and make disciples of all nations, baptizing them in the name of the Father and of the Son and of the Holy Spirit, and teaching them to obey everything I have commanded you. And surely I am with you always, to the very end of the age.'"

Jesus urged his followers to 1) go; 2) make disciples of all nations; 3) baptize these new disciples in the name of the Trinity; and 4) teach them to obey all of Jesus's commands. He ended his brief charge with a promise of his presence with them "to the very end of the age." Clearly, our disciple-making efforts should center on Jesus.

We should exclaim with the author of Hebrews, "Let us fix our eyes on Jesus, the author and perfecter of our faith" (12:2a, NIV1984). But the truth is we sometimes lose the focal point of Christian disciple-making. In his letter to the Philippians Paul's comments showed this shift is not a new problem: "For everyone looks out for his own interests, not those of Jesus Christ" (2:21). In the next chapter of Philippians Paul appealed to his readers to follow his example of keeping the focus on Christ: "But whatever was to my profit I now consider loss for the sake of Christ. What is more, I consider everything a loss compared to the surpassing greatness of knowing Christ Jesus my Lord" (Phil. 3:7–8a, NIV1984).

How can we keep Christ at the center of our disciple-making? Here are some suggestions. First, emphasize from the beginning that the leader's role (in the duo, trio, small group, etc.) is to facilitate faith and growth in Christ, not to have all the answers. Resist the tendency for the leader to become the "know-it-all" in residence, because this easily leads participants to think of the *leader* as the Master (see Matt. 23:8–12).

> "As we become more like Jesus, we reach out. As we reach out, we become more like Jesus."[3]
> —Robert Logan and Charles Ridley

Second, to the extent possible and appropriate, open the Scriptures every time you meet. This is a crucial part of the group living out its dependence on Jesus.

Third, pray together often. To the extent possible, replace "I'll pray for you" with "Let's lift that up to the Lord right now." Again, this is how a person dependent on Jesus lives.

Fourth, don't pray just for the personal concerns of the participants. Pray also for the concerns of Christ, especially those related to making disciples. Ask: Where do we see the Holy Spirit already working?[4] What dangers or opportunities for Christianity exist in our community?

Fifth, continually look for opportunities to serve other disciples in practical ways as they journey toward spiritual maturity.

Sixth, regularly study the life of Jesus from one of the Gospels. Always answer the question "What does this mean for *our* lives as disciples of Jesus?" Disciples personally relate to Jesus, not to a book or set of rules. We pray to a *person*, we trust a *person*, we worship a *person*, we love a *person*, and we obey a *person*. Our love for Jesus must mean more than a commitment to the *concept* of a sacrificing Savior. It must also include a *personal relationship* with the living Christ, who promised to be with his followers to the end of the age (Matt. 28:20). This change of perspective will change our faith walk!

The Disciples

Μαθητής (disciple) is used 261 times in the New Testament, but is found only in the Gospels and Acts.[5] The word is found in Classical and Greco-Roman literature from Herodotus (fifth century BC) onward, where it was used to describe either a *learner*, an *adherent* to a master, or a *pupil*.[6] By the late Hellenistic period, the majority of uses of "disciple" referred to adherence to a great master, with "the type of adherence [to be] determined by the master himself."[7]

Jesus used the existing concept of "disciple" in that sense and clearly defined the type of adherence required. John 6 gives us a good example of this usage with some would-be disciples in Capernaum. After Jesus healed the sick man at the pool of Bethsaida (John 5:1–14), he explained the power and authority connected with his divine sonship and then listed reliable witnesses to the truth of what he had said: the witness of his works, the witness of John the Baptist, the witness of the Father, and the witness of the Scriptures (5:31–40).

Many who saw the healing at Bethsaida hoped to see more miracles, so a large crowd followed him to the other side of the Sea of Galilee. There Jesus miraculously fed more than five thousand people using only five loaves and two fishes. Amazed by this, the people determined to make him their king by force. Jesus gave the crowd the slip but they soon found him in Capernaum.

At this point Jesus launched into a discourse calculated to "weed out" counterfeit disciples. He explained that he had not come to pass out free bread, but rather to offer himself as the spiritual "bread of life." When Jesus asserted that he had come down from heaven to do the Father's will, his listeners began to grumble. He repeated his comments and added: "I am the living bread that came down from heaven. Whoever eats of this bread will live forever. This bread is my flesh, which I will give for the life of the world" (John 6:51). At this, the listeners began to argue about the meaning of these words. In response, Jesus asserted that his hearers must feed on his flesh and blood. Some of his "disciples" complained, "This is a hard teaching. Who can accept it?" John records: "From this time many of his disciples turned back and no longer followed him" (John 6:60–66).

How could disciples of Jesus stop following him? D. A. Carson offers this insight:

> [Just] as there is faith and faith (2:23–25), so are there disciples and disciples. At the most elementary level, a disciple is someone who is at that point following Jesus, either literally by joining the group

that pursued him from place to place, or metaphorically in regarding him as the authoritative teacher. Such a "disciple" is not necessarily a "Christian".... Jesus will make it clear in due course that only those who *continue* in his word are *truly* his "disciples" (8:31). The "disciples" described here do not remain in his word; they find it to be hard teaching…and wonder who can accept it…. These "disciples" will not long remain disciples, because they find Jesus's words intolerable. (original italics)[8]

A model from the 1970s, known as the *Engel Scale*, is a good visual help in sorting out discipleship terminology (see Figure 3.1). The columns (in this adaptation, moving from bottom to top) are meant to represent a simplified and idealized picture of a person's spiritual journey.

> "Picture yourself having lunch with the Lord today. Just imagine that he invited you to join him, and as you sit across from him at that table set for two, he slides a piece of paper toward you. Imagine him looking into your eyes and saying, 'I know you love me more than anybody else in your life. I know this because of your actions and your attitudes. Here—I've made a list of all the ways you show that I am your highest priority.' *Your eyes fall to the slip of paper he's pushing toward you. And now I ask you: **What's on the list?**"[9]
> —Mark Bailey

Figure 3.1 Engel Scale[10]

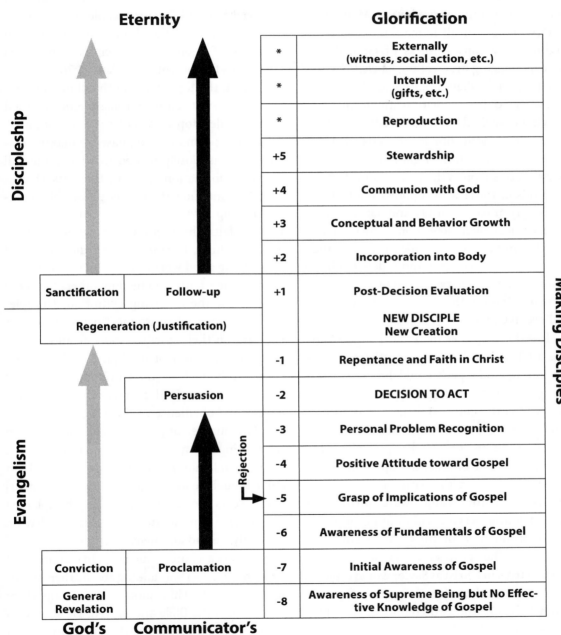

The rationale behind the arrangement of terms in the *Engel Scale* comes from the Great Commission mentioned previously (Matt. 28:16–20). First, note that all humankind starts with a rudimentary consciousness of God, derived from experiencing his creation, labeled "General Revelation" in the diagram. At a number of junctures, when confronted with truth gleaned from observing what God has made, reading the Bible, etc., people are faced with decisions [labeled "DECISION TO ACT" in the right hand column] to either seek or suppress the truth (Rom. 1:18–32). The minds of those who suppress the truth are increasingly mired in futility and darkness (seen by the vertical label "Rejection" which shows a regression from -2 to -5), while the lives of those who, by God's grace, seek and follow truth will be more and more characterized by purpose and light (Rom. 2:3–11). Thankfully, God allows some to believe in Christ.

How do the pieces fit? First, I suggest anything a Christian does to help others successfully follow God's path could be classified as *making disciples* (see right side of scale—the entirety of both columns). Whether as an individual or as a group, whether in a formal class or informal discussion, the disciplemaker's task is always a matter of seeking opportunities for helping others along the path, beginning with salvation, then progressing toward spiritual maturity, including service and multiplication (labeled "reproduction" on the scale—2 Tim. 2:2).

Second, the process of helping a non-Christian trust in Christ as Savior would typically be called *evangelism* (see left side of scale—bottom halves of the two columns). Acts 14:21 records that Paul and Barnabas went to Derbe and after preaching the gospel there "made many disciples." Evangelism is the first of two phases of making disciples. Of course, this is not all Paul and Barnabas did: "So for a whole year Barnabas and Saul met with the church and taught great numbers of people. The disciples were called Christians first at Antioch" (Acts 11:26b).

Third, the top half of both columns corresponds to what many call *discipleship* (see left side of scale—top halves of the two columns). This is the second of two phases of making disciples and is closely related to what some call "spiritual formation."[11] As in the Acts 11 passage just mentioned, in this phase fellow believers help new or immature Christians grow in their faith through receiving good teaching and preaching, learning to use their spiritual gifts, doing good works for Christ's sake, boldly sharing their faith, and helping others to do the same. I use the following definition: Disciple-making occurs when we meet people wherever they are on their spiritual journey and do our best, by the power of the Spirit, to help them successfully navigate the Christian walk (trust in Christ, be baptized, increase in their knowledge of and obedience to God's word, etc.).

Any number of people might participate in the making of any given disciple. For example, a young man I know heard the gospel preached as a child, though he was not brought up in a religious home. Years later a colleague at his job explained the gospel to him. He trusted in Jesus as his Savior. Suddenly, he had an intense interest in the Bible. He went to a church, but he didn't understand what the preacher was talking about. Then his co-worker friend told him about a men's group where they studied the Bible and prayed. He started to grow in his faith. He married a Christian woman and they started attending a good church and joined an adult study group. A good number of Christian individuals and groups helped this man on his journey from darkness to light.

The Enemy

The Bible makes more than two hundred references to Satan (also known as the devil, the tempter, Lucifer, etc.) and his evil helpers. These references come primarily from statements by Jesus (Luke 10:18—"I saw Satan fall"), Peter (1 Peter 5:8—"your enemy the devil prowls around"), and Paul (Eph. 6:11—"take your stand against the devil's schemes"). Unfortunately, many of our contemporaries reject the Bible's teaching on the supernatural, including Satan and evil spirits.

The biblical record of diabolical opposition to God and his people goes back at least to the garden of Eden and continues up to the present. Disciple-makers must take this threat seriously and prepare for battle, starting with an awareness of the various aspects of the enemy's *anti-disciple-making campaign*. This is briefly summarized in the following paragraphs.

Temptation

Since the beginning, the enemy has sought to tempt humans to sin. Not every temptation comes directly from the devil himself, of course. Demons tempt us (1 Tim. 4:1), as do our own sinful desires (James 1:14), and the world around us (James 2:27).

God has made provision for us to resist temptation. One of the most stunning promises in the Bible (1 Cor. 10:13b) relates to this: "God is faithful; he will not let you be tempted beyond what you can bear. But when you are tempted, he will also *provide a way out* so that you can stand up under it." In addition, Luke

records that Jesus twice advised his disciples in Gethsemane to *pray* so that they wouldn't fall into temptation (Luke 22:40, 46). Furthermore, Jesus demonstrated the power of *God's Word* against temptation when "the tempter" tried three times to lure Jesus into sin after the Savior had just finished fasting forty days and nights in the desert. Jesus's only response to the enemy was to quote appropriate Scriptures—"…it is written…"—and the devil left him.

Deception

Jesus called the devil "a liar and the father of lies" (John 8:44b). A priority for the enemy's evil campaign is to fool humans into thinking that there is no invisible realm in life. Satan works hard to convince even Christians that their struggle against sin only involves the world and other human sinners (Eph. 6:12).

One of the subtlest maneuvers of the enemy concerns his efforts to encourage us to break the first commandment, "You shall have no other gods before me" (Exod. 20:3). These false gods include, but are not limited to, idols and other cult objects. Timothy Keller rightly asserts, "Anything can serve as a counterfeit god, especially the very best things in life.… It is anything more important to you than God, anything that absorbs your heart and imagination more than God, anything you see to give you what only God can give."[12] Family, good health, safety, a good job, an enjoyable hobby, friends, entertainment, etc. are wonderful gifts of God … but they are horrible gods!

Disruption

God allows the enemy, in certain situations, the power to disrupt the life and ministry of individuals, groups, and the whole church. For example, he may cause us physical problems (Job; 2 Cor. 12:7–10), take God's Word from people's hearts (Mark 4:15), blind the minds of unbelievers (2 Cor. 4:4), or thwart the ministry plans of even his choicest servants (1 Thess. 2:18). Scripture also exposes other enemy inspired disruptions. The devil plants false "believers" amongst real ones (Matt. 13:39; Jude 4). He masquerades as an "angel of light" (2 Cor. 11:14). Scheming demons work hard to influence Christian teachers toward destructive false doctrines (Eph. 4:14; 1 Tim. 4:1; 2 Peter 2:1). One can see from these threats the importance of being prepared for spiritual battle as we go about making disciples (Eph. 6:10–18).

Intimidation

We have a powerful and intimidating foe, whom the archangel Michael did not dare accuse. Instead he said "The Lord rebuke you" (Jude 9). We would do well to show the same kind of restraint.

Of course, Satan has been defeated at the cross and the empty tomb, so we can serve Jesus without fear. We are specifically promised that the enemy cannot separate us from God's love (Rom. 8:35–39). The "shield of faith" is our special protection against the enemy's flaming arrows (Eph. 6:16). But we are human, and will naturally be afraid at times. Interestingly, no less a missionary than the apostle Paul twice asked the Ephesians to pray that he would be fearless in his proclamation of the gospel (Eph. 6:19–20).

Exploitation

The enemy looks for weaknesses to exploit—for example, people who are not alert and mindful of the spiritual danger around

them (1 Peter 5:8). Peter tells us to be on our guard (1 Peter 3:17). That means we habitually put on our armor (Eph. 6:13–18) and regularly check our lives for footholds that can be exploited by the enemy (Eph. 4:27). It is so easy for us to be blind to our own sins. Thus, our daily prayer should echo David's petition in Psalm 139:23–24: "Search me, God, and know my heart; test me and know my anxious thoughts. See if there is any offensive way in me, and lead me in the way everlasting."

Subjugation

Habitual sins can result in a downward spiral that serves the enemy's purposes in his quest to subjugate people. Paul warns against "godless chatter" because "those who indulge in it will become *more and more ungodly*" (2 Tim. 2:16). In 1 Timothy 6:9, Paul writes about the danger of greed: "Those who want to get rich fall into temptation and a trap and into many foolish and harmful desires that plunge people into ruin and destruction." Any sin can become a destructive habit and the enemy works hard to encourage that process.

The Human Facilitators

If the church is to make disciples, someone must exercise leadership. But the key issue is the *kind* of leadership. If our purpose is to help people come to faith and grow spiritually, then it stands to reason disciple-makers (especially those in a leadership role) should be progressing in the following areas.

Learning from and Living by God's Word

In the first chapter of his gospel, John identifies Christ as the Word of God incarnate.

Though we struggle to understand this, it seems reasonable to conclude that keeping the Word of God at the center of our disciple-making is essential to keeping Christ at the center of our disciple-making. Pause and think about that. What does that look like? Colossians 3:16 sums up some of the main aspects of discipleship centered on the Word: "Let the message of Christ dwell among you richly as you teach and admonish one another with all wisdom through psalms, hymns, and songs from the Spirit, singing to God with gratitude in your hearts." Let's look at that verse more closely.

"the message of Christ"—The idea here is to remember to link our teaching with Jesus's person, work, and message. This also applies to worship. Contemporary worship music can easily deteriorate into "feel-good" ballads that minimize the message of Christ. Our music should feature the Savior and his Word.

"dwell among you richly"—This message of Christ must live in or inhabit individuals and groups through which God wants to make disciples. The Gospel of Christ amongst Christians must dwell richly and fully, not sparsely and partially. It is "at home" in and among disciple-makers. Talking and singing about Jesus and the Word of God is typical, not exceptional, for them.

"as you teach and admonish one another with all wisdom"—Clearly, Paul is not describing a "club" where everyone tells you what you want to hear. Good teaching and effective admonishing will challenge the participants to repentance and transformation. At the same time,

this teaching and learning must be done carefully, with wisdom, rather than with anger, mixed motives, hypocrisy, harshness, and so on (James 3:17).

"through psalms, hymns, and songs from the Spirit, singing to God with gratitude in your hearts"—Dunn believes that these final two phrases round out a description of Christian worship.[13] Another possible interpretation is that the teaching and admonition took place "through" or "by means of" the singing. When our daughters were little, our church introduced us to recordings of kids' music that taught Scripture and doctrine through songs. They were well done and before long, I believe everyone in the family could sing along. In a similar way, hymns and choruses I sang in church, at retreats, and at Christian meetings have remained in my memory. Not only the melodies but the teachings stuck and I have included this music countless times in personal and family prayer.

Motivated by an Unselfish Heart

A striking example of making disciples with an unselfish heart is found in 1 Thessalonians 2:1–12:

> You know, brothers and sisters, that our visit to you was not without results. We had previously suffered and been treated outrageously in Philippi, as you know, but with the help of our God we dared to tell you his gospel in the face of strong opposition. For the appeal we make does not spring from error or impure motives, nor are we trying to trick you. On the contrary,

we speak as those approved by God to be entrusted with the gospel. We are not trying to please people but God, who tests our hearts. You know we never used flattery, nor did we put on a mask to cover up greed—God is our witness. We were not looking for praise from people, not from you or anyone else, even though as apostles of Christ we could have. Instead, we were gentle among you. Just as a nursing mother cares for her children, so we cared for you. Because we loved you so much, we were delighted to share with you not only the gospel of God but our lives as well. Surely you remember, brothers and sisters, our toil and hardship; we worked night and day in order not to be a burden to anyone while we preached the gospel of God to you. You are witnesses, and so is God, of how holy, righteous and blameless we were among you who believed. For you know that we dealt with each of you as a father deals with his own children, encouraging, comforting and urging you to live lives worthy of God, who calls you into his kingdom and glory.

One way to see the contrast between the "unselfish heart" (the good ministry of Paul, Silas, and Timothy described above) and the "selfish heart" (the opposite, which Paul warns against) is to list the elements of both in corresponding columns, inferring the opposite characteristic when it is not directly stated (see Figure 3.2).

"Take a quick look at the Five Contexts, remembering that the following is more descriptive than prescriptive:

- The Public Context exists where people gather in a large group (70+) around a shared outside resource (event, concert, speaker, etc.). In this environment the focus is on engaging with the outside resource rather than building relational depth with others.

- The Social Context has a range of 20–70 people where we build neighborly relations, we identify people we'd like to get to know better, and we reveal elements of our identity and journey.

- The Personal Context involves groups of 4–12, where we feel safe sharing private information about thoughts, feelings, and relationships. The members have built a genuine depth of friendship.

- The Transparent Context involves a group of 2–4 people. Ideally, complete honesty and candor characterizes the relationships and communication at this depth of human interaction.

- The Divine Context represents God's encounters with us as individuals. We delude ourselves if we believe we can hide anything from the Lord in some secret inner place. In this context we come face-to-face with our true selves as reflected in the loving eyes of our heavenly father."[14]

—Bobby Harrington and
Alex Absalom

Figure 3.2 Unselfish vs. Selfish Heart Disciple-Making

"Unselfish Heart" Disciple-Making	"Selfish Heart" Disciple-Making
Faced strong opposition to the gospel for the Thessalonians' sake	Compromised the gospel in the face of resistance
Based appeal on truth	Appeal based on false teaching
Didn't try to trick Thessalonians	Appeal based on trickery
Made appeal with pure motives	Did not make appeal out of pure motives
God approved them to be entrusted with the gospel	God did not approve or entrust them with the gospel
Never used flattery	Used flattery
Weren't secretly greedy	Concealed secret greed
Didn't look for praise from people	Looked for praise from people
Were gentle	Were harsh
Cared for people like a nursing mother cares for her children	Didn't care for the people
Loved so much, shared life as well as gospel	Shared the minimum, not their lives
Worked hard under difficult conditions 24/7 in order not to be a burden	Burdened the people to whom they preached
Behaved righteously, with holiness, and blamelessly toward the believers	Their behavior toward the believers was unholy, unrighteous, and blameworthy
Like a loving father, encouraged, comforted, and urged toward lives worthy of God	Like a father who discouraged, ignored needs, and didn't urge toward godliness

A key aspect of the disciple-maker's unselfish heart is the need for love to guide the relationships between disciples. Once I was planning for a discipleship meeting when I became aware of anger down inside me because of the continuing critical attitude of one of the participants. As I sat there stewing over this, the words of Jesus from Matthew 5:44 came to mind, "love your enemies and pray for those who persecute you." I thought, "But this person's not an enemy." Then it occurred to me that, although this person wasn't the typical "bad guy," he opposed and criticized me at every turn. Thinking about this verse, I was motivated by the Lord to pray for this person's blessing and good.

What an amazing, transforming process began! After a short while, I was able to pray for this person's flourishing in every aspect of life and really mean it. God changed my heart and enabled me to love an enemy. Too easy? Believe me, I'm still in the learning process!

A Person Praying as a Way of Life

Disciple-makers need a lot of wisdom to answer the many questions that present themselves. When and where to meet? What portion of Scripture to study? What can be done when disciples travel for their work? Do the participants understand how small groups work? Do I? What exactly is the commitment we're asking? How could we serve Christ? Are any emotional problems hindering growth? If so, what can be done? These and many more questions arise in the course of disciple-making, and supernatural wisdom is needed. God offers this wisdom to those who ask with faith (James 1:5–8).

We also need to pray regularly for our fellow-disciples. This practice is not based on a ritual or rule but on the simple fact that no lasting fruit will result from our labors without constant dependence on God! When we become disciples, we join God's army to battle for souls. This is why John Piper reminds us:

> God has given us prayer because Jesus has given us a mission. We are on this earth to press back the forces of darkness, and we are given access to headquarters by prayer to advance this cause. When we try to turn it into a civilian intercom to increase our conveniences, it stops working, and our faith begins to falter. We have so domesticated prayer that for many of us it is no longer what it was designed to be—a wartime walkie-talkie for the accomplishment of Christ's mission.[15]

Taking on the Role of a Servant

Matthew 23:11–12 records Jesus's warnings to his disciples about self-exaltation: "The greatest among you will be your servant. For those who exalt themselves will be humbled, and those who humble themselves will be exalted." John records Jesus's washing of the disciple's feet, giving them a powerful and unforgettable demonstration of serving. Jesus explains, "Now that I, your Lord and Teacher, have washed your feet, you also should wash one another's feet. I have set you an example that you should do as I have done for you" (John 13:14–15).

Jesus's example of washing the disciple's feet reminds me of the messiness of disciple-making. Jesus came to call sinners to repentance, as he said in Mark 2:17b, "It is not the healthy who need a doctor, but the sick. I have not come to call the righteous, but sinners." Making disciples requires spending time with the spiritually sick. I remember a young man saying to me, "If you knew the kinds of things I've done, you wouldn't want to be near me." Tragically, he knew Bible verses like those just quoted above, but somehow couldn't believe his sins could be forgiven.

Some want to make disciples with no problems. It's easy to forget real people are sinners. The church may be like an army, but armies have field hospitals with servant-hearted people who work very hard to heal the sick and wounded. Some who have failed need to be graciously mentored in order to give them another chance, as Barnabas did with John Mark (Acts 15:36–39).

Learning to Flex and Follow God's Plan When It Differs from Our Own

In this world, disciple-makers need to maintain flexibility. The key to doing this is our view of God. Do we believe God is omniscient, good, wise, and sovereign? If so, then Proverbs 16:9 is good news: "In their hearts humans plan their course, but the LORD establishes their steps."

A moving account of flexibility in disciple-making comes out of the 1956 massacre in Ecuador of five young missionaries by the Auca Indians. They had heard stories about the "feared Indians who had never been tamed," and God gave the five twenty-somethings a burning desire to bring the Aucas to faith in Jesus. So they did extensive research and "made careful plans."

Then came the day for a more formal meeting of the two groups. One of the missionaries radioed his wife, "Pray for us. This is the day!" But it was not the day they had envisioned. All five were killed by the Aucas. For all the careful planning, they never even got past the beach.

Many asked, "Why these needless deaths?" But others, remembering God is all-knowing, good, wise, and sovereign, looked for the path of faith. They asked, "What is God doing?" and "How can I be a part of it?" The wives of the martyrs belonged to the second group.

One month after the deaths of the five young men, two of the widows went with their small children to live among the Indians. They remembered God's purpose despite the failure of the original plan and the loss of their husbands. Talk about flexibility and focus! All six of the actual killers eventually accepted Christ. Christian Aucas began to reach out to enemy tribes. Soon mission organizations were inundated with people applying to "take the place" of the martyrs. The flexible faith of the widows helped the Good News ripple outward—in articles, films, books, and especially in an increased army of indigenous and foreign missionaries, resulting in thousands of new disciples.[16]

Being Willing to Suffer for the Gospel

The story of the Aucas brings me to the issue of suffering in a disciple-maker's life. Dietrich Bonhoeffer saw it as an important and inevitable part of being a disciple in the service of Christ:

> Suffering, then, is the badge of true discipleship. The disciple is not above his master. Following Christ means *passio passiva* [passive suffering], suffering because we have to suffer. That is why Luther reckoned suffering among the marks of the true church.... If we refuse to take up our cross and submit to suffering and

rejection at the hands of men, we forfeit our fellowship with Christ and have ceased to follow him. But if we lose our lives in his service and carry our cross, we shall find our lives again in the fellowship of the cross with Christ.[17]

The What of Disciple-Making

Doing Evangelism

Some Christians think of discipleship as an inwardly focused project with no organic connection to evangelism. This is a serious mistake. As we saw previously, Matthew 28:16–20 presents evangelism and discipleship together as subphases in the overall disciple-making process. This chapter began with a brief look at that passage. Similar commands are found elsewhere, as seen in the following.

- Mark 16:15–16—"He said to them, 'Go into all the world and preach the gospel to all creation. Whoever believes and is baptized will be saved, but whoever does not believe will be condemned.'"
- Luke 24:46–48—"He told them, 'This is what is written: The Messiah will suffer and rise from the dead on the third day, and repentance for the forgiveness of sins will be preached in his name to all nations, beginning at Jerusalem. You are witnesses of these things.'"
- John 20:21—"Again Jesus said, 'Peace be with you! As the Father has sent me, I am sending you.'"
- Acts 1:8—"But you will receive power when the Holy Spirit comes on you; and you will be my witnesses in Jerusalem, and in all Judea and Samaria, and to the ends of the earth."

One can hardly miss the prominence of giving witness to the gospel in these passages. Clearly, the witness of our lives is not enough—words are needed.[18]

Two of these "commission" passages mention baptism. This should remind us of the public witness to faith in Christ, the solemnity of the participation of the Triune God, and the identification with other disciples, both in a local assembly and in a worldwide fellowship.

Teaching Them to Obey All That Christ Commanded

Every chapter of this book deals with some aspect of bringing the life of the church in line with Christ's teaching. This has a couple of implications for making disciples. The obvious first step in the process is to pass on to disciples the teachings of Jesus.[19] Second, Christ requires us to go beyond knowledge of his teachings to instructing disciples how to obey his teachings.[20] And finally, the community of disciples is crucial for the success of this project.[21]

The local church is the source of the ingredients needed for teaching obedience to Christ's commands. There are the parents, teachers, pastors, theologians, and evangelists. There are the ones who will encourage and hold new disciples accountable. At the church are one's fellow learners to bond with, pray for, and serve.

For the last four decades, "spiritual disciplines" have come to dominate discussions about spiritual growth. How do they fit in with learning to obey Christ's commands? Consider carefully these observations by Dallas Willard:

But more than anything—and most important for our goal of understanding the disciplines for the spiritual life—we must recognize that Jesus *was* a master of life in the spirit. He showed us that spiritual strength is not manifested by great and extensive practice of the spiritual disciplines, *but by little need to practice them and still maintain full spiritual life.* To have misunderstood this point was the fundamental and devastating error of Christian asceticism in the Western church from the desert fathers up to the time of the Reformation. Yet when we look closely and continually at Jesus, we do not lose sight of this one fundamental, crucial point—the activities constituting the disciplines *have no value in themselves.* The aim and substance of spiritual life is not fasting, prayer, hymn singing, frugal living, and so forth. Rather, it is the effective and full enjoyment of active love of God and humankind in all the daily rounds of normal existence where we are placed. The spiritually advanced person is not the one who engages in lots and lots of disciplines, any more than the good child is the one who receives lots and lots of instruction or punishment.

People who think that they are spiritually superior *because* they make a practice of a discipline such as fasting or silence or frugality are entirely missing the point. The need for extensive practice of a discipline is an indication of our *weakness*, not our strength. We can even lay it down as a rule of thumb that if it is *easy* for us to engage in a certain discipline, we probably don't need to practice it. The disciplines we need to practice are precisely the ones we are *not* "good at" and hence do not enjoy.[22]

Multiplying Disciples

The apostle Paul urged Timothy: "And the things you have heard me say in the presence of many witnesses entrust to reliable people who will also be qualified to teach others" (2 Tim. 2:2). The concept of multiplying God's family is obviously not a new one (see Figure 3.3). The ideal multiplier is not necessarily an accomplished theologian, but rather a faithful person, a person of character, and one who has the same message and strategy as those who helped make a disciple of him or her.[23]

In this connection Scott Morton admonishes us to "keep the third generation in mind":

What is the goal of one-to-one ministry? Is it to reach the second spiritual generation? … we cut the process short unless our mentorees are faithfully reaching and discipling the people in "their" world—the third spiritual generation … In John 17, Jesus's famous final prayer … shows a "both–and" combination that is often overlooked: "I ask on *their behalf*; I do not ask on behalf of the world, but of those whom You have given ME…I do not ask on behalf of these alone, but for those also who believe in Me *through their word*" (vv. 9, 20, emphasis added). Reaching the third generation was in his mind from the beginning.[24]

Figure 3.3 Multiplying Disciples

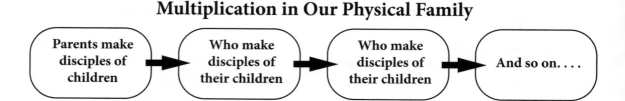

Multiplication in Our Physical Family

| Parents make disciples of children | → | Who make disciples of their children | → | Who make disciples of their children | → | And so on. . . . |

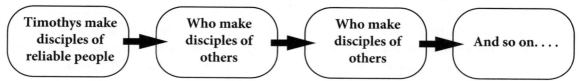

Multiplication in Our Spiritual Family

| Timothys make disciples of reliable people | → | Who make disciples of others | → | Who make disciples of others | → | And so on. . . . |

The When of Disciple-Making

The best time for disciple-making is now. Disciple-making is always appropriate. As Paul wrote in 2 Timothy 4:2, "Preach the word; be prepared in season and out of season; correct, rebuke and encourage—with great patience and careful instruction." This includes times when the Lord has clearly opened up an opportunity for the gospel to be communicated (2 Cor. 2:12), as well as those times when the disciple-maker faces strong opposition (1 Thess. 2:2).

This doesn't mean we should be passive. For example, at a church I pastored, our outward-focused ministry efforts seemed to lose steam, so we changed the Wednesday night prayer meeting into a time to pray for the salvation of the family, friends, neighbors, coworkers, etc. of the participants. Using first name only or initials, we made note cards that were updated and used for prayer every Wednesday. We began to notice God opening up opportunities for spiritual conversations with those for whom we prayed. Some of these came to faith in Jesus as Savior. We saw more results from these Wednesday night prayer meetings than any outreach program we'd ever had. I was reminded of the old saying: "Talk to God about people before you talk to people about God."

Deuteronomy 6:6–9 speaks to the when of disciple-making, especially as related to the family context:

These commandments that I give you today are to be on your hearts. Impress them on your children. Talk about them when you sit at home and when you walk along the road, when you lie down and when you get up. Tie them as symbols on your hands and bind them on your foreheads. Write them on the doorframes of your houses and on your gates.

The Where of Disciple-Making

The answer to where to make disciples is everywhere. Looking at Jesus's instructions about making disciples, one is struck with the all-encompassing words and phrases describing where disciples should be made: "Jerusalem, Judea, the uttermost parts of the earth"; "all nations, beginning at Jerusalem"; "into all the world"; and "all nations." There is no limit to the gospel enterprise, which has a centrifugal character, spreading further and further out from the starting point.[25]

> "If the leadership of our church said to me today, 'Randy, you have to choose between continuing in the pastorate as a preacher or discipling men life-on-life. You cannot do both,' I wouldn't think twice about it. I'd give up the pastorate. That's not because I don't love pastoring. I do. But I am keenly aware that discipleship has the greater kingdom impact."[26]
> —Randy Pope

Deuteronomy 6:4–9 not only addresses the when of disciple-making, but also the where. The passage contains four pairs of words which speak figuratively of the where of disciple-making, namely *everywhere*:

1. At home, along the road;
2. Lying down, getting up;
3. With the truth tied on one's hands (symbolic of doing?) and bound on one's forehead (thinking?);
4. Attached to the doorframes and gates.

Whereas the Deuteronomy 6 passage feels more private and spontaneous, Jesus and Paul also taught publicly (John 18:20; Acts 20:20). Both taught in synagogues and other places connected to religious or philosophical discussions (Mark 11:15–18; John 18–20; Acts 17:22).

We should note also that Jesus and Paul made disciples in the context of groups of all different sizes. Paul taught small gatherings from house to house (Acts 20:20), as well as great numbers of people (Acts 11:26). Jesus made a disciple of one woman (John 4:7–42), but he also taught the crowds (Matt. 5–7). The where of making disciples is very diverse.

The Why of Disciple-Making

Disciple-making is a command of God. As we've already seen, God has commanded us to spread the gospel to every corner of the earth. The power of the message, the gracious gift of forgiveness of sins and eternal salvation to all who trust in Jesus, should produce in us a sense of holy obligation, eagerness, and boldness to share the gospel (Rom. 1:14–16). Moo explains Paul's zeal to spread Christ's message:

> Paul's plan to have a harvest among the Roman Christians has its source not in a desire for personal aggrandizement but in his sense of missionary "obligation." Paul is deeply conscious of his calling, of his being "set apart for the gospel" (1:1), and it is this divine obligation to

use his gift (Eph. 3:8) that motivates Paul—"Woe to me if I do not preach the gospel!" (1 Cor. 9:16b).[27]

The How of Disciple-Making

By Studying the Scriptures Together

Years of sharing God's truth with others have produced in me the firm conviction that it is best presented directly from the Bible, regardless of which phase of disciple-making we are in. This approach reminds us of the authorship of the message and helps keep the conversation on track. It is, after all, Christ's *message* people must believe in order to be saved.

All believers need instruction in how to read and study the Bible. This helps them learn to feed themselves from the Word, helps them evangelize from the Word, and helps them avoid false teaching because they have the means to assess it. Bible study methods should be the first study disciples make.

In this connection one always hears questions about a plan of study for disciples. Many options present themselves: study a book of the Bible, purchase a ready-to-use study from a denomination or independent publishing house, read a Christian book and discuss it (some have participant workbooks available), use an online program, etc. As you choose, be careful (1) that the lessons are short enough to cover in the allotted time (you may have to split the lessons or passage in half); (2) that you and your fellow-disciple(s) commit to do the study and attend faithfully for the weeks needed to complete it; and (3) that you are intentional in your choice of materials.[28]

The key in teaching is to think of interesting ways for a disciple to engage with the content of the lesson. In most cases lecturing is not a good solution! However, you will find help for this challenge in the rest of this book. The Teaching and Learning Grid in Figure 3.4 is a simple chart that can be used to plan a study sequence. I'm sure all of us have finished a study feeling that it was interesting, but a bit random in the context of where you are at the moment. The grid shows where you've been and where you're going. This is one way for you to keep from just choosing favorite topics based on personal preference rather than on real need.

"Symptoms of decreasing quality and impact of disciple-making small groups:

- Blurred vision: in many churches, the purpose of small groups is confused, with competing expectations for members and leaders.

- Sheep-pen mentality: small groups in many places have become a safe haven for pastoral care and community building…. These are not groups that purposefully and effectively move people … towards maturity in Christ.

- Deficient leadership: Small groups don't make disciples; disciples make disciples. If we give the leadership of small groups to people who are not learning Christ themselves, the group members will have no shepherd to follow."[29]

—Colin Marshall and Tony Payne

Figure 3.4 Teaching and Learning Grid

HEAD *What you need to know*	HEART *How your attitude needs to change*	HANDS *How your behavior needs to change*	
			In Your Relationship with Triune God
			In Your Relationship with God's People
			In Your Relationship to Yourself
			In Your Relationship to Family
			In Your Relationship to Humankind
			In Your Relationship to Visible Creation
			In Your Relationship to Invisible Creation

So, how does one use it? The column on the right shows a general list of the entities to which every person must relate. The head, heart, and hands row represents the traditional divisions of learning: change in knowledge, change of attitude, and behavioral change. For example, suppose you are working with an older person struggling with how to relate to kids, grandkids, siblings, and so on. You choose "In Your Relationship to Family" and find a book on the subject that gives insight on what an older person needs to *know* about family (head), what *attitudes* an older person needs with regard to family (heart), and what an older person needs to *do* in the constantly changing setting of their family (hands).

Most of the items in the right column are self-explanatory, but others are perhaps not, like "In Your Relationship to Yourself." It may surprise some that John Calvin's *Institutes of Christian Religion* begins with the sentence, "Our wisdom, in so far as it ought to be deemed true and solid wisdom, consists almost entirely of two parts: the knowledge of God and of ourselves."[30] Clearly, Calvin saw one's relationship to self as crucial.

Two other items need explanation. First, "Visible Creation" refers to all creation humans can see, other than themselves, namely sky, stars, bodies of water, dry land, animals, fish, etc.[31] Second, "Invisible Creation" refers to the unseen world: good and evil angels (including Satan and the demons), heaven and hell, etc.

By Praying with Each Other and for Others

The New Testament presents prayer in a very serious light. In First Thessalonians 3:10, Paul writes, "Night and day we pray most earnestly that we may see you again and supply what is lacking in your faith." Paul addresses the Ephesians in the most sweeping terms on the subject:

> And pray in the Spirit on all occasions with all kinds of prayers and requests. With this in mind, be alert and always keep on praying for all the Lord's people. Pray also for me, that whenever I speak, words may be given me so that I will fearlessly make known the mystery of the gospel, for which I am an ambassador in chains. Pray that I may declare it fearlessly, as I should (Eph. 6:18–20).

By Sharing Life Together

It's clear that the task of making disciples takes more than a single person. We need coworkers just like Paul did (Phil. 2:25; 4:3). Serving together offers opportunities to learn from each other, to pray for each other, to encourage one another, and so on.[32] Sharing meals together has always been a great way to get to know fellow believers. You want to spend time with a friend or get to know a stranger? Have a meal or cup of coffee together. Informal time together at a sports event, concert, or a museum can lead to some deep conversation. The sky's the limit here. I knew two men who used to regularly take a "field trip" to the hardware store Saturday morning just to hang out and talk.

If possible, attending church together is an ideal place to share life. You've always got something to discuss. You can join the same Sunday school class or small group. Of course, if you don't live reasonably close to each other or if you have significantly different backgrounds, the church may not help you to draw together. In such cases, it may be that your places of work are near each other and your sharing of life happens at breakfast or lunch.

By Practicing a Healthy Mutual Transparency and Accountability

James wrote a challenging word in James 5:16— "Therefore confess your sins to each other and pray for each other so that you may be healed. The prayer of a righteous person is powerful and effective." This verse is simultaneously one of the most difficult to practice and one of the most healing. When is the last time you confessed your sin to another Christian? When is the last time someone confessed their sin to you? We can be a safe person in another's life. But it takes time to build the mutual openness we're talking about here.[33] The goal is that God-seekers feel "safe" to be themselves. Bill Hull devotes a whole book chapter to this matter of building mutual openness through a "disciple-making environment" that includes trust, grace, humility, submission, and affirmation.[34]

Conclusion

Millions wake up every day in despair. They need redemption and a new life as disciples of Jesus. I remember a young man named Ken. He was like that, so full of hopelessness that he prayed something like this: "God help! If you don't, I'm going to commit suicide. I know you've got your people. Please send one!" Right then two strangers showed up and asked if they could join him at his café table. One said, "We didn't want to startle you, but you looked like you were in trouble." They asked Ken questions and eventually heard his story, which was very sad. They told him about Jesus offering forgiveness and hope and he grabbed God's grace like a drowning man—he became a disciple of Jesus. The two Christians, over time, helped Ken learn to read the Bible, to pray, and to pass on his faith to others—they discipled Ken. He didn't get a free ticket to a life without challenges, but he did experience forgiveness and freedom through Jesus Christ.

That's what making disciples is all about. God has already made the preparations for you to join him in the work, just like he did for those who introduced you to Jesus. Will you show up?

Discussion Questions

1. What kind of discipleship ministry, if any, transformed you into the kind of disciple you are today? Do you tend to promote that method as "the best" because it worked for you? Why do you think the author desires to "abandon comparison games and get back to biblical basics"?

2. According to the author, who and what should be at the core of any discipleship ministry? Do you agree or disagree? Why?

3. What must drive a disciple-maker's heart? What characteristics of this quality ooze from 1 Thessalonians 2:1–12? Which quality is most difficult for you to live out? Why?

4. Discuss the methods suggested by the author in the "how" section of the chapter. Which ones have you included in your discipleship ministry? Would you add anything to the author's suggestions?

5. What aspect of the chapter was particularly helpful to you? Why?

Resources for Further Study

Books

Adsit, Christopher B. *Personal Disciplemaking: A Step-by-Step Guide for Leading a Christian from New Birth to Maturity.* Orlando, FL: Campus Crusade for Christ, 1996.

Boice, James Montgomery. *Christ's Call to Discipleship.* Chicago: Moody Press, 1986.

Bowland, Terry A. *Make Disciples! Reaching the Postmodern World for Christ.* Joplin, MO: College Press, 1999.

Coleman, Robert E. *The Master Plan of Evangelism.* 2nd ed. Old Tappan, NJ: Fleming H. Revell, 1964.

Dodson, Jonathan K. *Gospel-Centered Discipleship.* Wheaton, IL: Crossway, 2012.

Hodges, Herb. *Tally Ho, The Fox!* 2nd ed. Memphis, TN: Spiritual Life Ministries, 2001.

Koessler, John. *True Discipleship: The Art of Following Jesus*. Chicago: Moody, 2003.

Malphurs, Aubrey. *Strategic Disciple Making: A Practical Tool for Successful Ministry*. Grand Rapids: Baker Books, 2009.

Ogden, Greg. *Transforming Discipleship: Making Disciples a Few at a Time*. Downers Grove, IL: InterVarsity Press, 2003.

Spader, Dann, and Gary Mayes. *Growing a Healthy Church*. Chicago: Moody, 1991.

Study Guides, Materials, etc.

The list below is meant to be suggestive and not comprehensive. A thorough Internet search should produce all the materials you need. The ministry of making disciples is very dynamic and is constantly producing new books and programs. Note that any program or study plan must be adapted to local people and conditions.

Some books have *separate* accompanying workbooks or guides
   e.g., John Koessler. *True Discipleship: A Companion Guide*. Chicago: Moody, 2003.

Some books *contain* a study guide at the end
   e.g., Dann Spader and Gary Mayes. *Growing a Healthy Church*. Chicago: Moody Press, 1991.

Some books contain a discipleship program *outline*
   e.g., Randy Pope and Kitti Murray. *Insourcing: Bringing Discipleship Back to the Local Church*. The Leadership Network Innovation Series. Grand Rapids: Zondervan, 2013.

Some publishers offer a *complete* program
   e.g., Navigators 2:7 Series (http://www.navigatorchurchministries.org)

Some books have *questions* for reflection and discussion for every chapter
   e.g., Aubrey Malphurs. *Strategic Disciple Making: A Practical Tool for Successful Ministry*. Grand Rapids: Baker Books, 2009.

Some books are step-by-step training *guides*
   e.g., Christopher B. Adsit. *Personal Disciplemaking: A Step-by-Step Guide for Leading a Christian from New Birth to Maturity*. Orlando, FL: Campus Crusade for Christ, 1996.

Websites

e.g., Replicate.org

Author Bio

Dr. Mark Heinemann and his family were missionaries with Greater Europe Mission for fifteen years, during which time he taught practical theology at the Freie Theologische Akademie in Germany and was a member of the mission's European field leadership team. He also has served as a pastor and as a staff member with Campus Crusade for Christ. Currently, he is Professor of Educational Ministries and Leadership at Dallas Theological Seminary. Dr. Heinemann's research and teaching interests include learning outcomes assessment, theological education, foundations of educational ministry, and discipleship.

Endnotes

1. Mark Dever, *Discipling: How to Help Others Follow Jesus.* 9Marks: Building Healthy Churches (Wheaton, IL: Crossway, 2016), 36.

2. The content of this chapter is meant to be broadly applicable to any discipleship context, whether one-on-one, small group, etc.

3. Robert Logan and Charles Ridley, *The Discipleship Difference: Making Disciples While Growing as Disciples* (Los Angeles, CA: Logan Leadership, 2015), 186.

4. Henry T. Blackaby and Claude V. King, *Experiencing God: How To Live the Full Adventure of Knowing and Doing the Will of God* (Nashville: Broadman and Holman, 1994), 73–82.

5. Paul R. Trebilco, *Self-Designations and Group Identity in the New Testament* (New York: Cambridge University Press, 2012), 208–209.

6. Michael J. Wilkins, *Discipleship in the Ancient World and Matthew's Gospel*, 2nd ed. (Grand Rapids: Baker, 1995), 11.

7. Ibid., 42, 217.

8. D. A. Carson, *The Gospel According to John* (Grand Rapids: Eerdmans, 1991), 300.

9. Mark Bailey. *To Follow Him: The Seven Marks of a Disciple* (Sisters, OR: Multnomah Publishers, 1997), 47–48.

10. Adapted from James Engel and Hugo W. Norton, *What's Gone Wrong with the Harvest? A Communication Strategy for the Church and World Evangelization* (Grand Rapids: Zondervan, 1975), 45.

11. Evan B. Howard, *The Brazos Introduction to Christian Spirituality* (Grand Rapids: Brazos Press, 2008), 267–289.

12. Timothy Keller, *Counterfeit Gods* (New York: Dutton, 2009), xix.

13. James D. G. Dunn, *The Epistles to the Colossians and to Philemon: A Commentary on the Greek Text* (Grand Rapids: Eerdmans, 1996), 235–241.

14. Bobby Harrington and Alex Absalom, *Discipleship that Fits: The Five Kinds of Relationships God Uses to Help Us Grow* (Grand Rapids: Zondervan, 2016), 52–53.

15. John Piper, *Let the Nations Be Glad! The Supremacy of God in Missions,* 3rd ed. (Grand Rapids: Baker, 2010), 41.

16. James and Marti Hefley, *By Their Blood*, 2nd ed. (Grand Rapids: Baker, 1996), 614–622.

17. Dietrich Bonhoeffer, *The Cost of Discipleship*, trans. R. H. Fuller (New York: Simon & Schuster, 1995), 100–101.

18. See the chapter "Curious: Not Yet Christians" by A.J. Rinaldi for further discussion of evangelism.

19. Michael Wilkins writes, "While Jesus bore some similarity to other Jewish masters of the first century, his distinctive teachings marked him off from the religious authorities of Israel (cf. Mt 7:28–29). Therefore, knowing Jesus's teachings would mark his disciples off from other kinds of followers.... But knowing these teachings was not enough. Jesus's disciples were called to 'obey' or 'observe' all that Jesus commanded (Mt 28:20)." Michael Wilkins, *Following the Master* (Grand Rapids: Zondervan, 1992), 274–275.

20. Ibid., 274–275.

21. Ibid., 275.

22. Dallas Willard, *The Spirit of the Disciplines* (San Francisco: HarperSanFrancisco, 1988), 137–139.

23. Bill Hull, *The Complete Book of Discipleship: On Being and Making Followers of Christ* (Colorado Springs: NavPress, 2006), 287–288.

24.   Adapted from Scott Morton, *Down to Earth Discipling: Essential Principles to Guide Your Personal Ministry* (Colorado Springs: NavPress, 2003), 109–110.

25.   George W. Peters, *A Biblical Theology of Missions* (Chicago: Moody Press, 1972), 21, 174.

26.   Randy Pope and Kitti Murray, *Insourcing: Bringing Discipleship Back to the Local Church* (Grand Rapids: Zondervan, 2013), 177.

27.   Douglas J. Moo, *The Epistle to the Romans* (Grand Rapids: Eerdmans, 1996), 61.

28.   Naturally, there isn't a good book or study out there for every subject. But don't write your own discipleship program unless you have to. Writing your own from scratch is much more difficult than one might think. A better idea, at least at first, would be to collect a set of relevant Scripture passages and study them week after week in a logical sequence.

29.   Colin Marshall and Tony Payne, *The Vine Project* (Sydney, Australia: Matthias Media, 2016), 348–349.

30.   John Calvin, *Institutes of the Christian Religion*, one-vol. ed. (Grand Rapids: Eerdmans, 1989), 37.

31.   In 1997, 700,000 square kilometers of debris was discovered in the North Pacific. Is this the kind of "rule over the fish of the sea" (Gen. 1:26–28) God had in mind when he made humankind in his own image? Should disciples be concerned about that? See scientificamerican.com.

32.   Also see the chapter "Facilitating Transformative Small Groups" by Joye Baker and the chapter "Mentoring the Next Generation" by Barbara Neumann for additional information and ideas.

33.   Again, see the chapters "Facilitating Transformative Small Groups" and "Mentoring the Next Generation" for additional information and ideas.

34.   Hull, *The Complete Book of Discipleship*, 155–162.

Chapter 4

THE INFLUENCE OF TECHNOLOGY ON EDUCATIONAL MINISTRY

John Dyer

The LORD said to Moses, "See, I have called by name Bezalel the son of Uri, son of Hur, of the tribe of Judah, and I have filled him with the Spirit of God, with ability and intelligence, with knowledge and all craftsmanship."

—Exodus 31:1–3, ESV

Though I have much to write to you, I would rather not use paper and ink. Instead I hope to come to you and talk face to face, so that our joy may be complete.

—2 John 1:12, ESV

IN 1928, LEWIS SPERRY Chafer, the founder of Dallas Theological Seminary, wrote to his protégé about a new teaching technology he had just recently encountered:

Here you will find a school where the teaching is centered around the Bible. Regarding our line of instruction, we have fearlessly adopted some 1928 methods of approach to vital subjects to take the place of outdated methods. We are not modernists in material, though we certainly are in method.[1]

Though written almost a century ago, Chafer's excitement about the potential of new technology to transform education doesn't sound terribly different from how we feel today when we see a promising new technology.

But if you've been around education long enough, you know that not every technology delivers on its promise. In fact, it sometimes seems as if technology is threatening to overtake education and distract our people from truly learning. And yet as frustrated as we can become with people distracted by their phones or companies peddling expensive but not terribly useful new tech, who can deny that today's paper and pens are better than the chalkboards of early colonial America? And who among us doesn't recognize that the Internet, warts and all, has opened up new learning opportunities that were impossible a few decades ago?

As technology rapidly evolves and educators and ministers face a dizzying array of choices of what to implement and what do avoid, the question before us is—how can we think in a distinctly Christian way about the proper role of technology in our educational ministry environments? Should we just Google "great new educational technology" or is there unique wisdom in the Scriptures about the role of language and tools in our pedagogy that we can pair with the best modern thinking on learning?

In this chapter, I hope to work toward answers to these questions by doing three things. First, I will lay out the basic approaches to technology that we see broadly in our culture and specifically in Christian education. This is to reset our notions of high tech and low tech and help us think differently about how technology actually works. Second, since this is a book about educational ministry, I want to give us some theological grounding in the biblical story for valuing human creativity and using alternative ways of communicating and helping people be transformed in their learning. Finally, in the later part of the chapter, we will look at some current and forthcoming issues in educational technology.

Approaches to Technology

Before we think about specific technologies and how they work in education, it's worth taking a step back and thinking about how people, particularly Christians, think about and employ technology in general. In a study of how religious people have historically conceived of media, John Ferré outlined three basic categories: (1) conduit, (2) mode of knowing, or (3) social institution.[2] For our purposes, we'll rename these categories as (1) instrumentalism, (2) determinism, and (3) social shaping.

In the *instrumentalist* way of thinking, every media technology is considered a neutral "conduit" through which a person can transmit any message. It doesn't matter what means of communication you choose—in person, the printing press, radio, television, the Internet—all that matters is that the message going through the conduit of media is good. You can hear echoes of this idea in popular phrases like, "The means change, but the message never does." This assumes that the technology itself is simply neutral, and that it has no effect on the one using it or on how the people at the other end of the communication receive the message. In this view, one can simply swap out one media for another and it has no effect other than potentially reaching more people. This is clearly a very pro-technology outlook, allowing Christians to embrace every new technology as an opportunity for communicating the gospel. If critiques of a new technology do arise, the instrumentalist approach tends to redirect those worries away from the tool toward the people using it.

At the other extreme is *determinism* which sees technology as a nearly unstoppable force changing everything around it. When it comes to communication media, Ferré called this view a "mode of knowing" because advocates of this position attribute the technology itself with the power to overwhelmingly shape the ideas and values of a culture. Technology is embedded with a set of internal values that impress themselves upon the user and those around them. It probably won't surprise you to know that many writers with a determinist bent worry that technology is making human life worse. However, there are also those who see technological determinism in a more positive light, arguing that technology will eventually bring humanity into a kind of utopia where everyone has long, trouble-free lives. This kind of thinking shows up in headlines that follow the formula, "Technology is making us [bad thing X]," where the author is attributing to technology a powerful, almost human-like agency to control our lives.

It shouldn't be too hard to find problems with both of these extremes. At one end of the spectrum, instrumentalism is overly simplistic in its understanding of technology and communication. From experience, we know that there is more to communication than transmitting sets of objective data through neutral conduits. Our words are always understood contextually, and a host of factors around our words affect how a message is understood. In person, we find that our tone of voice and body language communicate powerfully. And when we use technology to communicate, we know that there is something different between teaching in person and watching a video online or between receiving an email and receiving a handwritten note.

At the other end of the spectrum, the determinist view seems to ignore the human side of technology, and give too much agency to technology itself. It's far too easy to see a problem in society and to blame a recent technology as its primary cause. For example, Columbia researcher Dana Boyd found that teenagers prefer face-to-face time with their friends over technologically mediated communication, but they spend more time on technology not because they are addicted to it, but because the current generation of parents do not allow kids to have as much unstructured free time to visit friends as previous generations had.[3] Because their parents require them to be at home more often, technology is the only means they have to reach one another.

Media Inventory

One helpful way to think about the place of technology in education is to perform an inventory of all that is available to you, starting with the things you normally take for granted like a well-lit, air conditioned classroom, and continuing through to projectors, PowerPoint, YouTube, discussion forums, 3D printing, text polls, and so on. After you complete the inventory, spend some time thinking about the obvious things—what each tool is good for—but then move deeper and consider (1) what kind of education does this tool value? and (2) how can I reshape the use of this tool in an unexpected way?

What Boyd's research points out is that neither a determinist nor an instrumentalist viewpoint fully captures the reality of the relationship between people and technology. A mediating position between the two is the idea of *social shaping* of technology (SST) which accepts that technology has certain embedded values, but also that people and cultures have a role in shaping their use.[4]

One example of this shaping process was the Segway, which was supposed to revolutionize all human transportation. Rather than deterministically changing the world, society decided that Segways were good in certain cases like city tours or for police patrols, but they didn't take over the world. Social forces shaped the technology itself, encouraging the makers to adjust the tool to fit how people were using it. Twitter, too, evolved over time from its original idea of 140 characters and broadcast texting. No one uses the texting part any more, so Twitter quietly let that part fade away even while it incorporated features like @replying and retweeting that were originally invented by users of the platform.

In a social shaping model of technology, we recognize that choosing one tool or method over another opens some doors and closes others, but also that we have agency in our own lives and in our classrooms to decide and adjust as we come to better understand a new technology. Sociologist Heidi Campbell summarizes the view this way: "This approach of seeing media as a social institution, therefore, advocates that religious groups should not shy away from media because a community can purposely shape and present media content in light of its own beliefs. Yet it also requires that religious community to critically reflect on how the nature of media technology may impact their community."[5]

One of the primary challenges in accomplishing this in today's world is that technological development moves so fast that it takes us a while to fully grasp how a technology will eventually be used. One cannot simply see a pop-up ad for a new technology and immediately understand all its benefits and potential downsides. It often takes society a few years (or decades) to really understand and adjust to a new tool. In his book *The Inevitable*, Kevin Kelly gives the example of cell phones which, in their early days, were always going off at inappropriate times and places.[6] Eventually, the problem was solved by the silent vibrate setting, and today most everyone knows to keep their phone on silent most of the time. To take Kelly's example a step further, soon after the silent vibrate became the accepted standard many smartphone users stopped using their devices primarily for calls and moved on to other socially shaped uses, first with texting, then with apps like WhatsApp, Snapchat, and Match.

The point here is that as educational ministry leaders we need to be careful not to fall into the traps of either seeing technology as completely neutral and value-free or believing that technology is taking over the world. Affirming the social shaping power of technology frees us to try new technology, both learning as we go and listening carefully to critiques of technology. This helps us discover the embedded values in the mediums we might choose to employ and helps us shape their usage according to what we value in a learning environment. The more willing we are to experiment with new technology, the better we can understand it, and the better choices we can make in shaping its use and development.

The other good news is that with technological development moving so fast, everything we are doing today is already obsolete, and no one understands new technology any better than anyone else. In other words, everything is obsolete, and everyone is a newbie.

The Place of Technology in the Story of God

Since this is a book not just on education, but on specifically Christian educational ministry, let us now take a turn to lay down the theological foundations of our general optimism about technology.

In one sense, the Bible doesn't say much about modern technology. The machines of the Industrial Revolution and the electronics and interconnectivity of our present age would be unimaginable to those living in the biblical world. And yet, there are two ideas found throughout the biblical story that can inform our use of technology today.

First, the importance of creativity expressed through the making and using of tools and media shows up all throughout the biblical story, and God seems to go out of his way to incorporate the things people make into his redemptive plan. Second, although the Bible doesn't directly address today's media technology, there are several stories in which the form of communication makes all the difference.

God's original commands to humanity were to be fruitful and multiply, to subdue the earth, and to cultivate and keep it. That word "cultivate" carried the sense of tool usage, and it pictures humans not just living in the garden of Eden, but actively developing it, moving things around, trying out new schemes and tools that will help them better fulfill the command to be "fruitful."

While we don't see Adam and Eve using shovels or backhoes, we do see God creating one of humanity's most powerful tools—language. In Genesis 1 we see God creating the world with language, and in Genesis 2 God asks Adam to name the animals, giving Adam a chance to create the terms that would shape the way his offspring viewed those creatures for generations. It has been said that if you want to get to know a new culture, the best way is to learn their language because it helps you see the world the way that culture sees it. Conversely, differences in language (and even regional accent) often separate cultures and create divisions. When an evangelical uses the term "love offering," those in the know feel included, while those new to evangelical culture scratch their heads wondering what that term might mean. God even used this to his advantage in the Tower of Babel when he created new languages with the express purpose of causing humanity to fulfill his command to "fill the earth."

This idea extends to digital culture as well, where new words, language, and ideas about the world are constantly being created and remixed. To truly understand this world, one has to be in it and a part of it. But as we saw in the concept of social shaping of technology, we also have the chance to shape the language of the people in our ministries, to show them how to form and be formed by the technologies we use. Perhaps the best example of this in Scripture is in the nation of Israel to whom God gave an entire set of language, rituals, and symbols all of which were designed to communicate or reinforce the ideas Moses had written down in Scripture.

In fact, the first time Scripture records the Spirit of God descending on a person is in the story of Bezalel, the man God had chosen to take all of the abstract theological principles given to Moses and create visual ways to capture and communicate that to a largely illiterate people. The priests were charged with teaching God's Law to the people, but in God's eternal wisdom this wasn't done with mere words and lectures to fill their ears. Rather, worship and teaching in Israel was a multimedia experience of hearing, sights, smells, tastes, and textures. The Law taught and communicated, but the tabernacle's walls and fabrics, the priests' garments and gems, the shape of the offering pyre, and the smell of blood running throughout were each designed to inculcate a sense of God's holiness and splendor that cannot be captured in a lecture.

Beginning in Exodus 31, when we meet Bezalel (whom we might dub the patron saint of technology and art), and through the Pentateuch we find that God is intentionally using every media available at the time to communicate who he is. Even the Ten Commandments contain a statement about the importance of *not* using graven images to represent God because doing so would communicate that Yahweh was just like all the other gods. Again, the media we use (or don't use) matters deeply to God, so much so that it's baked into the Ten Commandments. As Neil Postman wrote, the commandment prohibiting images "is a strange injunction to include as part of an ethical system unless its author assumed a connection between forms of human communication and the quality of a culture."[7]

There are dozens of places in Scripture where God makes his point or gets the attention of a person using something other than simple words. Think of Balaam who refused to listen to God directly, and was only shocked into listening when God used a donkey as the "medium" to talk to him (Num. 22:28–31). And consider creation itself where the Psalmist says, "The heavens *declare* the glory of God.... They have *no speech*, they use no words.... Yet *their voice goes out* into all the earth" (Ps. 19:1–4). God, it seems, is rather practiced at using media other than words to instruct us about his character and beauty.

In addition to using his own creativity, God also makes human inventiveness part of the salvation process in stories like Noah and the Ark where God gives detailed instructions (Gen. 6:14–16) on how to build a device that would save the human race. This God who could have done any number of other miracles to preserve Noah's family from his wrath, chose, in his wisdom, to make human ingenuity an essential ingredient on the pathway to redemption.

We even see this in the life of our savior, Jesus. We have been taught that his father Joseph was a carpenter, but the Greek word for carpenter is actually *tektōn* (Matt. 13:55; Mark 6:3) which literally means an artisan or craftsperson, someone who makes something with his or her hands. Through the years this Greek word became the root of our own English word *technology*. How fitting that the infinite God-man who came to fulfill the law of Moses also had as his occupation something very much like what Adam was originally commanded to do—to make things from the world that God made. And just as Jesus created humanity and humanity turned on him (John 1:3, 11), he worked with wood and nails and wood and nails were turned against him. As with Noah, God could have used any number of ways to cause Jesus's death, but in both stories a righteous man is put on a human crafted wooden object, hovering above death and destruction in order to save God's image-bearers.

The Purpose of Parables

Why did Jesus use so many parables in his teaching? The common answer is that these were illustrations he used to help everyone understand what he was saying. But if you look closely, Jesus actually says he uses parables to *hide* his meaning from some and make it clear to others (Mark 4:11; Luke 8:10). At times, the disciples were in the know, and other times the Pharisees understood but the disciples did not (Matt 15:12–15). Explaining this theologically requires more than a sidebar, but educationally, Jesus is an example of using media in intentionally unexpected ways to deepen his communication.

The presence of Jesus's human body in the world also serves as a kind of medium that tells us something about God without using words. God has said, "I am with you," but the little baby whose name was Immanuel communicated that same idea in a wordless physical form. God gave us strongly worded laws that reflect his character, but Jesus's life is a concrete illustration that powerfully tutors us in his kindness and grace.

The images of the future in Scripture are likewise replete with human creations. Unlike the portraits of the afterlife where saints float among the clouds, the biblical writers offer us tantalizing glimpses of a "heavenly city" (Heb. 11:15) beautifully engineered using the finest materials cultivated from creation and full of man-made things including roads and trumpets, banners and books, and even the very throne of Jesus (Rev. 21:3–5). As the prophet Isaiah taught us, "They will beat their swords into plowshares and their spears into pruning hooks" (Isa. 2:4; cf. Joel 3:10); God seems less interested in destroying our creations, than in redeeming them and refashioning them for human flourishing. N. T. Wright summarized the final state in this way: "God is not going to abolish the universe of space, time and matter; he is going to renew it, to restore it, to fill it with new joy and purpose and delight, to take from it all that has corrupted it."[8]

So what are we to do with our media and technology before this time when Jesus wipes away every tear and abolishes every Blue Screen of Death? Thankfully, the authors of the New Testament offer some models for us. Certainly, they seemed willing to embrace the Roman road system and Koine Greek as methods of transmitting their message. They also embraced a new form of media called the codex. In the first century, serious philosophical and religious literature was only written on scroll. In contrast, the codex (a handcrafted early book) was only used for personal letters, shopping lists, and everyday information. It is strange then that the disciples who so revered the Hebrew Bible would embrace this new technology as the means by which they recorded and transmitted the gospel. In fact, no scroll of any New Testament text has ever been found, leading scholars to debate over why exactly the disciples chose this new tool. Was it simply easier to read and teach from because one could turn pages? Was it that codices were easier to travel with? Or was it that a scroll could not hold all the four recognized canonical Gospels while a codex easily could? Or was it that the new media itself communicated a new way of relating to God?

Again, no one is certain why they made this counter cultural move, but we do see places where the New Testament authors wrestled with which media would best communicate to their audiences. In both 2 and 3 John, we find the old saint discussing his theology of media when he says, "Though I have much to write to you, I would rather not use paper and ink. Instead I hope to come to you and talk face to face, so that our joy may be complete" (2 John 1:12, ESV). Paper and ink were the communication media of his day, and he seems to have thought long and hard about which messages were best delivered via letter and which were best in person.

Paul, on the other hand, in his second letter to the Corinthians, goes into great detail about why he did not feel it best to come to them in person, but rather thought that a strongly worded letter would be more redemptive even if it caused them temporary sorrow (2 Cor 1:15–24; 2:1–4; 7:8). Today, we lament how people often allow technology to overtake face-to-face time, so it is surprising to see Paul argue that there are cases in which technologically mediated instruction is actually more redemptive than an in-person encounter.

What we see in the examples is that both Paul and John avoided the traps of instrumentalism and determinism, because they avoided the simplistic idea that media is simply a neutral conduit which would make being together in person exactly the same as sending a letter, and at the same time they didn't avoid new technology because it might be too dangerous to be beneficial. Instead, they appear to have carefully thought through the embedded values of both face-to-face and mediated communication, choosing the appropriate medium for the task at hand, and in so doing they effectively socially shaped the way the early Christians would use the codex and other media to build the church.

What I hope we can see in this view of Scripture is a balance where God has intentionally made media and technology part of the story he is telling, freeing us to avoid hopelessly fearing or uncritically adopting every new tool, and instead to faithfully embrace them and learn from them.

Educational Issues with Technology

With a basic critical and theological framework, we can now look at some of the issues facing educational ministry leaders. I will warn you that these are not simple checklists that if implemented will make you the champion of education. Instead, I offer three broad challenges and three broad opportunities that technology brings.

Challenge 1: Allowing Technology to Drive Education

There is an old saying about technology that goes like this, "To the man with a hammer, everything looks like a nail." The idea is that once we have a tool in hand and we begin to understand its merits there is a tendency for us to begin taking on some of its value system and seeing the world and its problems though that lens. This doesn't mean there is anything inherently wrong with the hammer itself, but that if there is no critical process for understanding and evaluating the hammer, we run the risk of falling into a "hammer mindset."

In an educational ministry context this can happen we when become so enamored with a tool that we attempt to fit our round education into the square peg of the media we know best. Sometimes this happens when a teacher wantonly uses new media in such a way that it becomes more of a spectacle than a true enhancement (think jazzy PowerPoint animations).

The more subtle issue is when we begin seeing a single technology as the solution to all our educational needs. For example, I had to give a lecture in which I felt I needed quite a bit of visual support. So naturally I fired up PowerPoint and constructed what I consider to be an educational experience that was much clearer than if I had simply lectured. After that success, the next time I had to teach something I immediately began thinking about how to "PowerPoint it." When that day's lecture did not seem to go over very well, my first thought was, "I need to make better slides." However, when I stepped back and thought about the material (in this case, how people of other faiths understand the doctrine of the Trinity), I realized that a five-minute group discussion would create a much more powerful learning experience than attempting to visualize the points on a slide.

At Dallas Theological Seminary, we are working through a similar issue in the way we teach preaching. For several decades the methodology has been to ask young preachers to stand up in front of the classroom and deliver a sermon while a professor sits in a sound room in the back and records both the preacher and a second audio track of comments and reactions. These reactions were delivered to the student first on a VHS tape, then a DVD, then on a USB drive. When we began to consider how we might teach preaching via online education, the first question was, "How do we replicate the preaching and voiceovers experience in an online context?" But as our discussion continued someone asked, "Is the voiceover system the best way to teach preaching, or is it just the technology we know so we're trying to replicate that online?" These are hard questions to ask especially if you've been teaching in a certain way for more than a few years. At the same time one of the great benefits of online education has been that it continually prompts us to reflect not only about how to teach online, but also on what we've been doing in the traditional classroom and ask if we're truly using the best methods.

Challenge 2: Resistance to Change

Studies on the effectiveness of teachers say that it takes three to four years for new professors or teachers to really hit their stride. In these early years teachers improve continuously, but then after three to five years, many plateau and are no more effective ten or twenty years out than they were at year four or five.[9] It can be challenging for any teacher to break out of this cycle, but this problem is especially acute today in light of the speed of technological change. Just when you're hitting your stride, connecting with your people and forming their minds and souls, a new technique or tool comes along and makes you look obsolete.

This can create tension between older and newer teachers, and lead to frustrations for both teachers and their people. When I began at DTS,

I was the twenty-something "tech guy" who was always using some new-fangled device or Internet tool. But as it tends to happen I eventually crossed into my thirties and found myself not reacting as quickly to new technology. This hit me hard when I discovered that when a new social network came along, I was too slow to get my preferred username (I'm @johndyer on Twitter, but alas, not on Snapchat). As I cross into my forties, I'm realizing that I need to embrace the idea I mentioned earlier that everything is obsolete, and everyone is a newbie. If I take the posture of a continual learner, I see new things less as a threat and more as an opportunity to stretch my own mind and connect with my students in new ways.

By taking the posture of learner myself, I hope to function as a kind of medium, an embodied illustration of the learning process. Technological change provides an opportunity either to express frustration with change or to model a "let's figure this out" attitude to learning. One of the challenges in doing this is that many educators feel that technological experimentation is outside the scope of their job description, which brings us to the next point.

Challenge 3: Lack of Training and Time

A study by the New Media Consortium identified "professional development" to be one of the key challenges in education in general and specifically with regard to technology. They summarize the problem this way, "All too often, when schools mandate the use of a specific technology, teachers are left without the tools (and often skills) to effectively integrate the new capabilities into their teaching methods. The results are that the new investments are underutilized, not used at all, or used in a way that mimics an old process rather than innovating new processes that may be more engaging for students."[10]

This skeptical part of me would like to point out that this very study was sponsored by HP, a company that just so happens to sell many wonderful new technologies and training for said new media. And yet, the point they make is still quite valid. Most of us would never ask a volunteer to lead a ministry effort without some training or teach a passage of Scripture without any preparation. And yet educational ministry leaders are often asked to do new things with technology without much guidance on how to use it or how to improve over time.

Offering technology training is challenging, though, because most of us have precious little time to train our leaders and volunteers as it is. We often need to cover so much in the way of content and relational issues, it might seem difficult to find additional time to work through technology and media issues. But technology training doesn't need to be treated as a completely separate topic. Instead it can be worked in as a part of the preparation you're already doing. For example, when you talk about discipleship and relationship building, it's a perfect time to remind everyone that technology is the air our people are breathing. You can then discuss ideas and etiquette for connecting with your people and discuss how you can build them up online in interims between when you meet in person.

Opportunity 1: Blended Education / Continuous Contact

In early discussions about the Internet and spirituality, many researchers and pundits talked in terms of a dichotomy between the online world and the offline or "real" world. There was a sense that the Internet was an entirely new place where a person could create a completely separate identity. However, as the social shaping process took place, the relationship between online and offline became more fluid. A group of friends might organize a get together using their phones, then spend time in person, then post about that time on social media, and then laugh about the posts in person the next day. This back and forth between mediated and non-mediated experiences is not without its problems, but it can also create strong ties between friends.

Similarly, in educational ministry, the technologies built on the Internet and mobile devices offer teachers more opportunities than ever to connect with students outside the classroom. Pastors are no longer limited to the ninety minutes on Sunday, and teachers don't have to remain within the confines of the classroom. Studies of college students comparing the effectiveness of online vs. classroom education often conclude that it is actually hybrid classes and programs that prove to be the most effective.[11] In a church context, this means that a combination of live, in-person time supplemented with ongoing touchpoints through technology may offer better chances for our people to grow and mature.

I studied science in college, and I always enjoyed classes that had both a lecture and a lab component, because the lab offered us a chance to see how the theory from the classroom actually worked. In the lab, we could try things and get immediate feedback which solidified the truths we learned in class. In a sense, our real lives are the labs for what we learn in educational ministry. Online technology allows us to connect and blend what we do in the classroom with our people's day-to-day spiritual lives, and it can help us move them from learning information to incorporating it into their everyday experiences and choices.

Opportunity 2: Resources and Best Practices

As educational ministry leaders, we need to continually remind ourselves that learning is more than just passing on information. That said, having great information is indeed a key part of education, and this is where technology has the potential to shine. I say "potential" because many of us have experienced information overload where there just seems to be a never-ending fire hydrant of data. But take heart, even Solomon felt this way when he said, "Of the making of books there is no end" (Eccl. 12:12) as did thinkers in the Enlightenment like Leibniz (1646–1716) who wrote, "the horrible mass of books keeps growing."

The important thing to keep in mind is that we don't just have more information, we have a different relationship to information. As new media evolved in the past few decades, our first instinct was to simply transfer the old way of doing things to the new tool such as the move from multi-volume print encyclopedias to multi-CD sets. But as the Internet evolved and matured, the source of information also changed from companies like Britannica where professional authors created summaries of human knowledge to sites like Google that used machine learning to read and organize Internet data and sites like Wikipedia filled with user-generated content. In recent years we've seen another shift where video sites like YouTube are being used as instructional resources for everything from how to fix a faucet to how to lead a small group. And educational sites like Khan Academy test various ways of teaching the same idea over and over again until they find the one that resonates with the most users.[12]

Where do grades come from?

William Farish (1759–1837) was a British scientist at the University of Cambridge. As a professor he pioneered a drawing technic called "Isometrical Perspective." But it was during his time as a tutor in 1792 that he came up with his most revolutionary idea. He decided to stop evaluating students in descriptive, qualitative ways, and switch to using a quantitative, numeric system. Thus the first grade from 0–100 was born. We don't think of "grading" as technology, but it is a technique and a way of both thinking about and of perceiving students, and it has dominated education ever since.

What this means is that we have the opportunity not just to provide our people with a better, more up-to-date book or website, but to incorporate tools that let people see the world in a different way and learn in a form of community. Educational ministry leaders also have the opportunity to find new ways to teach, not just in theory, but by watching others do it. Sometimes it will be appropriate to bring a video from an expert into the learning environment, and sometimes it will be better to take what you learned and make it appropriate to your context.

Opportunity 3: Emerging Technologies

There are also emerging technologies on the horizon that might not quite be ready for your ministry today, but that might be soon. 3D printing, for example, has the potential to allow people to download models of historical objects, such as a first-century coin (Mark 12:17), and print them out for the class to interact with. In the early days, the Internet was thought of as a "virtual" place, but 3D printing turns this on its head and has the potential for a more physical, visceral learning experience.

Similarly, various forms of augmented reality promised a kind of immersion not possible by looking into a screen. Almost every large tech company from Facebook to Microsoft has recently demoed visors that add holographic-like objects to the wearer's field of vision. Unlike a fully immersive, video game-like experience which projects a completely artificial world onto the eye of the user, augmented reality adds detail to the physical world. For example, a user could look down at a table and see virtual papers, books, Bibles, and other objects. An engineering student would no longer move a mouse to manipulate an 2D onscreen version of the object he or she is creating, but rather could see it projected into space and walk around it, examining it from every angle.

While these technologies might have limited application, I am personally looking forward to technology that allows me to create more customized learning for people. I don't mean individualized in the sense that it only caters to their interests, but rather that it has the capacity to provide them immediate feedback on what they are learning. If a person watches a video, such technology would be able to evaluate immediately the learning to see what made sense and what didn't and then provide feedback based on areas where the person needs additional work or simply wants to go deeper than what a traditional class usually offers.

Opportunity 4: The Value of Face-to-Face Time

Finally, it's worth remembering that in this fast-moving, always-connected world, where people are endlessly bombarded by advertisements and notifications, it's incredibly rare to find a fully present person willing to offer his or her full attention. That means that you and your presence may be the most valuable part of any educational ministry.

We live in a world where if people simply wanted information, they can just Google it and read the Wikipedia (or Theopedia) article. And if they want to hear perfectly delivered sermons, there are plenty of them on YouTube. Even if all they want is just a little shallow conversation, Siri, Cortana, or Alexa can handle that.

But people are not coming to your educational ministry for Googlable data and one-sided chatter. They are making room in their busy lives because somewhere deep down inside, God has hard-wired us (notice the tech metaphor) to crave more than skimming along the surface. Instead he created us to desire those difficult-to-define things we call "community" and "formation." People need to know Scripture and theology, and the latest and greatest technology can help us communicate those truths, but it's our embodied presence, our attention, and our godly lives that, through the Spirit of God, transforms knowledge into wisdom and stories into character.

Conclusion

In this chapter I hope I have presented a general case for being both sober and excited about technology. From the worlds of sociology, media ecology, and philosophy of technology, we have learned that technology has embedded values that can shape people and society. But we've also seen that we humans have the agency to shape the use of technology in our own lives, work, and ministries. From theology, we learn that God cares deeply about human creativity and tools, so much so that he made it a point to include tools in just about every part of the biblical story.

We cannot tell the story of our faith without talking about the cross, a human tool meant for destruction, but which God has transformed into a symbol of hope. We also see that when biblical characters, authors, and indeed, God himself, want to communicate, they thought carefully about which media to use and how it would shape what was received and what was learned.

This should give us the freedom to learn from both those who are critical of technology and those who are excited about it. We can learn to take advantage of the benefits of technology, while avoiding its downsides, and shape it in ways that conform to the values of the gospel. At the same time, we remain humble, always remembering that whatever we know today will be obsolete tomorrow. As Kevin Kelly says, when everything is obsolete and everyone is a newbie, there's no better time to learn.[13]

Discussion Questions

1. Has technology influenced your ability to learn, interact, or focus? If so, in what ways?

2. Why are both the instrumentalist way of thinking and the determinist way of thinking about technology flawed? How does Christian theology offer a mediating position that takes into account individual choice and technological formation?

3. How does technology benefit educational ministry?

4. What are some dangers educational ministers must take seriously when creating learning experiences for their students?

5. How can Christians think in a distinctly Christian way about the proper role of technology in our educational ministries?

Resources for Further Study

Books

Dyer, John. *From the Garden to the City: The Redeeming and Corrupting Power of Technology.* Grand Rapids: Kregel, 2011.

Gardner, Howard and Katie Davis. *The App Generation: How Today's Youth Navigate Identity, Intimacy, and Imagination in a Digital World.* New Haven, CT: Yale University Press, 2014.

Hamilton, Boni. *Integrating Technology in the Classroom: Tools to Meet the Need of Every Student.* Eugene, OR: International Society for Technology in Education, 2015.

Postman, Neil. *Amusing Ourselves to Death: Public Discourse in the Age of Show Business.* New York: Penguin, 1985.

Websites

Church Tech Today—www.churchtechtoday.com
EdTech—www.edtechmagazine.com
Edudemic—www.edudemic.com

Author Bio

John Dyer is the Dean of Enrollment Services and Educational Technology and Adjunct Professor of Media Arts and Worship at Dallas Theological Seminary. John has been a technology creator for more than twenty years, building tools used by Facebook, Google, Apple, Anheuser-Busch, the Department of Defense, and the Digital Bible Society. His open-source code is now used on more than thirty percent of websites. He has written on technology and faith for a number of publications and websites including Gizmodo, *Christianity Today,* The Gospel Coalition, and in the book *From the Garden to the City: The Redeeming and Corrupting Power of Technology.* John and his brilliant wife Amber have two bright and hilarious children, Benjamin and Rebecca.

Endnotes

1.   Dr. Reg Grant of Dallas Theological Seminary found this letter in a box while cleaning out an area under the DTS chapel. It is now archived in the DTS library.

2.   John Ferre, "The Media of Popular Piety," in Jolyon Mitchell and Sophia Marriage, eds., *Mediating Religion: Conversation in Media. Religion and Culture* (New York: T. & T. Clark, 2003), 83–92.

3.   Dana Boyd, *It's Complicated: The Social Lives of Networked Teens* (New Haven, NY: Yale University Press, 2014), 21.

4.   There have been many attempts at creating mediating positions, such as Social Construction of Technology (SCOT) and specifically religious versions like Religious Social Shaping of Technology, each with their own nuances.

5.   Heidi Campbell, *When Religion Meets New Media* (London: Routledge, 2010), 48.

6.   Kevin Kelly, *The Inevitable* (New York: Viking, 2016).

7.   Neil Postman, *Amusing Ourselves to Death* (New York: Penguin Books, 2005), 9.

8.   N. T. Wright, "The Road to New Creation," Durham Cathedral, Saturday, September 23, 2006. Available at http://ntwrightpage.com/sermons/Road_New_Creation.htm.

9.   Charles Clotfelter, Helen Ladd, and Jacob Vigdor, "Teacher-Student Matching and the Assessment of Teacher Effectiveness," National Bureau of Economic Research Working Paper No. 11936, January 2006. Available at http://www.nber.org/papers/w11936.

10. New Media Consortium. "NMC Horizon Report > 2013 K-12 Edition" (2013). Available at http://www.nmc.org/pdf/2013-horizon-report-k12.pdf.

11. William G. Bowen, Kelly A. Lack, Matthew Chingos, Thomas I. Nygren. "Interactive Learning Online at Public Universities: Evidence from Randomized Trials," Interactive Learning Online at Public Universities, May 22, 2012. Available at http://sr.ithaka.org/?p=22464.

12. Khan Academy was created in 2006 by Salman Khan from videos he created to help tutor his cousin. Today, Khan Academy provides thousands of "micro lectures" through YouTube in sixty-five languages.

13. Kelly, Kevin. *The Inevitable*, 11, 15.

WHO:
THE PEOPLE

Chapter 5
FORMATIVE: PRESCHOOL AND CHILDREN

Jerry Lawrence

...until we all reach unity in the faith and in the knowledge of the Son of God and become mature, attaining to the whole measure of the fullness of Christ. Then we will no longer be infants, tossed back and forth by the waves, and blown here and there by every wind of teaching and by the cunning and craftiness of people in their deceitful scheming. Instead, speaking the truth in love, we will grow to become in every respect the mature body of him who is the head, that is, Christ.

—Ephesians 4:13–15

IT HAD BEEN A long, dry spell without any extended one-on-one conversation time with children. Okay, maybe it had only been about a month or two. But when you are a children's person and you thrive on talking and interacting with children, that's an eternity. Being with children gives me joy.

So, when Claire and Joe Joe, children of dear friends, were on campus, we struck up a great conversation. We went to lunch together—my two new short friends, their parents, and grand-parents. Part of the fun of our lunchtime was the french-fry game with the objective to guess how many french fries each player was holding in their hand. Playing along and making crazy guesses was just as much fun for me as it was for them. I enjoyed getting to know these two great kids as well as catching up with my good friends.

The next day, Joe Joe and Claire came to my office for an extended visit. They were so excited to come see where a seminary "teacher" worked and were surprised and overjoyed to find toys in my office. Claire immediately remarked that when she grew up, she wanted to have an office just like mine, complete with toys. Of course, I call them "educational tools" because I believe all children learn through play. In contrast to the typical seminary professor's office lined with scholarly books, I have pop-up books and Bible storybooks. My scholarly books are at home. I purposefully designed my office to be kid-friendly. As a result, when any child comes through the door, all items are fair game for them to look at, touch, read, and play with.

So we pulled out the modelers clay and got down to business. They decided we should each make a Bible story and try to guess each other's stories. And because I believe in learning through guided conversations, as we were rolling out dough and making our stories, we talked and got to know each other better. I asked them all sorts of questions about their lives, their favorite colors, etc. We laughed and pondered life together and then we guessed which Bible stories were depicted by our modelers clay creations. And we talked a little bit about the truths of those Bible stories and why they chose them. It was a wonderful afternoon. At the end of our time together, I was blessed by Joe Joe's declaration that I was not like most adults because I still had "most of the kid left in me." Smile.

Maturity in Christ—Our Goal

Maturity in Christ—that is what we desire for all of the children in our children's ministries. It's a formidable task. These first twelve years comprise the most drastic developmental changes they will experience throughout their lifetime. Our goal is to take newborn babies, completely dependent and unable to speak or reason and partner with their parents to shape them into walking, talking disciples of Christ (hopefully) by the time they graduate into our student ministries. And, while we do

not expect complete maturity by the time they leave us, the nursery, preschool, and elementary years are formative. They are meant to lay a solid spiritual foundation on which to build for the rest of their lives.

Ephesians 4:14 describes what we want for children as they grow in maturity, that they would "no longer be infants, tossed back and forth by the waves, and blown here and there by every wind of teaching." The grounding we give them in God's Word will provide the stable footing they need to address the challenges they face now and in the future. As they grow in their knowledge of Scripture, we desire that our teaching does not just give them head knowledge, but it moves that knowledge from their heads to their hearts. As the Holy Spirit speaks to the heart of each child, life transformation is possible.

> "By age 9, most children have their spiritual moorings in place.... Your spiritual condition by the age of 13 is a strong predictor of your spiritual profile as an adult."[1]
> —George Barna

In the next few pages, we will look at the characteristics and learning needs of our children, the challenges to learning they face, and how to reach our learners. But I would be remiss not to mention the foundation from which I base my philosophy for ministering to children. As Scripture clearly states in Deuteronomy 6:4–9, parents bear the primary responsibility for the spiritual growth and development of their children. Parents are first to know and love God themselves (vv. 4–6) and then they are to teach his commands to their children during the daily rhythms of life (vv. 7–9). Yes, the time we spend at church teaching children is important. No doubt. But it cannot compare to the day-to-day, hour-by-hour, and minute-by-minute learning opportunities that happen as part of everyday life.

Our families need to know and believe how valuable and important they are to the process of passing down their faith to the next generation. We are privileged to walk beside parents and their children in this learning and maturing process. I view this as a vital partnership, with us both having different roles and responsibilities, but with the overarching goal of helping the children God has entrusted to us come to know the Lord as Savior and grow in that relationship. The church's role can be seen as a more formal one, where teaching takes place in an organized setting with scripted stories and planned activities. In the home, the teaching is much less formal and more spontaneous. Working in partnership, what is taught on Sunday morning can be reinforced during the week through intentional interactions and teachable moments. As we both do our parts, we help our children to mature in Christ.

The Learning Needs of Our Children

In order to understand the learning needs of our children, we must become students of the different stages of development. Physical, mental, social, emotional, and spiritual development stages are all intertwined. In the church or parachurch setting, we are wise not only to understand spiritual development but also to understand its interplay with other areas of development. Countless books have been written regarding the developmental theories of Jean Piaget (mental or cognitive), Erik Erikson (social-emotional), and James Fowler (spiritual).[2] We benefit from their research and theories when we identify how these stages work together to form the children who appear in our classrooms. By understanding what children are generally like at each age level, we can best determine how to help them learn. A more detailed list of characteristics and needs is included at the end of the chapter, but for now let's look at a few examples for each age group.

> "Parents are the key faith developers for their children—they can have either a positive or a negative impact on their kids' faith growth. But either way, they'll have the biggest impact. You can have strong faith-shaping programs for kids at church, but if you're not partnering with homes, you risk producing kids who have weak faith."[3]
> —Ben Freudenburg and Rick Lawrence

Infants and Toddlers (Infants: 0–18 months; Toddlers: 19 months–2 years old)

Even before birth, parents experience the miracle of development that takes place in the mother's womb. The heart starts to beat at twenty-one days, toes form at ten weeks, and all organs are developed by thirty-eight weeks, with lungs that continue to mature until birth. Once they are born, their development continues and is no less amazing.

Physically

Infants grow rapidly and move through the milestones of turning over, sitting up, and crawling. Toddlers can best be described as "wheels in motion." They begin to perfect the art of "toddling" and then move on to walking. All of these activities take up a lot of space, which is why your nursery needs to occupy the larger rooms in your children's area. To determine how much square footage for each room, use the following chart as a general rule.[4]

Table 5.1 Floor Space Per Person[5]

Age	Square Feet per Child
Birth–5 years	30–35 sq. ft.
1st–3rd grade	25–30 sq. ft.
4th–6th grade	20–25 sq. ft.

Mentally

As children learn to speak, their vocabulary is still quite limited, so we need to talk on their level. Their attention span is very short. For children in nursery and preschool, my general rule is one minute for every year. So, a two-year-old has about a two-minute attention span. This means you will need to introduce your main point of the lesson at the very beginning before you lose their attention. It also helps to provide a variety of activities—songs, hand motions, etc.—that relate to your Bible story. Toddlers learn best through their five senses, so help them feel, see, and taste the story. They also have very limited ideas of time and space. Instead of saying "Jesus lived two thousand years ago" you might say, "Jesus lived

a long, long, long time ago." As they grow older you can fill in the specific details.

Socially

After birth, infants spend most of their time with their parents and perhaps a few caretakers. It is important to establish a sense of trust in the first year of a child's life. Whenever they cry, their needs are met and so it is natural that they are self-centered. But as they grow, they become more aware of others and increase in friendliness. This is our opportunity to encourage sharing and provide more group activities during our class time.

Emotionally

Babies and toddlers have strong emotions and may be insecure in their feelings. Because they have no sense of time, they don't know that when their parents drop them off they will be back before long. They need reassurance that mom or dad will be coming back soon. The security of a schedule and a variety of activities that occupy their time helps them not to focus on their fear of abandonment.

Spiritually

The first eighteen months of life are crucial to a child's healthy development. As identified in Eric Erikson's stage of Trust vs. Mistrust, children are learning whether they can trust the adults in their life.[6] If a child lives in an environment where she is nurtured and cared for, she begins to believe that the people in her life can be trusted. This can set the stage later for her to believe she can trust a loving God with her future.

Can infants really learn anything spiritually? Many would say they are too young to learn.

Is that really true? Let me offer you a few examples. In the nursery of my childhood church, still today, the dedicated caregivers sing songs and speak biblical truths while they change diapers! With each individual child, they say, "God loves you so much. He created you very special." While babies may not understand the words, they sense the feelings behind the words. In my current church, we begin having a Bible lesson in the 7–8-month-old class. The children sit in their bucket seats at the table and alternate between two lessons. One month they learn that "God made the world" and the next month the lesson is "God made me." We begin each lesson by saying, "This is the Bible. It is God's letter to us and every word in it is true." Then we'll ask, "Can you say Bible?" and they will repeat the word. The lessons are filled with songs and manipulatives (toys they can see and touch). For example, when we explain that God made the fish and the sea, we bring out a fish bowl with plastic wind-up fish that swim in the water. Then we take them out of the water and let them hold the fish. By repeating the same two lessons over and over again, they begin to know and eagerly anticipate what comes next at each part of the story. It's really quite remarkable. One parent confided to me that one of their child's first words was "Bible."

Preschoolers (3–5 years old)

As children enter the preschool years, their rapid growth continues. Each day brings both challenges and accomplishments. Keep in mind that, while they do follow general guidelines, every child will grow and develop at his or her own rate. It is wise to encourage their development, but not push them too hard.

Physically

Preschoolers become confident in walking and begin climbing, jumping, running and skipping. Their large muscles and gross motor skills are still developing, so we want to provide them with large materials and toys such as balls and building blocks. Once their gross motor skills are more fully developed, they will be able to not just throw a ball, but to catch it as well. As they work with their hands, their fine motor skills are strengthened. In time they will be able to work puzzles and cut paper with better precision. Smaller crayons and pencils will eventually replace the box of jumbo crayons as they begin learning how to write.

Mentally

Preschoolers are like sponges, soaking in everything they are learning. They are still acquiring their vocabulary, so choose simple stories and short action words. They are also literal thinkers, so when introducing a new song or a Bible verse, consider what words might need to be explained. Otherwise you will hear humorous stories of kids who think the words are "up from the gravy a rose." They are familiar with flowers like roses and gravy for the turkey at Thanksgiving, but they probably do not know what a grave is or what "arose" means. Take time to explain the words, so they will learn. Repetition is helpful at this age and preschoolers don't mind hearing the story over and over again. This is why I always recommend when parents volunteer to serve in the second hour of Sunday school, that their preschool children stay in their own class to hear the lesson again. It helps with their recall of the story. Another helpful practice is to review from week to week what you are learning. Ask them, "What did we learn about last week?" This works especially well when the lessons build on each other or are part of a unit.

Socially

Up until now, their world has generally been small. But as they enter preschool, their world begins to expand. They generally like solitary play and many times you will see three-year-olds playing alone side-by-side. In the next couple of years they will begin to play interactively with their buddies. We can encourage this type of play by providing small group experiences. You might have them work together to make a meal in the play kitchen and serve it to each other.

Emotionally

They have gained a certain sense of independence and want to do things for themselves. You'll hear them say, "I can do it." Frustration comes when they are not quite able to do a certain task, such as putting a lid on a jar. And because they can't always communicate their feelings, they might melt down from the frustration. As much as you can, make it possible for them to do that task. Give them the jar with the lid already started and ask them to finish tightening it. Help them feel a sense of accomplishment.

Preschool kids can also be pretty sympathetic. You hear it in their prayers for people who are sick or hurt. That's a great time to capture their hearts to be kind and empathetic toward others. I would love to see more service projects at this age level, maybe one project a semester with a little time spent each week to build their understanding of the project and how they can help someone in need.

> "Parents whose children receive Christ as their Savior at the age of four or five may occasionally wonder if those youngsters' conversions are genuine. But the genuineness of that experience need not be doubted if the child clearly understood the awfulness of his sin and genuinely trusted in Jesus to forgive his sins and to take him to heaven."[7]
>
> —Roy B. Zuck

Spiritually

At this age, children are naturally curious about God. They have a fascinating wonder and awe regarding God's creation. I believe this to be a built-in sense of knowing there is a Creator who made this world for us to enjoy. As we treat the Word of God reverently, holding it in our hands while telling our Bible story, we impress on our children that God speaks to us through his written word. He has given us a map in the pages of his book and from its instructions we can know how to live our lives according to his plan.

They are also beginning to know the difference between right and wrong. Children who grow up in strong Christian homes and attend church regularly hear the plan of salvation early in life. From a very young age, children can understand a simple explanation of the gospel put into age-appropriate language. They can understand these basic truths:

1. God loves us (John 3:16).
2. We have all sinned (Rom. 3:23).

3. Because of our sin, we cannot be with God (Rom. 6:23).
4. Jesus died in our place and came back to life to save us from our sins (Rom. 5:8; 10:9).
5. We each need to trust Jesus to save us so we can live with him forever one day (Rom. 4:5; 6:23).

Preschoolers can also experience heartfelt worship. One of my favorite worship services of all time occurred in the threes-and-fours class. Those kids knew how to worship! Led by Mr. Gary and his guitar, they sang song after song loudly and enthusiastically. I couldn't help but feel we were in the presence of the Lord.

Younger Elementary Kids (Kindergarten– 3rd grade, 6–9 years old)

Kindergarten is a big milestone for children and their parents. As they venture off to school, their social circles widen even further. They are growing in friendliness and will be introduced to new experiences that will challenge them. By the time they reach third grade (age 9), they will become more confident in their abilities, especially in areas that are of interest to them.

Physically

Even as they grow older, kids remain susceptible to contagious diseases. It is important to maintain a healthy, germ-free environment and adhere to our written health and wellness policies. These kids are energetic, yet they tire easily. To help with their changing levels of energy, plan for a balance of active and quiet activities. They can control their large muscles much better than smaller ones, so plan activities requiring the use of large muscles. But also encourage activities such as cutting paper or writing which help develop their small muscles.

Mentally

Our younger elementary kids are literal-minded, concrete thinkers. They believe whatever you say and take it at face value, literally! But they also enjoy a great imagination and love stories. It is important to emphasize that our Bible stories are not imaginary, but are completely true. Kids at this age also have the ability to memorize quickly and easily. What they learn when they are young will stick with them for the rest of their lives. This is a time when they can hide God's Word in their hearts. So, even if the curriculum does not emphasize this, make it a point to weave Bible memory verses throughout your lessons on a regular basis.

Socially

Kids at this age prefer adult approval to the approval of their peers. They can be very imitative of adults who are important to them. When Macy, my friend's daughter, went to school she began wearing her hair in a ponytail and drinking from a tall cup with a straw simply because she loved her kindergarten teacher and wanted to be just like her. This is a great reminder of how essential it is for us to set a good, Christlike example for these impressionable kids. Girls and boys remain friendly toward the opposite sex until about the third grade, so at that time provide some separate activities for third grade boys and girls.

Emotionally

Kindergarteners are working out the challenges of their new world. It is important to give them personal attention and a listening ear as they confide the happenings of their life. They respond well to stories that give a sense of security and include a resolution of any conflict. Children at this age are noncompetitive. They prefer group activities with no competition to individual ones. We can begin to introduce a few competitive activities as they get older and are better able to handle their emotions. For now, encourage the whole group to work and play together cooperatively, and be careful not to force all children into the same mold.

Spiritually

These children's hearts are sympathetic toward others. We often hear it in their prayers for family and friends. Now is a good opportunity for them to participate in worthwhile service projects for children in need locally or in other countries. In doing so, we teach them God's heart for the world.

As we faithfully teach our children truths about God from week to week, each child can begin to know that he or she is a sinner—not able to please his or her parents, much less a perfect and holy God. They come to a realization they need Christ to save them, finally understanding the familiar words "Jesus loves me, this I know." They can place their faith in Christ and personally accept him as their Savior. My caution at this age is to give them regular opportunities to accept Christ, but to avoid group invitations. Because they desire approval from others, they might raise their hand to be polite, to please their teacher, or because their friend raised their hand. Instead, once you present the gospel, you could say, "We're going to move on to our next activity now. If you have questions

about what I explained, I would love to talk with you." This allows the opportunity to talk with them privately. You will also want to let the parents know what you talked about in class, so they can have further conversations during the week with their children.

Older Elementary Kids (4th grade–6th grade, 10–12 years old)

Depending on when your church promotes or moves kids on to the youth ministry, you have two, maybe three years with this age group. These are the last years we have to train our children towards maturity in Christ before we hand them over to the youth group. In these older elementary years, if our children have not already accepted Christ, we want to help lead each student to a personal acceptance of Jesus Christ as Savior and Lord. While salvation is our goal, we recognize that it is only by God's grace, through the conviction of the Holy Spirit. Once they have trusted Christ for salvation, we want to help them become like him in living their daily lives. External motivation to obey parents and other authority figures should be replaced by an internal motivation of wanting to live a life that is pleasing to the Lord.

Physically

Kids at this age are usually healthy. Growth spurts and hormonal changes are a normal part of their growth. They are bubbling over with energy and may shows signs of getting out of hand in class. Skillful teachers can guide their excess energy into useful ends—helping in the room, participating in the program, and finding answers in their Bibles. They may quickly lose interest in Sunday school if they experience "the same old thing" every week. We need to inject freshness and variety in our teaching with varied methods like visual aids, discussion, role-plays, etc.[8]

Mentally

As is true for younger elementary kids, preteens also like to memorize because they do so easily. This is the time to lead them in learning Bible verses that answer their questions, help them with problems, and encourage them to express their feelings about God and Jesus. They want to discover answers for themselves; so let them experience the joy of finding answers in God's Word. By treating them in a grown-up way and asking their opinions, you can help them to recognize their ability to think for themselves.

Socially

Preteens are growing more independent and relationships are becoming more important to them. They are loyal to their own "gang" and are learning about true friendships. They are also hero worshipers, but need help in choosing heroes that have biblical values. Friendly competition with classmates gives them a sense of challenge and accomplishment. This is a good age to encourage them to compete with themselves in memory work, daily Bible reading, and attendance, by keeping a record. As they begin to mature physically, they also mature socially. The old saying, "girls rule, boys drool" or vice versa, will no longer be their cry. Antagonism toward the opposite sex will be replaced by curiosity and interest. To alleviate some of the distraction this causes, it is a good idea to have separate classes for boys and girls with teachers of their own gender when possible. Stress teamwork within each class, but also provide for some competition between classes.

Emotionally

As their social circles widen, they begin to navigate their world of friends, enemies, bullies, etc. We, as adults, may wish for the perceived carefree life of a preteen. But think back to what it was like for you at this age. These kids actually do have many problems, such as getting along with their peers, doing what their parents and teachers want, navigating their parents' divorce, getting good grades, playing better in sports, doing more things on their own, and becoming their own person. One minute they may be celebrating a particular triumph or accomplishment. The next minute they may experience the anger or heartache of a friend who betrays them. Though they may not want to admit their problems, be sensitive to their needs. Depend on the Holy Spirit to help you to speak biblical truth into their lives and help them learn how to address their problems in ways that honor the Lord. In our fifth and sixth grade class we had a "pickle jar" with various situations written on the back of a pickle-shaped piece of paper. When we had time at the end of class, we would pick a "pickle" out of the pickle jar and discuss that problem together as a class. It was a great way to discuss real-life situations and guide them toward finding the answers in God's Word.

Spiritually

For the children we've been teaching from birth, they may have accepted Christ at an earlier age. But it is important to remember that we must regularly share the good news of Christ to our kids at every age level. We can never take it for granted that they have already come to a saving knowledge of Christ. Our kids who regularly attend may think they are Christians because their parents are or because they go to church or because they've heard about God and Jesus all their lives. Each child needs to recognize his or her own sinfulness. It's one thing for a child to know Jesus died for the world and a whole other thing for that child to realize that Jesus died for him or her personally. We must emphasize over and over again that we are to have a *personal* relationship with Christ. The same Jesus, who loved us enough to die for us, loves us enough to want to have an ongoing, deepening relationship with us. Our task is to help our kids understand and grow in their relationship with Christ.

As children reach adolescence, they begin a process of redefining what their faith means to them personally apart from their parent's beliefs. This searching process is a normal part of faith development. As children go through this period of questioning and testing, the strong biblical foundation that was laid during the earlier years is beneficial in helping them come to understand what their faith means to them personally.

While they grow and mature in Christ, we also want to help children discover God's purpose for them in the world. Encouraging and teaching children to have devotional, quiet times with the Lord gives them the opportunity to reflect and talk with God about who they are, who he is, and where they fit within the world. We also want to train our students to serve Christ using the spiritual gifts, talents, and abilities he has given them. As they learn more about themselves and the world in need of Christ, they

exercise and grow in their faith. Our children's program had a missions emphasis one summer and incorporated countries into the lessons, using information from *Operation World*.[9] We had a Bible lesson, games, crafts, and snacks related to that country and learned what God was doing in that part of the world. The kids loved it!

The Challenges to Learning for Our Children

The children we minister to have been entrusted to us by God. We have the privilege of guiding and teaching them in their faith journey. It is important to remember that this teaching does not happen in a vacuum. We cannot just stand up in front of our children from week to week and share Bible facts and knowledge about God and expect for our teaching to change their lives. If we are to teach kids with any hope of life transformation, we must understand their world. We must know who they are, what their daily lives are like, and the challenges they face in order to speak into their hearts. Today, more than ever, the children in our classrooms come from a wide variety of backgrounds and abilities. As we better understand the environmental and developmental challenges they face, we can find more effective ways to reach and teach them.

Environmental Challenges

When a child steps into our classroom, it is helpful to know a little about their background in order to teach according to their needs. At face value, we cannot always tell the environment each particular child is coming from. Many factors may impede their learning process. Let's consider some of those factors.

Home Environment

All growth in children, including spiritual, happens best in the context of a loving relationship where children have learned they can trust their adult caretakers. As parents build a home filled with love and trust, their children will be far better adjusted and secure as they mature and move out into the world. They will also be more inclined to develop a healthy and personal relationship with God when the time comes.

However, consider the children in our ministries that come from families with different life circumstances. Children who have experienced divorce or the death of a parent struggle to process what's happened to their world and to adequately express their emotions. This can come out in frustration or behavior problems during the teaching time. If the teacher knows about that child's family, they can better respond to those distractions. Teachers must understand and be sensitive to their physical, mental, and emotional needs as much as their spiritual needs. Our Bible lessons are important, but so are the relationships teachers nurture with their students.

What does home look like for children of single parents? Single parents have the challenging task of working, managing a household, and raising children, most likely on a limited budget. These parents would welcome a support system that cared for them and their kids. One life group I was part of recognized the need of one of our single mothers. Her job was outside of the city to the east and her kids attended school in the southern part of the city. Our group arranged to pick up and take her kids to school each day, so that she could make the hour drive to and from work and be home when we dropped the kids off after school. It was a small thing for the five of us that each took one day of the week, but it meant she could have the extra time to bake some chocolate chip cookies or get supper ready for her kids. On other occasions, the men in our group would help fix their car and sub-in as father figures to meet their dates when her daughters went to prom.[10]

Economic Environment

Finances may be tight for some of our children's families. Hunger is such a developmental issue for children that schools across the country have lunch programs, sometimes breakfast too. If a child is hungry they may have a difficult time paying attention during school. This is true in church as well. I recall a time when I was substitute teaching in a class. One little girl kept coming back for more goldfish crackers during our snack time. After about the fourth cup of crackers, I told her that was enough. It did not dawn on me until later to consider her home situation. She may not have had breakfast that morning! If I had been her regular teacher I might have known more about her circumstances. Keeping this in mind, I would recommend that teachers be trained to be aware of these possibilities. If the situation called for it, I would see what we could do to meet that family's need and perhaps send food home with them on a regular basis. I also see the value in having food at children's events, such as vacation Bible school. This type of neighborhood outreach allows children to come and be fed and learn about Jesus in a welcoming and supportive environment. We seek to meet both their physical and spiritual needs.

School Environment

It is important to know what our school environments are like for our children. The demands of academics and school testing may cause anxiety and stress. As they get older, relationships with their peers get more and more complicated. The kids in our classes may silently be struggling with an issue of bullying. Or, with the reality of social media, their disagreement with a friend or enemy could quickly become a public attack through media with damaging effects. Other realities our kids face are depression and suicide. We must be more aware of these issues in order to speak into the lives of these children and help them navigate their world. As we teach, we can help make the Bible relevant to their situations only if we understand their situations.

Outside Influences

Today's society and the media are loud voices vying for the attention of adults and children alike. Christians are not immune to the noise. As adults we may be able to drown out the voices, but children need help discerning right and wrong within our society today. The intolerance and disdain for Christians is alarming and increasing. Sports heroes and superstars tout lifestyles that may not align with Christian values. And yet, these are people our children look up to. We can easily be mesmerized by materialism and commercialism. How can we help our kids have the proper perspective? We must be diligent to teach them to listen to the Lord's voice above the noise of the crowd.

Biblical Literacy

Perhaps, in the past, we could expect a certain level of understanding concerning biblical concepts. However, in today's world, we cannot expect that all of our children come from biblical homes. Our students may come to us with incorrect beliefs concerning Christianity. They may not have grown up in the church or their attendance may have been sporadic. We need to take that into consideration as we plan our lessons each week. Does the curriculum allow for different levels of biblical knowledge? Teachers may need to include additional explanation about a specific Bible story if they think children might not understand the context.

Inconsistent Church Attendance

For some churches, regular attenders are considered those who attend at least twice a month. In other words, they only attend twenty-six Sundays a year! Adults and kids are stretched and pulled in so many directions today. Busy weekly schedules of extracurricular activities and homework and Saturdays filled with sports and birthday parties leave families exhausted by Sunday morning. In general, society used to see Sundays and Wednesdays as "sacred" time and did not schedule extra activities on those days. This is no longer the case. Sports practices occur on Wednesdays and tournaments are regularly scheduled on Sundays without regard to team members who attend church activities. The dilemma becomes whether to skip church or skip the game, neither being good options for the children involved. Children, whose parents are divorced but have shared custody, may only attend your church twice a month. These children find themselves straddling between two worlds, two homes, and perhaps two churches. In all of these instances we need to ask, how does the spiritual formation of children fit into these parameters? How can we systematically teach them given the sporadic nature of attendance?

Developmental Challenges

In addition to the environmental challenges we've discussed, we need to consider developmental challenges. The children in our care are individual and unique creations of our Heavenly Father. He has gifted them with special personalities and abilities. It is our responsibility to meet them where they are and teach them God's truth on their specific levels and learning abilities.

Age-level Learning

Our teaching should be done in age-appropriate ways, according to what each age group is able to handle. For the preschoolers, we should use short sentences that match the child's language ability. Also, keep in mind there may be children who are new to church and may not know the "language." We need to be sensitive to words they may not know and explain their meaning. Because of their limited attention spans, we need to plan for a change of activity three or four times during the hour. This keeps them interested and on their toes. For all ages, when teaching the lesson, explain to the kids that this is a true story from the Bible. Tell, do not read the story. The Bible story should only be part of the group time. Everything you do in the hour should relate back to the truth of the Bible story. For the older ages, remember that children are still concrete thinkers. In cognitive development, they do not begin thinking abstractly until their teen years. So, avoid the use of symbolism, because children are literal-minded.

Teaching to Different Learning Styles

Every student learns differently. As you get to know the children in your class, be sensitive to their different learning styles. A good curriculum will take different learning styles into consideration and will use a variety of materials and activities to teach. While studying your lesson each week, modify the lesson plans, if needed, according to what will best reach your children. Small children learn from sensory experiences. And most students learn best by doing. Ask yourself, "How can I involve them in the learning process?" Learning centers, where activities are set out simultaneously at specific learning stations, are a great way to incorporate different learning styles. For example, an auditory learner can spend time at the music station and listen to a song that relates to the Bible lesson. Allow the child extra time at an activity that appeals to him. Help him finish with that activity before moving to another learning station.[11]

Accommodations for Special Needs Kids

Perhaps the most unreached people in our neighborhoods are families with special needs. The challenges they face on a day-to-day basis can be difficult and lonely at times. If your church does not have accommodations for special needs kids, I would encourage you to put some in place. Start small. Reach out to one or two families you may be aware of and find out their needs. Before they even come to your church, ask the parents, "What can we do to best help you and your child?" These children are "fearfully and wonderfully made" by our Lord and we would be blessed to have them in our churches.[12]

Understanding How to Reach Our Learners

Now that we have an understanding of the characteristics and needs of children and the challenges to learning that they face, how do we reach them so that actual learning takes place? Ultimately, how do we reach their hearts? I'd like to invite you to sit in on a teacher training session I gave my teachers as we prepared for the new school year.[13] Listen in.

Teaching Tools for the New Year

How many of you have been shopping at the back-to-school sales? I just love this time of year. It's filled with hope and anticipation of what the new school year holds. Do you feel that way? Or maybe you feel caught between the excitement of a new year and the anxiousness of not being ready for what is ahead. Do you have those conflicting feelings?

As with any major undertaking, you need the proper tools. I found this toolbox in my back-to-school shopping this year. And there may be some things in this toolbox that might help you. Let's take a look.

Prayer

It has been said, "Effective teaching begins on your knees." Before we ever enter the classroom we begin by praying for our students and ourselves that God would work in our hearts and our lives through this new year. Here are a few suggestions:

Pray for your lesson—Early in the week, pray through the lesson plan as you begin to study each week. Ask God to teach you his truths and guide you as you prepare. Then ask God to

help you effectively teach and communicate his truths to the children in your class.

Know the Children in Your Class

1. Full Name:
2. Age:
3. Birthdate:
4. Parents' First and Last Names:
5. Brothers and Sisters, Younger or Older?:
6. Interesting Circumstances of Family:
7. Most Frequent Playmates in Class:
8. Outside Interests (sports, reading, etc.):
9. Favorite Topic of Conversation:
10. Prayer Requests:

Pray over your class roster—Each one of those names on your class list represents a person God has entrusted to you for the year. You may know some of them already. You may even think you know their family and their situation. But take some time to get to know each child individually. Ask them questions and listen to them. They will reveal to you who they are and what they need from you. It helps me personally to keep a written record for each child (see sidebar). Learn what they like (sports, reading, etc.) and learn what is in their hearts. Follow up and ask them about those things. You could mail them an actual postcard before promotion Sunday to introduce yourself and perhaps send them other notes throughout the year. Adults seldom get handwritten letters anymore, but kids almost never get mail, so this would make a lasting impression.

Make prayer part of your class time—Take prayer requests during class and pray for them during class. This may seem impractical and you may feel like you don't have enough time for this if your curriculum is already planned. However, this could easily be incorporated during snack time for the younger kids (see sidebar example). For the older kids, this could happen at the beginning while you are gathering or during the first five minutes of class.

Teachers, if you want your children to learn about God's love and God's Word, you must begin with prayer. God wants these children to know and love him even more than you do. And when we agree with God in prayer, we partner with him and allow the Holy Spirit to work in their hearts.

A Loving Welcome

First and foremost, we show our students love. A big smile and a warm hello when they walk through the door tell our children they are welcome and you are glad they are there. As we talk to them and listen to their stories, they identify church as a place where they are loved and affirmed. We need to see them as God's precious creations. In a world that does not value children, we need to be their advocates. Jesus knew this all too well when he reprimanded the disciples for keeping the children from him (Matt. 19:12–15; Mark 10:13–16; Luke 18:15–17). Instead of seeing children as a bother and an interruption, we need to see them as Jesus did.

When we welcome these children, we are being the tangible hands and feet of Jesus to them.

Teaching Three-year-olds the Value of Prayer

Every Sunday, in the three-year-old class amazing things happen during snack time. While the children sit at the table and eat goldfish crackers, their teacher asks if anyone has a prayer request or an answered prayer. Hands quickly shoot up in the air. As these little ones share the burdens of their hearts, the teacher asks, "Who would like to pray for Emily's request?" A classmate raises his hand. And because Levi can't write the request down and remember it for long, the teacher walks around to his side and helps him pray. She whispers in his ear, "Dear Jesus…" and Levi prays, "Dear Jesus." She whispers again, "Please help Emily's grandmom to get better." Levi repeats the prayer. Next, the teacher asks for other prayer requests. And they repeat the process one by one as requests are made and prayers are spoken. For answered prayers, they thank God for his kindness. Week after week, these children are learning wonderful lessons on the value of prayer—God wants to hear our prayers, we can help our friends by praying for them, God answers our prayers, we can thank him for the wonderful things he does for us.

Early Birds

Early birds do have an advantage. My mentor emphasized this over and over again: "Teaching begins when the first child enters your classroom." In order to be ready for that first child, we need to be there early, not just on time. Arrive before the children. Come already prepared with all of your materials ready. Set up your room and equipment before students arrive. This allows you the opportunity to greet the children at the door of the room when they walk in.

Main Point

Know the main point (the "big idea") of your lesson. What is the one thing you want your children to learn from this lesson? Keep that main point central to your teaching and repeat it throughout the lesson. You should have a clear starting point and an outline that helps guide your teaching. If using a published curriculum, the lesson is generally well mapped out in this manner. But you do need to personalize it to your teaching style. Also, be sure to know the lesson well enough that you do not have to read directly from the teacher's guide. Let the Bible be central to your teaching, always emphasizing the main point.[14]

Memorize Scripture Together

The psalmist knew the importance of hiding God's Word in our hearts (Ps. 119:11). In order to live out God's Word, we have to know his Word. And it's important for children to memorize scripture at an early age. Children's minds are like sponges. Whatever they memorize in their early life will stick with them their whole life. Take the opportunity to memorize Scripture *with* your children. Most curriculum companies provide memory verses for each lesson. If not, it is still easy to incorporate scripture memory with your lessons. What is the main Scripture that applies to this lesson? Try these tips to help with memorizing:

1. Repeat the verse frequently during the class hour.
1. Teach them the meaning of the verse— very important!
2. Review the verses from week to week.
3. Use a rhythm or song or hand motions to help children remember.
4. Write verses on posters, notecards, or post-it notes.
5. Send the verses home with the children.
6. Post them in your home where you will see them.

Application

To make the most of your lesson, send the lesson home with them. James 1:22 tells us that we are to be both hearers and doers of the Word. How do we make this happen? As we move toward the end of the lesson, we ask "So what? What does all this information mean to us? What are we to do because of this information?" Give your children a specific application, a response that you expect from the class members. Sometimes I will give them a fun application task or "mission" in a sealed envelope. They love the challenge! Then, most importantly, I follow up with them the next week to see if they carried out their application task.[15]

You Make the Difference!

You can make a difference in the lives of these children! The task we have ahead of us is huge—to help our children become more like Christ. You may not feel adequate for the task of teaching and training these children. Adopt the posture of learning together with your kids. Find ways to learn and become better yourself. Read books on the subject. Speaking from my own experience, God works through our weaknesses. He helps us. He just needs us to be willing. So, my question to you is, "Are you willing to allow God to use you this year in the lives of these children?" Remember… you can make a difference.

The Children

See the kingdom potential of every child in your class. God does. And he has given these children to you for the year. What is your vision for the children you see in your class each week? Do the little things we do from week to week matter in the grand scheme of things? Yes!! What we do really does matter. Picture these kids five, ten, twenty years from now. What does God want them to become? You have the opportunity, by God's grace and with the Holy Spirit's help, to speak into their lives.

Two Important Considerations

Safety

Safety is one of the key goals for children's ministry. I often tell my students that it doesn't matter what a great children's program we have if we haven't also taken the time to make our rooms, our policies, and our program safe. If first-time visiting parents don't think the environment is safe, they will not bring their children back. New parents, even if they have attended your church for years, will suddenly be concerned with how safe the nursery is for their firstborn child. They need assurance you will take care of their child as if he or she was your own.

Well thought-out, written safety and security policies are necessary. Your plans should include a well nursery policy, emergency evacuation plans, and a child abuse prevention policy, all outlining what to do should those situations arise.[16] It is a sobering realization that the world can be a dangerous place for children. Let's not let that be the case in our children's ministries! Let's give them a safe environment where they can learn God's truths.[17]

Table 5.2 Teacher-to-Student Ratio[18]

Ages	Teacher-to-Student Ratio	Max Number per Room
Infants	1:2–3	10–12
Toddlers	1:3–4	12–15
2–3 years	1:5	16–20
4–5 years	1:6	20–24
K–6th grade	1:6–8	24–30

Curriculum Selection

This is probably the question I am most often asked from people in the trenches: "We are considering changing curriculum, so what curriculum do you recommend for our church?" That is a loaded question! First, it's important to stay consistent with a curriculum and not switch from year to year and to be uniform throughout your age levels. The reason for this is that each curriculum company has a "scope and sequence" built into their lessons. They've designed their curriculum to cover all the different Bible stories (scope) in an established order over time (sequence). That being said, you may need to change companies to get every age group aligned. If you find yourself in that position, do a side-by-side comparison of your own curriculum and two or three others to see which one best fits your church's specific culture, spiritual needs, and environment.[19] What works for one church may not work for another church, and vice versa.

Conclusion

If you minister to children from week to week, you have a precious calling. You have the opportunity to make a difference in the lives of children for eternity. When we serve children,

we serve Christ. Matthew 25:40 reminds us, "Whenever you did one of these things to the least of these—you did it to me." Jesus sits in your classrooms, reaches up to hold your hand walking down the hall, and asks you endless questions—all in the form of a child, so that you can show that child what God is like. They cannot see God or know him or know what he is like, unless they first see him in you.

The journey of ministering to children is not without its challenges and obstacles. It takes dedication and determination to recruit, train, and schedule volunteers, and then prepare lessons and teach week after week. One of my favorite verses when I'm busy gathering supplies and getting ready to teach is Galatians 6:9–10: "Let us not become weary in doing good, for at the proper time we will reap a harvest if we do not give up. Therefore, as we have opportunity, let us do good to all people, especially to those who belong to the family of believers." This is my encouragement to you. Don't grow weary! We have a harvest field that walks through our doors every Sunday. What a blessing that God uses common people like you and me to show his love to children and introduce them to Christ as their Savior. Our part is to be available and watch him work through us!

Discussion Questions

1. Do you enjoy teaching children? If so, what is your favorite age to teach? What characteristics of that age make them your favorite?

2. How does understanding development help you teach children better?

3. Using age-appropriate language, how would you explain the gospel to a child?

4. Do you know the attendance patterns of the regular families who attend your church? What can we do to increase attendance?

5. How can the safety and security measures you have in place in your church be improved?

Resources for Further Study

Books on Children's Ministry

Anthony, Michelle and Megan Marshman. *7 Family Ministry Essentials: A Strategy for Culture Change in Children's and Student Ministries*. Colorado Springs: David C. Cook, 2015.

Clark, Robert E., Joanne Brubaker, and Roy B. Zuck. *Childhood Education in the Church*. Chicago: Moody Press, 1986.

Fuller, Cheri. *Opening Your Child's Spiritual Windows: Ideas to Nurture Your Child's Relationship with God*. Grand Rapids: Zondervan, 2001.

Haystead, Wes and Sheryl. *How to Have a Great Sunday School*. Ventura, CA: Gospel Light, 2000.

Jones, Christine Yount. *Sunday School That Works! The Complete Guide to Maximize Your Children's Ministry Impact*. Loveland, CO: Group Publishing, 2014.

Trent, John T., Rick Osborne, and Kurt D. Bruner. *Parent's Guide to the Spiritual Growth of Children*. Focus on the Family. Wheaton, IL: Tyndale House Publishers, 2003.

Wideman, Jim. *Children's Ministry Leadership: The You-Can-Do-It Guide*. Loveland, CO: Group Publishing, 2003.

Zuck, Roy B. *Precious in His Sight: Childhood and Children in the Bible*. Grand Rapids: Baker Academic, 1997.

Books for Children

Allen, Joey. *Big Thoughts for Little Thinkers*. Green Forest, AR: New Leaf Press, 2005.

Anderson, Debby. *Let's Talk about Heaven*. Colorado Springs, CO: Chariot Victor, 1991.

Lawson, Michael S. *Grandpa Mike Talks about God*. Ross-shire, Scotland, UK: Christian Focus Publications, 2007.

Lloyd-Jones, Sally. *The Jesus Storybook Bible: Every Story Whispers His Name*. Grand Rapids: Zonderkidz, 2012.

Tangvald, Christine Harder. *Someone I Love Died*. 3rd ed. Colorado Springs: David C. Cook, 2012.

Conferences

Children's Pastors' Conference, International Network of Children's Ministry—www.incm.org

D6 Conference, Randall House Publishing—www.d6conference.com

Websites

Group Children's Ministry—www.childrensministry.com

Focus on the Family—www.family.org

Heritage Builders—www.heritagebuilders.com

Kids Sunday School Place—www.kidssundayschool.com

Leaders in Training Ministries—www.leadersintraining.com

Author Bio

Dr. Jerry Lawrence has served in a variety of children's ministry venues over her past twenty-plus years of experience developing and overseeing children's ministries in a church plant and in small, medium, and large churches. Jerry teaches Children's Ministry courses at Dallas Theological Seminary. She has spoken at large conferences in breakout sessions and also loves conducting teacher and parent training at various churches across the country and internationally. On Sunday mornings, you'll find Jerry in the preschool area at her church, welcoming and interacting with children and families. She enjoys making crafts, antique shopping, and a relaxing cup of tea or coffee with friends. She also loves spending time with her twelve nieces and nephews and eleven great nieces and nephews any chance she can!

CHAPTER 5 APPENDIX:
CHILDREN'S CHARACTERISTICS AND NEEDS[20]

Nursery and Toddlers: Birth to Age 2

Because the child is like this:	The child needs us to do this:
Physical	
He is growing rapidly.	Provide ample room and choice of activities.
His large muscles are still developing.	Provide large materials and activities on his level.
He has much energy.	Allow him to move from place to place.
He tires easily.	Alternate activity with quietness.
Mental	
His vocabulary is still limited.	Talk on his level.
His attention span is limited.	Provide a variety of activities.
He has limited ideas of time and space.	Avoid specific concepts of time.
He is imaginative.	Tell stories with excitement.
He is literal-minded.	Avoid symbolism.
He responds to suggestions.	Avoid commands.
He learns through his senses.	Provide opportunities to see, touch, hear and smell.

Because the child is like this:	The child needs us to do this:
Social	
He is self-centered.	Encourage sharing.
He is increasing in friendliness and ability to play with others.	Provide more opportunity for group experiences.
He learns by imitation.	Be a good guide.
He wants approval.	Commend him for doing right.
Emotional	
He has strong emotions.	Control own emotions; have quiet atmosphere.
He has some insecure feelings.	Provide a feeling of security through activity.
He has some control over crying.	Encourage him to ask for things—not cry!
He may "explode" when angry.	Do not let tantrums be successful!
He may be jealous.	Avoid showing favoritism.
He is naturally sympathetic.	Teach sharing with the less fortunate.
Spiritual	
He thinks of God in a personal way.	Try to show him Jesus as his best friend.
He has a sense of awe and wonder.	Provide examples of God's creation.
He has simple trust in persons and in God.	Be trustworthy. Teach that God sometimes says, "No."

Preschool: Ages 3–5

Because the child is like this:	The child needs us to do this:
Physical	
She is active.	Provide ample room and activities.
She may not grow at the same rate as other children of her age.	Do not expect too much from her.
Her large muscles are developing.	Provide large materials and toys.
Her vocal muscles are not developed.	Provide songs on her level and range.
She can do only one thing at a time.	Provide simple activities one at a time.
She is susceptible to disease.	Keep rooms clean and sanitary. No unnecessary traffic.
Her senses are hungry.	Provide satisfying materials.
Mental	
She has a limited vocabulary.	Choose simple stories; use short action words.
She likes repetition.	Choose stories worthy of repetition. Repeat words. Have frequent recall.
Her attention span is short.	Use the first three minutes to the best advantage.
Her memory is not dependable.	Do not expect her to remember from one Sunday to another.
She believes everything she hears.	Tell her the truth.
She does not understand symbolism.	Avoid symbolism in any form.
She has no sense of time.	Use "long ago" or "when the piano begins to play."
She learns by doing.	Provide guided learning experiences.

Because the child is like this:	The child needs us to do this:
Social	
She is dependent.	Give her assistance if she needs it.
She is timid.	Provide small group experiences.
She is self-centered.	Teach her to share.
She likes to play alone.	Provide individual play experiences.
She has imaginative playmates.	Do not encourage her to give them up.
She desires attention.	Give attention within limits.
Emotional	
She is "excitable."	Avoid confusion. Plan with the child in mind.
She is afraid of the unfamiliar.	Provide stability.
She has many fears.	Provide stories with happy endings.
She frequently says, "No."	Provide choices.
She may have temper tantrums.	Try to avoid them; do not let them accomplish their intended purposes.
She needs security.	Visit her home. Be regular in attendance.
Spiritual	
She can be aware of God.	Provide worship opportunities on her level.
She "catches" her religion.	"Expose" her to good examples.
She can talk to God in her own way.	Provide opportunities for her to talk to God.
She is beginning to see the difference between right and wrong.	Teach her that wrongdoing is not pleasing to God.
She can experience real worship.	Provide times of group worship. Be alert for spontaneous worship!

Younger Elementary: Kindergarten—3rd grade, 6–9 years old

Because the child is like this:	The child needs us to do this:
He is energetic, but tires easily.	Provide occasional rest periods. Change activities about three times in an hour.
He can control large muscles much better than smaller ones.	Plan activities requiring the use of large muscles. Also plan activities (i.e. cutting, writing) that help develop his small muscles.
He is not persevering—his interests fluctuate.	Supervise his work and encourage him to finish what he starts.
He is impressionable and imitative.	Set forth the Lord Jesus as Savior and the One perfect example of what he should be and do. Set a Christlike example and live out the truths we teach.
He is eager for adult approval—prefers that over approval of his own age group.	Approve right conduct and efforts to do right, and disapprove as little as possible. Give him jobs such as putting away materials and commend him for helping.
He learns best through seeing, hearing, doing (sensory avenues).	Tell Bible stories vividly and personally so that he projects himself into the experiences of the characters. Have him retell the story with stick figures or through dramatic play.
He is non-competitive—prefers group activities with no competition to individual ones.	Encourage the whole group to work and play together cooperatively, but be careful not to force all children into the same mold.
He is sympathetic to others.	Interest him in doing things for others—for his family, friends, and far-off missionaries.
He is literal-minded: thinks in terms of the concrete, but enjoys the imaginary as well as the real.	Be careful to differentiate between Bible stories which are true, and imaginary, made-up stories. Present Bible miracles as wonders that show God's great power. Avoid abstract symbolism and generalities. Give him simple problems to solve so he can reason accurately. Show him how to go to the Bible to solve personal problems.

Because the child is like this:	The child needs us to do this:
He is curious and alert to many interests in his vastly expanding world.	Listen to and learn about his interests and needs. Use these as an illustration or to apply Bible truths. Aid learning by using interesting pictures, nature objects, souvenirs from mission fields, etc. Let him handle, explore, and experiment with these items.
He is responsive to teaching: The third grader is much more able to grasp and retain facts than the first grader.	Make teaching simple for the first grader, challenging enough for the third grader, and give the second grader all the child is capable of doing. Make spiritual truth such an integral part of the Bible story that there is no need for a moral to be tacked on to the end.
He is accountable: Most younger elementary kids have reached the age of accountability (they understand the difference between right and wrong and are sensitive to sin). They are able to grasp the plan of salvation and the simpler rules of conduct from God's Word.	Help him to see his need for a Savior by letting him realize he cannot obey by himself. Present the plan of salvation in a variety of ways. Plan the invitation for salvation so he trusts Christ because he wants to, and not merely to please us. Give him practice in discriminating between right and wrong. Explain to the Christian that if he sins he displeases God and should confess his sin in order to be forgiven.
He is able to memorize well.	Give each word in the memory verses a rich background of meaning. Weave Bible verses naturally throughout all activities.
He is capable of heartfelt worship.	Choose songs he can understand and sing joyously. Teach him to pray naturally, expressing praise and needs in his own words.
He is trustful, having a simple faith in God. Open to Bible truths on his age level. Willing to give himself wholeheartedly to the Savior when properly motivated.	Emphasize God's love, care, forgiveness, presence, and all-powerfulness. Teach, by example and instruction, reverence for our holy God and respect for the church in which we worship the Lord. Encourage him to do things for others because he loves the Lord and wants to please him. In all activities relate Bible truths to daily life, encouraging him to conform to God's will in what he thinks, says, and does.

Older Elementary: 4th–6th grade, 10–12 years old

Because the child is like this:	The child needs us to do this:
She is bubbling over with energy and shows signs of getting out of hand in class.	Guide excess energy into useful ends—helping in the room, participating in the program, finding answers in her Bible.
She loses interest in Sunday school if she gets "the same old thing" every week.	Inject freshness and variety with visual aids, discussion, role playing, drills, reading from missionaries' letters.
Her reasoning powers are growing, but she still thinks literally and needs help to understand the many figurative and symbolic references in the Bible.	Explain Bible words and figures of speech. Use pictures and objects, perhaps films, to clarify foggy impressions. Don't take her understanding for granted.
She likes to memorize because she does it easily.	Lead her in learning Bible verses that answer her questions, help her with problems, and encourage her to express her feelings about God and Jesus as Savior.
She is growing more independent. Wants to discover answers herself.	Treat her in a "grown-up" way, asking her opinions, recognizing her ability to think for herself. Suggest a problem and ask how she'd tackle it. Let her experience the joy of finding her own answers in God's Word.
She wants to plan things herself. Desires responsibility.	Make her feel important and useful. Let her plan class projects and outings, with just enough guidance to insure completing what is started. Show her that she can be useful to the Lord.
She likes to read adventure and hero stories. Identifies herself with heroine (or hero).	Discuss together the qualities of Bible heroes. Encourage her to read Christian biographies and missionary stories on her level.

Because the child is like this:	The child needs us to do this:
She shows considerable respect for authority and a high sense of honor and justice.	Keep her respect by controlling the class with authority that is consistently fair. Encourage her to take more responsibility as she shows she is ready for it. Stress the authority of Christ as God's Son and the Bible as God's Holy Word.
She is alert and eager to learn.	Keep ahead of her. Stimulate her curiosity. Show her how to use a Bible concordance to find verses that help her grow in Christ.
She likes competition and a sense of self-accomplishment.	Involve her in friendly competition with classmates. Also encourage her to compete with herself in memory work, daily Bible reading, and attendance by keeping a record.
She has many problems—getting along with boys and girls, doing what parents and teachers want, getting good grades, playing well in sports, or doing more things on her own.	Be sensitive to her needs. Depend on the Holy Spirit to help you to teach Bible truths that will be what God claims—a sword to pierce, food to nourish, light to illumine, and seed to grow.
She may "horse around" to cover up the fact that her heart has been touched.	Provide an outlet for her feelings by transferring her feeling to doing—helping, sharing, obeying, etc.
She wants to be part of a "gang."	Concentrate on winning the gang leaders and work through them to reach others, through group projects.
She is antagonistic to the opposite gender.	Plan separate classes for boys and girls with teachers of his/her own gender. Stress teamwork within each class and provide for some competition between classes.
She recognizes her own sinfulness and realizes her need of help to do right.	Present Christ as God's Son and the only Savior from sin. Stress his great love and his longing to help all who trust and obey him.

Endnotes

1. George Barna, *Transforming Children into Spiritual Champions* (Ventura, CA: Regal Books, 2003), 47.

2. Jean Piaget and Bärbel Inhelder, *The Psychology of the Child* (New York: Basic Books, 1969); Erik H. Erikson, *Childhood and Society*, 2nd rev. and enl. ed. (New York: Norton, 1964); James W. Fowler, *Stages of Faith: The Psychology of Human Development and the Quest for Meaning* (San Francisco: Harper & Row, 1981).

3. Ben Freudenburg and Rick Lawrence, *The Family-Friendly Church* (Loveland, CO: Group Publishing, 1998), 77.

4. Also see the chapter "Educational Ministry in the Smaller Church" by Lin McLaughlin for discussion of issues related to overall church size and facility space.

5. Adapted from Wes and Sheryl Haystead, *How to Have a Great Sunday School* (Ventura, CA: Gospel Light, 2000), 201.

6. Erik H. Erikson, *Childhood and Society*, 2nd rev. ed. (New York: Norton, 1964), 249.

7. Roy B. Zuck, *Precious in His Sight: Childhood and Children in the Bible* (Grand Rapids, MI: Baker Books, 1996), 240.

8. Helpful examples for teaching creatively are included in the chapter "Creativity in Educational Minsitry" by Karen Giesen.

9. Jason Mandryk, *Operation World: The Definitive Prayer Guide to Every Nation* (Downers Grove, IL: InterVarsity Press, 2010).

10. See the chapter "Invisible: Single Adults" by Joye Baker for more information on ministry with single adults.

11. See the chapter "Creativity in Educational Ministry" by Karen Giesen for additional information on learning styles.

12. See the chapter "Overlooked: The Disabled" by Mike Justice for additional information on special needs ministry.

13. Teacher training is most effective if it is offered at a convenient time, is not just a "pep rally" but gives them information they don't already know, gives teachers a variety of workshop options, and furthers their knowledge in a systematic way. Make it worth their time to come. Raise the bar and help them see the privilege they have of teaching these young ones. Let them rise to the challenge of becoming even better teachers.

14. See the addendum by Sue Edwards on "The Big Idea" in Karen Giesen's chapter "Creativity in Educational Ministry."

15. See the addendum by Sue Edwards on "Hook, Book, Look, Took" in Karen Giesen's chapter "Creativity in Educational Ministry."

16. An example of a Safety and Emergency Procedures Manual can be found at http://fellowshipdallas.org/ministries/kids/im-new/.

17. Ministry Safe is an organization dedicated to educating and training the church for the purpose of preventing child sexual abuse. Their website is www.ministrysafe.com.

18. Adapted from Haystead and Haystead, *How to Have a Great Sunday School*, 201.

19. For a list of children's curriculum providers, see http://www.kidmintools.com/2014/06/30/the-huge-list-of-childrens-curriculum-providers/.

20. Information in these charts adapted from *The Christian Educator's Handbook on Children's Ministry: Reaching and Teaching the Next Generation,* by Robert J. Choun and Michael S. Lawson (Grand Rapids: Baker Books, 1998), 60–64.

Chapter 6
IN BETWEEN: ADOLESCENTS

Jay Sedwick

Don't let anyone look down on you because you are young, but set an example for the believers in speech, in conduct, in love, in faith, and in purity.

—1 Timothy 4:12

THREE MILESTONES IN MY life define my commitment to the Lord and service to his church. First, I remember my conversion at the age of six in the kitchen of our small town church where two devoted senior adult ladies loved us and pointed us to Jesus during "children's church." Mrs. Davis and Mrs. Fenstemaker are with Jesus now, but their faithfulness made a difference to this young boy. Second, I responded affirmatively at the age of twelve when the speaker at summer camp asked if anyone sensed God calling them to fulltime ministry. I tucked that decision away for years, though I never forgot what I had done. Our church had a strong and vibrant youth ministry with solid teaching, worship and fellowship. I distinctly remember encouraging relationships with adult leaders and friends throughout my teenage years that helped me navigate my way through the challenges of teenage life. Third, at the age of twenty-one, sitting in my hotel room in Chicago one evening after spending a few days attending engineering lectures, God reminded me of my earlier commitment when I was twelve. I was convinced that night he wanted me to serve in the local church as a vocational minister. I quit my engineering job and moved to Dallas, Texas, to attend seminary.

Upon arrival I quickly joined a local church where the tenured youth minister took me under his wing. During the next four years I participated in organizing and leading ministry for youth that really made a difference. I saw lives radically changed. When I realized how vitally important reaching teenagers with the gospel of Jesus Christ was for their survival and the future of the church, I decided to devote my energy to youth ministry for the long haul.

> Here's an intriguing thought—Jesus may have been the first youth minister. In Matthew 17:24 Jesus was challenged with the requirement to pay the temple tax, which all male Jews between the ages of twenty and fifty years were required to pay. The Lord instructed Peter to go fishing for a shekel. In order to not "offend" those in authority, he and Peter paid the tax with that shekel. Certainly the other disciples were present, which has led some commentators to suggest Peter was the only one of the twelve disciples who paid the tax because he was the only one over the age of twenty. Intriguing possibility, indeed.

Why Youth Ministry?

When I speak on the critical importance of youth ministry in the church, I usually ask my seminary students, by show of hands, how many in the group trusted Jesus Christ as Savior before the age of thirteen? About 50 percent of the class raises their hands. I then ask those who trusted Christ by the age of eighteen to add their raised hands to the group. Typically, around 85 percent of the students' hands will be raised. The other 15 percent in the room (they are all Christians; it's a seminary class) trusted in Jesus during their adult lives. Although not a scientific survey, this anecdotal evidence is consistent semester after semester. Incidentally, Barna found thirteen

to be the most common age for conversion, with half trusting Christ before thirteen.[1]

Then I ask students, if they ran a business and 85 percent of the success, or "return on investment," occurred in a particular product division, where would they put their best resources and expend the most energy to produce even more? Likewise, if the return on investment in evangelism is highest when working with children and teenagers, it's reasonable that the church should invest its best resources (people, facilities, money) into this area of ministry. A more recent Barna study concluded that the chances of trusting Christ as Savior dramatically diminish throughout adult life after nineteen years of age.[2] Given this strong evidence, every church must make youth ministry a high priority.

Adolescence

Little is known about Jesus's early life before he began public ministry around age thirty. The birth narratives in Matthew's and Luke's gospels give us pertinent details about his early childhood which are critical to proving that he fulfilled Old Testament prophecy and was, in fact, the promised Messiah. Scripture skips over the next ten years or so of his life to the Passover narrative in Luke 2. Jesus, now twelve years old, was inadvertently left behind in Jerusalem for several days before his parents realized their mistake. Luke's commentary in verse 52 on Jesus's development serves as a helpful outline for the dramatic changes that dominate the typical teenager's life: "And Jesus kept increasing in *wisdom* and *stature*, and in *favor with God and men*" (emphasis mine).

I equate "wisdom" with cognitive development—the ability to process information and make decisions. "Stature" refers to physical development—the biological changes that take place mainly throughout the teenage years. I identify "favor with God" with spiritual development—a sensitivity to spiritual truth and God's leading. "Favor with men" corresponds to sociological and emotional development—the ability to relate well to yourself, others, and the world around you through relationships. These four distinct categories of growth and development seem to highlight Jesus's humanity and his ability to personally identify with each one of us. The writer of Hebrews points this out as well when he says, "For we do not have a high priest who cannot sympathize with our weaknesses, but One who has been tempted in all things as we are, yet without sin" (4:15, NASB). As a youth minister, I've encouraged many teenagers with this thought—that Jesus knows and understands what they are going through. He can relate to their struggles, their pain, and their successes as well. They can "cast their cares upon him."

Luke 2:52 describes what we call adolescence today—the transition from childhood to adulthood that begins with the onset of puberty and ends with the assumption of adult responsibilities and prerogatives. It startles many to consider that Jesus went through adolescence. The origin of the word is Latin, so it would not have been called that in Jerusalem in his day. Many sociologist and developmental psychologists assert that adolescence is a relatively new phenomenon created by Western cultural forces and became an identifiable life stage in the late nineteenth century with the publication of G. Stanley Hall's magnum opus in 1904 entitled *Adolescence: Its Psychology and Its Relations to Physiology, Anthropology, Sociology, Sex, Crime, and Religion.*[3]

David Setran and Chris Keisling discuss the five cultural factors that help explain why some adolescents may not emerge as adults.

1. Delayed marriage—The average age for first marriage is now 27. It was 21 in 1960.

2. Expansion and extension of higher education—Today that number is nearly 3/4 with 1/3 continuing on to graduate school. Just over 1/3 of high school graduates went to college in 1960.

3. Student loan debt and the inability to gain financial stability most feel they need for marriage and starting a family—Job-hopping is common often resetting the starting point for earning.

4. Enabling safety net provided by parents—Young adults are increasingly returning home to live underwritten by their parents.

5. Growing cultural tolerance for premarital sexuality. Marriage is no longer necessary for sexual intimacy, and easy access to birth control has removed reproductive consequences. As a result, the assumption of adult responsibility, like a stable career path, marriage and parenting, are all put on hold.[4]

—David Setran and Chris Keisling

While not causal, around the same time in history, the passage of mandatory education laws, juvenile justice laws, and child labors laws played a significant role in the focus on adolescence as a distinct phase of life-span development. However, a literature review shows this life stage was identified, discussed, depicted in story, denounced, and even extolled by countless observers throughout centuries.[5] Evidently, adolescence has been a part of human development for a very long time. Interestingly, the term most often used throughout history to describe those engaged in navigating adolescence has been simply "youth."

Today a huge industry studies adolescence with the implied goal of helping society make sense of this transition (and making as much money as possible through target marketing). Extended adolescence, a fairly new term, refers to the lengthening of adolescence beyond when most in society feel adult responsibility should be assumed. Jeffrey Arnett, in a widely circulated article in *American Psychologist* from 2000, established an entirely new field of research based on his identification of emerging adulthood. He argues that what we are seeing is not an extension of adolescence, but instead a separate life stage never before seen in history.[6] Many researchers are clamoring to study this intriguing proposition. The Millennial generation, those born between 1982 and 2004 according to generational researchers Neil Howe and William Strauss, are the newest designated segment of the demographic spectrum.[7] Interestingly, according to their brackets, some Millennials are adolescents and some are emerging adults.

Adolescent Development and Identity Formation

Dramatic changes take place in every person's life during adolescence. The transition from childhood to adulthood is often fraught with serious challenges. It is extremely helpful to understand the basic characteristics of teenagers from early to late adolescence, but that is beyond the scope of our discussion (see Table 1 for a brief overview of stages in adolescent development). It is important to make sure that your youth ministry programming is developmentally appropriate for the intended audience.

Table 6.1 Stages in Adolescent Development[8]

Stages of Adolescent Development	Early Adolescence Approximately 10–14 years of age	Middle Adolescence Approximately 15–16 years of age	Late Adolescence Approximately 17–21 years of age
Identity Development and Movement toward Independence	Emerging identity shaped by in/external influences	Self-involvement, alternating between unrealistically high expectations and worries about failure	Firmer identity
	Moodiness	Complaints that parents interfere with independence	Ability to delay gratification
	Improved speech to express oneself	Extremely concerned with appearance and body	Ability to think through ideas

Stages of Adolescent Development	Early Adolescence Approximately 10–14 years of age	Middle Adolescence Approximately 15–16 years of age	Late Adolescence Approximately 17–21 years of age
Identity Development and Movement toward Independence	More likely to express feelings by action than by words (may be more true for males) Close friendships gain importance Less attention shown to parents, with occasional rudeness Realization parents not perfect Identification of own faults Search for new people to love in addition to parents Tendency to return to childish behavior during times of stress Peer group influence on personal interests and clothing styles	Feelings of strangeness about one's self and body Lowered opinion of and withdrawal from parents Effort to make new friends; strong emphasis on the new peer group Periods of sadness as the psychological loss of parents takes place Examination of inner experiences, which may include writing a diary	Ability to express ideas in words More developed sense of humor Interests and emotions become more stable Ability to make independent decisions Ability to compromise Pride in one's work Self-reliance Greater concern for others
Future Interests and Cognitive Development	Increasing career interests Mostly interested in present and near future Greater ability to work	Intellectual interests gain importance Some sexual and aggressive energies directed into creative and career interests Anxiety can emerge related to school and academic performance	More defined work habits Higher level of concern for the future Thoughts about one's role in life
Ethics and Self-Direction	Rule- and limit-testing Experimentation with cigarettes, marijuana, and alcohol Capacity for abstract thought.	Development of ideals and selection of role models More consistent evidence of conscience Greater goal-setting capacity Interest in moral reasoning	Useful insight Focus on personal dignity and self-esteem Ability to set goals and follow through Acceptance of social institutions and cultural traditions Self-regulation of self-esteem.

Identity formation, a major task of adolescence, permeates all aspects of the four categories of development—wisdom (cognitive), stature (physical), favor with God (spiritual), favor with men (social/emotional). Youth are asking three basic identity questions. First, "Who am I?" This question is the most critical to answer correctly, for it directly influences the answers to the next two. Scripture tells us we are created by God in his image (Gen. 1:27). Psalm 100:3 says, "It is he who made us, and we are his; we are his people, the sheep of his pasture." The answer for every teenager needs to be, "I am a child of God. He made me on purpose. He did not make a mistake." Accepting who we are as a purposeful creation by the God of the universe is critical for healthy development in every other area.

The second identity question is, "Why am I here?" Why did God create me in the first place? The correct answer to this question is reflected in the Westminster Shorter Catechism, which asks, "What is the chief end of man?" The proper response is, "Man's chief end is to glorify God, and to enjoy him forever."[9] Paul tells us in 1 Corinthians 10:31, "So whether you eat or drink or whatever you do, do it all for the glory of God." We were created by God on purpose in order to glorify him with our lives. What better way to glorify him than to point others to him? As his ambassadors we are to represent Christ well in every sphere of influence (2 Cor. 5:20). I pray this over the guys in my small group Bible study every week as they walk out the door.

The third identity question, "Where am I going?" is not an eschatological question about eternal destination. Rather, this question deals with the chosen life path for the individual. Essentially, this is the same question as, "What do I want to be when I grow up?" I want every teenager to understand that he can glorify God through his work, his job, and his profession. No dichotomy should exist between church life and work life. Colossians 3:23 states, "Whatever you do, work at it with all your heart, as working for the Lord, not for human masters." I want teenagers to conform every aspect of their lives to the will of God. True fulfillment comes when we are doing what God has designed us to do.

Let me briefly explain the more formal approach to understanding what the broader field of researchers mean by identity formation. Building on Erik Erikson's work in the 1960s in developmental psychology, James Marcia focused on adolescent identity development and proposed four possible identity statuses—Identity Diffusion, Identity Foreclosure, Identity Moratorium, and Identity Achievement.[10] These are not sequential stages but choices adolescents make in committing to various aspects of their identity in response to normal identity crisis:

- Identity Diffusion: A teenager experiencing identity diffusion has neither investigated nor made a commitment to a faith tradition or an occupational direction and may seem careless and apathetic.
- Identity Foreclosure: Identity foreclosure describes an adolescent who has made a commitment to a faith tradition and occupational direction without exploring the many possibilities available and may feel threatened when her commitments are challenged.
- Identity Moratorium: When a teen is actively exploring the realm of possible options for faith and work he is said to

be in identity moratorium. Most adolescents are experiencing this status as a part of their normal development.

- Identity Achievement: Those who navigate the choices and possibilities and make a commitment to a faith tradition and occupational direction have established their identity, hence their classification in identity achievement.

> The formation of one's sexual identity normally takes place during adolescence as well. Since the culture is often at odds with the church on this issue, youth ministry leaders need to learn how to provide a safe environment where teens can talk to those they trust. "In youth ministry, this means that we intentionally seek to care for and minister to young people who are navigating sexual-identity questions and concerns—rather than alienating them or dismissing them…. If anything, our failure to discuss the topic in meaningful and relevant ways is one of the things that drives young people toward greater isolation and the consolidation of a new sexual identity."[11]
> —Mark Yarhouse

I like to use the term "faith ownership" as the most significant aspect of identity achievement. Most children believe what their parents taught them to believe. Their faith resembles their parents' faith. At some point in their lives, teenagers must transition to a personal faith commitment

to Jesus Christ, owning their own faith; not because someone they know and trust told them to, but because they have responded to the Holy Spirit's leading. Even if others fall away because they never truly "owned" their faith, those who own their faith will persist. If teenagers enter young adult life without achieving faith ownership, they will often struggle for years and sadly may fall away. One of the main purposes of youth ministry is to help teenagers achieve faith ownership.

Youth Culture

Knowing and understanding youth culture will enhance the effectiveness of youth ministry. Living in the Western culture, youth experience what could be classified as a "subculture" with distinct characteristics from the broader culture. Walt Mueller, founder of the Center for Parent Youth Understanding, argues the church needs to approach youth ministry as a cross-cultural missions venture.[12] When missionaries seek to minister among a "foreign" people group, regardless of geographic location, they must learn about that group's dress, food, music, rituals, language, and values. Similarly, youth ministry leaders need to learn about these characteristics in the lives of the church youth and surrounding community. Youth ministry leaders do not have to "experience" all aspects of youth culture to understand it better, but they need to be aware of those experiences through research, paying attention to the news and current events, general reading, noting trends, watching and listening to various forms of media, and simply talking with youth about their lives. That way, when youth ministry leaders get up to speak to students, they will use current events and relevant stories to contextualize the Bible and the gospel message.

The message never changes but the teaching methods, for example delivery and illustrations, must relate to the audience.

In John 17:15 Jesus prayed for all of us: "My prayer is not that you take them out of the world but that you protect them from the evil one." Jesus knew the culture was evil and it would not improve until he returned. Youth ministry leaders have a responsibility to discern their way through the youth culture, rejecting all that contradicts and violates Scripture, and wisely using what remains to effectively communicate God's Word to this generation.

Media Influence

Collectively, media is one of the strongest influences on youth, shaping youth culture. They listen to persuasive music. They play video games that condition their responses. They watch movies that shape their worldviews. Many are devoted to TV shows that shape their language and behavior. Large media conglomerates will stop at nothing to motivate teenagers to buy advertised products.[13] The Kaiser Family Foundation conducted research from 1999 to 2010 to measure media use among eight- to eighteen-year-olds in the United States. Their last report discovered that the average user consumed 7 hours, 38 minutes of media every day.[14] Common Sense Media conducted its own research on media use. Even though their research design was somewhat different, the study revealed a higher average media usage per day for thirteen- to eighteen-year-olds: 8 hours, 56 minutes. The study grouped eight- to twelve-year-olds and found their daily average media usage to be 5 hours, 55 minutes.[15] No one can dispute the power of the media over our youth. Many adults can't fathom spending that much time in a single day

consuming media. But before we get too smug, another study by Common Sense Media found that parents spend 9 hours, 22 minutes every day consuming media![16]

Not only has the media become more sophisticated (e.g., algorithmic target marketing by Facebook and Google), but the technology used to deliver and consume content has also changed rapidly. Youth ministry leaders, as a part of their youth cultural awareness, need to stay informed on what their youth are watching and listening to on their smartphones, tablets, laptops, and desktops. Video streaming services continue to innovate and don't just deliver programming from other sources. Now they create their own content. Social media applications push information and events in front of our youth's eyes and ears. The almost universal acceptance and usage of these various types of social media shape the thinking and behavior of our teens in ways we haven't even considered or discovered. Many research studies are underway attempting to identify the effects of social media usage. Technology and media companies are constantly imagining new ways to deliver content. You can be sure technology on the horizon, yet to be revealed, will amaze us all.

Here are a few suggestions for managing media consumption.

- Help parents learn to discern the worldview behind media messages that are both overt and covert.
- Encourage parents to regularly engage their teens in discussion about the media they consume, and to ask their teens about both the beneficial and detrimental aspects of spending time consuming various media.

- Since time is one commodity we never get back, help parents set sensible rules limiting the amount of time their teens spend with media. Make sure that youth don't have a television, a computer, or a smartphone in their bedrooms. Access to pornography has never been easier, and many teens struggle with this temptation in the privacy of their bedrooms. Services like Covenant Eyes (www.covenanteyes.com) help teens (and adults) learn to defeat this temptation.
- Finally, parents should consider their own habits and the examples they set for their teens who will typically adopt these habits themselves.

Given the power and influence of media in all of our lives, we must learn to leverage its use for the glory of God and our benefit. Media is neither good nor evil, per se. We can use social media in creative ways to effectively communicate with youth and their families. A major weakness of many youth ministers is poor communication. A number of software applications are available to enhance effective communication. Use group texting to keep everyone up to date on what's happening in the youth group. Create websites to let people know who you are, and as a landing place for all things youth related at your church, i.e., your calendar of events and the information about each one. You can even create interactive web pages to get those permission forms filled out and turned in on time. Technology has opened up so many avenues to creatively and effectively do youth ministry.[17]

Teens and Pornography

Teens' access to pornographic material has never been easier. "A Barna study in partnership with Josh McDowell Ministry shows that the proliferation of high-speed internet and internet-enabled devices has fundamentally altered the ways people view and interact with pornography.... The web has by far eclipsed all other avenues for accessing pornography. Smartphones offer new and dynamic means of accessing and distributing pornography.... Apps and text are an increasingly popular option, especially among teens and young adults. While just 12 percent of adults 25 and older view porn mostly on their phone, teens and young adults are three times more likely to do so (38%)" (*Barna Trends 2017*, p. 23).

"What is particularly disturbing is the apparent lack of conviction that viewing pornography is morally wrong. Thirteen percent of teens say they talk about porn in a positive way, and 40 percent accept and assume that all teens are viewing porn ... that it's no big deal" (*Barna Trends 2017*, p. 87). Parents, keep those media devices out of the privacy of your teenager's bedroom as a precaution.

The History of Youth Ministry and Parental Responsibility

In America, the short history of the roots of organized youth ministry can be traced back to the student movements on New England college campuses in the eighteenth century.[18] Several significant parachurch ministries formed later, like Youth for Christ and Young Life in the early twentieth century. Denominations established their own forms of youth ministry organizations and strategies in response to these parachurch youth groups. Prior to the advent of these organizations, parents were primarily responsible for the spiritual development of their children, whether they were doing it or not. These new strategies tended to move parents out of that primary role, delegating it instead to the "professionals."

Through the late 1980s, many churches followed an "attractional" youth ministry model, focusing on the charisma of the youth minister (i.e., the "professional") to plan and execute creative programming that would draw students to the church. They viewed the youth minister as the youth's primary spiritual leader. He or she planned, organized, and directed the teen's spiritual development. For many larger churches, the youth ministry evolved into a church within a church with its own building, ministers, musicians, leadership structure, and significant budget. Most parents "outsourced" the responsibility to teach their children reading, writing, and arithmetic to the public schools. In a similar way, many parents became accustomed to outsourcing the spiritual development of their children to the local church's children and youth ministries. The parents trusted the church to do the job that Scripture

clearly placed on their shoulders. Fortunately, in the early 1990s, the pendulum began to swing in the other direction.

Many parents, and the churches they attend, now realize parents must take the lead in their children's spiritual development. After all, "Children are a gift of the LORD" (Ps. 127:3, NASB). He put children in the right families at the right time in order to accomplish his purposes in their lives. God doesn't make mistakes. He intends for parents to teach their own children what they need to know about him.

To help us understand the parents' role, God instructed Moses to deliver the commandments in Deuteronomy 6. Even though he delivered these commandments to the whole nation of Israel, they also apply to individual families. Moses states:

> These commandments that I give you today are to be on your hearts. Impress them on your children. Talk about them when you sit in your house and when you walk along the road, when you lie down and when you get up. Tie them as symbols on your hands and bind them on your foreheads. Write them on the doorframes of your houses and on your gates.
> —Deuteronomy 6:6–9

In other words, parents should saturate every part of their family life with God's Word and stories of his faithfulness. The parents are responsible to ensure this happens. To be sure, the community of faith also has some corporate responsibility, but parents carry the primary responsibility of creating the proper environment to cultivate spiritual growth. Parents need to leverage everything they can because they are still the strongest overall influence in the lives of their teens. Sure, the media makes a difference. Peers make a difference. But parents are still the most influential … for better or for worse. Unfortunately, some parents don't take their responsibility seriously, either because they don't care or they don't know how. The church family and the youth ministry leadership have the responsibility to help these families succeed.

Many of the "problems" of adolescence can be traced back to the dysfunction of families. When the home is not conducive to experiencing the love of God, can we really be surprised when teens end up in trouble? In these situations, the community of faith needs to step in and provide support and assistance for teenagers who may not have the best situation at home. Families with strong marriages should be encouraged to "spiritually adopt" teenagers who need healthy parental role models to guide them.

An additional complication is divorce, leading to broken homes and the prevalence of weary single parents struggling to provide for and lead their families. I believe God has a special place in his heart for single parents who desperately want the best for their kids but who are disadvantaged sometimes through no fault of their own. Single parents need the support and love of the church community and the partnership with the youth ministry leadership to help them fulfill their responsibilities.[19]

A healthy "partnership" should exist between parents and youth ministry leaders. God calls youth ministry leaders to come alongside the parents and assist them in any way possible as they seek to raise their teens to honor the Lord. However, these leaders should not try to take the place of the parents or come between parents and teens as a mediator.

The Youth Minister

Just as youth ministry as an intentional programming strategy is relatively new historically, so too is the position of the youth minister. My students are surprised to hear that only around 10 percent of churches in America employ a youth minister. Also, my students are surprised to find out the average church membership size in America is around one hundred people. This country is dotted with thousands of churches that can barely afford to pay their pastor let alone support an additional minister on staff. The economics simply don't work. In most churches, volunteers do the youth ministry.

Group Magazine has published data about the profession of youth ministry for many years. They conduct an annual salary survey of youth ministers around the United States that helps churches when hiring a youth minister. One trend they've identified is nearly half of all youth ministers need extra income from outside sources. The average paid youth minister salary in 2015 was $43,000 for men and $28,000 for women working a forty-four-hour workweek.[20] A little more than half of all youth ministers say they have additional responsibilities in their churches besides youth ministry.[21]

Lack of tenure or longevity in youth ministry has been bemoaned for years and partially blamed on the low salaries available for the profession. An anecdotally based belief exists that youth ministers only stay at a church for eighteen months and then move on, but that is not based on any reliable study. The average tenure of a youth minister at a church is around four years. However, *Group Magazine* also found almost a quarter of all youth ministers have ministered at the same church for twenty or more years.[22] I believe it takes at least five years to learn the systems, people and culture of a church, in addition to building relationships with the families and their teenagers, to become really effective in the position. Sadly, many youth ministers leave for another position before really "hitting their stride."

> "...the more intentional a church is at building a sustainable youth ministry, the more likely it is that its staff will choose to stay for the long haul. Longevity does not happen by chance. It is undeniably impacted by the overall climate of the youth ministry. Churches with youth ministries that are appropriately funded and that have clear, measurable expectations tend to have momentum, and staff members just tend to stay longer. But in churches where the structure and goals are fuzzy or where each successive youth worker is expected to build the ministry from scratch, youth workers are much more likely to become entangled in conflict. And conflict turns out to be, far and away, the number-one reason youth workers give for leaving. Far too many youth workers find themselves moving on much sooner than expected."[23]
>
> —Mark DeVries

For those churches with enough size and budget to justify hiring additional staff, often a youth minister is the first position to fill. What qualifications should a church look for in a youth minister? Here is a list of characteristics to consider. He or she must:

- Have a vibrant personal relationship with Jesus Christ as Savior and Lord.
- Demonstrate dependence on God through a consistent prayer life.
- Show evidence of the fruit of the Spirit in everyday life.
- Exhibit a love for God's Word and study it regularly.
- Demonstrate an evangelistic heart for the lost.
- Obtain formal training in ministry, preferably a seminary degree.
- Be able to communicate God's Word with relevance.
- Be teachable and a lifelong learner.
- Exhibit humility.
- Love working with and be able to relate well with teens and their families.
- Demonstrate successful emergence from adolescence.

I'm describing mature Christian men or women who live out Philippians 2:5–8 and don't think too highly of themselves. Notice I did not list characteristics many churches look for when hiring a youth minister like young, athletic, plays the guitar, physically attractive, outgoing, etc. These stereotypical "rock star" qualities may seem important but really aren't. In fact, I believe the most effective youth ministers are in their forties and fifties with more life experience, often from raising their own teenagers and with greater spiritual depth from years of walking with God. Parents have greater respect for other parents and tend to discount the advice, usually dangerous to offer anyway, from a recent unmarried college graduate with no children.

The last characteristic on the list, "successful emergence from adolescence," is more important than most think. Relatability with youth is not tied to age but has more to do with one's love and concern for youth. Remember our previous discussion about the duration of adolescence? Most college students and many college graduates are still adolescents themselves, according to the definition previously stated. Youth ministers who are still dealing with issues of their own adolescence are not going to be as effective as ones who have emerged as responsible adults. Teens don't need additional friends to "hang out" with. Teens need adults with more life experience who set a proper example and provide biblical guidance and answers to their questions.

The youth minister should function as the coordinator of all ministry related to the youth of the church. A youth minister friend found himself in the middle of a difficult scenario. The church had a youth choir, an AWANA program for teens, and a youth Sunday school program, all with their own structures and adult leadership teams. And then there was the youth minister and his attempts to lead the "youth ministry" in total competition with the other three ministry groups. The adults involved in the four programs were different people, and the youth minister had no authority over anything other than his own youth ministry. The calendar was a nightmare! The only paid person in this scenario was the youth minister.

I suggested the senior pastor put the youth minister in a supervisory role over every aspect of ministry related to youth. The ministry would be far more efficient concerning facility space, time, finances, and especially adult volunteer leadership. And a coordinated discipleship strategy would be more effective in producing teens who are Christ-followers for life.

Also, the youth minister should be an effective communicator in a variety of both public and small group settings. Mark Senter suggests one of the "axioms" of an effective and growing youth ministry is directly tied to the youth minister's speaking skills in front of the youth group.[24] While I affirm the value of the youth minister's speaking skills, other factors also affect the growth of the group. One of the most significant is the overall health of the church. If the church is growing spiritually and numerically, then the youth group will be too. If excitement and enthusiasm characterize the church body, then the youth group will benefit as well. However, the most important factor is the depth of spiritual life and commitment of the youth minister. The list of youth minister characteristics presented earlier really does make a difference in the overall health and growth of the youth ministry.

Stereotypical youth ministers spend the majority of their time with the teenagers in their church. However, when I was a student in seminary years ago, one of my professors, Dr. Wes Black, suggested we divide our time into thirds—one third with the teenagers in our churches, one third with the adult leaders in our youth ministries, and one third with the parents of the teenagers in our youth groups. His words were wise.[25]

Figure 6.1 Ministry in Thirds

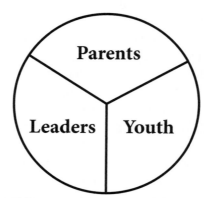

How you spend your time

Most youth ministers are very comfortable with teens and fairly comfortable with adult leaders. Where they usually falter is with the parents. One of the best ways to develop relationships with parents is to spend time with them in their homes. I suggest my youth ministry students set a goal and make it a habit to visit one home each week. Depending on the size of the youth group, this could take most of a year. If they complete the task early, start back through the list again. Remember to visit new families coming to your church and the families that graduate from the children's program. Make it a formal strategy so everyone is aware and no one feels threatened. Make appointments, not "cold calls." People will appreciate the chance to put their homes and apartments in order before you arrive. Don't stay too long, either. Tell parents your only purpose is to know them better so you can serve them best. God called you to assist families with the spiritual development of their teens. You will do that more effectively if you know the families better.

Adult Leadership in Youth Ministry

Ninety percent of churches rely on adult volunteers to lead the youth ministry strategy. Even if your church has a paid youth minister, he or she will need the help of trained adult volunteers to accomplish the assigned tasks. When teens feel they belong, they are part of a group, and people there care about them; they tend to stay involved. Relationships with friends and adults in the youth ministry are vitally important. This sounds obvious but the youth ministry will not grow beyond the number of teens who can be effectively connected in relationships. So much of the Christian life is caught through spending time with more mature believers who have lived more and walked longer with God. Teens greatly benefit from adult role models who demonstrate an exemplary Christian life.

The generally accepted ratio of adults to students is one for every five. Leaders find it difficult to stay informed and connected to more than five teenagers simply because of our busy lives. The math is simple. If you have forty youth in your group, the average size nationally, then you need eight committed adult leaders. Divide those forty teens into groups of five for regular follow-up, encouragement, and accountability. If you have one hundred youth in your group, you need twenty committed adult leaders. Of course, guys need male leaders and girls need female leaders.

Chap Clark's research has turned the five-to-one ratio upside down.[26] He found the best ratio was five adults for every one teenager. His study showed youth who were well adjusted (i.e., successfully navigating adolescence, doing well in school, staying away from substance abuse, maintaining respect for authority, obeying the law, etc.) had on average five significant adults speaking into their lives. As the number of influential adults dropped, all of the typical teenage problems we lament increased dramatically. Clark argued that our adult population has "abandoned" (his term) its youth to be raised and guided by the youth culture. I am not talking about having twenty-five adults in a small group with five teenagers. But the youth ministry must make sure the teens in the youth group have multiple adults who love them, believe in their success, and will invest a significant amount of time in their lives. Hopefully their parents are two of the five. The others may be the youth minister, a small group leader or a Sunday school teacher, a coach or teacher at school, an aunt or uncle, an older sibling, a grandma or grandpa. Involved adults become even more crucial if the parents abandon their sons or daughters or if a teen attends church without any other family members.

Youth Specialties and YouthWorks commissioned The Barna Group to study several areas of youth ministry and to discover the parents' perspective. The report revealed the state of youth ministry is cautiously better than many believed. "Given an opportunity to rate their satisfaction with their church's youth ministry, more than nine out of 10 parents whose teen attends regularly report they are 'very' (57%) or 'somewhat satisfied' (39%). A similar proportion say their teen is 'very' (58%) or 'somewhat satisfied' (39%). Parents are also overwhelmingly satisfied with their youth leader: More than nine out of 10 say they are 'very' (59%) or 'somewhat satisfied' (36%) with her or him. Interestingly, a high level of satisfaction with the youth leader correlates to more interaction between the parent and the leader. Nearly half of parents report 'a lot' of interaction with the youth pastor (45%), and these highly involved parents are more likely to be 'very satisfied' with their youth ministry leader (62% vs. 39% with less interaction). So, if parents in your program seem dissatisfied, consider asking them to volunteer!"[27]
—The Barna Group

Where do these adult leaders come from? Recruiting leaders is the ongoing task of any minister who directs programming strategy. I tell my students they should always be in "recruiting mode." The character qualities needed for effective adult leaders are not much different from those of youth ministers listed previously. They should be faithful, available, teachable, and responsible. Always be on the lookout for adults with these qualities. Also, properly screen and train all adult volunteers to protect minors from sexual abuse. *Church Law & Tax Report* found the number-one reason churches ended up in court for five years in a row (2011–2015) was because of the sexual abuse of a minor.[28] You are responsible to do everything within your power to ensure the safety of the teenagers involved in your ministry. I highly recommend MinistrySafe and the resources they provide to train and prepare your adult leaders to address this issue.[29]

Parents are a great resource and should be considered for adult leadership positions. Also, college students and young adults can be great youth leaders. Often overlooked, but invaluable in my experience, are senior adults. I remember serving with "Granny" in one of my churches. Granny was a successful commercial chef. We ate like kings and queens at all of our events, especially youth camp, turkey dinner with all the "fixin's." But Granny was also a grandmother who cared for the youth in a special way. Her life was priceless for our teenagers to watch. Many in the group sought her wisdom.[30]

One of the best ways to find adults to work in youth ministry is through the referrals of those already involved. Trust is a commodity that can't be taken lightly. If those you already trust recommend another adult based on their relationship, that carries a lot of weight. One caution, never announce from the pulpit you are in need of adult leaders. If you do, you'll be inviting people who should never be youth leaders to get involved.

Now your problem becomes telling some of them why they can't, which can be very uncomfortable.

Once recruited, challenge adult leaders with specific responsibilities and give them the training and authority to do what you've asked them to do. Leaders will become frustrated if they don't understand why they are serving and how to accomplish their ministry well. They want to contribute and make a difference. You must help them do so. I recommend, at minimum, a monthly adult leadership meeting to cultivate relationships among the team, offer instruction and training, provide accountability, and share joys and burdens.[31]

A Great Commission Youth Ministry

In recent years, ministers have tried many different approaches or "models" in their attempt to do effective youth ministry. Interestingly, they have all enjoyed success at different times and in different contexts. From studying these models I have learned none of them is guaranteed to work in every place and time. Too many variables exist in different contexts.[32] A passionate and theologically sound argument can be made for each of them.

One unhealthy organizational approach I alluded to earlier is called the One-Eared "Mickey Mouse"[tm] (see Figure 6.2). In this approach, the youth ministry operates outside the larger church community as a separate entity, operating essentially as its own mini-church. It has its own pastor, worship band, adult leaders, building, etc., and functions wholly independent of the church. When the family arrives at church on Sunday morning, the teenagers go to "Youth Church" and the adults to "Big Church." The only point of contact with the main church body is the youth minister.

> "…the larger body of Christ should include the emerging generations as it assembles for worship, mission, fellowship, education and service. In other words, we must stop our destructive practice of separating the body of Christ along generational lines. For example, we must ask ourselves why we are so quick to remove teenagers from the opportunity to worship with the older, wiser and spiritually gifted members of our congregation by starting a separate culturally relevant 'youth worship.' Doing so robs the body of Christ of its ability to function properly."[33]
>
> —Walt Mueller

Figure 6.2 One-Eared "Mickey Mouse"™

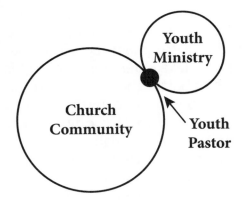

Among other issues, this approach segregates teens from their parents during worship, disrupting the natural modeling that takes place when the family worships together. A sixteen-year-old son watching his father sing praises to the Lord makes a huge impression. "*This is very important to my dad. He highly values his time of worshipping God.*" Now the teen may not verbalize his thoughts, but over time he will most likely adopt his father's value of worship. If a fourteen-year-old girl watches her mother place an offering in the plate when it comes by every Sunday, don't you think that she will realize how important it is to give to the church as an act of worship? Won't this experience influence her as she learns to be a good steward of all that God gives her? When the parents pay attention, maybe even take notes and interact with the pastor's sermon, the teens sitting next to them will catch the vital importance of studying, understanding, and applying God's Word to their lives, too. This won't happen if the youth are off in their own setting with their peers, who are also trying to figure out these values … but without the most important role models to watch. Adult leaders can and do play a vital role, but they don't have as much influence in the lives of teens as parents do. This approach isolates teens from the very people who have been charged in Scripture with guiding their discipleship.

A healthier perspective is reflected in Figure 6.3. In this variation, the youth minister is an integral part of the total leadership of the church, and the youth are incorporated in the overall life and ministry of the congregation. The church needs to "own" the youth ministry. There is still a role for age-segregated biblical instruction based on an understanding of developmental issues. For instance, a seventh grade girl (11–12 years old) and a twelfth grade girl (17–18 years old) do not think and process information in the same way. The developmental differences between early adolescence and late adolescence are well known. Small group Bible study where the teens are grouped with their peers for interactive learning is very effective. However, teens should be together with their families in corporate worship. The typical youth seating section in the balcony also needs to go. Teens need to be worshipping alongside their parents. If teens come alone, they can sit with a friend's family.

Figure 6.3 Healthier Model of Youth Ministry

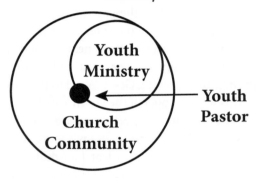

The most robust youth ministry model I've ever experienced and used can be contextualized to any cultural or socioeconomic group. This helpful model is patterned after the discipleship progression of the believer. First, conversion happens when lost people hear the gospel and trust in Jesus Christ to pay for their sins. Second, sanctification begins as the convert learns the basics of the Christian faith in a nurturing environment. Third, discipleship deepens as maturing disciples exercise their gifts in an ongoing commitment to become more like Christ. And fourth, mature disciples disciple others as they take responsibilities for different aspects of ministry. It seems so simple, and it's not a new approach. In fact, it's based on the Great Commission in Matthew 28:18–20.[34]

"[Jesus's] life was ordered by his objective. Everything he did and said was a part of the whole pattern. It had significance because it contributed to the ultimate purpose of his life in redeeming the world for God. This was the motivating vision governing his behavior. His steps were ordered by it. Mark it well. Not for one moment did Jesus lose sight of his goal.

That is why it is so important to observe the way Jesus maneuvered to achieve his objective. The Master disclosed God's strategy of world conquest. He had confidence in the future precisely because he lived according to that plan in the present. There was nothing haphazard about his life—no wasted energy, not an idle word. He was on business for God (Luke 2:29). He lived, he died and he rose again according to schedule. Like a general plotting his course of battle, the Son of God calculated to win. He could not afford to take a chance. Weighing every alternative and variable factor in human experience, he conceived a plan that would not fail."[35]
—Robert Coleman

Dann Spader, founder of Sonlife Ministries and influenced by Robert Coleman's classic work *The Master Plan of Evangelism*, argues the subtle strategy of ministry Jesus demonstrated in the Gospels can be identified by these four broad levels of maturity for a disciple—from being lost to being a trained spiritual leader.[36] Other ministries have likewise identified this and given the four-level progression memorable labels. Cru has used win, build, equip, and send.[37] Sonlife Ministries has used outreach, growth, ministry training, and leadership multiplication.[38] Doug Fields, in *Purpose Driven Youth Ministry,* uses community, crowd, congregation, committed, core (he divides the first level into two).[39] I've also used curious, convinced, committed, and commissioned. These labels have been illustrated in the form of concentric circles, a time line, an incline, and an upside down funnel. The

"wedding cake" diagram (see Figure 6.4) illustrates the discipleship journey in a way that can be easily explained to ministry staff, parents, adult leaders, and teens as well.

The numbers on the left of Figure 6.4 relate to the size of the groups to which Jesus ministered in different contexts during his ministry. He demonstrated his love for the *curious* when he fed five thousand men plus the women and children who were present in Matthew 14. He sent out seventy *convinced* believers who told others about him in Luke 10. The twelve *committed* disciples enjoyed more intentional time and training with Jesus over the course of his earthly ministry, as the Passion week events culminating in the Last Supper show in John 12–17.

Figure 6.4 The Great Commission Youth Ministry

A Great Commission Youth Ministry challenges teenagers at their level of spiritual interest

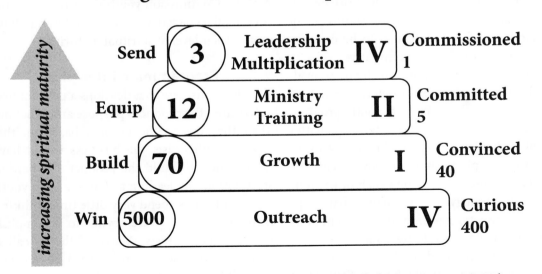

The Great Commission: "make disciples" (Matt. 28:18–20)

Peter, James, and John were the *commissioned* leaders who had an even more intimate relationship with Jesus demonstrated by their exclusive invitation to go up the mountain with him in Mark 9 and further into the garden of Gethsemane in Mark 14. Jesus was ministering to and with all these people at different levels of spiritual interest and maturity. He did that by intentionally managing his time with each group for maximum effectiveness. We can learn from this pattern.

The numbers on the right of the figure are related to the typical size of a church youth group, which is forty *convinced* teenagers growing in their faith. Each of those teenagers knows at least ten people who have not yet trusted Jesus, leading to the four hundred who are the *curious* and ongoing potential prospects for the youth group. There should be five to seven *committed* teens from among the forty who have responded to the leading of the Spirit of God to do the work of ministry. On occasion, a teen will rise up and demonstrate exceptional wisdom, stature, favor with God, and favor with man to be *commissioned* to lead ministries and initiatives.

Youth ministers can use this figure to evaluate their own ministry to determine if they have a "balanced" discipling youth program that can minister to any teenager no matter what his or her level of spiritual maturity. Every youth ministry program should have at least one primary purpose from among each of the four levels of the strategy. The problem is that a typical youth ministry has around 85 percent of its programming designed for teens who are at the build/growth/convinced level of spiritual maturity. They have accepted Christ as Savior and are now growing in their faith through Sunday

school, midweek Bible study, Sunday evening small groups, camps, retreats, service projects, and mission trips. These are important programs, but too many resources are being used up on the forty at that level. Only 15 percent of the remaining programming is then focused on the other three levels. Most youth ministries need to be rebalanced so that all programming is intentionally targeted for one of the four broad levels of spiritually mature teenagers.

You can measure the long-term effectiveness of your youth program by observing how the youth move through these levels of spiritual maturity. Paul tells Timothy, "And the things you have heard me say in the presence of many witnesses entrust to reliable people who will also be qualified to teach others" (2 Tim. 2:2). The goal is to make disciples who will make disciples. After all, the imperative command in the Great Commission is not to "go." That was assumed. The command is to "make disciples." A Great Commission youth ministry can minister to all teenagers who come to the church no matter their level of spiritual maturity.[40]

Programming Principles

Every business that develops a product first determines the product's purpose and function. Then they design the product based on this "target." Otherwise, the business would have no idea how to build the product or where to start, eventually leading to failure. Most youth ministry leaders spend very little time thinking through what they are trying to accomplish through their efforts. Many of the so-called "drop-out" studies claim between 50–85 percent of high school teenagers drop out of church involvement after they graduate from high school. If any company had a 50–85 percent failure rate on a product, that company would be quickly bankrupt with a lot of explanation due its customers. If teenagers spend six years in your youth ministry, how have they changed? When they graduate from your program, could any of them be called "mature in Christ?" What do mature teenage disciples of Jesus Christ exemplify? I encourage youth ministers to "draw a target" for their teens. What should they know? What should they value? What should they be able to do? The answers to these three main questions inform the design of the Discipled Student Profile (DSP).[41]

The DSP consists of key qualities or characteristics based on Scripture that spiritually mature teenagers should exemplify by the time they graduate from high school. The source for these key qualities is the Bible. What characteristics does God say he wants his disciples to exhibit? Paul provides a great list in Galatians 5:22–23 (NASB), "But the fruit of the Spirit is love, joy, peace, patience, kindness, goodness, faithfulness, gentleness, self-control; against such things there is no law." Also, in 1 Timothy 3, Paul discusses the character qualifications of elders and deacons. While not all of them are applicable to teenagers, many of the listed qualities can be emulated by teens. Other qualities can be listed from throughout Scripture, but the key is to develop a profile that is manageable and reachable for youth involved in the ministry.

To help you think through your own list, consider some of the following examples. Steve Miller identified nine key qualities for every disciple after an extensive study of the sermons and writings of Charles Spurgeon:

1. A passion for prayer
2. A faith that endures
3. A commitment to holiness
4. A heart for service
5. A love for the Lord and his Word
6. A willingness to suffer
7. A zeal for proclaiming God's Word
8. A passion for lost souls
9. A singular focus—Jesus[42]

Each of these is worthy of our attention and could form the solid basis of a healthy profile for youth.

Another example comes from Search Institute. Search Institute has spent years researching and testing what they call "developmental assets" for the purpose of helping faith-based organizations draw a target for their youth. Search Institute identified forty developmental assets they believe are critical for teens to internalize in order to be productive and responsible members of society.[43] While the number is a little overwhelming and aimed at a diverse audience, these "assets" can be helpful in identifying the characteristics of discipled teenagers.[44] Also, Search Institute produced a list of "evidences" or "observable criteria" of a mature Christian teenager in the *Exemplary Youth Ministry Study.*[45] They are:

1. Seeks spiritual growth
2. Possesses a vital faith
3. Practices faith
4. Makes the Christian faith a way of life
5. Lives a life of service
6. Reaches out to others
7. Exercises moral responsibility
8. Speaks publicly about faith
9. Possesses a positive spirit[46]

These nine behavioral characteristics are observable and can help measure progress in the discipleship process.

In an attempt at drawing a target for youth, Andy Stanley and Stuart Hall offer another example describing what they call "seven checkpoints." They believe these are principles every teenager should know. They are:

1. Authentic faith—putting your trust in God
2. Spiritual disciplines—seeing with God's eyes
3. Moral boundaries—paving the way for intimacy
4. Healthy friendships—choosing friends for life
5. Wise choices—walking wisely in a fool's world
6. Ultimate authority—finding freedom under God
7. Others first—considering others before yourself[47]

Stanley and Hall have also developed curriculum that corresponds with each of the "checkpoints" so that youth ministers can systematically teach these key qualities to their youth in a discipleship context.[48]

These and other lists are helpful to use for reference or a starting point, but the best target is the one the youth minister draws after researching his own present ministry context and the families and teens who are a part of it.

Once the target is drawn, then every programming decision should be governed by this intentional focus of producing a student disciple. All of the curriculum that is either purchased or created will assist youth ministry leaders and families in moving the youth closer to conformity with the profile. Every programmed activity must help teens develop the key character qualities in the DSP. Whenever parents or youth ask the youth ministry leader the purpose of the mission trip that summer, he or she will be able to clearly explain how the goals of the trip help the youth develop in one or more of the key character qualities. If anyone asks why the youth should go to camp the answer will be simple—because students will likely develop this "key" quality during the focused time away from distractions. In other words, the DSP guides all program decisions.

Conclusion

You may have heard someone say the youth of today are the leaders of tomorrow. I happen to think they are capable of accomplishing far more than many adults believe they can. Alvin Reid makes a strong case for "raising the bar" for teenagers.[49] He argues that he has seen youth rise up to the challenge of spiritual maturity time and time again. If we set the bar low, we should not be surprised when teens accomplish little. But when we set the bar higher, we will see teens rise to our expectations and often exceed them.

The discipleship process is not confined to the adult experience. Teenagers can and will make significant progress in becoming like Christ if we organize our youth programs to minister to all teenagers regardless of their level of spiritual interest and maturity. Understanding and implementing a balanced program based on the strategy Jesus demonstrated in the gospels can work in any context, with any culture, with any ethnicity, and with any socioeconomic group. So, go and make disciples … of teenagers.

Discussion Questions

1. Why should every church make youth ministry a priority?

2. What questions do youth ponder related to their identity? Why is identity formation so important in youth ministry, and how can you help them grasp who they are in God's eyes?

3. Describe ways media influences youth today. Name strategies to help young people overcome unhealthy media addictions and distractions.

4. Name several difficulties youth ministers and volunteers face today. How can you support and encourage them?

5. Who is ultimately responsible for the spiritual formation of teenagers? Name ways the church and the family can cooperate for the benefit of young people today.

Resources for Further Study

Books

Cannister, Mark. *Teenagers Matter*. Grand Rapids: Baker Books, 2013.

Clark, Chap, ed. *Adoptive Youth Ministry*. Grand Rapids: Baker Books, 2016.

Clark, Chap. *Hurt 2.0: Inside the World of Today's Teenagers*. Grand Rapids: Baker Books, 2011.

DeVries, Mark. *Sustainable Youth Ministry*. Downers Grove, IL: Intervarsity Press, 2008.

Fields, Doug. *Purpose Driven Youth Ministry*. Grand Rapids: Zondervan, 1998.

Lawrence, Rick. *Jesus Centered Youth Ministry*. Loveland: Group Publishing 2007.

Mueller, Walt. *Engaging the Soul of Youth Culture*. Downers Grove, IL: Intervarsity Press, 2006.

Stanley, Andy and Stuart Hall. *The Seven Checkpoints for Student Leaders: Seven Principles Every Teenager Needs to Know*, rev. ed. New York: Howard Books, 2011.

Yarhouse, Mark A. *Understanding Sexual Identity*. Grand Rapids: Zondervan, 2013.

Websites

Center for Parent/Youth Understanding—www.cpyu.org

Dare 2 Share—www.dare2share.org

Group Magazine's Youth Ministry—www.youthministry.com

Lifeway Publishing—www.lifeway.com

Sonlife Ministries—www.sonlife.com

Youth Ministry 360—www.youthministry360.com

Youth Specialties—www.youthspecialties.com

Periodicals

Group Magazine

The Journal of Youth Ministry

Youthworker Journal

Author Bio

Dr. Jay Sedwick is Department Chair and Professor of Educational Ministries and Leadership and has served on the faculty at Dallas Theological Seminary for twenty years. Jay has more than thirty years of youth ministry experience as a volunteer, part-time, and full-time youth minister. He and his wife Laurie have been married for thirty years, during which time God blessed them with four children, one son-in-law, and their two grandsons. An ordained minister who teaches youth at a large Dallas-area church, Dr. Sedwick is also a popular conference and seminar speaker. His research and teaching interests include youth development, biblical education for youth, curriculum design, and legal and financial issues in ministry.

Endnotes

1. Barna Group, *Generation Next: What You Need to Know About Today's Youth* (Ventura, CA: Regal Books/Gospel Light, 1995).

2. Barna Group, *Transforming Children into Spiritual Champions* (Grand Rapids: Baker, 2003).

3. G. Stanley Hall, *Adolescence—Its Psychology and Its Relations to Physiology, Anthropology, Sociology, Sex, Crime, and Religion* (New York: Appleton and Company, 1904).

4. David Setran and Chris Keisling, *Spiritual Formation in Emerging Adulthood: A Practical Theology for College and Young Adult Ministry* (Grand Rapids: Baker, 2013).

5. Crystal Kirgiss presents strong evidence in her historical review of volumes of related literature on the subject of adolescence. Her book *In Search of Adolescence: A New Look at an Old Idea* (San Diego: The Youth Cartel, 2015) presents a strong challenge to the widely accepted view that adolescence is relatively new.

6. Jeffery Arnett, "Emerging Adulthood: A Theory of Development from the Late Teens through the Twenties," *American Psychologist*, 55. no. 5 (May 2000): 469–480.

7. Neil Howe and William Strauss, *Millennials Rising: The Next Great Generation* (New York: Vintage Books, 2000).

8. Sedra Spano, "Stages of Adolescent Development," *Research Facts and Finding*, ACT for Youth Update Center of Excellence, Cornell University, Ithaca, NY: May 2004. More information can be found at http://www.actforyouth.net/resources/rf/rf_stages_0504.pdf.

9. See http://www.pcaac.org/resources/wcf/.

10. James E. Marcia, "Development and Validation of Ego-Identity Status," *Journal of Personality and Social Psychology*, 3, no. 5 (1966): 551; James E. Marcia, "Identity in Adolescence," *Handbook of Adolescent Psychology*, 9, no.11 (1980): 159–187.

11. Mark Yarhouse, *Understanding Sexual Identity* (Grand Rapids: Zondervan, 2013), 30, 67–68.

12. Walt Mueller, *Engaging the Soul of Youth Culture* (Downers Grove, IL: IVP, 2006), 110. More information on the Center for Parent Youth Understanding can be found at www.cpyu.org.

13. For a chilling exposé of the power and manipulative techniques used by the large multi-national media conglomerates, watch the Frontline special *The Merchants of Cool* (2003) available at PBS (http://www.pbs.org/wgbh/pages/frontline/shows/cool/. Although it is dated, the program reveals tactics that are still in use today. Caution: The video is not censored very well and contains some offensive material.

14. Kaiser Family Foundation, *Generation M2: Media in the Lives of 8 to 18 Year Olds* (2010), 2.

15. Common Sense Media, *The Common Sense Census: Media Use by Tweens and Teens* (2015), 13.

16. Common Sense Media, *The Common Sense Census: Plugged in Parents of Tweens and Teens* (2016), 7.

17. See the chapter "The Influence of Technology on Educational Ministry" by John Dyer for additional information on the topic of technology and media.

18. For a thorough presentation of the historical roots and development of youth ministry in America see Mark Senter's *When God Shows Up: A History of Protestant Youth Ministry in America* (Grand Rapids: Baker, 2010).

19. See the chapter "Invisible: Single Adults" by Joye Baker for additional information on working with single parents.

20. The disparity of pay between the male and female youth workers in this survey is dismaying. Without access to the raw data and further analysis to investigate additional variables that could explain it, I have to conclude there is significant gender bias in the pay scale.

21.   *Group Magazine*, "The 2015 Youth Ministry Salary Survey," *Group Magazine*, Fall 2015, 26–34.

22.   Ibid.

23.   Mark DeVries, *Sustainable Youth Ministry* (Downers Grove, IL: IVP, 2008), 127.

24.   Mark Senter and Richard Dunn, *Reaching a Generation for Christ* (Chicago: Moody Press, 1997).

25.   Dr. Wes Black was Professor of Student Ministry at Southwestern Baptist Theological Seminary from 1983 to 2012.

26.   Chap Clark, *Hurt* (Grand Rapids: Baker Academic, 2004).

27.   The Barna Group, *The State of Youth Ministry* (2016), 26.

28.   Richard Hammar, "The Top 5 Reasons Religious Organizations Went to Court in 2015," Church Law and Tax, http://www.churchlawandtax.com/web/2016/august/top-5-reasons-religious-organizations-went-to-court-in-2015.html.

29.   Ministry Safe is an organization dedicated to educating and training the church for the purpose of preventing child sexual abuse. Their approach is the best I've seen. Their website is www.ministrysafe.com.

30.   See the chapter "Forgotten: Senior Adults" by Sabrina Hopson for additional information on senior adults.

31.   See the chapters "Administering a Healthy Educational Ministry" by Jim Thames and "Educational Ministry in the Smaller Church" by Lin McLaughlin for additional information on working with volunteers.

32.   Mark Senter and Richard Dunn reviewed the most common models at the time when they published *Reaching a Generation for Christ* (Chicago: Moody, 1997). Several attempts have been made since then to suggest newer models or variations of the models such as Mark Senter, ed., *Four Views of Youth Ministry* (El Cajon, CA: Youth Specialties, 2001) and Chap Clark, ed., *Youth Ministry in the 21st Century: Five Views* (Grand Rapids: Baker, 2015).

33.   Walt Mueller, *Engaging the Soul of Youth Culture* (Downers Grove, IL: IVP, 2006), 193.

34.   See the chapter "The Heart of Making Disciples" by Mark Heinemann for more on discipleship.

35.   Robert Coleman, *The Master Plan of Evangelism* (Grand Rapids: Revell, 1964), 18–19.

36.   Coleman, *The Master Plan for Evangelism*.

37.   Cru was formerly known as Campus Crusade for Christ. See more of Cru's strategy at http://www.cruhighschool.com/resource/understanding-win-build-send/.

38.   See more of Sonlife Ministries' strategy at https://www.sonlife.com.

39.   Doug Fields, *Purpose Driven Youth Ministry* (Grand Rapids: Zondervan, 1998).

40.   See the chapter "The Heart of Making Disciples" by Mark Heinemann for more information on discipleship.

41.   This is my personal adaptation of a tool that was developed and used by Sonlife Ministries called the Description of a Discipled Student or DDP.

42.   Steve Miller, *C.H. Spurgeon on Spiritual Leadership* (Chicago: Moody Press, 2003).

43.   Peter C. Scales and Nancy Leffert, *Developmental Assets* (Minneapolis: Search Institute, 1999).

44.   This list is broken down into external assets (support, empowerment, boundaries/expectations, constructive use of time) and internal assets (commitment to learning, positive values, social competencies, positive identity). The full list of the forty developmental assets from Search Institute can be found at http://www.search-institute.org/content/40-developmental-assets-adolescents-ages-12–18.

45.   Information on the *Exemplary Youth Ministry Study* can be found at www.vibrantfaith.org/project/eym. The research is also discussed in *The Spirit and Culture of Youth Ministry* by John Roberto, Wes Black, and Roland Martinson (St. Paul, MN: EYM Publishing, 2010).

46. *Exemplary Youth Ministry Study.*

47. Andy Stanley and Stuart Hall, *The Seven Checkpoints for Student Leaders: Seven Principles Every Teenager Needs to Know*, rev. ed. (New York: Howard, 2001).

48. Andy Stanley and Stuart Hall, *The Seven Checkpoints: Student Journal* (New York: Howard, 2001).

49. Alvin Reid, *Raising the Bar: Ministry to Youth in the New Millennium* (Grand Rapids: Kregel, 2004).

Chapter 7
OVERWHELMED: ADULTS

Sue Edwards

Then Philip ran up to the chariot and heard the man reading Isaiah the prophet. [The man is an Ethiopian eunuch in charge of his nation's treasury.] "Do you understand what you are reading?" Philip asked.
"How can I," he said, "unless someone explains it to me?" So he invited Philip to come up and sit with him.

—Acts 8:30–31

Introduction

GOD RECRUITED PHILIP, a Jesus-follower in the early days of the church, to teach this lone student, sharing a seat in his chariot as it snaked its way through the arid wasteland on the Ethiopian's way home from Jerusalem to Nubia, modern-day Sudan. We don't know how long the lesson lasted, but we do know that Professor Philip culminated this divine encounter with an appropriate activity to cement the meaning of the lesson deep into his pupil's mind and heart. Philip baptized the eunuch.

Adults down the block and around the world need teachers willing to meet them where they are, understand their unique needs, create learning environments that work for them, and walk with them as they grow into fully formed disciples equipped to love, serve, and woo a desperately needy world to transformative faith in Jesus. If you are privileged to teach adults, your classroom may not be four walls with rows of desks and a teaching lectern where you will stand at the front. Instead you will find adults eager to learn in living rooms, at dining tables, coffee shops, restaurant booths, workplaces, stairwells and hallways, campgrounds, parks, maybe even sitting in a chariot, in spaces you've never thought of as the typical classroom. God may give you that sacred space to teach, whether it's through his Word, illustrating with a related incident in your own life that attests to God's faithfulness, listening well to your students' stories so you can teach in a highly personal way, or challenging them to risk and adventure for the glory of God. Broaden your view of teaching.[1]

> "We see the Word of God as revealed, as true information from God. And so it is. But we tend to see it as information *only*! We neglect the personal dimension. And when a person tries to obey the Bible as pure information, as rules for living or standards to live up to, he slips into an unconscious and fruitless legalism. When the Bible is understood and taught as information in which we meet God, when our goal in teaching and reading is to be responsive to the One who speaks to us, then we move beyond information and beyond law into the realm of personal relationship. And it is only this—personal relationship with God—that can transform."
> —Lawrence O. Richard

Just as God orchestrated this divine encounter between Philip and the Ethiopian eunuch, God looks for teachers to follow up with what he's already doing in the lives of adults everywhere. And the most effective educators of adults take the time to discern the differences between teaching children and teaching adults.

Beginning in the 1970s, secular educators tackled this complex subject (Malcolm Knowles, Stephen Brookfield, Jack Mezirow, Sharan Merriam and Rosemary Caffarella, Raymond Wlodkowski, and others). Before that, educators made little distinction between teaching children and teaching adults. Building on their findings, Christian educators have attempted to discern how this research might enhance the way we minister to adults in churches and parachurch organizations, and the way we teach adults the Bible.

I've joined in the quest, partly due to my concern for the escalating state of believers' biblical illiteracy and partly because recent studies reveal serious moral and ethical deterioration in the church. Consider the following:

> Fewer than half of all adults can name the four gospels. Many Christians cannot identify more than two or three of the disciples.... According to 82% of Americans, "God helps those who help themselves," is a Bible verse. Those identified as born-again Christians did better—by one percent.[2]

> Fueling my doubts were experiences with other Christians whose lives were generally no different from a nonbeliever. They lusted after the same materialistic things; they complained and got angry over trivial matters; they backstabbed and slandered other Christians (especially leaders in the church); and they harbored life-sapping pride. Much of this I experienced directly through the church's women's ministry or with individual women in the church. Worse, I realized my own attitudes and thoughts were not any better.[3]

"I emphasize an approach to teaching adults where you, the teacher, engage your entire personality, how you think, what you know and how you know it, and how you feel and why you feel that way. I emphasize a teaching approach that involves all of the learner, too—feelings, thoughts, relationships, backgrounds, values, beliefs—everything that makes a person unique."[4]
—Jerold W. Apps

I've also personally witnessed the moral decline in the church over my forty plus years ministering there and in parachurch contexts. Too often, sadly, we observe similarities between church attendees and those who never darken the sacred door. In addition to the experiences just mentioned, examples include:

- Families destroyed through divorce, abuse, and addictions
- Women undergoing abortions under pressure from spouses or parents, and then either shutting down their hearts to live with the guilt or caving emotionally under the stress of what they've done
- Dads in bondage to pornography, thus losing their wives' affection due to the horrendous sense of rejection, as intimacy wanes or even disappears

In a joint venture commissioned by Proven Men Ministries and conducted by the Barna Group, researchers found that 77 percent of Christian men between the ages of eighteen and thirty view pornography at least monthly, and 36 percent look at it at least once a day. Thirty-two percent of these men admit having an addiction to porn, while 12 percent think they do. These epidemic numbers infiltrating the church confirm that much work needs to be done so that marriages, families, and the very foundation of American society aren't undermined by something that the Bible repeatedly warns believers about.[5]

What we see on the streets we see equal measure in the pews. How can this be? Many of these dear people sit weekly under the teaching of a high-powered godly pastor who communicates the Bible well, and yet, for too many, real-life transformation eludes. What's missing?

Yes, ministers must train to preach the Bible inductively with oratory skill, love, and boldness. But regardless of a sermon's excellence, people need more than a great message once a week. To be transformed into fully formed disciples of Christ, adults require additional opportunities for connection, participation, and service, according to their gift-mix and wiring. The key to understand what that "more" is lies in our understanding of who adults are, how they learn, how to help them connect with God and each other, and how to teach them so that the teaching sticks and moves from head to heart to hand. It's far more than the transfer of information, even more than feeling included in a community, although both are important parts of the process. Christian teachers who are serious about becoming sharp tools that God can use to transform and sanctify adults must team teach with Jesus and prayerfully seek to know the adults that he will entrust to them. They must become skilled andragogists.

Andragogy—What Is It?

Malcolm Knowles, the most influential scholar in awakening educators to the need to understand adults as learners, coined the term.[6] Andragogy, in contrast to pedagogy (teaching children) simply means the art and science of helping adults learn. For us as Christian educators, teachers, and preachers, it means *the art and science of helping Christian adults grow strong in Christ, as together, teacher and student, we seek and depend on God's enabling power and direction.*

Knowles and others described characteristics of adult learners that can help us in this quest to know, understand, love, and challenge our students. And in ministry, "our students" means *everyone* that God sends our way:

> He is the one we proclaim, admonishing and teaching *everyone* with all wisdom, so that we may present *everyone* fully mature in Christ. To this end I strenuously contend with all the energy Christ so powerfully works in me.
> —Colossians 1:28–29
> (emphasis mine)

We teach the intellectually gifted and the intellectually challenged; those who loved school and those who hated it; those who grew up in affluent neighborhoods and those from poverty-stricken areas; adults who grew up in Christian homes and those who came to faith later in life; eager students who are easy to love and resistant students with sour attitudes; those who look like us and those who don't; those who grew up feasting on Bible stories and those who watched cartoons on Sundays.

Also, we teach the whole person for life change. Teaching with the goal of spiritual transformation is different from teaching subjects like mathematics and geography. If a math teacher succeeds in teaching you algorithms and you ace the test, she's done her job well. If our students can name all the books of the Bible in proper order and can tell you the general theme of each, and they even make a higher test score than anyone else, still we have only just begun. The cognitive is crucial as life change begins in the mind, but knowing isn't growing. The heart and the will, the affective domain, must be transformed in the sanctification process. Finally, only when pupils behave and live differently can we say they have truly learned. Head, heart, *and* hand.

> Therefore, if anyone is in Christ, the new creation has come:
> The old has gone, the new is here!
> —2 Corinthians 5:17

Our task is more challenging than rocket science or cancer research, and more important. How can we possibly measure up?

> Such confidence as this is ours through Christ before God. Not that we are competent in ourselves to claim anything for ourselves, but our competence comes from God. He has made us competent as ministers of a new covenant—not of the letter but of the Spirit; for the letter kills, but the Spirit gives life.
> —2 Corinthians 3:4–6

So, again I say, empowered by the Spirit, team-teach with Jesus!

General Characteristics of Adult Learners

Generally adult learning is self-directed, multi-faceted, practical and problem-centered, built on prior and varied experiences, and divided up by life tasks while also connecting adults in meaningful relationships with people of other generations. As we consider general characteristics of adult learners, remember not to pigeon-hole people. Each is unique and complex, yet examining general truths about most adults, as distinct from children, will help you become more skilled at reaching the adults God sends your way.

> "The adult learner is a neglected species," observed the noted adult education leader Malcolm Knowles some years ago. In Christian education we have been especially slow to change. Somehow we persist in teaching adults as though they were children, devoid of experience and lacking ability to think and learn for themselves. Church educational programs continue to feed strained food rather than sirloins, to disregard creativity and capability."[7]
> —Howard Hendricks

Self-Directed

As people enter adulthood, their priorities shift. For children, school is compulsory. Unless children are homeschooled, if they don't show up at school, a truant office searches for them and contacts their parents, involving legal penalties if they don't comply. Children are dependents preparing for the future, requiring years of education. Once they reach adulthood, school is voluntary. Some professions require continuing education but anything offered in a church or parachurch organization is a matter of choice. And you'll be teaching without grades, test scores, or academic awards as incentives.

If you offer a Bible class in a church, typically it's free, or at most there is a small fee for a workbook or study guide. Ministries sometimes charge a nominal fee to attend their workshops, seminars, and conferences. But even there, adults vote with their feet. If they find the class helpful, they show up again. If not, you probably won't see them the next time you meet. Unlike some children and teens, adults usually aren't rude if they don't like your teaching. They seldom pass notes or talk when you're talking, but if they don't find the course helpful, interesting, or challenging, they quickly drop out. Adult life is complex and full of choices, and they generally won't take time for anything that's not feeding them.

Many adults are hungry to learn and will be a joy to teach. But others shun learning the Bible for different reasons. Some older adults see their age as a hindrance. They believe the old adage, "You can't teach an old dog new tricks." Some adults grew up where education wasn't valued. Some feel inadequate and don't want to risk embarrassment. Since you are reading this book, I'm assuming you want to become an effective minister, teacher, or preacher, either as a vocation or as a volunteer. You probably enjoy learning and have a fairly positive attitude toward school. Many of you excelled there. Some of you are pursuing higher education and hope one day to teach in the academy. Others of you are gripped with a passion to help adults grow strong in their faith in the church or parachurch organizations. If any of these descriptions fit you, the first thing you must understand is that *the typical adult today is not you!* Most churches and parachurch organizations are full of adults who would never pick up this book and read it.

Consider how these statistics from the American Literacy Foundation will affect your Bible class:

- In a study of literacy among twenty "high income" countries, the US ranked twelfth.
- Illiteracy has become such a serious problem in our country that 44 million adults are now unable to read a simple story to their children.
- Fifty percent of adults cannot read a book written at an eighth-grade level.
- Forty-five million are functionally illiterate and read below a fifth grade level.
- Forty-four percent of American adults do not read a book in a year.
- Six out of ten households do not buy a single book in a year.[8]

The adults who left school murmuring a new mantra, "I'm never going back there again," won't be the first to sign up for your Bible study or Sunday school class. They may love the Lord and desire to know him, but delving into a thick ancient book with lots of strange words isn't on their bucket list. Those with poor educational backgrounds often lack interest and confidence in their ability to learn. When they walk into a learning environment, if it looks and feels like "school," negativity sets in, even unconsciously. What can you do? Create a different ethos. Take

your classroom into the community by meeting in a coffee shop, library or recreation center meeting room, or your own living room. Brown bag a Bible discussion group in your workplace. Make the learning space look and feel more like a welcoming home than a school.

Some adults resist learning because, unlike children, they think they have life figured out already. They are more open to change at times of crisis when they realize they need help, but we can't wait around for a crisis to strike so that they're more open to learn. We must find ways to reach adults now:

> They have usually found a way to successfully cope with life and have formulated a set of strongly held convictions. New learning often asks them to become temporarily dependent, to open their minds to new ideas, to rethink certain beliefs, and to try different ways of doing things. This is somewhat threatening to them, and their attitudes can easily lock in to support their resistance.[9]

How do we persuade adults to stick around? In my experience, most Christian adults do want to grow in their faith, learn the Scriptures, live to please God, and step out to tackle new and meaningful Christ-centered opportunities. They respond well to teachers who respect and believe in them, who prepare well, and who live what they teach—again, all reasons to team-teach with Jesus!

Multifaceted

Unlike formal schooling, generally adult learning is not a sequenced set of steps like a degree plan. Adults aren't checking off required courses to graduate. Instead, their learning looks like a life-long web that adults design for themselves. It might include listening to a favorite radio preacher on the way to work, attending a midweek Bible study, pulling up a favorite blog as a quick-start to their day. They might attend a seminar or conference if the topic is especially appealing. They might read a book. They might join a small group in an attempt to build community, and often small groups study a Bible curriculum. Typically adults create their own learning experiences by selecting from a smorgasbord of choices throughout life, often without much scope (what they will learn) and sequence (when they will learn it).

About now you may be feeling a little discouraged. In light of these realities, can you really become an effective teacher partnering with God to grow adults so that they become all-in mature Christ-followers? Yes, you can. Think quality rather than quantity, and consider my story.

I grew up an unwanted only child in a pagan home. By the time I went off to college I was a mess. After college, I married a backslidden Baptist. We know that because he married me, a nonbeliever. The Lord blessed us with two beautiful baby girls, eighteen months apart. However, we were both immature, and under the stress of trying to figure out life and be a good wife and wise parent, I fell into a dark depression. Our marriage was crumbling when a neighbor invited me to a parachurch women's Bible study. There I found Jesus, a caring community, and soon was invited into the leader's group where I discovered God had gifted me with a love for teaching the Bible and helping other women find Jesus and the transformation he endows.

I spent about six hours a week investing in this Bible study, two in my home study and four meeting with others for quality group discussion, Bible teaching, leader training, and authentic community. In time, as deep relationships developed I spent additional time with women who became my spiritual mothers and sisters. But compared to the hundreds of weekly hours that culture bombarded me with diametrically opposed messages, you'd think I'd have been another one of its victims. But I wasn't, because women covered the ministry with prayer, they invested in one another's lives creating real community, they provided excellent leadership training that produced women passionate about stepping out of their comfort zones to serve, and they taught the Bible with relevance and skill.

Over the next ten years I grew like mushrooms in the rainy season. In time our family joined a healthy Bible-based church, thus clocking more hours learning about God and his Word. Weekly we heard stellar preaching. We made friends with other Christian families and joined a small group, all helpful. But my core spiritual strength resulted from that midweek Bible study—a time of honest engaging, serving, praying together, intentional listening, accepting leadership opportunities, and later teaching the Bible to women. I needed more than just sitting and listening to a weekly sermon.

Others may find what they need to grow strong in their faith within church communities or in a variety of other Christian venues. Choices abound, and the Lord guides all his yielded children to the people and places they need to grow. But for any of us to become fully formed disciples, we must actively engage and not just passively receive.

Practical and Problem-Centered

Pedagogy is subject-centered. If I'm teaching science, my teaching outcomes center on my students learning information and principles related to the subject of science. In contrast, andragogy is problem-centered. Why? Because adults are plagued with problems. While the major task of childhood is to prepare for adult life, the major tasks of adults revolves around work and relational connections, usually family and friends. Adults are busy with life—bills to pay, people and stuff to care for, and problems to solve. The washer breaks down, teenagers rebel, the boss lays you off, your spouse wants a divorce.

As a result, most adults demand practical Bible teaching that links to life. Your teaching must be life-related with lots of life-application. Your typical adult student thinks, "I don't have time for this unless you can show me how it will help me navigate life now."

Please don't misunderstand. I'm not saying you should water down or sugar-coat God's Word. Adults are smart, so don't insult their intelligence. Teach them the Bible, book by book, or thematically, and not just topically, so they understand the essential doctrines of the faith. Don't shy away from exposing them to difficult passages. They expect you to go deep into the meat of the Word. Give them the tools to unravel unclear problem passages. Present various views when godly respected scholars disagree. Help them discern the differences between pillars of orthodoxy and grey issues. Equip them with sound reasoning and useful apologetics so they are ready to give a reason for the hope that they have in Jesus. Warn them about the devastating consequences of habitual sin. Challenge them to take the kinds of risks that often yield abundant harvests both in their own lives and the lives of others. But link the Bible to their everyday lives in the real world. Fortunately, the Bible was written to be understood and interpreted carefully, but also to be applied—to change our lives.

Those of us who love to debate topics like the sovereignty of God versus the free will of people need to realize that, although these issues are important to theologians, the typical adult doesn't care. To them it's theological navel-gazing. Nor are they impressed with your Greek and Hebrew expertise unless it legitimately adds to what they need to know. Leave the theological jargon behind. I've heard it said that both the original biblical languages and theological jargon are like underwear. It's nice to have it, but don't go around showing it to everyone.

I learned these lessons the hard way. My first year out of seminary, back in the early 1990s, my church invited me to teach in their new equipping ministry called "Tool Box." I choose my own version of my favorite seminary course—Howard Hendricks's *Bible Study Methods*.[10] That course was life-changing for me and my seminary friends. We dreamed of teaching and preaching God's Word, and this was the course that initially trained renowned Bible communicators like Chuck Swindoll, David Jeremiah, Andy Stanley, Jennie Allen, Chip Ingram, Tony Evans, and Priscilla Evans Shirer. I was thrilled at the opportunity to share what I learned in my church. About ninety people enrolled in the class. I assigned the same reading and class assignments as Dr. Hendricks. Admittedly, I'm not Dr. Hendricks, but still the joy of acquiring these critical Bible study skills should have been enough to keep all of my students enthralled, at least that's what I thought. But they weren't. Week by week attendance dropped until at the last session I think maybe eight loyal friends showed up, assignments in hand, but exuberance lacking. The evaluations awakened me to the reality—most adults today don't care about pure theory, or even skill development, if it's not linked to their everyday lives.

Of course, exceptions abound. In every faith community God has endowed people with gifts like teaching and leadership, those with academic bents, and those who would love to earn a seminary or advanced degree but for multiple reasons probably never will. My responsibility is to identify, train, and provide opportunities for them to serve in sync with their gifting and wiring. They would have loved my *Bible Study Methods* class, but they don't represent the vast majority of adults today.

One word of caution, however. In ministry I've observed that some people who complain and ask for more "advanced" training aren't using what they've already received. They mistake maturity for head knowledge and I sense an undertone of pride in their demands. I'm tempted to quote 1 Corinthians 8:1, "knowledge puffs up while love builds up," but more often I alert them to the church's need for people like them to minister to others, hoping they will reevaluate what the Christian life is about.

The experience with my *Bible Study Methods* class flushed away my naiveté to the reality that most adults find academic, abstract topics like Bible study methods useless in their raw form. Now that doesn't mean they don't want to learn how to study the Bible with skill and accuracy. I learned to teach these important skills in tandem with books of the Bible that do relate to real life. While they are learning how to live joyfully in the midst of hardships (Philippians) or how to live courageously in a pagan culture (Daniel or 1 Peter), I incorporate lessons that arm them against Scripture-twisting and help them observe the text before they interpret or apply it. I learned the hard way that adults go home to problems, and they need teachers and preachers who understand and want to help them navigate the tough realities of living in a fallen world.

I've found that my teaching becomes far more effective when I'm teaching someone who wants to learn. For example, I raised two delightful daughters, and I felt one of my responsibilities as a mother was to be sure that before they left our home they knew how to cook. Rachel, our younger daughter, enjoyed whipping up a tasty dish, but our older daughter, Heather, loved academics, athletics, and music. She made it known that you can lead a girl to the kitchen but you can't make her cook—until her junior year in college. Her high school beau proposed and suddenly she turned into the famous French chef Julia Child. In a couple of months, she learned everything I knew about cooking and today she's a better cook than I am. Readiness matters. Adults first choose what they are eager to learn.

I also learned to include praxis in my teaching—opportunities to practice with reflection. When learning about serving others in the Gospel of Mark, we might break out of our regular schedule and tackle multiple community projects with paintbrushes, lawn mowers, and dish towels. Afterwards, we would debrief about what we learned. Go deep and give adults the meat of the Scriptures but link it to life, keep it practical, because adults are plagued with problems and they need the wisdom of the Word to live a life that pleases God and encourages others.

General Characteristics of Healthy Educational Ministries

Build on Prior and Varied Experiences

Unlike children, adults come into the learning environment with a lot of experience. For example, in my seminary classroom, students attend from all generations, all walks of life, and from all over the world. If I added up the years of ministry experience, in some classes, we would clock thousands of hours. I've been in ministry for over forty years, and that's valuable. But I only bring the experience of one person. I'd be foolish not to open up the conversation and draw on the multiple experiences of others. Opening up the conversation means I must listen well, be skilled at directing the discussion, and ask good questions that facilitate rich interaction.

> "Many adults who grew up in church confess with regret that their patience has been sorely tried by being expected to sit through so much talking that now, even though they want to listen, their minds automatically turn off whenever a person starts. We train our church people to be professional listeners rather than leaders. The Scriptures declare that teaching is more than talking, though it sometimes is talking."[11]
> —Lois E. Lebar

Not all, but many adults learn by interacting, participating, and collaborating. Many of us assume that everyone learns the way we do, and we tend to teach the way we personally learn. But over fifty research studies support the fact that adults learn differently. So, although you may not especially like an interactive learning environment, many other people do. It's not just about you. I hate aimless discussions that waste time and go nowhere. So I've worked hard to become skilled at guiding profitable discussions. And I'm careful to vary what we do, so everyone has the opportunity to learn the way that works best for them.

In addition, quality discussions benefit adults because they create connections between students that foster a web of robust relationships that not only enrich our time together but often spill over into deep friendships, some lasting a lifetime. I know of a number of ministry partnerships, future job opportunities, as well as marriages that took root in my classroom as a result of our interactions.

I find interactive conversations stimulating and I learn from them, even though I've been teaching the same topics for many years. In these conversations, sometimes a group member from another country, occasionally a prominent church leader, shares a global perspective we had not considered. If I'd spent the entire time lecturing, we'd never have known. Some of us travel overseas either as a tourist or on a mission trip to minister and to become more globally literate. We spend extravagant amounts of money and invest valuable blocks of time, and certainly we often experience great reward. But sometimes we could benefit just as much if we were to walk across the room and introduce ourselves to the interesting people God puts right under our noses. We just might learn more by initiating meaningful conversations with the diverse group of people who sit across from us rather than if we'd made an expensive trip as a tourist but never rubbed shoulders with nationals.

> "Participation in the learning process stimulates learning and encourages growth. Negatively, when the teacher is in total control of the class's activities, his or her ego may be the only growing thing in the classroom."[12]
> —Marlene D. LeFever

Often, in class discussions or collaborating on a project, we come in contact with people of other generations who think and act quite differently. These intergenerational exchanges should mimic what we find in our ministries, communities, neighborhoods, and families. I understand my children and grandchildren better as I hear from men and women of different age groups.

As a woman, I benefit greatly from hearing men's take on different topics and they benefit from hearing women's perspectives. Gender awakenings benefit us all, not just in the classroom, but for a lifetime as we go out together to serve our Christian brothers and sisters as well as nonbelievers, both male and female.

However, quality conversations in the classroom require teachers skilled at guiding those interactions. For decades, I've observed, studied, and tried to emulate professors, pastors, leaders, and teachers who excel at creating quality connections where students feel safe and comfortable contributing while avoiding tiresome rabbit trails, dominating students who waste everyone's time, and contentious students attempting to impress others by arguing their agenda.

If you want to become an expert communicator, learn to listen well, lead quality conversations, and ask good questions in the classroom. It's as essential as learning to lecture well and use creative methods. Adults bring many years of life experience into the learning context with them. Capitalize on this and watch a learning community thrive because you are drawing from the deep well of their combined life experiences. You are also teaching those entrusted to you to communicate their ideas with clarity, building their confidence that God can use them "out there."

Creating a positive discussion ethos isn't achieved easily or overnight. You set the tone. The way you interact with students creates patterns for the way they will interact with each other, so take the responsibility to create that environment seriously. Build a learning community where everyone feels safe speaking up but understands that wasting time and foolishness won't be tolerated. How? Consider these suggestions.

Love Your Students

Some aren't easy to love but God loves them and he can enable you to love them too. Pray over your students by name and ask God to enable you to love *all* of them. They sense you genuinely care, and this affects their attitudes in class.

Be Personable

Transformational teaching is not just information dump. Share yourself and your life with them enough so they feel they know you personally. The course is about them and not you, but letting them know a little about your family, your failures, your passions, your desperate dependence on the Lord, and your intense love for him makes you real, approachable, and shows them that God uses ordinary people to do his extraordinary work. I usually spend part of our first session together introducing myself, along with a short slide show of my family, including grandchildren, my ministry, and my life outside my vocation. If the class is small enough I give them a little time to introduce themselves to the class. In larger classes I often end with a five- to ten-minute time for them to introduce themselves to a couple of people they don't know. It's fun to see those conversations extend down the hall as they leave class talking or result in an invitation to meet for a cup of coffee.

Learn Their Names

In large classes this can be challenging, but our memories are like a muscle. The more you use it the stronger it becomes. I try to know their names the first time we meet. (Our seminary provides rosters with student pictures.) If that's not possible, learn their names as fast as you can and call them by name in class. Soon many of the students will know one another's names, a building block of a positive learning community.

Take the Learning Space with Your Voice

As a teacher I'm not an autocrat. I'm partnering with the Holy Spirit and team teaching with Jesus. God has given me this space for this time with the privilege and responsibility to oversee learning with a group of adults made in his image, precious to him and to me. I'm accountable to God for what happens, to the best of my ability, during the hours we spend together. My role as professor/teacher is to protect

the more tender students from toxic influences of others, whatever the reason. My role is also to reach those who act out in unhealthy ways, but that sometimes requires tough love on my part. I usually give out discussion guidelines the first day we meet to clearly set boundaries so everyone knows what to expect. Probably most important is how I treat students myself. Early on I'm open and caring, but not smothering or overly sentimental. I never embarrass or humiliate a student, especially for brain freeze, a mistake, or misunderstanding. But neither do I allow students to humiliate one another or to negate the classroom ethos by rudeness or lack of civility. I love them too much to let anyone poison what God wants to do through our time together, but that love goes beyond just making sure no one shuts down anyone else. It extends to the difficult student to try to find out what's going on that's showing up negatively. As a teacher you can always request to meet with your students, not with punitive intentions but just to get to know them and find out what's going on in their lives. I'm often surprised by what I learn one-on-one over a cup of coffee.

Remember: Gender Affects the Discussion

I teach all-women courses and mixed-gender courses. Sometimes a woman student takes both courses the same semester. Often she's quiet, sometimes silent, in the mixed gender setting, but when it's all women, she's one of the first to contribute. I can usually coax her to speak up when men are present but the difference is easily detectable. My goal is to create a space where both men and women are comfortable interacting. Women sometimes articulate different perspectives from men, and since in many congregations 60 percent of the church is female, everyone and the Lord's work benefits when both male and female voices are heard. Men and women are different, but not as different as some insist. One isn't from Mars and the other from Venus. It's more like one is from North Carolina and the other South Carolina. Foremost, we are both made in the image of God, and equally precious to him.[13] As brothers and sisters in the family of God, we are called to support one another and work together. Positive discussions in a learning environment further these understandings and promote peace and respect. However, if the men begin to take charge of the discussion in an ultra-aggressive manner, typical of what I've observed when leaders' meetings become competitive, women generally shut down. I can see them withdraw from the discussion by their posture and facial expressions. I remove this kind of interaction in the guidelines that I hand out the first session because I want both men and women to feel comfortable interacting. I'm not saying that we need to forbid differences of opinion. Those differences season a healthy robust discussion where insight and deep learning are often achieved. I'm simply asking for an irenic tone, where we can all learn from the prior and varied experiences of everyone.

Divide Up Adults by Life Tasks? Yes and No

The best way to be formed in Christ is to sit among the elders, listen to their stories, break bread with them, and drink from the same cup, observing how these earlier generations of saints ran the race, fought the fight, and survived in grace.[14]

Over the last hundred years, research studies focused on differences in peoples' cognitive, psychosocial, moral, and faith development (Jean Piaget, Erik Erikson, Abraham Maslow, Lawrence Kohlberg, Carol Gillian, James Fowler).[15] Life-span specialists emphasized the different life tasks that challenge people as they age. As educators applied these findings to schools, ministry educators implemented age-graded ministry structures in churches and parachurch organizations. For example, in many churches today, groups like children, youth, singles, young marrieds, and seniors are so segregated that their paths seldom if ever cross. Certainly the needs of single twentysomethings adjusting to their first job differs vastly from the needs of their grandparents adjusting to retirement. But as a result, many churches, particularly megachurches, have unintentionally created age-specific mini-congregations within the church so that the single twentysomething and the retiree never even meet, much less converse, serve together, or enjoy a mentoring relationship.

> "Mentors and apprentices are partners in an ancient human dance, and one of teaching's great rewards is the daily chance it gives us to get back on the dance floor. It is the dance of the spiraling generations, in which the old empower the young with their experience and the young empower the old with new life, reweaving the fabric of the human community as they touch and turn."[16]
>
> —Parker J. Palmer

I've observed that adults do need to be part of groups divided up by life tasks to grow strong in their faith. Newlyweds benefit from interaction with other newlyweds. New moms and dads need the friendship of other young parents dealing with the same challenges. Singles need other singles and widows enjoy the companionship of other widows—but not to the exclusion of intergenerational connections.

We find support for life-stage ministry in the educational research but we find support for intergenerational ministry in the Bible. Today adults need both. The Bible pictures intergenerational ministry in the pastoral epistles. For example:

> Teach the older men to be temperate, worthy of respect, self-controlled, and sound in faith, in love and in endurance. Likewise, teach the older women to be reverent in the way they live, not to be slanderers or addicted to much wine, but to teach what is good. Then they can urge younger women to love their husbands and children, to be self-controlled and pure, to be busy at home, to be kind, and to be subject to their husbands, so that no one will malign the word of God. Similarly, encourage the young men to be self-controlled. In everything set them an example by doing what is good. In your teaching show integrity, seriousness and soundness of speech that cannot be condemned, so that those who oppose may be ashamed because they have nothing bad to say about us.
> —Titus 2:2–8

Within this text we observe valuable models of mentoring that should be commonplace in the church.[17] In addition, Paul invested in younger men who traveled with him on his missionary journeys. Typically, he left them to oversee churches as he moved on. Jesus's mother Mary left immediately for the home of her older relative Elizabeth as soon as she learned she would bear the Messiah, where she found comfort, trust, and support.

Through the pages of Scripture, families, communities, and churches naturally involved people of all ages and stages. Boys apprenticed alongside their fathers as one generation passed on their vocation to the next. In the biblical family, children worked alongside their mothers and fathers in the fields or the village store that they ran together and lived above. I recall my parents sharing stories of their early years in farming communities where they grew up surrounded by great grandparents, grandparents, aunts, uncles, nieces, and nephews, kinfolk ranging in age from ninety-five to six months. These natural connections evolved into mentoring relationships in family, church, and community. However, today most nuclear families have splintered all over the nation and even the world. These natural connections are rare, making a mix of ages in Christian communities and churches all the more valuable.

New dads not only need other new dads to share their experiences. They also need experienced dads to help them raise healthy families. Young career women need older working women who've navigated those complex boardrooms. A class full of new parents can sit around and bemoan struggles with their willful two-years-olds, but hearing from parents who've weathered that season well is priceless, providing both encouragement and insight. Adults today need both same-social-stage connections and intergenerational relationships to thrive.

As you attempt to provide both life-task and intergenerational connections to people God entrusts to your care, remember *the peril of the pendulum*. In reaction to a growing awareness of the unintended consequences of generational segregation, some churches have committed what Dr. Howard Hendricks called *the peril of the pendulum*. He argued that typically we humans respond to a negative with such extreme reactions that we sometimes end up creating other negatives. Whenever you make changes, think carefully, strategically, attempting to foresee unintended consequences. Here is an example of a new church trend that serves as an example, but, in my opinion, could go too far.

This approach terminates all age-specific ministries and requires everyone, including children and youth, to attend the adult worship service, eliminating most age-appropriate teaching. Families are instructed to worship together and sometimes required to participate in neighborhood small groups. All age and gender-specific ministries are shut down or left with little support. Certainly there are benefits to families worshipping together. However, completely disregarding what we've learned about developmental and learning readiness may produce unintended consequences in the future. Toddlers simply will not benefit from a sermon aimed at adults.

The Peril of the Pendulum

Sometimes by attempting to correct one set of problems we create others. Ministry is messy

and similar to herding cats. Bottom line—make changes on your knees with your ministry team or fellow teachers, and listen to a variety of voices. Remember that adults need *both* opportunities to connect by social stage and intergenerational relationships. You must figure out how to do that within the given context that God assigns to you. Then with God's help, your investment, and their willing hearts, learning and spiritual maturity will skyrocket.

> "A teaching style is not something you go looking for and then copy. Every teacher has one. You have a teaching style, and it is distinctive for you. No other teacher works in the same way you do, even with the same materials and the same learners."[18]
> —Jerold W. Apps

Conclusion

Teaching adults well requires a willingness to look at teaching from an andragogical perspective. If you've been a successful student in the typical western school or university system, you may love sitting in rows, hearing a stellar lecture, taking a test, and making the grade. As a result, you may be tempted to transplant that model to teaching in ministry or parachurch contexts with adults. You'll make the mistake of thinking that every other adult is like you! And if you do, you may teach them a lot about the Bible but unless they live out what they know, they won't really progress in the sanctification process. Andragogy, from a Christian perspective, is *the art and science of helping Christian adults grow strong in Christ, as together, teacher and student, we seek and depend on God's enabling power and direction.*

You need to understand that teaching adults is different from teaching children, and you need to know what sets adults apart. Anytime we attempt to categorize people we run into exceptions but generally adult learning is self-directed, multifaceted, and practical and problem-centered. Healthy educational ministries for adults are built on their prior and varied experiences and divided up by their life tasks while also connecting them to meaningful relationships with people of other generations.

In addition, we need to master basic educational concepts such as understanding: different learning styles and creative methods; how to listen well, guide quality discussions, and ask good clear questions; how to lecture effectively; and how to develop healthy appropriate relationships with our students. These are skills, just like playing a musical instrument, excelling at a sport, or becoming an expert writer or chef. Mastery takes time. But God empowers men and women to herald his Word so it sticks deep into the minds and heart of his people so they go out and live to their full potential in him. Is God calling you to be part of this process? If he is, you are embarking on a grand adventure. You'll find it challenging, and hard work, but also satisfying and glorious, a delightful privilege when you team teach with Jesus.

Discussion Questions

1. When you envision yourself teaching, what do you see? Has this chapter challenged your view of teaching, and if so, how?

2. Consider the different general characteristics of the adult learner described in this chapter. Which ones, if any, fit you? How are you different or the same as the typical adult learner?

3. Have you experienced someone teaching adults well? Why was their teaching life-changing?

4. Have you experienced someone teaching adults poorly (no names, please)? Why do you think their teaching was not effective? What should they have done differently?

5. What changes do you need to make in your thinking and/or skill-building to become a master teacher of adults?

Resources for Further Study

Allen, Holly Catterton and Christine Lawton Ross. *Intergenerational Christian Formation, Bringing the Whole Church Together in Ministry, Community and Worship*. Downers Grove, IL: InterVarsity Press, 2012.

Bruce, Barbara. *7 Ways of Teaching the Bible to Adults: Using Our Multiple Intelligences to Build Faith*. Nashville: Abingdon Press, 2000.

Gangel, Kenneth O. *Ministering to Today's Adults: A Complete Manual for Organizing and Developing Adult Ministries in Local Congregations*. Eugene, OR: Wipf and Stock Publishers, 2006.

Merriam, Sharan B., Rosemary S. Caffarella, and Lisa Baumgartner. *Learning in Adulthood: A Comprehensive Guide*. San Francisco: Jossey-Bass, 2007.

Palmer, Parker J. *The Courage to Teach: Exploring The Inner Landscape of A Teacher's Life*. San Francisco, CA: Jossey-Bass, 1998.

Wlodkowski, Raymond J. *Enhancing Adult Motivation to Learn: A Comprehensive Guide for Teaching All Adults*. San Francisco: Jossey-Bass. 2008.

Author Bio

Dr. Sue Edwards has more than thirty-five years experience as a Bible teacher, overseer of several megachurch ministries, and author. Now, as Associate Professor of Educational Ministries and Leadership, she teaches full-time at Dallas Theological Seminary. She has trained women leaders in Russia, Africa, and Germany. Sue is the coauthor of five leadership books including: *Organic Mentoring: A Mentor's Guide to Relationships with Next Generation Women, Leading Women Who Wound, Mixed Ministry: Working Together as Brothers and Sisters in an Oversexed Society,* and *New Doors in Ministry to Women.* Women everywhere enjoy learning the Scriptures using her Bible studies, the *Discover Together Series* (DiscoverTogetherSeries.com). Married for forty-five years, she and David are the proud parents of two married daughters and the grandparents of five. David is a retired computer engineer who serves the Lord as a lay prison chaplain, and is now taking courses at DTS.

Endnotes

1.   Lawrence O. Richard, *Creative Bible Teaching* (Chicago, IL: Moody Press, 1970), 57.

2.   Albert Mohler, "The Scandal of Biblical Illiteracy: It's Our Problem," January 20, 2016, www.albertmohler.com.

3.   Mary Jo Sharp, *Defending the Faith, Apologetics in Women's Ministry* (Grand Rapids, MI: Kregel Publications, 2012), 20.

4.   Jerold W. Apps, *Mastering the Teaching of Adults* (Malabar, FL: Krieger Publishing Company, 1991), 1.

5.   Michael F. Haverluck, "Survey: *Alarming Rate of Christian Men Look at Porn, Commit Adultery,*" October 9, 2014, www.onenewsnow.com, accessed on July 4, 2016.

6.   Malcolm Knowles, Elwood Holton, and Richard Swanson, *The Adult Learner*, 11th ed. (New York: Routledge, 2015).

7.   Howard Hendricks, DTS Professor (from the Preface/Foreword of *The Christian Education of Adults*, ed. Gilbert A. Peterson [Chicago, IL: Moody Press, 1984]).

8.   Literacy Project Foundation, "Staggering Illiteracy Statistics," www.literacyprojectfoundation.org/community/statistics. Original source material comes from the National Institute for Literacy, the National Center for Adult Literacy, The Literacy Company, and the US Census Bureau.

9.   Raymond J. Wlodkowski, *Enhancing Adult Motivation to Learn: A Guide to Improving Instruction and Increasing Adult Learner Achievement* (San Francisco, CA: Josey-Bass Publishers, 1993), 82.

10.   See the chapter "What Makes a Great Teacher?" by Bill Hendricks for more on Howard Hendricks.

11.   Lois E. Lebar, *Education That Is Christian* (Colorado Springs: Cook Communications, 1995), 27.

12.   Marlene D. LeFever, *Creative Teaching Methods: Be An Effective Christian Teacher* (Colorado Springs, CO: Cook Communications, 1996), 9.

13.   For more insight on understanding and teaching men, dig into the chapter "Men: Stressed" by Paul Pettit. For women, see the chapter "Undervalued: Women" by Sue Edwards.

14.   James Frazier, "All Generations of Saints at Worship," in *Across the Generations: Incorporating All Ages in Ministry: The Why and How,* eds. Vicky Goplin, Jeffrey Nelson, Mark Gardner and Eileen Zahn (Minneapolis: Augsburg, 2001), 56–63.

15.   Michael J. Anthony, ed., *Evangelical Dictionary of Christian Education* (Grand Rapids, MI: Baker Academic, 2001), 31–34.

16.   Parker J. Palmer, *The Courage to Teach: Exploring the Inner Landscape of A Teacher's Life* (San Francisco, CA: 1998), 25.

17.   Barbara Neumann's chapter on "Mentoring the Next Generation" provides more insight on the critical need for mentoring today.

18.   Apps, *Mastering the Teaching of Adults*, 23.

Chapter 8
STRESSED: MEN

Paul Pettit

Be on your guard; stand firm in the faith; act like men, be courageous; be strong.

—1 Corinthians 16:13

MANY MILITARY VETERANS ARE returning from recent conflicts in Afghanistan and Iraq with heroic stories of unbelievable and dangerous battles. Best-selling movies and books describe fire fights, grenade launches, hand-to-hand combat, and air-to-land warfare skirmishes. And yet, long after the shooting has slowed there is one area of danger that has caused unlimited damage and destruction: unexploded landmines, often referred to today as an improvised explosive device (IED). An IED is a bomb constructed and deployed in ways other than in conventional military action. It may be constructed of conventional military explosives, such as an artillery round, or attached to a detonating mechanism. They are commonly used as roadside bombs.

IEDs are generally seen in heavy terrorist actions or in unconventional warfare. In the second Iraq War, IEDs were used extensively against US-led invasion forces, and by the end of 2007 they were responsible for approximately 63 percent of coalition deaths in Iraq. Also, in Afghanistan, they have caused over 66 percent of coalition casualties since 2001.[1]

Landmines Facing Men Today

What are the landmines keeping many men today from becoming fully functioning members of their families, faith-communities, and even society at large? What do we know about men today that will help us build effective ministries to and for them? The one-word emphasis of this chapter on men's ministry is: *stressed*. Just as military personnel who return from battle are often stressed, so too men today are stressed out trying to hold down a well-paying, full-time job, serve as an active member of their community, carry out their role as loving husband, as well as attempting to be the best dad for their children. All of us hear about the dangers of PTSD (post-traumatic stress disorder). Similarly, many men today are traumatized by the stressful challenge of fulfilling all of the roles they are asked to take on.

> "Courage is contagious. When a brave man takes a stand, the spines of others are often stiffened."
> —Billy Graham

This chapter, however, provides answers. It details ways the church of Jesus Christ can help men lower their stress levels and avoid landmines. Churches with effective men's ministries can point out the dangerous IEDs along the pathway to godly manhood and Christian masculinity. In fact, research shows reaching out to men with the gospel message of Jesus Christ helps build churches. *Focus on the Family* engaged research demonstrating the importance of churches becoming more intentional in their development of ministries to and for men. Their findings show if a child is the first person in a household to become a Christian, there is a 3.5 percent probability everyone else in the household will follow. If the mother is the first to become a Christian, there is a 17 percent probability everyone else in the household will follow. But, if the father is first, there is a 93 percent probability everyone else in the household will follow.[2]

And yet, something is keeping men from filling the rooms where our men's ministries meet. So let's jump right into the problem:

Why are so many men stressed out these days? Men today are expected to become competent workers in the marketplace who earn a healthy wage while advancing in their career or chosen profession. In addition, they are applauded if they are romantic husbands and nurturing fathers. Also, men are asked to volunteer in their community or place of worship. Many men serve as little league baseball coaches, Boy Scout leaders, or National Guard volunteers. Despite this continual flurry of activity, the average male still tries to fit in time watching television or movies, enjoying hunting or fishing, or indulging in a hobby such as restoring an old car or flying drones. There's just not enough time to be a man these days!

Although some men are able to juggle all of these balls, avoid the many IEDs along the road, and leave a lasting legacy as an honorable man, many men fall through the cracks of this regimented, demanding schedule society lays out for them. Statistics show there are real dangers at every turn along the journey from boyhood to manhood in North America. Ugly addictions and social ills trip up men, much like improvised explosive devices stop military personnel from completing their mission. These traps stall many men from becoming fully functioning members of faith communities and even society at large. The following six problems are all landmines for men and areas where today's evangelical men's ministries should plan to offer guidance and assistance. Let's look at these one by one.

Alcoholism

One of the most dangerous pitfalls facing men is the overconsumption of alcohol. Men are disproportionately more likely to suffer from alcoholism than women. Among adults, 16.3 million adults ages 18 and older had an Alcohol Use Disorder in 2014. This includes 10.6 million men (9.2% of men in this age group) and 5.7 million women (4.6% of women in this age group). Statistics show that 1.5 million adults received treatment at a specialized facility in 2014. This included 1.1 million men and 431,000 women. When it comes to alcohol-related deaths nearly 88,000 people (approximately 62,000 men and 26,000 women) die from alcohol-related causes annually.[3]

Drug Abuse

Obviously, drug addiction is equally devastating for both men and women. Drug abuse destroys families and ruins careers. Nationwide surveys continue to show that males abuse drugs at higher rates than females. The 2013 National Survey on Drug Use and Health indicated that close to 12 percent of American males age twelve and older were currently using illegal drugs, compared with just over 7.3 percent of females in the same age group. Multi-drug use was also more common in males than in females. Comparative studies from the 1980s and 1990s showed that drug addiction was more common among men than among women.[4] In addition:

- Males start using drugs at an earlier age.
- Males abuse drugs more often and in larger amounts.
- Males are more likely to abuse alcohol and tobacco.
- Males are more likely to engage in binge drinking (the consumption of five or more drinks in a short time period).

Pornography

Most pornography is targeted toward men and is degrading to women. Dawn Hawkins, Executive Director of the National Center on Sexual Exploitation, says the harms of pornography are becoming clear in light of overwhelming scientific and social research. "In addition to its negative impacts on public health, pornography damages the equality of women in society," Hawkins added. "A study analyzing scenes from popular pornography films revealed that 88 percent of the scenes depict acts of aggression against women. It is time for Americans, no matter their political affiliation, to take a stand for women's equality and for human dignity. There can be no true equality in America when violence against women is considered sexy."[5] According to data taken from Internet users who took part in the General Social Survey, the following are predictors of online pornography use:

- Men are 543 percent more likely to look at porn than females.
- Those who are happily married are 61 percent less likely to look at porn.
- Those who had committed adultery are 218 percent more likely to look at porn.
- Those with teen children are 45 percent less likely to look at porn.[6]

Human Trafficking

Another social danger keeping men from becoming effective husbands, fathers, and friends is prostitution or human trafficking. It is now a $32 billion a year industry, which is $7 billion dollars more than the restaurant McDonalds makes in a year.[7] When most people think of prostitution, they normally think of a male customer and a female client. Identification of male victims is difficult not only due to the lack of awareness, or focus, from law enforcement and service providers, but also the reluctance of boys to speak up. Still, males remain a largely invisible population within the dialogue on sex trafficking. According to a 2008 study by the John Jay College of Criminal Justice, in fact, boys comprised about 50 percent of sexually exploited children in a sample study done in New York, with most being domestic victims. However, the percentage of male victims may be higher due to the underreported and subversive nature of the crime. Summar Ghias, program specialist for the Chicago-based International Organization for Adolescents, states, "We're conditioned as a community to identify female victims more readily," she said, "because that has been the more prominent focus of the anti-trafficking movement."[8]

There are many reasons why prostitution is a horrible practice. These include:

- It promotes human trafficking and child prostitution.
- It increases the risk and spread of HIV/AIDS.
- It increases the abuse and displacement of immigrants.
- It increases the number of women who turn to drugs and alcohol in order to cope with the things done to them.
- It increases the number of unwanted pregnancies and, therefore, abortion rates rise.[9]

Unemployment

Most men gain a sense of purpose and strengthened identity based upon the work they perform. Labels are tossed around to describe men who fail to secure work. "Bum," "drifter," "lazy," or "jobless" are all derogatory names for men who don't work. Men don't work for numerous reasons. Lack of available jobs, injury, inadequate training, and particular lines of work becoming obsolete or even fear of failure can all enter into the equation of un- or underemployment. Whatever the reason, lack of work can reap devastating consequences on men and families. Job loss is associated with elevated rates of mental and physical health problems, increases in mortality rates, and detrimental changes in family relationships and in the psychological well-being of spouses and children. Compared to stably employed workers, those who have lost their jobs have significantly poorer mental health, lower life satisfaction, less marital or family satisfaction, and poorer physical health.[10]

Loneliness

Henry David Thoreau famously wrote, "The mass of men lead lives of quiet desperation. What is called resignation is confirmed desperation. From the desperate city you go into the desperate country, and have to console yourself with the bravery of minks and muskrats. A stereotyped but unconscious despair is concealed even under what are called the games and amusements of mankind. There is no play in them, for this comes after work. But it is a characteristic of wisdom not to do desperate things."[11] Many men are busier than ever but also report feeling lonely.

The problem of loneliness can be worse for men than women. More elderly men experience high levels of social isolation and almost a quarter of men over fifty have less than monthly contact with their children compared to just one in seven women. Nearly one in five older men admitted to having less than monthly contact with friends compared to one in eight for women.[12] Men need healthy friendships. The unhealthiest man in any community is the isolated, unattached male who lives disconnected from family, friends, or neighbors.

Summary

Each of the six landmines described above wreak havoc on men and families. Any one of these problem issues alone can derail a man from becoming all that God desires. Why bring up these issues at the outset of a chapter on men's ministry? My contention is that any effective men's ministry must be keenly aware of these problems and have readily available resources to assist struggling men. Obviously there's no such thing as a perfect man. God's plan for the connected, healthy male is outlined in section two of this chapter. Bottom line: many men in the United States are stressed! And, the church is well-positioned to welcome in these men to help them discover and implement their purpose in life.

> "Every man dies. Not every man really lives."
> —William Wallace in *Braveheart*

God's Plan for Biblical Manhood

As mentioned previously, it is unhealthy for men to live unconnected, isolated lives. That is, unless they have experienced a specific, Christian vocational call to live a life wholly devoted to prayer and service. Some Christian men live in supervised monasteries or godly, monastic communities. But the vast majority of men choose to marry and live as active members of a civilized society. Although our society promotes this romantic notion, it is important to remember that the highest ideal of love is not necessarily married love. Many choose to live a life of singlehood. Jesus was certainly single and perhaps also the apostle Paul. Did they not experience the incredible love of God? The highest form of love is the love God demonstrates to each of us, married or single.

> "The world has yet to see what God will do with, and for, and through, and in, and by the man who is fully and wholly consecrated to him."
> —Dwight L. Moody

That being said, a large part of God's enculturation process for moving boys into manhood involves leaving the comforts and conveniences of home and striking out into the world. God describes this "break" from a young man's father and mother this way: "That is why a man leaves his father and mother and is united to his wife, and they become one flesh" (Gen. 2:24).

Especially for many who have never wed, marriage remains a life goal.[13] About six in ten (61 percent) men and women who have never married say they would like to get married, according to a 2010 Pew Research survey. Only 12 percent say they do not want to marry and 27 percent are not sure.[14]

Family is God's idea. The notion of a man and woman marrying in a lifelong, exclusive covenant of oneness is the manner in which

God first established family. It's interesting to note that the husband and wife enter into a one-flesh relationship. Parents are not in a one-flesh relationship with their children. Children will one day leave the home and start the process anew. But, parents are to remain in their one-flesh state of marriage till death do them part. Marriage unites a man with one woman, out of all possible women, in a life-long, sacrificial relationship. In this way men are socialized and encouraged to live in an ordered, civil society. Sins of rape, adultery, and domestic violence militate against a civil society in the worst way.

> "A real man is one who rejects passivity, accepts responsibility, leads courageously, and expects the greater reward, God's reward."
> —Robert Lewis

The institutions of marriage and family also bind men to their children. Throughout the Scriptures God shows his kindness and compassion toward the widow and the orphan. "A father to the fatherless, a defender of widows, is God in his holy dwelling" (Ps. 68:5). Cultural anthropologist David Blankenhorn states it this way, "A good society celebrates the ideal of the man who puts his family first."[15] While not all men feel called to marriage, effective men's ministries devote considerable time and attention to men who are husbands and fathers. Much time should be spent in encouragement, training, and modeling for how a man can serve his wife and children.

Men as Husbands

In Ephesians 5 the apostle Paul upset the apple cart and went against the grain of his current culture. At that time, husbands ruled with absolute authority in their home and could "put away" or divorce their wives for any reason. Paul commanded Christian men in this manner, "Husbands, love your wives, just as Christ loved the church and gave himself up for her" (Eph. 5:25). This was indeed radical advice for the times. Husbands, Paul said, are to lead in the same manner in which Christ served his bride, the church. And how did Christ serve his bride? He lovingly laid down his life. What a high calling! Too often men act as frustrated drill sergeants in the home stomping their foot, throwing up their hands, and crying out *submit*! Healthy, effective men's ministries teach men to be the type of men who are worthy of being submitted to. It should be remembered the term Paul uses for submission in this passage is defined as, "willingly aligning oneself under." The word does not carry with it any idea of inferior value. Did you catch that? Wives do not have to submit to their husbands ... but they can choose to.[16]

> "At the heart of mature masculinity is a sense of benevolent responsibility to lead, provide for and protect women in ways appropriate to a man's differing relationships."
> —John Piper

Most critics of this often quoted passage mistakenly believe that Paul is asking all women in the church to submit to all of the men in the church. Not so. Paul urges each wife to respect and follow the loving leadership of her *own* husband. The best men's ministries will spend much time and energy teaching men how to be excellent husbands. In a real sense communities are impacted by healthy homes. Healthy homes are made up of solid marriages. Marriages are only as effective as the people in them. Thus, teaching men to be loving, servant leaders in their marriage and home helps build stable communities. The late New York senator Patrick Moynihan summarized his landmark report on families by noting, "A community that allows a large number of young men to grow up in broken families, dominated by women, never acquiring any stable relationship to male authority … that community asks for and gets chaos."[17]

To summarize, the loving husband is to lay down his life for his wife. This self-sacrificial lifestyle cannot be accomplished without adhering to Paul's injunction that Christian husbands (and wives) be filled with the Spirit (Eph. 5:18). So that their prayers are not hindered, husbands also are called to live with their wives in an understanding manner (1 Peter 3:7).

I love what one of my mentors, Chuck Swindoll, wrote concerning his own marriage:

> Cynthia and I, for several years now, have determined to strengthen our relationship by declaring our permanent commitment to each other. This is something we took for granted far too long. It is no longer something we assume. Periodically, through the year (especially on New Year's Day, our anniversary, and each other's birthday), we affirm our commitment, eyeball to eyeball, stating our love and devotion to each other. This really helps! We do not consider separation even an option, no matter how hot the disagreement—and, believe me, it gets awfully hot at times. This is all part of cleaving to each other. Regardless of the difficulty or the problem we are working through, the bond God sealed in June 1955, is not ours to break.[18]

Men as Fathers

Men's ministries can do much to train and encourage men in their role of effective fathering, which is a learned behavior. Many men grow up without the benefit of a healthy father role model. Thus, mistakes and sins of the past are repeated and carried into the newly formed family. Young men often need education and encouragement in the basics of child care. While many young girls grow up role-playing *family*: complete with dolls and pretend marriages, most boys don't know the first thing about diapers or bottle-feeding. An effective men's ministry can and should offer training for first-time dads, fathers of adolescents, single dads, and even incarcerated fathers.

> "When Christ calls a man, he bids him come and die."
> —Dietrich Bonhoeffer

No other activity is more important for the witness and effectiveness of the church than its leaders ministering to widows and orphans. The pastor of the first church put it this way, "Religion that God our Father accepts as pure and faultless is this: to look after orphans and widows in their distress and to keep oneself from being polluted by the world" (James 1:27). Encouraging men to be effective fathers who are physically and spiritually present with their children is spiritual work of the highest order.

A wonderful strategy cutting-edge men's ministries are using is pairing older men with younger men in the practice of generational discipleship. Since we are now ministering essentially to a fatherless generation and within a culture of broken families, younger men desperately need the advice and wisdom that older, godly men can impart. I have met countless young men who are ready for this type of small group or one-to-one training, but are simply waiting for a pastor or minister to help the interactions get organized. Older men tell me they are ready to befriend younger husbands or new dads … and young men express a desire to meet with and learn from seasoned husbands and fathers who have been around the block and learned from their mistakes. A keen men's minister helps facilitate these strengthening relationships.

> "He is no fool who gives up what he cannot keep to gain what he cannot lose."
> —Jim Elliot

The goal of fatherhood training is men becoming the leading servants in their home. A high value for the *worldly* in the marketplace is ascending to places of authority and privilege where they can *be the man* and *pull rank* over those under them. Not so in the Christian community! Our Lord instructed his closest followers in a new and different way. "Jesus called them together and said, 'You know that the rulers of the Gentiles lord it over them, and their high officials exercise authority over them. Not so with you. Instead, whoever wants to become great among you must be your servant, and whoever wants to be first must be your slave—just as the Son of Man did not come to be served, but to serve, and to give his life as a ransom for many'" (Matt. 20:25–28). The best Christian servants make the best dads.

> "Fathers are to sons what blacksmiths are to swords. It is the job of the blacksmith not only to make a sword but also to maintain its edge of sharpness. It is the job of the father to keep his son sharp and save him from the dullness of foolishness. He gives his son that sharp edge through discipline."
> —Steve Farrar

Allow me to quote my friend, Steve Farrar, who shares strong words on fathering:

God has hardwired us from the womb. And he has hardwired us for relationships. And one of those relationships is a father and his children. Kids in America are in trouble because many of them have lost this central connection to their dads. They've got a dish, a receiver, and a television. But somehow the wiring has gotten messed up and they are not getting a clear picture. They are getting clothes, money, and cars, but they are not getting what they need. That's why they are so depressed and confused. They are not wired into Dad. Dad's too busy building his kingdom to build into them.[19]

Men as Friends

"Most men lead lives of quiet desperation and go to the grave with the song still in them."[20] It's true many men have no other men in their lives that they would classify as a great friend. One study published in the *Journal of Personality and Social Psychology* showed men generally felt less lonely when their friend groups were more "dense," whereas women showed little correlation between loneliness levels and friend group density. As the authors put it, "It is suggested that men may use more group-oriented criteria in evaluating loneliness, whereas women focus more on the qualities of [one-on-one] relationships."[21] In other words, men feel less lonely when they are at a stadium full of people watching a football, baseball, or soccer match or with a group of guys working on a car. When they are with a group of men they don't feel lonely. But men often have fewer *close friends* than women. For many men, talking about their feelings or frustrations with other men makes them feel feminine.

> "No man is an island."
> —John Donne

Add to this that in the Westernized, rugged-individualistic, go-it-alone culture of the United States, men are expected to pull themselves up by their bootstraps and young boys in little league baseball are told that crying is illegal. Boys are told at a very young age, "There's no crying in baseball!" For many boys, the demonstration of emotion is seen as less than masculine. Even if a boy is injured or hurt he is often told, "Stop crying … you're not a girl!" Boys learn at a very young age to stuff their emotions inside and not let anyone see the chinks in their *masculine armor*.

A healthy men's ministry can offer genuine friendships and opportunities where men can be encouraged to be open and authentic in transparent, safe men's small groups. A gifted men's minister understands the importance of men being involved in healthy friendships where masks can come off and hurts can be healed through the power of authentic, Christ-centered community. As a reminder, family research experts mention caution when discussing the *unattached male*. Men need the socializing benefit derived from both a healthy marriage and authentic friendships with other healthy males. Socialized men serving their homes and families form the bedrock foundation of a civil society.

Men at Work

Many men struggle with confusing their identity with their work. It is a common fault. Besides, what's the first thing someone asks when meeting a man for the first time? "Glad to meet you, what do you *do*?" If a man falls into this trap of thinking he *is* what he *does* for a living he can expect a roller coaster ride of emotions. If things are going well at work, promotions and pay-raises are coming his way, a man can feel like a winner. If the economy changes, resulting in layoffs or pink slips, a man can feel like a loser. How can men's ministries encourage men in the workplace? Two emphases ought to be taught on a regular basis.

The first is the idea of *calling* or *vocation as ministry*. Every generation has to struggle with the notion that work is good and has been ordained by God. God did not curse work after the fall, God cursed *the ground* as a result of the fall. In addition, God encourages men to work to provide for needs. The apostle Paul wrote: "For even when we were with you, we gave you this rule: 'The one who is unwilling to work shall not eat'" (2 Thess. 3:10). And further, Paul wrote, "Anyone who does not provide for their relatives, and especially for their own household, has denied the faith and is worse than an unbeliever" (1 Tim. 5:8). So, men's ministries should help men find and keep full-time employment.

> "Do not pray for easy lives, pray to be stronger men…. Do not pray for tasks equal to your powers, pray for powers equal to your tasks."
> —Phillips Brooks

Some men wrongly believe that spiritual work is ministry and secular work is not related to ministry. However, it is important to teach our men that all work is ministry in God's eyes. It does not follow that only those involved in full-time vocational Christian ministry are involved in spiritual or Christian work. The reformer Martin Luther wrote, "the works of monks and priests, however holy and arduous they may be, do not differ one whit in the sight of God from the works of the rustic laborer in the field or the woman going about her household tasks … all works are measured before God by faith alone."[22] So, all work is holy to God. The idea of *calling* is not for those in ministry alone.

Calling and vocation are terms that should be used by all workers everywhere.

A second idea to emphasize is practicing *integrity* in the workplace. Men should work hard at whatever they find to do and perform their work with excellence. A young boy needed a pen to complete his homework assignment on honesty. After a fruitless search throughout the house his dad piped up, "Oh don't worry about finding a pen, son, I can bring home a whole handful from work!" The irony of writing a report on honesty with his dad's purloined pen was surely not lost on the son. Hopefully Christian men in the workplace are the ones who show up on time and don't leave early. The best witness for Christ in the marketplace is the man who conducts his life and work with honesty and integrity.

Building an Effective Men's Ministry Structure

In every church, several different on-ramps into the men's ministry, which provide opportunity for involvement, need to exist. Men often enter into the life of the church for varying reasons. Some attend out of habit or tradition. On one end of the spectrum are leaders in a church who are heavily involved in providing spiritual oversight and active ministry to others. On the opposite end of this yardstick are men who are involved at a low commitment level. They may attend a worship service one Sunday a month and little else. How does an active, effective men's ministry capture the attention of all of the men along this spectrum, as well as those who are not yet attending or interested in the church? The following three-pronged approach is a winning strategy for attracting and involving men in ministry.

Come and Listen Events

Some think the entirety of men's ministry is simply a monthly breakfast held on the first Saturday of the month or a time of service where men do chores for the church. And indeed, these types of activities do constitute many church's men's ministries. But so much more can be accomplished with an effective, well thought out strategy. The first type of activity to consider is the *come and listen* event. This meeting is open to all. The only *ask*, the only commitment requested is that men attend and be open to what the speaker or presenter has to say.

Some folks call this type of gathering a flagpole event. Why? Because it is open to all and the event raises the flag for this particular ministry. During this event we are waving the flag of men's ministry. This is the type of meeting where food is served and a guest speaker or teacher might present an introductory type of lesson. Maybe the gospel is explained in a clear manner and men are invited to investigate the truth claims of Christianity. Worship music may or may not be included but if so the songs are often brief and upbeat. At my home church this event is held seven times a year and is called Man Church. The speakers address the needs of men. Maybe your church determines to hold one of these events four times a year, once a quarter.

In my travels and work consulting churches on developing effective men's ministries, I have heard of *come and listen* type of events where muscle cars, motorcycles, or hot rods are displayed. Others serve grilled hamburgers or thick steaks. Lots of churches hold wild game nights where hunters and fishermen are encouraged to attend by serving fish, pheasant, quail, and venison.

There is no set formula for these events. Men's ministry teams should hold events they believe will appeal to the men in their particular geographic community. To reiterate, this is an entry-level, low commitment type of event. What is being asked of the men? That they simply attend and maybe that they invite and bring a neighbor, friend, or colleague from work. The best guest speaker at this event is someone who can connect with men. Effective choices include a successful thinker from the marketplace, a former or current professional athlete, a military or political leader, or a man with an outstanding testimony of overcoming adversity. I have heard amazing presentations from men who have overcome addictions, clear speakers who present the complexity of the gospel message in simple, easy to understand ways, and godly Bible teachers with long track records of healthy marriages and families.

Obviously, Jesus Christ is our highest role model. And ultimately, all men are frail and but dust. But there is also nothing wrong with learning from other men who are fighting the good fight of faith and striving to be godly men. The apostle Paul encouraged men to give honor to whom honor is due (Rom. 13:7). The *come and listen* large event is a foundational mainstay of an effective, growing men's ministry.

Come and Learn Events

This second type of event builds upon the first and asks men for a bit more involvement and commitment. This type of gathering often features worship and Bible teaching. Men may be broken up into small groups for reflection and discussion. The men are asked not only to attend (*come and listen*) but also to study their lesson beforehand or come prepared to discuss the answers they came up with during the week. An example of this style of event is the popular Bible Study Fellowship groups that meet across the country.[23] Another *come and learn* gathering is called Men's Fraternity.[24]

This type of event is held more frequently than the first and requires deeper levels of commitment and learning. Perhaps an introductory book on a spiritual topic or Bible lesson is the starting point. Men can be challenged to complete specific Bible studies or learn about the doctrines and theology of their faith. Some men's ministries offer elective or "hot topic" classes on marriage or fathering.

These *come and learn* events may not be the best starting point for a visitor. Perhaps a first-timer would feel more welcome at a *come and listen* meeting. But over time, challenge men: we want you to get involved in the men's ministry at our church. It may sound something like this: "Men, some of you have been attending our monthly rallies for quite a while, and for you guys, the next step would be to check out our learning events which are held every other Tuesday night (or whenever they are held). At this time, we're going to pass out a flyer which provides all the details for this event. Again, if you are a first-timer tonight, we're simply glad you decided to attend!"

Offering varied meetings, gatherings, and events with different levels of commitment and challenge reflect the growth men encounter when they step out in faith and determine to become stronger in their faith.

Come and Lead Events

These meetings involve the highest level of commitment from the men in the men's ministry. In this ongoing meeting, men are involved in praying for and planning all of the other events. Men are challenged to make sure they are involved in a mentoring or discipleship relationship with mature, godly men in the church. Men are selected to become involved in these gatherings by older, wiser men who have walked with Jesus Christ and shown maturity in their faith. Some call these men elders. Others refer to this as a leadership council. Leadership in the church is a serious calling. James warned, "Not many of you should become teachers, my fellow believers, because you know that we who teach will be judged more strictly" (James 3:1). In addition, in 1 Timothy 3:1–7, Paul lays out the guidelines for those who would provide servant-leadership for the church:

> Here is a trustworthy saying: Whoever aspires to be an overseer desires a noble task. Now the overseer is to be above reproach, faithful to his wife, temperate, self-controlled, respectable, hospitable, able to teach, not given to drunkenness, not violent but gentle, not quarrelsome, not a lover of money. He must manage his own family well and see that his children obey him, and he must do so in a manner worthy of full respect. (If anyone does not know how to manage his own family, how can he take care of God's church?) He must not be a recent convert, or he may become conceited and fall under the same judgment as the devil. He must also have a good reputation with outsiders, so that he will not fall into disgrace and into the devil's trap.

Table 8.1 Effective Men's Ministry Structure

What?	Come and listen	Come and learn	Come and lead
When?	Once a month	Biweekly or a season of time	Biweekly or monthly
Who?	For the visitor or new Christian	For the growing Christian	For the maturing Christian
Why?	Topical presentation	Biblical study / table discussion	Doctrine or leadership lessons

Retreats

One of the best ways to connect men is to offer a weekend retreat.[25] If possible a three-day retreat over a Friday through Sunday works best. However, smaller churches, where many of the participants are volunteers in the church's Sunday services, may need to use a Friday and Saturday weekend format. There are at least three wonderful reasons to hold a men's retreat.

> "Paul commanded Timothy to find faithful men and teach them and they'll be able to teach others. What God is looking for is what every woman is looking for—not a man of great power, but a man who will be faithful. When we develop faithful men, we develop mature men."
> —Paul Cole

First, a retreat provides an excellent opportunity for men to gather in a casual format outside of the normal "church building" interactions. Men need to see their friends in a setting where they are offered extended time for conversation, recreation, meals, and fellowship. Second, an offsite retreat is one of the best ways to involve visitors. Many men don't feel comfortable getting up early on a Sunday morning and checking out a church for the first time, where they don't know the lingo or the words to the hymns. Author David Murrow wrote a best-selling book explaining this phenomenon in *Why Men Hate Going to Church*. On the other hand, a neighbor or coworker feels less threatened when invited to a getaway that involves fishing, skeet shooting, golfing, watching *man movies*, or countless other masculine, recreational activities. Some men's retreats feature an effective businessman or former professional athlete as a speaker. Others incorporate outreach themes or activities that appeal to men who are not heavily involved in church. And, there are retreats with spiritual formation themes inviting committed Christ-followers to go deeper in their walk with their Savior.

The third reason men's retreats are effective is because men are often stressed and distracted, the theme of this chapter. Men often worry about whether they are doing enough at work to keep their job or earn a promotion, whether the family home or car needs repair, or how they can *keep up* with other men in their neighborhood. At an off-site retreat location, often set at a camp near a lake or out in a beautiful nature setting, men are able to let down their guard, decompress, and reflect on their own life and legacy. Hold offsite retreats at reoccurring times such as each fall or every spring so that memories and traditions can be built and passed on to younger men. Normally, these events are open to young men eighteen and older. Other highly effective events are father-son or father-daughter retreats.

A caution is in order here: These events should be planned with excellence well in advance of the retreat weekend. A haphazard retreat with an obvious lack of detailed planning can be frustrating to all involved. Even smaller-size churches can partner with other like-minded fellowships to hold an outstanding event.

Conclusion

There are dangerous landmines which must be avoided in order that men become the men God wants them to be. Regular, active involvement in a healthy men's ministry helps men avoid these ugly explosions. Men's ministry serves as a critical component of a healthy, local church. Even though training and encouragement for men is often overlooked in the structure of the local church, men are often expected to serve in time-consuming leadership roles. In addition, many local churches provide few on ramps for men. Women's groups often hold luncheons or other events where guests are welcome. However, few churches offer effective outreach activities where men can invite their neighbors, friends, or coworkers. The effective, well-rounded church offers both: ongoing training for men and outreach events where guests and new attenders feel welcomed to the life of the church.

In summary, men in the church should not be overlooked or taken for granted. Even though most men have a difficult time expressing their need for friendship and spiritual encouragement, church staff play a critical role insuring that programmatic efforts are offered for men in various states of Christian growth—from the first-time visitor to the maturing grandfather.

Discussion Questions

1. Why do you think men's involvement in churches and Christian organizations is so critical?

2. Is your church intentional about its ministry to men? Can you discern any results either positive or negative?

3. The author lists six "landmines" for men today and suggests that churches help men overcome these problems. Did any of these "landmines" surprise you? How might local churches better serve men struggling in these areas?

4. What did you learn about men as husbands, fathers, and friends, that will help you minister to men more effectively?

5. What do you think a transformational men's ministry looks like? How might you help this type of ministry flourish where you worship?

Resources for Further Study

Books

Arterburn, Stephen and Fred Stoeker. *Every Man's Battle: Winning the War on Sexual Temptation One Victory at a Time*. Colorado Springs: Waterbrook, 2000.

Downer, Phil. *Effective Men's Ministry*. Grand Rapids: Zondervan, 2001.

Edwards, Sue, Kelley Mathews, and Henry Rogers. *Mixed Ministry: Working Together as Brothers and Sisters in an Oversexed Society*. Grand Rapids: Kregel, 2008.

Evans, Tony. *Kingdom Man: Every Man's Destiny, Every Woman's Dream*. Colorado Springs: Focus on the Family, 2015.

Feldhahn, Jeff and Shaunti. *For Men Only: A Straightforward Guide to the Inner Lives of Women*. Portland, OR: Multnomah, 2013.

Getz, Gene. *The Measure of a Man: 20 Attributes of a Godly Man*. Ada, MI: Revell, 2004.

Hendricks, Howard and William Hendricks. *As Iron Sharpens Iron: Building Character in a Mentoring Relationship.* Chicago: Moody, 1999.

Hughes, R. Kent, *Disciplines of a Godly Man.* Wheaton, IL: Crossway, 2016.

Köstenberger, Andreas and Margaret Elizabeth Köstenberger. *God's Design for Man and Woman: A Biblical-Theological Survey.* Wheaton: Crossway, 2014.

Mason, Eric. *Manhood Restored: How the Gospel Makes Men Whole.* Nashville: B & H Books, 2013.

Medinger, Alan. *Growth into Manhood: Resuming the Journey.* Colorado Springs: Shaw Books, 2000.

Morley, Patrick. *The Man in the Mirror: Solving the 24 Problems Men Face.* Grand Rapids: Zondervan, 2014.

Murrow, David. *Why Men Hate Going to Church.* Nashville: Thomas Nelson, 2011.

Omartian, Michael and Stormie Omartian. *The Power of a Praying Husband.* Eugene, OR: Harvest House, 2014.

Strauch, Alexander. *Men and Women, Equal Yet Different: A Brief Study of the Biblical Passages on Gender.* Littleton, CO: Lewis & Roth Publishers, 1999.

Websites

Celebrate Recovery—www.celebraterecovery.com

Christ in the Tetons—www.christinthetetons.com

Dynamic Dads—www.dynamicdads.com

Family Life—www.familylife.com

Focus on the Family—www.focusonthefamily.com

Iron Sharpens Iron—www.ironsharpensiron.net

Man in the Mirror—www.maninthemirror.org

Men's Fraternity—www.mensfraternity.com

National Association of Men's Ministries—www.ncmm.org

National Center for Fathering—www.fathers.com

New Commandment Men's Ministries—www.newcommandment.org

Pure Desire Ministries—www.puredesire.org

Author Bio

Dr. Paul Pettit serves as Director of Career Services at Dallas Theological Seminary, and teaches in both the Pastoral Ministries Department and Educational Leadership & Ministries Department at the seminary. Paul's background includes experience as a sportscaster, author, and speaker. He and Pamela have five children, and he has authored several books on parenting, marriage, and spiritual formation. He enjoys developing emerging leaders, golf, and barbecue.

Endnotes

1.   Rohan Gunaratna, *Suicide Terrorism: A Global Threat,* http://www.pbs.org/ frontlineworld/stories/srilanka/glo-balthreat.html (October 2000). Rohan Gunaratna, PhD is Senior Research Associate, Centre for the Study of Terrorism and Prevention of Political Violence at University of St. Andrews.

2.   Robert Horner, *The Promise Keeper at Work* (Colorado Springs: Focus on the Family Publishing, 1996).

3.   National Institute on Alcohol Abuse and Alcoholism, "Alcohol Facts and Statistics," January 2017, https://pubs.niaaa.nih.gov/publications/AlcoholFacts&Stats/ AlcoholFacts&Stats.htm.

4.   Tammy Anderson and Lynn Bondi. "Exiting the Drug Addict Role: Variations by Race and Gender," *Symbolic Interaction* 21, no. 2 (1998): 155–74.

5.   Dawn Hawkins, "GOP Considering Pornography as a Public Health Crisis," National Center for Sexual Exploitation, July 12, 2016, http://endsexualexploitation.org/articles/statement-gop-considering-pornography-public-health-crisis/.

6.   Steven Stack, Ira Wasserman, and Roger Kern, "Adult Social Bonds and Use of Internet Pornography" *Social Science Quarterly* 85 (March 2004): 75–88.

7.   State of California Department of Justice, Office of the Attorney General. "Human Trafficking," https://oag.ca.gov/human-trafficking.

8.   Yu Sun Chin, "Trafficked Boys Overlooked," *Juvenile Justice Information Exchange*, April 14, 2014, http://jjie.org/trafficked-boys-overlooked-underrepresented/106688/.

9.   Purposefully Scarred, "Dangers in Legalizing Prostitution," August 12, 2012, https://purposefullyscarred.com/2012/12/08/the-dangers-of-legalizing-prostitution/.

10. Frances McKee-Ryan, Zhaoli Song, Connie Wanberg, and Angelo Kinicki, "Psychological and Physical Well-Being During Unemployment: A Meta-Analytic Study," *Journal of Applied Psychology* 90 (2005): 53–76.

11. Henry David Thoreau, *Walden* (London: Bibliolis Books, 2010), 6.

12. James Banks, James Nazroo, and Andrew Steptoe, eds., "The Dynamics of Ageing: Evidence from the English Longitudinal Study of Ageing 2002–2012," *The Institute for Fiscal Studies* (October 2014).

13. See the chapter "Invisible: Single Adults" by Joye Baker for more information on singleness.

14. D'vera Cohn, "Love and Marriage," *Pew Research Center, Social and Demographic Trends*, February 13, 2013, http://www.pewsocialtrends.org/2013/02/13/love-and-marriage/.

15. David Blankenhorn, *Fatherless America: Confronting our Most Urgent Social Problem* (New York: Harper Collins, 1995), 5.

16. For a fuller discussion of this topic, see *Man and Woman in Christ: An Examination of the Roles of Men and Women in Light of Scripture and the Social Sciences* by Stephen Clark (Ann Arbor, MI: Servant Books, 1980).

17. Daniel Patrick Moynihan, *The Case for National Action.* Office of Policy, Planning and Research. United States Department of Labor, March 1965.

18. Charles Swindoll, *Strike the Original Match: Rekindling and Preserving Your Marriage Fire* (Portland, OR: Multnomah, 1980), 30.

19. Steve Farrar, *King Me: What Every Son Wants and Needs from His Father* (Chicago: Moody, 2005), 36.

20. Henry David Thoreau, *Civil Disobedience and Other Essays* (Mineola, NY: Dover, 1993).

21. Joe Stokes and Ira Levin, "Gender Differences in Predicting Loneliness from Social Network Characteristics," *Journal of Personality and Social Psychology* 51, no. 5 (Nov 1986): 1069–74.

22. Martin Luther, *The Babylonian Captivity of the Church* (Minneapolis: Fortress Press, 2016).

23. Bible Study Fellowship, 19001 Huebner Road, San Antonio, Texas 78258. (210) 492–4676. See: https://www.bsfinternational.org/.

24. Authentic Manhood, 12115 Hinson Road, Ste. 200, Little Rock, AR 72212. (800) 446–7228. See: http://www.mensfraternity.com/.

25. See the chapter "Utilizing Retreats, Camping, and Outdoor Ministries" by Dan Bolin for more information about retreats.

Chapter 9
UNDERVALUED: WOMEN

Sue Edwards

Do not rebuke an older man harshly, but exhort him as if he were your father. Treat younger men as brothers, older women as mothers, and younger women as sisters, with absolute purity.
—1 Timothy 5:1–2

M R. ASKEW LOOKED OVER his wire-rimmed spectacles with a wry smile and a twinkle in his eye, exhorting my eighth grade English class, "Listen to this." He read my entire essay out loud. Then he asked the class, "Who do you think wrote this?" They all turned to look at me, and with an affirming grin, he nodded, "Yup, she's the one." He had done this once before, and again the cool water of his encouraging words nurtured my thirsty soul. I was little-girl-lost that crossroads year, and those two readings spurred me on toward the better path.

Attitudes and Actions toward Women That Affect Your Teaching

I missed the first half of that school year. I'd been hopscotching around Europe with my mom and dad on our return trek from Rhodes, Greece,

an island in the Aegean Sea, where we lived for three years. My father, a Coast Guard officer, had been stationed there on a ship that broadcast behind the iron curtain. You may be thinking, *what a grand adventure for a thirteen-year-old girl*, and I probably should have appreciated the opportunity more. But, I entered my teen years anxiety-ridden, the perpetual new kid, terrified that I wouldn't fit in at school. My pagan mother derided her "silly, oversensitive" daughter, and the more she made fun of me, the more my apprehension grew. I adored my father, yearned for his attention, but he had practically disappeared from my life, barely present even when he was home. Several "bad boys" started hanging around, but as much as I craved their attention, I was pretty sure Mr. Askew wouldn't approve— the titanic power of a "father's" influence!

Two years earlier, while living on that Aegean Greek island, I attended sixth and seventh grades in a small American school provided by the Coast Guard for the dependent children of the crew. Mrs. Glanville, a senior spinster from the United Kingdom, oversaw my education both grades. Dour, no-nonsense, and demanding, she marched all five of us students to the docks where she set up easels and taught us to paint with water colors. Under her supervision, we made clay models of Stonehenge, wrote a play from Dickens's *Great Expectations*, and acted out Shakespeare's *Macbeth*. She set my heart afire for the beauty of God's earth and the wonder of words. The titanic power of a "mother's" influence!

> "Accept one another, then, just as Christ accepted you, in order to bring praise to God (Romans 15:7). The world offers only tolerance, but the Christian community is one of acceptance, recognizing one another's differences while valuing their presence as brothers and sisters in Christ."[1]
> —James R. Estep Jr., Michael J. Anthony, and Gregg R. Allison

The Family of God

Throughout the New Testament, the Bible uses family language to describe Christians' relationships with one another. God doesn't picture the Church as a business, a military platoon, or a sports team. We are family, mothers, fathers, sisters, and brothers. The ramifications are numerous but in this chapter, I'm focusing on what this means for Christian educators and the women in our classrooms and ministries. In the previous chapter, Dr. Pettit talked about teaching and ministering to men. In this chapter, I'll be addressing how to teach and minister to women. In several sections, I'll specifically address men, assuming that men might need a little additional insight into the needs of female students.

Who Is Your Audience?

As you prepare to teach or preach, the first question you might ask is, "What am I going to say?" However, a preaching professor would counsel you to ask this entirely different question: "Who is my audience?" Likewise, the first question a teacher needs to ask is, "Who are my students?" According to Barna's groundbreaking study in 2000 (*Women Are the Backbone of the Christian Congregations in America*, March 6, 2000), typically, if you are teaching in a church in the U.S.A., almost sixty percent of your students, and an even higher percentage in many other countries, will be female. Will that matter? Absolutely, if you want your women students to become all-in, fully mature disciples of Jesus Christ.

Your Goal When Teaching Women

What does an all-in, fully mature female disciple of Jesus Christ look like? The answer depends on your views about Christian women, even if you are one. What would you like to see your biological daughter, sister, or mother become? If we are the family of God, what are our aspirations for our *spiritual* daughters, sisters, and mothers? In education, teachers constantly evaluate learning outcomes. What learning outcomes do we want to see in the Christian women and girls we teach?

First, Jesus's Great Commandment (Matt. 22:37–39) and the fruit of the Spirit come to mind: "Love the Lord your God with all your heart and with all your soul and with all your mind. This is the first and greatest commandment. And the second is like it: Love your neighbor as yourself." We want her to love God with all she is and has, and to love others well. And we want her life to first exhibit love, then joy, peace, forbearance, kindness, goodness, faithfulness, gentleness, and self-control—the fruit of the Spirit listed in Galatians 5:22 and 23.

Second, we want women to become biblically literate. What does this mean? Jen Wilkin, in her book *Women of the Word: How to Study the Bible with Both Our Hearts and Our Minds*, defines it this way:

> Bible literacy occurs when a person has access to a Bible in a language she understands and is steadily moving toward knowledge and understanding of the text. If it is true that the character and will of God are proclaimed in Scripture, then any serious attempt to become equipped for the work of discipleship must include a desire to build Bible literacy. Bible literacy stitches patchwork knowledge into a seamless garment of understanding.[2]

I would add to Wilkin's emphasis on knowledge and understanding that we are not biblically literate until we apply what we know.

Third, since she receives the same kinds of spiritual gifts as all other Christians, we want her to discover, develop, and use those gifts to serve others. Since the entire Bible was written to her just like to all Christians, we want her to know, believe with conviction, and live out a godly lifestyle, in accordance with biblical truth and parameters. We want her to be rightly and passionately related to God in an intimate relationship, to think of others first, and to be secure in her identity in Christ. Then she can carry out God's purposes for her life with God-dependence and strength. Imagine the extraordinary boost to God's work if the majority of Christian women were empowered to live like this.

Come to think of it, we desire the same learning outcomes for our male students. Imagine the kingdom impact, if strong, gracious, and godly men *and* women, brothers and sisters in Christ, served side by side and worked together for the glory of God!

The Positive Power of "Fathers" and "Brothers" in Women Students' Lives

Examples from my own life and the lives of women I know might clarify what I mean when I say "The Positive Power of Fathers and Brothers." Besides Mr. Askew, a number of Christian men, in addition to my dear husband, have equipped, encouraged, blessed, and opened ministry doors for me. Specifically, how might male teachers relate to women in ways that would facilitate this kind of positive impact?

I attended Dallas Theological Seminary in the eighties, while ministering to my husband and children, and teaching the Bible to women. Also, I served as Parent Teacher Association and band presidents to earn a voice in my children's schools. I was a busy wife and mother, attending classes on the side. Back then, the campus was still "a man's domain" although no one mistreated me. I felt grateful to be there, but invisible, and, as a result, I never spoke up in class—until Dr. Bill Lawrence's Spiritual Life course.

I savored every minute and worked hard on my assignments. I usually slipped into the back, but the day we focused on Romans chapter 7, I arrived a bit late, requiring me to sit in the front row. In the midst of a dynamic class discussion, Dr. Lawrence asked us a difficult question. Before I could catch myself, I barely raised my hand and then quickly jerked it back down. He walked over to the side of the room where I was seated, looked at me with a rather stern expression, and said, "Yes, Mrs. Edwards." After I recuperated from the shock of being called by name, I gulped and then stammered out my answer. He drew closer, almost nose to nose, and with a scowl on his face, he boomed, "Don't you ever hesitate to give an excellent answer like that again." A dozen words broke my campus silence and launched me in a new direction full of new possibilities—the power of a "father's" words.

Fast forward twenty years, the chair of the Christian Education department, fearless and fired-up Dr. Mike Lawson saw the jump in the enrollment of women students on our campus and the need for more equipped women in the Church. He decided to include women on his faculty team and create enhanced training for them. He chose Dr. Joye Baker and me to lead this endeavor, but we had not yet completed our doctorates. Rather than wait on us to teach seminary courses until we were done, and because a credentialed professor must be in the room, he sat with us in the classroom for two years. He taught occasionally but more often, he used the time to coach, encourage, and sponsor us—the power of a "father's" actions.

Additional "father" and "brother" figures abound in my life—Howard Hendricks, George Hillman, Lin McLaughlin, Jay Sedwick, Mark Yarbrough, Mark Heinemann, Rodney Orr, David Cotton, Andy McQuitty, Steve Roese, and others. I could give examples for each. I trust and am indebted to these godly men.

The Negative Power of "Fathers" and "Brothers"

Sadly, however, I could list, but won't, other men with contrasting stories who've hurt me and other women deeply. I listen to these women's accounts, dry their tears, and pray with them for forgiveness and healing. The majority of these men are well-intentioned and clueless that their words, actions, and attitudes wounded, discouraged, and scarred their sisters, causing some to give up on themselves or the Lord.

"I think too often churches either avoid the topic or settle for an unbiblical 'strategy of isolation' where men deliberately separate themselves from women as a means of temptation avoidance. This leads to a loss of biblical community, lost opportunities for the development of leadership gifts, and doesn't even help in avoiding sin. For God's intent is that we aim at becoming *the kind of persons* who treat one another as brother and sister."[3]

—Dr. John Ortberg

What do women who have left churches due to the failings of male authority figures have to say? Bill Hendricks published a series of exit interviews that tell us. Here's a summary of his findings related to women:

If some of the comments from the women I spoke with are any indication, the church has a time bomb on its hands. Women are angry and getting angrier. I would not presume to characterize all women in the church this way. But the message is loud and clear: when it comes to issues like language, opportunities, praise and rewards, authority, staffing, expectations, marriage and sexuality, and justice, women increasingly see the church as dominated by a male perspective. Many feel that Christianity as represented by its institutions and leaders comes across as insensitive. Certainly they would say there are exceptions, but overall it feels like a system that does not respect women.[4]

If current research is any indication, the time bomb is already exploding. In a recent Barna study, researchers reported what we all know—Americans are leaving the church in larger and larger numbers. In the early 1990s, only 30 percent of adults were unchurched. In 2015, the number reached 45 percent and the trend shows no indication of slowing. But what you may not know is that the largest group of adults walking away is women. Eighty-five percent of unchurched women are labeled *de-churched*. This means that the vast majority of these unchurched women, nine out of ten, have attended church, but at one point they decided that church was no longer for them.[5]

Consider these examples of the negative power of male leaders. Two of my students, a married couple with the same master's degree in cross-cultural ministries, relayed their angst

to me after they investigated missions agencies in order to select one as their sending organization. Only two of the eighteen they talked to had any interest in *her* future ministry or part on the team. Most didn't even ask to see her résumé or interview her. The couple chose one of the two that did, but both communicated shock and dismay at the experience.

Dr. Pam MacRae, Associate Professor of Pastoral Studies at Moody Bible Institute, writes about a similar experience in *The Moody Handbook of Preaching* in her chapter on "How Women Hear the Sermon":

> Recently a pastor was speaking with my husband and me about his family. During that part of the conversation, I was very much included in what was being said. Then he began to talk about a theological question he was pondering, related to a topic that had been discussed in one of his seminary classes. At that point, the conversation shifted and was solely directed at my husband. Even his body turned slightly to shift away from me and more directly face my husband. Ironically, I was probably more interested in the particular topic he was discussing than my husband was. I would have enjoyed having a conversation with him about the subject, but was not included, nor expected to be included, in the discussion.[6]

Another of my female students shared her professor's comment in class after he pointed out that the Bible calls Isaiah's wife a prophetess. "I'm thinking maybe she is called a prophetess because she is the wife of a prophet," he surmised, as if the idea that his wife might actually be considered a prophetess on her own merit impossible, even though Deborah, Huldah, and Philip's three daughters were referred to as prophetesses in their own right. The women in the class winced.

I've experienced well-intentioned men addressing women with doctoral degrees as "sweetie" and formally introducing women with impressive credentials on their staff "as the prettiest face on the team" while ignoring their accomplishments, but fully listing the academic achievements of all the men. Once when several of us professors were interviewing a single woman for one of our doctoral programs, the professor teased her, saying, "What's wrong with all those men where you live, letting a cute girl like you get away?" No doubt, he meant it as a compliment, but later she confided in me that she heard yet another message asking why she wasn't pursuing her assigned role in life, to snag a man rather than pursue what she believed to be God's calling in her life. Would he have ever talked to a male candidate like that?

Yes, these examples may seem petty taken alone. However, a steady diet of this kind of rhetoric, accompanied by constant biblical language using "his" and "man's" and preaching that only includes football and fishing illustrations—all this together sends a clear message to many women. It's not a message that motivates them to become all-in, fully devoted disciples of Jesus Christ, our hoped for outcome as we teach.

If you are a man, think about how you talk to and treat women. Your attitude toward women will color how you teach them. Are you respectful and encouraging toward them or do you exclude, ignore, or unintentionally use offensive words?

Do you consider yourself emotionally healthy in your relationships with spiritual daughters, sisters, and mothers? Have you investigated how Jesus interacted with women? Your answers profoundly affect your teaching ministry to over half your students. Before you step into a teaching role, remember that you wield influence that will impact your future female students either positively or negatively. The next section will explain how to teach women well and you'll also find useful resources at the end of this chapter.

Realities to Remember When Teaching Women

1. Be Aware of Many Women Students' Tendencies to Underestimate Their Abilities and Value

In her book on motivation, Deborah Stipek paints caricatures of some female students as "Hopeless Hannah" or "Safe Sally." "Hopeless Hannah" exhibits a firm view of herself as incompetent, with a "why try" attitude, and assumptions that there is simply no domain where she can excel. Stipek labels her as a classic example of "learned helplessness," which I'll talk about later. "Safe Sally" makes straight As, meticulously follows directions, is well-behaved and highly motivated, as long as the learning requires no risk of failure. She systematically plays it safe, resists trying anything new or tapping into her creativity. Learning is something you do in school, brings no joy or excitement, and the desire to become a life-long learner will be abandoned upon graduation.[7] If "Hopeless Hannah" or "Safe Sally" become Christ followers and you become their teacher or minister, you'll need to help them overcome obvious hindrances to grow strong in Christ.

> *How, then, can they call on the one they have not believed in? And how can they believe in the one of whom they have not heard? And how can they hear without someone preaching to them? And how can they preach unless they are sent? As it is written, "How beautiful are the feet of those who bring good news."*
> —Romans 10:14–15

> "Every last Christian today is under the same order of our heavenly Commander-in-Chief as were the disciples in Jesus's day. You and I do not know those whom God has chosen in grace to be saved and whom he will powerfully call by the inner summons of his Spirit. Therefore, we must faithfully preach the Word and trust the ministry of effectual calling to the sovereign Spirit of God. The task to which we are called is to be diligent and faithful in presenting the verbal call and to leave to the Spirit the internal call that effectively brings sinners to Christ.... May this task of delivering the gospel call be our constant delight and joy."[8]
> —Bruce Demarest

Certainly not all women fit these descriptions but, as a professor, often I observe women who do. In various ways, they underestimate their abilities, while many of my male students tend to overestimate theirs. If she does poorly on an exam, she's quick to label herself "stupid." If she does well, I hear her tell a friend that the test was "easy." On the other hand, if he does well on the test, he easily puffs up with pride: "Whoop, I am so smart." And if he does badly, I'm not surprised to hear him blame the test or me. In addition, I constantly hear women second guess themselves. How many men do you hear making excuses for a bad hair day, constantly qualifying their opinions, or refusing to take credit for a task well done?

I cannot explain why so many women act this way. Some say this tendency is simply the way God wired women, nature. Others insist it's because of the way women are socialized, nurtured, influenced by the messages women get as little girls, especially in some Christian families: *Be nice, take care of people, keep the peace.* Personally, I think it's both nature and nurture.

However, David Neff, *Christianity Today* editor-in-chief from 1985–2012, cited a fascinating study at Ontario Bible College that gives weight to the socialization argument that nurture is highly influential. The college measured what entering women students at nine Canadian Bible colleges thought about their personal competence, and the researchers compared the results with what women in secular institutions thought about theirs. Researchers found that in the secular institutions, women fell about 7 percent behind the entering male students in their confidence in their own abilities. But in the Christian institutions, the gap between the men and the women was an appalling 40 percent. And the Bible college men rated 15 percent above their secular counterparts in their confidence levels. The confidence gap existed in both secular and Christian research studies, but why was the gap so much greater between Christian men and women?[9]

Regardless of the reasons, for typical women who easily find fault with themselves and lack confidence, your influence as a teacher/minister, what you say, how you say it, and what you do, carries tremendous weight for both good or ill, especially if you are male. Realize that for women without a strong male voice in their lives, women who yearn for encouragement and to feel valued by a man they respect, you could be a "Mr. Askew."

> "Teaching, like any truly human activity, emerges from one's inwardness, for better or worse. As I teach, I project the condition of my soul onto my students, my subject, and our way of being together. The entanglements I experience in the classroom are often no more or less than the convolutions of my inner life. Viewed from this angle, teaching holds a mirror to the soul. If I am willing to look in that mirror and not run from what I see, I have a chance to gain self-knowledge—and knowing myself is as crucial to good teaching as knowing my students and my subject."[10]
> —Parker Palmer

Learned Helplessness

Eleanor Maccoby grew up in a remote rural area in which many families had difficulty transporting their children to the county school. To solve this problem the state allowed teens as young as thirteen to get their drivers' licenses, and their parents provided an ancient vehicle with limited potential for speed, so they could drive themselves to school. Eleanor was one of these fortunate teens. Her car was a 1934 Ford with a top speed of forty miles per hour, a radiator that both leaked and boiled, and a fuel pump that sometimes suddenly ceased to function.

One fall, her father overheard the car give a suspicious hiccup as it rattled into the yard that evening. As a result, he placed a new fuel pump in the trunk of her car after he taught her how to replace it. And this was a good thing, because the next afternoon on the most remote part of her trip home, the car coughed, ran an erratic half mile, and then stopped dead. Her dilemma was clear: either repair the car or walk home. She might have chosen to walk if it had not been that particular Friday. She had a date with the captain of the football team. He was an overwhelmingly handsome young man ardently pursued by most of her female classmates.

And she had chores to do when she got home. Family rules forbade her to leave the house until her chores were done. Clearly, she had no choice but to change out the fuel pump, speed for home, persuade her sister to help with chores, hoping meanwhile that her date would be late.

She did exactly that, and was totally out of breath but ready by the time her date arrived. Her long hair was curled, her white blouse starched and ironed, and her skirt carefully pressed.

During their date, she waited sedately while he opened the car door and helped her into the car. He helped her climb the bleachers, took the cap off her bottle of soda, helped her with her sweater, and at the end of the evening helped her out of his car and back into her house. Had the fuel pump in his car expired anytime during the trip, she confessed that she would have sat properly in the car, looking helplessly feminine, and acting as though she had no earthly idea what a fuel pump was.[11]

Please don't misunderstand. Chivalry isn't dead. I love it when men open the door for me and I graciously thank them. But at the same time, I don't believe God wants women to hide their competence, pretending helplessness when their abilities are needed to live well and serve Jesus effectively. Think about the difference in Eleanor's behavior when she was alone grappling with a fuel pump, when she was seeking to persuade her younger sister to help her with her chores, and then consider how she acted on her date. She was practically a different person when she was with that young man whose company provided her with the excitement of courting and the prestige of social rank. Where did she learn to act that way? Who is the real Eleanor? Which Eleanor will be prepared to face the challenges in life that she'll undoubtedly face? Certainly, Eleanor needs to embrace her God-given femininity, but how can she do that while still developing into a fully competent all-in disciple of Jesus Christ?

I remember a woman telling me about a time when she and her husband were lost and late for an important appointment. She knew exactly where they needed to go but refrained from offering this knowledge and instead sat quietly while they drove in circles looking for their destination. I work with many bright young women students at Dallas Theological Seminary and more than a few have confided that they hide their intellectual capacity, thinking it makes them less attractive to men. This unhealthy thinking carries serious ramifications for relationships and challenges women face in adult life.

It also leads to some strange situations in ministry. A woman who led a thriving ministry to women in a megachurch recently confided in me that her pastor told her to rein in the ministry quality because he didn't think the men could "keep up." He even forbade her from accepting a publisher's offer to write a book to help other women leaders. She's since left the church for another leadership position.

> "The world as it has evolved has become more and more intolerant of environments that don't bring in a woman's voice. For example, my daughters—ages twenty-one and twenty-six—would never enter a world where a woman's voice was not represented in the church. I see a growing presence of women in the postmodern world, and the environments that do not include women will die."[12]
> —Dr. Dan Allender

I'm not saying that women should be domineering or aggressive, or act like men, but learned helplessness results in unintended consequences for women, their families, and communities. Women fail to develop themselves or their spiritual gifts. They shut down their potential and easily become passive aggressive, silent, weak, and overly dependent or needy. This shackles half of the church and confuses many women. And if women act this way long enough, people can mistakenly believe that women are "less than" their Christian brothers, damaging women and hindering our attempts to teach them.

2. Expunge Harmful Reductionist Stereotypes

Two grave errors exist as we consider masculinity and femininity. If you want to help women become fully devoted all-in disciples of Christ, resist both.

The first error exaggerates the differences between men and women. Have you seen the long lists of theoretical masculine and feminine characteristics? Often the list describes qualities like: men are thinkers and women are feelers, men are independent and women are dependent, men are initiators and women are responders. If these lists suggest or imply that God created men and women this way, then it sounds like deviation from that norm goes against God's intentional design. The problem is that every man and every woman is a unique creation made in the image of God, and none fits the cookie-cutter lists that make all men very much alike and all women very much alike. These lists cause great inner conflict and guilt to people who don't fit the list, and in one way or another, that's most of us.

Lumping all women and all men together is actually harmful because these stereotypes mess with people's identities. If they believe "the list" is true, and if they are not like the list, they may mistakenly believe something is wrong with them. With so many young people confused about their sexual identities today, these lists are not helpful. They box people into "roles" that may not fit their God-given design, wiring, personality, and gift-mix. They may try to "play" roles that cause them to shut down and deny their full personhood. Think through the ramifications and disguised consequences that easily accompany this kind of

people pigeonholing, especially since many of the characteristics on the list are exaggerated and not based on dependable unbiased research.

Helpful research on women's epistemology:

1. *Women's Ways of Knowing: The Development of Self, Voice, and Mind* by Mary F. Belenky, Blythe M. Clinchy, Nancy R. Goldberger, and Jill M. Tarule, New York: Basic Books 1986.

2. *In a Different Voice: Psychological Theory and Women's Development* by Carol Gilligan, Cambridge, MA: Harvard University Press, Thirty-sixth printing 2000.

3. *Why Gender Matters: What Parents and Teachers Need to Know about the Emerging Science of Sex Difference* by Leonard Sax, M.D., Ph.D., New York: Broadway Books, 2005.

4. *Preaching That Speaks to Women* by Alice Mathews, Grand Rapids: Baker Academic, 2003.

Over the last forty years, researchers produced mountains of literature on women, and some shed light on how women learn, although again we must be aware of the dangers of overgeneralization. For example, a common and important finding in an overwhelming percentage of the studies is that women are collaborative learners. And many are. However, certainly not all women. How do I know that?

Almost every semester I teach an introductory course on educational ministries. One of the sessions exposes students to varied learning styles so they will use creative methods to reach the different people God will entrust to them in their future ministries. To prepare for our time together, I ask each student to take a learning style assessment to acquaint them with their own predominant learning style. At the conclusion of the session, I divide them up into groups according to their learning styles and ask each group to explain to the other groups how to best teach them according to their particular bent. I tell them they are representing all the future students those future teachers will teach. The groups create insightful presentations that inform and inspire the other groups, cementing the concepts we've studied in theory, and we have lots of fun.

One of the groups represents collaborative learners. Collaborative learners are caring compassionate people who like to discuss what they are learning. Through a decade of teaching this course, I've observed the gender breakout, expecting to see the collaborative group packed with females, and plenty end up there. But we usually have an equal number of men in the collaborative group. And a fair number of women test out as other types of learners. Some are analytics, more focused on analyzing information. Others are common sense learners, insisting the learning be useful and practical. Still other women are dynamic learners, dreaming of new ways to use what they've learned. Again, we must be careful not to pigeonhole people. Each is unique.

Nevertheless, some generalizations can be worth considering as we attempt to teach the women within our learning communities.

On the other hand, the second error denies *any* difference between men and women, except for physiology, and some go even further to suggest that gender is a manmade concept that doesn't matter. Those who teach this view say everyone would be happier and get along better if we adopted a unisex attitude or a multi-sex attitude. *Let people mix it up any way they want. Forget gender and be a woman today and a man tomorrow.* These bizarre ideas, adopted more and more in the broader culture, are repugnant to most Christians today. We see these ideas leading to wild behavior, confusion, disorder, and anarchy. Many of us are confused and distressed by these new trends but we are uncertain about what to do. Certainly, God is never the author of confusion, but we must be careful not to overreact and embrace the distortion of these errors in our uncertainty.

The truth is that God designed men and women to be different, and it's beautiful. However, we are not nearly as different as we are sometimes portrayed. Gender differences are real, complex, and the result of a variety of different factors including heredity and biology, our family of origin, and the culture and environments where we live. We must be careful not to adopt a reductionistic approach to gender. Research confirms that there is as much diversity *within* a group of women or *within* a group of men as there is *between* men and women. He's not from Mars and she's not from Venus. We have much more in common than we have differences—first we are human beings, brothers and sisters in the family of God.

"How does a healthy family function? The best working model is when Mom and Dad work together using their gifts, valuing one another's ideas, and respecting each other in the process. They listen to each other and make better decisions together. As a result, the children feel safer when Mom is empowered and Dad is respectful. The same principles apply in the church. Just as we need both a dad and a mom in the home, we need men and women working together in ministry. When they do, the congregation feels safer, and the church thrives."[13]
—Dr. Michael Lawson

Neither do our differences imply inferiority or superiority. However, with the explosion of brain research, we now see that male and female brains are organized differently. And some physical differences are undisputed. For example, the male retina is substantially thicker than the female retina, true in every male and every female including animals.[14] But other long-held assertions, such as the familiar notion that all men have superior navigational abilities, turn out to be false. Women typically navigate using landmarks while men often prefer maps, true for me and my husband, but false for my friend Kay, the map guru, who drove us around Boston without a hitch. It's complicated. Many of the stereotypes that we held onto were merely a reflection of personal beliefs or political or religious agendas that have been disproven.

The bottom line is that the brain is just organized differently in females and males. The tired argument about which sex is more intelligent or which sex has the "better" brain is about as meaningful as arguing about which utensil is "better," a knife or a spoon. The only correct answer to such a question is: "Better for what?" A knife is better than a spoon if you want to cut through a piece of meat, while a spoon is better if you're facing a bowl of chicken broth.[15]

You are not teaching stereotypes. Approach each student, whether male or female, as first a person made in the image of God and uniquely designed. As we teach, research reveals some similarities that you will likely observe among many of your women students. We will examine them further as we conclude this chapter. But exceptions abound. Our task as a minister or teacher is to see each one as a daughter, sister, or mother in our spiritual family, all placed under our care for a time, to love, nurture, and challenge as she takes another step on her journey to becoming an all-in, fully devoted disciple of Jesus Christ.

3. Educate Yourself on Changing Demographics

The women's world that I lived and taught in thirty years ago has radically changed. But some Christian teachers still envision "the way things were" as the ideal and teach to an audience that no longer exists. Back then, we planned and programmed midweek Bible studies for stay-at-home moms. Today almost 60 percent of Christian women work outside the home and over half the women in America are single.[16] Women marry and start families later. As a result, we need to create teaching experiences that work when and where most women can participate, which isn't on a weekday morning any more. We need to broaden our thinking to include working and single women as well as married women and stay-at-home moms.

We are in the midst of an era shift, moving from a print era to a technological era, exacerbating generational differences. You may find yourself teaching a new widow from the World War II generation who is sitting next to a millennial attempting to figure out how to live for Christ in her new work environment. Both need Jesus and both need to grow stronger in their faith. Bringing them together to learn from one another benefits both, but you'll need to understand how differently these two women view the world. Educate yourself on demographic and generational differences today, remembering that everyone is unique, and you'll be a far more effective teacher.

4. Watch Words, Jokes, Expressions, and Illustrations

Remember the examples from the *Negative Power of "Fathers" and "Brothers"* section earlier in this chapter? The missions agency that wasn't interested in the wife's abilities or potential contributions, even though she had the same calling and equipping as her husband—the female college professor who was included in a conversation about family but excluded when the conversation turned to theology, the male leader who introduced his female colleague as "sweetie" and the "prettiest face on the team" while ignoring her academic credentials, even though he listed all the men's? These words, actions, and attitudes are part of the reasons we

are losing more women from our churches than any other demographic.

> ## Toolbox on Generational Differences:
>
> 1. *Intergenerational Christian Formation: Bringing the Whole Church Together in Ministry, Community, and Worship,* by Holly Catterton Allen and Christine Lawton Ross, Downers Grove, IL: IVP Academic, 2012.
>
> 2. *One Church, Four Generations: Understanding and Reaching All Ages in Your Church,* by Gary L. McIntosh, Grand Rapids: Baker Books, 2002.
>
> 3. *Generations: The History of America's Future, 1584 to 2069, by* William Strauss and Neil Howe, New York: Quill, 1991.

Many Christian women have learned to do the mental gymnastics required to constantly turn male pronouns and stories into applications that work for women. We know men who speak and act this way are usually well intentioned, we love our brothers, and we give them the benefit of the doubt. But women who can do that are usually mature, grace giving, and confident. Many grew up in Christian families and the church. However, with the breakdown of the nuclear family and the secularization of the culture, more and more women come out of unhealthy homes and skewed environments. Fewer grew up in Christian homes. Some are disappointed in the men in their families who should have been there to protect and nurture them but instead took advantage of them, marginalized them, neglected them, or even worse, abused them. For many of these women, trust comes slow, offense quickly. And this is true for some Christian women as well as nonbelievers.

How might we unintentionally offend some women? Consider these examples:

- An off-color or demeaning joke about "dumb blondes" or other silly women
- Reading Bible verses that seem to apply only to "brothers"
- Off-the-cuff comments like "It will make a man out of you"
- Stories that always feature topics of interest to men
- Only talking about male heroes from Scripture
- Only quoting male authors

To overly sensitive women of the culture, these words, actions, and attitudes only reinforce what they've been hearing for years: "*Stay away from Christianity—it's a hierarchical male-dominated institution that doesn't care about women.*" But Jesus loves these women and wants them to come into an intimate relationship with him. Why would we want to erect unnecessary hindrances for these women to come to faith even if it means reevaluating any prejudices and giving up some of our own preferences?

I remember well the Monday morning a lovely professional woman dropped by my office. I was the minister to women at a Dallas megachurch that she had visited the day before. "Why would I ever want to join a church like yours?" she remarked candidly. "I didn't see a single woman doing anything anywhere. Men welcomed me at the door, men handed out bulletins, men ushered me to my seat, men did the announcements, men passed the plate, a man led worship, a man read the sermon passage, and a man preached." She was right. I was there and it hadn't bothered me at all, I suppose because I knew that our church valued women. I led a staff of two full-time women, excluding myself, and one part-time woman, all to minister to the women of the church and the community. I knew the heart of the male leadership, but I suddenly realized that this reality was not evident to a visitor. I did my best to explain all the ways our church valued women, hoping she would give us and Jesus another chance. We had not represented Jesus well. I don't think she believed me. I only hope she tried another church who represented our Lord better.

Afterward, however, I shot down the hall into our executive pastor's office and immediately relayed the conversation. He listened intently and it was if a light came on for both of us. She was right. Although we were a church that valued women, to an outsider and even most pew-sitters, we hid that reality well. We were a Bible church, evangelical to the core, and yet we had been erecting unnecessary roadblocks for women to give their lives to Jesus—but never again. My boss acted quickly to remedy the oversight. Well-intentioned ministers and teachers can create environments that either powerfully welcome women to thrive and grow strong in their faith or to walk away, disillusioned, disappointed, or angry.

Only Jesus can heal their brokenness and calm their outrage, but he needs an army of godly Christian men to step into the roles of fathers and brothers. These women need to see different kinds of men, evangelists, preachers, teachers, and ministers who truly value their sisters, teaching and treating them with the brotherly care they've yearned for. In the Gospels, women flocked to Jesus because he treated them with dignity and respect, and godly men who treat women like sisters in Christ today continue to exert this kind of healing power in their female students' lives.

5. Expect Many Women, More Than Men, to Desire Affiliation with the Teacher and Peers

Although women score all over the map on lots of different kinds of learning, personality, and leadership inventories, I have observed that most women seem to view life through a relational lens, thus supporting the broad findings that many women live in a relational web while many men see life from a more individualistic separate perspective. I'm a good example. I'm an even mix of analytic/dynamic on the learning styles assessment. On leadership inventories, I score off the charts on whatever term they use to describe the strongest natural leader. I love people but I'm an introvert and need my time alone. People exhaust me and I can hold up in my office for days on a writing project that I'm passionate about. I'm type A, bottom line, goal-oriented, all qualities often on the list of masculine traits, but I'm feminine in my appearance and demeanor. However, when I view my life, I see it through a relational lens, first with my beloved Lord, then with my husband, children, and grandchildren, then with my students and colleagues at work and my church family.

As a result, I love to learn in community and, during my student days, I valued relational connections with my teachers and professors. Thus my point that when you teach, you may find that your women students desire an appropriate affiliation with you. If you invest in those personal connections, you will create a culture where they will learn better. You will find that they will stop thinking so much about the impression they are making on others, relax, and begin taking risks in their thinking. They'll be open to trying out new ideas, delving deep into dynamic discussions, helping others learn, searching for answers together, listening respectfully to opposing viewpoints, and enjoying the process. You'll start to hear comments like, "The time in our class just flies by" and "I never knew this could be so interesting." These kinds of cultures are Petri dishes for learning that move most female students, and some men, into becoming all-in fully devoted disciples of Christ.

If you are male, personal relationships with female students may scare you. Were you taught that they are "taboo temptresses" and you better ignore them and focus on the guys? I understand your concern for your reputation, but notice I said appropriate relationships. Navigating that balance is beyond the scope of this book, but I'll give you a resource at the end of the chapter if you need help figuring out what healthy relationships with sisters look like.

6. Beware of Her Response to High-Pressure Ethos

Over the years, I've observed the differences in what motivates most men and most women in learning environments. Many men are more energized by a confrontational in-your-face approach and by time-constrained tasks. Fewer women thrive in high-pressure, do-it-in-thirty-seconds-or-you-lose activities. Although some women love competition, many find it stressful, even juvenile, and prefer an ethos where everybody works together and everybody wins. Research backs up these findings and may be why men generally score higher than women on time-constrained stressful standardized tests while women often make better grades, engage more quickly in the classroom, and are quicker to ask for a teacher's help. Both are smart; they simply excel in different ways.[17]

Conclusion

How you view women will dramatically influence how you teach them, and if you teach in the USA, up to 60 percent of your students will likely be female, with a higher percentage in many other countries. How does the Bible describe the relationships between Christian men and women in the church? With familial language. We are fathers and brothers, sisters and mothers. Learning to view women as part of your spiritual family dramatically effects how you teach them.

What learning outcomes do we want to see in the women and girls we teach? We want them to love God and others well and to develop the character qualities that reflect the fruit of the Spirit in Galatians 5:22 and 23. We want them to be biblically literate, to develop their spiritual gifts and serve others, to live what they profess, to be rightly related to God, secure in their identity in Christ, and to carry out their life purposes with God-dependence and strength. Come to think of it, that's what we want for men too.

As a teacher/minister, you are God's representative and he uses your influence for titanic good or ill in the lives of women. For positive impact, be aware of certain realities when teaching women or a mixed group. Be aware of many women students' tendencies to underestimate their abilities and value. Understand the dangers of learned helplessness in women. Expunge harmful reductionist stereotypes from your thinking. Educate and keep up with the changing demographics regarding women, and watch your words, jokes, expressions, and illustrations. Are they about men all the time? If so, without meaning to, you'll project an insensitive and dismissive attitude toward women that will likely shut them down and hinder their sanctification. Expect that many women, more than men, will desire affiliation with you, their teacher, and peers, and learn how to engage with women appropriately and effectively. Not only are most women quicker to ask for help, they are highly influenced by your appropriate personal attention, words of encouragement, and affirmation. When you communicate that God cares for women, values their contributions, and calls them to develop their gifts to serve Christendom in various capacities, and you do too, God uses you to heal and empower over half of the body of Christ. Make the effort to understand women well, hone your skills to reach them, and watch God use you to raise up a generation of godly women all-in and on fire to serve our great God. Through the power of the Holy Spirit, that life-transforming teacher can be you!

Discussion Questions

1. Jesus describes Christian relationships in family terms in Matthew 12:46–50, and Paul does the same in 1 Timothy 5:1–2. Do men and women see one another as family in your ministry, church, and classroom? What are the ramifications of Christian men and women seeing and treating one another as family?

2. What kind of ethos did Paul foster in the church at Thessalonica (1 Thess. 2:6–8, 10–12)? How might you apply what Paul modeled in these verses to your teaching ministry?

3. Do you view Christians of the opposite sex through sibling eyes? If not, what attitude changes and action steps might correct your eyesight?

4. Has someone of the opposite sex either defended or offended you? If so, what happened and how did you feel (no names, please)?

5. What did you learn about gender differences in this chapter that may impact your teaching ministry in the future?

Resources for Further Study

Edwards, Sue, and Kelley Mathews. *New Doors in Ministry to Women: A Fresh Model for Transforming Your Church, Campus, and Mission Field.* Grand Rapids: Kregel Publications, 2002.

Edwards, Sue, Kelley Mathews, and Henry Rogers. *Mixed Ministry: Working Together as Brothers and Sisters in an Oversexed Society.* Grand Rapids: Kregel Publications, 2008.

Hislop, Beverly White. *Shepherding a Woman's Heart: A New Model for Effective Ministry to Women.* Chicago: 2003.

James, Carolyn Custis. *Half The Church: Recapturing God's Global Vision for Women.* Grand Rapids: Zondervan, 2010.

Mathews, Alice P. *Preaching That Speaks to Women.* Grand Rapids: Baker Book House, 2003.

Sax, Leonard. *Why Gender Matters: What Parents and Teachers Need to Know about the Emerging Science of Sex Differences.* New York: Broadway Books, 2005.

Scott, Halee Gray. *Dare Mighty Things: Mapping the Challenges of Leadership for Christian Women.* Grand Rapids: Zondervan, 2014.

Tannen, Deborah. *You Just Don't Understand: Women and Men in Conversation.* New York: HarperCollins, 2007.

Author Bio

Dr. Sue Edwards has more than thirty-five years experience as a Bible teacher, overseer of several megachurch ministries, and author. Now, as Associate Professor of Educational Ministries and Leadership, she teaches full-time at Dallas Theological Seminary. She has trained women leaders in Russia, Africa, and Germany. Sue is the co-author of five leadership books including: *Organic Mentoring: A Mentor's Guide to Relationships with Next Generation Women, Leading Women Who Wound, Mixed Ministry: Working Together as Brothers and Sisters in an Oversexed Society,* and *New Doors in Ministry to Women.* Women everywhere enjoy learning the Scriptures using her Bible studies, the *Discover Together Series* (DiscoverTogetherSeries.com). Married for forty-five years, she and David are the proud parents of two married daughters and the grandparents of five. David is a retired computer engineer who serves the Lord as a lay prison chaplain, and is now taking courses at DTS.

Endnotes

1. James R. Estep Jr., Michael J. Anthony, and Gregg R. Allison, *Theology for Christian Education,* (Nashville, TN: B & H Publishing Group, 2008), 259.

2. Jen Wilkin, *Women of the Word, How to Study the Bible with Both Our Hearts and Our Minds* (Wheaton, IL: Crossway, 2014), 36–37.

3. Dr. John Ortberg (M.Div., Ph.D., Fuller Seminary) is senior pastor at Menlo Park Presbyterian Church in Menlo Park, California.

4. William D. Hendricks, *Exit Interviews* (Chicago: Moody Press, 1993), 261.

5. Barna Group, "Five Factors Changing Women's Relationship with Churches," Barna Group, June 25, 2015.

6. Pam MacRae, "How Women Hear the Sermon," in *The Moody Handbook of Preaching*, ed. John Koessler (Chicago: Moody Press, 2008), 96.

7. Deborah J. Stipek, *Motivation to Learn: From Theory to Practice*, 2nd ed. (Boston, MA: Allyn and Bacon, 1993), 2–5.

8. Bruce Demarest, *The Cross and Salvation: The Doctrine Of Salvation*, ed. John S. Feinberg (Wheaton, IL: Crossway, 1997), 233.

9. David Neff, *Christianity Today*, July 22, 1991, 13.

10. Parker Palmer, *The Courage to Teach: Exploring the Inner Landscape of a Teacher's Life* (San Francisco, CA: Jossey-Bass Inc., Publishers, 1998), 2.

11. Story adapted from M. Gay Hubbard, *Women: The Misunderstood Majority, Contemporary Concerns in Counseling Women* (Nashville: Word Publishing, 1992), 124–25.

12. Dr. Dan Allender, President of Hill Graduate School, Seattle, Washington from 2002–2009, Dan continues to serve as Professor of Counseling Psychology at The Seattle School. Dan is the author of *The Wounded Heart, The Healing Path, To Be Told*, and *God Loves Sex*, and he has coauthored several books with Dr. Tremper Longman, including *Intimate Allies, The Cry of the Soul, Bold Love*, and *Bold Purpose*.

13. Dr. Michael Lawson, Senior Professor of Educational Ministries and Leadership at Dallas Theological Seminary, An interview for *Mixed Ministry: Working Together as Brothers and Sisters in an Oversexed Society,* by Sue Edwards, Kelley Mathews, and Henry Rogers (Grand Rapids: Kregel Publications, 2008), 84.

14. Leanord Sax, *Why Gender Matters: What Parents and Teachers Need to Know about the Emerging Science of Sex Differences (*New York: Broadway Books, 2005), 20, 21.

15. Ibid., 32.

16. Margaret Weigel, "Women, Work and Work/Life Balance: Research Roundup," October 20, 2013, Journalist's Resource, Harvard Kennedy School, Shorenstein Center, http://journalistsresource.org/studies/society/gender-society/women-work-research-roundup.

17. Sax, *Why Gender Matters,* 77–92.

Chapter 10
UNDER ATTACK: FAMILIES AND MARRIAGES

Michael S. Lawson

> *For this reason I kneel before the Father, from whom every* family
> *in heaven and on earth derives its name.*
>
> —Ephesians 3:14–15 (emphasis added)

"WHAT PLACE DOES A course on the 'Christian Home' have in theological education?" grumbled the seminary professor whose name I will not cite. I had no answer, being only two years old in the Lord and brand spanking new to seminary education. In 1965, some leaders apparently assumed everyone knew what a Christian marriage and family was all about. My conversations with classmates (100 percent male in those days) indicated that most of us were wandering in the dark. The litany of classmate family wrecks since then testifies that I was not too far off.

I have thanked God over and over again for Dr. Howard Hendricks, who stood against the grumbling, and Dr. John Walvoord (the former president of Dallas Theological Seminary) who backed him.[1] Dr. Hendricks' "Christian Home" course set the foundation for my marriage, my

family, and everything I would develop in the field of family ministry.[2]

So, today I would answer Dr. Grumble with a big smile and these words, "Family is the centerpiece of creation! Why shouldn't we study something so central to the Bible?[3] Family is everywhere in the Bible from the creation of mankind to the wedding feast of the Lamb. Since family has such a prominent place in the Bible, I believe it deserves a prominent place in theological education." Moreover, I would continue with an animated voice, "Family, and most particularly marriage, is intended to teach theology. If we relegate theology to books and classrooms, we rob the family of her proper role as the incubator of theological education.[4] How will young pastors train their families to be theological educators unless we help them formulate some clear plans for their own family?"

Over the years, theological education has adjusted pastoral training by offering courses in premarital and marriage counseling. However, these needed approaches are poorly timed or remedial. What new church leaders really need in their training is a proactive educational model. That, dear reader, is the subject of this chapter because I honestly believe that too many marriages in the church today resemble that collection of seminary men in 1965 … wandering in the dark.

For the purposes of a single chapter on family ministry, I propose to guide our thinking together using seven questions about:

1. Foundations: What makes you think family is the centerpiece of creation or that marriage was intended to teach theology?
2. Reality: What current conditions suggest family ministry ought to be a major priority in the church?
3. Potential: What if we could change the expectations and conversations within the church?
4. Philosophy: What principles should guide a church-based family ministry?
5. Focus: In what ways should the church coordinate her efforts?
6. Process: How can a church get started in family ministry?
7. Assessment: How can a church know whether she is moving forward?

Although there might be endless approaches to a chapter on Family Ministry, I have chosen these so when you are finished reading, you might have an action plan built on a solid biblical, philosophical, and practical base. My hope is that this chapter will help birth hundreds of church-based family ministries in days to come.

Foundations of Family Ministry

Family: The Centerpiece of Creation

The assertion that family is the centerpiece of creation leads us immediately into Genesis. God has the entire plan of creation in his mind before he begins. Had he chosen, he could have performed the creation instantaneously. However, he chose to develop the creation sequentially with the creation of the human race culminating his creative activity. Only after God positions everything else in its proper place does he take up humankind (Gen. 1:26). Then, God distinctively and deliberately creates humans, both male and female, in his personal image—a serious deterrent to anyone who might consider damaging his image in either its male or female form. We will learn later that everything in creation reflects his eternal power and divine nature though females and males alone bears his image (Rom. 1:20).

The human race's central role as divine image bearers helps us understand later commands. For instance, Moses emphasizes God's prohibition of making, carving, or worshiping images (Exod. 20:4; Lev. 26:1; Deut. 4:16; 5:8). That prohibition makes perfect sense given God's creation of living images. There were no mirrors in Eden. Adam and Eve only had each other, yet each should have been able to see the image of God in the other. God designed living reminders of himself in Adam and Eve.

In addition, God makes a puzzling affirmation of his newly created couple. He blesses them (Gen. 1:28). How curious. Adam and Eve are brand new, bear God's personal image and currently live without sin. Why do they need to be blessed? Why not give them simple clear instructions about their responsibilities? If the blessing and the following command to bear fruit (children) are connected as so many commentators indicate, then this truly is the family moment. God's mantle of blessing covers the family. How could family be anything other than the centerpiece of creation having come under God's first blessing (Gen. 1:22, 28)?

If the creation account were not persuasive enough, certainly the reader of the Bible would get the point when God saves several families not merely individuals from the great flood (Gen. 6:18). And, when God cements his covenant with Abram, he says,

> And I will bless those who bless you,
> And the one who curses you I will curse.
> And in you all the families of the earth
> shall be blessed (Gen. 12:3, NASB).

In addition, God seamlessly weaves family protection and instruction into his ten core commandments (Exod. 20:1–17). Honoring father and mother, avoiding adultery, and not coveting your neighbor's wife all protect the family. Who could forget the Sabbath day which I view not only as a day of rest but also family time.[5] Clearly, no one, including servants and children, was to work. However, the text says nothing about play.[6] In rural Israel, "Daddy's home" on the Sabbath and God won't let him work! Children need not compete with television, Internet or newspaper. Could there be a more obvious opportunity for family time each week? God's grace and goodness deserved

generous thanksgivings as families enjoyed restful time together as a gift from God.

Israel's central feast, the great Passover, was the only sacrifice offered in the family (Exod. 12). The entire festival, from the cleansing of the house, to dressing in travel clothes and standing during the meal buried Israel's historic redemption by God deep in everyone's memory. What child could ever forget watching her father cut the throat of a helpless lamb and smearing the blood around the doorway. God goes on to heap up instructions for parents and children in the Proverbs and punctuates his final words in the Old Testament with a warning to heed Elijah's calling to fathers who had been neglecting their children (Mal. 4:6).

The New Testament carries forward the same family emphases. God's son is now born into a human family with real brothers and sisters not to mention extended family (Luke 1; John 7; Mark 3). Luke links Jesus to his royal family ancestor David, the great patriarch Abraham, and the human race's origin in Adam. By no accident, Adam is called the "son of God," an obvious family term (Luke 3). Jesus performs his very first miracle at a family gathering celebrating the marriage of an unnamed young couple from an obscure village (John 2). His generous provision of wine (approx. fifty gallons) obviously blessed the whole marriage celebration. The apostle Paul clearly declares that those who would lead Christ's church must have stable families (1 Tim. 3; Titus 1). Paul goes even further by warning men to not only care for their own household but also their extended family. To neglect these duties classifies a man as worse than an unbeliever (1 Tim. 5). No one should overlook the conclusion to God's great redemptive story by blessing all those invited to the great wedding supper of the Lamb (Rev. 19). So, I repeat, family is the centerpiece of creation.

> "I wish to suggest that marriage (and family) was among the most basic guidelines for understanding God's Word."[7]
>
> —J. Lanier Burns

Marriage: Intended to Teach Theology

Jesus's words, "it was not this way from the beginning," must have jolted those men who thought they could divorce their wives for any reason (Matt. 19:8). In addition, Jesus points everyone to Genesis for an understanding of God's intention about marriage. The two image bearers were living reminders of God as together they ruled and replenished the earth (Gen. 2).[8] Had children been born under those conditions, they would have understood God first from the smiling faces of mommy and daddy and experienced God through the image-bearers tender care.

Although sin damaged this perfect scenario, God pushes his theological teaching agenda once again in Deuteronomy 6. Here, the marriage team (mommy and daddy) must become impassioned lovers of God first. They are the living examples of loving God. Nothing less than complete exertion of heart, soul, and strength will suffice. Now, as living lovers of God, they must "impress" their love for God and his teaching on their children.[9] Nothing speaks louder than living examples. In addition, their instructions blended smoothly into all the daily doings. If a love for God burns deep in your heart, he most assuredly will be part of your conversations. Amazing.

These Old Testament texts lay a sturdy framework for their New Testament counterparts. Perhaps the most potent passage to emphasize that marriage was intended to teach theology comes in Paul's letter to the Ephesians. Chapter 5 of that epistle has been used and misused for a variety of purposes. Without trying to undo anyone's point of view, let me simply add to the conversation by pointing out some very obvious features:

1. Chapter 5 opens with these words, "Therefore be imitators of God, as beloved children" (Eph. 5:1 NASB).[10] The imitation of God refers more to reproducing his character/behavior (love in this case) than passively bearing his image.

2. As Paul wraps up Chapter 5, his next to last concluding thought is "This is a profound mystery—but I am talking about Christ and the church" (Eph. 5:32). The marriage partners provide a visible reflection of the invisible reality of Christ and his church. Some might call this a metaphor and in writing, they would be accurate. But a real live marriage functions more like an icon with the focus on the invisible reality of Christ and the church.

3. Chapter 5 sets up the perfect case scenario where each partner embraces their given role. No exceptions for errant, uncooperative, or unbelieving partners are mentioned here. In fact, Paul reaches back (even as Jesus does) to the beginning in citing Genesis 2, "For this reason a man will leave his father and mother and be united to his wife, and the two will become one flesh" (Eph. 5:31).

4. I conclude from this passage that husbands teach Christology as they love/care for their wives while wives teach ecclesiology as they respond to their husband's love. Both teach theology proper as they imitate the God who loves them. When marriage partners do not observe these imperatives a great deal of heresy spreads among family and friends. Marriage is serious business for many reasons but especially because it teaches at least these elements of theology.

> "What if God designed marriage to make us holy more than to make us happy?"[11]
> —Gary Thomas

The apostle Peter adds soteriology to the list of theological subjects taught in marriage. In 1 Peter 3:1–2, he says, "Wives, in the same way submit yourselves to your own husbands so that, if any of them do not believe the word, they may be won over without words by the behavior of their wives, when they see the purity and reverence of your lives." This woman with an unsaved husband offers a silent movie version of soteriology but the picture comes in vivid color and high definition! Theology has no better spokesman than a life lived in utter devotion and loving dedication to God. In fact, in another time and place I might argue that the best apologetic we have for the Christian faith is a healthy marriage and family.

If you have been persuaded that family is the centerpiece of creation and marriage was intended to teach theology, then we have our work cut out for us. Although theological education and the church have rightfully placed a great deal of emphasis on our verbalizing the gospel, we have neglected the training of marriage partners for their rightful place as theological educators. We have urgent business in correcting our oversight by developing thoroughgoing family ministries. But if that were not enough, the current state of marriage in the United States ought to motivate a serious reconsideration of our priorities.

Reality of Families

American money-makers have a strange fascination with horror movies. Personally, the real horror lies in America's current attitudes and values toward marriage, cohabitation, same-sex marriages, divorce, and sex before marriage.[12] If you want some chilling reading, consider what the United States government surveys reveal.[13] Here are a few of their conclusions published in the public domain:

- In 2011–2013, 60 percent of women and 67 percent of men agreed, "Living together before marriage may help prevent divorce."
- In 2011–2013, 36 percent of women and 32 percent of men agreed, "Marriage has not worked out for most people I know."
- In 2011–2013, three-quarters of women (74.7%) and men (75.9%) agreed, "It is okay to have and raise children when the parents are living together but not married."
- The percentages of women and men who agreed, "Sexual relations between two adults of the same sex are all right," increased over the survey periods, from 42.3 percent in 2002 to 51.2 percent in

2006–2010, and to 60.2 percent in 2011–2013 among women, and from 39.7 percent in 2006–2010 to 48.9 percent in 2011–2013 among men.

In stark contrast to public opinion comes amazing research from scholars at public universities. Their collective pedigrees leave little room to criticize. Their collaborative research efforts surface through the Center for Marriage and Families at the Institute for American Values. Their stated objectives are:

> The Institute is a nonprofit, nonpartisan organization that brings together approximately 100 leading scholars—from across the human sciences and across the political spectrum—for interdisciplinary deliberation, collaborative research, and joint public statements on the challenges facing families and civil society.[14]

In one particular document, they publish thirty conclusions which point more toward a biblical model of marriage and family than the one represented by public opinion. Here are a few of their conclusions, but I highly recommend you read the whole document to energize your thinking:

- Cohabitation is not the functional equivalent of marriage.
- Marriage is associated with better health and lower rates of injury, illness, and disability for both men and women.
- Cohabitation is associated with higher levels of psychological problems among children.

- Family breakdown appears to increase significantly the risk of suicide.
- Boys raised in non-intact families are more likely to engage in delinquent and criminal behavior.
- A child who is not living with his or her own two married parents is at greater risk of child abuse.[15]

If the church actually reaches a significant proportion of this generation for Jesus Christ, they will come in with the attitudes and values cited in the government surveys. Those attitudes and values are unlikely to change unless submitted to a vitamin-enriched educational program. I am not convinced the average American pastor, even with good seminary training, is prepared to embrace couples with these notions or behaviors.

One young pastor moved to Seattle because one registry described it as the "least churched" city in the United States. He and his team set out to evangelize a section of that city and through their efforts planted a church of first-generation believers. One couple, who had come to faith through their efforts, shared how they had been living together for over a decade and had children from their cohabitation. They wondered what they should do which precipitated his phone call to me. He was ill prepared to help them navigate the second wave of decisions that needed to be made after their conversion.

One of my doctoral students proposed to study how churches in his community dealt with domestic violence. He hoped to compare ten to twenty different policies to compile a list of best practices. Of course he would need the help of various local pastors. Before he could begin, a police officer in his church warned him that many of the pastors he would need were personally guilty of domestic violence. He abandoned his study. I sometimes wonder whether pastors' marriages are any better than those in the community around them.

On a positive note, many churches now offer some kind of premarital counseling for those considering marriage. While highly commendable, the timing could not be worse. I find young couples in this high state of emotional attraction adorable but almost incapable of seriously considering the roles and responsibilities that accompany the commitment they are about to make. I rejoice at the numerous marriage and family conferences being offered in churches today. These occasional emphases bring worthy opportunities to renewed efforts on the part of marriage partners and parents. I worry that they function like so many retreats where people make strong commitments to renewed spiritual lives. But, upon returning home, the tyranny of everyday responsibilities saps all their strength and resolve. In addition, I am very grateful for the whole field of marital counseling that bloomed in recent decades. Even these wonderful remedial efforts often catch married couples too late.

No one wants to give up any of these well-intentioned efforts to serve the marriages and families in our care. But, what if there was a way to harness potent educational forces within marriages and families themselves? Here is your personal invitation to dream a bit with me in this next section.[16]

Potential of Family Ministry

My early understanding of role as Pastor of Christian Education at Metropolitan Baptist Church in Oklahoma City, Oklahoma resembled that of "truth dispenser." After all, I had just completed a four-year, 126-semester-hour Master of Theology degree. So, family ministry involved whatever I did to the married couple, which mostly involved some form of instruction accompanied with some well-meaning advice about what I perceived needed changing. Unfortunately, some precious couples who endured my instruction—followed by premarital and/or postmarital counseling—still failed in their marriage. Many times I grieved over their divorce more than they did. What was wrong?

I consulted a psychologist friend of mine about his experience. Obviously troubled couples came to me but those who came to him needed life support and time in the emergency room. I wondered how many of those marriages he counseled could be put back together if *both* parties really wanted to make the marriage work. His answer surprised me, "Oh, 90–95 percent." During my years as pastor, I never really figured out how to find and help those before they got waist deep in trouble. The frustration never left me. I'm convinced at least part of my failure originated from my perceived role as "truth dispenser." Somehow, if I could just get to them early enough and dispense enough correct information, their marriage would not end in disaster.

But what really needed to happen was my role image needed to change. Here I embark on a series of what if questions that occurred over a much longer period of time than it will take you to read them. These have helped me change the direction and planning for family ministry.

First, what if my role was not so much an information dispenser but more like an orchestra conductor? As orchestra conductor my role would be to know the whole piece of music to be played, to know which instrument should be beckoned into the performance, when to elevate everyone's effort to crescendo, when to soften the performance to cause the audience to listen more closely, and how to guide everyone to a triumphant ending.

If that were my model, then I would have to do different things. In the past our church had provided a lot of good ministries to help marriages and families but they were like an orchestra without a conductor. Different instruments tooted, honked, beeped, and thumped at random with no particular end in mind. Those ministries did not move in a coordinated way toward a common goal. Someone needed to be in charge of them all and call them into play when needed and not before. No instrument would be allowed to honk or thump unless in concert and moving toward the common goal. But what should the common goal be?

Second, what if the common goal was to make marriage partners more intentional in their care for one another and families more intentional about the transmission of the faith?[17] Then the acid test for everything done in the church that related to marriage or family would have to answer one of two questions: "How does this help couples be more intentional about their marriage?" or "How does this help couples be more intentional about the transmission of the faith to their children?" Finally, I had an organizing principle around which to build the music. No more random beeping or honking.

Third, what if we were successful—so successful that couples at church would begin to talk about their experiences? I began to wonder just how attractive and fun we could make these experiences. Would it be possible to change the average conversation after church from football or shopping to positive marriage and family encounters? What if wives began to brag on their husbands love and care for themselves and the children? That is a worthy objective—changing the conversations.

Fourth, what if we could elevate successful experiences in the eyes of the whole congregation? Would that along with other things actually begin to raise everyone's expectations about marriage and family? Would such an effort motivate people to move from where they are to the next level of marital intimacy and family satisfaction? The social pressure of group expectations offers powerful allies in our efforts to motivate people from complacency and into action.

Finally, what if the expectations about marriage and family became so naturally obvious that guests and visitors would begin to notice? What if the small gatherings of adults seemed to all be talking about marriage and family? Would we in some way become the city on a hill that Jesus spoke of in Matthew? If so, then that might validate my assertion that the best apologetic we have for the Christian faith in this culture is a healthy marriage and family. These goals always seem just out of reach until submitted to the rich design manual of the creator.

These wonderings create a vague image of what an individual church might envision as their long-term goal. But in order to reach that goal, they will need a guiding philosophy of family ministry.

Philosophy of Family Ministry

The first time I heard about a "family altar" a cold chill ran down my spine, as I wondered how in the world anyone could replicate something so formal sounding in a family with small children? Then I began to read some of the early books on marriage which made me feel drenched in syrup. Everything they described seemed flawless. My marriage had warts and lumps. So, my wife and I decided to just stumble along the best we could, caring deeply for one another, adjusting to life's realities, and including Christ in everything with our children. Without articulating it as precisely as I did in the former section, we were very intentional about our marriage and transferring the faith to our children. But I still had no idea how to formulate a church-based educational program until I met Kurt Bruner and John Trent and interacted with those in their Innovation Alliance.[18]

Kurt spent many years with Focus on the Family and their research teams, rising to vice president.[19] He left Focus on the Family to join the staff of Lakepointe Church in Rockwall, Texas.[20] He wondered if he could design, implement, and evaluate a church-based family ministry. John Trent, noted Christian psychologist, author, and conference speaker also sought more sustainable emphases on family through the church.[21] Their Innovation Alliance challenged a select group of church leaders to see what their creative imaginations could envision. From their experience and insights, I gleaned the following philosophical principles for family ministry in a church.

I now turn from my role as theologian and practitioner to a reporter of best practices. Here is what I learned. First, family ministry is not so much about what the church does for or to families and family members as it is about shaping what families do internally among their members. Are husbands and wives being more intentional about nurturing their relationship? Are parents being intentional about the transference of the faith to the children/youth?

Second, every ministry of the church must embrace their role in helping grow healthy marriages and families. Programs must work in concert with each other rather than ministry silos acting independently.[22] When everything from the pulpit to the nursery emphasizes a similar theme, church members have nowhere to hide.

Third, the emphasis on family ministry cannot add to the pastor's already overloaded job description. However, his cooperation and endorsement are essential. Without the pastors' endorsement, family ministry quickly fades like cheap wall paper. Everyone knows whatever gets pulpit time on Sunday morning is what church members consider vitally important.

Fourth, family ministry must reach out to the least engaged church attender as well as the most neglected family member. The first lacks basic motivation believing everything is "OK." The second requires specific solutions for particular issues. These require a wide range of approaches from entry-level activities to in-depth directives. One ministry to families with special needs children provides a twenty-four-hour care package that allows couples time for internal refreshing.[23]

Fifth, the best family ministries take a comprehensive approach. They account for the widows and orphans without losing their central mission of strengthening marriages and families.[24] Family ministry must focus her energy on education rather than remediation. Though counseling ought to be available in house or through referral, family ministry must never cease to ask the two central questions, "How does this cause marriage partners to be more intentional about nurturing their relationship? How does this cause parents to be more intentional about transferring the faith?"

Sixth, each aspect must undergo regular and rigorous effectiveness assessment. As any initiative enters the planning phase, leaders should ask, "How will we know if we succeeded?" If we are evaluating the success of a conference, we generally look at attendance. But what we really want to know is whether something about the inner workings of the family experienced sustained change. Designing that assessment device may be the most important part of the plan. If you cannot figure out whether your plan was successful, how can you know whether the effort was worthwhile?

When I present this philosophy to students, I use a graphic (see Figure 10.1).

Every philosophy of family ministry needs a central focus around which to form a constellation of activities and emphases. This leads to the next question in our discussion.

Focus of Family Ministry

Our church did many things over the years to address marriages and families. Sermon series, marriage conferences, couples retreats, parenting classes, library resources, and special speakers all made the list. I was always really happy with what our church did to and for marriages and families. I never knew whether any real changes were being made internally. What I had not seen until the Innovation Alliance was an attempt to rally the programs and resources around a singular focus and measure the change in the internal workings of marriages or families. In addition, I never figured out how to reach the very marriages that avoided the conferences, retreats, classes, and resources. They appeared to be the most needy but least willing to make any special effort.

No single program or combination of program emphases result in a finished product: i.e. the perfect Christian family. Christian families are always works in progress. But, by asking how each emphasis contributes to making healthier internal workings more likely, family ministry can have a sustained focus over time.

Figure 10.1 Philosophy of Family Life Education

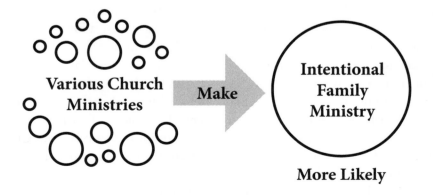

Here is how Lakepointe Church in Rockwall, Texas, began to reach out to their least motivated.[25] Several times a year they promote a churchwide emphasis from the pulpit and among the various ministries. One of their first challenges targeted husbands. They said, "We challenge husbands to do one thing in the next ninety days to be intentional about nurturing your marriage." Husbands who found themselves at a loss to generate even one idea could visit the resource center and look through business sized cards containing a single idea.[26] They could take the card to remind themselves to take action. Each idea was simple and doable but more importantly represented an intentional activity to nurture the marriage relationship.

In addition, they capitalized on a potent motivational tool. The designers of this emphasis reached out to the children's department who were asked to tell the children, "If you see daddy doing something really special and nice for mommy, tell us and we will give you a prize." If you forget everything else I have written, remember this: The biggest stakeholders in a healthy marriage are the children. No one has more to lose if the marriage breaks apart. They can be recruited as motivational allies.

Note how this activity functions internally within the family. The time period of ninety days provides planning and breathing space in our time-crushed schedules and provides a wide range of options. By limiting the challenge to one thing, husbands are more likely to make the effort. Whatever we plan for husbands, wives, or parents to do, those activities must be "doable" within the context of modern living and sustainable over time. This is where the liturgical "family altar" failed. A modern family might pull it off once, but it is too complicated to sustain over a long period of time.

This activity also represents something that can be assessed. At the end of the ninety days, a card inserted in the bulletin can simply ask, "Did you do something intentional to nurture your marriage during the last ninety days?" That anonymous card can be dropped in the offering plate and the results tabulated.

Not everything you try will be successful. Not everything Lakepointe has tried has been successful. For instance, the leadership sought to help parents be more intentional about the transference of faith to their children. Their first venture involved asking fathers to pray with the family once a week. Men pushed back. Many said they had never prayed out loud with anyone … ever! This task was not "doable." In my past experience, when leaders experience resistance, they double down by playing the guilt card. Lakepointe chose to listen to their men. As a result, they reformulated the challenge for men who have never prayed with their family. They asked men to gather their family together, hold hands, and have a brief period of silent prayer together for known needs inside the family.[27] Note how their change is both doable and sustainable.[28]

Quality family ministries must continue to promote entry-level activities for those whose marriages and families are slowly calcifying. Although every Christian leader I know would love each family to be fully functional and healthy, that simply does not represent reality. We know the ideal. Our job is to help marriages and families begin heading toward that ideal. Just being intentional seems to be a great place to start.

The approach at the HomePointe resource center at Lakepointe has another feature that makes sense. They take a long-range approach looking out in their planning over three to five years. Advertisers know you have to say something many times before you get a positive customer response. Their plan represents a slow drip model that keeps the emphases in small doses but coming regularly over a long period of time.

Lastly, they have taken the time to video positive responses from those who have followed through with the suggested activities. Those are shown in the morning service from time to time. Has the church overworked the salvation testimony and undervalued the duty-bound husband and wife just trying to make their marriage better?

Let me help you glean from Lakepointe's experience. While there is a great deal to learn from them, the following help shape their focus:

- They consistently try to make intentional marriage and family changes *more likely.*
- The promoted church-wide activity is "doable," sustainable, coordinated, periodic, and evaluated.
- They record and promote positive outcomes.
- They recruit motivational help from various ministries.
- They offer timely help through their resource center.

Their family ministry is highly sophisticated. They have had years to fine tune and develop their various approaches. The question remains for you, "Where do we begin?"

Process of Family Ministry

The process has at least four parts. These may be sequential, simultaneous, or a blend of the two. They are:

- Preliminary research
- Initial and long-range planning
- Phased implementation
- Assessment and evaluation

Look with me at some particulars within each of these parts.

Preliminary Research

First, the church's leadership must work through their vision of family ministry. Do they see it functioning alongside children, youth, singles, couples, men, and women's ministries? Preferably they envision family ministry enriching, recruiting, facilitating, and coordinating the church's move toward strengthening families. Without any apology, the pastor represents the key person in this vision. Without his support, family ministry will never possess the strength to challenge the largest number of people in the congregation. It will only be one in a long list of ministries and services mostly helping the highly motivated.

Second (or is this first?), if the leadership sees the need for family ministry, that ministry needs a champion. He or she can be a volunteer or paid staff but this must be their personal dream as well as their responsibility. Enough obstacles appear along the way that only a deep desire can overcome.

Third, if the pastor and official board(s) envision family ministry as a systemic addition to ministries throughout the church, then ministry leaders must be surveyed and hopefully recruited as full participants. Here both caution and diplomacy serve the champion well. Ministry leaders, whether they are volunteer, part time, or full-time staff usually face overloaded schedules. If they perceive that family ministry basically adds to their workload, then expect resistance. Sometimes there are philosophical issues to resolve when ministries have functioned as silos for a very long time.

One youth minister did not trust parents to provide proper and consistent training of youth. He perceived their role as outsourced to the church and that was fine with him. He alone had the training anyway. I would be critical but it sounds like me in the early days. To suggest that some responsibility, not to mention primary responsibility, be returned to parents seemed out of the question. Of course the primary responsibility does belong to parents whether they assume it or not. The best results come when ministry leaders embrace the idea that everyone has a place at the planning table and collaboration brings needed insight to the big picture of strengthening families. This is a proactive rather than a remedial model.

Fourth, an inventory of current ministry and communication tools need to be made. What does the church already have that can be recruited and coordinated from time to time to assist in promoting intentional marriages and families? Your list might look something like Figure 10.2.

Figure 10.2 Inventory of Current Ministry and Communication Tools

Communication Tools	Ministry Tools
Email	**1. Sermon series**
Group texting	**2. Special speakers**
Church bulletin	**3. Sunday school**
Pulpit announcements	**4. Small groups**
Videos (sanctuary and hallway)	**5. Fellowship ministries (men, women, singles)**
Testimonies	**6. Youth ministry**
Bulletin boards	**7. Children's ministry**

Communication Tools	Ministry Tools
Web site	**8. Library**
Bulletin insert	**9. Resource center**
Etc.	**10. Retreats**
	11. New churchwide emphases

Initial and Long-Range Planning

If I have learned anything about church ministry over the last fifty years, it is that churches move at glacial speed. Whatever you want done, plan for it to take a long time. Committees take forever to make decisions but are more committed to the overall goals when thoughtfully consulted and engaged. Planning requires the marriage of calendar, communication, and ministries. The most effective ministries utilize a backdated calendar. To use a common model, if vacation Bible school occurs in June, a timeline of planning, recruiting, training, communicating, and promoting begins the previous January. The

difference between vacation Bible school and the family ministry model we are talking about is that the family ministry model enlists the cooperation of all the various ministries utilizing all the communication devices available.

In essence, every lesson, event, or emphasis needs to work in concert. In this systemic model, we avoid having the marriage retreat on the same weekend that the pastor begins his sermon series on marriage or the couples Sunday school class begins a special emphasis on relationship building. For purposes of illustration, note how I have brought the gray scale-coded ministries into the calendar in Figure 10.3.

Figure 10.3 Yearly Church Planning Calendar

	Jan	Feb	Mar	Apr	May	June	July	Aug	Sept	Oct	Nov	Dec
Week 1		1			11							
Week 2	10	1			11		4			11		
Week 3		1		3	11		4			11	1	
Week 4				3			4	2		11	1	
Week 5?			2	3					10		1	

This calendar represents an arbitrary alignment of various ministries. But it is spread out across the calendar in such a way that something about marriage and family is being promoted throughout the year. The sheer, gentle, ongoing promotion communicates the church's unrelenting vision and concern. Remember, each of these must use every communication vehicle available.

Phased Implementation

A start date a year or two away is recommended, but you can still do things in the interim. Whatever is done ought to go on a larger planning calendar to begin the coordinating process. A delayed start date allows time for focus groups to discuss various possibilities; field-testing various activities; anticipation to build; and all the ministry leaders have time to buy into the model.

Figure 10.4 Long-Range Church Planning Calendar

	Year 1	Year 2	Year 3	Year 4	Year 5
Sermons					
Retreats					
Special Speaker					
Sunday school					
Church wide emphases					
Small Group					
Resource Center	ASAP				

The shadings show which years each ministry might begin their emphases. While the various ministries are reaching out to different segments within the church or the church as a whole, the resource center fills in needed gaps by helping address specific needs. People do not attend every event for a variety of reasons. Or, they may have such special needs that only a particular video series, book, pamphlet, or recorded sermon may address. Once again, I highly recommend the HomePointe center at Lakepointe church.[29] Their model resource center provides a well thought through inventory of resources.

Assessment and Evaluation

Sometimes people use these two terms synonymously. However, they do provide two different steps that help close the education cycle as well as provide guidance for the future. Assessment accumulates data. In church ministry, questionnaires need to be kept short and simple. All of us are survey weary but we need to find out whether couples and/or parents acted on the recommended activity. Instead of surveying the parents, you might also survey the children or youth. A simple yes/no will get the job done. If you really want more information, ask for volunteers to serve on a focus group to evaluate the exercise.

Evaluation looks at the data to determine whether the activity was worthwhile. Should this be repeated, modified, or abandoned? Churches are like individuals; no two are alike. What really works well in one cannot be sustained in another. Evaluation is not an easy process. Sometimes a program works but we assume it works for the wrong reason.[30]

Conversely, an emphasis may fail and we assume people aren't interested. But, we failed to pick a good date, promote adequately, or utilize supporting motivational help. Evaluation involves using wisdom and discernment to interpret the facts gathered in assessment. Without good assessment and evaluation, you cannot build on your successes and minimize your failures.

I hope this last discussion catapults you and your church into action. I predict that a church full of healthy marriages is a healthy church.

Conclusion

The verse that captions this chapter traces family names, not just families, back to God himself. In our highly individualized American society we frequently forget to nurture the most basic of all human relationships, the family. At the same time, our government and media promote every possible distortion of the biblical model. This is exactly the right time for the church to live out an incarnational model that reflects the deep satisfaction that comes from following the creator's plan.

I began this chapter by asserting that family was the centerpiece of creation and that marriage was intended to teach theology. From those assertions I briefly described the need for a stronger emphasis on family ministry in the church. For those churches wishing to design a systemic family ministry program, I cited one of the most comprehensive models and suggested some immediate steps that can be taken.

Now, may God help you and your church leaders bow before your sovereign Lord to determine what needs to be done in your context.

Discussion Questions

1. In what sense is family the centerpiece of creation?

2. What does biblical marriage teach us about theology? Suggest specific passages.

3. What cultural conditions today make strong marriage ministries in the church a high priority?

4. What general principles did you learn in this chapter that might guide you in creating a dynamic family ministry?

5. What specific methods would you like to see implemented in your church?

Resources for Further Study

Books

Anthony, Michael and Michelle Anthony. *A Theology for Family Ministries*. Nashville: B&H Academic, 2011.

Hess, Richard S. and M. Daniel Carroll R. *Family in the Bible: Exploring Customs, Culture, and Context*. Grand Rapids: Baker, 2003.

Hynes, Brian. *Shift: What It Takes to Finally Reach Families Today*. Loveland, CO: Group Publishing, 2009.

Jones, Timothy Paul. *Family Ministry Field Guide: How Your Church Can Equip Parents to Make Disciples*. Indianapolis: Wesleyan, 2011.

Kimmel, Tim. *Connecting Church & Home: A Grace-Based Partnership*. Nashville: Randall House, 2013.

Websites

Drive Faith Home by Kurt Bruner—www.drivefaithhome.com

Family Life by Dennis and Barbara Rainey—www.familylife.com

Family Matters by Tim Kimmel—www.familymatters.net

Focus on the Family—www.focusonthefamily.com

HomePointe by Kurt Bruner—www.lakepointe.org/homepointe

Marriage Core by Chip Dickens—www.marriagecore.com

Strong Marriages by Dewey Wilson—www.strongmarriages.com

Author Bio

Dr. Michael S. Lawson is Senior Professor of Educational Ministries and Leadership at Dallas Theological Seminary and Coordinator of the Doctor of Educational Ministries Degree. At Dallas Seminary, he teaches doctoral cohorts in Family Ministry and Academic Ministry. For more than thirty years, he has conducted faculty development seminars and taught courses for Christian Colleges and Seminaries in North America, Europe, Africa, Central America, Eastern Europe, Asia, and the Middle East.

CHAPTER 10 APPENDIX:
INFERTILITY AND CHILDLESSNESS

Julie Shannon

I ALWAYS WANTED TO be a mom, and the motherhood expectation wove itself through most of my life. We experienced seven years of active infertility challenges, including three miscarriages. The motherhood dream I nurtured never came to fruition; emotional and spiritual paralysis were the outcome. The pain, disappointment, and bitterness took time to work through and my confusion lived in the question of why, when he calls us to be fruitful and multiply (Gen. 1:28), did God not allow any of my babies to enter this world. I desperately sought someone or some read that would encourage me in what looked to be a bleak future if I did not live out the purpose and role of mom. I struggled to understand my value and to determine what activity or action could fill the purposeless hole within.

Infertility and miscarriage are silent topics in a noisy world. As time passes with no pregnancy or with pregnancy and a miscarriage, emotions rise and despair can follow. The more couples try, and—in their minds—fail, the more they require emotional and spiritual support. Unfortunately, the pain and humiliation of infertility may create a cocoon of privacy and disconnection that isolates them from friends, family, and their faith community.

The church and Christian ministry in general often emphasize the importance of marriage and family in order to gain true meaning and purpose. Those who experience fertility challenges or involuntary childlessness may exist on the fringes of life, feeling unworthy, isolated, and neglected.

Church communities must gain an understanding of the infertility impact in order to minister to couples' hurt and need, to act as God's instruments of healing, and to love one another. Historically, the Christian church emphasizes the growth of the nuclear family, and the fertility of couples as an answer to "be fruitful and multiply." Throughout the Bible, the barrenness stories of Hannah, Sarah, and Elizabeth are held up in today's sermons as evidence of God's blessing through the matriarchs' eventual fruitfulness in bearing children.

The body of Christ is called to love God, love one another, and make disciples. Loving one another requires undergirding fellow believers in their pain of infertility and childlessness through guidance and hope, encouraging vitality in a well-lived life, spiritual transformation, and discipleship. God's purposes are achieved by using his children and their gifts and talents to glorify himself, and give them personal satisfaction and fruitfulness. He often uses family, friends, coworkers, and church members to help identify and encourage gifts they see in others.

What the Church Can Do

- Be aware. The church must become acquainted with the experience of infertility and involuntary childlessness.
- Be intentionally inviting and ask couples to serve in their giftedness. God's family members should personally reach out to their brothers and sisters and invite them to serve in mission opportunities and participate in church activities and fellowship. Please act with caution, care, and sensitivity and avoid asking women to serve in the nursery or in any glorified babysitter opportunities.
- Be the hands and feet of Christ. During someone's active infertility season, provide a meal, schedule a time to sit and read or watch a movie with them, invite them to an art museum, show, non-child-related event, or take them on a nature walk. When a surgical procedure takes place, show up and quietly sit in the waiting room with the spouse.
- Show interest, not judgment and avoid offering opinions or "biblical truth" about a couples' infertility treatment, adoption, or any other personal choices.
- Listen; do not probe. Hear their story while exercising thoughtful care with any questions.
- Invite and clearly offer grace. Communicate pregnancy and birthday events but keep expectations of involvement to a minimum. Women in the midst of fertility challenges might want an invitation to a baby shower or toddler birthday, but they also desire the freedom to politely decline.
- Include, do not ignore. Create non-mom space and activities for the childless women in your church to participate in discipleship and growth. Build additional opportunities that are not mom- or family-focused.
- Remember these couples during special seasons and events. Mother's Day, Father's Day, and Christmas create opportunities to lovingly incorporate them into prayer or message.
- Offer relationship, not advice. Walk with these couples without giving opinions, sharing "success" stories, or offering third-party medical tips. They spend time desperately searching for answers and are well aware of opportunities in treatments. Success stories only offer false hope and possibly add to feelings of failure.

The church family promotes awareness of infertility and childlessness by educating from the pulpit, through church leadership, and in various forms of communication. Personal interactions and relationships enable trust and support. Church members lovingly reach into the lives of couples in the midst of infertility or childlessness and similarly, these couples must be willing to extend a hand back to accept the love and care.

Church family and friends welcomed us into their lives and children's activities. Opportunities to mentor teenagers, attend musicals and dance recitals, and support parents and their children added meaning and purpose to our lives. Family retreats at a Christian camp enabled us to spend time with families in an organic way, which increased bonds of friendship and added depth to our faith relationships. Love and service between disciples of Jesus strengthens fellowship, grows ministry, enlightens purpose, and undergirds spiritual growth. When the church remembers and includes couples, in the midst of infertility and those who experience involuntary childlessness, the family of God multiplies ministry and bears fruit for his kingdom.

Julie Shannon, author of *Infertility and Involuntary Childlessness: Traveling the Terrain*. More information at www.drjulieshannon.com.

Endnotes

1. See the chapter "What Makes a Great Teacher?" by Bill Hendricks for more information on Howard Hendricks.

2. Today, Dallas Theological Seminary offers concentrations in family ministry in our MA in Christian Education, Master of Theology, and Doctor of Educational Ministry degree programs. In addition, the seminary offers a MA in Biblical Counseling.

3. Notice I did not say family is the centerpiece of the Bible. Clearly, Jesus himself is the centerpiece of the Bible.

4. See Timothy's initial theological training through his mother and grandmother. I do not believe the Holy Spirit accidentally connected Timothy's reminder to everyone's favorite verse on inspiration. See 2 Timothy 3:14–16.

5. The Sabbath is unique to Israel. All other civilizations worked seven days a week. "The quest for the origin of the Sabbath outside of the Old Testament cannot be pronounced to have been successful. It is, therefore, not surprising that this quest has been pushed into the background of studies on the Sabbath in recent years." Gerhard F. Hasel, "Sabbath," ed. David Noel Freedman, *The Anchor Yale Bible Dictionary* (New York: Doubleday, 1992), 5:851.

6. We hear very little about good play in the Bible until God fills Jerusalem's streets with children playing in Zechariah 8:18.

7. J. Lanier Burns, "The Biblical Use of Marriage to Illustrate Covenantal Relationships," *Bibliotheca Sacra* 173, no. 691 (2016): 274.

8. I sometimes wonder whether Jesus was hinting at this unique quality of man when, as the only sinless human on the planet, he said, "If you have seen me, you have seen the Father" (John 14).

9. The Hebrew word "שׁנן" means whet or sharpen. Richard Whitaker, Francis Brown, Samuel Rolles Driver, and Charles Augustus Briggs, *The Abridged Brown-Driver-Briggs Hebrew-English Lexicon of the Old Testament: From A Hebrew and English Lexicon of the Old Testament* (New York: Houghton, Mifflin and Company, 1906).

10. I prefer the New American Translation of Ephesians 5:1, as it does justice to the Greek word "μιμηταί" (imitator).

11. Gary Thomas, *Sacred Marriage* (Grand Rapids: Zondervan, 2000), 13.

12. This chapter has a decidedly American slant. A short chapter on family ministry does not allow room for a thorough analysis of the state of marriage around the world. However, having traveled extensively for over thirty years, I have yet to visit a place where a marriage and family are understood in their full biblical richness.

13. Copen Daugherty, "Trends in Attitudes about Marriage, Childbearing, and Sexual Behavior: United States, 2002, 2006–2010, and 2011–2013," *National Health Statistics Reports*; no. 92, Hyattsville, MD: National Center for Health Statistics, 2016. http://www.cdc.gov/nchs/data/nhsr/nhsr092.pdf (accessed September 26, 2016).

14. Bradford Wilcox, ed., *Why Marriage Matters: 30 Conclusions from the Social Sciences*, 3rd ed. (New York: Institute for American Values, 2011).

15. Ibid.

16. In this section and through the remainder of the chapter, I acknowledge my deep debt to Kurt Bruner and John Trent. My first encounter with them together involved attending one of the final meetings of their Strong Families Innovation Alliance. At that meeting, various churches reported on their creative strategies recently implemented in their churches. Out of these meetings emerged a network of churches attacking family ministry with renewed energy. My one encounter with that group in 2009 energized the formation of the Dallas Theological Seminary Family Ministry Cohort offered in both Doctor of Ministry and Doctor of Educational Ministry degree programs.

17.   See *Innovation Alliance Executive Summary* at http://johntrent.publishpath.com/ Websites/johntrent/images/ InnovAllianceExecSummary.pdf. These seem so relatively simple but they are based on the assumptions that families need some basic starting places. Research on families bears this out.

18.   The Innovation Alliance was a short-term ad hoc group of cutting-edge church leaders charged with creating their best vision of a family ministry and reporting the successes and challenges to the whole group for research purposes.

19.   More information on Focus on the Family can be found at www.focusonthefamily.com.

20.   More information on Lakepointe Church can be found at www.lakepointe.org.

21.   More information on John Trent's ministry can be found at www.strongfamilies.com.

22.   Some youth ministers were skeptical about entrusting the spiritual formation of youth to the parents.

23.   More information on Jill's House (a ministry of McLane Bible Church in Vienna, Virginia) can be found at www. jillshouse.org.

24.   Philip H. Towner, *1-2 Timothy & Titus: The IVP New Testament Commentary Series,* ed. Grant R. Osborne (Downers Grove, IL: Inter Varsity Press, 1994), 116–123.

25.   Lakepoint Church has now made its program available to other churches. I highly recommend this model. If I were pastoring a church today, we would most certainly adopt and implement its first rate design. See www. lakepointe.org/homepointe.

26.   The resource center is filled with both general and specific help for any husband, wife, or parent. Its location near the children's ministry makes it a convenient stopping place. The warm cookies and friendly volunteers create a welcoming atmosphere. The child-sized table and chairs provide a convenient place to wait until daddy or mommy finds what they need.

27.   Sixty seconds of dead silence feels like "forever" to small children … and many adults. Try it.

28.   See the chapter "Stressed: Men" by Paul Pettit for additional information on ministering to men.

29.   More information on HomePointe can be found at www.lakepointe.org/homepointe.

30.   Many American pastors offer conferences in Eastern Europe. They measure success by the number of pastors who attend. Those same Eastern European pastors have told me they love the conferences but not for the teaching which does not fit their setting. They love the nice hotels and meals paid for by generous American church members.

Chapter 11
INVISIBLE: SINGLE ADULTS

Joye Baker

An unmarried man is concerned about the Lord's affairs—how he can please the Lord.... An unmarried woman or virgin is concerned about the Lord's affairs: her aim is to be devoted to the Lord in both body and spirit.... I am saying this for your own good, not to restrict you, but that you may live in a right way in undivided devotion to the Lord.

—1 Corinthians 7:32–35

I MEET WITH MANY single women at seminary as they pursue their studies toward vocational Christian ministry. Many of them have never been married. Our conversations often turn to their desire to find a godly husband and have children. As I listen to the longings of their hearts and wipe away their tears, I try to comfort them and encourage them to trust God and surrender to his plan and purposes for their lives. I find it important to explain to them that my singleness is not the same as their singleness. I shared life with a wonderful Christian husband, raised three children, and enjoy the happiness of grandchildren. Though the painful, sudden loss of my husband in a car accident after eighteen years of marriage shattered my world, God graciously allowed me to experience the blessed fulfillment of marriage and children.

One day I woke up happily married, and hours later I found myself a widow and single parent. Though my life changed in an instant, it took years to transition from marriage to singleness. The grief overwhelmed me as my heart exploded into a million pieces. I felt helpless as I tried to console my children who would now spend the rest of their lives without their devoted father. Thankfully we all had a deep faith in God, and he sustained and comforted us as we stepped into an unexpected and unknown future.

No one knows one day to the next what God's plan for us may be. Some of you reading this wake up to a spouse, while others of you wake up with no one beside you. Whatever your circumstance, we all have one thing in common: God is always with us. We may feel lonely during certain times in our lives, but we are never really alone. Just before the disciples abandoned Jesus as he headed towards Calvary, he reminded them as he reminds us today: "Yet I am not alone, for my Father is with me" (John 16:32). Whether married or single, this is a wonderful promise to cling to. As we look at singleness, we must first discover what the Scriptures say about life as a single person.

A Biblical View of Singleness

Many single people have a sense of being "invisible" because marriage and family have been given priority in so many churches. Messages on Sunday morning often emphasize marriage through biblical teaching, sermon illustrations, and references made to husbands and wives, fathers and mothers. Church budgets often reflect the low priority given to singles by much higher financial support for children and youth ministries, parenting classes, marriage counseling, and family events.

Many churches do not offer a separate ministry for singles, or if a singles ministry does exist, its leadership consists of volunteers rather than someone on the pastoral staff. Singles often feel marginalized, ignored, undervalued, and given the message that marriage holds a higher value and importance in God's plan for the world.

It is true that singles have unique needs and a lifestyle that differs from married people. It is also clear throughout the Bible that marriage represents a key means by which God has unfolded his plan for mankind as seen for example in the first two chapters of Genesis and Ephesians 5:22–33. But Scripture also upholds singleness as a means to reach the world for Christ. Many of the significant men and women in the Bible were single some or all of their life such as Joseph, Ruth, Daniel, Nehemiah, Jeremiah, Anna, Mary, Martha to a name but a few. V. M. Sinton summarizes it well when he states,

> The Christian perspective on the biblical material is that, while the first created human beings, Adam and Eve, were a married couple, in the new creation the second Adam, Jesus Christ, was a single person. Singleness and marriage are parallel routes for loving and serving in the world and preparing for life in the resurrection community.[1]

Jesus and Paul represent two of our greatest examples of men who were single and they each guide us in a biblical view of singleness.

Jesus's Teaching on Singleness

Jesus holds marriage in very high regard and addresses the issue of divorce when he is questioned about it (Matt. 5:31–32; 19:3–9; Mark 10:6–12; Luke 16:18). Only two places in the Gospels record that Jesus refers to singleness. The first account occurs in Matthew 19:10–12 in response to the disciples when they question the validity of marriage based on Jesus's explanation that adultery is a justification for divorce. Jesus responds by saying, "Not everyone can accept this word, but only those to whom it has been given" (Matt. 19:11). He goes on to use the example of single men called "eunuchs." He explains that men can be eunuchs in one of three ways: They were born that way and unable to physically reproduce; they were castrated sometime in their life; or they voluntarily chose to forego marriage, remain single, and practice sexual abstinence. Jesus particularly focuses on the third example. "The eunuch for the kingdom is the one who voluntarily refrains from marriage and family so as to guard his or her freedom for the sake of serving the Lord in whatever way he should call."[2] Jesus commends those men or women who deliberately choose to remain single in order to further the kingdom of God.

The second time Jesus touches on the subject of singleness is found in Luke 20:27–36. Here he responds to a scenario the Sadducees present to him about a woman who has been a wife and widow of seven brothers. The religious leaders ask, "Now then, at the resurrection whose wife will she be since the seven were married to her?" (Luke 20:33). In Jesus's response, he explains that in heaven people will not marry. All believers will essentially be single in heaven "like the angels" (Luke 20:36b). Jesus elevates singleness by emphasizing that marriage fulfills some of God's purposes on earth, but singleness reflects the heavenly state all believers will one day experience.

Paul's Teaching on Singleness

No other chapter in the Bible says more about singleness than 1 Corinthians 7. In this letter the apostle Paul responds to Corinthian believers who lived in a time when some people taught marriage was God's will for all people while others believed singleness represented the

highest spiritual state. Paul goes to great lengths to compare marriage and singleness, emphasizing that each represents a gift from and a calling by God (1 Cor. 7:7, 17, 24). Paul clearly teaches both marriage and singleness hold equal value to God (1 Cor. 7:1–2, 7–9, 17, 24, 27–28). Men and women have the freedom to choose to marry or remain single as long as they marry another believer (1 Cor. 7:38). As we consider the biblical view of singleness, Paul exhorts single believers in three particular ways: Be content; be pure; and be fully devoted to God.

Be Content (1 Cor. 7:17, 20, 24)

In the early verses of 1 Corinthians 7, Paul focuses on the husband/wife relationship. The rest of the chapter moves into comparing marriage and singleness. It is evident by Paul's words that his letter comes in response to two groups of people: those who think marriage is God's ultimate desire for all people and those who think singleness is the greater, more spiritual way to be used by God. These contrasting teachings confused new believers. If they accepted Jesus as their Savior while single, they thought they needed to get married in order to most please God. If they accepted Jesus as their Savior when already married, they concluded that they needed to divorce their spouse in order to please God more as a single person. Neither way was correct.

To address this misunderstanding, Paul uses circumcision and slavery as examples to challenge all believers to "remain" in whatever marital state they found themselves. God values both married people and single people equally and can use either marriage or singleness for his glory. Paul uses this concept of "remaining" to urge the Corinthians to "be content" whether married or single.[3] In regards to singleness, Paul admonishes each single man and woman to accept and embrace their current state of singleness and seek ways to maximize the opportunities afforded them during their years as a single person. He urges single men and women to find contentment in the fact that they are currently in the center of God's will, and to faithfully seek ways to use this particular time in their life to honor and serve God.

Be Fully Devoted (1 Cor. 7:32–35)

Secondly, Paul spends the last half of 1 Corinthians 7 using a number of examples to contrast marriage and singleness with the emphasis on the advantage single people have to be "fully devoted to God." Here he explains that never-married singles have more time to devote to God because they are free from the "troubles" of married life because "one who is married is concerned about the things of the world, how he may please his wife and his interests are divided (7:33) … [and a wife is concerned about] how she may please her husband" (7:34). Paul is not criticizing husbands and wives who focus on their responsibilities towards one another, and their children if they are parents, because the Scriptures are filled with directives for people who are married. Their time must be divided between their earthly family needs and their availability to God. However, Paul builds a case for the advantages of being single without children because singleness affords a person more time dedicated to the things of God. Single men and women don't have the demands and expectations inherent in marriage and parenting. A single person does not have all the distractions that come with a family. He or she is free

to make independent decisions and choose how they will live their life. But Paul is careful to communicate in 1 Corinthians 7 that since single people have more discretionary time, they have greater opportunities to devote more of their life in service to God. Paul sees this to be a great advantage for singles. He admonishes them to stop dwelling on the fact that they are not married and pray for God to show them how they can maximize the time they have to invest their lives in ways that will have spiritual benefits and serve the needs of others.

> "First Corinthians 7 is filled with the benefits of singleness. As a single adult, you have the ability to serve God more 'singularly' and whole-heartedly than the married adult whose interests are necessarily divided."[4]
>
> —Doug Rosenau and Michael Todd Wilson

Be Pure (1 Cor. 7:1–2, 9)

The third way that Paul specifically addresses single men and women relates to their sexual lives. He states very clearly that sexual intimacy is only permissible within the bounds of marriage. I remember the early months after my husband died. We had enjoyed a very fulfilling physical relationship. I missed his companionship, his protection, his support, his unconditional love, and his very presence. But, my body also missed his tender touch and closeness that had been so satisfying. I have a very clear memory of a conversation I had with God based on my understanding of many scriptural passages, including those in

1 Corinthians 7. I told God that I understood that unless I was to remarry I would never experience the pleasure of a sexual relationship again. I knew from 1 Corinthians 7:39–40 that as a widow I was free to remarry but I also read Paul's admonition to remain single so I could be more devoted and available to the Lord. Although I have always been open to God's will for my life, for the past twenty-five-plus years I have not remarried. Through these many years of singleness, I have discovered much to my surprise and delight how sufficient and fulfilling God's love can be as I have trusted and depended on him as my "husband" (Isa. 54:5). God offers to be a devoted and intimate partner to every single man and woman who entrusts their lives to him and his will for their life.

Single men and women are to remember the words of Jesus and Paul and be content, fully devoted to God, and sexually pure in order to fulfill God's plan and purposes during their years of singleness.

> "Abstinence is a response to outside circumstances, whereas celibacy is inner-driven, a response to a calling. Celibacy ... could be described as 'purpose-driven abstinence.'"[5]
> —Dr. Abraham Kuruvilla

A Calling to Singleness

Jennifer Marshall's book *Now and Not Yet* offers an excellent perspective on singleness. Though the book focuses on single women, its principles are just as applicable for men. She offers a very helpful discussion on the difference between God's call on our life and the various callings we experience throughout our lives.[6]

All believers have the same general call to follow Christ and accomplish his purposes.

Jesus is our example. In John 4:34 he explains to his disciples, "My food is to do the will of him who sent me and to finish his work." Then again in John 6:38, he declares, "For I have come down from heaven not to do my will but to do the will of him who sent me." All believers whether married or single have the same call on their lives to accomplish God's plan for them.

> "Our highest calling is to love God and to live in obedience exactly where he currently has us."[7]
> —Jennifer Marshall

At the same time, we each have different callings throughout our lives. In my college and young adult years, my calling was to singleness. My calling changed to that of wife and mother after I married. Years later, my calling instantaneously changed to that of a widow and single parent. In each of these seasons of my life, God wanted me to maximize the opportunities I had to accomplish his purposes and plan for me. Instead of bemoaning what I did not have during each period of my life, I was to pray and ask him to show me how to leverage the years of marriage or singleness to best honor and glorify him. As Marshall reminds us:

> Callings ... are made up of what God has put before us to do *right now*.... We don't have to worry that we've missed a calling—and that includes marriage. As long as we live attentive to the first call to Christ and the personal callings he has

put in our lives, we can be confident that we aren't in a holding pattern just because twenty-five (or thirty, or forty) is around the corner and marriage is nowhere in sight…. A person's callings *may* include, but will not be limited to, marriage. Even for those who do marry, the marriage relationship is not the sum total of their callings. To reduce the idea of callings to a single relationship—even one as central and life-changing as marriage—is to miss the point. Getting married, in other words, shouldn't be the measure of any woman's [or man's] success in life.[8]

For a man or woman to embrace the gift of singleness does not mean it is necessarily for a lifetime, but to accept it as a calling to faithfully serve God during that season of being single.

Single Adults: Who Are They?

Over the last one hundred years there has been a huge demographic shift in the United States. In 1900, 95 percent of the adult population was married.[9] By 1996, 43 percent of the American population was single.[10] In 2014, a milestone was reached when it was announced that 50.2 percent of adults in America were single. Research revealed that 124.6 million people over the age of eighteen were single.[11] Of that single population, 62 percent have never married, 24 percent are divorced or separated, and 14 percent are widowed.[12] Of this number, 47 percent are men and 53 percent are women.[13] For the first time in history, there are more single adults than married adults and that percentage continues to climb each year. This raises many challenges for the church and requires a paradigm shift as we

seek to address the needs of those who are single inside and outside the church.

In the years before 1900 and well into the next fifty to sixty years, marriage was the norm and young people were taught to plan for and expect to get married and have children.[14] Those who remained single were looked down upon, criticized, and often questioned as to the reason for their singleness. Terms such as "old maid" or "confirmed bachelor" were used in a derogatory way to address those who were single. Tragically, even their sexual orientation was questioned if they were still single in their mid-twenties or older. Since God commanded men and women to be "fruitful and multiply" in Genesis 1:28, it has generally been assumed throughout the ages that men and women were expected to marry and bear children.

Yet, we now have a majority of adults who are not married. As we study our single population, we find not all singleness looks the same. We have those who have never married, divorced, widowed, and single parents. Within each of these four broad categories, we discover a troubling statistic: from 1960 to 2010, the number of cohabiting adults climbed from 439,000 to 8,100,000. As if these high numbers aren't startling enough, research has revealed that when people were asked, "Do you think marriage is obsolete?" in 1970, 28 percent agreed, but that number jumped to 39 percent in 2010.[15]

When these numbers related to the low value placed on marriage were broken down by generations, we see an even more disturbing trend in our general adult population: 32 percent of our oldest adults (65+), 34 percent of those 50–64, 41 percent of those 30–49, and almost half (44 percent) of young adults ages

18–29 believe marriage is obsolete.[16] Added to this, 3.5 percent of US adults identify as gay or lesbian.[17] That number steadily grows as a result of the Supreme Court decision in June 2015, which declared same-sex marriage legal.[18]

The fact many millions of American adults no longer value the sanctity of marriage, often choose to live together unmarried, and disregard the biblical teaching of marriage between a man and a woman presents many challenges for those in church leadership. It's beyond the scope of this chapter to address all these issues, but one thing we can know for sure: Singleness is reflected in many different ways. This means that the needs of one particular single man or woman will differ from another. Let's take a brief look at some of the unique characteristics of those who have never married, are divorced, widowed, or are a single parent.

Never Married

As mentioned previously, statistics in 2014 reveal that 64 percent of the American single population had never been married. That percentage of never-marrieds jumps to 74 percent for those who are 18–29 years old.[19] The high number of young adults who remain single reflects the change in the median age for marriage. In 1960, the median age for men to marry was twenty-two and twenty for women. As of 2014, that number had grown to twenty-nine years old for men and twenty-seven years old for women.[20] There are a number of reasons why young adults may be postponing marriage: they want to travel and see the world, gain further training and postgraduate work, attend medical school, join the military, establish their careers, enjoy the freedom of singleness, grieve the loss of a spouse, focus on raising their children, are unable to find a suitable mate, or cohabitate before making a commitment to marry.[21] Whereas in the past, most single people longed to marry, more young men and women intentionally choose to remain single well into their thirties and beyond with a growing number preferring to never marry. In addition, about a quarter (twenty-four percent) of never-married young adults ages 25–34 live with a partner.[22]

> "It is time the church sees the 'singling of America' as an *opportunity to be seized* rather than only a problem to be solved!"[23]
> —Dennis Franck

In addition, many young adults delay marriage for financial reasons. This is supported by the fact that in 2014, 31 percent of young adults ages 18–35 were living with their parents. This is up significantly from 1960 when 20 percent of this age group lived with their parents.[24] Many young men and women leave college with high debt and often find it difficult to secure a decent paying job. They choose to live with their parents in order to lower their expenses until they can be financially independent. Until that time, they normally do not seek marriage.[25]

Statistically, as mentioned previously, the vast majority of those in their twenties have never been married. But another shift has occurred with more and more people in their thirties and forties having never married. Whereas in the past it was expected young adults would marry in their early twenties, many of these young men and women are now content in their singleness, enjoying their independent lifestyle and in no hurry to marry.[26] However, as they move into their thirties, many of their attitudes change, particularly for women since many women want to marry and have children and they realize their biological clock is winding down. This is not a factor for men, so we see more and more men delaying marriage well into their thirties and even into their forties.

Young adults in their twenties are more inclined to describe themselves as "not yet married" rather than "single." But once men and women enter and move through their thirties, their perspective changes as the reality sets in that they are still single. For many of them who want to marry, this can be a time of crisis. Panic begins to set in, accompanied by the fear that they might never marry. Longtime friendships can no longer substitute for the intimate connection marriage offers, and many of their friends have married. Some older singles experience deeper feelings of loneliness and fear, more occurrences of depression, and a sense of desperation to find a husband or wife and settle down to raise a family.[27]

Older singles who have never married represent a challenging demographic for the church, yet there exists a great opportunity to help these men and women find their deepest need for love and acceptance in Christ alone. Elizabeth Woodson, the Singles Minister at Oak Cliff Bible Fellowship in Dallas, Texas emphasizes discipleship and the need for singles to realize first and foremost their call to follow Christ and to find their greatest fulfillment and security in their relationship with Jesus.[28] She explains, "Marriage is part of the conversation but not THE conversation." It is fine to acknowledge and desire marriage, but it should never be the source of life for

a person.[29] The most important lesson a single person needs to learn and remember, no matter his or her age, is that fulfillment and completeness will never be found in a marriage partner. We were created to enjoy an eternal relationship with God and he alone is adequate to meet our deep needs for unconditional love, acceptance, value, and security.

Divorced

Since 24 percent of the American adult population identified as divorced in 2014, they represent the second largest group of single adults. The vast majority of those divorced are over the age of thirty-five and more women (57 percent) than men (43 percent) are divorced.[30] Many have children, some do not. Singleness as a result of divorce varies greatly depending on whether or not children are involved. As difficult and painful as divorce is, most will say divorce is much easier and less complicated when the couple has not had children together. When couples share children, custody and child support issues can often be very complex and painful with the children often caught in the middle of the conflict between parents.

Thankfully, many churches offer divorce care ministries. A good example is Watermark Community Church in Dallas, Texas.[31] Under the leadership of Lonnie Smith (Director of Single Adults) and Lindsey Lauderdale (Single Adults Coordinator), they offer ministries to adults, teens, and kids who have been impacted by divorce. Their adult divorce ministry meets one night a week for thirteen weeks. It is available to the wider community, and 50 percent of the men and women who take part in the program are either from other churches or unchurched. Leaders address topics such as depression, loneliness, finances, sexuality issues, forgiveness, and reconciliation along with testimonies of those who have gone through the program. Men and women are placed in separate small groups for the purpose of more personal discussions. The DivorceCare curriculum has a strong emphasis on biblical teaching related to marriage, divorce, and remarriage.[32] The goal is spiritual growth. As Smith explained, "DivorceCare is not a destination ministry but one more step to grow spiritually."[33]

Whenever a person or couple contemplating divorce contact a church for help, the first step in caring for them should always be to offer counseling or recommend a Christian counselor with the hope of reconciliation. If the couple decides to move forward with the divorce, support groups are designed to help men and women process their pain, answer questions, address fears, provide emotional support, offer financial and legal advice, and guide in the transition from marriage to singleness.[34]

If a church has the staff and budget available, it should also consider offering support to children and teens impacted by divorce. Elizabeth Oates, a graduate of Dallas Seminary, offers help for hurting children in her book, *Dealing with Divorce: Finding Direction When Your Parents Split Up.*[35] She provides participant and leader guides as a resource for parents and churches to "walk teens through various issues of their parents' divorce, including God's feelings about divorce, reasons why parents divorce, communicating with parents, and living with stepfamilies."[36]

With a fourth of our population experiencing the sorrow and heartache of divorce, churches must consider what kind of support they can offer to these men and women. Many feel like they now have a scarlet letter representing guilt, shame, and failure. Divorced adults need to know and experience God's love and forgiveness. They need support and guidance to move into their new life of singleness and discover how God desires to redeem their pain, restore their life, and set them on a new path of spiritual growth and a God-honoring life.

> "Divorce is much more than two people parting. I had plans for my family that stretched out for the next forty years. Suddenly I was separated from my wife, her family, her friends, my friends, my lifestyle, and my future. You don't divorce a person; you *lose a life.*"[37]
> —Mike Klumpp

Widowed

Traditionally in a wedding ceremony, the bride and groom pledge their commitment and love to one another "til death do us part." Jesus taught, "at the resurrection people will neither marry nor be given in marriage; they will be like angels in heaven" (Matt. 22:30). God designed marriage only for life on earth. Unless a couple divorces, one or the other of them will eventually experience the loss of their spouse and statistics confirm that most wives will outlive their husbands.[38] As noted earlier in this chapter, widows and widowers account for 14 percent of the adult population in America. This number continues to grow as life expectancy increases.

These truths echoed deep in my heart when I was told at the age of forty-one my husband had been in a fatal car accident. The word "fatal" kept ringing in my ears as the reality of death and separation invaded my life and suddenly plunged me into widowhood and single parenting. I have remained a widow for over twenty-five years, having chosen to follow Paul's advice in 1 Corinthians 7:39–40,

> A woman is bound to her husband as long as he lives. But if her husband dies, she is free to marry anyone she wishes, but he must belong to the Lord. In my judgment, she is happier if she stays as she is—and I think that I too have the Spirit of God.

The loss of a spouse can come unexpectedly as in my case, or be anticipated as a result of a terminal health issue. In either case, the loss of a spouse involves a wide variety of emotions that include deep grief, sadness, fear, anxiety, anger, hopelessness, confusion, worry, depression, despair, and loneliness.[39]

Many larger churches will offer a grief recovery ministry. Often the ministry falls under the oversight of the pastoral care ministry rather than the singles ministry. Normally this ministry will address all kinds of losses: death of a child or parent, loss of a job, infertility, empty nest issues, cancer recovery, as well as the death of a spouse. Grief is not a journey meant to be walked alone. If a church is too small to offer a means to support widows or widowers, then they should be prepared to suggest other churches in the community that are equipped to support and assist men and women who have lost their spouse.

From my observation, it is more common for older widows and widowers to want to stay connected with their married friends or participate in a senior adult ministry if one is offered in their church.[40] Younger widows and widowers are more inclined to want to participate in a singles ministry where they can enjoy the company of peers and have some of their social and spiritual needs met.

Single Parents

In 1970, one ninth of households were led by a single parent. By 2000, that percentage had grown to one third of households.[41] God's ideal design for children consists of a mother and father who love one another and are committed to teach their children how to love God and follow his commandments. When a father or mother is missing from a home, the challenges of child-rearing can be overwhelming.

Sue Birdseye found herself as a single mother after a very painful divorce. She offers this description of single parenting in her book *When Happily Ever After Shatters:*

> Although sometimes I am physically tired and emotionally drained, I believe the mental fatigue is what really gets to me. I get weary of trying to figure out all the details, of having to make all the decisions, and of second-guessing myself. It is exhausting.[42]

Because of these challenges, many single parents who desperately want and need to be involved in singles ministry cannot find the time.

Single parenting can occur in a number of ways: an out-of-wedlock pregnancy, divorce, adoption of a child by a single person, or death of a spouse. Although the circumstances are quite different, many of the challenges and needs of the single parent are the same. They often experience financial pressures, lack of personal space, feeling overwhelmed with their children's emotional issues, little time for peer friendships, exhaustion, loneliness, and their own personal feelings of grief, guilt, fear, anger, and anxiety. The fracture of their family can best be addressed through the love and support of the family of God within a local church setting.[43] Often their needs are met through the children's and youth ministry of a church since a single mother or father will usually prioritize their children over their own personal needs. The singles ministry can best meet the needs of single parents if they on occasion offer "family-friendly" events that allow single parents to bring their children.[44]

When my husband died, our daughter was out of school and working in another city, but our boys were fourteen and eleven. Each of the three of them responded to the loss of their dad in different ways and challenged me to find the balance between addressing my own grief while offering them the support and love they needed. Thankfully, the men in our church as well as those in our small town stepped in to father my sons and helped me meet the unique needs of teenage boys. I was also blessed and encouraged by family-oriented activities in the church or when a family included my children for a meal and fellowship in their home. I rarely had time to take part in activities in the evenings or on weekends because of the needs of my children. Most single parents face these same challenges.

Although mothers head up a majority of single parent households, a growing number of fathers are gaining full responsibility of their children. In 1960, about 14 percent of single parent households were headed by fathers. By 2011, almost one-quarter (24 percent) were.[45] Resources for single dads are scarce, but Mike Klumpp offers a comprehensive look at the difficulties faced by a single father, such as anger management, facing emotional pain, parenting a daughter versus a son, applying discipline as well as tenderness, swallowing pride and asking for help, and developing a committed, dependent relationship with God.

Klumpp sums up the role of a single parent (mother or father) well when he says,

> I view it a privilege that I am trusted with the lives of my children. When cabin fever sets in and I'd rather be out with the guys, I remind myself that the lives of my children are of utmost importance. They will someday grow up, and that's when I'll pursue my hobbies and other diversions. For now, however, I have a higher priority—the welfare of my kids.[46]

A single mother or father may on occasion be able to slip away from their parenting responsibilities and attend a singles event, but any singles ministry that wants to minister to the needs of single parents will have to design a few activities that include children. When they do, single parents will enjoy the opportunity to get better acquainted with other men and women who understand and live with the daily issues of single parenting.

> "I feel so obviously single when it comes to parenting and I feel so obviously a parent when it comes to being single. The rhythm of my life revolves around parenting so it is a unique type of singleness."
> —Kristen Jackson,
> Dallas Seminary student

A Rationale for Ministry with Single Adults

Dennis Franck has done extensive ministry with singles. He reports, "Over the course of history single adults have only comprised 2 to 3 percent of the adult population. Marriage was the norm and the expectation of almost all adults. It has only been since the early 1900s that the awareness of single adults has increased and attitudes have changed."[47] For the first time in American history the adult population has more single adults than married adults.[48] During the 1970s and 1980s, this steady increase of single adults became more and more apparent and churches began to investigate ways to address the unique needs of single adults. "By the late 1980s singles ministries had become a staple at many churches."[49]

This significant population shift impacts churches and yet "according to a recent Barna study, less than a quarter of active churchgoers are single (twenty-three percent). Comparing the national average, the 2014 U.S. census estimates that more than half of Americans (fifty-four percent) between the ages of 18–49 are single (either never married or divorced)."[50] This reveals a large number of single adults who need to know Jesus Christ as their Savior or grow in their relationship

with God. Their lives are very different from those who are married. Singles will benefit greatly when a church prioritizes their unique needs and also create ways for single men and women to integrate into the life of the church and find opportunities to serve the needs of others.

> "A successful single is one who maximizes his or her singlehood for the betterment of others, the advancement of God's kingdom, and the manifestation of his glory."[51]
> —Tony Evans

Developing a Single Adults Ministry

As the singles population grows in number, churches everywhere are faced with the challenge to discover how to best minister to and involve singles into their local body of believers. Four different types emerge related to ministry to singles. One advocates for the establishment of a separate ministry to singles to address their unique needs in the context of big events and small groups which I call a "Singles Only" ministry. A second type, "Diversified Single Adult Ministry," holds to creating two separate groups made up of younger and older singles within the singles ministry to address the broad span of ages now in our singles population. The third type represents the belief that there should not be a separate, distinct ministry to singles, but rather they should be included with the married adults. This has the title of "No Singles Ministry." A fourth type integrates the first three types and can be described as an "Integrated Singles Ministry." It calls for a specifically designed ministry for single adults that addresses both their unique social and personal needs while also encouraging single adults to involve themselves in any of a number of other ministries in the church such as intergenerational small groups, service opportunities, and leadership roles. Most churches will reflect one of these four types or a combination of them.

Single Adults Only Ministry

The first singles ministries tended to separate single adults from other adult ministries by offering social events, Bible studies, small groups, and service projects that would exclusively appeal to them and allow them to connect with other singles. As the single adult population grew, singles in the church began to feel marginalized within a separate ministry rather than be accepted as an integral part of the total church family. At the same time, the makeup of the single population was radically changing. The median age of marriage (the lower number for women and the higher number for men) had shifted from approximately 20–22 in 1960 to 24–26 in 1990 to 27–29 in 2015.[52] In addition, 20 percent of eighteen- to twenty-nine-year-olds were married in 2010, compared with 59 percent in 1960.[53] This translates into a demographic shift where most of your young adults between the ages of eighteen to twenty-nine are unmarried and many more of those age thirty to fifty are now also single. No longer were single adults satisfied to have a ministry focused only on singleness since the needs, interests, and desires of single adults between the ages of eighteen to fifty vastly differ.

Diversified Single Adult Ministry

One solution to the growing singles population that surfaced involved offering two tiers within the singles ministry: one for young singles in their twenties and one for older singles, ages thirty to fifty. The majority of the younger singles have never married whereas the older singles are much more diverse: never married, divorced, widowed, and single parents. This two-tier option for singles takes into consideration the vast differences in the needs and interests of a twenty-two-year-old versus a forty-five-year-old. This type of ministry still leaves many singles feeling separate and "different" from married adults and marginalized within the church body as a whole. Often churches that encourage singles to primarily find their needs met in the company of other singles fail to emphasize the personal value of singles and the contribution they can make within the broader church family.

"Thirty-somethings across the nation are missing in our churches (single and married). Singles who live alone, have a job, a home are less likely to feel they need Christ in their lives. Churches have done such a great job of reaching older singles as well as young singles, but somehow, the ones in between are missing. Thirty-somethings to maybe mid-40s are a special group of single adults. They have the most flexible use of their time and money due to most of them having never been married. They have the possibility of being the hardest workers for our churches, for our missions programs, yet, they are least reached."[54]

—Kris Swiatocho

No Single Adult Ministry

North Coast Calvary Chapel in Carlsbad, California is one example of a church which chose to eliminate their singles ministry.[55] In 2005 they hired Adam Stadtmiller to "explore ministering to thirty-to-fortysomething adults in an integrated construct of married and singles."[56] He created a young adult ministry for singles and marrieds who are in their twenties. Stadtmiller had surveyed many churches and found that their initial large single ministries many years ago had dwindled in number considerably to a point where many churches no longer could justify a designated singles pastor. "In the end, singles ministry had proven unsustainable for all of these churches, even though there was still an often-vocal singles contingent clamoring for a ministry they could call their own."[57] Some churches have found this model of only offering different types of adult ministries that include both singles and marrieds to most effectively provide opportunities for singles to grow spiritually and be involved in a local church.

Integrated Single Adult Ministry

Through my reading, research, and interviews with men and women who either oversee ministry to singles or are singles who participate in their local churches, I have come to the conclusion that the best way to reach singles involves offering both a designated singles ministry and adult ministries that include both singles and marrieds. This allows for singles to have a choice based on their individual needs and preferences.

Often singles will involve themselves in multiple ministries, some that are single only and others that allow them the opportunity to enjoy intergenerational gatherings that include both singles and marrieds. Today singles are a diverse group. Some have on the forefront of their minds to be married and so prefer to primarily interact with other singles. Some desire to be married, but are content in their singleness and find enjoyment with both singles and marrieds. Others have become comfortable and satisfied as a single adult and want to fully engage in many of the various ministries within a church and prefer not to participate in singles-only groups. A local church is wise to provide options and let singles choose where they want to participate as well as serve.

Two good examples of an integrated type of singles ministry can be found at Watermark Community Church and Oak Cliff Bible Fellowship, both in the Dallas, Texas area. Each of these churches offers large events for singles to gather together as well as small group and service opportunities to enhance personal spiritual growth in the context of community. Watermark has recently launched a specific ministry focus for single adults in their thirties through fifties in addition to their weekly young adult gathering. In addition, their hope is to build relationships among the singles and encourage them to also take part in other aspects of church life.

Designing a Single Adult Ministry

Church size and budget often determine the feasibility of a singles ministry. A small church of under a few hundred members most likely will not offer a separate ministry for single people. Most small churches have very few single adults in their twenties and thirties. Singles in this age group tend to gravitate to larger churches where there are more single adults unless they live in a small town where there are no large churches.

In small churches, single adults tend to integrate into intergenerational adult ministries and enjoy the sense of "family" that smaller churches offer. The church my late husband and I attended in the small town of Borger, Texas near Amarillo had a membership of about 150–200. We had very few younger singles and a number of older singles, primarily widows. Everyone came together on Sundays, as well as to weekly small groups and Bible studies. We were more like a family with the older men and women functioning as godly fathers and mothers and younger men and women as brothers and sisters. It was closer to what the early church would have looked like and was a wonderful environment not only for the adults but also for the many children in our congregation.

The best-case scenario for a successful ministry to single adults requires a full-time or part-time salaried minister to direct the ministry along with a committed lay leadership. The following presents a number of key components to consider when establishing a singles ministry.

> "A specific ministry for single adults can provide an atmosphere of acceptance and openness where people can discover others with the same hopes, hurts, issues, and interests, and where they can establish relationships and friendships in a Christian context."[58]
> —Dennis Franck

Establishing a Singles Ministry

When you consider the development of a singles ministry, a number of key components must be considered. You need to involve the pastoral leadership, recruit and train lay leadership, and design large and small group gatherings.

Pastoral Leadership Support

As with any successful ministry, the entire pastoral staff and core lay leaders must offer full support, both through the budget and with verbal acknowledgement of the value and contribution of singles. This can be demonstrated most significantly by the senior pastor who regularly includes references to singles in his Sunday morning messages rather than exclusively mentioning marriage and family, promotes single activities from the pulpit, occasionally attends singles' events, acknowledges the contribution singles make through volunteering in a variety of church ministries, and thanking them privately and/or publicly for their participation in service and missions projects.

Other church leaders should also show their support for the single members of their congregation. They can reflect this by inviting singles to hold leadership roles in various church ministries, selecting a single as a member of the governing board, befriending singles, and inviting singles into their homes for meals, fellowship, Bible study, intergenerational small group gatherings, and one-to-one mentoring. Because many single men and women do not have their own families, the local church needs to embrace them as a significant and valuable part of the family of God. Paul states it best when he advises Timothy, "Do not rebuke an older man harshly, but exhort him as if he were your father. Treat younger men as brothers, older women as mothers, and younger women as sisters, with absolute purity" (1 Tim. 5:1–2). God designed the church to function as the family of God with marrieds and singles along with children all contributing and relating to one another equally as family members.

Recruiting and Training Leaders

The leadership of a singles ministry determines the success of the ministry. The team should consist of men and women who are either single or married couples who understand the unique needs of single adults. If the church is large enough, the leader of the singles ministry should be paid and included on the pastoral team. For smaller churches with limited budget and a good number of single adults, hopefully someone within that singles community will volunteer their time to oversee the ministry.

Should the lead pastor of the singles ministry be a man or a woman? Dennis Franck *offers* an insightful observation: "Men will usually attract both genders better than women, especially for groups targeting people thirty-five years of age and older. This is because men born in the 1960s or earlier were raised to be more comfortable with men than women in visible leadership positions."[59] This does not mean women are less competent or gifted to lead a singles ministry, but acknowledges most men tend to more readily follow a man and be influenced by a male role model. This being said, a singles ministry can be led by a woman, but it is critical the broader lay leadership team consists of both men and women. The ideal scenario would be a man and woman co-leading a singles ministry if a church is large enough to budget for two people or a married couple where both the husband and wife are engaged in the ministry.

Although the leader holds a key role, lay volunteers are also vital to ministry health. An enthusiastic team determines the level of outreach and participation from other singles. This lead team needs training and should share in important ministry decisions and the oversight of the ministry. Most singles ministries will offer both large and small gatherings.

> "Maturing, passionate leadership is the main ingredient for ministry to single adults and to growing an effective ministry that reaches and retains people. The wise pastor/director will invest much time into recruiting and developing leaders to assist in ministry to single adults."[60]
> —Dennis Franck

Large Group Gatherings

Single adults should be encouraged to participate in various aspects of the wider church life, but they also have unique social needs that are different from their married friends. Many Christian singles want to socialize with other Christians in a biblically focused setting. Some churches offer monthly social gatherings, others plan fellowship events every two or three months. The purpose is to provide a fun environment for singles to meet and enjoy time together. Often there will be annual one-day conferences or weekend retreats. These bigger events offer the opportunity to invite their unsaved friends.

Some churches hold a weekly large group time for the purpose of worship, teaching, and fellowship to target young adults. For example, "The Porch" is sponsored by Watermark

Community Church in Dallas, Texas on Tuesday nights and Grace Bible Church in College Station, Texas offers "Junction" on Thursday nights.[61] Biblical messages focus on topics relevant to young adults and singles with the purpose of challenging men and women in their Christian walk or sharing the gospel with unbelievers. These large group gatherings can draw singles from throughout a city, much like a Sunday morning worship service, but real spiritual growth rarely can happen until people connect in smaller group gatherings.

Small Group Gatherings

The heart of any singles ministry rests in small group gatherings that meet regularly, weekly or twice a month. These are often either women's, men's, or coed groups that meet to grow spiritually, often studying the Bible together. They also enjoy connecting at a deeper, more intimate level, sharing openly, praying and supporting one another, and sharing fellowship and meals together. In addition, the groups have an outward focus through service projects.[62]

Topics related to sexuality need to be addressed both in large group settings in a more general way and in small groups where more intimate conversations and specific personal questions can be discussed. In the final section of this chapter, a few insights are offered related to the unique relational and sexual issues singles face in relationships.

Sexuality Issues for Singles

Albert Hsu offers a detailed look at the history of singleness in his book *Singles at the Crossroads*. He summarizes the diverse perspectives related to singleness:

The history of Christian singleness has been that of a pendulum swinging back and forth between two equally unhealthy extremes. Jewish society elevated marriage and family to the extent that it marginalized the single person. Religious leaders were always married. Then New Testament Christian teaching raised singleness to an equal level with marriage. Then the early church, influenced by Gnosticism, advocated an asceticism that taught singleness as the better way. Only worldly people married, while holy monks and nuns forsook marriage. In reaction to the abuses of enforced chastity, the Protestant Reformers rejected clerical celibacy and instead elevated marriage and family over singleness.... Just as the Catholic doctrine of clerical celibacy incorrectly overemphasized celibacy as the Gnostics did, so also does Protestant "family theology" incorrectly overemphasize marriage and family as the Jews did.[63]

As we move into the early decades of the twenty-first century, it is time to stop the pendulum swings and settle back into the New Testament teaching of the equal value of marriage and singleness. But, I see one major obstacle that has impeded single adults from faithfully honoring God in their sexuality. Traditionally throughout history, men and women married in the early years after puberty so sexual abstinence was only for a short time. This is not to say no young men and women entered into sexual relationships outside of marriage, but the broader population married at a young age and thus avoided an extended time of sexual temptations.

Today, the vast majority of children do not grow up working side-by-side with their parents teaching and training them in the knowledge and skills required for adulthood. Instead, most young people spend years in an educational setting preparing for adulthood. We describe this time between puberty and adulthood as "adolescence"[64] and the time seems to be growing longer and longer as young adults delay marriage.[65]

During this ten to fifteen year span, young people are expected to remain sexually pure in the midst of a very oversexualized society that constantly exposes children and single adults to sex of every kind through TV, media, movies, the Internet, advertisements, pornography, and social media. Beyond just the exposure, the message of our culture promotes and encourages sexual experimentation of every kind. In the midst of this current time, people have "exchanged the truth of God for a lie, and worshiped and served the creature rather than the Creator" (Rom. 1:25). Christian singles face the temptation to give into their fleshly tendencies and struggle to practice self-control and honor God with their bodies.

It is impossible to provide a relevant ministry to singles without addressing the sexual challenges that face young adults. Sexuality should not be the overriding message of a singles ministry, but various topics related to sex and God's plan within the context of marriage need to be included both in large and small group gatherings. *Soul Virgins* by Doug Roseau and Michael Todd offers one of the best resources I have found to address the complex issues surrounding singleness, dating, and sexual temptation. They explain the purpose of the book in this way:

Our heart's desire is to help Christian single adults sort through and find better answers about their sexuality—to not just repress or tolerate their sexuality but to redefine and celebrate it! ... We desire to help you create a theology that goes beyond mere "do's and don'ts," providing practical explanations of why and how to wait within the Creator's awesome plan. We want to take you on a journey of growth and healing as you learn to experience our true sexual identity in the context of wonderfully intimate relationships that are both healthy and godly.[66]

Many books for singles focus on how to find a marriage partner and subtly or not so subtly communicate the incorrect notion that singleness is a "temporary time" before the long-awaited and anticipated reality of marriage. Instead, single adults need to settle into and embrace their time of singleness as a gift from God and learn ways to successfully navigate through the landmines associated with sexuality and Christian relationships.

> "Jesus our Lord ... never married or experienced sexual intercourse. Yet he was and is the perfect model of humanness. His example teaches us that it is perfectly possible to be single, celibate and human at the same time!"[67]
>
> —John Stott

Conclusion

Single adults now make up just over half of the American adult population. Some have never married, others are divorced or widowed, and many are single parents. It is time for our churches to acknowledge, affirm, and address the unique needs of these men and women who are made in God's image and who are of equal value and worth as those who are married. Sunday morning messages need to include illustrations and examples of both married and single people. Singles should be part of governing boards, church committees, pastoral staffs, and lay leadership in order to tap into the significant contribution and perspective offered by singles. Although single men and women want to integrate into many different aspects of the church, they also have social and relational needs that can best be addressed by specific singles ministries especially in larger churches. Most importantly, singles need to be encouraged to see their season of life as an opportunity to live their lives fully devoted to God.

Discussion Questions

1. What is a biblical view of singleness? Support your answer with Scripture.

2. What has been your experience as a single adult? What challenges did you face?

3. What opportunities accompany the single lifestyle that married people cannot enjoy?

4. How can a church affirm and encourage single adults? Discuss ways your church could reach singles in your community.

5. The author suggests four different types of singles ministries. Which of these models do you think might work best where you worship? Why?

Resources for Further Study

Birdseye, Sue. *When Happily Ever After Shatters: Seeing God in the Midst of Divorce and Single Parenting.* Carol Stream, IL: Tyndale House, 2013.

Danylak, Barry. *Redeeming Singleness: How the Storyline of Scripture Affirms the Single Life.* Wheaton, IL: Crossway, 2010.

Evans, Tony. *Living Single.* Chicago: Moody, 2013.

Franck, Dennis. *Reaching Single Adults: An Essential Guide for Ministry.* Grand Rapids: Baker Books, 2007.

Gorman, Julie A. *Community That Is Christian: A Handbook on Small Groups,* 2d ed. Grand Rapids: Baker, 2002.

Klumpp, Mike. *The Single Dad's Survival Guide: How to Succeed as a One-Man Parenting Team.* Colorado Springs: WaterBrook Press, 2003.

Leman, Kevin. *Single Parenting That Works: Six Keys to Raising Happy, Healthy Children in a Single-Parent Home.* Carol Stream, IL: Tyndale House, 2006.

Marshall, Jennifer. *Now and Not Yet: Making Sense of Single Life in the Twenty-First Century.* Colorado Springs: Multnomah Books, 2007.

Rosenau, Doug and Michael Todd Wilson. *Soul Virgins: Redefining Single Sexuality.* Grand Rapids: Baker Books, 2006.

Swiatocho, Kris and Dennis Franck. *Everyone Knows a Single Adult: The FAQs of Single Adult Ministry.* Garner, NC: Yes! Marketing and Design Services, 2015.

Yarbrough, Julie. *Inside the Broken Heart: Grief Understanding for Widows and Widowers.* Nashville: Abingdon Press, 2012.

Author Bio

As Adjunct Professor and Women's Adviser in the Educational Ministries and Leadership Department at DTS, Dr. Joye Baker advises and mentors women students, teaches Educational Ministry courses, serves on the staff of the DTS Spiritual Formation small groups program, and team-teaches in the Doctor of Ministry Women in Ministry cohort. She has trained women in Russia and speaks at various women's events. She provides leader training, teaches, and leads a small group in the weekly women's Bible study at her local church in Dallas. She was widowed at a young age and has a daughter and two sons, one daughter-in-law, and two grandsons.

Endnotes

1. V.M. Sinton, "Singleness," in *New Dictionary of Christian Ethics & Pastoral Theology,* eds. David J. Atkinson, David F. Field, Arthur Holmes and Oliver O'Donovan (Downers Grove, IL: InterVarsity, 1995), 791.

2. Barry Danylak, *Redeeming Singleness: How the Storyline of Scripture Affirms the Single Life* (Wheaton, IL: Crossway, 2010), 162.

3. Peter Naylor, *A Study Commentary on 1 Corinthians* (New York: Evangelical Press, 2004), 181.

4. Doug Rosenau and Michael Todd Wilson, *Soul Virgins: Redefining Single Sexuality* (Grand Rapids: Baker Books, 2006), 245.

5. Dr. Abraham Kuruvilla, interview by Kelley Mathews, *Kindred Spirit,* Spring/Summer 2015, 6.

6. Jennifer Marshall, *Now and Not Yet: Making Sense of Single Life in the Twenty-First Century* (Colorado Springs: Multnomah, 2007), 103–125.

7. Ibid., 52.

8. Ibid., 116.

9. Albert Y. Hsu, *Singles at the Crossroads: A Fresh Perspective on Christian Singleness* (Downers Grove, IL: Inter-Varsity, 1997), 15.

10. Ibid., 14.

11. Single Adult Ministry of the UPCI, "Single Adult Statistics," http://www.upcisam.com/about/singles-statistics/ (accessed December 10, 2016).

12. Ibid."

13. Ibid.

14. Hsu, *Singles at the Crossroads,* 14.

15. Pew Research Center, "The Decline of Marriage and the Rise of New Families: Marriage," *Social and Demographic Trends*, November 18, 2010, http://www.pewsocialtrends.org/ 2010/11/18/iii-marriage/ (accessed December 4, 2016).

16. Ibid.

17. Pew Research Center, "Record Share of Americans Have Never Married," *Social and Demographic Trends,* September 24, 2014, http://www.pewsocialtrends.org/ 2014/09/24/record-share-of-americans-have-never-married/ (accessed December 4, 2016).

18. Supreme Court of the United States, "Obergefell et al. V. Hodges, Director, Ohio Department Of Health," June 25, 2015, https://www.supremecourt.gov/opinions/ 14pdf/14-556_3204.pdf (accessed December 4, 2016).

19. Pew Research Center, "Millennials in Adulthood," *Social and Demographic Trends,* March 7, 2014, http://www.pewsocialtrends.org/2014/03/07/millennials-in-adulthood/ (accessed December 10, 2016).

20. Stephanie Hanes, "Singles Nation: Why So Many Americans Are Unmarried," *Christian Science Monitor,* June 14, 2015, http://www.csmonitor.com/USA/Society/ 2015/0614/Singles-nation-Why-so-many-Americans-are-unmarried (accessed December 4, 2016).

21. June Hunt, *Singleness: How to Be Single and Satisfied* (Torrence, CA: Rose Publishing, 2014), 29.

22. Pew Research Center, "Record Share of Americans Have Never Married."

23. Dennis Franck, *Reaching Single Adults: An Essential Guide for Ministry* (Grand Rapids: Baker, 2007), 54.

24.   Pew Research Center, "For First Time in Modern Era, Living With Parents Edges Out Other Living Arrangements for 18- to 34-Year-Olds," *Social and Demographic Trends*," May 24, 2016, http://www.pewsocialtrends.org/2016/05/24/for-first-time-in-modern-era-living-with-parents-edges-out-other-living-arrangements-for-18-to-34-year-olds/ (accessed December 4, 2016).

25.   For a more detailed look at young adults, see the chapter "In Between: Adolescents" by Jay Sedwick.

26.   Hanes, "Singles Nation."

27.   Hunt, *Singleness*, 15–21.

28.   More information about Oak Cliff Bible Fellowship can be found at www.ocbfchurch.org.

29.   Elizabeth Woodson. 2016. Interview by author. Oak Cliff Bible Fellowship, Dallas, Texas. August 12, 2016.

30.   Pew Research Center, "The Differing Demographic Profiles of First-Time Married, Remarried and Divorced Adults," *Social and Demographic Trends*, November 14, 2014, http://www.pewsocialtrends.org/2014/11/14/chapter-3-the-differing-demographic-profiles-of-first-time-married-remarried-and-divorced-adults/ (accessed December 11, 2016).

31.   More information about Watermark Community Church can be found at www.watermark.org.

32.   More information about DivorceCare can be found at www.divorcecare.org.

33.   Lonnie Smith and Lindsey Lauderdale. 2016. Interview by author. Watermark Community Church, Dallas, Texas. September 8, 2016.

34.   Smith and Lauderdale.

35.   Elizabeth Oates, *Dealing with Divorce: Finding Direction When Your Parents Split Up* (Grand Rapids: Zondervan, 2009).

36.   Elizabeth Oates, "Books," http://www.elizabethoates.com/books/.

37.   Mike Klumpp, *The Single Dad's Survival Guide: How to Succeed as a One-Man Parenting Team* (Colorado Springs: WaterBrook, 2003), 12.

38.   Julie Yarbrough, *Inside the Broken Heart: Grief Understanding for Widows and Widowers* (Nashville: Abingdon Press, 2012), 75.

39.   Ibid., 10.

40.   For more information related to the unique needs of older adults, see the chapter "Forgotten: Senior Adults" by Sabrina Hopson.

41.   Franck, *Reaching Single Adults*, 41.

42.   Sue Birdseye, *When Happily Ever After Shatters: Seeing God in the Midst of Divorce and Single Parenting* (Carol Stream, IL: Tyndale House, 2013), 133.

43.   Kevin Leman, *Single Parenting That Works* (Carol Stream, IL: Tyndale House, 2006).

44.   Kristin Jenn. 2016. Interview by author. Dallas Theological Seminary. April 28, 2016.

45.   Pew Research Center, "The Rise of Single Fathers," *Social and Demographic Trends*, July 2, 2013, http://www.pewsocialtrends.org/2013/07/02/the-rise-of-single-fathers/ (accessed December 4, 2016).

46.   Mike Klumpp, *The Single Dad's Survival Guide,* 118.

47.   Franck, *Reaching Single Adults,* 36–37.

48.   Single Adult Ministry of the UPCI, "Single Adult Statistics."

49.   Adam Stadtmiller, "Whatever Happened to Singles Ministry?" *Leadership Journal*, (Summer 2012): 77–80.

50.   Joyce Chiu, "A Single-Minded Church," *Barna Trends 2017* (Grand Rapids: Baker Books, 2016), 163.

51.   Evans, *Living Single*, 51.

52.   Marni Feuerman, "Estimated Median Age of First Marriage by Gender: 1890 to 2015," About.com. October 2, 2016, http://marriage.about.com/od/statistics /a/medianage.htm (accessed December 6, 2016).

53.   Ibid.

54.   Swiatocho, *Everyone Knows a Single Adult,* 46.

55.   More information on North Coast Calvary Chapel can be found at www.northcoastcalvary.org.

56.   Stadtmiller, "Whatever Happened to Singles Ministry?" 78.

57.   Ibid.

58.   Franck, *Reaching Single Adults*, 79.

59.   Ibid., 179–180.

60.   Ibid., 151.

61.   More information about Grace Bible Church can be found at www.grace-bible.org.

62.   More specific details on the structure and implementation of these small groups can be found in the chapter "Facilitating Transformative Small Groups" by Joye Baker.

63.   Hsu, *Singles at the Crossroads*, 46.

64.   Hanes, "Singles Nation."

65.   For a more detailed look at young adults, see the chapter "In Between: Adolescents" by Jay Sedwick.

66.   Rosenau and Wilson, *Soul Virgins*, 20–21.

67.   John Stott, an interview with Hsu, *Singles at the Crossroads,* 179.

Chapter 12
FORGOTTEN: SENIOR ADULTS

Sabrina Hopson

Even when I am old and gray, do not forsake me, my God, till I declare your power to the next generation, your mighty acts to all who are to come.

—Psalm 71:18

SEVERAL YEARS AGO, I joined a small close-knit church whose primary membership consisted of several family groups. Many of these members were descendants of the original church founders. Over the course of a few years, I had the opportunity to observe the matriarch of one of those families, Sister Dorothy Drew. She was an older woman, stout and strong in stature. Every Sunday, you could count on her to enter the sanctuary impeccably dressed in a sequin-embellished suit, with a large matching hat, and heels. Even when I could not see her, her incredibly robust voice and hearty laughter immediately gave her identity and location away. An active member of the church, she served as a deaconess, a greeter, and in the church choir. She was the embodiment of hospitality and passionate about making sure the needs of her family, friends, and church family were met.

Our first verbal encounter occurred as she was planning the menu for a meal we were preparing for a grieving family. I asked her what she needed me to bring. She laughed and said, "You young people don't know how to do anything." Finally, she relented and said I should just bring some cucumbers. I smiled as I walked away, as I was known to be a pretty good cook. Our paths diverged at this point.

As I became more heavily involved in the education ministry of the church, I simply failed to notice that her presence was not as big as it had once been. It was during this time that I entered seminary, following God's call to better myself in teaching his Word. I was also teaching a weekly women's Bible study class, directing my church's literacy ministry, and singing in the church choir. Once again, I didn't realize that she was not attending church and that her name was regularly listed on the sick and shut-in list. During the time I was oblivious to her absence, God was preparing me to minister to her and preparing her to accept and receive my care. During this time my women's class rolls grew, primarily with older women. It was then that I realized that Sister Drew was missing. Sadly, I discovered that she was now completely bedridden and unable to do much on her own. Knowing her love for the church, I decided that since she couldn't come to class at church, I would take the class directly to her at her home.

When I arrived, her husband let me in and ushered me to her bedroom at the back of the house. He put a chair beside her bed and then left us alone. She apologized for her condition, the clutter in the small room, and asked if I was okay. I assured her that everything was fine; and we chatted a bit about the church and our families. Finally, I asked her to consider becoming part of my women's class, to study the women in the Bible. Initially hesitant, she finally agreed. I left her the class workbook and the assignment for the week and told her I'd see her next week during my lunch hour. Given her condition, I honestly expected our time together to be more like friendly visits than Bible study; but I was okay with that. About midweek I called her, just like I did all my students, to see if she had any questions about the assignment and she said she had finished it all.

When I arrived for our first lesson, her husband walked me to her room and disappeared to another part of the house. To my surprise, I found her lying in the bed with a big smile, her Bible and assignment laid out in front of her. We talked a bit, went through the lesson, and prayed together. After which, I confessed that I had expected her to cancel the whole thing. Ironically, she confessed that she hadn't really believed that I was going to come back at all; but come back I did, week after week.

Within a few weeks, her husband, who had also doubted my commitment, became a beneficiary of the lessons, as he began to sit closer to the room and listen. Eventually, he would sit on the front porch waiting for me to drive up, asking what we were going to study that day. Our bond of trust was now well established.

At the end of the first twelve weeks, I brought a certificate of completion and a certificate of perfect attendance, issued by the church, and presented it to her. Her smile quickly turned to tears. "Thank you, thank you," she said. "Thank you for doing this for me. I thought the church had forgotten about me.... I thought that no one cared." Our lessons continued for another seventeen weeks until her declining health prohibited them. Our final visit was in the hospital about a week before her death. She thanked me again for bringing the lessons to her and for being her friend.

Isolated and Forgotten

I hope my story illustrates just how easy it is for senior adults to become isolated and forgotten. And also, how important it is for the church to be sensitive to the needs, expressed or not, of its senior members. Walter N. McDuffy, minister to senior adults at First Baptist Church in Fargo, North Dakota, states "Sometimes seniors feel that their fellow members and even God has forgotten them, because they can no longer do it faster. They want others to feel their pain, but they don't want to be a drain on others' compassion. Sometimes they feel they have been placed on a shelf and forgotten." McDuffy states further that it is his mission "to remind them that God loves them, that they are accepted, and that they are not forgotten."[1] I think this should be the mantra of all pastors, ministry leaders, and teachers in the church. Seniors want to be active members of the church, to the extent they can. My experience with Sister Drew, her eagerness and excitement to study God's Word, shows that seniors want and need to feel connected to the body of Christ.

Regrettably, with the push to keep Millennials in the church, many ministry leaders have chosen to focus more heavily on ministries to reach them and keep them actively involved. As I've aged, I've become all too aware of this shift of focus in church services. I recently visited a church in which the sanctuary was extremely dark, like you might expect in a movie theater. The sound system was so loud that it was difficult to hear or understand the words in the praise music. And the speaker's message contained periodic quips about church practices that were an integral part of my Christian experience. Though the people were very warm and friendly, the environment, with its poor lighting and extreme noise, made it difficult to focus on what was going on.

Additionally, the insensitivity to tradition gave me the feeling that the church's target audience was clearly not an older adult like me. Please understand that I am not disparaging this style of worship. I would just ask you, as ministry leaders, to be mindful of the senior adult members and guests who will sit in your pews and classrooms. They are a large and vibrant part of our churches; with many years of experience and testimonies that can benefit everyone. As ministry leaders we would do well to see and value senior adults as God does; as the true and beautiful assets they are. "The righteous will flourish like a palm tree, they will grow like a cedar of Lebanon; planted in the house of the LORD, they will flourish in the courts of our God. They will still bear fruit in old age, they will stay fresh and green, proclaiming, 'The LORD is upright; he is my Rock, and there is no wickedness in him'" (Ps. 92:12–15).

Demographics

The importance of making certain your church and ministries are senior sensitive cannot be overstated, as the number of senior citizens is rising every day. With all the technological advances in healthcare and the heavy emphasis on wellness, seniors are living longer, more active lives than ever before. Consider that in the next thirty to thirty-five years the senior adult population will have doubled,[2] such that the number of people aged sixty-five to eighty-five years old will be greater than those under age eighteen years.[3]

> Teach us to number our days, that we may gain a heart of wisdom.
> —Psalm 90:12

With these trends in mind, ministry leaders need to prepare to handle the sheer numbers of this growing population present in their churches. They also need to make conscious decisions to identify, target, and engage senior adults, and create ministries geared to their specific needs. Amy Hanson wisely points out that God, "in his great sovereignty and wisdom, chose this time to raise up an army of older adults for his purposes" and that "they are seeking meaning and purpose, and are capable of contributing their time and talents to the Kingdom efforts."[4]

> "Though I've always been active in the church, when I retired, I thought hey, I can be more involved. The opportunity to serve is there but seniors have to decide to do it. It's a choice not to serve; so leaders must make deliberate and concerted efforts to value and encourage seniors."
> —Joyce Guthrie (age 69)

Understanding the Needs of Senior Adults

The needs of senior adult learners do not change simply because they age, nor are their learning expectations any different. To effectively minister to senior adults, it is important to know how they learn and see themselves as learners.

> For this God is our God forever and ever; he will be our guide even to the end.
> —Psalm 48:14

Need to Learn

First, begin by understanding adults need to know why they need to learn something.[5] I can't tell you how many times I've found myself sitting in classrooms, meetings, or at conferences uninterested in a subject or assignment, because I saw no need for it. And until someone could explain what was in it for me, I felt learning the material was pointless. One might think senior adult learners in Bible study classes would understand the importance of lifelong learning, but this thinking could be a mistake. Senior adults need to know that by continuing to learn they will develop a closer relationship with God and present a stronger testimony for others around them. The writer of Proverbs has provided an excellent response to anyone, including senior adults, who would question the importance or value of learning. "Blessed are those who find wisdom, those who gain understanding, for she is more profitable than silver and yields better returns than gold. She is more precious than rubies; nothing you desire can compare with her. Long life is in her right hand; in her left hand are riches and honor" (Prov. 3:13–16).

Life Experience

Second, senior adults will bring their life experiences to the learning context and many will delight in new learning that enriches their current understanding. In many cases, senior adults have been walking with and trusting God for decades, making their experiences and the knowledge they've gained valuable to others. God expects them to share their knowledge. In fact he commands it. "Hear this, you elders; listen, all who live in the land. Has anything like this ever happened in your days or in the days of your ancestors? Tell it to your children and let your children tell it to their children, and their children to the next generation" (Joel 1:2–3). God also exhorts ministry leaders to provide opportunities for senior adults to share their knowledge, expertise, and experiences with others. "Remember the days of old; consider the generations long past. Ask your father and he will tell you, your elders, and they will explain to you" (Deut. 32:7).

Different Approaches

Finally, as they do in any classroom, senior adult students will have different approaches and responses to learning. Each student is unique and will bring different things to the table. I have observed that some senior adult students are quite content to listen to an instructor lecture the entire time, particularly those of the "Silent Generation."[6] They are happy to follow their ministry leaders and respect their decisions. However, other senior adults, typically those in the Baby Boomer category, want to be active participants not only in the classroom but in the formation of the ministry itself. They earnestly desire to take your ministries to new heights, in a transformative way, when given the opportunity to do so. Though different in their responses to ministry, both groups are equally important and you will want to listen well to hear and meet their specific needs.

The students in the women's course I taught demonstrate how important it is to understand the needs of your older students or ministry participants. On one occasion, I asked how many had worked on the lesson for the week. I was very surprised when one of my students politely informed me that she had no intention of doing homework assignments for the class. In her words, "I come to class for you to tell me what I need to know; you're the expert, so teach me." While I could easily have categorized her as a negative person, her statement probably revealed the typical way in which she had been taught. When she and

I were younger, there was a general assumption that it was the teacher's responsibility to relay accurate information, primarily through lectures, and the student's responsibility to sit quietly, listen, and learn. Students were allowed to ask questions for clarification, but it was never okay to present a thought different from that expressed by the teacher. My student didn't sound like a very teachable person, but given the right care, in time, she began to participate in class as much as the others. In the process we became close friends, but she never completed one homework assignment. You too may find that you have senior adults like this in your ministries, but do not assume that they are not enjoying or learning.

Conversely, I found that many of my students were fully engaged in the class and some even wanted more depth. They were actively involved in the lessons and eager to discuss what they had discovered each week in preparation for the class. One student, to my delight, still uses the lessons as outlines for ministry speeches she gives across the country. Whenever I hear her speak, I marvel at how much deeper she has developed my simple lessons.

The bottom line is that after listening to my students and seeing what was needed, I evaluated and redesigned my lessons, including more time and methods for them to interact with the material and each other. In making these small adjustments I was able to meet the needs of both the Baby Boomers and the Silent Generation.

Understanding the Challenges Senior Adults Face

As we age, normal vision loss occurs and can become a challenge to senior adult learning. My vision isn't what it used to be and though I love to read, my eyes tend to strain more easily when doing so. Reading is my vehicle of choice for keeping up with world events and technological changes, and it is also my preferred method of relaxation. Therefore, I tend to ignore the eyestrain and suffer the consequences later. All adults will experience a decline in vision at some point, which may make reading more challenging.

> Therefore we do not lose heart. Though outwardly we are wasting away, yet inwardly we are being renewed day by day.
> —2 Corinthians 4:16

Older adults may also experience more difficulty processing visual information, such as that from printed material and computer screens.[7] As many churches now use large screens in church services, care should be taken to make sure the font size used is appropriate for senior adults. Making large-print Bibles available is also an option.

As adults age, hearing is also affected. About one-fifth of senior adults have at least some difficulty hearing and/or processing the sounds they hear. It may appear that older students are not interested in the lesson, when in fact they simply cannot hear or understand what you are saying. Senior adults with hearing difficulties may also face the following challenges:

1. Understanding someone who talks very quickly or speaks with an accent.
2. Knowing where sound is coming from.
3. Identifying who is talking in a group conversation.
4. Understanding quickly what a person is saying.
5. Figuring out what people are saying when listening conditions are poor, such as in noisy rooms.[8]

I make a concerted effort to speak more slowly when I address a group of people, especially senior adults. This is not an easy task for me, and while I am not always successful, slowing down tends to decrease the number of questions asked afterward. Welcome feedback from your senior adults; ask if you are moving too fast for them to understand. Also, a good rule of thumb is to remove as many external distractions to learning as possible. Small adjustments to noise levels, lighting, room temperature, and seating arrangements can make all the difference for senior adults.

One of the most significant and troubling challenges that senior adults face is the myth that as they age, they become incapable of learning. This couldn't be further from the truth. Research suggests that while some people may experience a small decline in their ability to learn new things, remember certain things, or recall specific details, they can often make up for this if given time to think.[9] Additionally, just because some senior adults may seem reluctant to enter the world of computers and the Internet, it is not because they don't see the need to be lifelong learners.[10] All one has to do is look around, in your communities and in your churches, and you will find senior adults actively working in new careers, serving in different areas, and learning new things every day. Don't assume all seniors lose the ability to learn.

Coupled with the previous myth that senior adults lose the capacity to learn is its sister myth that senior adults no longer *desire* to learn or serve. Many seniors want to remain active and will if given the opportunity. For example, when my children were small, I took them to vacation Bible school at a local church in my community every summer for about six years. Each year, the same two older gentlemen greeted us. They smiled and talked to each of the children as they helped them cross the four-lane street to the church. Once inside, we observed a host of senior adults diligently working with other generations, registering children, and escorting them to their respective classrooms. I remember appreciating that the church brought different generations together like this. Then one year, I noticed that one of our friendly crossing guards was not at his post. But then as we got closer to the door to the church, we saw him. He had the same smile and the same cheery attitude, but he was seated in a wheelchair. Though he was no longer able to help the children cross the street, he used his chair to prop the door open for the children as they entered.

My parents are another example. Both in their eighties, they continue to be active in their church. In addition to attending Sunday worship services and Bible studies, mom leads a variety of special programs and dad serves on the church's finance committee. They are surpassed in dedication only by the matriarch of their church, who, at ninety-four, arrives for Sunday school early and ahead of them.

Howard Hendricks, long-time professor at Dallas Theological Seminary, wisely points out,

"Physical limitations do not necessarily signal mental deficiencies. Because our society tends to marginalize elderly people, try to include them in appropriate activities, but be mindful of limitations. When seniors opt out of anything, it can often be because of hearing loss, failing eyesight, arthritic pain, or something very personal. Perhaps even the noise or confusion of an event, or just plain weariness may not be an affront, but simply a fact of life."[11] So if some of your seniors decide that it's time to slow their active service, that's okay too.

> "I think it is important for seniors to keep doing something. There is so much that we can do, with kids and young adults because they need guidance. We can be examples so that when they see us involved they will want to get involved. That's why I can't just sit around. God gives me the strength to work and I'm going to work until I can't."
> —Lilly Hopkins (age 85)

As I reviewed the challenges senior adult learners face for this chapter, I found myself looking at my own challenges. As I have grown older, I have experienced various aches and pains that sometimes slow me down. And like many seniors I am forced to face the fact that these changes will continue and new ones will crop up. I am confronted with my fear that I might become immobile and thereby lose my independence, my fear that I won't be financially stable when I retire, my fear of being alone in my old age. And of course, I struggle with the fear of losing my treasured memories to the dreaded disease Alzheimer's. Who will be there for me and who will help me when the time comes? And while I trust that my children will be there to assist me, I don't want to be a burden to them, and thus, I still have those concerns.

> "I don't drive at night because I don't see too well anymore and my overall health is not too good. Sometimes I get tired just doing my laundry; so I think it would be helpful to have someone from the church check on seniors to see if they need anything, like shopping, getting gas, cutting grass, or just changing a light bulb. Health services are available but most of us are not comfortable with strangers in our house. A simple visit would be nice too."
> —Herma "Tiny" Walls (age 81)

Like me, many older adults consider their self-reliance essential to their well-being. Therefore, physiological changes can be a source of anxiety for seniors. For those seniors without a support system, ministry participation and church attendance may decrease. Amy Hanson states that one of the most important things that ministry leaders can do to address these very real fears is to gently remind seniors of God's promises, provision, his faithfulness, and loving kindness.[12] The apostle Paul reminds us, "Do not be anxious about anything, but in every situation, by prayer and petition, with thanksgiving, present your requests to God. And the peace of God, which transcends all understanding, will guard your hearts and your minds in Christ Jesus" (Phil. 4:6–7).

Biblical Motivation for Serving Senior Adults

The senior adult population in and out of our churches is growing. As Baby Boomers continue to age, ministry leaders must prepare for this unavoidable reality. Senior adults have always been important to God and vital to the body of Christ. With God's help, they have been the builders, sustainers, transmitters, and keepers of the most hallowed traditions of the faith. While new facilities, special programs, and volunteer recruitment are part of the required elements to accommodate their growing numbers, there are simpler things that are equally important.

> Be shepherds of God's flock that is under your care, watching over them—not because you must, but because you are willing, as God wants you to be; not pursuing dishonest gain, but eager to serve.
> —1 Peter 5:2

Value and Encourage

First, value and encourage them. The Word of God says that "Gray hair is a crown of splendor; it is attained in the way of righteousness" (Prov. 16:31). Show seniors how important they are to you and your church body, ministry group, or Bible class by providing opportunities for them to serve and succeed. When they are absent make sure they know that their presence is important and that they were missed. And when they are ill or hurting, let them know that just as God will stand with them, so will you. By doing this you will avoid the possibility that any of them feel left out.

Respect

Second, respect them. Ask seniors for their opinions and advice, and include them in making decisions. Though they may not have formal Bible training, God admonishes you to inquire of past generations, and consider the things searched out by their fathers (Job 8:8). The words of senior adults contain wisdom formed by their long experience of believing and serving God. If problems arise, respect is still in order. "Do not rebuke an older man harshly, but exhort him as if he were your father. Treat younger men as brothers, older women as mothers, and younger women as sisters, with absolute purity" (1 Tim. 5:1–2). Demonstrate that you care about what's important to them and respect their feelings. One consistent theme I hear from seniors is the failure of leadership to consult them or consider their feelings when making changes, especially involving worship styles and music. As one senior put it, "It is okay to sing older hymns so our history is not completely forgotten. Hip-hop is good, but sometimes when you're going through something, you just need to hear 'I Need Thee Every Hour.'"

Honor

Third, honor them. Here again God guides ministry leaders. "Stand up in the presence of the aged, show respect for the elderly and revere your God. I am the LORD" (Lev. 19:32). When a senior adult excels, take time to acknowledge it

with a simple private thank you or a public affirmation during church service. Not only will this honor the specific individual, but it will show other seniors that their accomplishments are important too.

Love

Finally, love them. The Bible admonishes all Christians to love one another multiple times. This is especially true for senior adults. No matter how blessed one is to have made it to one's senior adult years, those years will not only be filled with joy but also a significant amount of loss. Loss of employment through disability or retirement, loss of friends and loved ones through death, and loss of independence can lead to loneliness and possibly depression. God instructs us all to love seniors in both good and bad times and to remind them of his promise "Even to your old age and gray hairs I am he, I am he who will sustain you. I have made you and I will carry you; I will sustain you and I will rescue you" (Isa. 46:4). The old African proverb states "It takes a village to raise a child." That same village must also stand ready to care for its seniors as well.

Recommendations for Senior Adult Ministry Leaders

When the subject of ministry to senior adults comes up, who do you see? Is there a certain age you think of? Do you see little gray-haired ladies covered with shawls or bald men with bulging bellies seated around bingo tables? Do you envision daily trips to hospitals or nursing homes? Few senior adults fit these stereotypes, with only a small portion of them living in institutional settings.[13] Many seniors are still employed full- or part-time and lead active lifestyles.

> Carry each other's burdens, and in this way you will fulfill the law of Christ.
>
> —Galatians 6:2

While much of the research and census data uses age sixty-five as the designated age for a senior adult, my experience has been that senior adult ministries typically begin at age fifty to fifty-five. But remember, just because they fit your chronological designation for a senior adult doesn't mean they see themselves that way. Anyone over the age of fifty can join AARP, yet many senior adults, though chronologically eligible, are reluctant to join.[14] It's as though joining means that they have somehow given in to the fact that they are old, and being old still carries some negative connotations. For others the realization that they are indeed seniors comes as a surprise. Retired Dallas Theological Seminary professor Dr. Eugene Merrill states, "I feel like I've always been the same age," while retired professor Dr. Stanley Toussaint states, "Younger people begin to call you older when you don't expect it."[15] Therefore, in planning your ministry consider calling it something other than Senior Adult Ministry. The old saying that age is just a number literally rings true for some seniors.

When planning a ministry to senior adults, you are wise to enlist a designated staff member or volunteer to assist you. The largest generation you'll probably serve are the Baby Boomers, the newest generation of senior adults.[16] The Barna Group points out four factors about Boomers that ministry leaders will need to address:

1. Church attendance plummeted by 12 percent, dipping to 38 percent in 2011.
2. Sunday school attendance by Boomers fell by nine points, from 23 percent in 1991 to just 14 percent in 2011.
3. Volunteering at churches was less likely among Boomers in 2011 than was the case twenty years ago, declining from 28 percent in 1991 to 18 percent in 2011.
4. The percentage of unchurched Boomers has risen dramatically, jumping up 18 points! At 41 percent, they are now the generation most likely to be unchurched.[17]

Be sure you include Boomers on your leadership teams to be sure you meet the challenges and needs of this unique group of senior adults.

Don't take Barna's fourth point about unchurched Baby Boomers lightly for two reasons. First, learning to live in the likeness of Christ is best done in fellowship with other believers. Therefore, make every effort to bring these unchurched senior adults into the fellowship of the church. Second, don't assume that unchurched senior adults are believers. Though they may have attended churches before, their salvation is not a given. Therefore, evangelism for this group of senior adults is also important. I will never forget the Sunday that my great-aunt rose from her seat and went to the front of the church. Honestly, I thought she intended to go to the ladies room and had made a wrong turn, but in reality, she had decided to become a believer and join the church. She had been living with my family for about eight years and thus attended Sunday school and church with us. Based on my observation, she had been a faithful member of her home church her entire life, so naturally I assumed she was a believer. When I asked why she'd come forward, she said that if she was going to attend the church that she needed to be part of the church. She was eighty-nine years old that day.

> "God has been awfully good to allow you to become a senior adult. If God does nothing more, he has done enough; and we will serve him all of our days. We seniors have so much to offer. We have seen the Scriptures fulfilled in our lives. You won't be able to speak to everyone but they will see your example. We know people are watching us and we want what they see to be of Christ."
> —Ed (age 69) and Doris Charles (age 73)

Remember that all seniors are not mentally slow or senile. For a long time people assumed that senior adults could not think as well as they once did. Though plenty of evidence to the contrary, the idea can become a self-fulfilling prophecy for senior adults, if they believe it applies to them.[18] Therefore, leaders need to build confidence in senior learners by providing ways for them to succeed. Senior adults may take longer to process information but for many, their memories are very much intact and they are eager to contribute what they know to the mix. One useful strategy is to relate lesson elements to familiar generational or life experiences to help them understand and contribute.

Respect for their knowledge and life experiences keeps seniors engaged. They will know when you are talking down to them and they will not appreciate it.

Avoid the trap of prioritizing young adult over senior adult ministries. With the intense emphasis on bringing young people into the church and retaining them, many churches have exchanged all traditional worship service elements for the more contemporary. Older adults may feel that they are no longer valued, being cast aside, and their responses can vary. One group may readily accept the changes as progress; another group may pull away from the church or leave altogether; and still others will fiercely fight the leadership to remain relevant. All three groups still have something to contribute to the body of Christ.

Titus 2:2–3 provides good reasons for older people to work with and mentor young people. Senior adults, who have already experienced the good and bad that life offers can and should guide the young, to show them the path of righteousness, goodness, and wise priorities and values. In return young people can teach the old about new technologies and generational differences so they can relate well to their children and grandchildren. Leaders would do well to provide avenues for the young and old to come together.

Additional misconceptions about senior adults to guard against include the following:

1. Older people are all the same.
2. Older people have nothing to say.
3. It is not worthwhile encouraging older people to engage in learning.
4. Older people live in the past and don't like change.

5. Older people are not interested in today's world.
6. Older people do not like to go out.
7. Older people aren't interested in learning.
8. Older people are not interesting in learning anything new.
9. Older people are not interested in learning information technology.
10. Older people only want to learn with other older people.[19]

Recognize the some seniors may be reluctant to ask for assistance because they do not want to be a burden to anyone. To counteract this, the thoughtful leader will schedule regular service events specifically designed to honor or assist senior adults. For example, ask senior adults to lead the entire worship service quarterly or create and prominently display a senior-of-the-month photo wall. Consider offering events designed to provide basic wellness and medical screenings, legal assistance clinics, including will preparation, Medicare information workshops, and long-range housing planning, including assisted living options. Finally, plan simple home repair events to help senior adults, which could include topics like biannual smoke alarm battery changes. Even something as simple as regular home visits just to sit and talk would go a long way in combating the loneliness many seniors experience.

Conclusion

This chapter focused on ways to assist you in serving the senior adults in your church or ministry. The demographic data suggests that the senior adult population will grow for the next several decades. Thus, church ministries will be affected for some time. Accordingly, this chapter sought to debunk some of the myths about the ability or willingness of senior adults to learn and serve. Senior adults love God and desire to be active participants in ministry. However, despite their willingness, they can become isolated and alone due to prolonged illness, physical disability, or the normal challenges associated with aging. Recent trends of focusing on the young may cause some seniors to feel unheard, left out, and unwanted.

> Follow God's example, therefore, as dearly loved children and walk in the way of love, just as Christ loved us and gave himself up for us as a fragrant offering and sacrifice to God.
> —Ephesians 5:1–2

Senior adults are important to the life and ministry of the church, so it is vital that leaders make a conscious and concerted effort to pay attention to them. This chapter gives practical examples, tips, and recommendations that will help you enhance or create a ministry environment that is sensitive to senior adult needs. It also offers a biblical perspective on how to think about, engage, serve, and care for senior adults. My desire is that no senior adult feels forgotten. And I believe that your hard work, through the power of the Holy Spirit, will make that desire a reality.

Discussion Questions

1. Why is a vibrant ministry to senior adults becoming more and more important every day?

2. How can a church honor its senior adults without alienating younger generations?

3. What specific needs and challenges do senior adults face today?

4. How can healthy seniors benefit churches today?

5. What ministries should churches create to minister to senior adults in deteriorating health?

Resources for Further Study

Books

Haemmelmann, Keith. *Ministry with Boomers: Growing Older, Thinking Younger*. Cleveland: Pilgrim Press, 2012.

Hanson, Amy. *Baby Boomers and Beyond*. San Francisco: Jossey-Bass, 2010.

Houston, James M. and Michael Parker. *A Vision for the Aging Church: Renewing Ministry for and by Seniors*. Downers Grove, IL: InterVarsity Press, 2011.

Merriam, Sharan B., Rosemary S. Caffarella, and Lisa Baumgartner. *Learning in Adulthood: A Comprehensive Guide*. San Francisco: Jossey-Bass, 2007.

Wlodkowski, Raymond J. *Enhancing Adult Motivation to Learn: A Comprehensive Guide for Teaching All Adults*. San Francisco: Jossey-Bass, 2008.

Woodward, James. *Valuing Age: Pastoral Ministry with Older People*. London: Ashford Colour Press, 2008.

Websites

Administration on Aging—www.aoa.gov

American Association of Retired Persons www.aarp.org

American Society on Aging—www.asaging.org

Centers for Disease Control and Prevention, Aging—www.cdc.gov/aging/data

National Academy on an Aging Society—www.agingsociety.org/agingsociety

National Council on Aging—www.ncoa.org

National Institute on Aging—www.nia.nih.gov

United States Census Bureau—www.census.gov

Author Bio

Dr. Sabrina Hopson has worked in Christian education for more than thirty-five years and is an advocate for lifelong learning. She has served as a children's ministry leader, family ministry and literacy director, vacation Bible school coordinator, and Sunday school teacher. She has served Dallas Theological Seminary students, faculty, and staff as a member of the Registrar's Office team since 2004; and in the Educational Ministries and Leadership Department as an adjunct professor since 2014. In her spare time, she enjoys cooking, reading John Grisham novels, watching old westerns, Star Trek, and NFL football. She is a lifelong and avid Dallas Cowboys fan. Dr. Hopson especially loves spending time with her husband Robert, her five children, their spouses, and her grandchildren.

Endnotes

1.   Walter N. McDuffy, First Baptist Church, Fargo, ND, http://www.firstbaptistfargo.com/page/staff (accessed May 25, 2016).

2.   US Census Bureau, "Fueled by Aging Baby Boomers, Nation's Older Population to Nearly Double in the Next 20 Years," *Census Bureau Reports*, May 06, 2014., Release Number, CB14-84 http://www.census.gov/newsroom/press-releases/2014/cb14-84.html (accessed 16 March 2016).

3.   Jennifer M. Ortman, Victoria A. Velkoff, and Howard Hogan, "An Aging Nation: The Older Population in the United States," Report Number: P25–1140, May 6, 2014, http://www.census.gov/library/publications/2014/demo/p25-1140.html (accessed 16 March 2016); Sandra L. Colby and Jennifer M. Ortman, "The Baby Boom Cohort in the United States: 2012 to 2060," Report Number: P25–1141, May 6, 2014 http://www.census.gov/library/publications/2014/demo/p25-1141.html. (accessed 16 March 2016).

4.   Amy Hanson, *Baby Boomers and Beyond* (San Francisco: Jossey-Bass, 2010), 8.

5.   Malcolm Knowles, Elwood Holton, and Richard Swanson, *The Adult Learner: The Definitive Classic in Adult Education and Human Resource Development*, 5th ed. (Houston: Gulf Publishing, 1998), 64. Also see the chapter "Overwhelmed: Adults" by Sue Edwards for more on adult learning.

6.   Josh Sanburn, "How Every Generation of the Last Century Got Its Nickname," *Time*, December 1, 2015, http://time.com/4131982/generations-names-millennials-founders/ (accessed 31 December 2016).

7.   C. Pesce, et al., 2005, as cited in Raymond Lodkowski, *Enhancing Adult Motivation to Learn: A Comprehensive Guide for Teaching All Adults* (San Francisco: Jossey-Bass, 2008), 37.

8.   Patricia B. Kricos, "Audiologic Management of Older Adults With Hearing Loss and Compromised Cognitive/Psychoacoustic Auditory Processing Capabilities." *Trends in Amplification* 10, no. 1 (2006): 13.

9.   National Institute on Aging, "The Changing Brain in Healthy Aging," Alzheimer's Disease: Unraveling the Mystery, September 2008, https://www.nia.nih.gov/alzheimers/publication/part-1-basics-healthy-brain/changing-brain-healthy-aging (accessed 9 March 2016); David Crawford, "The Role of Aging in Adult Learning: Implications for Instructors in Higher Education," Johns Hopkins School of Education, http://education.jhu.edu/PD/newhorizons/lifelonglearning/higher-education/implications/ (accessed 11 April 2016).

10.   James Houston and Michael Parker, *A Vision for the Aging Church: Renewing Ministry for and by Seniors* (Downers Grove, IL: InterVarsity Press, 2011), 155.

11.   Kelley Stern, "Age With Vitality," *DTS Kindred Spirit* 35, no. 1 (2011): 6–7.

12.   Amy Hanson, *Baby Boomers and Beyond* (San Francisco: Jossey-Bass, 2010), 160.

13.   Mark Kahrs, "Senior Ministry: A Look at the Growing Number of Senior Citizens and How to Effectively Minister to Them" (thesis, Wisconsin Lutheran Seminary, 2015), 10.

14.   James L. Knapp and Charles D. Pruett, "The Graying of the Baby Boomers: Implications for Senior Adult Ministry," *Journal of Religion, Spirituality, and Aging* 19, no 1 (2006): 6.

15.   Stern, "Age with Vitality," 6–7.

16.   Keith Haemmelmann, *Ministry with Boomers: Growing Older, Thinking Younger* (Cleveland: Pilgrim Press, 2012), 49.

17.   George Barna, "Religious Changes Among Busters, Boomers, and Elders Since 1991," *Faith & Christianity*, July 26, 2011. https://www.barna.org/barna-update/faith-spirituality/506-barna-describes-religious-changes-among-busters-boomers-and-elders-since-1991#.V5PIrjX95n0 (accessed 4 April 2016).

18.   Sharan Merriam, Rosemary S. Caffarella, and Lisa Baumgartner, *Learning in Adulthood: A Comprehensive Guide* (San Francisco: Jossey-Bass, 2007), 386–387.

19.   James Woodward, *Valuing Age: Pastoral Ministry with Older People* (London: Ashford Colour Press, 2008), 136–140.

Chapter 13
OVERLOOKED: THE DISABLED

Mike Justice

The LORD said to him, "Who gave human beings their mouths? Who makes them deaf or mute? Who gives them sight or makes them blind? Is it not I, the LORD?"

—Exodus 4:11

Making Connections

I WAS DIAGNOSED WITH Type 1 diabetes as a ten-year-old child.[1] I learned quickly that kidney failure, heart attack, stroke, and blindness were just a few of the possible complications of the disease. At the age of twenty-five, I began to experience some blurred vision due to hemorrhaging in both of my eyes. An ophthalmologist diagnosed me as having Diabetic Retinopathy.[2] He recommended a laser treatment on the right eye because it was the worst. After I entered the hospital, the doctors did one of the early forms of laser eye treatment. Unfortunately I went totally blind in my right eye three weeks later. When the doctors suggested using the laser treatment on my other eye, I refused— perhaps more out of fear than anything.

Those early days of blindness were scary, to say the least. My wife and I prayed often in desperation, begging God to heal me of this problem. We expressed great faith in God's healing power. We believed he would be glorified if he did. Still the problem of diminishing eyesight remained.

Suddenly I couldn't drive, couldn't read, couldn't pay bills, and couldn't write a check. I was teaching school at the time and I couldn't grade my students' papers. I couldn't tell my best friend's face from my wife's face until one of them spoke. I had to walk much slower since I as yet had no mobility training (with a white cane).[3] I used the most powerful magnifying glass, along with bifocals, to read even the largest of words. But it rarely helped. Through all the grief and hassles, I attempted to get help so I could learn to read Braille and travel independently.

However, finding assistance seemed impossible at the time. My wife and I experienced grief in the forms of fear, anger, sadness, and depression. We bargained with God a lot.

My wife and I desperately needed emotional and spiritual support. When we sought this support from our church family, many of our closest friends unfortunately just pulled away and kept their distance. We never realized that they were grieving too, and probably didn't know what to say or do to help.

New challenges were introduced into the mix. Church attendance and involvement, although not impossible, became one disconnect after another for me. While I could get into the church building, I couldn't read the morning worship bulletin or the music. I served as the church's minister of music at the time. As my eyesight grew worse, the typical matters of church life seemed to become impossible, especially if I wanted to remain on the staff.

Questions overwhelmed us each day. How would I read the Bible? How would I sing the songs if I couldn't read the words? How would I learn the Bible study material if I couldn't see to read? How would I know one person from another without seeing faces? How would I locate the correct restroom in the building? How would I travel back and forth to church? Overall, how would I participate in the normal activities of church life? Would others merely feel sorry for me and think they must do everything for me? Would they only see me as an object of ministry or also see me as an avenue for ministry? And what about others who lived with challenges different from my own? Would they be welcomed to be integral servants in our fellowship, or would they be marginalized and seen as liabilities?

For the first time in my life, I realized many others with different disabilities faced the same or similar issues. Each issue raised various questions concerning accessibility into the ministry and assimilation into the various activities of local church life. Ministry methods often feel rigid and unaccommodating when those affected by disabilities want to serve. How can they fit in and become ministers of God's grace as he works in the midst of their weaknesses? How can they use the giftedness that the Holy Spirit has sovereignly given them to serve in the local body of Christ? How can they connect in light of the many daily challenges? The questions seemed endless, but not impossible to problem-solve if the following saying is true: The common denominator of disability is *how,* not *can* or *can't*! With this in mind, I offer some of what I've learned to help Christian workers minister through the Spirit to those who live with all kinds of disabilities.

Defining Disabilities

In Exodus 3 and 4, Moses raised several objections when God called him to go into Egypt to deliver the Israelites out of bondage. His final objection was his inability to speak well. Moses said, "I am slow of speech and tongue" (Exod. 4:10). To this final protest from Moses, God replied with a series of probing questions to help his servant gain a proper perspective on his speech impairment. God asked, "Who gave human beings their mouths? Who makes them deaf or mute? Who gives them sight or makes them blind? Is it not I, the LORD?" (Exod. 4:11). One might suppose God would have chosen an eloquent ambassador to approach the mighty Pharaoh, but he did not nor did he heal Moses of his disability. Instead, God used Moses with his disability and gave him a helper, his brother Aaron. God made Moses's mouth. God made the mouth of every human being. He made some deaf, some mute, and some blind. He even made some sighted. No matter their challenges, God used them all to do his bidding. None thwarted his plans or purposes.

This passage in Exodus names a few disabilities but never really defines disability. Some disabilities are obvious while others are hidden. The Americans with Disabilities Act (ADA) defines a disability or disabled person as any physical or mental impairment that substantially limits one or more major life activities, a person who has a history or record of such impairment, or a person who is perceived by others as having such impairment.[4] But the law does not offer an exhaustive list of specific disabilities. Such a list exists online for United States government agencies, but not

every country uses the same or even similar definitions and laws. Typically, disabilities fall under the four categories of physical, sensory, mental, and cognitive. Disabilities vary as to the extent of limitation they put upon individuals.

Physical disabilities usually mean an individual needs to use a particular piece of adaptive equipment like a brace, white cane, wheelchair, or prosthesis. Sensory disabilities affect the senses with blindness, deafness, or speech impairments as examples. Mental disabilities include disorders such as bipolar disorder, schizophrenia, and dissociative disorder, and are known as invisible disabilities. Cognitive disabilities cover a broad spectrum of limitations. Learning disorders like dyslexia and dysgraphia, for example, fall under the category of cognitive disabilities. Obviously, this is not an exhaustive list.[5]

Churches and the *Americans with Disabilities Act*

Congress passed the *Americans with Disabilities Act* (ADA) in 1990. The act prohibits discrimination against individuals with disabilities. The Act, along with its 2008 amendments, is codified at 42 U.S.C. §12101, et seq. Many states have adopted accessibility regulations and building codes that meet or exceed the ADA.

The Act defines a "Covered Disability" broadly to include both physical and mental impairments. Originally, the Act provided that such impairment "severely or significantly restrict" one or more major life activities. The 2008 Amendments broadened the coverage to impairments that "substantially limit" a major life activity. The impairment can be temporary (episodic) or permanent. A very long list of conditions and disorders have been determined to be impairments covered under the Act.

The Act protects the disabled in two broad areas. Employers with more than 15 employees (deemed "Covered Entities" under the Act) shall not discriminate against a qualified individual with a disability in employment matters. If a disabled person is qualified to perform the essential functions of the job with a "reasonable accommodation," then the employer is required to provide the accommodation so long as the accommodation does not represent an "undue hardship." "Undue hardship" is defined as one with significant difficulty or expense.

The second area of protection involves the disabled's "full access" and enjoyment of public buildings and transportation. This includes commercial facilities such as theaters, restaurants and retail stores. New construction must comply with extensive ADA Accessibility Guidelines (federal and state). Existing construction must remove architectural barriers so long as the removal is deemed "readily achievable."

While much has been made of the exemption afforded religious organizations under the Act, caution is warranted. The religious exemption of Title VII, Civil Rights Act of 1964, does allow a religious organization to discriminate in hiring on the basis of *religion* for those positions that perform religious functions. Nevertheless, with respect to two equally qualified pastoral candidates, the ADA would prohibit discrimination against one who was disabled.

The "full access" provisions of the ADA expressly do not apply to religious organizations or places of worship, despite being public. After much lobbying from church organizations that such guidelines would interfere with religious liberty, Congress exempted religious organizations from removing barriers in their facilities. This includes worship centers, church schools, and daycares. Nevertheless, the exemption does *not* apply to a nonreligious organization that might *use* the church facilities (e.g., a Boy Scout troop). Further, in many states (e.g., Texas), the exemption does *not* apply to "common areas" (parking, entrances, hallways, bathrooms, etc.). In practice, it is recommended that all new church construction comply with federal and state accessibility standards. *Jesus certainly practiced "full access." Shouldn't we, as Christians, want the same?*

by Steve Forman, Private Practice Lawyer and
Director of Business Development for Camino Global Foundation

Dealing with Disconnects

Depending upon the severity of the limitation, those who live with disabilities soon learn that life, while not necessarily impossible, is full of disconnects. This is certainly true in many churches with their inaccessible buildings, educational classrooms, restroom facilities, and sanctuaries.[6] However one must make sure access is not limited to merely being able to enter a building. Ministry access is also important. Disconnects can occur when disabled people try to participate in various kinds of ministry endeavors. Connections have to be made both on the part of people with disabilities and those who seek to engage them. This level of involvement demands both understanding of some of the unique problems associated with any particular impairment as well as the ways it produces a disconnecting effect from the nondisabled world.

Ministry to and through someone with a disability involves the making of several meaningful connections. This process is definitely a two-sided coin for those who live with impairments. They need to hear the gospel, be under good Bible teaching, and be able to use the spiritual gifts that the Holy Spirit has sovereignly given to them (1 Cor. 12:7). The following connections demonstrate this.

An Informational Connection

There are all kinds of misconceptions out there about disability:

- A person who is hearing impaired automatically reads lips and understands sign language.
- Talking loudly and slowly helps a visually impaired person function better.
- An individual with dyslexia has a vision problem so he or she should visit an eye doctor.
- If a blind person cannot see to read, therefore he/she must be illiterate.
- A person with paralysis never feels pain.
- Using different study habits easily solves a learning disability.

- A person with autism cannot communicate.
- A person who has experienced paralysis from a stroke will usually regain the use of the paralyzed limb.
- A person who loses his/her eyesight tends to become a great musician.

And the list goes on....

These misconceptions could not be further from the truth and represent only a few individuals. Unfortunately, many will probably stay in the safe confines of ignorance about any given disability. Even a person who has one or more disabilities does not know everything about his/her own disability. Whatever the Christian worker can learn about such issues will certainly provide furthering understanding in making accommodations so disabled individuals can read the Bible and comprehend it in a manner that connects with their unique problems. For example, not everyone can see a hymnal, song sheet, or PowerPoint slide; however, reasonable accommodations can help the disabled engage in a worship service.

Gaining a basic knowledge of any particular disability can certainly be helpful if one desires to understand the unique disconnects of an individual with that impairment. The Internet is full of websites about various disabilities, their adaptive solutions, and answers to various questions.[7] These websites often dispel common misconceptions about impairments both in work settings and the public arena. Testimonials offer helpful information on various impairments. Frequently Asked Questions (FAQs) sections on these websites usually cover most of the issues of any curiosity-seeker.

However the best information comes directly from a disabled person, or indirectly from the family of that individual. These are, after all, the people living with the daily challenges. They know best what they need.[8]

Awkwardness may certainly occur when one tries to communicate with someone who lives with a disability. What to say, not to say, the language used or avoided seems ever changing in the world. What results often is a large lack of communication to the disabled community simply because of the fear of offending that person.

The following are two ideas that often work well. First, use people first language. It is much better to say, "This is my friend Jane," rather than, "This is my paraplegic friend Jane." Usually, there is no reason to even mention that person's disability, so why bother? He or she can mention it if needed. Personhood is emphasized by the first statement ("This is my friend Jane"), while the disability is emphasized in the second statement ("This is my paraplegic friend Jane). Jane is not a disability with a person; she is a person who is affected by a disability.

Second, ask if someone needs help. Do not assume he or she does need help or wants help. Sometimes it is unsafe for others to help, especially when that person has not even solicited it. If you do ask, consider this method: "Sir! I realize that you are independent and can do what you need for yourself but may I be of some assistance to you?" If that person accepts your offer, then follow the directions given; but if he or she rejects the offer, please honor the request without pushing your help. Giving credit to the disabled person edifies him or her and the offer is given in kindness. Pushing one's help, though not meant to be cruel, often comes across as if the disabled individual has no abilities at all. Each one needs the opportunity to be independent, as much as possible.

A Relational/Emotional Connection

Grief is waiting in the wings for anyone who has suffered a loss. The ability to physically or mentally function normally is often taken for granted until one suddenly learns he or she has multiple sclerosis or muscular dystrophy, faces an amputation, experiences paralysis, or has a head injury after a trauma or an accident. At some point, a discipler must begin to engage the disabled person in his/her grief process. Without engagement, it's doubtful much of a relationship will form, particularly one of a spiritual nature. The daily hassles of any disability may be enormous, depending upon the newness and extent of the condition. Many onlookers will not engage the grief, believing it to be weakness on the part of the sufferer. God, however, is an emotional God. Human beings are made in his image and therefore are emotional beings. Emotions are God-given mechanisms that aid human beings in facing traumatic events.

To suddenly learn that one must face the rest of life with a disability may bring intense grief, no matter how much one might attempt to bottle it up. And in a society where we're often told to "keep a stiff upper lip," "be tough," or "don't act like a baby," the misunderstanding of grief responses pressures one to deny the pain and difficulties of living in an imperfect world. Sometimes the pressure goes so far as to cause the denial of emotions of any kind, forgetting that God has provided emotions for many reasons, including the ability to help cope with loss.

Responses such as shock, denial, fear, anger, bargaining, sadness, depression, and eventually some measure of acceptance are absolutely normal reactions to the losses and challenges of the disabled. Although coping with the issues of a disability go far beyond mere acceptance, understanding that everyone grieves differently also plays into how each disabled individual deals with challenges. Some describe grief as a process experienced off and on for a lifetime, while others reach a point of acceptance with the dawn of each new day.[9]

Wanting to give up is common when a person faces the future without an arm or a leg. Intense fear and anger may be the reaction of a newly impaired individual when facing the loss of career for which he or she spent thousands of dollars in educational preparation. Intense feelings of alienation might accompany the loss of hearing, as one suddenly experiences the struggle of being left out of normal conversations. In the case of disability due to a chronic illness, one might be able to work through a period of grief, only to face it again six weeks later as the illness progresses. Some may just want to throw in the towel over a new loss that requires more enormous adjustments to cope. A disability is not something one gets over but a lifestyle one learns to embrace. No matter where in the journey an individual is with regard to a disability, that person must adapt and conquer. Time, training, friendships, and emotional support usually help the individual to learn that life isn't over, it's just changed.

An Experiential Connection

The Christian worker must engage the disabled individual where that person struggles. To stay aloof from those struggles will affect the depth of any discipling relationship. To engage, however, will usually bear fruit, for the very attempts create a more level ground. It's one thing

to observe someone with a disability. It's quite another to experience life with that impairment.

The following are ways one might try to connect experientially or help others to connect with someone living with a disability:

- Secure a person's arms and legs with cloth bands to a wheelchair to mimic quadriplegia, or just the legs to mimic paraplegia.
- Blindfold a person to mimic blindness or visual impairment.
- Place rifle-range ear covers over a person's ears to mimic pronounced hearing loss.
- Secure an old shoe to a ten-inch piece of wood and then have the person walk around with one leg that is longer than another.
- With a hand-held mirror, ask a person to hold a printed piece of paper in front of him/her so that the print faces away. Then have that person try to read the text by looking into the mirror to mimic dyslexia.
- Take a left-hand glove and have a person wear it on the right hand, or vice versa. Then use masking tape to bind various fingers and make them useless to mimic partial paralysis from a stroke.
- Construct a padded hook and suspend a heavy fishing sinker weight from a person's lip so that it pulls the lip downward to mimic facial paralysis or palsy.

Variations of this list may help to demonstrate other disabilities.

Once the person is "temporarily disabled" (using one of the previous techniques in the list), try several typical church scenarios. To further help the nondisabled person relate to the disabled person's world, ask the "temporarily disabled" person to do simple exercises to mimic what he/she might experience in a typical worship service, Sunday school class, home Bible study, women's ministry meeting, student ministry gathering, as examples. Pretend the "temporarily disabled" person is in a worship service and is asked to leave one's seat and greet three other people in the worship center. Ask the person using the mirror to simulate dyslexia to read a Scripture passage in front of other people in a classroom context. Ask the person with the heavy fishing sinker to teach a brief lesson from that same Scripture passage. If the participants are willing, have them spend one day with that particular impairment both at home, work, and church.

The "temporarily disabled" person will learn quickly that they cannot easily connect with what they are being asked to do. They may very well experience new frustrations and formerly easy tasks may suddenly seem monumental. And it will be up to them to problem-solve the awkwardness.

Awareness will skyrocket as they experience their different limitations. The limitations are not necessarily impossible, but they do require some brainstorming on how to cope. The important thing to remember is that these exercises are by no means the same as actually living with that impairment. After all, the "temporarily disabled" person eventually will remove his/her restriction and return to normal life, but those who actually live with a disability cannot.

The flip side of the coin is that God desires to use the disabled in Christian service to help others and glorify himself. Moses possibly had a speech impairment (Exod. 4:10). Isaac's eyes were dimmed in his old age (Gen. 27:1). Mephibosheth had crippled feet, yet ate at King David's table (2 Sam. 9:13). In the gospel accounts, we see Jesus interacting with a man with a withered hand (Matt. 12:10–13), people with leprosy (Mark 1:40–45; Luke 17:11–19), people who were deaf and mute (Matt. 9:32–33; Mark 7:31–37), people who were paralyzed (Matt. 8:5–13; 9:1–8), people who could not walk (John 5:1–9), people who were blind (Matt. 9:27–31; 20:30–34; Mark 8:22–26; John 9:1–38) a woman with internal bleeding (Luke 8:43–48), a woman who could not stand up straight (Luke 13:10–17), and many who lived with illnesses of all kinds. God used all of these people in different ways. Some were healed to demonstrate God's power and Jesus's messianic authority, while others were never healed. They went on to serve God and be used of God in mighty ways to accomplish his plans. Whatever their roles, God used them.

Adequate Resources

For a disabled individual to serve may only require a simple adaptive solution. Not every adaptive tool has to be purchased. Whatever that individual needs can often be made or simply adapted from what is already there. For example, attach an easily obtainable tray table to the arms of a chair to help a disabled individual use a laptop or Braille device, or the tray table can serve as a book holder. Often a disabled individual may know exactly what is needed or what may be adapted from another device. Some disabled people use a labeling system to mark audiotapes, DVDs, or CDs. Labeling devices come in both English and Braille formats. Others may use book holders to aid them while they read. Magnifying glasses come in all sizes with powerful and varied magnification for those with low vision.

I Had a Stroke

"I had a stroke right after the fact I had a heart attack. I was out of ministry for ten months. The only lasting effect was my inability to communicate all that was in my mind. I have apraxia. Apraxia is caused by brain damage related to conditions such as head injury, stroke, brain tumor, and Alzheimer's disease. The damage affects the brain's ability to correctly signal instructions to the body. Forms of apraxia include the inability to say some words or make gestures.

My life has changed. To get over the disappointment, I go to three fellowship groups at church which include a couple's home group and two men's accountability groups. The support I get from them is awesome. The group members have to be patient with me as I try to communicate with them. I have trouble saying what I would like to say, and they give me the time I need to get the words out of my mouth. They allow for my inconsistencies. I have found it is good to have fellowship like that. Without it, I was would be a prisoner in my own world of intense grief.

My life at work in ministry has changed, too. I was involved in many committees, was travelling to recruit new students for the seminary, was conducting orientation sessions, and I had the responsibility in all fifty states to authorize all of the online classes the seminary was producing. When it was time to me to return to work after my stroke, my supervisors made the decision to hire me again! It was tremendous! I was asked to come back and take the form of an advisor. They accepted me back with all my deficiencies and limitations as if nothing had happened. When I go to work, I feel significant! I feel I have an influence in the decisions people make with their lives.

In David Jeremiah's book *A Bend in the Road*, he quotes a letter. In the letter, the author says of the Lord, 'THIS THING IS FROM ME.' That is why I press on. Whatever difficulty comes my way, it comes from the hand of God. You are in control, God, and you have allowed this to happen in my life!"

by John Contoveros, External Studies Advisor at Dallas Theological Seminary

Those with reading or learning disabilities may require learning or study aids to thrive in a class environment. Their methods may also involve other adaptive pieces of equipment to enhance their abilities and skills. Powerful hearing aids are available provided that one can afford them or has the insurance or agency to cover the cost. Volume enhancement is also available for church services or special meetings. Virtually anything can be used as an adaptive tool.

Many denominational and curriculum publishing company websites provide Bible study materials in Braille, large print, or audio formats. A creative teacher using these formats may succeed in attracting the disabled to learn more about the Christian faith and possibly become a Christ-follower.

Not all hearing-impaired people are totally deaf. This has to do with the levels of pitch the individual can actually detect and understand. As with visual impairment, hearing impairment levels vary widely. Using voice synthesis can enable an individual to choose a voice that is pitched for bettering understanding. Several good voice synthesizer software packages exist, including JAWS (3) and Zoom Text (Zoom Text is primarily a powerful screen enlargement program).[10] Both offer pitch manipulation as well as numerous preset voices from which to choose. Even those with learning disabilities use these programs to help listen to large portions of text. These programs easily read words, phrases, sentences, and even punctuation if the user wants to do editing.

Voice recognition software has been refined to more user-friendly levels. A person wanting to write or keep track of notes may find this type of tool helpful. It does, however, require the use of a computer and a special piece of software called Dragon Naturally Speaking, which will type what the user speaks.[11] Being able to give commands to that computer allows the user to keep track of study notes to use for sermon and lesson preparation as well as many other practical uses.

Opportunities to Try

Ministry opportunities for the disabled are often relegated to a few one-time occasions. People tend to think that the disabled cannot do what the nondisabled can. If a disabled individual tries but doesn't live up to the expectations of the group, he or she may never again be given the chance to develop skills and giftedness. Everyone needs time, training, and plenty of room to learn. Otherwise they may never accomplish the work God has wired them to do. One of the best ways to encourage the disabled to develop their gifts is to start small. Ask them to lead in prayer, quote or read a passage of Scripture, help organize an event, lead music, or even team-teach with a more experienced teacher. Working with the disabled benefits the nondisabled to learn compassion and patience as they observe the courage and perseverance of their disabled brothers and sisters.

The disabled individual's first attempts may seem awkward, but that is normal. That may very well be what God uses the most to demonstrate his power. God's strength is perfected through our weaknesses or disabilities (2 Cor. 12:9).

When the disabled sense little room for failure, they may easily become deeply discouraged and refuse to try again. Perhaps the adage "it's not a matter of can or cannot, it's merely how" will help that person to try again. Few of us do things exactly right the first few times we try. Most able-bodied people make mistakes and fail, so allowing the disabled disciple to try again is the best plan.

Working with Special Needs Families

"Often, when families come to our church for the first time, they come in with their 'tail between their legs.' They are just waiting to be told 'I'm sorry, we don't have a place for you here.' How is it acceptable for Christ's representatives to turn someone away? I will never get tired of seeing their relief and hope when we tell them, 'Come in! We are so glad you're here.' Churches should not simply 'tolerate' individuals with special needs, including them out of pity or a sense of sacrifice. We should be seeking them out and begging them to come! Jesus made it clear that his body is diverse. Each person is made in the image of God and conveys something unique about his character. Each person is endowed with gifts that are necessary to the functioning of the body and the furthering of the kingdom. Special needs ministry is not something only certain churches are called to—as believers we are all called to welcome all people and help them live out their unique purpose God has prepared in advance for them to do. There are thousands if not millions of families out there who desperately need the hope of Christ. They need to hear they are valued and desired just the way they are. But they are cut off from this hope. Jesus tells us to 'Go out to the road and country lanes and compel them to come in, so that my house will be full.' Let's do it!"

by Shannon Miller Pugh, Director of Special Needs Ministry
at Irving Bible Church in Irving, Texas

Opportunities to Shine

Ask the disabled in your church to put together a Disability Awareness Sunday service. Use those who already live with disabilities to do the behind the scenes preparation. They can plan it, set it up, direct it, be an integral part of it. If available, one of them can preach the sermon, perhaps on some aspect of how God uses the disabled to glorify himself. During the Sunday school or adult Bible community hour, several may want to share from their experiences what it means to serve Christ in the midst of living and coping with their challenges. Some may

also choose to create a display featuring their particular disability.

Recruit more severely disabled individuals to participate in the following small ways, as appropriate:

- Memorize or read a verse or passage of Scripture to open up a Bible study. Be sure to consult this individual concerning how much time he/she reasonably needs to prepare.
- Involve a disabled person in a service project. If the disability prohibits such

involvement, that person might be given the task of phone calling people who have recently visited the church to welcome them, to share information about various ministries in the church, or to answer questions.

- Enlist a disabled person who can read and speak clearly to record digital books for children or adults who have reading disabilities. These resources may help others process this information more quickly, allowing them to engage in more classes.

- Ask a hearing impaired person to share his/her personal testimony with the men's or women's ministries. You may also need to engage a sign language interpreter, adding clarity and fun for listeners.

- Encourage people with disabilities to write lessons, devotionals or mentoring materials that others can use. While an individual may struggle with speech impairment, he or she may be well equipped to both write and evaluate learning curriculum.

- Invite disabled people to participate on a panel. Use a few preplanned questions, giving panelists the opportunity to consider their answers ahead of time. Then allow the audience to ask whatever they would like to know. The panelists will be living proof of God's grace amidst enormous difficulties.

- Plan a summer discipleship project where youth spend an hour or so each week helping someone who is disabled with specific needs such as buying groceries, fixing meals, mowing lawns, or do-it-yourself projects. Ask each youth to commit to the project for four to eight weeks, or however long the disabled individual requests. Both the youth and the disabled person should benefit from relational connections as well.

Conclusion

People with impairments serve as pastors, teachers, missionaries, conference speakers, retreat organizers and speakers, writers, soloists, professional readers, seminary professors, evangelists, musicians, moms and dads, engineers, politicians, judges, lawyers, and practically anything one might imagine. All they need to succeed are people who attempt to understand, people who will be a friend during the rough days, and people who will try to relate—plus the needed resources, the room to try, and the opportunities to shine. God isn't limited by their impairments, so why not give them a chance?

Discussion Questions

1. What misconception have you held about a particular disability? Did correct information change your thinking, and if so, how?

2. Has someone in your family struggled with a disability? If so, what has this experience taught you?

3. Do you tend to offer unasked for advice to those with disabilities? If so, can you discern why? After reading this chapter, do you believe this practice harms or helps the disabled?

4. What often hinders families with disabled children from attending church? How can local churches provide more welcoming atmospheres?

5. What resources are lacking in your local church that make it difficult for people with disabilities to minister to others?

Resources for Further Study

Carder, Stan. *A Committed Mercy: You and Your Church Can Serve the Disabled.* Grand Rapids: Baker, 1995.

Hubach, Stephanie. *Same Lake, Different Boat: Coming Alongside People Touched by Disability.* Phillipsburg, NJ: P&R Publishing, 2006.

Tada, Joni Eareckson. *Beyond Suffering: A Christian View on Disability Ministry.* Agoura Hills, CA: Joni and Friends, 2012.

Tada, Joni Eareckson. *Joni: An Unforgettable Story.* Grand Rapids: Zondervan, 1996.

Newman, Gene, and Joni Eareckson Tada. *All God's Children: Ministry with Disabled Persons.* Grand Rapids: Zondervan, 1993.

Sheetz, Timothy. *Reaching the Disabled for Christ.* Upper Darby, PA: Handi*Vangelism, 1988.

Waters, Larry and Roy Zuck, eds. *Why, O God?: Suffering and Disability in the Bible and the Church.* Wheaton, IL: Crossway, 2011.

Wolf, Jay and Katherine Wolf. *Hope Heals: A True Story of Overwhelming Loss and an Overcoming Love*. Grand Rapids: Zondervan, 2016.

Author Bio

Mike Justice has worn many hats: pastor, associate pastor, music minister, hospital chaplain, and music teacher—remarkable because, as a Type 1 diabetic, he is totally blind in one eye and severely legally blind in the other. He also endured two kidney transplants, the second donated by his wife Terri. Mike teaches sessions on ministry to the disabled at DTS, where he earned a Masters of Theology degree. His classes prepare future pastors and ministers to welcome the disabled into their flocks with compassion, insight, and skill, ensuring the likelihood that future churches will glorify God by ministering to everyone God redeems and calls to serve.

ADDENDUM A: DISABILITY BEATITUDES

Autism Beatitudes

- Blessed are you to realize that autism is a spectrum disorder. The population of people with autism is much like the rest of the world's population. Some have special talents, some are intellectually challenged, but most are average.
- Blessed are you to understand that autism is a bio neurological disorder that affects the functioning of the brain. It is not a mental illness.
- Blessed are the pure in heart who recognize that it is often difficult to ascertain the cognitive level of individuals on the autism spectrum due to behavioral challenges expressed.
- Blessed are you to understand that autism impacts the normal development of the brain in the areas of social interaction, communication, and cognitive function.
- Blessed are those who appreciate the splinter skills in the life of one with autism.
- Blessed are those who treat individuals with autism uniquely. People with autism are not all alike. Autism is a spectrum disorder.
- Blessed are the peacemakers who offer assistance rather than judgment with the following: slowness in understanding messages; problems of the sensory system (touch, taste, and smell), hearing and language disorders, inappropriate social responses (screaming, unprovoked tantrums, laughing, crying, and resisting touch, cuddling, and eye contact); sleep disturbances, and in severe forms the child may injure themselves, constantly move various body parts, show an apparent insensitivity to pain and/or constantly isolate themselves from their parents and all others.
- Blessed are those who appreciate interdependence on this earth. We can all help one another. There is no cure for autism, but there are a wide variety of treatments that are effective at treating its symptoms.
- Blessed are the visionaries who respect the person with autism to see the world through a different lens.
- Blessed are you to understand that making eye contact during a conversation may be difficult for me.
- Blessed are those who give the gift of time and listen to passionate interests.
- Blessed are you to realize that I may be nonverbal, but I can communicate with intent.
- Blessed are those who hunger and thirst after friendships and befriend a person on the spectrum. And teach reciprocity within the friendship.
- Blessed are those who reach out to someone different than they are and appreciate those distinctions.
- Blessed are you to treat me as if I were a part of your family. My feelings get hurt, too.

- Blessed are the pure in heart who recognize that people with autism feel emotions and develop personal attachments. Sometimes it is demonstrated idiosyncratically.
- Blessed are you to not judge my parents as bad parents; my autism is not a result of bad parenting.
- Blessed are you to understand that autism cannot be fixed by punishment or strict discipline.
- Blessed are you to understand that I may not honor your physical space, but would kindly appreciate it if you would honor my space.
- Blessed are those who separate fact from fiction when it comes to autism.
- Blessed are those who realize that it is very rare for a person with autism to act violently out of malice, in spite of what you've seen on the news.

Blind Beatitudes

- Blessed are you when you speak normally to me, for yelling only damages my hearing!
- Blessed are you who identify yourself to me, for I may not know who you are!
- Blessed are you who use verbal description, for you paint the world so the blind can see it!
- Blessed are you who ask rather than assume, for in asking me if I need assistance, you show me dignity!
- Blessed are you when you tell me you're leaving, for it humiliates me to talk to the air!
- Blessed are you who express your feelings in sound, for I cannot hear your smiles.
- Blessed are you who observe and learn from me, for it's easy to give unwarranted advice!
- Blessed are you when you respect my guide dog or white cane, for both are effective ways of doing mobility!
- Blessed are you who believe that I can, for it frees me to figure out how!
- Blessed are you when you connect to me through the senses of hearing and touch, for both give light to the blind!
- Blessed are you who speak to me instead of my guide dog, for she really doesn't understand your instructions!
- Blessed are you who learn that blindness is not a liability, for that discovery helps you to see that I'm just like you!
- Blessed are you when you don't leave me stranded, for your commitment to give me a ride home seemed genuine!

Deaf Beatitudes

- Blessed are you when you face me directly, for that is an easier way for me to read your lips!

- Blessed are you who don't mock me by trying to use made up signs, for this does not help me to understand you!
- Blessed are you when you realize that the way I sing is through sign, for I demonstrate that praise is communicated in all forms!
- Blessed are you who use printed letters and emails to me, for this is another way for me to connect with you!
- Blessed are you when you shake my hand in greeting, for that gesture communicates universal friendship!
- Blessed are you who recognize that your facial gestures and body language are welcome, for they are definitely a good way for us to mutually connect!
- Blessed are you when you give me opportunities to serve at church, for I can share my heart and what God has taught me (provided I have a sign-language interpreter)!
- Blessed are you who try to learn sign language to speak to those who are deaf, for even the attempt communicates love and acceptance!
- Blessed are you when you allow me to pray for you in sign, for though you have no idea what I'm saying, God completely does!
- Blessed are you who communicate your emotions outwardly, for your expressions shout volumes about your heart!

Hard of Hearing Beatitudes

- Blessed are you when you speak more clearly and slowly to me instead of yelling, because yelling only blows away my ears through my hearing aids!
- Blessed are you who don't get irritated with me for asking you to repeat yourself.
- Blessed are you who don't talk too fast for me to hear what you're saying.
- Blessed are you who explain things to me patiently in a group conversation if I miss something.
- Blessed are you who face me directly when speaking, so I can pick up all the visual cues I can.
- Blessed are you who are willing to patiently tell me something I missed during a movie or TV show.
- Blessed are you who allow me to joke about my disability before you do.
- Blessed are you who recognize that hearing loss is a disability, and that my hearing aids will never give me "normal" hearing.
- Blessed are you who don't think I'm unfriendly if I'm quiet sometimes. I may just not be following the conversation, and don't want to burden someone with repeating too much.
- Blessed are you who want to learn more about hearing loss and how to help others who are affected by it.

Learning Disability Beatitudes

- Blessed are you who make eye contact when speaking to me, to ensure I understand.
- Blessed are you who don't overuse the word "No," but instead use a creative alternative.
- Blessed are you who repeat oral instructions, as I may act like I understand, but don't.
- Blessed are those who don't make assumptions.
- Blessed are you who don't judge me by my lack of ability to spell.
- Blessed are you who genuinely encourage me, for I often have a poor self-image.
- Blessed are you who provide consistent rules and directions, so I know what to expect.
- Blessed are you who are flexible with me, for the ways I use to study may differ drastically from yours.
- Blessed are you who understand that dyslexia is not an eye problem.
- Blessed are you when you realize that my learning problems are not contagious.
- Blessed are you who accept that I don't feel comfortable reading, for I'm not trying to be lazy as some falsely assume.

Paralysis/Amputation Beatitudes

- Blessed are you when you sit down to converse with me, for you and I are surely equals.
- Blessed are you who do not push my wheelchair without being asked, for I may not want to go where you think I should.
- Blessed are you when you don't cut in front of me, for my manual wheelchair won't stop on a dime.
- Blessed are you who engage me with your eyes and your smiles, for in doing so, you make me feel worthwhile.
- Blessed are you when you observe that I cannot shake your hand, for your kind words and gestures also communicate friendship.
- Blessed are you who sit and read to me, for it keeps me from feeling obsolete.
- Blessed are you when you leave the handicapped parking spaces open, for I need the extra room to get in and out of my van.
- Blessed are you who include me in your events, for it helps me to feel wanted and needed.
- Blessed are you when you stay seated with me during a standing ovation, for I too would like to honor the individual but must stay seated.
- Blessed are you who don't mind my slower pace, for walking alongside me helps me to feel a part of the group.
- Blessed are you when you offer to push my wheelchair up the ramp, for I don't always have the strength to do it myself!

- Blessed are you who allow me to be transparent with my emotions, for you give me grace to cope!
- Blessed are you when you don't stare at my missing legs, for I'd like for you to meet the rest of me!
- Blessed are you who don't ask, "Have you ever thought about getting prosthetic limbs?" for not all amputees can afford or even wear them!
- Blessed are you when my adaptive extension crutches are not a bother, for they are my means of getting around!
- Blessed are you who engage me intellectually, for my leg was amputated, not my brain!

Special Needs Beatitudes

- Blessed are you who respect me and accept me just as I am and don't make me your target for jokes and bullying, because I won't or can't fight back!
- Blessed are you who accept me just as I am, because we **all** have things we can and cannot do. That's why we are all different!
- Blessed are you who do not see my accommodations as cheating, but just as a way to help me show what I know and to help me do my best!
- Blessed are you who do not expect me to be cured when I am mainstreamed into your class. My special education teacher is good, but cannot cure me of my disability to make me "normal"!
- Blessed are you who realize I can learn, maybe in a different way and maybe by taking more time. I am not stupid!
- Blessed are you who are happy when I can do something really well, and maybe even better than you!
- Blessed are you who measure my progress by what I am doing, and not by measuring my progress by comparing me to everyone else who is not disabled!
- Blessed are you who believe in me and encourage me to be the best I can be. Thank you for those nudges and pushes because you knew I could do it!
- Blessed are you who pick me to be on your team or ask me to help, instead of ignoring me or assuming I can't. I will do my best and will not let you down!
- Blessed are you who talk with me and not about me or as if I am not there. I may need to communicate in a different way, but I have thoughts and feelings, too!
- Blessed are you who accept me as I am and do not treat me differently when you cannot see my disability, like the person who is in the wheelchair!
- Blessed are you who are not shocked that you cannot pick me out of a crowd because I don't look differently while having a disability!

- Blessed are you who do not use me in the name of friendship to do your dirty work. Being a friend is precious, not manipulating!
- Blessed are you who are not afraid to ask questions about my disability so you can understand me!
- Blessed are you who do not equate every disability with being retarded, and instead treat me like an intelligent human being who happens to have a disability!
- Blessed are you who do not laugh at me, but include me in the fun times so we can laugh together!
- Blessed are you who do not assume I cannot understand fairness because I have a disability. Thank you for treating me just like you would anyone else acting like me. Thank you for not pitying me!
- Blessed are you for allowing me to try instead of automatically assuming I can't do it.

Speech-Impairment Beatitudes

- Blessed are you when you allow me to finish my own sentences, for I just need a little more time to share my thoughts!
- Blessed are you who don't answer your own questions, for I really do have valid opinions!
- Blessed are you when you include me in conversations, for I do have other ways to communicate!
- Blessed are you who accept my stuttering, for you help me to feel more confident!
- Blessed are you when you encourage me to use technology to speak, for that allows me to be a part of meaningful discussion!
- Blessed are you who greet me, for you make me feel more valuable and significant!
- Blessed are you when you don't use sign language to me, for I'm not deaf but speech-impaired!
- Blessed are you who talk to me normally, for when you shy away, I feel rather cheap!
- Blessed are you when you don't try to mimic my speech problems, for you have no idea how hurtful that is!
- Blessed are you when you write an email to me in normal size print, for I have trouble speaking, not seeing!
- Blessed are you who let me pray in my own way, for God can understand me even though you may not be able to!
- Blessed are you when you realize that worship can easily be done without saying a word, for my best worship is coming from my heart!

ADDENDUM B: DISABILITY PROBLEM SOLVING

Break into groups of four or five, and strategize how you would solve the following problems with regard to a church's educational program.

1) A fifteen-year-old year old girl, who is totally blind, recently joined the youth group. On her first visit to the youth group, she felt left out of the group because the other kids already knew one another.
   - Strategize creative ways for her to learn the names and voices of the other youth in the class.
   - How might the other kids give her clues to help her identify their voices?
   - What can the quiet youth do to help this blind girl identify them?
   - What connections could the other girls make to experience this girl's situation and help her feel included?

2) Some parents express some concern about their youngest son and the way in which the fifth- and sixth-graders have treated him in his Bible study class on Sundays. He's a fifth-grader and walks very awkwardly, due to a birth defect where one of his legs is about two inches shorter than the other. The other kids laugh at him and mock him when he walks.
   - What might you do to teach the other children in his class to treat him with respect?
   - How might you handle those children who poke fun at him?
   - What might you do to create an experiential connection for the other fifth- and sixth-graders?

3) A lady who has suffered with painful rheumatoid arthritis desires to be a part of a women's Bible study class but has difficulty climbing the stairs to the floor where it meets.
   - What solutions can you offer to solve the accessibility issue?
   - How might that women's Bible study class build some connections with this woman?
   - What encouragement might you offer to this lady that would help her to feel like she is definitely worth the time and effort of solving this problem?

4) When the Bible study teacher training seminar meets at the end of the month, three new people sign up. One is a man who has a learning disability and will struggle with reading class materials. Another is a woman who has multiple sclerosis and is confined to a wheelchair. The third is a college student who wants to work with junior high kids but has a hearing impairment.
   - What would you do first to learn what the challenges would be for each person to be able to work with a class?
   - What roles might you initially give these three people to let them get started?
   - What personal fears and/or hesitancies would you have in allowing them to continue?

5) A senior adult who suffered from a stroke the year before loves kids and wants to be a helper in one of the children's classes on Sunday. Her left arm is completely paralyzed, and she has some labored speech but is understandable.
   - What ways could you use her as a helper in one or more of the children's classes?
   - What could you do to teach the children in this class about this woman's disability?
   - What might you do to handle the parents who pulls their child out of the class because they are scared to have their child around this lady?

6) A man who is deaf wants to work in the youth department as a helper, especially when they go on retreats and to summer youth camps.
   - List the resources you think he will need to do these.
   - How would you go about communicating with him to discuss problems that often arise with the teenagers?
   - Come up with two ways that the youth can make relational and experiential connections with this man.
   - If a youth Bible study teacher got sick, would you let the man teach? Why or why not?

7) A lady who had her right leg amputated after a serious car accident and a college student who has multiple sclerosis asked if they might be of service in the children's ministry. Both were fairly outgoing and both used a wheelchair as adaptive equipment to accomplish mobility. In that same department, there were several children who dealt with different learning disabilities.
   - Strategize ways the two could be used in the department.
   - What could they do to help the learning disabled kids to function better in their classes?
   - Come up with a game of some sort that would help the nondisabled kids and adults to begin to grasp the problems of both learning and physical disabilities.

8) A woman with severe learning disabilities, a man who lost his leg on the battlefield, and a young lady who was born with no right hand desire to be used in Christian service.
   - How might you use them in the various Sunday school age groups, to teach lessons of faith and endurance?
   - What questions do you think the kids would ask with regard to that individual's disability?
   - What do they have to offer the kids that nondisabled people rarely have?

9) Two college females express their desire to disciple younger girls. Two girls have also asked for someone to disciple them. One is dyslexic, while the other has bipolar disorder.
   - How might you advise the college-age disciplers to proceed?
   - What accommodations do you think will be needed for the relationships to occur?

- Since a book on some aspect of Christian growth will be used by the college students to help the two girls, what must be done for both to engage the material?

10) Some concerned parents asked to meet with you over issues regarding several questions on the value of those who are disabled. The questions are raised: 1) Are disabled people under the judgment of God? 2) What examples in the Bible show that God uses someone with a disability? 3) How can a disabled believer have and use his or her spiritual gift(s) in the church?
   - How might you prepare for such a meeting considering five people with disabilities are currently attending that church?
   - Though speculative, what issues do you think underlie such a meeting, for the concerned parents?
   - If one or more folks are disabled in the church are willing to attend, how might you use them to answer the questions raised?
   - What Scriptures would counter those who feel that the disabled lack value in God's sight?

ADDENDUM C: IQ TEST ON DISABILITIES

A man with a speech impairment goes into a drugstore to buy a toothbrush. By using the gesture of brushing his teeth, the storekeeper helps him find a toothbrush and the purchase is completed. Think through what each person would do.

- What would a hearing-impaired woman do to buy a toothbrush in that drugstore?
- What would a paraplegic do to buy a toothbrush in that drugstore?
- What would a visually impaired woman do to buy a toothbrush in that drugstore?
- What would a person who had facial paralysis do to buy a toothbrush in that drugstore?
- What would a college student with schizophrenia do to buy a toothbrush in that drugstore?
- What would a woman who had rheumatoid arthritis do to buy a toothbrush in that drugstore?
- What would a man who had one leg amputated do to buy a toothbrush in that drugstore?
- What would a woman with dyslexia do to buy a toothbrush in that drugstore?
- What would a man with multiple sclerosis do to buy a toothbrush in that drugstore?
- What would a teenager with muscular dystrophy do to buy a toothbrush in that drugstore?
- What would a professor who had polio do to buy a toothbrush in that drugstore?
- What would a woman who had bipolar disorder do to buy a toothbrush in that drugstore?

Endnotes

1. Type 1 diabetes is simply defined here as an autoimmune disease where the pancreas is unable to produce insulin to break down simple sugars like glucose so the cells can use it. It is treated by giving daily insulin injections based upon blood sugar monitoring, a balanced diet, and exercise. Type 2 diabetes is different because the pancreas produces insulin but the body is resistant to a percentage of it. Diet and exercise are the most important treatments, but blood-sugar monitoring may dictate the use of certain medications. Excessively out of control blood sugars may demand the use of insulin.

2. Diabetic retinopathy is an ocular condition where new, fragile blood vessels on the retina have burst resulting in blood hemorrhaging into the fluid portion of the eye. Early treatment is crucial but still may eventually lead to blindness.

3. Mobility training is the instruction an individual with blindness receives as he or she learns to use a white cane to navigate. Usually, white cane training is the basic mode of maneuvering, but it may also lead to further training using a guide dog.

4. The United States Department of Justice maintains an excellent website with the very latest information on the Americans with Disabilities Act and its implications. More information can be found at www.ada.gov.

5. More information can be found on websites like Joni and Friends (http://www.joniandfriends.com); Bartimaeus (http://www.bartimaeus.com); Optasia Ministry (http://www.optasiaministry.org); Autism Society (http://www.autism-society.org); nonPareil Institute (http://www.npitx.org); or Handi*vangelism Ministries (http://www.hvmi.org/).

6. Places of worship are not legally bound by ADA law, but ethically they should be aware of the requirements to create fewer disconnects. Joni and Friends website (http://www.joniandfriends.com) offers a simple checklist that can be downloaded for free and used to evaluate the accessibility of your own place of worship.

7. A great website to start with is Joni and Friends International Disability Center (http://www.joniandfriends.org).

8. Refer to the Disability Beatitudes at the end of this chapter. These demonstrate some of the typical and most likely well-meant things that the general public does to try to help those with disabilities. Often, however, these ideas may be unsafe, confusing, and unwarranted.

9. More information can be found in Elizabeth Kübler-Ross's book On *Death and Dying* (New York: Scribner, 2014).

10. Information on JAWS can be found at http://www.freedomscientific.com. Information on Zoom Text can be found at http://www.aisquared.com.

11. Information on Dragon Naturally Speaking can be found at http://www.nuance.com/dragon.

Chapter 14
CURIOUS: NOT YET CHRISTIANS

A. J. Rinaldi

...so is my word that goes out from my mouth: It will not return to me empty, but will accomplish what I desire and achieve the purpose for which I sent it.

—Isaiah 55:11

"That Is So Cool!"

IS THERE A MOVIE you enjoy watching so much you've seen it many times? There is usually a memorable scene or line you have memorized, and it impacts you every time you see it. Then there are those scenes you take for granted; perhaps after watching them multiple times you forget how special or moving they really are. Now imagine watching it with a friend who has never seen the movie at all. Their passionate reaction to those scenes you have been overlooking can serve as a reminder of why you fell in love with the film in the first place.

I had a similar experience profoundly relevant to understanding Scripture from a new perspective. One of my curious, but not yet Christian, friends was having a personal crisis. As unfortunate as the situation was, it opened the door for some valuable conversation time focused on spiritual things.

Surprisingly, he asked me to explain the constant unrest in the Middle East. After a brief hesitation, I said something like, "You know the deal with Abraham and Isaac and Ishmael? You know that story, right?" His head moved side-to-side with an expressionless face, as he said "Nope." I thought, here's a great opportunity to do some storytelling about the greatest story you can tell!

Well, I proceeded to tell my friend Kevin about the Old Testament. I went through the story of Abraham and Israel, the Exodus, even touching on the Assyrians, Babylonians, and Persians and how all the nations' turmoil, the depth of which we can glimpse through the prophets, enlightens the Bible's metanarrative—the big story about Christ revealed throughout the whole Bible.

Inwardly, I began grinning to myself; "Wow—I actually learned some things in seminary."

Kevin was familiar with Moses, of course, having seen Charlton Heston portray him in the movie *The Ten Commandments*. And Kevin was also vaguely familiar with the story of Joseph. Musical theatre performances of *Joseph and The Amazing Technicolor Dreamcoat* have placed the biblical narrative in pop-culture consciousness. Although some in ministry would undoubtedly disagree with me, I believe placing God's Word creatively in the spotlight is a good thing. Even when the expression takes liberties with the story, it allows us the opportunity to engage with *individuals*. Spiritual conversations must start somewhere. When the Bible, God, Jesus, etc., are already in the public forum, it makes it easier for us to talk to people one-on-one in private.

As I was telling Kevin the story about Joseph, something happened that shook my thinking about how we communicate the biblical narrative to non-Christians. It is important to note I was not reading from a Bible. I was recounting stories I had read, heard, and written about for years. Although I tend to be animated when I speak, in this instance I was essentially storytelling in a slightly more subdued, academic fashion—which is one reason for my surprise at Kevin's response to a very particular part of Joseph's story.

Upon the death of Jacob, as you may recall, Joseph's brothers were desperately afraid for their lives (Gen. 50:15–21). Therefore, after securing an audience with their now very powerful brother, they begged and pleaded for Joseph to have mercy on them. Here's where it gets interesting. Perhaps you're familiar with the story, or even if you've never thought too much about it, you may know what Joseph's response was: "You intended

to harm me, but God intended it for good to accomplish what is now being done, the saving of many lives" (Gen. 50:20). Which I paraphrased for Kevin as something like this: "You idiots! Do you still not get it!? What *you* intended for evil, *God* intended for good."

After a slight pause, Kevin leaned back in his seat and simply said, "That is so cool."

"Well, yeah. I guess that *is* cool," I replied—somewhat taken aback at the sincere, fresh observation. That is *so* cool! Yes, it is. It's cool, it's deep, it's revelatory, it's impactful, it's life-changing, and it's awesome! Here he was connecting with an infinitely difficult theological tension, and calling it cool!

When was the last time you thought to *intentionally* engage with someone who knows little to nothing about the Bible or the gospel, telling him or her life-changing stories with a renewed perspective? This wasn't intentional for me—God put Kevin in my life perhaps not to teach *him* something, but to teach *me*.

Our Role in Evangelism

The primary function of the church, and therefore the preeminent role of Christian education is to make disciples. The first step in discipleship is conversion.[1] Reaching the non-Christian is at the center of our mission. So how can you, as an educational leader, most effectively implement that directive?

First, you must set aside any delusions your brilliant program, initiative, or study will be responsible for someone's salvation (John 6:44, 63–65; 2 Cor. 4:1–6; Gal. 3:3). Conversion itself is always, in every context, the work of the Holy Spirit. Contact is our job, conversion is God's.[2] It is also imperative you inculcate this message within every outreach or evangelism program you lead. Once you've settled the fact that ultimately the eternal results are God's work and not yours, you can set about implementing a strategy for effective outreach and evangelism.

It should be clear there are as many ways to reach non-Christians as there are non-Christians. It is essential to recognize there can be specialized methods for reaching numerous people groups—based on race, religion, socioeconomic position, gender, geography, family history, etc.[3] However, finding relevant published resources to fit all the various people groups is difficult, and there is always room for you, as the educational leader, to be innovative and creative in your own outreach and equipping efforts. In fact, if I tried to lay out detailed programmatic instructions in this chapter, by the time it went to print they would probably be outdated, and certainly not necessarily relevant to your sphere of influence. Hopefully the materials at the end of this chapter will help you find some resources and inspiration helpful to your ministry.

Increasingly, as John Piper states, "The dividing line between missionary tasks and the tasks of near-neighbor evangelism are sometimes unclear."[4] How we define an unreached people group was much easier in the recent past, often limited to the foreign mission field. In the progressive society of today, however, we might find not only individuals but entire families and even communities in any region of the United States with absolutely no point of reference to the Bible; let alone the gospel or authentic Christianity. So, in some cases, near-neighbor evangelism is no longer much different from foreign mission work.

As I am sure you have heard so many times before—the message doesn't change, the method has to. It is my sincere prayer that what I have to share in the next few pages, through real-life examples, will help stir your thoughts and feelings about how God is leading *you* to reach the unsaved in your community. In addition, you will have biblical, practical guidance for developing and implementing educational initiatives relevant to your specific situation.

Figure 14.1 Outreach and Evangelism Strategy

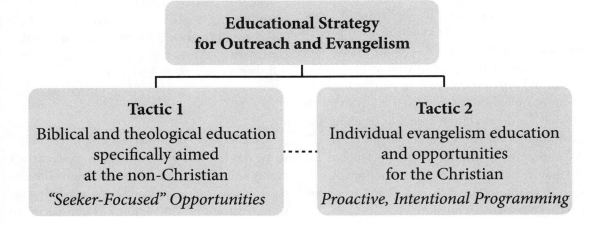

Outreach and Evangelism Strategy

That said, I believe we can establish a two-fold advance where a strategy for outreach and evangelism is concerned. This is not to suggest there are only two plans, or that only two philosophies exist. Rather, I propose two techniques—or tactics—you as an educational leader could employ toward a more intentional model of contact. Both approaches necessarily require teaching, training, and equipping your people. Even though the training would look different for each, they would complement and strengthen each other.

Biblical Education for the Non-Christian

Tactic 1 is biblical education specifically aimed at reaching the non-Christian through learning. People in general are curious about *spirituality*, perhaps now more than ever. And despite the concerning statistics about biblical literacy, many are still inquisitive about the Bible.

Our goal is to draw curious nonbelievers into a learning experience where they willingly seek truth through personal discovery. Therefore, we must be keenly aware to recapture the awe that comes from reading or hearing God's Word from a fresh perspective. In *The Heavenly Good of Earthly Work*, Darrel Cosden issues this relevant warning: "if we are not careful we could bog ourselves down yet again in church-based programs and activities rather than putting the bulk of our energies into the mission itself … so much of what we do at church seems to be about the institution of the church, and that is worrying."[5] As important as church programs tailored for the mature believer are, we must not limit our efforts to an inward focus thereby completely overlooking our primary mission.

Christians have exponentially increasing opportunities to engage with people who may have no exposure whatsoever to biblical truth. Within our places of work, where we do our shopping, playing, and any other facet of everyday life, preparing for the reality outside the walls of the local church must be at the forefront of our efforts. Understanding the interdependent nature of workplace and other social relationships can help change the mindset of fear and task-oriented evangelism and foster a true relational approach many claim, yet few really practice.[6] Pursuing Bible study with an intentional focus toward our unsaved friends is a prime example.

"You're Freaking Me Out, Man!"

For several years, I held a leadership position with a rapidly growing healthcare business. During that time, I had the privilege of engaging in multiple conversations of a spiritual nature. One such discussion took a turn illustrating the confusion some may have toward historical theology.

> For the time will come when people will not put up with sound doctrine. Instead, to suit their own desires, they will gather around them a great number of teachers to say what their itching ears want to hear.
> —2 Timothy 4:3

A colleague of mine, an employee whose name was Jeff, had been asking me about current events and their relationship to religion. The discussion was somewhat loaded and escalating toward frustration. Although it was nonspecific to the gospel, I saw an opportunity to engage with Jeff about his understanding of Jesus.

I point-blank asked him this question. "Jeff," I said calmly, "why do you think Jesus was crucified?" At this point, anyone reading this story will most likely realize I was looking for a spiritual answer—or at the very least a historical one with some validity. However, I will never forget how he answered me. With absolute confidence and no hesitation, he replied, "Because he was speaking out against the *Roman Catholic Church*!"

After taking a deep breath, I quietly yet firmly said, "No—actually let's back up a bit." I told him although I wasn't looking for a historical answer, clearly there was a need to explain the actual events of Jesus's ministry and last week prior to the crucifixion. However, Jeff was insistent not only was he correct, but he indeed had read the Bible for himself.

Finally, after a bit of friendly debate, I was able to convince Jeff his understanding of the life and death (and subsequent resurrection) of Jesus was not based on the biblical narrative. In an effort to lay out the gospel for him, I simply said Christ died to pay the penalty for our sin so we could be reconciled with God, our Creator and Father! I explained (clumsily I'm sure—I had no benefit of any evangelistic training or biblical education at this point) all of humanity is in a sinful state, separated from God and we could only be reconciled by grace through faith in Christ and him crucified.

"So, you're telling me you believe we are born bad?" was Jeff's reply. When I answered him in the affirmative, he literally threw his arms and hands in the air and loudly exclaimed, "You're freaking me out, man!" He emphatically stated his belief was in the "blank slate" theory; the idea

we are born with no point of reference or pre developed morality, ethics, knowledge, etc. We are literally a product of our environment, which Jeff assumed had pretty much been proven by psychology.[7] My initial response was to remind him I had toddlers and he did not. Once you have a two- or three-year-old running around, the idea of *tabula rasa* quickly loses its credibility!

My interaction with Jeff illustrates the reality of the concept you may be familiar with—the unsaved have to have a felt need for salvation, understanding their lost state and need for a savior, before they can accept the sacrifice of Christ. Lewis Sperry Chafer plainly and accurately points out, "The examples of soul-winning in the New Testament present a conspicuous contrast to some examples of present-day evangelism. So far as the divine record shows there seemed to be little urging or coaxing, nor was any person dealt with individually who had not first given evidence of a divinely wrought sense of need."[8]

Biblical Illiteracy

Although Jeff's story illustrates how assumptions based on inaccuracies and misunderstandings can distort perceptions of the Bible, this is not to say unbelievers have completely forsaken Scripture as something worthy of consideration. As George Barna states, "Americans' relationship with the Bible is complex. Despite its hallowed past and historical role as a cornerstone for the nation, people have been slowly weaning themselves from it over the past quarter century, though they are not likely to abandon it altogether."[9] Hence my friend's willingness to debate an issue concerning Scripture, even though he was clearly uninformed of the biblical truth.

Nevertheless, biblical illiteracy is always worse than you think. One might safely assume that within the relatively faith-friendly borders of certain geographical areas of the United States, that most people at least have some basic knowledge of the Old and New Testaments. They may even understand the differences between the two. Increasingly, cultural geography is dissipating in the United States. Indifference to the Bible has become less of a regional issue and more of a contemporary one.

Studies on the relevance and accuracy of the Bible illustrate the ever-decreasing significance of Scripture in American culture. The importance of the Bible to those polled decreased by 8 percent over just five years (see Figure 14.2). In that same time span, the perception of the Bible as a reliable text decreased by 15 percent![10]

The truth is Christians who care about studying the Bible are beginning to accept their coworkers and neighbors probably know little to nothing about it. The illusion the general populace still values Scripture is fading. As ministry leaders, your outreach efforts should start with the assumption there is no biblical foundation upon which to begin.[11]

Again, the first tactical approach of outreach and evangelism leadership is our response to biblical literacy. How do we inform and inspire the unbeliever toward a better understanding of the content of Scripture? There is most definitely power in the Word of God and how we use it to reach those as-yet unaffected by it.

Figure 14.2 The Bible in America: Six-Year Trends[12]

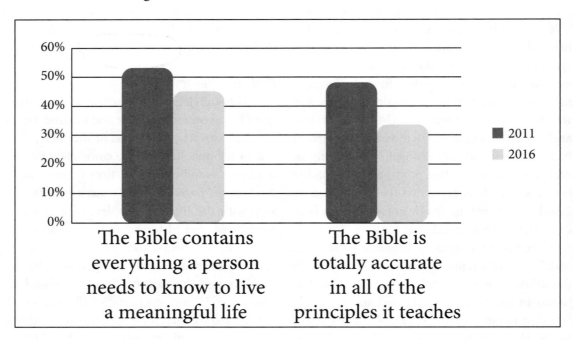

"I Don't Know What Those Words Mean"

From the Old Testament to the Gospels and to the Epistles, for some the Bible is one long, confusing piece of literature. My encounter with Melissa taught me even more about just how much work we have in biblical education for the non-Christian.

> How, then, can they call on the one they have not believed in? And how can they believe in the one of whom they have not heard? And how can they hear without someone preaching to them? And how can anyone preach unless they are sent? As it is written: "How beautiful are the feet of those who bring good news!"
>
> But not all the Israelites accepted the good news. For Isaiah says, "Lord, who has believed our message?" Consequently, faith comes from hearing the message, and the message is heard through the word about Christ.
> —Romans 10:14–17

College ministry has been a passion of mine for a long time. I have the privilege of leading our college ministry as part of my responsibilities with adult discipleship at my church. One thing I love about the ministry are the visitors. The students will invite friends from all walks of life throughout the summer when we have a weekly time of fellowship and devotion.

Not long ago, we had a young lady visit our midweek gathering and sit in on my lesson on redemption. Melissa had come one or two other times, but I never really had an opportunity to engage with her until this particular night.

As the evening was winding down and we were preparing to leave, I was enjoying a quiet discussion with Melissa and two of the students who had invited her. She began to share about some difficulties she was facing and was clearly seeking some peace. During the discussion however, she shared how, despite her efforts, she found reading the Bible to be very difficult because of the words. Now this is a smart girl. So, I asked her what she meant, using specific examples like grace, forgiveness, redemption, etc. Clearly she understood those concepts—and even more difficult ones.

At one point in the conversation, I began to quote the book of Ephesians, reciting a passage I had used earlier that evening. That's when she stopped me and exclaimed, "That's it! That's what I'm talking about! Those words!" She slowly and tentatively said, "Ephesians." It was then a light bulb went on in my head as she was saying, "What does *Ephesians* mean?"

So we began a whole new dialogue about how the Bible is structured and exactly what the book titles mean. She literally had no point of reference. I explained how Ephesians was written to the church at Ephesus, Colossians to the church at Colossae, Corinthians to Corinth, etc. Finally, as she was getting the idea, I asked her, "So, based on that information, who do you think the book of Romans was written to?" Her halting response, "Romanians?" I delighted in her answer because she was trying to get the idea and sincerely processing. After revealing the true audience of the church at Rome, she shook her head and acknowledged that made more sense. We all had a healthy laugh at that because it was a healthy environment.

What the Words Mean

Is it important she understand what those "words" mean? Absolutely! Context is king! Any understanding of a biblical passage begins with a basic knowledge of the context in which it was written. Without it, the biblical text can easily be misunderstood to convey ideas never intended.[13] Not that Melissa would be able to competently exegete Scripture because she now knows the epistles were actually letters written to churches in specific places—but every bit matters![14]

This is key, because educating nonbelievers about things we take for granted requires tremendous patience as well as a sense of humor. Imagine how Melissa would have felt if the other students or I got frustrated with her, were condescending to her, or simply apathetic. Instead, it was an engaging, lively discussion resulting in a next level of understanding for Melissa. She could now open her Bible the other students had given her and at least have some way of identifying what she was reading. Prior to that night, she had no idea.

Furthermore, the gospel was completely alien to her. As much as I love the approach of "can I show you what the Bible says about...", it won't work with someone like Melissa.[15] Who we are (anthropology), who Jesus is (Christology), what he did for us and how we should respond (soteriology), are foreign concepts to her. They are not clear, simple principles. It is easy for believers to take this for granted. Although we shared the gospel with her that night, there was so much rolling around in her brain—including conflicting notions about other world religions—that it was difficult to land on a solid invitation to trust in Christ.

The reality is: This is the new normal. Increasingly, the upcoming generations have no or limited exposure to the Bible or biblical ideas. Therefore, we must expect new challenges when reaching out to younger demographics, regardless of culture.

I'm not going to belabor the point of generational disconnect. Gabe Lyons and David Kinnaman have already done an excellent job and continue to with that subject matter.[16] The Barna Group also always has valuable, up-to-date statistics and information available at their website and by subscription.[17] If you're going to lead a multigenerational outreach ministry, you must become familiar with the new normal—if you're not already.[18]

Addressing a common negative stereotype in *God Space*, Doug Pollock points out:

> To many people in our culture, Christians are considered the "disagreement people." We've worked hard to earn this label, one reaction at a time... Many times, not-yet-Christians will say or do things just to see how we'll react. This is often a test to determine whether or not it's safe enough for them to engage with us in real conversations ... what we need are supernatural responses—"love, joy, peace, patience, kindness, goodness, faithfulness, gentleness and self-control" (Galatians 5:22–23)—that communicate radical acceptance, if we hope to create space for spiritual conversations to happen naturally.[19]

Maturity, and especially spiritual maturity, is a prerequisite for this type of awareness.

Eight Guidelines for Developing and Presenting Bible Studies for Nonbelievers:

1) Assume nothing—Your target audience likely has little to no reference point to the Scriptures or true Christian theology.

2) Maintain a safe and healthy environment—People will be much more open to asking questions and engaging in lively discussion if they feel you care about and respect them. You want to develop and encourage real relationships.

3) Keep it simple!—This is not a seminary course. Avoid the temptation to show off how much Greek and Hebrew you know; same goes for in-depth exegetical demonstrations.

4) Be patient—Remember all the principles you've learned about education in general and Christian Ed in particular. Everyone learns at a different pace; and although you may be teaching concepts so ingrained in your consciousness, see point #1! Also, keep in mind your role and the role of the Holy Spirit—contact and conversion.

5) Begin with the Gospel of John—Ask yourself: "What's the purpose of Bible studies for non-Christians?" If the answer is anything other than "to see them trust in Christ for salvation," then check your motivation. This is not an academic exercise. Try not to begin with Genesis or Revelation!

6) Be prepared—If you don't know the answers to difficult questions, that's alright. Just have a wealth of apologetics and other resources available at your disposal. And of course, make sure your basic material is clear and that you are very familiar with it.

7) Be creative—Utilize illustrations, multimedia: anything and everything available to you. Don't teach to one type of learner.

8) Pray—Any initiative must be covered in prayer. This should always be a given!

Relational and Personal

Much of what I'm espousing here is an informal, casual approach to biblical education for non-Christians. There is much about the new normal of outreach and evangelism that is nebulous, primarily because it *necessarily has to be more relational*—and therefore more personal and affectual. Unashamed, authentic expressions of Christianity on a personal level will help us break out of the ever-increasing stereotypes perpetuated by popular culture about Christianity in general and evangelism in particular.

By focusing on outspoken, boisterous, and often misguided "leaders," the media have helped present evangelical Christians as a gross caricature, stoking the prejudice of large segments of the nonreligious population.[20] Unfortunately, this is counter-productive to winsome, effective evangelism. In *The Gospel & Personal Evangelism*, Mark Dever addresses the issue of changed hearts influencing society: "Evangelism is not declaring God's political plan for nations nor recruiting for the church—it is a declaration of the gospel to individual men and women. Societies are challenged and changed when, through this gospel, the Lord brings individual men and women together in churches to display his character and to pursue their own callings in the world."[21]

Does this mean there is no place for structured, methodical education concerning the gospel and evangelism in the church? Absolutely not! It is still essential to acknowledge the need for intentional training and programmatic approaches in certain contexts.

Biblical and theological classes, workshops, or discussion groups for non-Christians are a very effective way to accomplish contact, and easier to grasp for those whose personality types are more linear and concrete, as opposed to abstract and random. There are several good programs available for non-Christians to study the Bible and learn more about Christianity. A few of those are listed at the end of this chapter.

In addition, there is perhaps now more than ever a great need for evangelism training in your educational programs within the church. That brings us to the second tactic in your approach to evangelism and outreach education: training for the believer.

> Preach the word; be prepared in season and out of season; correct, rebuke and encourage—with great patience and careful instruction. For the time will come when people will not put up with sound doctrine. Instead, to suit their own desires, they will gather around them a great number of teachers to say what their itching ears want to hear. They will turn their ears away from the truth and turn aside to myths. But you, keep your head in all situations, endure hardship, do the work of an evangelist, discharge all the duties of your ministry.
> —2 Timothy 4:2–5

Biblical Training for the Believer

In *Questioning Evangelism*, Randy Newman articulates what so many of us think and feel when we hear about the abundance of successful efforts from well-known evangelists: "People don't as readily 'pray the prayer' with me as they do with famous speakers I've heard. Those natural evangelists are always sitting down next to someone and sharing the gospel. And they always lead every person to a salvation decision. (And it's always on an airplane!)"[22] If those stories tend to discourage you, don't let them. Many people react the same way—including me. However, solid biblical evangelism training can go a long way in equipping believers to feel more confident when the opportunity arises to share Christ with someone.

> Always be prepared to give an answer to everyone who asks you to give the reason for the hope that you have.
>
> —1 Peter 3:15

"Why Aren't the Churches Teaching That?"

I was on a long plane ride, chatting with a pleasant young doctoral student. She shared how she was disillusioned with the church's response to homosexuals. As many believers do, she had several gay friends, and the tension caused by the often-caustic public discourse made it difficult for her to engage in open, spiritual discussions with them. She was always fearful of coming off as just another "bigoted" Christian. In response, I was able to tell her about a time I shared the gospel with a friend of mine and his homosexual partner. The story is too long to recount here in detail, but it clearly struck a nerve with her.

I explained to her how I had applied simple principles anyone can learn and went as far as articulating the actual gospel presentation I used. After describing how the whole encounter unfolded, she exclaimed, "I couldn't have done

that. No one has ever made me think I could share the gospel that way. Why aren't the churches teaching that?"

> "…frustration might be the most common emotion that Christians associate with evangelism (followed closely by guilt, confusion, and despair)."[23]
>
> —Randy Newman

The reality is you can substitute any profile or demographic of an unbeliever in place of homosexuality. Post-Christian culture continues to put labels on Christians and will continue to intimidate many believers with a desire to share their faith. It is our job as Christian leaders and educators to ensure our people are equipped and confident in a way that is winsome and graceful without sacrificing truth.

Equipping for Clarity

Equipping for evangelism is not the same as equipping for service. As Duane Litfin emphasizes in *Word vs. Deed*, "The gospel is inherently a *verbal* thing, and preaching the gospel is inherently a *verbal* behavior. Thus the implication of this saying—that we are daily 'preaching the gospel' with our deeds—is seriously misguided."[24] Those you are called to lead should have a keen understanding of the biblical gospel by which we are saved and how to present it through words. There must be no ambiguity about the difference between evangelism and service; both of which, in their own way, can be integral to outreach. The initiatives developed to impact and improve culture and society can be awe-inspiring or completely ineffective. But from best to worst, none of them are the gospel of Jesus Christ.[25]

Clarity must be at the center of any effective evangelism training initiative. Clarity of the message, clarity of the methods, and clarity of the expectations—yours and of those you are equipping. Larry Moyer, founder of EvanTell, has been teaching this worthwhile phrase for years, and it's still relevant today: "Be Clear, Be Clear, Be Clear!"[26]

Recently, I introduced an evangelism training course to our church entitled "It's Not as Hard as You Think!" Within the course we covered several key elements any evangelism training program should include, as well as a few interesting topics to help engage the learners. I believe there is a lot of room for creativity and innovation, to develop a course for your specific audience.

For example, you may want to include the topic of turning a conversation to spiritual things, overcoming objections and questions, addressing fear, etc. My personal favorite to teach is "How to Be Assertive without Being Obnoxious."[27] There are many relevant, yet peripheral subjects complementing and enhancing any evangelism course. However, there are essential core principles and practical applications any program should include. Next is a basic outline to illustrate how you can begin to structure the core of your evangelism training.[28]

Essential Components of Evangelism Training for Christians

1. The Importance of Evangelism

Before learning how to do something, knowing why one ought to do it often leads to a more diligent and concerted effort. Learning to evangelize is no different. Understanding the eternal implications of what happens when we share God's most important message will help believers grow in ways that could otherwise be overlooked. The proclamation of the gospel is essential to understanding our purpose, the problem that keeps us from fulfilling that purpose, and God's ultimate solution.

Essential Components of an Evangelism Training Initiative:

1. The Importance of Evangelism: Why, Who?
   A. Motivation
   B. Calling

2. The Gospel: What?
   A. Definition
   B. Clarification

3. Methodology: When, Where, How?
   A. Content
   B. Style

A. Evangelism Is Fundamental to Our Ultimate Purpose

Humanity's purpose for living begins and ends with knowing our Creator. Unless people are told about God and shown how they can know him personally, they will never fulfill their ultimate purpose. This is not only temporal, as in the here and now, but also eternal as we worship him forever. Evangelism is how God uses his people—believers—to accomplish his will for all people.

> "Humanity's chief end is to glorify God, and to enjoy him forever."
> —The Westminster Shorter Catechism

B. Evangelism Addresses Our Problem— Separation from God

An understanding of why we need to be reconciled to God in the first place is essential. Unless we see ourselves as sinful, we will not see our need for a Savior. However, since sin did enter the world through Adam and is present in each one of us, the perfect sacrifice—Christ— was necessary as the substitutionary atonement for all our sins.

C. Evangelism Declares God's Solution

God's mission is to reconcile his creation into a loving relationship with him. His means to do so was Christ dying for our sins and being raised from the dead. His method of communicating the mission and the means is by declaration from person to person: evangelism.

> "...most often we have not integrated our belief that Christians are called to be salt and light ... with what we believe and practice concerning 'real' missions.... And it is hard to believe that we really are full-time 'salt and light' when only visiting missionaries are asked to come up front in church and visit our small groups to talk about the ups and downs of their ministries."[29]
> —Darrell Cosden

2. Understanding the Gospel

A. The Importance of Clarity

From the most knowledgeable theologian to the newest believer, the gospel must be understood in its clarity and simplicity. If the Christian does not clearly understand it, how could we ever expect the unbeliever to understand it?

Therefore, we need to make the gospel clear. Larry Moyer says, "Many Christians don't share the gospel; they try to share the whole Bible! Instead of receiving the gospel message, the lost person receives everything from Genesis to Revelation. Although the entirety of scripture encompasses 'good news', the gospel by which we are saved is not 66 books ... the message of the gospel can be communicated in ten words!"[30]

B. The Simple Message of the Gospel

The actual message of the gospel by which we are saved is not hidden in secret code, nor is it something that requires biblical scholarship to articulate. The biblical clear gospel can easily be found in Scripture and expressed in ten words: Christ died for our sins and rose from the dead (1 Cor. 15:1–8).[31]

In 1 Corinthians 2:2 (NKJV) Paul emphasizes, "I determined not to know anything among you except Jesus Christ and Him crucified." It cannot be overstated. The message cannot change; the method has to. There is a stark difference between pre-Christian and post-Christian paganism. Today, the gospel, rather than being greeted as a relevant idea worthy of consideration, is more likely to be dismissed with sarcasm and even hostility. The broad appeal of Christianity in culture, like so many other things, belongs to a past many believers long for, but which we must accept is anachronistic to many.[32] Hence the grave importance of effective methodology when presenting the gospel!

3. Methodology

I have heard it said learning and memorizing a method to present the gospel leads to a "wooden" or "canned" delivery. The fact is the opposite is true. When someone is so sure and confident of what he or she will say when given the opportunity, he or she will be able to relax and be real in any conversation without worrying about what to say when the window opens for the gospel.

Furthermore, most methods simply provide a framework allowing for the user to "customize" the presentation and make it one's own. Empowering and equipping the individual to really embrace his or her unique approach to a gospel presentation is vital. The methodology of Jesus was Jesus. Gimmicky tricks or slick tools never overshadowed his message. He used brilliant illustrations—yes—but always clearly relevant and supportive of the point, not distracting or entertaining for its own sake or the listeners' amusement.[33]

A method can follow Scripture, and it can also be illustrative. Some of the most effective presentations are formed around and within personal testimonies. Whatever the case, the important thing is to cover the essential elements of a gospel presentation.

A. Content

The first essential element of any presentation is awareness of our standing before God— we refer to this as sin. Sinfulness is our condition, as people alienated from God through the fall. It

is the consequence of our state of being. It must be understood we are damaged people living in a damaged world. Most people will readily admit something is "off," that everyone falls short of God's perfection (Rom. 3:23). This point is not about repentance, it's about acknowledgement—personal accountability of one's need to be reconciled to their creator.

The issue is recognizing we are imperfect, fallen, messy people. Working toward a more sinless life is the result of repentance, not a condition of salvation. It demonstrates our desire to follow Christ. Although we should "bear fruits worthy of repentance" (Matt. 3:8, NKJV), turning from sin is not a biblical prerequisite for salvation.[34]

The second essential element of a presentation is the aspect of substitution. It is the understanding Christ died *for* us in our place while we were in that sinful state (Rom. 5:8; 1 Cor. 15:2–5). Although Jesus demonstrated a perfect life for us to follow, that's a function of our spiritual formation *following* salvation.[35] Above all, he willingly gave his life so we could have eternal life.

We must make it clear discipleship is essential following conversion. However, salvation is not offered on a condition we give anything to God. It is extended solely on the basis of the provision he made for us and our belief and trust in that provision.[36] Though well worn, it is an accurate phrase: Don't put the cart before the horse! Which leads us to the final essential component of a presentation.

Trust in Christ alone for salvation is the third essential element of a gospel presentation (Eph. 2:8–9). Every presentation should lead to the point in which the listener is invited to place their trust in Christ. Trust is an effective term to use because it is biblical and easy to understand. While not necessarily harmful, some commonly used phrases should be avoided because they are not clear on the issue. Some examples of these are: "Invite Jesus into your heart," "Give your life to God," and "Make Jesus your Lord and Savior" (something that happens anyway when you place your trust in him).

B. Style

In support of substance is style. It is common for substance to take a back seat to style in many areas of life: fashion, music, art, movies, sports; unfortunately, even church. When presenting the gospel, it's all about the substance (Gal. 1:6–10). Although creativity and innovation are absolutely necessary, and constant adaptation to the language, symbolism, and context of culture is essential; it should never come at the sacrifice of a clear presentation with biblically accurate content.

That said, what do we mean by style when choosing a presentation to learn? Although, as I mentioned earlier, there are as many ways to share the gospel as there are unbelievers, we can categorize presentations into certain types. These aren't the only types, but they are easily recognizable and will help the learner drill down to a method they prefer.

First, and most accurate, is the biblical or "verse-by-verse" style (Isa. 55:11). The user walks the listener through Bible passages arranged in a way that tells the gospel story. As such, there is complete scriptural accuracy with little room for error. Another advantage is, given the proper training, this method is easy to memorize. In addition, it is adaptable for the user to utilize their original illustrations without straying from the message.

However, the biblical method is not without disadvantages. While we must not overlook the primacy of God's Word and the authority of Scripture, the reality is a presentation purely comprised of Bible verses may not speak to the biblically illiterate. Furthermore, in today's post-Christian and pluralistic culture, some equate "Bible-thumping" with the hostile "religious right" and it could provide an additional barrier to those who see the Bible as archaic and obsolete.

Although there are many methods using a direct, verse-by-verse style, some familiar examples include: The Four Spiritual Laws, The Romans Road, and The Bad News/Good News.[37]

There are also methods to utilize storytelling or illustration conveying the gospel message in a creative way while adhering to biblical accuracy. With this style, there is prime opportunity for you to develop your own using any type of medium. It has the potential to transcend cultural and socioeconomic barriers by its adaptability to multiple contexts. Just as significant of an advantage, creative arts often attract listeners who would otherwise not be receptive to the message.

Of course, with creativity comes risk. It is much easier to stray from the core message of the gospel and you may have the temptation to develop style over substance. Even if you have developed or discovered a biblically accurate creative presentation, it may not be easy for everyone to learn or memorize.

While the storytelling, illustrative, or creative style of presenting the gospel has the most room for fresh, innovative ideas, there are examples to help inspire you. Just a few that are biblically accurate include The Evangecube, The Story, and Big Story Gospel Presentation.[38]

A third style is a different kind of storytelling: personal testimony. Everyone has a story about how they came to put their trust in Christ for salvation. The problem is most people don't really know how to clearly articulate the gospel within the context of their story. Teaching believers how to integrate the gospel message is key to using their testimony as an evangelistic presentation.

Although our personal testimony is a powerful tool for sharing our faith, ultimately the truth of the gospel is based on historical fact. It is foundational to everything we believe (1 Cor. 15:14–17). Therefore, any training regarding personal testimony must be centered around the gospel itself.

> "It is worth noticing that the New Testament Christians never attempted to establish the truth of Christianity by appealing to their inward experiences. Other people may have taken note of a change in their lives, but that is another matter. To be sure they would not have rested content with the resurrection simply as a fact of bare history. Paul claimed that he had experienced the risen life when, for example, he declared 'Christ lives in me' (Galatians 2:20). That, however, does not mean that he ever advanced this experience as the ground on which others ought to believe. To put it another way, never do we find him trying to prove the truth of Christianity to others 'because of the difference it has made to my life.'[39]
> —Kenneth Prior

A personal testimony does, however, have some specific advantages when used properly. It is *your* story. No one can question what you believe and how you came to believe it. And because it's yours, it's easy to remember and you can rely upon it in any situation. With the proper amount of preparation, it is possible to share it quickly and succinctly.

Of course, as any method does, the personal testimony has potential pitfalls as well. It may come off as too "experiential" or "touchy-feely," which is another reason to be certain it is centered around a clear gospel. There is always the risk of not presenting a clear gospel message when telling it through story, perhaps especially when it's our own with which we are so familiar. We should avoid becoming lengthy and rambling, which happens easily without proper preparation.

Most methods of developing a personal testimony reference the same idea of using a three-part approach which includes a before Christ section, explanation of how one came to put their trust in Christ, and a since salvation description as the third piece to conclude. I find the "Three-Word" Testimony to be an easy and effective way to teach most people how to construct their testimony (see sidebar).

Christ-followers from all backgrounds, education, and experiences need continuing training in evangelism. Any effective program will include the importance of evangelism, a clear understanding of the gospel, and an overview of methodology. As uncomfortable a word as "evangelism" has become, there is no other word that so encapsulates our calling. Every Christian in your sphere of influence should be able to present the gospel confidently, clearly, and winsomely when the opportunity arises.

Three-Word Testimony

Your testimony is an effective way to share the gospel because it's your story—edited by you, filtered by you, qualified by you, and told by you. You can tell it anywhere, and it includes how you came to Christ and how others can come to Christ, too.

Here are steps you can use—or teach others to use—to craft a personal, three-word testimony.

1. First Word—Should describe your life, feelings, situation, thoughts, etc., before you placed your faith in Christ. Consider: angry, independent, manipulative, miserable, hopeless, empty, addicted, aimless, restless, striving, confused, insecure.

2. Second Word—Should describe how you came to place your faith in Christ. Consider: creation, studied, concert, grew, Bible, friend, trouble, observation, evangelist, spouse, loved.

3. Third Word—Should describe your life, feelings, situation, thoughts, etc., after you placed your faith in Christ. Consider: approachable, peaceful, generous, loving, brave, teacher, servant, elder, hopeful, compassionate, confident.

Once you have your three words, come up with one to two sentences for each word. Provide a brief explanation of how each word relates to your story. For the second word, be sure to include a clear presentation of the gospel.

Three words … 1–2 sentences per word … 3–6 sentences to tell your story.

Example Three-Word Testimony

"Although I believed in the existence of a God and even knew the story of Jesus, I didn't fully understand how it all fit together. I was *ambiguous* about the nature and character of Jesus as God and how he had provided a way for me to be reconciled to the Creator of the universe! Through a series of conversations with new Christian friends in college, as well as exposure to some Christian music with meaningful lyrics, I came to understand Jesus as Savior. I was *awakened* to the reality that Christ died for my sins and rose from the dead. Now I am *assured* that through my trusting in Jesus Christ for salvation, I have an unbroken relationship with God. This relationship is for eternity, and my life with him will not end when my time on earth does."

Figure 14.3 Gospel Presentation Methods Styles-at-a-Glance

Presentation Style	Advantages	Disadvantages	Examples
Biblical/ Verse-by-verse	Little room for error Easy to memorize Adaptable	Limited to biblically literate Vulnerable to negative stereotypes	Four Spiritual Laws Romans Road Bad News/Good News
Illustrative/ Story	Transcends cultural and socioeconomic barriers Adaptable Creative	Risk of straying from the core message Temptation to develop style over substance Could be difficult to learn or memorize	Evangecube The Story Big Story Gospel Presentation
Personal Testimony	It's *your* story Easy to remember Concise	May seem experiential or overly emotional Risk of unclear gospel Could become too lengthy	Three-part structure "Three-Word" Testimony

Conclusion

It is our job as educational leaders to keep that torch burning and spearhead initiatives aimed at perpetuating this skill within our congregations, assemblies, parishes, etc. The more creative you can be with your programs, the better. People are naturally scared of evangelism and hesitant to enter any situation where they are learning to share Christ, let alone they might be called upon to actually present the gospel one day. However, by implementing training born

of grace, not guilt, with an emphasis on contact, not conversion, and a clear understanding of the message and how to present it, I am confident you will see amazing results.

The crucial role of educational ministry is to make disciples. Reaching the non-Christian is at the center of our mission. As we've seen, there is more than one way to accomplish this task. Any effective strategy should include an initiative to intentionally provide instruction for those who know little to nothing of the Bible—a demographic which is rapidly increasing. Much like foreign missionaries introduce new people groups to scripture, you may be introducing it to your friends, coworkers, and neighbors.

> "A person unwilling to fail in the determination to find some way to get the job done will never get started, nor will the one afraid to try and try again make much progress."[40]
> —Robert Coleman

In addition to our tactical, outreach-driven response to biblical illiteracy, those within the faith need effective preparation to reach their spheres of influence. Evangelism training and programs must be intentional and comprehensive. It is a privilege for us to serve by equipping them to be clear and confident.

Engaging with a broken world and inspiring others to do so is difficult. Although there are numerous complexities to understanding our fallen nature, and the gospel by which we are reconciled to God, the core message is simple and full of hope. As an educational leader, if you are unwilling to fail in the determination to find some way to connect with nonbelievers and equip your people to do the same, you will never get started. Even when you fail, if you don't keep trying, you will never make much progress.[41] So I pray that you will be bold in your initiatives as you reach out and within to reach the world.

Opportunities for Continuing Evangelism Education Initiatives

- Personal evangelism
- Evangelistic speaking
- Youth and student evangelism
- Child evangelism
- Workplace evangelism
- Specialized evangelism
  - Disaster relief
  - Urban/inner-city
  - International/short-term missions
  - Holidays
  - Specific world religions-focused

Discussion Questions

1. The author shares personal conversations with nonbelievers. What kind of conversations have you experienced with nonbelievers? How did you feel before, during, and after the conversation?

2. Name some incorrect ideas about a Christian's role in the conversion of a nonbeliever that hinders personal evangelism. How can correct thinking help Christians become less fearful in their interactions with non-Christians?

3. The author recommends two primary strategies for outreach and evangelism in any local church. What are they? Why are both critical in reaching nonbelievers?

4. What did you learn about outreach and evangelism from the author's conversations with his non-saved friends?

5. What did you learn from this chapter that will help you relax and make evangelistic conversations simply a natural part of your life?

Resources for Further Study

Books

Cecil, Douglas M. *The 7 Principles of an Evangelistic Life*. Chicago: Moody, 2003.

Chafer, Lewis Sperry. *True Evangelism: Winning Souls Through Prayer*. Grand Rapids: Kregel, 1993.

Coleman, Robert E. *The Master Plan of Evangelism*. 30th Anniv. ed. Grand Rapids: Revell, 1993.

Dever, Mark. *The Gospel & Personal Evangelism*. Wheaton, IL: Crossway, 2007.

Moyer, R. Larry. *21 Things God Never Said: Correcting Our Misconceptions about Evangelism*. Grand Rapids: Kregel, 2004.

Newman, Randy. *Questioning Evangelism: Engaging People's Hearts the Way Jesus Did*. Grand Rapids: Kregel, 2004.

Pollock, Doug. *God Space: Where Spiritual Conversations Happen Naturally.* Loveland, CO: Group, 2009.

Root, Jerry and Stan Guthrie. *The Sacrament of Evangelism.* Chicago: Moody, 2011.

Yaconelli, Michael. *Messy Spirituality.* Grand Rapids: Zondervan, 2002.

Studies and Resources Aimed at the Curious, Not-Yet Christians

Coleman, Lyman. *Serendipity Bible for Personal and Small Group Study.* Grand Rapids: Zondervan, 1996.

Community Bible Study—http://www.communitybiblestudy.org/

Cru: Investigative Bible Study—https://www.cru.org/content/dam/cru/legacy/2012/02/Jesus-Study.pdf.

Intervarsity: Groups Investigating God (GIGs)—https://intervarsity.org/bible-studies/gigs-index

Poling, Justin, and Mark Mittelberg, eds. *The Journey: The Study Bible for Spiritual Seekers.* Rev. ed. Grand Rapids: Zondervan, 2014.

Scazzero, Peter. *Introducing Jesus: Starting and Investigative Bible Study for Seekers.* Downers Grove, IL: InterVarsity Press, 1991.

Search Ministries—http://www.searchministries.org/.

Resources for Evangelism Training Programs and Curriculum

Billy Graham Evangelistic Association—www.billygraham.org/grow-your-faith/how-to-share-your-faith/tools

Dare 2 Share—www.dare2share.org/mobilize

EvanTell—www.evantell.org/training

The God Test—www.thegodtest.org

The Story—www.spreadtruth.com/thestory

Author Bio

A. J. Rinaldi is the Associate Pastor of Adult Discipleship at Frisco Bible Church in Frisco, Texas. He served for nine years as a Ministry Director with the parachurch organization *EvanTell*. A. J. has published over fifty articles related to evangelism and outreach in print and online, and is a guest lecturer and featured speaker at colleges and universities nationwide. His contributions to curricular development, as well as practical evangelism tools and materials, are being used in a variety of applications. A. J. and his wife Dana, an accomplished Worship Leader, have been serving together in ministry since the early 1990s. Prior to entering full-time ministry, A. J. enjoyed a diverse career in the healthcare industry which began when he served as a Combat Medic with the U.S. Army's 82nd Airborne Division. A. J. is a graduate of Belmont University and Dallas Theological Seminary.

CHAPTER 14 APPENDIX: A PROFILE IN OUTWARD FOCUS: SADDLEBACK IRVINE NORTH

The Saddleback Irvine North campus launched in 2015 in Irvine, California. Within one year attendance more than doubled. All their Sunday services, as well as their ministries, focus toward the unchurched.

Worship Services

The worship service style is contemporary music; the language is plain and direct, lacking "insider" terms that only those within the church would understand. The messages are practical, but also biblical. Only people who call Saddleback their church home partake in the offering. The worship service is positioned as a gift to unchurched guests.

Student and Children's Ministries

Saddleback Kids Ministry and Student Ministries (Youth) have a similar format. Kids walk away with Bible stories, as well as games, crafts, and prizes that bring the lessons to life.

First Impressions Ministry

The first impressions ministry—which includes hospitality, greeters, connection center, healthcare, and security—are trained to proactively engage with guests. The emphasis is on recognizing that for many who attend, this could be their first church experience.

Seeker Sensitive vs. Seeker-Focused

The Purpose Driven Church Model Saddleback Irvine North incorporates is one of being seeker-sensitive, not seeker-focused. Seeker-sensitive is different. It is sensitive to where the unchurched person may be in their spiritual journey while not completely seeker-focused, which abandons spiritual truth at any cost to attract an unbelieving crowd.

Evangelistic Leadership

The campus pastor, instructors, and any other ministry leaders—staff or volunteer—are chief evangelists. Saddleback Irvine North's leadership show by example how to witness by word and deed.

Strength in Diversity

At Saddleback, they say "every member is a minister." This calling is reinforced through messages, educational leadership, and personal invitation. As with many communities across the country, Irvine is increasingly diverse. Therefore, one of the tasks is to engage ministry leaders from multiple cultural backgrounds and ethnicities. This has proven to be both challenging and fruitful. Community outreach becomes more effective and "family-oriented" when lay leadership reflects the diversity of the community.

Quality vs. Quantity

Although Saddleback Irvine North will certainly continue to grow in attendance, they have a commitment to maintain intimacy and a warm and welcoming environment upon which they have built the ministry. Quality over quantity is the emphasis. When effective ministry and outreach is the focus, size just doesn't matter.

Changing Lives

- People trusting in Christ
- Baptisms
- Marriages restored
- Addictions overcome
- God replacing idols
- The church—the body of Christ truly coming together to support and minister to one another. That is what matters.
- Changing lives through Jesus is what motivates Saddleback Irvine North's staff and volunteers to continue reaching out to the community, and caring for those who find God's message and mission being lived out here.

Special Thanks to D. J. Crawford, Irvine North Campus Pastor, for providing their story.

Endnotes

1. See the chapter "The Heart of Making Disciples" by Mark Heinemann for further discussion of discipleship and specifically the Engel Scale.

2. As so succinctly stated by my friend, mentor, and former employer Dr. R. Larry Moyer of EvanTell (www.evantell.org).

3. Method is not a bad word—it's an essential tool!

4. John Piper, *Let The Nations Be Glad! The Supremacy of God In Missions*, 2nd ed. (Grand Rapids: Baker Academic, 2003), 195.

5. Darrell Cosden, *The Heavenly Good of Earthly Work* (Peabody, MA: Hendrickson, 2006), 139.

6. Cosden, *The Heavenly Good of Earthly Work*, 140–141.

7. The official term for this theory is *tabula rasa*.

8. Lewis Sperry Chafer, *True Evangelism: Winning Souls through Prayer* (Grand Rapids, MI: Kregel, 1993), 58.

9. George Barna, *America at the Crossroads: Explosive Trends Shaping America's Future and What You Can Do About It* (Grand Rapids: Baker, 2016), 36–37.

10. The Barna Group, "The Bible in America: 6-Year Trends," June 15, 2016, https://barna.org/research/faith-christianity/research-release/the-bible-in-america-6-year-trends.

11. Kenneth Briggs, *The Invisible Bestseller: Searching for the Bible in America* (Grand Rapids: Eerdmans, 2016), 6.

12. Ibid.

13. Duane Litfin, *Word vs. Deed: Resetting The Scales to a Biblical Balance* (Wheaton, IL: Crossway, 2012), 17.

14. For more on this subject, see Leland Ryken's excellent book *How to Read the Bible as Literature: and Get More Out of It* (Grand Rapids: Zondervan, 1984).

15. This is not to diminish, in any way, the power and authority of God's Word. It's recognizing that many unbelievers have no connection to Scripture, and therefore need to be eased or educated into it by illustration and personal connection.

16. David Kinnaman and Gabe Lyons, *UnChristian: What a New Generation Really Thinks about Christianity ... and Why It Matters* (Grand Rapids: Baker, 2007); Gabe Lyons, *The Next Christians: The Good News about the End of Christian America* (New York: Doubleday Religion, 2010).

17. More information from the Barna Group can be found at www.barna.com.

18. Also see the chapter "Mentoring the Next Generation" by Barbara Newman and the chapter "In Between: Adolescents" by Jay Sedwick for additional insight on working across generations.

19. Doug Pollock, *God Space: Where Spiritual Conversations Happen Naturally* (Loveland, CO: Group, 2009), 31.

20. Michael Gerson and Peter Wehner, *City of Man: Religion and Politics in a New Era* (Chicago: Moody, 2010), 66.

21. Mark Dever, *The Gospel & Personal Evangelism* (Wheaton, IL: Crossway, 2007), 76.

22. Randy Newman, *Questioning Evangelism: Engaging People's Hearts the Way Jesus Did* (Grand Rapids: Kregel, 2004), 23, 24.

23. Ibid., 24.

24. Litfin, *Word vs. Deed*, 13.

25. Dever, *The Gospel & Personal Evangelism*, 75.

26.   Evangelism training through EvanTell can be found at www.evantell.org.

27.   For more information, additional tips, lesson plans, or help with content, please feel free to contact the author at aj.rinaldi@outlook.com.

28.   For additional information and resources, visit www.evantell.org where much of this material was initially developed and is used here with permission.

29.   Cosden, *The Heavenly Good of Earthly Work*, 136–137.

30.   R. Larry Moyer, *You Can Tell It!* seminar available at www.evantell.org.

31.   Ibid.

32.   Kenneth Prior, *The Gospel in a Pagan Society* (Ross-shire, Scotland: Christian Focus, 1995), 96.

33.   Robert Coleman, *The Master Plan of Evangelism*, 30th aniv. ed. (Grand Rapids: Revell, 1993), 74.

34.   R. Larry Moyer, *21 Things God Never Said: Correcting Our Misconceptions About Evangelism* (Grand Rapids: Kregel, 2004), 97.

35.   See the chapter "The Heart of Making Disciples" by Mark Heinemann for more information on discipleship.

36.   Moyer, *21 Things God Never Said*, 127.

37.   The Four Spiritual Laws evangelistic presentation was originally created by Bill Bright of Cru (formerly Campus Crusade for Christ). Tracts using this method can be obtained at http://crustore.org/four-laws-english; The Romans Road evangelistic presentation is used by many organizations (Rom. 3:23; 5:8; 6:23; 10:9–10, 13); The Good News/Bad News evangelistic presentation was originally created by Larry Moyer of EvanTell. Tracts using this method can be obtained at http://www.evantell.org/gospel-presentation/.

38.   The Evangecube evangelistic presentation was developed by e3 Partners and can be found at http://www.e3resources.org/; The Story evangelistic presentation was developed by Spread Truth and can be found at http://spreadtruth.com/thestory; Big Story Gospel Presentation was developed by Intervarsity and can be found at http://evangelism.intervarsity.org/how/gospel-outline/big-story-gospel-presentation.

39.   Prior, *The Gospel in a Pagan Society*, 79.

40.   Coleman, *The Master Plan of Evangelism*, 108.

41.   Ibid.

HOW:
THE PROCESS

Chapter 15
FACILITATING TRANSFORMATIVE SMALL GROUPS

Joye Baker

> *Let us hold unswervingly to the hope we profess, for he who prom-*
> *ised is faithful. And let us consider how we may spur one another*
> *on toward love and good deeds, not giving up meeting together, as*
> *some are in the habit of doing, but encouraging one another—and*
> *all the more as you see the Day approaching.*
>
> —Hebrews 10:23–25

I ARRIVED AT DALLAS Seminary (DTS) on a hot, August day in 1996. I was a widow of seven years, having lost my husband in a car accident after eighteen years of marriage. My three children were college age and older and I was following the dream my husband and I shared to go into full-time vocational ministry. I became aware of the Spiritual Formation (SF) program at DTS, and joined a group of five other women.[1]

I quickly began to look forward to the weekly meetings where we shared the highs and lows of our lives and encouraged and prayed for one another. My past experiences with small groups had been mainly centered on Bible study or discipleship, with little emphasis on the creation of a safe place where members of the group openly shared personal issues of struggle. That concept of vulnerability was foreign to me and yet my heart longed to connect deeply with other believers.

We learned a process to develop and share the story of our lives. At first apprehensive, I shared the details of my past with my group and peace flooded my soul as I experienced unconditional love and acceptance in the midst of confessing my past wrong choices.

The small group curriculum guided us through a process to identify one particular area of our life that hindered our relationship with God and ultimately would negatively impact our effectiveness in ministry. God revealed to me a fear that had taken root in my heart during my years as a teenager. As I shared this discovery with my sisters in Christ, I realized a false fear enslaved me. Through my years as a Christian, I had embraced God's forgiveness and was no longer that teenager who desperately needed and wanted to be loved. And yet, this fear had affected all my relationships for thirty years! My dear friends prayed for me and I no longer experienced the fear and in its place came a sense of freedom and peace.

After my first SF group, I have led other groups of women through our small groups program, served as a mentor/coach to women group leaders, joined the SF staff, and ultimately began to teach a master's level course on developing and leading small groups.

These experiences led to a deeply held conviction. We will never fulfill God's plan for our lives without connecting with other believers in a small group context—not just any small group, but one that creates an environment that invites transparency, acceptance, and unconditional love. It's a challenge in our very private, individualistic culture to be open and honest with others, yet critical in order for the body of Christ to survive and thrive.

Biblical Foundations of Small Groups

Any ministry that describes itself as Christian must have a biblical foundation. Biblical principles are at the core of the educational cycle as explained in Chapter 21. As we consider the validity of developing a means to gather believers together in small groups, what biblical truths support the establishment of small groups in a local church setting?

The Trinity

First, our God is described as the Trinity because he exists in the form of three persons: Father, Son, and Holy Spirit (Gen. 1:26–27; 3:22; John 3:16–17; 16:7; 2 Cor. 13:14). God is essentially a small group! He expresses himself in unity as all three Persons in the Godhead are equally God and in diversity because all have unique functions. A small group ministry allows for the people of God to experience and reflect the equality and differences of the God in whom they have put their faith. Todd Speidell, a noted theologian, aptly states, "Humans find their true being as a communion of persons whose mutual personal relations mirror, however imperfectly, the triune life of God."[2] Small groups are certainly not the only way believers can image God, but they represent one way the world can witness the unity and diversity found in the Godhead and group members can experience the unity and intimacy God created people to enjoy with one another.

> "God is triune—Father, Son and Holy Spirit—and lives in eternal unity as three persons in one being. God is a social unity, a community of love, while at the same time each person in the Trinity is unique."[3]
> —Scott Boren

Relationships

We learn from Jesus that the basis of human life is rooted in relationships. When asked, Jesus declared that the greatest commandment involved loving God and loving others (Matt. 22:37–40). The Christian life is "a journey *with*

Christ rather than a journey *to* Christ."[4] God calls us into a love relationship which begins at the moment we trust Christ as Savior. But Jesus emphasizes that the Christian life is also characterized by love for others. As former professor Howard Hendricks often said in his classes at Dallas Seminary, "You can impress people at a distance; you can only impact them up close. The general principle is this, the closer the personal relationship, the greater the potential for impact."

Designing ways for people to connect in small groups creates opportunities for them to give and receive the love of God and share it with one another. Centuries ago, people experienced close contact on a daily basis. Families lived near one another, worked beside those in other families, and gathered in various ways to enjoy time together. Our fast-paced, technology-driven culture seldom fosters an environment where deep relational connection occurs among people. Attending a Sunday morning service, though very important for the purpose of corporate teaching, worship, and casual conversation, seldom allows people to connect in a way that fosters loving others as Jesus commands. God designed us for an intimate, trusting relationship not just with him but also with other people.

Community and Fellowship

Since our relationship with God and with others characterizes the foundational components of small groups, community and fellowship lie at the heart of small groups. New Testament writers admonish believers to enjoy *koinonia*. Jerry Bridges notes, "In both Acts 2:24 and 1 John 1:3, the New English Bible translates *koinonia* as 'sharing a common life.' This is the most basic meaning of *koinonia*, or fellowship. It is sharing

a common life with other believers—a life that, as John says, we share with God the Father and God the Son. It is a relationship, not an activity."[5]

Small groups are a catalyst for people to enjoy Christian community and fellowship with one another. It's more than just a social time together. It's an opportunity to penetrate below the surface, connect at a heart level, and speak truth motivated by love into one another's lives.[6] God designed us for relationship and we cannot find true fulfillment and satisfaction outside of significant relationships with him and with others. "Community becomes God's nurturing, caring, revealing, supportive means of displaying himself as a personal relational being in our culture."[7]

> "Even in the last moments of his life, Jesus was concerned about community. In fact, community is the very essence of his character. The complex doctrine of the Trinity demonstrates to us that God exists in community with himself. Scripture proclaims that God is love because he is inherently relational."[8]
> —Heather Zempel

Old and New Testament Models

To further support the value of small groups, we find evidence in the Scriptures where God sanctioned the need for small groups. First, in the Old Testament, Moses's father-in-law Jethro urges Moses to distribute the responsibility of leadership into small groups. Jethro explains, "That will make your load lighter, because they will share it with you. If you do this and God so commands, you will be able to stand the strain, and all these people will go home satisfied" (Exod. 18:22–23). Although this example particularly addresses the need for delegation, the broader message emphasizes the benefits gained when people join together in small groups.

Second, Jesus provides a model in the New Testament. Although he often addressed the masses, his strategy to reach the world came primarily through a small group of twelve men with whom he spent constant and intentional time over a period of three plus years. At Christ's ascension, these men along with other faithful followers of Jesus received a commission to spread the gospel.

Finally, the book of Acts chronicles the early church and establishes the framework of small groups: "They devoted themselves to the apostles' teaching and to the fellowship, to the breaking of bread and to prayer.... All the believers were together and had everything in common" (Acts 2:42–44). We don't find small groups mentioned per se in the New Testament, but evidence of people meeting together in small groups happened many times as they went "house to house" (Acts 20:20) and Jesus travelled with a small group of disciples along with other men and women with whom he shared life. "The way of Jesus is the way of small groups."[9]

The Scriptures present multiple examples which inform us of the importance and value of creating ways for small groups of people to gather together within the local church. But, what exactly does the term "small groups" mean?

Defining a Small Group

During my forty-plus years since I accepted Christ as my Savior, I have participated in numerous small groups. These varied in number according to the purpose of the group. Some were as small as three women meeting together regularly for prayer and accountability, to a midweek discipleship group of twelve men and women, to a weekly Bible study group of fifteen, to a Sunday school class, to a support group that addressed various emotional struggles. I've served on church and ministry committees and shared mission trips with a small group of women. People gather together regularly in multiple types of groups whether in families, recreational activities, classrooms, board meetings, or coffee shops. Except for when we find ourselves alone, life is essentially a series of group gatherings.

As we consider small groups in a local church, they vary greatly according to the needs of the people in a local body of believers. No matter the group, its design should provide opportunities for people to experience a deeper relational connection with others that goes beyond the surface connection that normally happens at large gatherings during weekend worship services. The groups can consist of married couples, singles, men, women, families, youth, or intergenerational mixed ages. For many years, small groups of people have met on Sunday mornings in classes called Sunday school. In addition, many churches now have a designated staff position to oversee a specific small group ministry which encourages the membership to join a small group that meets weekly most often in homes or sometimes at the church. These particular small groups are described as cell groups, life groups, community groups, care groups, fellowship groups, grace groups, home groups, or flocks. Churches give their small groups a variety of names, but they all serve a similar purpose: to move people into a smaller, more intimate setting to deepen relationships and enhance spiritual growth.

No one way defines a small group ministry in a local church. In the broadest sense, *a Christian small group seeks to facilitate spiritual growth by regular time together, shared discovery of God's Truth, open and honest communication, and mutual encouragement and love.* Each church leadership team needs to prayerfully determine the distinctive way in which a small group ministry would enhance the overall mission of their local body. Every church should include a means to help people experience life together outside of the weekly Sunday morning worship service. As stated at the beginning of this chapter, the writer of Hebrews encourages believers to meet together regularly. Jerry Bridges explains in more detail the broader message of these verses when he states:

> The admonition of Hebrews 10:24–25— "not giving up meeting together"—is not fulfilled by attending church on Sunday morning, as is often supposed. Rather, it is fulfilled only when we follow through with the instruction to encourage, spur on, or stimulate one another. This cannot be done sitting in pews, row upon row, listening to the pastor teach. It can be done only through the mutual interchange of admonishment and encouragement. This is not to diminish the importance of the teaching ministry of pastors....But we need both the public teaching of our pastors and the mutual encouragement and admonishing of one another [which

is accomplished best in a small group setting]. It is the latter that seems to be the main thrust of Hebrews 10:24–25.[10]

Harley Atkinson describes four different categories of small groups:

- Process-oriented—friendship and home fellowship groups
- Content-oriented—Bible study and discussion groups
- Task-oriented—committees, work, evangelistic, and ministry groups
- Need-oriented—encounter, growth, support, twelve-step recovery, spiritual formation groups[11]

No matter what the purpose of a group, there exists the potential to contribute to their members' spiritual transformation. The content of this chapter applies to any kind of small group, but I want to particularly focus on groups which often meet during the week and normally in homes. But some groups may choose to meet in the church building during the week or on Sunday mornings to accommodate people's schedules or to access childcare. Yet, the overall intent remains the same: an opportunity for small groups of people to connect together outside of the large-group weekend worship service.

With this in mind, Bill Donahue and Russ Robinson offer these church distinctions related to small groups: "There are three ways to describe the role of group life in a local church: the church *with* small groups, the church *of* small groups, and the church *is* small groups."[12] The insights I will share relate primarily to a "church of small groups" where multiple types of small groups make up a church body and people are encouraged to find biblical community through regular connection through regular connection with other people, but all the principles in this chapter are applicable for any small group setting.[13]

The Goal of Small Groups

As the title of this chapter indicates, the overarching goal of small groups should be "to transform." The driving purpose of all small groups should contribute toward the spiritual transformation of the group members. As Sam O'Neal clearly articulates, "The goal of a small group is spiritual growth. It's transformation. It's helping participants move away from that first gasping breath they took as born-again children of God, still wallowing in their sin, and toward their ultimate identity as fully glorified disciples of Christ."[14] We should see this lived out in Bible studies, support groups, on missions trips, outreach opportunities, sports ministries, and other times when people connect in a small group setting.

At the same time, I emphasize that small groups can "*contribute* towards the spiritual transformation of the group members" because there certainly exist other ways besides the participation in a small group that can enhance a person's spiritual growth. Sunday morning worship and teaching and other church-wide large group gatherings can and should positively impact people spiritually. But it has been my experience and observation that regular, intentional community in a small group setting on a weekly basis, with other believers who offer open and honest dialogue with one another, often provides the rich soil needed to produce spiritual growth.

> "The core idea behind this ministry we call 'small groups' is that disciples of Jesus are not meant to follow after him alone. God is a divine community, and we are made in his image—created to live and learn and love and serve in community as well."[15]
>
> —Sam O'Neal

Hindrances to Building Community

Now that we know that the Bible mandates Christians to gather in small groups and that they benefit from intentional community, the big question becomes, "Why are so many people reluctant to join a small group?" What hinders the development of authentic Christian community through small groups? These include individualism, busyness and priorities, mobility and change, and lack of trust and commitment.

Individualism

Biblical community requires people to value the group over the individual and have an other-centered mindset rather than a me-centered focus. This flies in the face of the American values of independence and self-sufficiency. I remember as a child hearing my mother remind me countless times, "Joye, when you get down to it, you only have yourself to depend upon." I learned at home, in school, and through the media that I needed to study hard, go to college, and in my own strength make a life for myself. Though a people-person at heart, I often saw people as means to an end to accomplish my own agenda and make my way in the world. We have millions of adults who have bought into the same mindset and so often resist the basic components of biblical community. As Julie Gorman states:

> While the concept of community is deeply rooted in biblical soil, we live in the land of the self-made individualist. "Meism" is nurtured as a cardinal virtue. Self-centered individualism is considered an essential right of being a person. This is the principal language of our time.[16]

In order for a small group to function well, it has to have a communal focus. The people within the group must prioritize the needs of others in the group over their own wishes and desires. The apostle Paul reminded the early church: "Do nothing out of selfish ambition and vain conceit. Rather, in humility value others above yourself, not looking to your own interests but each of you to the interests of the others" (Phil. 2:3–4). Unless we set aside individual rights and personal autonomy, it becomes very difficult if not impossible for a small group to function in a biblical way.

Busyness and Priorities

People have massive amounts of options as to how to spend their time, especially in our larger cities. Many represent good choices, but too many "good" choices can crowd out the best things that God might want for us. Families enroll their children in multiple activities, men and women work long hours each week, people choose to spend time watching television, surfing the Web, checking social media, going to movies, attending sporting events, traveling here and there, and indulging in other distractions.

Some are single parents with no time to spare after holding down one or two jobs, caring for their children, taking care of all the demands of a home, and often battling exhaustion and lack of sleep. With only twenty-four hours in a day, attending a small group quickly becomes crowded out of an already full calendar.

Mobility and Change

People tend to hold down a number of different jobs in their lifetime which often require multiple moves. This mobility impacts relationships because committed friendships take time to develop and a mobile society does not create the extended time required for people to connect deeply with one another. In the women's Bible study small group I lead on Wednesday evenings, usually half of the group members drop out every six months due to a move or job change. Or such things as work schedule, family responsibilities, or other options in the evenings factor into their decision. We live in a society that experiences change at warp speed now that technology affords us on-demand information and instant gratification. These quick and constant changes tend to hinder involvement in small groups.

Lack of Trust and Commitment

Finally, development of a successful small group involves trust and commitment, two characteristics that people often find difficult. Our twenty-first-century population consists of many adults who come from broken homes and dysfunctional families. They have experienced sexual relationships outside of marriage, divorce, infidelity, and abuse of all kinds. These negative experiences tend to create distrust, fear, anxiety, addictions, and self-protection which often contribute to a lack of commitment. Trust and commitment are foundational to the success of a small group. Honesty, transparency, and vulnerability represent key ingredients for spiritual growth. Despite the fact that many Christians have allowed the complexity of twenty-first-century life to crowd out the importance of connecting in a small group, church leaders need to make small groups a priority and then prayerfully seek ways to design groups that can meet people's relational needs, even if the people fail to recognize it. The first step involves strategizing how to best develop an effective small group ministry.

> "People who have reservations or fears of entering a church sanctuary may be willing to join a small group in a home or participate in a lay-led support group. The small group, often serving as a kind of a halfway house, provides a nonthreatening opportunity to become part of a church."[17]
> —Harley Atkinson

Developing a Small Group Ministry

To successfully develop a small group ministry, the educational cycle found at the end of this book offers a good guide with accompanying worksheets at the end of the chapter. Before you begin, make sure the church leadership support and will enthusiastically promote the value and benefits of small groups for the people in the congregation. Once the leadership pledges support, a select group of people within the church, often made up of both pastoral staff and lay people, should form

a committee to begin the process of designing a small group ministry.

Each local church reflects uniqueness in its location, size, ethnic, and gender mix, theological doctrines, core values, and mission. Proverbs 3:5–6 declares both the starting point and the continual focus of any ministry: "Trust in the LORD with all your heart and do not lean on your own understanding. In all your ways acknowledge him, and he will make your paths straight." Prayer becomes key as only through the guidance of the Holy Spirit can all the components of a ministry be successfully formed and carried out. "In their hearts humans plan their course, but the LORD establishes their steps" (Prov. 16:9). Human planning remains important and necessary, but God gives the wisdom for each decision.

Foundational Issues

First, write biblical principles, core values, mission and vision statements. Then conduct an environmental scan of both the church and the local community.[18] Clarify the overall purpose and goal of your small group ministry.[19] Your groups will usually meet in homes or at the church, though some groups may choose to meet in a coffee shop or the back room of a restaurant. Normally twelve to fifteen people constitute the maximum number for a small group to enable all the people in the group to have the opportunity to take part in meaningful conversation.

Meeting Times

Determine how often the groups will meet. Different churches select one of two options: weekly or twice a month. The weekly format offers the best opportunity for group members to get to know one another and develop regular community. But if you discern that the people in your church seem unwilling to commit to more than twice a month, then that becomes the better option. For some churches, a third arrangement involves the offer of some weekly and some biweekly groups to allow people to select according to their schedules and availability. Try to avoid the option to meet once a month. People can rarely build a close relationship with one another on a monthly basis. Plus, if anyone misses a meeting, a two-month lapse in attendance occurs which creates the probable loss of interest and commitment.

Open and Closed Groups

Now decide whether your groups will be closed or open. This depends on the purpose of the group. Open groups welcome new members into existing groups at any time with an understanding that once a group grows to about twenty members, consideration must be given to birth a new group.[20] Closed groups are not open to newcomers. The group members begin together on a certain date and stay together. As new people want to join a group, the leadership of the small group ministry forms a new group. Jim Egli and Dwight Marable offer this explanation:

> Proponents of closed groups have argued that closing the membership of a group allows people to become closer to one another, to develop deeper friendships, and to share more deeply. Proponents of open groups have contended that small groups are the more effective way to reach new people, so it is counterproductive to have closed groups.[21]

Open groups tend to emphasize evangelism and focus on ways to welcome new people into existing groups. Those who favor closed groups emphasize discipleship and spiritual growth by creating an environment of intimacy and deeper personal sharing. Often the acceptance of new people into groups that have already shared intimately with one another will disrupt the deep connection that has been developed among the group members. One isn't better than the other. They serve different purposes. Some churches offer both depending on the overall goals of the small group ministry.

Meeting Format

As a small group ministry develops, give thought to what to include in each small group meeting. Structure your group meeting according to the focus of the group. Some components to consider include fellowship, worship, prayer, biblical discussion, service, and outreach. Rarely will a group meeting contain all of these activities at the same time, though some may choose to include various ones at different meetings. For instance, the women's Bible study group I lead discusses our lesson for three or four weeks and then takes a break for one week and we enjoy a time of fellowship and informal conversation. Sometimes we select a service project and join together outside of our scheduled meeting time to package gifts for a pregnancy crisis center or assist in an event to support our local refugees. One year, we reached out to an overseas missionary and included her in our group through email and Skype. We also sent her birthday and Christmas gifts.

Other small groups may be strictly service-oriented or evangelistically focused so much of their meeting time will include discussing and planning their outreach projects. Support groups will often include time in God's Word, sharing openly about issues in which the members struggle, and offering encouragement and support to one another. No matter the group, prayer should always have a place when a group of believers comes together. Prayer enables our hearts to join together in grateful acknowledgement of the presence of God in our midst, with thankfulness and humble dependence.

In addition, small group meetings need to provide at least a short amount of time for informal fellowship as the meeting begins and ends. Relational connection through casual conversation demonstrates genuine interest and care for one another. Some groups like to start with a song or short devotional or testimonial, and prayer. Often groups end their time with prayer requests. Suggestions on how to include prayer requests can be found later in this chapter under the section entitled "Leading a Small Group Discussion."

When you consider the establishment of groups which serve as "home" groups or "community" groups, the members of the group often determine the format of their group time. Fellowship, prayer, and some type of refreshments should always be included. Some groups will have a structured Bible study, others will include a devotional to focus on God and biblical truth. Some groups will have three meetings a month and the fourth meeting might include some kind of service project. Or they might include a service project every two to four months. I have also observed groups which meet twice a month all together, once a month the men and women meet separately,

and then the fourth time together they share a service-oriented or fellowship time. Many creative and different ways exist to structure a small group according to the needs and interests of the group members.

Curriculum

Small groups should prioritize God's Word so that group members remember the central place biblical truth belongs in their lives. Some churches designate what their groups will study. Other churches give their groups freedom to select their biblical focus. Different options include the following.[22]

Sermon-Based Studies

The church assigns someone the task to design questions based on the Sunday sermon and then make the questions available to groups to use as a basis of discussion at their group meeting. People have the opportunity to ask questions and discuss the key points from the pastor's weekly teaching and consider ways to apply biblical truth in their personal lives. Someone in the group summarizes the Sunday message for those who were unable to attend the church service.

Video Studies

The church makes available a selection of Bible studies taught by respected teachers of God's Word. The group members view the message on the video together and then discuss the suggested questions that accompany the teaching.[23]

Church-Written Studies

A selected team of men and women in the church write curriculum for the small groups. In this format, someone in the small group may provide a short teaching time, but discussion fills the majority of the group time. Often with this approach, group members answer a series of questions individually during the week, in preparation for the discussion when the group meets back together.

Published Curriculum Studies

Many biblical scholars have written excellent Bible studies. The church provides a list of various studies which have been evaluated to make sure the content aligns with the theological position of the church. Group members discuss the options and select a particular study from the list that best meets the needs of the group.

Books-of-the-Bible Studies

Some groups choose to study a particular book of the Bible. The church offers a list of recommended video or book studies to choose from or the group members select a video or book and submit it to the church leadership for evaluation and approval.

Topical Book Studies

Some groups desire to study a Christian book. Each member of the group purchases the selected book, reads a designated portion, and when the group meets together they discuss what they have read. Some books will include questions at the end of each chapter to use as a basis of the discussion. If not, the one who leads the discussion can develop some questions to use in the group discussion. The church can provide an approved list of books or ask groups to submit their choices for evaluation and approval.

> "As people process aloud, they become instruments of change in one another's lives."[24]
> —Julie Gorman

Selecting and Training Leaders

The success of a small group depends on a skilled leader. The selection and development of leaders must have a high priority in any small group ministry.

Selecting Leaders

The ideal scenario to select leaders calls for the leader of the small groups ministry to personally identify and invite men and women as potential small group leaders. Ask the current leaders of small groups to watch for potential new leaders. In our Spiritual Formation program at Dallas Seminary, we challenge our small group leaders to be on the alert for qualified men or women in their group whom they can recommend as future leaders. As we start to recruit new leaders for the following year, they are encouraged to "leave us a leader." Potential leaders should demonstrate the following characteristics: spiritual maturity, dependability, availability, faithfulness, teachability, humility, commitment, and a love for people. In addition, look for those who actively involve themselves in the church and participate in a small group where others have also observed these qualities in them.

First, design a one-page description of a small group leader's responsibilities such as coordinating group meetings, facilitating discussions based on the curriculum, overseeing or delegating fellowship and service opportunities, conducting times of prayer, meeting one-on-one with members, and identifying needs for pastoral care. Also create a list of benefits available to each potential small group leader which include opportunities for training, coaching, and personal development.

Second, contact potential leaders. Ask if they would consider serving as a small group leader. If so, arrange a time for an interview. Do not allow anyone to lead a group without a vetting process in place to make sure all group leaders have the qualifications needed for leadership. During the interview, get to know potential leaders, explain the responsibilities of a small group leader, ask them why they desire small group leadership, what they hope to gain personally, and answer any questions they might have. I do not recommend that a final decision be made at the conclusion of the interview. Suggest everyone involved pray and seek God's guidance with the understanding that a follow-up contact will be made soon after the interview to confirm whether or not to extend an invitation to lead.

Training Leaders

After the selection of leaders, consider how you will train, develop, and support leaders. Many people are reluctant to lead because they have little experience leading a group. They may meet all of the stated qualifications, but lack the confidence to take on the responsibility. In many cases, potential leaders misunderstand what is required of them. It becomes very important to assure them that they will be given training to prepare them to lead their group.

Some prospective leaders erroneously think they must possess the ability to teach in order to lead a small group. On the contrary, their main responsibility involves facilitation of a discussion,

not teaching the Bible. Eddie Mosley explains, "Our initial training spent a lot of energy on helping leaders move from seeing themselves as the teacher to seeing themselves as more of a facilitator." The following section in this chapter details how to effectively facilitate a discussion.

When you want to start a small group ministry but lack experienced group leaders, consider training through a "turbo group." Potential leaders meet together as a group over an established period of time and receive training in small group leadership skills. They become leaders of newly formed groups.[25]

Provide leader training a number of times a year when most convenient for group leaders. Normally these training events occur in the evening or on weekends since the majority of people work weekday jobs. Consider offering the same training two different times to accommodate leaders' schedules. In addition to training, set aside an annual time to show appreciation and express thanks to group leaders. Consider such things as a handwritten thank-you note, a dinner, a picnic, an invitation to a sporting event, or a gift card, depending on the budget of the church.

Coaching Leaders

To best support and encourage small group leaders, each leader should have a "coach." In large-size churches, each coach oversees five or more small group leaders. In smaller churches, the person who directs the small group ministry functions as a coach for all the small group leaders. Select coaches who have previously led a small group and qualify to give guidance and support to newer, less experienced group leaders. Jim Egli and Dwight Marable explain:

Coaches meet personally with their leaders to encourage them in their spiritual growth and leadership, they are aware of their leaders' needs and are praying for them, they gather their leaders for ministry and problem-solving, and occasionally they visit their groups.... Our research demonstrates that coaching is the most pivotal factor in the health of small group ministries.[26]

Co-Leaders

Most people who serve in various ministries emphasize the value of shared leadership where two people share the responsibilities of a leadership position. Small group leaders particularly benefit from co-leadership. It provides a way to share the responsibilities of leading a group. I co-led a small group Bible study with another woman. I enjoy facilitating the weekly discussion and she loves staying in touch with the group members and planning fellowship times and refreshments. Our gifts complemented one another as we worked together to meet the needs of the group. In addition, one of the best ways to develop inexperienced, yet qualified group leaders involves placing them as a co-leader in a group. By doing so, they learn through observation and practice how to lead a group which prepares them to oversee their own group in the future. "Apprentice leaders" represent another name for leaders-in-training.[27] A church that implements a process for existing leaders to team with potential leaders will create opportunities for people to develop their gifts, grow spiritually, and experience the benefits of transformational community.[28]

Creating a Safe, Caring Environment

As mentioned earlier in this chapter, God created people for relationship with one another. Men and women desire to know others and connect at a deeper level than what they experience at a weekend worship service. Small groups create the opportunity for greater connection, but an environment must be created where members of a small group feel accepted, loved, and encouraged. A leader should consider these suggestions when leading a small group.

Establish Guidelines

At the first meeting of a small group, discuss how to structure the group so that all members benefit from the discussion and time together. Some groups establish a group covenant agreed upon by all the members. See the addendum at the end of the chapter for an example of a group covenant. Ask group members to share their ideas first. The group leader can add other guidelines for the group's consideration from the following list:

- Determine the length of time of the meeting.
- Commit to confidentiality.
- Decide whether or not to allow babies and children to attend and discuss how to provide for childcare if needed.
- Agree to keep comments during discussions brief and concise so more people have the opportunity to contribute to the conversation.
- Avoid critical or judgmental statements towards one another.
- Allow and respect differences of opinion.

- Encourage questions during discussions.
- Refrain from "fixing" other people's problems.
- Accept and encourage one another in the midst of personal struggles.
- Offer unconditional love and acceptance to one another.

Model Authenticity

A leader must be honest and transparent in group discussions in order to encourage group members to share openly. Group members will normally only share as deeply as the leader shares.

Prepare Ahead

Be very familiar with the discussion material and assigned questions, so that you can focus on the group members and your role as facilitator.

Be Focused and Present with the Group Members

Put away or silence cellphones and show interest and encouragement through body language and eye contact.

Forget Yourself

Your responsibility centers on helping others learn and grow spiritually. Yes, you are a member of the group and should be open to the Holy Spirit's work in your own life, but remember you should first focus on the needs of your group members.

Honor People's Time

Start and stop the meeting at the determined time. Come early and stay afterward to engage in casual conversations and random questions and comments. Some people are more comfortable and willing to talk privately, one-on-one rather than in the group.

Don't Call Attention to Those Who Come Unprepared

Group members will benefit most if they do assigned reading and answer related questions in between meeting times. Some people will do the work, others may not. Just be glad each person has come to the meeting. When it seems appropriate, privately remind them of the value gained from the completion of the Bible study or reading assignment.

Be Enthusiastic and Welcoming

Always let group members know you are happy to see them and follow up with a phone call, email, or text when they miss a meeting.

> "Give me broken leaders over those who lead out of bravado and strength any day. Broken leaders know their limitations. They do not live a lie by trying to be perfect. Only a broken heart can love. Only a person who has come to end of self can be real."[29]
>
> —Scott Boren

Facilitating a Small Group Discussion

Oral communication of God's truth happens primarily through lecture or discussion. Picture in your mind a motor boat and a sailboat. Which boat would you say more closely represents "steering" a small group? It would be a sailboat. In a motor boat, the driver controls and steers the boat in a particular direction. The same happens for a Sunday morning sermon, a Bible study lecture, or teaching in a Sunday school setting. The speaker develops and delivers the message, while the audience listens.

Facilitating a small group discussion looks more like a sailboat guided by the wind and sails. It follows a less direct and unpredictable path. An effective group leader's goal centers on encouraging a conversation among the group members in order to create a stimulating discussion. Once you ask a question, you can't predict where the conversation will lead. Hopefully, stimulating and challenging dialog will engage the hearts and minds of the group members through the leading of the Holy Spirit. The key to successfully leading a small group discussion centers on listening well and asking good questions. In addition, the following tips will help you facilitate a meaningful group discussion.

Pray

Always pray before the group meeting that your heart and the hearts of those in the group will be open to learn what God has for each individual. Also pray silently during a group meeting for God's guidance. I call these "flare prayers" which I silently shoot up to God when I need his help to know how to direct the conversation when it suddenly goes in an unanticipated direction. The leader needs God's wisdom to guide the discussion so that it profits those participating.

Include Icebreaker Questions

Icebreakers are an effective, non-threatening way to help group members become better acquainted with one another and lead into the topic of the discussion. With a new group, use questions that focus on basic information such as, "If you could travel anywhere in the world, where would it be?" or "What is your favorite movie, and why?" As the group connects more deeply, then use more personal questions like, "What is your favorite Bible verse and why?" or "What is your greatest fear about death?" You can search for "icebreakers" online for many helpful suggestions as well as find lists of icebreaker questions in books by O'Neal and Donahue.[30]

Affirm Every Comment

Nothing feels more awkward and hurtful than to express an answer to a question or share an idea and have it ignored. Each time a group member says something the leader should acknowledge it with a response such as: "Great insight," "Thanks for sharing something so personal," "I like the way you thought that through," "Excellent observation!" The only exception is if another member of the group affirms a comment. Even if someone gives an incorrect answer or comment, a response should be given. For example, "I never thought about it like that" or "That's an interesting way to look at it." By affirming a comment, a person feels heard and appreciated for the contribution made to the conversation. Wrap up the discussion of a question with an encouraging comment to the group, and then move on to the next question.

Equalize Participation

A discussion leader needs to regulate participation in a way that allows for everyone in the group to contribute to the discussion. This becomes challenging given that some people want to dominate a conversation and others choose to remain silent. If some group members talk too much and monopolize the conversation, speak with them privately outside of the group time. First express your appreciation for their great insight and knowledge, but then ask them to defer to others in the group so that the quieter ones have an opportunity to contribute. A leader may need to call on quieter people to encourage them to share but always ask them nonthreatening questions and never ask personal questions.

Don't Call on Anyone for Personal Information

Hopefully the Bible study includes personal application questions. Always ask for volunteers to share their answers. If no one responds, the leader should be prepared to share with the hope that others will follow.

Never Say, "You're Wrong!" by Word, Gesture, or Facial Expression

Acknowledge an incorrect answer graciously and then call on other members of the group to offer their answers. When possible, allow the group members to give another more accurate perspective, rather than have the leader immediately respond to an incorrect answer.

Don't Spend Too Much Time on Observation Questions or Wild Speculations

Quickly move the discussion through obvious answers, random comments, and "rabbit trails" that do not contribute to the overall focus of the study. Allow the majority of time on thought-provoking questions and personal application questions. Hopefully group discussions will challenge as well as convict people to grow in their knowledge of and commitment to God.

Encourage Self-Disclosure

As mentioned, small groups need to provide an environment that motivates people to share deeply, creating an opportunity for spiritual transformation. "Life change happens in the context of community," reflects the mantra often repeated in our small groups at DTS. But in order for spiritual growth to occur, a group must develop a climate of personal sharing and transparency with a foundation of trust in order to give the Holy Spirit the freedom to do his transforming work.

Handle Emotional Responses Carefully

On occasion members of the group will express an emotional response during the discussion, often accompanied by tears or anger. If so, the leader needs to guide the group to respond in a helpful, supportive way. This normally involves letting people express why they feel as they do and then pray for them. If they are too upset or distraught to continue in the group discussion, ask someone in the group to leave the room with the person to follow up and offer needed support. Then continue the discussion. Later the group leader should check on the group member to further assess the situation and offer additional help.

Include Group Prayer

Prayer is an important component of a small group but often gets crowded out by other aspects of the time together. Besides opening and closing with prayer, group members should share personal prayer requests to intercede on behalf of one another. Avoid letting everyone verbally share their request as that often takes up a great deal of time. Instead, consider these options related to prayer requests: (1) Split into groups of two or three and share requests and pray together. (2) Pass out 3x5 notecards and have each person write down their prayer request. If time permits, pass the cards to the person on the left or right and then out loud, one at a time, each person prays the request on the card. (3) If there's limited time, collect the notecards and ask a volunteer to take the cards home each week, type them out, and email the requests to the group so that everyone can pray for the individual needs throughout the week.

> "The best spiritual leaders are not those who give the most right answers but those who ask the most powerful questions. Jesus asked approximately 307 questions in Scripture…. The right question at the right time can make someone unzip her or his heart and crave encouragement and correction."[31]
> —Heather Zemple

Conflict in Small Groups

It is not a question of *if* you will have conflict in a small group, but rather *when* you will have conflict. Peacemaker Ministries defines conflict as "a difference in opinion or purpose that frustrates someone's goals and desires."[32] Anytime you bring people together, the potential for conflict escalates. The goal is not to avoid conflict but to learn how to manage it successfully.

For most of my life, I thought all conflict was wrong. I did not grow up in a family that addressed conflict. I assume my parents had arguments because they ultimately divorced, but their disagreements happened behind closed doors. I never observed healthy confrontation, and rarely was allowed the freedom to disagree. Along with

this, my temperament tends toward harmony and peace at all costs. So, it was quite a revelation to learn during my seminary training that conflict can be "good." I have discovered that conflicts themselves should not be thought of in a negative way. They have negative consequences when they become destructive, but positive results happen when conflict is constructive.

How can conflict be constructive in a small group? It surfaces issues that need clarification, addresses and helps solve problems or confusion, allows expression of emotions, and reveals differences of opinions among group members. A conflict shows the leader what the members of the group believe in order to address any wrong thinking.

But on the flip side, conflicts in small groups become destructive when people say unkind or disrespectful comments that hurt others, when division occurs, when people accommodate or avoid conflict which leads to anger and bitterness, and when people become disillusioned with others and turn from God as they observe Christians speaking and behaving in unbiblical ways.

So, if we can anticipate that conflict will eventually surface in a small group setting, how should a small group leader respond? We need to remember Julie Gorman's words: "Generally, it is not the conflict itself that causes a fracturing of relationships but an inadequate way of dealing with the conflict."[33] I suggest you have a P.L.A.N.….

- Pray: Always ask God for guidance. You will need his help to prepare, facilitate, and respond to a conflict situation.
- Listen and learn: Let those involved share their opinions and perspectives. Listen carefully in order to learn the

details of the conflict and determine how you should respond.

- Answer with appropriate questions: Respond gently and respectfully, allow for differing thoughts and feelings, clarify opposing opinions, affirm each person's perspective, ask understanding and probing questions, brainstorm possible options and ideas, seek resolution and/or reconciliation. If resolution does not come, seek a third party for mediation. If necessary, agree to disagree.
- Note the underlying issues: Look past the conflict to the people involved and take into consideration any personal issues that might contribute to the conflict.

Always remember that Satan wants to use conflict to discourage, distract, disrupt, and destroy. God desires people to benefit from conflict as they follow a "plan" to discover an amicable resolution which can result in the spiritual blessings of unity and peace.

> "Community is messy because it always involves people, and people are messy. It's about people hauling their brokenness and baggage into your house and dumping it in your living room."[34]
> —Heather Zemple

Multiplying Groups and Group Placement

One of the biggest challenges within a small group ministry involves adding new groups and placing people into groups. No one way exists to expand the number of groups and different methods fit different churches. Some churches prefer to start new groups rather than disrupt existing groups. They hold to the concept of addition rather than division.[35] Other churches design a model that starts new groups from existing groups. Many of those who prefer this way agree to avoid using the term "split" when describing the multiplication of new groups from established groups. Instead, words like "reproduce," "birth," or "launch" characterize their method.

Placing people into groups also happens in a variety of ways. Some churches assimilate potential group members through what they call a *campaign strategy*,[36] while others incorporate "GroupLink"[37] where specific times a year people have an opportunity to sign up to join a group. Some churches prefer to structure their entire small groups program in an online format. See churchteams.com for an example of small group software. Finally, there are churches who choose to interview new group members and then place the people in an open group. Individual churches must decide which process of expanding groups and placing new members best fits the culture and structure of the church.

Conclusion

Ultimately, each local church needs to prayerfully determine not *if* but *how* to establish, strengthen, or expand ministry to their people through transformative small groups. Men and women are created to function best in committed, supportive relationships with others. Developing opportunities for them to gather in small groups will contribute toward their spiritual growth, enhance the Holy Spirit's work in each of their lives, and image our Triune God to a watching world.

Discussion Questions

1. What type of small groups have you been part of in the past? Were they positive or negative experiences? What made them so?

2. Do you agree that small groups are a necessary part of a local church? Why? Or why not?

3. If you have been in a small group in the past, what type(s) of curriculum have you found to be meaningful and helpful in contributing to your spiritual growth?

4. Have you experienced conflict in a small group? If so, how was it handled? Would you have handled it any differently? If so, how?

5. How has God used a small group of people to impact your spiritual life?

Resources for Further Study

Boren, M. Scott. *Leading Small Groups in the Way of Jesus.* Downers Grove, IL: InterVarsity Press, 2015.

Bridges, Jerry. *True Community: The Biblical Practice of Koinonia.* Colorado Springs: NavPress, 2012.

Donahue, Bill. *Leading Life-Changing Small Groups.* 3rd ed. Grand Rapids: Zondervan, 2012.

Donahue, Bill and Greg Bowman. *Coaching Life-Changing Small Group Leaders: A Comprehensive Guide to Developing Leaders of Groups and Teams.* Grand Rapids: Zondervan, 2012.

Donahue, Bill and Russ Robinson. *Building a Life-Changing Small Group Ministry: A Strategic Guide for Leading Group Life in Your Church.* Grand Rapids: Zondervan, 2012.

Gladen, Steve. *Small Groups with Purpose: How to Create Healthy Communities.* Grand Rapids: Baker Books, 2011.

Gorman, Julie A. *Community That Is Christian: A Handbook on Small Groups,* 2d ed. Grand Rapids, MI: Baker, 2002.

Mosley, Eddie. *Connecting in Communities: Understanding the Dynamics of Small Groups.* Colorado Springs: NavPress, 2011.

O'Neal, Sam. *Field Guide for Small Group Leaders.* Downers Grove, IL: InterVarsity Press, 2012.

Zempel, Heather. *Community Is Messy: The Perils and Promise of Small Group Ministry.* Downers Grove, IL: InterVarsity Press, 2012.

Author Bio

As Adjunct Professor and Women's Adviser in the Educational Ministries and Leadership Department at DTS, Dr. Joye Baker advises and mentors women students, teaches Educational Ministry courses, serves on the staff of the DTS Spiritual Formation small groups program, and team-teaches in the Doctor of Ministry Women in Ministry cohort. She has trained women in Russia and speaks at various women's events. She provides leader training, teaches, and leads a small group in the weekly women's Bible study at her local church in Dallas. She was widowed at a young age and has a daughter and two sons, one daughter-in-law, and two grandsons.

CHAPTER 15 APPENDIX: SMALL GROUP COVENANT

We seek to become more Christlike in all areas of our lives. Our small group can contribute to our spiritual growth by emphasizing several values. We endeavor to hold in common the following values:

1. _____

2. _____

3. _____

4. _____

5. _____

6. _____

7. _____

8. _____

When: _____

Where: _____

Duration: _____

Means of Communicating Absence: _____

Signatures of Group Members:

_____   _____

_____   _____

_____   _____

_____   _____

_____   _____

Endnotes

1.   Spiritual Formation (SF) is a two-year, peer-led small group program at Dallas Seminary. It promotes the belief that life change happens best in the context of community. The SF groups help to facilitate spiritual growth in the lives of the students as they meet weekly, follow a prescribed curriculum, and share and support one another on their individual spiritual journeys while in seminary.

2.   Todd Speidell, "A Trinitarian Ontology of Persons in Society," *Scottish Journal of Society* 47, no. 3 (1994): 283–300.

3.   Scott Boren, *Leading Small Groups in the Way of Jesus* (Downers Grove, IL: IVP Books, 2015), 88

4.   Kenneth Boa, *That I May Know God* (Sisters, OR: Multnomah Books, 1998), 13.

5.   Jerry Bridges, *True Community: The Biblical Practice of Koinonia* (Colorado Springs: NavPress, 2012), 10.

6.   Steve Gladen, *Small Groups with Purpose: How to Create Healthy Communities* (Grand Rapids: Baker Books, 2011), 55.

7.   Julie Gorman, *Community That Is Christian: A Handbook on Small Groups* (Grand Rapids: Baker Books, 2002), 15.

8.   Heather Zempel, *Community Is Messy: The Perils and Promise of Small Group Ministry* (Downers Grove, IL: InterVarsity Press, 2012), 18.

9.   Boren, *Leading Small Groups in the Way of Jesus*, 16.

10. Bridges, *True Community*, 61–62.

11. Harley Atkinson, *The Power of Small Groups in Christian Education* (Nappanee, IN: Evangel Publishing, 2002), 34–48.

12. Bill Donahue and Russ Robinson, *Building a Life-Changing Small Group Ministry* (Grand Rapids: Zondervan, 2012), 32.

13. Beyond the content of this chapter, smallgroups.com and smallgroupnetwork.com offer excellent resources to help develop, support, and strengthen small group ministry.

14. Sam O'Neal, *Field Guide for Small Group Leaders* (Downers Grove, IL: InterVarsity Press, 2012), 23.

15. Ibid., 15

16. Gorman, *Community That Is Christian*, 42.

17. Atkinson, *The Power of Small Groups,* 20.

18. See the chapter "Putting It All Together: The Educational Cycle" by George Hillman for a detailed explanation of these individual components in the educational cycle.

19. Chapter 1, "Clarifying Your Purpose." in *Leading Life-Changing Small Groups* by Bill Donahue and Russ Robinson addresses this well.

20. A discussion of birthing groups can be found later in this chapter.

21. Jim Egli and Dwight Marable, *Small Groups, Big Impact* (St. Charles, IL: ChurchSmart Resources, 2011), 36. Egli and Marable surveyed three thousand small group leaders in twenty-one countries with the purpose of discovering, "What are the factors that impact conversion growth through small groups?" Their emphasis was primarily evangelistic and their data strongly favors open groups.

22. See the chapter, "Putting It All Together: The Educational Cycle" by George Hillman for additional information on curriculum selection.

23. Some resources such as RightNow Media at RightNow.org have a large selection of video studies by excellent Bible teachers. They require a membership fee, but it is well worth the investment.

24. Gorman, *A Community That Is Christian,* 98.

25. Donahue and Robinson, *Building a Life-Changing Small Group Ministry,* 216.

26. Egli and Marable, *Small Groups, Big Impact,* 87–88.

27. Donahue and Robinson, *Building a Life-Changing Small Group Ministry,* 160–161.

28. Bill Donahue, *Leading Life-Changing Small Groups,* (Grand Rapids: Zondervan, 2012), 75.

29. Boren, *Leading Small Groups in the Way of Jesus,* 109.

30. O'Neal, *Field Guide for Small Group Leaders,* 89–104; Donahue, *Leading Life-Changing Small Groups,* 119–122.

31. Zempel, *Community is Messy,* 104.

32. Ken Sande, *The Peacemaker: A Biblical Guide to Resolving Personal Conflict* (Grand Rapids: Baker Books, 2004), 29.

33. Gorman, *Community That Is Christian,* 168.

34. Zempel, *Community Is Messy,* 24.

35. Steve Gladen, *Small Groups with Purpose: How to Create Healthy Communities,* (Grand Rapids: Baker Books, 2011), 33.

36. Ibid., 213–221. This is a strategy conceived by Saddleback Church in 2002. "A campaign is an intensive, church-wide focus on a particular aspect of spiritual growth that involves every age group … Over 30,000 churches have successfully used Saddleback campaigns, and the strategy has proven to be an amazing vehicle for spiritual growth and connecting people into groups" (213–214).

37. Andy Stanley and Bill Willits, *Creating Community: Five Keys to Building a Small Group Culture* (Sisters, OR: Multnomah, 2004), 125–130. "GroupLink" is a process of creating new small groups conceived by the leadership of North Point Community Church in Alpharetta, Georgia.

Chapter 16
CREATIVITY IN EDUCATIONAL MINISTRY

Karen Giesen

*So God created mankind in his own image, in the image of God he
created them; male and female he created them.*

—Genesis 1:27

"We Need a Pie!"

"MISS KAREN, WE NEED a pie. We are doing a skit and we need a pie!" Four eager nine-year-olds and I looked around at the shelves in the crafts building at the youth camp where I had been laying out supplies for the afternoon project. Spying an aluminum pie pan—the kind a neatnik would dispose of the minute the contents were eaten, we began to search for a "filling." Ultimately, we filled it with round beige carpet samples, "cut" into six slices and conveniently held in place by three crisscrossed rubber bands. Voila! Off they scooted with a "pie." Twenty-five years later, I remember how much fun it was!

You Are Creative—Yes, You!

Picture the most glorious sunset you have
· seen, pink and gold reflecting on clouds.

Now think of trees below where all sorts of outrageous and brightly colored birds are beginning to roost. And animals, like a star-nosed mole, the fastest-eating animal alive, who takes as little as 120 milliseconds to identify and consume a grub underground. Maybe this forest overlooks a body of water with another world of creatures below the surface, like a Japanese spider crab as much as twelve feet wide from claw to claw, or a goblin shark that eats by sensing electric fields associated with its prey. God, who created all this, created you in his image. You are creative. God made you that way. When you read God's Holy Word, you see that the Creator of Everything created *you* in his image (Gen. 3:27). To deny it is blasphemy. Yet many of us default to "some very creative ladies in my church," and miss out on all the fun. Ask yourself what Christ has called and gifted you to do? In what ways has God made you creative? Are you using all that God has given you creatively?

> "Creativity is intelligence having fun."
> —Attributed to Albert Einstein

God has assignments for you that no one else can do. Not your mentors, not your idols, not your favorite teachers. The late Howard G. Hendricks[1] convinced me that "If you are just like somebody else, we don't need you." One Sunday, after a lesson using pictures of unusual birds and animals to teach this principle, three kindergartners were talking, through puppets. One summarized the idea saying "It is nice to be different. If you were just like somebody else, one of you would have to be taken out, because there would be too many of one!" God doesn't need another like my husband, Barney Giesen, who is the most free-thinking, uninhibited, hard-working, fun-loving teacher ever! (Pardon my bias.) God doesn't need another Marlene LeFever, who continues to write my favorite books on creative teaching.[2] He doesn't even need another Howard Hendricks, who was for me, and hundreds of others, an enthusiastic indubitable encourager. Their influence permeates this chapter. As indebted as I am to this trio for their creativity, as well as for sparking mine, God needs me to be Karen. And he needs you to be *you*!

Your personality may not be silly, or perky, or quirky. What is it? Let it show. Your experiences and voice are unique. One friend describes her lifelong church attendance since "lying on the pew in ruffled panties." What's your story? Your tastes are your own. Maybe yellow is *not* your favorite color. What is? Your vocabulary, your sense of humor, your approach to life, all make you the only one for certain kingdom tasks. "For we are God's handiwork, created in Christ Jesus to do good works, which God prepared in advance for us to do" (Eph. 2:10).

> "Because of their courage, their lack of fear, creative people are willing to make silly mistakes. The truly creative person is one who can think crazy; such a person knows full well that many of his great ideas will prove worthless. The creative person is flexible; he is able to change as the situation changes, to break habits, to face indecision and changes in conditions without undue stress. He is not threatened by the unexpected as rigid, inflexible people are."[3]
> —Frank G. Goble

The following qualities are often attributed to creative people: dependent on the Holy Spirit, daring, willing to take risks, curious, receptive to change, unpredictable, colorful, fun-loving, silly, adventurous, uninhibited, childlike, vulnerable, flexible, making the most of every situation, breaking patterns, and hard-working. In our individuality, we will not all have or need every one of them. And we may have some not listed here. Which describe you? Which would you like to cultivate? Which will never be you?

Knowing you are creative, how will you uncover your gifts? Slow down. Rest is essential in the marathon of ministry. It also allows your mind to wander and new ideas to escape. Try lying in a hammock or lounger, gazing at the sky. Write down your daydreams or night dreams. Take a walk through a park, on a beach, or down the halls of your building. Go on excursions to a dollar store or a museum or a zoo. Observe creative people. Can you adapt an idea? Yours will be different, maybe better. Read. Travel. Browse art books. Take a painting class—even just one. Listen to music. Make up movements to songs. What inspires you? When do ideas come to you? Your creativity will differ from anybody else's. You are unique. Have a crazy idea? Try it!

Characteristics of Creative People

- Dependent on Holy Spirit
- Daring, willing to take risks
- Curious
- Receptive to change
- Unpredictable
- Colorful
- Fun-loving
- Silly
- Adventurous
- Uninhibited
- Childlike
- Vulnerable
- Flexible
- Making the most of every situation
- Breaking patterns
- Hard-working

Creative Programming

Most educational programming serves the congregation as well as others in the community. Whether you are thinking in-house or outreach, think of ways of make your events and programs more inviting and memorable.

Decorate the entry, the hall, the door, the stage, and the walls. Set the mood so participants are transported from the moment they step in. Nobody ever complained about too much color, clever design, or Scripture. Use paint, bright table cloths, balloons, bags, tissue, crepe paper, found objects, and dollar store treasures to set the tone. If your theme is "Road Trip," get discarded tires and hubcaps from the neighborhood flat repair shop. Spray paint some of the tires bright colors. Set the stage with empty Valvoline boxes. Buy steering wheel covers, windshield reflectors, and gas cans at the dollar store. Try the junkyard for old car body parts! Over-the-top is not too much!

Give each program a theme and a special name. This gives you a focus for decorating and promoting your event. (Remember, this is not your overarching purpose once you have excited the participants. Find your teaching theme in your Bible focus. Emphasize such principles as God's love for his people, his miracles, or his second chances, according to your teaching aims.) But to make it more fun, consider naming your event something special like "City Kids," "Men at Work," "Under Construction," or "Faith Connection," depending on your location, church name, and ministry focus. Choose a name that fits you and your unique ministry.

Now, if you are picturing only children, stop. This chapter applies to everybody. Adults enjoy fun (aka creativity) as much as kids do. Surprise them. If you host midweek Bible studies or adult Sunday morning activities, put on your thinking cap. Could refreshments relate to the lesson? Figs and dates, or seafood? Could the teacher wear a costume, or a funny hat? Could you put your chairs in a round, horseshoe, square, or diamond shape? Could you assign a few students to act out a portion of the lesson? Or just read a script in funny voices?

When you need volunteers, consider their schedules. How about VBS in the evening? Singles, parents, and retired folks will all be drawn by your passion, thoughtfulness, clear communication, and the impact of your ministry. Serving together yields the added benefit of building community while having fun. Add some adult activities to your children's vacation Bible school, such as Bible studies or games or service projects for parents during the same time period. Make it into an all-church "Summer-Rama." Schedule an SOS (Serving Other Souls) or Arts Camp during a midseason break. The adults may enjoy it more than the kids. Best of all, they could do it together.

Creative Teaching

How you teach reflects the material, your personality, and the people you teach. Will they remember the point of the lesson? Will it change them? How will your persona, your gifts, your experiences, and your "crazy" ideas contribute to the impact of God's Word? Understanding your students will spur your creativity in your quest to make a lasting impression.

Profile: Louann Blair Pepper

Louann Blair Pepper loves yellow. Her Converse shoes, her mini-backpack, her baseball cap, and her phone cover are yellow. So is "Buzbee," the Fiat with the sunflower license plate that reads LOUANN. If yellow meant "big, generous, and loving," then her heart would be yellow too. She tutors inner-city kids, leads chapels at Christian schools and daycares, and consults with small rural churches to improve their children's programs. Her bright, sunny clothing and accessories reflect her fun-loving, creative personality. As the children's ministries director for a small inner-city church, she brings light to a whole community. Combining children from her own church with those of a neighborhood preschool and a homeless shelter, she hosts Book Buddies for older children to read to younger ones, and Lunch Bunch using classic children's literature to teach biblical principles. When she observed that the number of children in her church was not growing, she added Sunday school in a nearby apartment complex. Volunteers from the church lead a class there every Sunday morning before returning for worship at their home church. Asked about the offsite Sunday school's diluting her volunteer staff at the church, she responded, "If you wait for sufficient staff, you will never do it."

The ways people learn have been characterized in two categories: how they receive information and how they process information.

Learning Modalities

How people receive information is generally called "learning modalities." According to the Swassing/Barbe Modalities Model, learners fall into three major groups (it is also possible for people to fall into more than one category).[4]

Visual Learners

Visual learners remember best what they see. They love to read, watch, write, draw, and organize. They tend to sit in the front and take numerous detailed notes. They may close their eyes to visualize or remember something. Since they like to see what they are learning, bring colorful pictures, film clips, handouts, or PowerPoints. Draw graphs and charts on the board.

Auditory Learners

Auditory learners complete their learning by re-telling what they have heard. They have excellent listening skills, catch subtle nuances in speech, and learn what they hear themselves say. They will sit where they can hear but may not appear to pay attention. They acquire knowledge by reading aloud and verbalizing lessons to themselves and complete their learning by telling someone else. Of the 20 percent who have this preference, more are women. Be sure to include chances to write, talk, sing, repeat, chant, and cheer.

Tactile/Kinesthetic Learners

Tactile/kinesthetic learners learn best through touch and experience. Because they

like to move while learning, they often have difficulty in a traditional classroom. Among the 40 percent who have this preference, more are men. Children love a flannelgraph and objects to pass around.[5] They may need a pipe cleaner or modeling clay to fiddle with during the lesson. For youth and adults, consider simulations, field trips, or case studies that give the sensation of being there. Some need to take notes. They will appreciate opportunities to stand up to answer a question, draw while they listen, or perform in a role-play. You may want them to sit near the door or somewhere they can easily get up and move around. Breaking occasionally into small groups or pairs gives everybody a chance to move, talk, listen, wiggle, stretch, and connect.

Learning Styles

How people process information is generally referred to as learning styles. Dr. Bernice McCarthy developed a Four-Step Learning Plan known as the 4MAT System.[6] Marlene LeFever, who expanded on that work, summarizes the different learning styles as follows:[7]

Innovative Learners

Innovative learners learn by listening and sharing ideas. They start with what they see, and generalize. They are wonderful people to have in your class because they work hard for harmony in the group.

Analytic Learners

Analytic learners enjoy learning by listening to a lecture. They are the thinkers and watchers in our classes. Their thinking patterns are rational and sequential. These students learn best in what could be called a traditional classroom setting. They can easily become "teacher's pets" because they defer to authority.

Common Sense Learners

Common sense learners learn through direct, hands-on experiences. They are skills-oriented; they need to know how what they are learning can be applied practically. In a classroom, they want step-by-step directions. They have no trouble following the steps, but they want to do the work themselves. They don't value the teacher's input as they are trying things out and experimenting.

Dynamic Learners

Dynamic learners enjoy taking what they have learned and trying to build something experimental from it. They don't start with ideas; instead they start with what they can see, hear, touch, and feel. This group bores easily. Dynamic students need to be given flexibility in which to learn. Teachers sometimes have trouble with this learning style because students not only have experimental attitudes; they also have experimental behavior.

Teacher Preparation

In addition to understanding your students, you will enhance your impact by your own diligent preparation. The following steps are adapted from Marlene LeFever's process of preparation:

1. Preparation. Learn how to study the Bible inductively as well as how to use reference tools.

2. Incubation. After some preparation, let ideas just sit in your head for a while. (Try reading over the lesson each evening before going to sleep.)
3. Illumination. The "light-bulb" moment when thoughts jell and ideas come.
4. Elaboration. Plan and write out the complete lesson. Be flexible as new ideas come.
5. Verification. Evaluate your plan. Does it meet your goals? Be willing to revise.
6. Practice. You cannot do it off the top of your head. Rehearse the lesson or sermon or story. Good teaching takes work! [8]

Teaching Methods

Of course, the learning task includes the student's participation, guided by the teacher. Our Master Teacher Jesus included stories, questions, object lessons, and emotion. Keep these in mind as you decide how to present the treasure—the Word of God.

The environment matters, too. If you are outdoors, relate your teaching to nature as much as you can. If you are indoors, try to regulate the cooling, heat, light, and cleanliness to make your space comfortable. Eliminating distractions allows you to focus your impact. Consider adding color, music, and name tags. Arrange the furniture so that your students face one another. Decide where and whether you will you sit or stand.

Lecture serves to convey information. It may be the only method of engaging a large unwieldy group. Some masterful speakers lecture with spellbinding results. Lecturing well takes preparation and practice. Whenever possible, combine discussion with your lecture. Invite and acknowledge comments and questions. Be sure to affirm a speaker, even when correcting. If the group is small and well-acquainted, comments and questions may become personal testimonies and life-changing applications. To open or to summarize your class, try a free-flowing group project using what Gabriele Rico calls "clustering"[9] and Tony Buzan calls "mind-mapping."[10] Use a white or blackboard or mounted paper tablet. Start with a circled word in the middle and work off in any direction to craft a synthesis of your lesson. Everyone who contributes takes ownership and remembers.

Stories may be the original teaching tool in centuries of oral cultures. I readily admit they are my personal favorite. Everybody loves a good story. Tell stories yourself, and invite class members to tell stories. Give yourself and your students a nudge by providing one or two props or costume pieces. Include enough data and detail to make them credible. Appeal to all five senses. Come full circle so that the end relates to the beginning. Include historical tales. Relate your own experiences, the element that only you can bring. Tell Bible stories with excitement that conveys your personal beliefs. With little ones, I hold up my Bible every time, saying, "This is my Bible and

Resources for Costumes, Props, and Object Lessons:

- Keep a special stash of interesting items that you have collected from thrift stores, garage and estate sales, dollar stores, and trash piles. Keep your teaching ministry in mind. Train your car to stop at every inviting sale.
- If possible, keep all your props and costumes in one place, where it is easy to go and find what you need or see what you have. Sometimes just looking through your stash will be God's way of giving you a creative approach.
- Invest in a pair of angel wings—the most often used costume piece we own. Angels show up at all the special events in the Bible. (Don't hog those wings. Let your students wear them, too.)
- Search your own closets, drawers, and garage.
- Borrow from friends and neighbors. Use social media or neighborhood email groups to send out the need. This may serendipitously witness to an unbeliever.
- Buy retail with the promise to return with receipt.
- Call schools, 4-H clubs, FFAs, feed stores to borrow animals, even in a big city.
- For makeup, try watercolors and dollar-store cosmetics. Flour works like powder.
- As a last resort, buy or rent. Check the Internet for suppliers.

the stories in it are true!" Bring along memory prompts, such as live chicks, dead bugs, fake snakes, or stuffed animals—and maybe some actual or replica artifacts from ancient times. How about individual cups of blue Jello with a gummy fish and whipped cream on top whenever your story includes large body of water?

Drama in various forms, in costume or partial costume and well-rehearsed, can keep audiences of all ages on the edges of their seats. Mime takes a special concentration from the viewer and skill by the presenter. Skits lend themselves to participation by willing amateurs. Costumed first-person narrative monologues allow the teacher or preacher to lecture without boring the students.[11] This is very effective, but takes a lot of preparation time to memorize the lines.

Role-play encourages participation from everybody. With costumes, kids will do the same story over and over, taking turns with the various parts and trading costumes, all the while benefitting from the repetition. Their hands-down favorite is angel wings, but they are happy with hats, capes, or the old shirt you were about to give away. Even just one costume piece transforms them into a character. If the lines are complicated, a narrator can read the script, holding a hand above the head of the character "speaking" the lines. Adults enjoy role-play and costumes, too, often revealing hidden desires or talents.

Games and puzzles, both physical and mental, with any age, can reinforce a lesson or provide an opening activity. Ask your class to compose rhymes, songs, chants, psalms, poems, acrostics, tag lines, mottos, or advertising copy. Done by individuals or by groups, these encourage reflection and synthesis of the subjects discussed and can be a catalyst to more reflection following the class time.

Art, whether drawing, coloring, painting, clay, or pipe cleaners, can be used to reflect or illustrate or make personal applications.

Sing! God puts songs in our hearts. Sing to glorify him, to reinforce the lesson, for joy. And songs are great memory aids. Think how often you sing the alphabet or the "Fruit of the Spirit," or for that matter Handel's "Messiah." If you don't readily know a song that teaches what you need, make one up. Add new words to familiar tunes. Figure out movements to accompany each song. This aids memory for all ages, not just young ones. If you are uncomfortable with singing and choreography, pretend you are a character in the song. Or make it a game by standing in a circle, asking students in turn to add a motion or different words. No criticism allowed. All singing is beautiful when it reflects our love.

Wake them up by having everyone move to a different chair. Or wear a mask. Masks often free up people, especially adults, to be more open, since their faces are hidden. To liven up a question and answer session, toss a beach ball, bean bag, or any soft object, to the one you want to answer (or ask) the next question. And I repeat, try these ideas with adults, youth, and children. We all like to have fun!

Dip Your Toe In. Just Start!

Pray—first, last, and along the way. Show your dependence by asking God to unbridle your creativity. Break patterns. Do not do it the way you have always done it or others have always done it. Wear a hat—or scarf—or headband. Plan an icebreaker. Bring an object. Rearrange the furniture. Reverse the order of your class. Change whether you sit or stand. Make the most of every situation. Be willing to fail. It will do no permanent damage. And the joy of seeing engaged students will feel so good that it was worth the risk.

I offer these suggestions not to give you something to copy but to stimulate your own creative juices. May they spark ideas for activities that are fun for you and edifying for those you influence, whether that is one class, one midweek activity, one segment of your congregation, your neighborhood, or your city. Unleash that wonderful creative self of yours. All to God's glory.

Ideas Successfully Tried by My Crazy-Creative Husband Barney

- To end a sermon to adults on Adam and Eve's big mistake, he took a bite of an apple and spit it out onto the floor.
- To experience a plague, young students crawled into a tent full of crickets, pretending they were grasshoppers. (Crickets are readily available online as fishing bait.)
- One church we attended still has fruit from the fig tree the middle school class planted.
- Dressed as an old fisherman, he brought a fish and octopus (from the grocery store) that "could have been in the big fish's stomach with Jonah."
- When a friend wrapped in old white sheets hid in a closet until Barney called, "Lazarus, come out," the little girl on the front row whispered, "Is he really dead?"
- "Nothing teaches like fire" has been our motto ever since we begged for and received an almost dead plant from a nearby nursery. Having taught about Moses's experience, Barney doused the plant with flammable liquid and lighted it—in the rain—as a class of elementary kids watched under shelter a good distance away.
- Since then we have learned that rubbing alcohol poured over sand in a Corningware bowl will burn and can be moved without sloshing.
- "Moses" led his class out of Egypt. Barefoot kids crossed through the desert of beach sand and fake snakes, led by a cloud of bed pillows tied with cord and then a bowl of flames at "night," with the classroom lights turned off, of course.
- For easier safer ambiance, use battery-powered candles.

Discussion Questions

1. When have you, because you were far from a store or lacking funds or short of time, created a much-needed item from resources on hand?

2. Do you believe you are a creative person? Why or why not?

3. What are some ways you can discover your creativity?

4. What was one creative thing you did in teaching that seemed to work well? Why did it work? How did you think of it?

5. People learn differently. Discuss learning styles and the variety of methods you can use to reach different students.

Resources for Further Study

Books

Barbe, Walter and Raymond Swassing. *Teaching through Modality Strengths: Concepts and Practices.* Columbus, OH: Zaner-Bloser, 1979.

Barrett, Ethel. *Storytelling, It's Easy!* Grand Rapids: Zondervan, 1965. Out of print but readily available online.

Buzan, Tony. *Use Both Sides of Your Brain.* New York: Plume, 1994.

deBono, Edward. *Lateral Thinking: Creativity Step by Step.* New York: Perennial Library, 1990.

Grant, Reg and John Reed. *Telling Stories That Touch the Heart.* Eugene, OR: Wipf and Stock, 2001.

Hendricks, Howard G. *Color Outside the Lines: A Revolutionary Approach to Creative Leadership.* Nashville: Word, 1998.

LeFever, Marlene D. *Creative Teaching Methods: Be an Effective Christian Teacher.* Colorado Springs: David C. Cook, 2004.

LeFever, Marlene D. *Learning Styles: Reaching Everyone God Gave You to Teach*. Colorado Springs: David C. Cook, 2004.

Rico, Gabriele L. *Writing the Natural Way*. New York: Penguin Putnum, 2000.

Von Oech, Roger. *A Kick in the Seat of the Pants: Using Your Explorer, Artist, Judge, & Warrior to Be More Creative*. New York: Harper Perennial, 2001.

Von Oech, Roger. *A Whack on the Side of the Head: How You Can Be More Creative*. New York: Grand Central, 2008.

Websites

75 Quotes on Creativity—www.american.edu/training/Profdev/upload/April-6-Quotes-on-Creativity-SCB-2.pdf

Storytelling that Moves People—www.hbr.org/2003/06/storytelling-that-moves-people

How to Tell a Great Story—www.hbr.org/2014/07/how-to-tell-a-great-story/

Modality Strengths—www.ascd.org/ASCD/pdf/journals/ ed_lead/el_198102_barbe.pdf

Culture and Learning Styles—www.ascd.org/publications/educational-leadership/may94/vol51/num08/The-Culture~Learning-Style-Connection.aspx

The End in Mind with Lori Lane. Four steps for teaching children – www.theendinmind.net/motivate-your-child-to-learn-using-these-four-steps

Bernice McCarthy explaining 4MAT System—www.youtube.com/watch?v=cpqQ5wUXph4

Swassing/Barbe Modality Strength Characteristics—www.touchmath.com/pdf/ Seminar_Swassing.pdf

Author Bio

As an Adjunct Professor in Educational Ministries and Leadership, Dr. Karen Giesen teaches, mentors, and advises students on the Dallas Theological Seminary Houston campus. Dr. Giesen has served as Director of Christian Education for her inner city, multiracial, economically diverse church. She leads a Girl Scout troop, enjoys entertaining friends, and loves sunsets. She and her husband Barney live in an older Houston neighborhood near their children and grandchildren.

CHAPTER 16 APPENDIX A:
THE NUTS AND BOLTS OF TEACHING—THE BIG IDEA

Sue Edwards

Before attending Dallas Seminary in the eighties, I attended a workshop on biblical communication taught by Haddon Robinson, known today as the Father of American Preaching. At the time I didn't know how privileged I was to sit under his teaching, but the tools he taught us, especially related to "The Big Idea," revolutionized my Bible teaching. Years later, he served as the second reader on my dissertation and his encouraging words still ring in my ears. His book, *Biblical Preaching, The Development and Delivery of Expository Messages* is still the primary text in my Dallas Theological Seminary course *Women Teaching Women*.

If I were limited to passing on just one teaching tip, I would teach you to pull out the one big idea from the passage you are teaching and then write that idea in a crystal-clear sentence in several forms:

- First, a sentence reflecting the main big idea the author intended for the original audience in its original context (the exegetical big idea),

- Then a sentence reflecting that same idea written as a timeless truth agreeing with the whole of Scripture (the theological big idea),

- Finally, a sentence reflecting the very same idea but with words that work for your audience today, pithy, provocative, creative, and memorable (the homiletical big idea).

Pulling out the main thrust of the text and taking it through this process—exegetical, theological, and homiletical—is often the most difficult but the most valuable and significant step you can take if you want Bible messages that truly transform.

The big idea principle is equally valuable whether you are preaching to a congregation on Sunday morning or teaching a group of adults or teens in a Sunday school, Adult Bible Community, or in a coffee shop. Whether you are lecturing or creating a learning experience full of creative interactive methods, the big idea principle still rules.

Imagine your students the day after you teach them. See them sitting in their cubicle at work, driving carpool, in the midst of their morning run, or standing at the sink cleaning up the kitchen. As their minds drift back to what you taught them, that one big idea should immediately pop into their heads and, we hope, make its way to their hearts, as they wrestle with the truths of the passage and its implications for how God wants them to live. That big idea serves as the cue that should blast forth the entire message into the mind and heart of the listener, or at least the part that the Holy Spirit wants to drive deep.

Consider this statement from J. H. Jowett in a Yale lecture:

> I have a conviction that no sermon is ready for preaching, not ready for writing out, until we can express its theme in a short, pregnant sentence as clear as crystal. I find the getting of that sentence is the hardest, the most exacting, and the most fruitful labour in my study. To compel oneself to fashion that sentence, to dismiss every word that is vague, ragged, ambiguous, to think oneself through to a form of words which defines the theme with scrupulous exactness—this is surely one of the most vital and essential factors in the making of a sermon: and I do not think any sermon ought to be preached, or even written, until that sentence has emerged, clear and lucid as a cloudless moon.
>
> J. H. Jowett, *The Preacher: His Life and Work* (Grand Rapids: Baker, 1968), 133.

Whether you are preaching a sermon or teaching a lesson, the Word of God, his Love Letter to his beloved, is deserving of the same preparation and effort. Hone your speaking skills by mastering the concept of the big idea.

For Further Study

Robinson, Hadden. *Biblical Preaching: The Development and Delivery of Expository Messages.* 3rd ed. Grand Rapids: Baker, 2004.

Newton, Gary. *Heart-Deep Teaching: Engaging Students for Transformed Lives.* Nashville: B&H Academic, 2012.

Willhite, Keith, and Scott Gibson. *The Big Idea of Biblical Preaching.* Grand Rapids: Baker Books, 2003.

CHAPTER 16 APPENDIX B: THE NUTS AND BOLTS OF TEACHING—HOOK, BOOK, LOOK, AND TOOK

Sue Edwards

To understand concepts, our minds naturally look for the flow of ideas; they crave structure. Strong teaching is strong in structure. I'm not saying that we must verbalize our form with *number one, number two, number three*. Many of my younger students verbalize disdain for hyper-structured messages that feel rigid and obstructive. I hypothesize their reaction is sourced in their attraction to the natural, organic, and authentic. Nevertheless, as John Stott writes in his book on communication *Between Two Worlds*, "Just as bones without flesh make a skeleton, so flesh without bones makes a jellyfish. And neither bony skeletons nor jellyfish make good sermons" (p. 229). To avoid jellyfish teaching, we must plan learning experiences that flow naturally from one concept to another, each section clearly supporting, explaining, illustrating, or applying the big idea.

One staple lesson plan template comes from Larry Richards' book *Creative Bible Teaching* (pp. 108–113). This easy-to-follow structure is composed of four parts that he labels: Hook, Book, Look, and Took.

Hook

You begin by "hooking" your students because although you may be excited about what's ahead, they are thinking about issues like overdue taxes, broken faucets, or sick children. You have about thirty seconds to grab their attention with an interesting question, story, or statistic—something that convinces them to leave their preoccupations and join you. Give them reasons to pay attention by showing them how this lesson will benefit them, not because you have the answers but because God's Word does.

Book

Once they are "hooked," it's time to communicate biblical information as a basis for life change. You may need to clarify the meaning of the text. You are simply helping students understand what's going on in the passage. Taking them deep into the text means transporting them to another culture, time, and place so they can correctly interpret what the passage meant for the original audience, and then what it means for people today. You can teach these truths either by lecturing, using charts and other visuals, or participative methods such as discussion, small groups, or related learning activities. Good lectures are the fastest way to cover content but additional methods help learning stick.

Too many teachers think that once they have introduced the topic well (hook), and taught the passage thoroughly (book), then they're done. Wrong. By including only the hook and book components, you're only half way there. To reach all learning styles and to ensure that your student actually apply the Bible, you also need the look and took components.

Look

The look portion of the lesson focuses on the implications for daily living in our contemporary world. What insight can students draw from the text that explores the relationship of the passage with life today? How does this text look in the culture where they live? What are some of the ways the Holy Spirit might apply these truths to people's lives right now? It's imperative that students consider these questions for God's Word to travel from their minds into their hearts where convictions form. Unless teachers guide students to "look" at life through a biblical lens, life change is unlikely.

Took

Finally, the took part of the learning experience hones in on the individual student—what does God want *me* to do with what I've learned? How can the teacher move what's learned inside the learning environment to outside the learning environment? Students may have good intentions but often as they walk away, without the teacher's and their own intentionality, they forget. Teachers can help students prepare an action plan, specifically how and when will they act on what they've learned. They help students pinpoint areas that need to change in their lives and think through how to implement that change. Teachers can hold students accountable by reviewing the took part of the lesson the next time the class meets.

You might provide these four components over a single session or, if you are teaching a series, you could use this creative pattern over a period of weeks. Whether you choose the Hook, Book, Look, and Took pattern; the classic introduction, body, conclusion structure; or some other creative combination of the various elements that comprise helpful structure, remember that our minds crave continuous systematic ideas that flow naturally to support clear, life-changing big ideas. Marry the two and you are on your way to transformational teaching.

For Further Study

Richards, Lawrence O. *Creative Bible Teaching*. Chicago: Moody Press, 1980.

Stott, John. *Between Two Worlds*. Grand Rapids: Eerdmans, 1982.

Swindoll, Charles. *Teaching Others with Your Words: The Art and Practice of Successful Speaking*. New York: FaithWords, 2012.

Wilhoit, Jim and Leland Ryken. *Effective Bible Teaching*, Grand Rapids: Baker Books, 2000.

CHAPTER 16 APPENDIX C:
THE CREATIVE TEACHING OF JESUS

1. Object lessons (John 4:1–42)—using familiar "water" to help the Samaritan woman understand the unfamiliar "living water"

2. Points of contact (John 1:35–51)—using opportunities to build relationships with people, Andrew, John, Peter, Philip, and Nathanael

3. Aims (John 4:34)—to move people to action

4. Problem-solving (Mark 10:17–22)—to move people to understand and apply Jesus's words

5. Conversation (Mark 10:27)—to move people to obedience

6. Questions—As recorded in the Gospels, Jesus asked more than one hundred questions for the purpose of provoking people to think and to seek the truth.

7. Answers—Jesus used his answers to move people from where they were to where they needed to be in order to grow spiritually. Jesus encouraged people to discover the truth.

8. Lecture (Matt. 5–7; John 14–17)—Jesus made use of discourse to instruct and convince the people in the truth.

9. Parables (John 10:1–21; 15:1–10)—Jesus taught by illustrating spiritual truth with familiar situations.

10. Scripture—Jesus quoted extensively from the Old Testament to teach people God's truth.

11. The teachable moment (John 4:5–26)—Jesus took every opportunity to make an ordinary situation a "teaching situation."

12. Contrast (Matt. 5:21–22, 33–34, 38–39, 43–44)—Jesus contrasted his kingdom with worldly standards, giving the listener a choice for obedience.

13. Concrete and literal examples (Matt. 6:26–34)—Jesus used the concrete to teach abstract truths such as trust, greatness, hospitality, discipleship, etc.

14. Symbols (Matt. 26:17–30; John 13:1–20)—Jesus used symbols, such as the Passover before his death and washing his disciples' feet, to teach great lessons.

15. Large and small groups (Matt. 5–7; John 14–17)—Jesus taught large groups (the crowds, the multitudes) and small groups (the disciples).

16. Individual teaching opportunities (John 3:1–21; 4:5–26)—Jesus took the initiative in reaching out to individuals, helping them understand who he was and what he was going to do.

17. Modeling (Matt. 15:32; Luke 18:15–17)—Jesus, the Master Teacher, was the Truth and modeled what it meant to be a Man who loved God the Father.

18. Motivation (Matt. 16:24–27; 20:21–28; Mark 1:16–18)—Jesus motivated his followers to action. He sparked a response from within the person to godliness and obedience to the Father.

19. Impression and expression (Matt. 4:19–20; 7:20)—Jesus used himself to impress and motivate his followers to act and obey. Jesus was God in the flesh, yet he helped his disciples decide for themselves.

20. Himself (Matt. 28:19–20)—Jesus possessed the qualities of a great teacher: a global vision, understanding of man, mastery of all knowledge, ability in teaching, and a life that was an example to those whom he taught.

Choun, Robert Joseph Jr. "Choosing and Using Creative Methods," in *The Christian Educator's Handbook of Teaching*, eds. Kenneth Gangel and Howard Hendricks, Grand Rapids: Baker, 1998, 166–168.

Endnotes

1. Dr. Howard G. Hendricks (1924–2013) was a legendary professor at Dallas Theological Seminary for over 60 years. He mentored many of today's Christian leaders, authored sixteen books, and ministered in over 80 countries. I was privileged to be among his students. See Bill Hendricks' chapter "What Makes a Great Teacher?" for more information on Howard Hendricks.

2. Marlene LeFever's books are available from David C. Cook Publishing or your local bookseller. See especially *Creative Teaching Methods: Be an Effective Christian Teacher* (Colorado Spring: David C. Cook, 1997) and *Learning Styles* (Colorado Springs: David C. Cook, 1995).

3. Frank G. Goble, *The Third Force: The Psychology of Abraham Maslow* (New York: Grossman, 1976).

4. Walter B. Barbe and Raymond H. Swassing, *Teaching Through Modality Strengths: Concepts and Practices* (Columbus, OH: Zaner-Bloser, 1979).

5. Flannelgraphs are still widely used and available in several sizes from "Betty Lukens—Learning Fun with Felt." www.bettylukens.com.

6. Bernice McCarthy, Four-Step Learning Plan known as the 4MAT System (https://www.4mat.eu/). Also see Bernice McCarthy and Dennis McCarthy, *Teaching Around the 4MAT Cycle: Designing Instruction for Diverse Learners with Diverse Learning Styles* (Thousand Oaks, CA: Corwin, 2005).

7. Marlene LeFever, "Learning Styles," PACE Conference, 1983.

8. LeFever, *Creative Teaching Methods,* 23–28. Also see the chapter by Bill Hendricks on "What Makes a Great Teacher?" for additional insights.

9. Gabriele L. Rico, *Writing the Natural Way* (New York: Penguin Putnam, 2000).

10. Tony Buzan, *Use Both Sides of Your Brain* (New York: Plume, 1994).

11. John W. Reed, workshop presentation (Dallas Theological Seminary, Houston, 2003).

Chapter 17
MENTORING THE NEXT GENERATION

Barbara Neumann

> *...we will tell the next generation the praiseworthy deeds of the*
> LORD, *his power, and the wonders he has done.*
> —Psalm 78:4

The Need for Mentoring

THE BUSTLING NEIGHBORHOOD COFFEE shop began to relax as customers dispersed for daily employment or chores. Seated at a tucked-away table, I watched for the arrival of a young woman. An energetic young employee, long dark ponytail swinging as she worked, bused tables nearby. Pausing at my table, she asked, "Can I get you something?" With a smile I responded, "No thanks. I'm just waiting to meet someone." As my second cup of coffee grew cold I realized she had forgotten to come. I collected my things to leave the nearly empty coffee shop when the young employee approached, "Would you like some company while you wait?"

My mind stalled momentarily because I didn't know her, she was an employee, and I didn't know what to make of this invitation. But I managed to reply, "Sure. Have a seat."

She plopped down and inquired, "What do you do?"

"I'm involved in Christian ministry. I was waiting to talk with a young woman but I think she forgot to come. Tell me about you—what do you do?"

Over the next few minutes I heard this twenty-something's story. She had recently arrived in the city, discouraged but hopeful for a new start in life. This job was temporary and would pay the bills while she got on her feet. She had no idea what was next for her, but she longed to know. With eyes darkened by frustration, she exclaimed, "Sometimes I wish God would just give me a road map so I would know what to do!" Her secret angst had abruptly forced its way to the surface.

Sensing the need to return to her job, she moved to the edge of the bench. Another unexpected invitation followed. "Would you be willing to talk to *me*?" Taken aback once more, I nodded, jotted down my email and told her to contact me when she was available. Pushing the paper in her apron pocket, she collected a few empty plates and headed toward the kitchen. I never heard from her. She disappeared from the coffee shop, possibly moving on after failing to find the new life she hoped for, her wandering journey prolonged.

Another Voice

This coffee shop encounter brings to life the urgent need to mentor. Alone and searching for guidance, this young person was willing to engage a stranger in conversation, longing for direction from someone a little further along in life's journey. Her tentative question, "Would you be willing to talk to me?" demonstrates that countless hearts, both male and female, are open and that the need for guidance is great.

> "…even the most positive stories about the emerging-adult years contain evidence of a powerful longing for spiritual companionship, community, and guidance on the journey."[1]
> —Richard R. Dunn and Jana L. Sundene

Many today grow up in broken homes, without the church, without the Bible. Holding a faulty compass, they try to find their way in a confusing world. Alone. As one next-generation person observed, "My friends and I are all dry sponges in need of encouragement, help, love, and listening ears. All of us want mentors."

Like the young woman in the coffee shop, many hunger for another voice to help them sort through life issues and make wise decisions.

Yet most say they can't find these mentors. Those more experienced in life don't have time for them or aren't interested. So they listen to the voices of their peers, or go it alone based on their own limited experience. Too many hit painful dead ends or struggle to construct a meaningful life. Many have adopted a "lessons learned" approach, where aching hearts are stilled with a no-regrets-allowed positivity and nonstop busyness. But underneath the positivity and busyness is often discouragement and anxiety. Too many feel like failures before they make it out of their twenties.[2]

This solemn reality challenges the church and Christian ministries to examine their approaches when it comes to mentoring. When it seems like so many are slipping away, what can faithful believers do to pass on the Christian faith? A careful look at God's ancient command to his people still offers help today.

God's Vision for Mentoring

After delivering his people from Egypt, God gave life-giving instructions for their forward journey, commands that were to dwell within them and shape their souls. Moses delivered these directives as the people stood on tiptoe at the Jordan ready to enter their new homeland. This was not new information; they'd heard it before but needed a reminder.

> Hear, O Israel: The LORD our God, the LORD is one. Love the LORD your God with all your heart and with all your soul and with all your strength. These

commandments that I give you today are to be on your hearts. Impress them on your children. Talk about them when you sit at home, when you walk along the road, when you lie down and when you get up.

—Deuteronomy 6:4–7

> "We have millions of men and women walking the halls of our churches who have the potential to invest powerfully in the life of a young adult but aren't doing it because they consider themselves inadequate and unqualified."[3]
> —Richard R. Dunn and Jana L. Sundene

The Israelites were to think beyond the personal benefits in store for them. God's soul-shaping truths were to be pressed on the hearts of the young ones in tow so they too would love God and prosper in his land. *"Impress them on your children,"* God directed. This is usually understood as a command to parents, and that is certainly valid. Parents are the primary source for their children's spiritual instruction. But careful examination of the historical context reveals a wider application.

Because the ancient Israelites prioritized community over individual lives, they would have understood "your children" to refer not just to individual sons and daughters, but to all the young people in their community. Passing faith to the next generation was a mission given to all God's people.[4] Some six centuries later Jesus gave an equivalent command to the few disciples with him. "Go therefore and make disciples of all nations ... teaching them to observe all that I have commanded you" (Matt. 28:19–20, ESV). In a similar manner, the church has always understood this command to apply not just to those eleven men, but to every believer in every age. Everyone is to do their part. Together the believing community accomplishes the goal of raising up godly generations.

How do God's people accomplish this essential but daunting goal? While Israel waited at the Jordan they first received formal instruction from Moses (Deut. 6:1). The Israelites were then to informally discuss God's commands while sitting or walking, rising up or lying down. This is a figure of speech that uses opposites to indicate an all-encompassing situation, or in this case, all of life's activity. The message: As all of you go about daily life, talk to the young ones about how to live righteously. Use routine events to integrate knowledge with life and pass on faith in God.

Notice that the method is simply talking, or conversation as life happens. This is how truth is impressed on hearts. Everyone who came in contact with Israel's younger generation—parents, farmers, herdsmen, cloth weavers, toolmakers, rabbis, grandmothers, merchants, teachers, shopkeepers, neighbors—could do this. It's a natural method that fits every personality and lifestyle.

This is God's vision for mentoring. As life is lived out, the more experienced believers talk to the less experienced so they might understand and live according to God's Word. Surprisingly, this simple type of conversation between younger and older is infused with transformational power.

God's people continue to need reminders that the Christian faith is more than an individual journey. Personal knowledge of God's Word first is a must, for it grounds believers in the truth. But there's more. Informal conversation about personal life experiences in light of God's Word still impresses truth on hearts, and passes faith to another generation. The final part gives practical suggestions for mentoring in the spirit of Deuteronomy 6, but first we must look at why the paucity of mentoring should concern Christian leaders.

> "Beginning with Jesus's earliest words to the men and women who would become his apprentices of faith, Christianity has understood itself to be a faith taught by one to another."[5]
>
> —Keith R. Anderson
> and Randy D. Reese

Why Mentor?

Mentoring Grows Disciples

Mentoring has always been a powerful way to shape people. The Uncommon Individual Foundation, a mentoring organization, tells us that mentoring is the third most influential relationship in a person's life.[6] The greatest influence comes from one's relationship with parents, the second is the relationship with a spouse, and the third is a relationship with a mentor. If this is true, mentoring can put people on the fast track to spiritual growth.

When they responded to the call to follow him, Jesus's disciples stepped on the fast track to spiritual growth. Countless conversations took place as they sat, walked, rose up in the morning, and retired at night. Questions were asked, ideas debated, and problems solved. Occasional challenges from their mentor required these men to change their thinking, accept responsibility, and sometimes even go beyond what was humanly possible. Understanding their God and confidence to live according to his Word grew as the disciples listened to Jesus's voice and participated in discussions about life and faith. Using the Deuteronomy 6 strategy, Jesus mentored his disciples and they experienced the impact.

Paul also harnessed the power of mentoring relationships as he spread the news of Jesus and his resurrection (Timothy, Titus, Epaphras, Tychicus, Onesimus, Priscilla and Aquilla, etc.). Though together a relatively brief period of time, those mentored by Jesus and Paul were forever influenced by that relationship. Both left behind a host of men and women who were able to pass faith to the next generation. Other instances of mentoring such as Moses and Joshua, Naomi and Ruth, Eli and Samuel, Samuel and David, Elijah and Elisha, Jehoiada and King Joash, and Elizabeth and Mary are sprinkled throughout the Bible. God's truths were pressed on these hearts, and the influence of mentors lasted a lifetime. People may move or lose touch with a mentor, but when God puts people together in a mentoring relationship the impact is usually lifelong.

Mentoring Is Personal

The seminary where I teach equips some students for ministry through an internship. When a student inquired about doing an internship with me, we met to discuss the possibility. With seminary requirements spread on the table, she realized she forgot to include specific options for her development and thought our conversation had to be postponed. I assured her everything was okay because I could see *her*, who she was, how she needed to be developed, and that was enough to guide us through the process. In the quiet pause that followed, tears filled her eyes. "You have no idea how I've longed to hear those words. I've felt like a number in the system. You're the first one to really see who I am."

In a mentoring relationship a person can be seen for who they are, and where they are in life. People hunger for this opportunity, and when it's present their hearts open to the acceptance it communicates. When someone feels seen by another, they often begin to see things about themselves, and become more receptive to the reflective thinking that's required to mature. And something else happens—they begin to see Scripture differently. It becomes more personal, and they hear God speaking into their life. This is the goal of mentoring, to promote attentiveness to God's truths and voice, and assist the less experienced to love God and respond appropriately in their own life situations. The personal focus that mentoring creates often leads to a more personal journey with God.

> "Growth is a gift given as we learn to attend to the presence of God in our lives."[7]
> —Keith R. Anderson and Randy D. Reese

Mentoring Is Timely Guidance

Natural mentoring as life unfolds captures teachable moments and turns them into life change. When a person contacts a mentor, they usually need to solve a problem, gain a new perspective, or think through a difficult situation. Life, in some way or another, brings this person ready to listen and learn.

A difficult boss prompted a young person to contact me for help. Exasperated, she wanted to quit a job she previously enjoyed. As we read selected Proverbs and discussed foolish people, she began to better understand the challenges she faced. This allowed her to calm down and focus on a solution. As we continued to work on the problem, she tried out godly responses week-by-week. What could she do to love God and her boss? A real-time problem that intersected with hands-on learning created insight that stuck with her, and she learned godly skills she now uses routinely. Mentoring often intersects with critical junctures in a person's spiritual journey, and what was once just information converts to learning that sticks. Attitudes change, actions change when truth is connected to life.

Mentoring Is Natural Follow-Up

If you've been in ministry for a while, you know that people (including me) don't always act on what they hear. The teacher's not to blame; biblical truth was faithfully communicated. Heads nod at these compelling truths, but most of it is deposited in the brain's storage closet by dinnertime. Out of sight, out of mind. Perhaps that's one reason God intends believers to function as parts of one Body. As much as we might love the idea of autonomy, we are incomplete without others. By God's design, one part helps another part do its work, or in this case, to remember.

I believe mentoring's great value lies in the opportunity to help another person *think* about what they've heard or know. Words that are heard or read flow by so quickly that deliberate thinking on the part of the listener is often rare. Mentoring facilitates conversations where biblical truth has an opportunity to marinate. Mentor and mentee pull convicting truths out of mental storage and examine them in a slower paced setting. The result is natural follow-up, or what we sometimes refer to as accountability. One person helps another to remember, or pay attention to their life before God. The simple act of meeting with a mentor brings truth out of mental storage and into active use.

A New Learning Style

If mentoring remarkably grows ordinary people through personal connection, timely guidance, and natural follow-up, why do many mentoring initiatives find fewer and fewer participants? Dedicated believers are ready to mentor, people seek mentors, but the two are not connecting. Obviously we have a problem. Research I carried out in 2010 revealed a few answers.[8] Part of the problem involves generational differences. Older mentors frequently prefer a method of mentoring that younger people think is unnatural or not worth their time. What happened? How did we get so far removed from the Deuteronomy 6 model? Let's look at what's behind this disconnect.

> "We are experiencing a mentoring crisis today. One key reason is that too many of us ... cling to an outdated formulaic idea of what mentoring is all about."[9]
> —Sue Edwards
> and Barbara Neumann

Something Changed

The next generation was born into a society undergoing a seismic shift. As adoring parents rocked their cradle, new digital technology led businesses, services, and institutions to retool for digital transactions. While those in the older generation scrambled to learn new ways to do almost everything, the younger generation never knew anything else. For them, the Internet has always existed and the way things get done.

Digital technology not only rearranged the way people do life in the twenty-first century, it impacted the way the next generation learns. Those born after 1980 grew up with two teachers—the person in the room, and the device in the room. Because the latter became a greater source of information, learning increasingly depended on the device. As a result, technology changed *how* the next generation learns and what they find valuable when it comes to mentoring.

Previous generations learned mostly through a teacher and structured curriculum. Since most who were believers hungered for knowledge about God, the Bible, or spiritual practices, the goal of the mentor was to impart their knowledge by teaching a Bible study, discipleship curriculum, or book. With information on any subject instantly accessible from the device that's always attached to their body, the next generation isn't interested in information. If they want to know the best practices for prayer, Google pops up pages of websites. With earpiece in place while jogging, they listen online to the best and brightest teach the Bible. Their inbox contains favorite blogs that update them on the latest Christian thinking. Phones beep with the forty million Bible verses tweeted every year.[10] Bible studies online connect them with believers around the globe. For younger people, knowledge and teaching has moved on-line. Everything they want to know is available on their device. When it comes to mentoring *they want what they can't get online.*

Instead of information, people want mentors who will listen to their life and help them make godly decisions. They want mentors who will point out God's presence and work in their life. They want healing from sin. They want to see grace move from theory to reality. They want to make a significant contribution to the kingdom of God. They want a bold faith that gives hope in a desperately broken world. This is the stuff that isn't available online.

> "If we really want to help someone grow, we will have to help them in a way that fits their wiring. Our great model for this is God himself, for he always knows just what each person needs…. God does not do 'one size fits all.'"[11]
>
> —John Ortberg

Practical Suggestions

How does the Christian community provide opportunities to grow this kind of faith? Natural mentoring relationships, such as those described in Deuteronomy 6, can open the door.[12] Instead of joining a program, being assigned a mentor, and going through a book, most people prefer to simply talk to someone they trust about what's going on in their life. They refer to these conversations as organic, or something that happens naturally. To get faith-passing conversations

going again, mentoring approaches must be more natural, or organic.

Keeping in mind that mentoring is a process that will look different for different people in different situations, the following are a few organic mentoring suggestions offered by those in the next generation.

Grow an Authentic Relationship

Life in a digital world both connects and disconnects. Momentary superficial connections through social media are easy to come by, but genuine relationships—not so easy. Overscheduled lives leave little room for solid relationships where one feels known and loved. Daily life in this culture often grows hunger for authentic, face-to-face relationships that accept, encourage, and allow them to be themselves.

> "…the humans we lead need to see it's normal to wrestle, have doubts, feel numb."[13]
>
> —Mandy Smith

This means the polite conversation and superficial concern that often gets us by as believers just won't do for the next generation. They desire a mentoring relationship where both people participate as pilgrims on a rigorous faith journey. Both learn from the other, encourage each other, pray for each other, and grow spiritually. It's a place where the real self can emerge and offer itself for renovation. The result is a relationship built on deep conversation, mutual trust, and shared wisdom—the desire of every heart, and the substance of transformation. Mentoring that takes place in an authentic relationship opens a heart to God's commands and fosters spiritual growth.

Exactly what do people mean when they say they want an authentic relationship? I recently asked a panel of Millennials what they want to learn from a mentor. Almost in unison they replied, "We want to know how you did it (lived the Christian life), and we especially want to hear about your mistakes." In other words, they want the real-life stuff. At this revelation several older mentors who were listening looked at each other and made a face. Not good news for those of us who grew up carefully camouflaging our weaknesses and believed that mistakes disqualified us as mentors.

> "[But] congregants in the emerging ... culture are hungry for leaders who are approachable ... transparent, and real. They want to connect with someone who is unscripted, unrehearsed, and not 'on.'"[14]
> —M. Rex Miller

I recently led a ministry in my church that wasn't going well. After a vigorous and successful start, some underground discontent seeped in slowly. What was previously a joy turned into a stressful duty that depleted me more each day. I began to doubt my competency, and God's call. It took courage to be vulnerable, but when I admitted to a mentee that I was hurting and why, a rich discussion about the difficulties of ministry and leadership took hold. The conversation not only balanced and encouraged me; the mentee learned how to engage similar problems in her life. Together we heard from God and grew in faith.

The mentoring critique I hear most often is the older generation needs to loosen up and be real. A carefully perfected persona signals that one is fake, the real person buried somewhere beneath a painted mask. Transparency about weaknesses and failure makes one real, and a person from whom less experienced people want to learn. They want a mentor who will share their faith journey transparently with all its ups and downs. Stories of doubt, struggle, pain, failure, perseverance, healing, restoration draw anxious people like a safe harbor in stormy seas. They want to see how another's faith works itself out in real life. They want to hear about "God moments" that transform. When this happens, they're all ears, and learn how to live out their faith. Sounds like an oxymoron to some of us, but it works.

> "Tell on yourself! Like Paul or the writers of the Psalms, let people know what's causing you pain, what makes you angry, what's difficult for you to overcome in your life—and how God and your closest friends are helping you deal with it."[15]
> —Gary Kinnaman

The Mentee Takes a Larger Role

Dan, a dynamic young engineer, business leader, and Christian mentor, received a call from the mother of a recent college graduate. Her son was at loose ends and she wondered if Dan would meet with him and give him a vision for engineering in the business world. The two men didn't know each other but they had similar professional interests so it seemed like a good idea. "Sure, I'd love to meet with him,"

Dan responded, "but I've found it works best if he contacts me." When talking with me about this mom's request he remarked, "Absolutely the mentee should have the larger role and take responsibility for initiating contact. I prioritize time to meet with younger men, but I'm really busy and I only want to meet with guys who are really interested. It's important to me that the time be meaningful." From Dan's next-generation perspective and personal experience, a potential mentee should make the first move.

> "Tell me and I forget, teach me and I may remember, involve me and I learn."
> —Benjamin Franklin

This is new thinking for many in the older generations. In the past the mentor would typically play the larger role and take the lead. But those born after 1980 bring a different perspective to the mentoring relationship. First, they are used to having a say in everything that concerns them, and think it's natural to choose their own mentors. Being matched with a mentor, whether mom or a pairing committee selects that person, is a frightening situation for many. They're scared of being paired with someone they don't like, relate to, or trust. Instead they want a relationship with someone they already know and admire. Attraction to a potential mentor is non-negotiable. Second, they want the relationship to be a partnership instead of one-way input, and this requires mentor and mentee to actively work together. Third, those whose mentoring is arranged for them are often unmotivated, resulting in a limp relationship that

benefits neither. Since dynamic relationships begin with the less experienced person's hunger to know and learn from one they respect, they should take an active role and make the contact.

This may seem intimidating to some in the younger generation, but it needn't be. A mentoring relationship can start naturally when a person brings a question or problem to a respected believer. It's as simple as, "Would you have time for coffee? I have a question I want to ask you." Or, "Do you have time to meet? I'm struggling with something and I'd like your input." When a mentee identifies the purpose for meeting, they take responsibility for the direction of the relationship, and it's much easier for a mentor to say yes and make time to meet.

But the mentee's larger role doesn't mean the mentor is passive. Many people hesitate to ask for a mentor's time because they fear rejection, so a mentor must also be active in communicating acceptance and interest, whether it's a friendly smile, brief inquiry about one's welfare, or an invitation to grab coffee. Once an interested person initiates, it's the mentor's responsibility to respond warmly and accept. Experienced believers are probably thinking, "But I'm too busy for this," and I get that. All of us are too busy; but if I look at my schedule one or two weeks ahead I can usually find thirty minutes or an hour to help someone think through a situation.

If a mentor receives an invitation, it often works well for the two people to meet informally for coffee or lunch. As conversation unfolds it usually becomes apparent whether or not additional discussions will follow. Perhaps one meeting meets the mentee's need. Perhaps a problem's complexity indicates another meeting. Perhaps it's obvious there's not a click between the two. If not, no problem—it was just coffee and no-one's embarrassed. When mentoring is organic there's freedom for the relationship to start, keep going, or stop according to the preferences of those involved.

> "In my own life, I've felt a strong desire to be in close relationships with older men and women. I desire to learn from them, be nurtured by them, and—maybe most importantly—have mutually beneficial relationships with them. I desire reciprocity in all my relationships, and I suspect that may be part of God's design for us as members of the body of Christ. However, the word 'mentor' brings forth images of a teacher teaching, of hierarchy, of one person taking from another with no option to give back. Honestly, I thought I was being prideful—that I didn't like being taught—even though that didn't make sense because I ask so many questions that people around me run out of time to hear them."
>
> —Holly (age 21)

A larger role for the mentee also doesn't mean an experienced believer can't initiate a relationship. If the Spirit prompts a mentor first, they can suggest coffee to express availability. But keep in mind it's possible a potential mentee won't feel the same attraction. Sometimes people can feel like a pursuing mentor has

an agenda, so when initiating it's a good idea for the mentor to move with sensitivity and allow the mentee to follow up if interested.

It's also appropriate for a mentor to bring a topic for discussion. The mentor might see something in the mentee's life that would benefit from examination and suggest a related conversation. Once a relationship is established, it's natural for both participants to contribute topics for discussion, keeping in mind the mentee has the larger role for determining the content.

Flexibility Is Key

Many in the next generation are busy people who operate on schedules designed to accommodate life as it happens. Weekly mentoring meetings often feel like an obligation they just can't manage. "The last thing I want is for mentoring to be an obligation," remarked one young man, "I want to meet when it makes sense. I have one mentor I see once every six months but he's still a major influence in my life." Another young woman commented, "I want to meet with a mentor, but not every Tuesday. I can't just schedule this stuff out." Some might want to meet every week, but for others there may be weeks or months between meetings. Mentoring isn't a preset program; it's a process that's built conversation by conversation as people sit, walk, rise up, or unwind. Sporadic meetings cause some in the older generations to question the effectiveness of this approach, but our next-gen folks insist that although meetings may be irregular they are still transformational.

Guide Instead of Teach

As those in our youngest generations moved forward—took their first steps, started school, played soccer, sat for the SAT, and came of age—the church at large moved downward. High profile Christian leaders failed morally, fewer people felt loyalty to a denomination, fewer people believed the Bible, intense church conflict over doctrine and gender roles became public, church attendance dropped off, and giving to charity frequently replaced tithing. Many people lost confidence in the Christian faith. As Millennials and Gen Z grew up, what had been a pillar of American society receded to minor status.[16]

As a result, fewer in these generations grew up in the church or Christian homes. Many admit they've never seen the Christian faith lived out, or have little idea how believers are supposed to be different. Those who choose to follow Jesus often ask questions like, "Why does my life need to change? How do I experience the presence of God? How do I change the way I feel? What does it look like to depend on Jesus? What do I do with doubt?" Most next-gen people hope a mentor will help process questions like these, show them what a Christian life looks like, and be a trusted guide instead of the Bible answer person.

> "...the emerging adult wants to be challenged, supported, and empowered."[17]
> —Richard R. Dunn and Jana L. Sundene

A trusted guide first understands where a person is, and then where they need to go. So it's important for a mentor to respond to questions by first listening carefully to grasp where this person is and what's happening in their life. People are unlikely to accept feedback if they don't first feel heard and understood. Listen for feelings that are driving behavior, faulty understanding of God or his Word, sin that's interfering, ignorance of biblical commands, etc.

The mentor can advance the discussion by asking questions such as, "What are the choices in front of you? Where will each choice lead? Is there anything about your thoughts or behavior that's causing problems? How do you see God present in this situation? Do you have any sense of what God might be saying to you?"

The goal is to guide the mentee to think and apply biblical truth. As the discussion progresses the mentor can introduce how the Bible speaks to the situation. It usually works best to explore the biblical text together instead of teaching it in a formal way. When a person discovers biblical truth and applies it to their situation, truth is impressed on the heart.

> "I am not a teacher, but an awakener."
> —Robert Frost

Allow Mentoring to Be a Community Effort

A young woman attempting to help older women understand how she wanted to be mentored held up her cell phone and said, "I want to 'Google' you. I want to find out who knows something about a problem I'm having and talk with her. I want to access the talents of multiple people depending on what I need."

Later, a mentoring book on my lap initiated a conversation with a college student seated next to me on an airplane. I asked for his opinion on mentoring, and he energetically replied that he would love to have a mentor. When I asked who that might be, he said, "I want lots of mentors. There're a lot of things I want to learn." Instead of the one-mentor/one-mentee model, next-gen people see mentoring as a community effort. Because they've been raised to expect lots of options, they want to learn from numerous people, and freedom to move among mentors feels only natural.

But moving from mentor to mentor doesn't feel so natural to the older generation. These believers often think it's more natural to be a mentee's only mentor, and a complete resource for that person's needs. While researching mentoring I heard over and over, "Oh no, I can't mentor—I don't have enough wisdom." The good news is that most people don't expect a single mentor to know everything. They generally admire a particular trait in a person and seek help developing the same characteristic. This brings mentoring down to something almost anyone can do.

For example, one who knows how to build a business on Christian principles can mentor another to do the same, or one who has experience coping with a special needs child can mentor a struggling mom. One who's worked through life/work balance, made it through a difficult pregnancy, or remained pure for marriage can mentor another to do the same. I know one person who has a mentor for ministry, another one for marriage, and still another for her special needs child. People look for mentors who can help them do particular things—not everything—in a way that lives out their faith. When experienced believers stop focusing on their deficiencies and share the responsibility, the pressure's off, and the next generation grows.

Mentor Those in Ministry

A twentysomething camp counselor took off his shoe and propped a sweaty foot on a stool. Since I was camp nurse for the summer, it was my job to hold my nose and treat the peeling skin on the bottom of his foot. During the foot soaks that followed, his love for God and plans for the future became the subject of conversation. He excitedly revealed that the fall would find him in seminary preparing for Christian ministry. "You know you've chosen one of the hardest professions, right?" I offered. His puzzled look told me this was news to him.

My young friend was unaware that 50 percent of those entering ministry will not make it five years, 90 percent of ministry staff people feel unable to meet the demands of their job, and 70 percent battle ongoing loneliness.[18] Ministry is joyful and rewarding in many ways, but also hard. Things happen that take divots out of souls and leave God's servants depleted and discouraged. In my years of ministry I have felt like unstable Swiss cheese more than once.

If you are in ministry, know that you need—no, you must have—at least one mentor. The above statistics alert us that no matter how much we love God, we're not likely to make it if we go it alone. God never means us to discern his character, purposes, or will by ourselves. Find a trusted believer and bring the questions you thought you'd never ask. Let someone help you process thorny problems that eat at your soul. I know you draw heavily from God's Word, but you must also hear another voice that brings truth, balance, and encouragement somewhere along the way.

If you are an experienced person in ministry, know that others need you—no, are desperate for you as a mentor. The above statistics indicate that someone around you is struggling right now, and frantically trying to make it alone. The optimistic start of a young leader who believed they could be anything and do anything may be colliding with the realities of ministry in a fallen world. It's possible your valuable ministry experience and spiritual maturity can keep another afloat and God's name respected.

Conclusion

In his book *The Mentored Life*, James Houston reminds ministry leaders why we all need to mentor and be mentored, "a tree planted in a clearing of an old forest will grow more successfully than when it is planted in isolation in an open field. The roots of the new planting will follow more easily and more deeply the hidden pathways of old root systems. Likewise, human beings thrive best when following the paths of life already taken by others before them…for beyond our own horizons there are those who have seen beyond us or have anticipated challenges and obstacles we may not yet have encountered on life's journey."[19]

Some of you are old forest people with deep roots; some of you are a new planting looking for the hidden paths of life. Whatever the case, mentoring is one of God's provisions for strong servants who finish well. The Deuteronomy 6 model offers a natural approach that works well for both generations. God's given us what we need; now it's up to us to pass it on.

Discussion Questions

1. Can you think of any people who mentored you as you went about life? If so, what was the lasting impact?

2. Why do you think many people fail to see themselves as potential mentors?

3. What one or two things would you like to gain from a mentoring relationship?

4. What do you find appealing about an organic approach to mentoring? What do you find challenging?

5. In what one area could you mentor a younger believer? Have you ever done this? If so, describe the experience.

Resources for Further Study

Books

Anderson, Keith R. and Randy D. Reese. *Spiritual Mentoring: A Guide for Seeking and Giving Direction.* Downers Grove, IL: IVP Books, 1999.

Dunn, Richard R. and Jana L. Sundene. *Shaping the Journey of Emerging Adults.* Downers Grove, IL: IVP Books, 20012.

Edwards, Sue and Barbara Neumann. *Organic Mentoring: A Mentor's Guide to Relationships with Next Generation Women.* Grand Rapids: Kregel, 2014.

Kinnaman, David with Aly Hawkins. *You Lost Me: Why Young Christians Are Leaving Church and Rethinking Faith.* Grand Rapids: Baker, 2011.

Long, Jimmy. *Emerging Hope: A Strategy for Reaching Postmodern Generations.* Downers Grove, IL: IVP Books, 2004.

Stanley, Paul D. and J. Robert Clinton. *Connecting: The Mentoring Relationships You Need to Succeed in Life.* Colorado Springs: NavPress, 1992.

Chapter 17 — Mentoring the Next Generation

Websites

Mentoring Helps through Dallas Theological Seminary—www.dts.edu/mentor

Author Bio

Dr. Barbara Neumann currently serves as adjunct professor in the Educational Ministries and Leadership Department as well as Academic Advisor at Dallas Theological Seminary. She teaches students attending the seminary's Houston campus. Her additional ministries include mentoring young leaders, church mentoring consultant, speaker, and Bible study leader. She recently published *Organic Mentoring: A Mentor's Guide to Relationships with Next Generation Women*. Barbara lives in Houston with her chemical engineer husband Ralph, but escapes to the Colorado mountains every chance she gets. She's mother of three, and grandmother to eleven perfect grandchildren.

Endnotes

1. Richard R. Dunn and Jana L. Sundene, *Shaping the Journey of Emerging Adults: Life-Giving Rhythms for Spiritual Transformation* (Downers Grove, IL: IVP Books, 2012), 23.

2. Alexandra Robbins and Abby Wilner, *Quarter Life Crisis: The Unique Challenges of Life in Your Twenties* (New York: Putnam, 2001).

3. Richard R. Dunn and Jana L. Sundene, *Shaping the Journey of Emerging Adults: Life-Giving Rhythms for Spiritual Transformation* (Downers Grove, IL: IVP Books, 2012), 50.

4. Moses was speaking to the entire nation when he made these remarks (Deut 1:1). This is underscored by the call "Hear O Israel" in Deuteronomy 6:4. Jews refer to this verse as the *Shema,* which comes from the Hebrew word "hear." Eugene Merrill points out, "The singular form of the verb (hear) emphasizes the corporate or collective nature of the addressee, that is, Israel. The covenant was made with the nation as a whole and so the nation must as a unified community give heed to the command of the Lord." Eugene H. Merrill, *The New American Commentary: Deuteronomy,* Vol. 4 (Nashville: Broadman & Holman, 1994), 162.

5. Keith R. Anderson and Randy D. Reese, *Spiritual Mentoring: A Guide for Seeking and Giving Direction* (Downers Grove, IL: IVP Books, 1999), 15.

6. Larry Kreider, *Authentic Spiritual Mentoring: Nurturing Younger Believers toward Spiritual Maturity* (Ventura, CA: Regal, 2008), 12.

7. Anderson and Reese, *Spiritual Mentoring,* 132.

8. Barbara Ann Neumann, "An Examination of Mentoring Programs for Serving the Needs of the Postmodern Christian Woman" (D.Min. diss., Dallas Theological Seminary, 2011).

9. Sue Edwards and Barbara Neumann, *Organic Mentoring: A Mentor's Guide to Relationships with Next Generation Women* (Grand Rapids: Kregel, 2014), 14.

10. Morgan Lee, "Spamming the Good News," *Christianity Today* 60, no. 5, June 2016.

11. John Ortberg, "Hand Craft Disciples," in David Kinnaman, *You Lost Me: Why Young Christians Are Leaving Church ... and Rethinking Faith* (Grand Rapids: Baker, 2011), 216.

12. Edwards and Neumann, *Organic Mentoring,* 97–101.

13. Mandy Smith, *The Vulnerable Pastor: How Human Limitations Empower Our Ministry* (Downers Grove, IL: IVP Books, 2015), 10.

14. M. Rex Miller, *The Millennium Matrix: Reclaiming the Past, Reframing the Future of the Church* (San Francisco: Jossey Bass, 2004), 154–155.

15. Gary Kinnaman, "Tell On Yourself," in Kinnaman, *You Lost Me,* 231–232

16. Gen Z is the generation following the Millennial generation. This generation was born after 1995.

17. Dunn and Sundene, *Shaping the Journey of Emerging Adults,* 48.

18. Bo Lane, *Why Pastors Quit: And What We Can Do to Change the Statistics* (CreateSpace: 2015), 16–20.

19. James M. Houston, *The Mentored Life: From Individualism to Personhood* (Colorado Springs: NavPress, 2002), 10.

Chapter 18

UTILIZING RETREATS, CAMPING, AND OUTDOOR MINISTRIES

Dan Bolin

The heavens declare the Glory of God.... The Law of the LORD is perfect, refreshing the soul.... May these words of my mouth and this meditation of my heart be pleasing in your sight, LORD, my Rock and my Redeemer.

—Psalm 19:1, 7, 14

Introduction

I WAS ONE OF about forty Christian leaders attending a training meeting where the host asked for volunteers to share how we came to faith in Christ. Seven brave souls agreed to tell their stories. When the dust settled, one had shared about a vacation Bible school experience, two told of conversations with family members leading to their conversions, and four recounted decisions made at camp: one as a child, two as young people, and another as a young adult.

Camp is a place for fun, challenge, adventure, rest, and relationships, but it is also a place where decisions are made; it is a place where transformation begins or accelerates. Not every emotional, end-of-camp commitment is a keeper—but many are. Around the world, pastors, missionaries, youth workers, counselors, professors, Sunday school teachers, and a host of others involved in ministry look back to a moment at camp where life changed forever.

Long before Michael Eisner was head of Disney, he was a camper. Not at a Christian camp, but he understood the powerful impact his camp experience had in shaping his adult life: "the planned deprivations are fun, exciting, the stuff from which character is built. As I've gotten older, they make more and more sense. Camp taught me a lot of things, and the experiences accumulated into some big 'stuff,'

stuff that builds backbone and teaches lessons that keep popping up in adulthood.... For me, camp really mattered."[1] Even in a secular camp environment, significant growth and positive change occurred. How much more a Christian experience that employs the same powerful tools within a Christian context.

Henrietta Mears invested much of her considerable influence into building the modern Christian camping movement and was instrumental in founding Forest Home, a leading Christian camp and conference center in Southern California. Her philosophy was, "If the Sunday school is the place where people are built up in the faith, then camp was where they made their decisions."[2] Campers and guests make life-changing and eternity-changing decisions at camp. Many make first-time decisions to follow Christ, others reaffirm earlier spiritual commitments; some find liberation from sins that have entangled their lives, and many more—especially staff members—develop into the next generation of Christian leaders.

Foundations of Camp

Camp is a place where decisions are made, but why? What is it about the camp experience that creates the context in which God works in remarkable ways? Three factors intersect to form the amazingly effective ministry setting for Christian camps, retreats, conferences, and adventure experiences.

Time Away

First is time away. The children of Israel were commanded to leave their homes, their flocks, their fields, and their shops three time a year to go to "Camp Jerusalem." "Three times a year all your men must appear before the LORD your God at the place he will choose: at the Festival of Unleavened Bread, the Festival of Weeks and the Festival of Tabernacles" (Deut. 16:16). This was not only a men's retreat, it was for the whole family—and beyond. The camp experiences that God designed were for everyone, young and old, rich and poor, rejoicing or in difficult circumstances. Time away was important for everyone. "Be joyful at your festival—you, your sons and daughters, your male and female servants, and the Levites, the foreigners, the fatherless and the widows who live in your towns" (Deut. 16:14).

> "People grow in their faith when they are exposed to God's still quiet voice through his creation. The noise of life tends to drown out our ability to hear God speak into our lives. That is why it is so important to immerse children, youth, and adults into God's creation. In the camp setting, people can unplug from their dependency on technology and plug into the Lord."[3]
>
> —Ray Schnickels

God understands the value of trusting him enough to take time away from the pressures, routines, demands, and distractions of our lives, so that we can clear the cobwebs and refocus our attention on things that really matter. Life has a way of crowding out the most important issues of personal refreshment, time with family, and intimacy with God. So, the Lord designed these breaks for the ancient Israelites

406 Chapter 18 — Utilizing Retreats, Camping, and Outdoor Ministries

to restore, renew, and refresh their lives. And today, he calls us to do the same.

Psalm 127 is a Psalm of Ascent, sung on the way to Jerusalem during the three national feast weeks. This little song was part of the repertoire that was sung as the "campers" went to "camp." Solomon begins this brief psalm by identifying two of the primary excuses people often use to avoid the important discipline of retreat: first, our desire for success, and second, our longing for security. His opening salvo is targeted toward those who want to pour everything into the successful completion of their current project. He said, "Unless the LORD builds the house, the builders labor in vain" (Ps. 127:1a).

Solomon knew what it was like to be a builder; he built a palace, a temple, and a lot more. He knew how easy it could be to stay focused on the immediacy of the project and skip Israel's version of "family camp." In essence he calls out those who say, "I'm too busy to go to camp" or "I can't leave now. I'm essential to the success of this project." Solomon reminded his readers then, and now, to trust God and take some time for soul-care and family relationships. He goes on to address those who are driven by security issues. "Unless the LORD watches over the city, the guards stand watch in vain" (Ps. 127:1b). This time Solomon confronts the timid souls who fear becoming vulnerable and facing the possibility of losing possessions, position, or power.

As they wound their way toward Jerusalem, the Children of Israel sang this song to remind themselves of God's power and provision while disconnecting from the projects they were building and the possessions they were protecting. With every step and every chorus, they remembered the importance of pulling back from life's responsibilities and focusing on their worship of God and their relationships with their families.

Stepping away from what we are building and protecting leaves us in a vulnerable position; it demands that we trust God. We can worry and fret about building and protecting and miss opportunities for retreat and reflection. But Solomon reminds us, "In vain you rise early and stay up late, toiling for food to eat—for he grants sleep to those he loves" (Ps. 127:2). God is in control of what we are striving to achieve and what we are trying to protect. We can relax, enjoy the rest he provides—and go to camp.

The psalm shifts its focus away from the excuses people employ to avoid joining the festival and locks the singers' attention onto family relationships and the importance and blessing of investing in the lives of the next generation. "Children are a heritage from the LORD, offspring a reward from him. Like arrows in the hands of a warrior are children born in one's youth. Blessed is the man whose quiver is full of them. They will not be put to shame when they contend with their opponents in the court" (Ps. 127:3–5). Camps, retreats, conferences, outdoor adventures all require that we trust God with what we are building and protecting. We need to step away from the routine and pressures to take a deep breath. Within the space that time away provides, we have the opportunity to worship God and invest in others we love. The return is significant, transformational, and eternal.

Lacking external stimulus, we tend to roll through life on autopilot, allowing the routines and rhythms of life to create an emotional and spiritual force field that obstructs deep, evaluative thought. God understands the powerful impact that occurs when people leave behind the security of their routine lifestyle and the comfort of their familiar existence to enter a world that is just a little off kilter. New beds, different food, strange people, and altered schedules create a disequilibrium that helps recalibrate our senses to "high alert." When the circumstances of life are altered, the "sameness" that inhibits reflection is removed, allowing us to gravitate toward self-examination.

At times, life grabs us by the scruff of the neck and challenges the ruts that we trudge through day after day. Often, harsh or painful interruptions force us to reexamine our lives. But camp experiences offer a less traumatic, and often enjoyable, pathway to change. From camp's new vantage point, campers and guests reflect on their daily lives and see their mistakes and missed opportunities. Life's routine and mundane distractions tend to obscure our most significant opportunities and mask our greatest threats. Time-away dissipates the haze and obliterates the distractions allowing us to see life with new clarity and focus.

God's Revelation

The second reason camps, retreats, conferences, and adventure experiences are so effective is because they operate in the sweet spot of God's self-revelation. God uses his creation to proclaim his glory. "The heavens declare the glory of God; the skies proclaim the work of his hands" (Ps. 19:1). The first six verses of Psalm 19 focus on God's revelation through creation. David reminds us that the message is being proclaimed all the time, "Day after day they pour forth speech; night after night they reveal knowledge" (Ps. 19:2). The clouds, blue sky,

sunshine by day, the moon and stars at night, not to mention sunrise and sunset are always proclaiming the glory of God. David also explains that his message supersedes the limits of language. God's self-proclamation through creation is not constrained by the curse of Babel; everyone can understand the proclamation. "They have no speech, they use no words; no sound is heard from them" (Ps. 19:3). Camp is effective in China, Russia, Brazil, and Kenya, in part because God speaks creation fluently. God's self-proclamation through creation is not bound by geography or topography. David goes on, "Yet their voice goes out into all the earth, their words to the ends of the world" (Ps. 19:4a). No ocean, mountain, river, or desert limits access to God's self-revelation. His proclamation is ubiquitous.

Camp ministry follows the teaching model set by Jesus. As the master teacher, Jesus understood the importance of the instructional context and the powerful impact of spending time in creation. Over half of Jesus's recorded teaching took place out-of-doors.[4]

General revelation from creation is only one part of the story. God has also chosen his Word to provide special revelation about what he expects and how we can know him. The second section of Psalm 19 focuses on revelation from the Bible. This section begins, "The law of the LORD is perfect, refreshing the soul" (Ps. 19:7a). David goes on to use six names for God's Word: law, statutes, precepts, commands, fear, and decrees. He adds six descriptions of God's Word: perfect, trustworthy, right, radiant, pure, and firm.[5] He also provides six explanations of the benefit or qualities of God's Word: refreshing the soul, making wise the simple, giving joy to the heart, giving light to the eyes, enduring for-ever, all of them are righteous.

Obviously, the intense and continuous time at camp allows extended opportunities for bib-lical instruction. But not only is camp a place where the Word of God is taught in a compressed timeframe; camp also allows the classroom and the laboratory experience to intersect. In a camp setting, what is learned can be applied immediately. Teaching and life are intertwined. David understands that application is essential for transformation so he concludes his powerful little psalm with the prayer, "May these words of my mouth and this meditation of my heart be pleasing in your sight, LORD, my Rock and my Redeemer" (Ps. 19:14). Camp is ultimately about transformation—not just knowing God's Word in our heads, but living it out in our lives. Camp allows campers and staff to interact with God's Word throughout the day in formal and informal encounters, and it also provides opportunities to live out what is learned in real time. How do campers treat their least attractive cabin mate? How do they wait in line when the meal is late? How do they win, and how do they lose? Every moment at camp—whether in Bible study or in the swimming pool—allows campers to apply in their lives, what they are learning in their Bible studies. Jim Badke, a thought leader in the Christian camping movement writes, "The point is, you teach your campers all day long, not just when you open the Bible with them … what you teach them from the Bible should recap what you have taught them all day."[6]

Camp, retreat, conference, and adventure ministries thrive because they employ two pow-erful methods that God has chosen to reveal him-self: his creation and his Word. These two areas of revelation reinforce each other and together create a transformational force in campers' lives.

Relationships

The third foundation is relationships. In ad-dition to using time away and God's revelation, camps are built upon human relationships. Be-fore Jesus sent his disciples out to do ministry, he called them to spend time with him (Mark 3:14). The Twelve were young men, probably in their teens or early twenties, who were called to sleep on the ground, cook over open fires, hike trails, and sail boats together.[7] Camp creates a tem-porary community that provides support and encouragement along with critique and account-ability. All this is done with trained role models in a challenging and high-trust environment.

The relational nature of the camp setting pro-vides a supportive and encouraging context where effort is honored and progress is rewarded. Camp also provides immediate feedback and loving ac-countability. Camp life, however, is not immune from the effect of sin: angry words, malicious acts, inappropriate behavior, and personal con-flicts can all find their way into cabin groups and camp activities. The wonderful thing about camp is that we have to deal with issues as they arise. Waiting until next Sunday, or avoiding a conflict altogether is impossible at camp. Resolving prob-lems, confessing sin, asking for forgiveness, and finding reconciliation is much more likely in the supportive environment of a Christian camp.

Due to the integrated nature of camp min-istry, every staff member becomes the embodi-ment of the Christian values and beliefs of the ministry. Counselors, lifeguards, dishwashers and wranglers provide real-life superheroes for campers to mimic. The fact that young, impressionable campers look up to the camp staff members demands that staff recruitment, selection, organizing, training, supervision, and evaluation be given utmost importance.

Trust is the bonding agent of all human relationships, and camps provide a context where trust can develop rapidly. Sometimes this accelerated growth is intentionally designed, but most often trust emerges naturally and effectively within the camp setting.

Several factors influence the development of trust; and camps provide many of the critical trust-building elements: demonstrated skills and competencies, godly character, transparency, and shared emotional experiences. The camp setting provides many elements but it uniquely provides the aspect of shared emotional experiences.

Pastors who tell a joke to start their sermons are doing more than entertaining their audiences, they are creating a context in which trust flourishes. Shared painful, traumatic moments such as wartime friendships create deep bonds of trust that last a lifetime. But the most common shared emotional experience is laughter, and camp is fun! Love, joy, happiness, security, and camaraderie make it hard for skepticism to survive for long. God uses the fun of camp to grow trust, and trust is critical to Christian commitment.

Camping ministries are effective because they utilize time away from the routines and distractions of life, immersion into God's revelation through creation and scripture, and deepening relationships through modeling, encouragement, and trust.

Styles of Camp

There are many expressions of Christian camping, and many of the terms used to describe outdoor ministries have similar or overlapping meanings. Definitions vary geographically and within select church and ministry groups. At the risk of oversimplification, confusion, or argument, some of the basic expression of outdoor ministries are:

Resident Youth Camps

Resident youth camps are traditional sleep-away experiences that require overnight accommodations, recreational activities, outdoor settings, and trained supervisory staff. Generally, resident youth camps serve children and young people for one or more weeks.

Retreats

Retreats also involve overnight experiences for children, youth, or adults. They are generally shorter and often relationally focused. The social structure of retreats (middle school, high school, women, men, singles, or couples) is often the defining focus. Retreats tend to be smaller, more interactive, and more intimate than larger camps and conferences.

Conferences

Conferences can target any age group. They tend to center around content such as: prophecy, Bible, missions, stewardship, or parenting. Conferences tend to be larger and focus significantly (but not exclusively) on the information that is being shared or the training being provided.

Family Camps

Family camps engage the whole family and there are many variations. One basic model keeps the entire family together most of the day. As a unit, they participate in activities designed for the entire family sharing biblical teaching times, sleeping in one cabin or dorm room, and eating meals together. Another model separates families into age-specific tracks and runs parallel, yet at times, intersecting programs. Most family camps borrow from both poles combining elements of family togetherness as well as some age-specific activities.

> "Family camping is one of the greatest catalytic ministry environments on earth…. With the staff as the agents of joyful service, the miracle of family camp happens through the cultivation of loving relationships and the modeling of godly living. Youth camping has this transformational impact on the individual child. Family camp impacts the entire family."[8]
>
> —Daniel Wallace

Adventure Experiences

Adventure experiences generally involve confronting the unknown, facing challenging physical circumstances, and overcoming perceived risk. They are often conducted in remote, wilderness areas. These outdoor adventures tend to engage small groups of canoers, hikers, climbers, sailors, spelunkers, or other adventure enthusiasts. Processing the adventure and learning experientially are generally critical elements. These events are often led by staff members who are trained in outdoor skills, interpersonal relationships, and spiritual transformation.[9]

> "In experiential learning, knowledge is gained and internalized when facilitated or incidental experiences are followed by intentional reflection."[10]
>
> —Muhia Karianjahi

Day Camps

Day camps provide a daytime camp experience but reduce some of the challenges, expense, and risks faced by those who operate overnight camps. Day camps are often suited for younger children who are not yet emotionally or physically ready for an overnight event but who are eager for a camp experience. In many parts of the world, day camps are growing because there is very little capital investment. They can be held in city parks, at farms, or any other suitable site. Day camping is expanding in the United States, as established resident camps are reaching out and holding day camps in urban settings.

> "As families' summer calendars become busier and more challenging, it is vital that camp be brought to the people. Sending the kids to camp needs to be an easy decision. Therefore, it needs to be reasonably priced and conveniently located. The answer—Day Camps. Day Camps can be put on in just about any location—churches, schools, recreation centers, etc."[11]
>
> —Reed Livesay

Mission/Service Camps

Short-term mission/service trips (at home or internationally) are generally camps with an outreach or service component. At times mission/service camps are sandwiched between weekend retreats or conferences that prepare the participants for the challenges ahead, and then debrief what has been experienced.

Specialty Camps

Specialty camps focus on a unique and very narrow area of interest, or serve a very specific population. Specialty camps can include quilting, English immersion, scrapbooking, basketball, trombone, or square dancing. Specialty camps can also involve focused planning, intense Easter cantata preparation for a choir, contemplative or silent retreats. At times, specialty camps can serve terminally or chronically ill children, children of military parents, or children of missionaries.

Camp Components

On first glance, camp ministry appears simple, but upon further examination it is actually very complex. There are many moving parts. Each outdoor ministry activity requires several levels of planning and implementation. Camp design and implementation must be intentional. Each aspect of the outdoor ministry is too important and involves too many variables to be left to chance. Because camp is complex, planning is critical, and it is essential that the plan includes both the philosophical foundation for *why* camp is happening and the practical outworking of *how* the event should unfold.[12]

Rob Ribbe, director of Wheaton College's HoneyRock Camp and Assistant Professor of Christian Formation and Ministry says, "Camp experiences have the potential to be truly transformational in all of their aspects. The 24-hour living-learning environment, if fully utilized, allows for the teaching, practice, and reflection that deeply embed cognitive, emotional, behavioral, spiritual, and relational growth. A reemphasis on involvement with the outdoors and maximizing the value of the temporary community seems critical to the future of the camping movement. This approach requires development and articulation of a sound philosophy of ministry that affects the practice of all program elements."[13]

That philosophy of ministry (the *why*) must be applied to four critical elements of each camp experience (the *how*): program, place, people and promotion. Each of these four aspects of camp requires prayerful attention and conscientious detail management.

Programming

Programming is what most people envision when they think about camp. There are two fundamental programming styles: centralized and decentralized.[14] Centralized programming generally consists of large group meetings, activities for the entire camp, meals in large dining halls, and dormitory housing. Decentralized programming employs small group activities, interactive Bible studies, and cabins that generally house six to ten campers.

Centralized programming works well in situations where the camp mission calls for an emphasis on proclamation. Great communicators, powerful worship leaders, exciting, large-group activities can be orchestrated well. Decentralized camps work well in contexts where the mission is more relational. Intimate discussions, deep interactions, and life-long friendships are often associated with decentralized camping.

Both styles have drawbacks. Centralized camp experiences create what has been called "church in the woods." This style may miss opportunities to build and strengthen relationships often allowing campers with needs and problems to go undetected and unassisted during camp. The effectiveness of decentralized camping depends on many committed, gifted, and trained staff members who are expected to provide instruction, care, and relational depth to the camp experience. Finding qualified, committed, enthusiastic staff members can be a daunting challenge. Too often, the staff members (paid or volunteer) are ill equipped to fulfill all the challenging role requirements. Recruiting, selecting, organizing, training, supervising, and evaluating camp staff members is especially critical in a decentralized style of camp.

Most camps adopt a hybrid program model employing aspects of the two extremes. They use some large group instruction to ensure that truth is articulated in an accurate and engaging way, but they also plan small group interactions to personalize the instruction. Large group activities generate excitement and energy, while smaller activities allow everyone to participate and go deeper.

Programming—whether centralized, decentralized, or a hybrid format—tends to look at camp through one of five programmatic lenses: In-between, Incentive, Instructive, Illustrative, or Integrative.[15]

In-between Programmatic Lens

This model looks at programming as what happens between meetings. Those who program around this design tend to draw a distinction between spiritual and secular aspects of camp. The heart of camp is the meeting times, but children cannot sit still forever. This style of programming allows them to play and burn off energy so that they can sit through another significant meeting.

Incentive Programmatic Lens

Programming, for some, provides an incentive for campers to attend. The newest and most exotic programming activity will entice children and young people to attend camp. Once there, God will go to work in their lives. The longest zipline in North America, the fastest ski-boats on the planet, the highest climbing wall. Did I mention jet skis?

Instructive Programmatic Lens

Learning new skills and gaining confidence is a big part of many camp programs, and it should be. Campers develop confidence as they accomplish the simple tasks of living independently from their parents, overcoming their fear of heights, learning to swim, or making new life-long friends. For many campers, camp provides first-time opportunities to ride a horse, repel (abseil), zipline, or roll a kayak. Learning new skills, especially those not generally accessible in an urban setting, breeds greater confidence and trust. These newfound forces often unlock chambers of the heart sealed by fear and insecurity.

Illustrative Programmatic Lens

Programming can also create opportunities for illustrations of deeper spiritual truth. Sail boating provides a wonderful opportunity to talk about Jesus's correlation of the Holy Spirit to the wind in John 3. The archery range can set the stage for a conversation about sin's meaning to "miss the bullseye." And a crafts class discussion can be turned to God's creation being his arts and crafts project, "the work of his hands." Bruce Dunning, director of Medeba Adventure Learning Center in Ontario, Canada writes, "No one argues that you are 'narrow minded' when teaching the correct use of climbing knots, because tying them incorrectly could result in death.... If we can have absolutes on a simple scale, don't you believe that it is true on an ultimate scale?"[16] The activities of camp provide a treasure trove of illustrative materials to deepen our awareness of who God is and what he expects from our lives.

Integrative Programmatic Lens

When my daughters were young, they loved to play with clay. We bought different colored canisters and let them go, rolling it into snakes, using cookie cutters to create flowers and elephants, and squishing it in their little fists. Then the clay had to go back in the canisters. As best we tried, the red, green, yellow and blue clays would not go back into their original tins. There was now one unified mass; the distinct colors still visible within the inseparable whole. That's the way camp truly is, distinguishable parts, but an inseparable whole. Life tends to compartmentalize our faith into Sunday mornings and maybe a Bible study during the week. Camp, however, creates an integrated experience where God invades every aspect of our lives.

Place

The place should support the mission of the event. A centralized philosophy of programming requires large-group meeting, eating, recreation, and housing. A decentralized philosophy calls for small breakout areas, round tables, cabin-style housing and small group program elements. Not all camp facilities are the same. Find a site that supports the style of camp program that best expresses your philosophy of outdoor ministry.

Meeting Space

The style and philosophy of ministry will determine the type of meeting space that best suits your group. On a backpacking trip the best meeting place may be around a fire in the evening darkness, a mountaintop overlooking miles of wilderness in all directions, or a grassy meadow along a babbling brook. Conferences may require large auditoriums with sound, lighting, and video equipment. Most groups require a point of assembly for large group meetings, breakout areas for small group discussions, and quiet areas for private conversations.

During the feeding of the five thousand, Jesus found ways to engage the entire five thousand, use small group techniques, and have personal conversations. Jesus modified his ministry style to meet the needs of his audience and to engage them in the most effective ways possible. He also had the people sit down in green grass (Mark 6:39). Apparently he wanted them to be comfortable and free of unnecessary distractions. Making campers and guests comfortable contributes to the trust-building experience and it removes distractions that can hinder a positive reception of the message. Few sites offer perfect meeting areas but they must meet the basic requirements to accomplish the camp's mission and fulfill its vision.

Dining

Dining space fulfills a critical operational function; therefore, it is easy to allow efficiency to dominate the design and operation of this space. However, feeding people is also a relational experience and a key contributor to the camp ministry.

Round tables support inclusive conversation whereas rectangular tables limit discussion to those seated nearby. Food can be served cafeteria style (served by staff), buffet style (self-served), family style (serving bowls and platters for the whole table), or banquet style (plate by plate). Cafeteria and buffet styles allow flexibility as to when campers or guests may arrive for meals, and this allows tables to be "turned" multiple times allowing more people to be fed than possible in one seating. But family style and banquet style allow everyone to start and end at about the same time. This provides programming options that engage the entire camp community. Singing, skits, games, entertainment, guided discussions, devotions, and prayer can all be incorporated into mealtime programming.

Housing

Camp housing comes in all shapes and sizes. Finding a site with housing that supports your ministry design is key. Large dormitories with bunkers for thirty to forty people provide sleeping accommodations that maximize a small space. This generally offers the lowest cost option but also limits conversations and small group interaction. Cabins provide housing for eight to twelve campers and allow for more small group identity and unity. Dormitories and cabins generally provide community restrooms. Most local governments maintain their own standards for bunk height and methods of egress as well as specifying ratios of floor space, toilets, sinks, and showers per camper.[17]

Recreation

Depending on the purpose for the event, recreation can be active or passive. Active recreation involves traditional swimming, horseback riding, hiking, archery, and crafts; but camps also provide ropes courses, creation care activities, jet skis, rock climbing, repelling (abseiling), and an assortment of team building activities.

Passive recreation includes picnic tables strategically located throughout the property to provide quiet places for private conversation. Rocking chairs situated on decks exploiting a panoramic view. Benches placed in peaceful settings for reflection or prayer.

> "God's people have always sought quiet and solitude in the outdoors. As we observe Moses on Mt. Sinai, Elijah in the cave or Jesus in the wilderness, the principle is the same: being quietly alone in the natural world is one of God's great teaching tools. This is why the camping movement so profoundly affects those who seek silence, and seclusion in the wilds. As we distance ourselves from the fast paced, manic, mechanized world, we finally can hear the still, small, whispering voice of the Creator."[18]
> —Bedford Holmes

People

Christian camping is a relational ministry and, as such, staffing is of utmost importance.

Whether paid staff or volunteers, assembling the best team possible is critical to the success of the camp ministry. This is true for many reasons: safety, role modeling, community modeling, ease of operations, and effectiveness of ministry. And camp is a place where the next generation of leaders cuts it teeth in ministry. For many Christian leaders, camp was the first place they taught a Bible study, shared the gospel message, learned hard work, and developed a servant's heart.

The summer staff experience is valuable on multiple levels and its impact can be felt throughout an individual's lifetime. When it comes to staff, five issues are essential: hiring, organizing, training, supervising, and evaluating.

Hiring

Selecting people based on both their character and competence is key. A formal application should be developed for potential staff members whether paid or volunteers. References and criminal backgrounds should always be checked. A code of conduct or a lifestyle covenant should be agreed upon before an invitation to serve is finalized. A letter of invitation should be issued and a formal commitment secured to solemnize the agreement.[19]

Organizing

Two tools are essential to organizing the people who are committed to serving with you at camp: job descriptions and an organizational chart.[20] The job description explains each person's role, addressing issues such as mandatory commitments, required and desired skills, authority in areas such as hiring, spending, or contracting, responsibilities of the job, and a clarification of compensation expectations. The organizational chart describes the relationships within the organization and explains the flow of information and where legitimate authority resides.

"Summer staffers are challenged physically, spiritually, mentally and emotionally on a daily basis and are provided an opportunity to have their life transformed by the experience. When paired with leadership that is willing to invest personally, the opportunity for personal growth is truly significant and life altering. From meaningful work experience to lifelong relationships, being a summer staff member can impact an individual for many years."[21]
—Tom Roots

Training

Each staff member deserves to be prepared to do the job that they are called to perform. Training should involve at least six areas:

Mission and Goals—The mission and goals of the camp should unify and energize everyone on staff. The overarching reason why the camp is being held should be emphasized in words and exemplified in behavior.[22]

Logistical Issues—Staff members need to know where to park their cars, where to pick up their mail, how to answer the phone, and where to do their laundry.

Relational—Camp is a relational ministry and, as such, opportunity should be given for staff members to get to know one another. Superficial "speed dating"-type conversations are a necessary start; but gaining information about social styles, personality types, learning styles, values, commitments, and beliefs will strengthen the relational core.

Policy and Procedure Issues—A policy is the answer to a question that will be asked again. A procedure is a standard response to a recurring situation. Policies and procedures may be related to communication requirements and channels, responses to dangerous or crisis situations, regulations that must be followed, along with the sanctions that will be enforced if the regulations are violated, and a host of other issues.

Job Responsibilities—Lifeguards will have different expectations than cooks; the work requirements for wranglers will be different than counselors. Whereas policies and procedures are shared throughout the organization, job responsibilities are specific to the requirements of the position. Understanding job responsibilities is especially important for those who lead Bible studies and provide spiritual instruction.

Spiritual Preparation—Everyone from dish room helpers to program directors participate in ministry. Peter reminds us, "If anyone speaks, they should do as one who speaks the very words of God. If anyone serves, they should do so with the strength God provides, so that in all things God may be praised through Jesus Christ. To him be the glory and the power for ever and ever. Amen" (1 Peter 4:11). Whether fulfilling a speaking role such as a counselor, program director or Bible study leader, or in a

serving role such as food service, maintenance, or housekeeping, camp ministry is still ministry and spiritual preparation should be taken seriously for every staff member. Bible study, prayer partners, times of reflection, and words of encouragement should be considered. Those in the serving areas may not see the direct spiritual impact of their efforts. Sharing life-change stories, positive evaluation comments, or reading thank-you letters helps give meaning to stacks of dirty dishes or clogged toilets.

Supervising

Camps provide powerful life-change experiences for the staff members because of the immediate, direct, and loving feedback. Jesus often taught, healed, fed, or confronted groups or individuals in authentic, compassionate ministry. However, he was always working on a secondary level, teaching and challenging his disciples. Camp staff members are not disposable resources that can be used up and thrown away in the name of ministry. Neither is camp an experimental laboratory to develop the next generation of Christian leaders at the expense of the campers. Jesus ministered to and through his disciples. Camps should design and implement authentic ministry programs for campers and staff alike.

Evaluating

In the parable of the talents, the master gives different levels of responsibility and opportunity to three servants. When the master returns, he evaluates each servant's performance. He begins examining their character; two are declared good and one wicked. He then makes an observation about their performance;

two are deemed faithful and one lazy. In camp ministry we have opportunity to assess both character issues and work-related performance. There should be a strong emphasis on developmental steps needed for staff members to grow in both areas.

Promotion

Promotion of camp involves a four-part structured process. Each is important and, although they are all interrelated, each should be considered carefully and independently.

Features

We tend to focus on the features of our camp ministries. Features include good food, beautiful setting, trained staff, swimming pool, waterfall or climbing wall. Features are the components that make up camp; they are important but they are not critical in the promotion process. For promotional purposes, one significant and unique feature should be selected to become a signature representation of the camp. This might be the world's best cinnamon rolls, the state's longest zipline, a spring-fed swimming hole, or an artificial ski slope. The most unique and attractive feature should qualify as the one to highlight and upon which to focus.

Benefits

Features focus on the camp, but benefits focus on the campers. Benefits address the needs and desires of the campers and guests. What will they gain from the weekend retreat, the canoe trip, or the week of summer camp? Spiritual transformation, lifelong friendships, joy, confidence, hope, forgiveness, and independence are just a few of the benefits that camp leaders pray

will accompany campers when they return home from their outdoor ministry experience.

Promotional Message

The promotional message should be a consistent and focused statement that is repeated and reinforced within all promotional communication. Ideally, three benefits and one feature will constitute the promotional message. It might be something like, "At camp this year we are going to have a blast, make new friends, deepen our relationship with God, and hike to the top of the highest mountain in the state." This concise message highlights an emotional, relational, and spiritual benefit and also mentions one key feature of the camp experience. Too often we show pictures of our new building or a plate of spaghetti; wonderful features, but not what grips the heart.

Promotional Methods

Many methods can be used to express the message. Pictures in brochures or on websites should be selected to express the central themes in the promotional message. Pictures of smiling faces, groups of campers involved in inclusive activities, campers bowed in prayer; these activities all reinforce the critical message of fun, healthy relationships, and spiritual growth. Social media, websites, church bulletins, announcements, videos of previous years, endorsements from "happy campers," and a host of other methods can be considered. By far the most effective marketing tools are the comments of a transformed camper or guest. "Let someone else praise you, and not your own mouth; an outsider, and not your own lips" (Prov. 27:2).

Camp Finances

Introduction

Money is essential in running camp; at times significant amounts of money are required. Renting facilities, buying food, providing honorariums for speakers and musicians, insurance, transportation, programming equipment, and promotional expenses must all be paid. The costs associated with camp must be covered through two income streams: the price charged to the campers, or donations of money, time, or in-kind gifts (products or services).

The expenses of camp can be divided into two broad categories: fixed costs (costs that do not change whether there are no campers or a thousand campers), and variable costs (costs that increase as attendance grows). Fixed costs include things like speaker and musician honoraria, climbing wall rental, graphic design work for a website, brochure or logo. Variable costs include things such as t-shirts, the price charged by the campsite, insurance based upon the number of campers, meal cost per camper, or Bible study materials.

Setting a fair and appropriate price is critical. A price that is too low will leave bills unpaid and can signal that the event may be low quality, while too high a price can turn people away. The four critical factors involved in finding the break-even-point are: fixed costs, subsidy, price, and variable costs. The formula is: break-even-point = (fixed cost—subsidy) divided by (price—variable costs), or $BEP=(FC-S)/(P-VC)$.

For example, you plan a middle school retreat for eighty campers and twenty staff. You have the following fixed costs equaling $3,000: $500 for speaker honorarium; $300 for musician honorarium; $200 for climbing wall rental; and $2,000 for bus rental. No outside donor steps forward to give any money to help cover the cost of camp. The price last year was $100, so that is what will be charged this year. The next list includes variable costs charged for each person who attends equaling $80: $55 for rental of the camp with meals; $2 for camper insurance; $3 for Bible study materials; $8 for special camp T-shirt; $5 for program supplies; $1 for name tags; $4 for snacks and drinks; and $2 for awards.

With these numbers, the formula would be:

$$BEP = (\text{fixed costs } \$3,000 - \text{subsidy } \$0) /$$
$$(\text{price } \$100 - \text{variable costs } \$80)$$
$$BEP = (3,000) / (20)$$
$$BEP = 150 \text{ campers.}$$

You would need 150 campers to break even financially.

The best guess is that you will only have eighty campers and twenty staff. There are four options: lower the fixed costs, increase the subsidy, increase the price, or lower the variable costs:

- Lower the Fixed Costs—Do you really need to bring in outside speakers and musicians? Can you find a better price for the climbing wall? Do you need buses?

- Increase the Subsidy—Can you find donors to help underwrite some of the cost? Would parents be willing to drive the campers to the site? Would the church provide the Bible study materials?

- Increase the Price—Would people be willing to pay more? Would people be able to pay more?

- Lower the Variable Costs—Can you find a lower-priced campsite that still meets your needs? Do you need camper insurance? Can you give away camp bandanas for $2 instead of camp t-shirts for $8?

After evaluating each area, revise your budget:

- Fixed Costs—You abandon the buses. You keep the speaker, musician, and the climbing wall. New total is $1,000.
- Subsidy—You find three donors who combine to provide $400. Parents, as donors of in-kind gifts, are willing to drive the campers to the site.
- Price—You keep the price at $100.
- Variable Costs—You go with $2 bandanas instead of the $8 t-shirts, and the church provides the Bible study materials and the name tags. The other factors remain the same, and the new variable cost becomes $70.

The formula is now, BEP = (fixed costs $1000—subsidy $400) / (price $100—variable costs $70):

$$BEP = 600/30$$
$$BEP = 20 \text{ campers}$$

You may consider adding back the t-shirts, lowering the price, or making other adjustments. But until you understand the critical factors that influence pricing, camp leaders will always default to asking, *What did we charge last year?* And hoping for the best.

Discounts, Premiums, and Scholarships

Providing a low price for camp is noble but it is not always wise. Once the price is set there will always be some families that cannot afford camp and many who will want a better price. Three similar—but very distinct—factors should be considered: discounts, premiums, and scholarships.

Discounts

Discounts are provided to encourage the camper (or the one paying for camp) to do something that will benefit you as the camp leadership. Do you want them to bring a friend? Give them an incentive by providing a discount for bringing a friend. Do you want them to register early? Give them a discount for signing up by an early-bird deadline. Do you want them to memorize scripture? Give them a discount for reciting their verses. Determine what it is worth to you for them to bring a friend, sign up early, or learn their memory verses, and then provide a discount to encourage that behavior.

Premiums

Premiums are discounts' wise cousins. Premiums are similar to discounts in that they provide an incentive for campers to do something that helps the camp leadership, but instead of lowing the price, premiums give away things of value. For instance, instead of a $20 discount for bringing a friend, why not give away $10 credit at the camp snack shop? Camps may give away t-shirts to the first fifty who register rather than a discount for anyone signing up early. Why not provide an ice cream social for everyone who memorized their verses? Even better are premiums that have nonmonetary value. Those who bring friends get to sign-up first to ride horses. Those who register early get to stay in the new cabins. Those who memorize their verses go first in the dinner line. Some of the nonmonetary premiums hold more value than material-based premiums or price-related discounts.

Scholarships

Charging people to attend camp will create some awkward situations, especially within a church context. In every group there is someone who is the least able to afford camp. So, what can be done to provide the camp experience to as many campers as possible? The tendency of many people in ministry is to keep the price of camp as low as possible, benefitting everyone. But an artificially low price for all participants limits the camp's ability to significantly help those who have legitimate needs. Maintaining a fair and reasonable price, while at the same time providing significant assistance to those who need it most, allows the camp to rifle the available resources most effectively. Generally, requiring the camper to pay a small portion of the price rather than providing the entire cost of camp, creates a sense of value for the scholarship recipient.

Determining which families will benefit from the limited scholarship funds can be challenging. A policy should be established to control the distribution of funds. Some of the question to ask might include: What is the family's financial situation? Is this due to unusual circumstances such as a medical problem, care for an aging parent, or the loss of a job; or is it due to poor planning or poor choices? How many children are in the family? Is the family

involved in full-time ministry? And, is this family involved in its church? What spiritual benefit may result from this camp experience? It may be best to set a scholarship application deadline and to hold one meeting to make distribution decisions. That way, all of the requests for financial assistance can be considered in relationship to one another.

Risk Management

Parents entrust what they hold most dear to camps and expect their child to return home happy and healthy. Camps must take this responsibility seriously.

Outdoor ministries face many and varied dangers. Safety concerns range from food allergies to sexual predators. Staff members should strive to make the experience as safe as possible. While pursing safety, they should be prepared for emergencies.

Some of the physical dangers that should be considered are waterfronts, cliffs, dangerous animals, poisonous plants, and current fire danger. Program activities are always more exciting if they involve perceived risk. There is a distinct difference between perceived risk and true risk. Bruce Dunning stated, "All adventure experiences must include risk to a certain degree. From a human perspective, our goal is to maximize the perception of risk and minimize the actual risk."[23] High ropes courses that are operated by trained and attentive staff members provide a great deal of perceived risk, while at the same time, a low degree of actual risk.

Emotional dangers and challenges such as fear of the dark, shyness, homesickness, bullying, or alienation by cliques should be addressed by adult leadership.

Each state, and many countries have facility standards that detail the ratios of campers to toilets, sinks, showers, cabin floor space, and a host of other standards. The most recent inspection reports may reveal potential problems.

Having a doctor, nurse, or other qualified and certified medical staff member will help with the routine concerns such as supervising the distribution of medications and responding to scraped knees and stomach aches. But the trained experts will be invaluable in moments of crisis when accidents or emergencies occur. Standard medical release forms are expected for all minor age campers. These forms should be required with each registration.[24]

Conclusion

Camp is a place where God changes lives. Select a style of camp that helps accomplish your purpose and then build a program that utilizes time away, immerses campers or guests into God's revelation through creation and the Bible, and create a context of modeling, loving, trusting relationships. Plan it well. Price it properly. Be safe. And watch God work in the hearts of campers and staff, and yours as well.

Discussion Questions

1. Has a time away at camp been instrumental in changing your spiritual life? If so, describe the experience and why it was important to you.

2. Why does a Christian camp experience have the potential to be so impactful?

3. What surprised you about the different kinds of camps described in this chapter? How might one of these outdoor ministries enrich and complement a ministry in your church?

4. What are some of the challenges facing ministers who create camps today?

5. How well does your church take advantage of the camping ministries available? How might you use a camp experience to heighten your ministry effectiveness?

Resources for Further Study

Badke, Jim. *The Christian Camp Counselor.* Vancouver, BC, Canada: Qwanoes Publishing, 1998.

Badke, Jim. *The Christian Camp Leader.* Mesachle Lake, BC, Canada: Jim Badke, 2013.

Denton, Ashley. *Christian Outdoor Leadership.* Fort Collins, CO: Smooth Stone Publishing, 2011.

Dunning, Bruce. *God of Adventure.* Belleville, ON, Canada: Essence Publishing, 2012.

Eisner, Michael. *Camp.* New York: Warner Books, 2005.

Louv, Richard. *Last Child in the Woods.* Chapel Hill, NC: Algonquin Books, 2005.

Mattson, Lloyd. *Christian Camping Today.* Wheaton, IL: Harold Shaw Publishers, 1998.

Venable, Stephen F. and Donald M. Joy. *How to Use Camping Experiences in Religious Education.* Birmingham, AL: Religious Education Press, 1998.

Author Bio

Dr. Dan Bolin is the International Director of Christian Camping International (CCI). CCI is an alliance of twenty-four autonomous associations of Christian camps and camping leaders around the world. These twenty-four associations serve camps, conferences and camping leaders in sixty-one countries who minister to 13 million campers and guests annually. Dan has served in Christian leadership for more than thirty-five years; twenty-five years at Pine Cove Christian Camps; eleven years on staff (1975–1983) and another fourteen as executive director (1983–1997). For nine years Dan served as the president of KVNE-KGLY Christian radio in Tyler, Texas (1998–2007). He has been the International Director of CCI since August 2007. Dan has served on the Board of Directors of numerous organizations including the Christian Management Association (now Christian Leadership Alliance) and the Christian Camp and Conference Association where he served as chairman for two years. (CCCA is the United States affiliate of CCI.) He served six years on the Board of Trustees of the Tyler Independent School District and for five years on the Board of Lifewind International. Dan also teaches as an Adjunct Professor of Educational Ministries and Leadership at Dallas Theological Seminary. He is the author of eight books and writes a weekly devotional blog entitled Fresh Bread. Dan speaks throughout the United States and around the world on family, leadership, marketing, management and other biblical and professional topics. He is married and has a married daughter. Dan enjoys reading, fly-fishing, jogging, most sports, and writing.

Endnotes

1. Michael D. Eisner, *Camp* (New York: Warner Books, 2005), xvi-xvii.

2. Earl O. Roe, *Dream Big, The Henrietta Mears Story* (Ventura, CA: Regal, 1990), 252.

3. Ray Schnickels, Former Christian camp director and President/CEO of Strategic Executive Tools.

4. Ashley Denton, *Christian Outdoor Leadership* (Fort Collins, CO: Smooth Stone Publishing, 2011), 22.

5. In verse 9, the word *fear* is an exception to the list but does not diminish the overall theme of the passage.

6. Jim Badke, *The Christian Camp Leader* (Mesachle Lake, BC, Canada: Jim Badke, 2013), 72.

7. Denton, *Christian Outdoor Leadership*, 32.

8. Daniel Wallace, Executive Director, Gull Lake Ministries, Hickory Corners, Michigan.

9. Educator David Kolb proposed an active learning cycle that begins with facilitated experience, followed by focused reflection, generalizing what is learned, and applying it to new experiences. David Kolb, *Experiential Learning* (Englewood Cliffs, NJ: Prentice Hall, 1984).

10. Muhia Karianjahi, Graduate Programs and Global Initiatives Manager, Honeyrock of Wheaton College, Three Lakes, Wisconsin.

11. Reed Livesay, President and CEO, Pine Cove Camps, Tyler, Texas.

12. For a comprehensive discussion on ministry planning, please see the chapter by George Hillman on "Putting It All Together: The Educational Cycle."

13. Rob Ribbe, "Redefining Camp Ministry as Experiential Laboratory for Spiritual Formation and Leadership Development", *Christian Education* 7, no. 1 (2010): 144–161.

14. Lloyd Mattson, *The Camp Counselor* (Duluth, MN: Camping Guideposts, 1981), 60–63.

15. Dan Bolin, "Programming," *Journal of Christian Camping*, January-February, 1983.

16. Bruce Dunning, *God of Adventure* (Belleville, ON, Canada: Essence Publishing, 2012), 47.

17. Generally, state health departments establish local camp health and safety regulations. The American Camping Association provides the most comprehensive industry standards for camp health and safety within the United States (www.acacamps.org).

18. Bedford Holmes, Executive Director, Zephyr Point Conference Center, Zephyr Cove, Nevada.

19. Consulting a local attorney with experience in non-profit personnel law is always wise.

20. Additional information on job descriptions can be found in the chapters on "Administering a Healthy Educational Ministry" by Jim Thames, "Educational Ministry in the Smaller Church" by Lin McLaughlin, and "Putting It All Together: The Educational Cycle" by George Hillman.

21. Tom Roots, Executive Director, Timberline Baptist Camp and Conference Center, Lindale, Texas.

22. See the chapter "Putting It All Together: The Educational Cycle" by George Hillman for additional resources on mission and goals.

23. Dunning, *God of Adventure*, 26.

24. Consult with your attorney or heath care provider for a specific form that meets your group's needs.

Chapter 19

ADMINISTERING A HEALTHY EDUCATIONAL MINISTRY

Jim Thames

We have different gifts, according to the grace given to each of us. If your gift is prophesying, then prophesy in accordance with your faith; if it is serving, then serve; if it is teaching, then teach; if it is to encourage, then give encouragement; if it is giving, then give generously; if it is to lead, do it diligently; if it is to show mercy, do it cheerfully.

—Romans 12:6–8

WHEN I TEACH ON Christian administration at my school, I always begin with a simple question, "How many of you enjoy, really enjoy, administration?" After I get a show of hands, I followup with a second question, "How many of you would avoid it at all costs?" I might ask those of you reading this chapter the same two questions, and I suspect if I did, your answers would pretty well reflect the answers I have received from my students over the years. Without fail, only a few will acknowledge that they truly enjoy administration. (I suspect a few are reluctant to admit they do.) Usually a greater number express they would avoid administration at all costs. The rest are somewhere in the middle, neither truly enjoying nor truly avoiding it at all costs.

What is the point of this exercise? Simply, I want students and you, the reader, to think about the answers, because the simple truth is this. Whether you like administration and think you have some gifting or aptitude for it or whether you would avoid it at all costs, if you are in ministry, you will need to organize, manage, and lead those ministries. Administration is inevitable. It is unavoidable. It is essential.

So, if ministry requires a level of organization and administration whether one loves or loathes it, then how does one accomplish the task? The answer to that question is training. Everyone can learn the basic principles of good administration, and like the proverbial "bag of tools," when you have those principles at your disposal, you can use them to effectively build, organize, administer, and lead the ministries over which God has placed you and for which you are responsible.

First, I acknowledge that for some people, organization and administration come naturally and easily. Some people are gifted by God in this particular area for the work of ministry. Note what Paul says in Romans 12:6–8:

> We have different gifts, according to the grace given to each of us. If your gift is prophesying, then prophesy in accordance with your faith; if it is serving, then serve; if it is teaching, then teach; if it is to encourage, then give encouragement; if it is giving, then give generously; *if it is to lead, do it diligently*; if it is to show mercy, do it cheerfully.

In verse 8, Paul mentions a gift of leadership (italics mine), implying that for some at least, leadership is a special ability given by God to accomplish the work of ministry. I prefer how the 1984 edition of the NIV translates 1 Corinthians 12:28. In this verse Paul again refers to the idea of gifting for the work of ministry, indicating that God "has appointed ... those with gifts of administration" (NIV1984).

I see myself as having a gift of administration. I have come to realize over the years that it is the way God has wired me for ministry. I truly enjoy planning and organizing things. "I love it when a plan comes together" to quote an old 1980s television character. I enjoy solving problems, organizing and managing processes, procedures, and events, and seeing success in the process. It is especially fulfilling to use that gifting in service to God and to see him bless those efforts on a regular basis. But that's me and not everyone is gifted in the same way. I can tell you that the majority of the faculty at my school are more than happy to let me do what I love to do so they don't have to! At the same time, they are gifted in ways I am not. It truly is amazing to see how God has uniquely gifted and equipped those in the church to accomplish his purposes in the world.

I can hear some of you say, "That's great; I agree with you, but I wasn't one of those given a gift of leadership or administration, and because I wasn't, that's why I avoid it!" Ahh! Not so fast. Another passage on gifts found in Ephesians 4:11 says: "It was he who gave some as apostles, some as prophets, some as evangelists, and some as pastors and teachers." Focus on the phrase "some to be evangelists." Paul is saying some have been given special ability as evangelists. When I think of evangelists I immediately think of Billy Graham, whose passion and calling was to preach the gospel to thousands and see innumerable people come to faith in Christ as a result of this calling. You may know someone like this, someone for whom sharing the gospel comes naturally and easily. People so gifted that when they share their faith God blesses them with bushels and bushels of fruit. It really is amazing, but then I am reminded of the rest of us, those who have not been "appointed to be evangelists." Does that let us off the hook? I don't think so!

Look at what Paul says to Timothy in 2 Timothy 4:5, "But you, keep your head in all situations, endure hardship, *do the work of an evangelist*, discharge all the duties of your ministry" (italics mine). Notice Paul summarizes for Timothy that he is to "discharge all the duties of [his] ministry." That includes doing the work of evangelism.

So what's my point? Simply this: not everyone is gifted to be an evangelist and yet each of us is called to do the work of an evangelist. How can we do that? Training! The same is true in the area of administration and leadership. Not everyone is gifted in these areas, but everyone is still responsible to discharge "all the duties of their ministries." So if we must organize, administer, and lead, then we must be trained to do it. Because, as I mentioned earlier, the simple truth remains: It must be done; ministry requires it.

The rest of this chapter will explore essential principles of good organization and administration, principles that if followed will help in the task of building, organizing, and leading ministries. These principles will also aid in the effective and efficient use of gifts and resources to accomplish God's purposes in ministry.

Christian Administration: A Definition

You will find countless definitions of administration in the literature today, even in literature that focuses primarily on administration in Christian contexts. The terms *administration, organization, management,* and *leadership* are often used to describe this aspect of ministry and the terms are sometimes used in different and confusing ways. A glance at any dictionary or thesaurus will often make distinguishing these concepts difficult and may often view them as synonymous. The truth is most people use these words interchangeably. In fact I do so quite frequently myself. But for my purposes here, I want to draw some distinctions between the terms in my definition of Christian administration.

First, I am going to assume a closer tie between the terms *organization* and *management*. In doing so, I am assuming that *organizing* is a function of *managing* and that these can be distinguished from *administration* and *leadership*. So, my definition of Christian administration is:

> a strategic combination of leadership and management, exercised by gifted and/or trained individuals to assist people, the church, and other Christian organizations in achieving God-given goals for his glory.

Leadership versus Management

I view administration as a strategic combination of leadership and management. That, of course, implies I see a distinction between leadership and management (which, as I mentioned earlier, is closely related to *organization*). The distinction is fairly obvious to most. I view leadership as that element of administration that is the vision-casting component. Leaders are people who have a clear idea of what God has called them to do. They are able to clearly articulate that calling and inspire others to follow and become a part of the vision. It requires passion. It also requires the ability to communicate clearly and to bring others along in the process. Administration without leadership can be mechanical and uninspiring. Good leadership is essential to good administration. However, some leaders can get so excited about the vision that they lose sight of the process that brings that vision to fruition. Many aspire to leadership, but not all are gifted to lead.

> "If you think you are leading, turn around and take a look behind you. If no one is following, then you are just out for a walk."
> —Attributed to Chuck Swindoll

Good leaders must stay in touch with those they lead. They must have eyes in the back of their head so to speak, so that they can keep an eye on where God is leading them while at the same time keeping an eye on those who follow. Some leaders lose sight of those behind them for two reasons. First, they may not have adequately cast a vision and inspired others to be a part of that vision. Second, they may be so far ahead that those whom they lead can no longer see them. Either reason results in the same outcome: ineffective leadership. If the first reason prevails, we might question the leader's ability. But God has provided a solution for the leader who is too far out in front of those he or she leads. That solution is management.

Management is that element of administration that puts feet to the vision. It is the process that makes sure the details and resources are in place to bring a vision into reality. It is the nuts and bolts aspect of administration. And while it may not be as glamorous as leadership, it is certainly as important.

But just as leaders can lose sight of those they lead, managers, too, may have a shortcoming. Managers like to make sure things work. They are happy to help good leaders accomplish what they believe God has called to do, to bring a dream, a vision, into reality. But, once they get the details worked out, managers tend to dislike change. After all, if it is working well, why change it! The problem is visionary leadership leads through change. So while leaders may need to be reined in, managers may need a swift kick to keep them moving forward. In other words, both are essential components of administration. The reality is that not every leader is a good manager and not every manager is a good leader. You are doubly blessed if you are good at both.

What Makes Administration Christian?

You can find numerous secular publications on administration, leadership, and management. The same distinctions noted earlier apply whether the leaders and mangers are responsible for a business or a ministry. What makes them uniquely Christian is their purpose and ultimate goal. As the definition earlier states, Christian administration assists people, the church, and other Christian organizations in achieving God-given goals for his glory. In other words, Christian administration is others-focused, not self-focused, and its ultimate purpose is to achieve God-given goals for his glory. Interestingly today, many secular leadership gurus are recognizing the importance of "servant-leadership," as if somehow the concept was new. Jesus Christ emphasized the servant element of leadership throughout his ministry. We see this throughout the Gospels and the entire New Testament. So, if you want to be a good administrator, don't forget the importance of serving for God's glory, not your own.

Biblical Principles of Administration

Educational ministry rests on a solid biblical foundation. Many of the principles I have learned over the years and seek to practice in my administrative role come from Scripture. My colleagues who have contributed to this book have identified many of these principles, but I want to focus on six biblical principles that I think are essential to those of us who want to be effective Christian administrators in local church and parachurch ministry.

Christian Administration Creates Order

The church in Corinth was plagued with many problems, including a chaotic approach to worship. To address this concern, the apostle Paul reminded the Corinthians in 1 Corinthians 14 that the self-focused and uncontrolled worship evident in the church was inconsistent with the character of God. Paul states those who speak in the church should do so in a controlled fashion in order to benefit the entire body, "For God is not a God of disorder but of peace" (1 Cor. 14:33). Paul closes the chapter by observing that "everything should be done in a fitting and orderly way" (1 Cor. 14:40).

What's the point? Very simply God cares that things be done in an orderly, organized, and well-managed way. Order reflects his character. It reflects how he does things. Good administration is the means by which order is accomplished. Our first principle then is that

biblical, Christian administration creates order. In turn, creating order in our ministries makes them more effective and efficient.

Christian Administration Depends on and Glorifies God

In speaking through the prophet Isaiah, God has strong words for the southern kingdom of Judah. The words are indicative of the sins of the nation that would result in their eventual captivity in Babylon. In Isaiah 30:1–2 we read:

> "Woe to the obstinate children," declares the LORD, "to those who carry out plans that are not mine, forming an alliance, but not by my Spirit, heaping sin upon sin; who go down to Egypt without consulting Me; who look for help to Pharaoh's protection, to Egypt's shade for refuge."

And again in Isaiah 31:1, God says:

> Woe to those who go down to Egypt for help, who rely on horses, who trust in the multitude of their chariots and in the great strength of their horsemen, but do not look to the Holy One of Israel or seek help from the LORD.

What was Judah's problem? Why were they chastised by God? Because they continually made their own plans rather than following God's and they continually depended on others to protect them rather than depending on God. Old Testament history reveals that this was a recurring problem for God's chosen people. It can also be a problem for Christian administrators today. What is the principle for those of us in administration and leadership? We need to make sure our administrative efforts, processes, procedures, and plans are ultimately designed and carried out to glorify God. These efforts also need to reflect our absolute dependence on him for outcomes consistent with his will and that ultimately bring him glory. So, good Christian administration glorifies and depends on God.

Christian Administration Protects People

In the story of Moses in Exodus 18, the children of Israel have miraculously escaped from Egypt. They are journeying to Mount Sinai as directed by God. Even though God has graciously provided for their needs, they have already begun the habit of complaining. In spite of their complaining, they still recognize Moses's leadership and that he is God's chosen leader for the nation. As a result we read beginning in verse 13:

> The next day Moses took his seat to serve as judge for the people, and they stood around him from morning till evening. When his father-in-law saw all that Moses was doing for the people, he said, "What is this you are doing for the people? Why do you alone sit as judge, while all these people stand around you from morning till evening?"

> Moses answered him, "Because the people come to me to seek God's will. Whenever they have a dispute, it is brought to me, and I decide between the parties and inform them of God's decrees and instructions."

Moses' father-in-law replied, "What you are doing is not good. You and these people who come to you will only wear yourselves out. The work is too heavy for you; you cannot handle it alone. Listen now to me and I will give you some advice, and may God be with you. You must be the people's representative before God and bring their disputes to him. Teach them his decrees and instructions, and show them the way they are to live and how they are to behave. But select capable men from all the people—men who fear God, trustworthy men who hate dishonest gain—and appoint them as officials over thousands, hundreds, fifties and tens. Have them serve as judges for the people at all times, but have them bring every difficult case to you; the simple cases they can decide themselves. That will make your load lighter, because they will share it with you. If you do this and God so commands, you will be able to stand the strain, and all these people will go home satisfied" (Exod. 18:13–23).

First, we observe that this passage isn't about wise in-laws and how we need to listen to them, although it is clear from the text Jethro was very wise. A cursory reading of this passage might also lead us to think that the principle for administration here is the principle of delegation. While that is certainly in view, a more important administrative principle results from the delegation Jethro is recommending—*good administration protects people.*

We see in this passage that Moses takes his seat to serve as judge for the people. We read that he does this "from morning till evening." The text does not state this is a daily occurrence, but the context would imply this is not an isolated incident.

Imagine this scenario. Mr. Ben-Judah and Mr. Ben-Simon have a dispute they can't resolve. They get up early in the morning to take their dispute to Moses. When they arrive, the line to see Moses already stretches almost beyond sight. The two men get in line and wait. The line moves, but at a snail's pace. The day wears on. As the sun continues to move across the sky and begins its downward descent toward evening, the men are getting closer, but realize it's possible they won't get to see Moses before the day is done. Closer … closer …almost there… they are next in line … and then the sun sets! Moses puts up the "closed" sign and leaves for the day. How would you feel if you were Mr. Ben-Judah and Mr. Ben-Simon? Probably like I feel when I get stuck in a long line at the grocery store. I have heard of people ending up in physical fights because someone tries to cut-in on a long line, especially at Christmas time.

And if it's hard for those waiting to see Moses, what about Moses himself? He's one man! He must have been worn out listening to people's disputes all day long. It's not like he doesn't have other important things to do as well. Jethro's advice to Moses isn't so much about delegation as it is protecting himself and others from "wearing out" (v. 18). Delegation is just the means of doing this. Jethro also observes that if Moses follows his advice he will "be able to stand the strain, and all these people will go home satisfied" (v. 23). Good administration protects people.

Christian Administration Preserves the Leader's Primary Role

In Acts 6 we see a related principle: Good administration preserves the leader's primary role. In this passage we see a dispute that arose in the early church about the fair distribution of food. As in the day of Moses, when people had a problem, they went to the person in charge for a resolution. Acts 6 was no different; word of the problem made its way to the apostles. The apostles' solution? Another example of delegation, but delegation that served a different purpose. The apostles realized they could not meet all the daily needs of the rapidly growing church. It wasn't that meeting the physical needs of people was unimportant or beneath them, but God had appointed them to handle other responsibilities. In order to preserve that primary function, they directed the church to select from among themselves capable, spiritually minded men to care for the need.

Preserving the primary role of those in ministry is an important administrative principle. Those in leadership positions can easily get embroiled in the daily needs of the body. The problem with this is that while they are caring for important things, they are things others could just as easily care for. And, as a result, they are not caring for the things that God has called them to care for. It's a matter of priority. However, those in positions of leadership walk a fine line. They don't want to give the impression that they are too important to be bothered with mundane ministry duties, nor do they want to imply that those other ministry duties are less important in the church. Nonetheless it is important to humbly acknowledge the calling of God in the life of the ministry leader. In short, good administration preserves the leader's primary role.

Christian Administration Involves Thoughtful Dependent Planning

I have encountered those in my years of ministry who seem to think planning does not reflect dependence on God. Their approach to planning appears to be praying only, then waiting for God to reveal what it is he wants them to do. Now don't get me wrong. I completely agree we need to be spending a great deal of time in prayer; asking God for wisdom in our planning is essential. I would rather err on the side of prayer than self-sufficiency! But having said that, believers still need to plan. God plans. Scripture is full of instances of this. God has plans for his people. Jeremiah 29:11 reminds us that God's plans for his people are for their good. This was certainly true of his promises to his chosen people. God's plans will not be thwarted, but ours certainly may be. Proverbs 16:9 has become a verse that means more to me today than it did in my earlier ministry. In that verse, Solomon tells us that people plan their way, but the LORD directs their steps. This is both comforting and terrifying. It reminds us that no matter what we plan to do, we have no guarantee it will work out as we plan because God's plans supersede ours. It is comforting knowing God's plans for us will prevail, especially when we realize his plans are best.

Notice, however, that Proverbs 16:9, as well as many other verses on planning in the Scriptures, never tells us we shouldn't plan. Such verses are reminders, however, that God's plans always supersede our own. We may not always understand this. We may not always like this. But, when you consider it carefully, we are always better off with the plans God has for us, even if they upset our own.

In summary, good Christian administrators plan well, but they also recognize God may change the best of plans and replace them with something even better.

> "Hold everything in your hands lightly; otherwise it hurts when God pries your fingers open."
> —Attributed to Corrie ten Boom

Christian Administration Functions according to Giftedness

Earlier in this chapter, we looked at Romans 12, 1 Corinthians 12, and Ephesians 4, when we talked about the various gifts God gives to his people for the work of the ministry. Those passages point out that God gifts believers in different ways for different works of service. Look around your local church or ministry and you will see people who are different from one another. Diversity has always been a good thing from God's perspective. We function better in unity when we celebrate our differences and acknowledge them as coming from God.

One of the most important functions for those in administration is to help people identify their unique giftedness and the strengths they bring to ministry. Nothing will be more empowering and encouraging to people in ministry than to serve in their areas of giftedness. Yet how many people serving in our churches are misfits? By this I mean they are serving in areas of ministry not related to their unique giftedness.

Effective ministry is ministry that functions according to giftedness, and good administrators make this a priority for themselves and for their people.[1]

Key Elements of Administration

If you have ever been involved in planning, organizing, and running an event, you are probably aware of the essential components necessary to successful administrative process. For those of you who are administratively gifted and geared, these elements will seem natural and obvious. For those who may not be gifted or wired for administration, employing these key elements will help you accomplish the administrative process with confidence. Many of the following key elements have been discussed in other places in this book, so I will only list those with a brief comment. Others I will develop in a little more detail. I and my colleagues who teach administration and administrative process have identified the following twelve key administrative elements that apply in almost all ministry contexts.

1. Knowing Your Mission

Consider the wisdom of the anonymous saying, "If you don't know what you are aiming at, you will hit the target every time!" Why? Because if you don't have a specific target, then you have a moving target, and if your target moves to wherever you aim, you will always hit it. This may work well for those who only care about hitting a target, but not so well for those whose target is fixed. Even if you don't hit a fixed target, you can make adjustments that will allow you to hit what you are aiming at.

Having a clear mission is like having a fixed target. It guides you, keeps you on track, and provides constant feedback when you wander off course. The question every administrator needs to ask, whether leading or managing, is "Do I know where I am going?" Do you, as a leader, have a clear understanding of God's call on your life that keeps you focused? Do you as a manager understand where you are going so that the details of the administrative process are moving you in that direction? Without direction and guidance, people are left with deciding for themselves where they think they should be going. Knowing your mission and having a clear vision of what it is that God is leading you to do is essential to good administration.[2]

2. Creating a Plan

As we already pointed out previously, it's good to plan. It is an essential component of administration. Good planning reflects the character of God and honors him when we depend on him in the process. Once mission and vision are clear, a good administrator must create a plan that will bring them to reality. The details of good planning are addressed elsewhere in this text, but the person who finds himself or herself leading and organizing a ministry had better have a detailed plan on how to proceed.[3]

3. Stating and Prioritizing Goals and Objectives

Goals are brief directional road signs. Objectives then develop the specifics of how to achieve the goals. They need to be directive, measurable, achievable, and oriented to time, otherwise administrators will never know if they are actually making meaningful progress in fulfilling the mission and vision God has set before them.[4]

4. Organizing and Supervising People

There are no loan wolves in ministry. Effective ministry is a team effort. Throughout the New Testament, we see that ministries are led by teams not individuals. The image of the body Paul so often refers to in his writings implies the body only functions well when all the parts do what they are designed to do. No one individual is capable of running a ministry alone. Ministry requires people working together, either paid staff or volunteers. The good administrator knows it is important to provide clear supervision and direction so people understand what is expected of them and how to accomplish their assigned tasks.

Leaders by default must supervise people. Many of the key elements of administration in this chapter apply to supervising people, but the following five guidelines will help a supervisor be more effective in supervising the people for whom he or she is responsible.

Supervisors Provide Direction

Don't assume those you supervise know what is expected of them. Good supervisors work diligently to make sure they provide clear, adequate, and timely direction to their staff or volunteers.

Supervisors Provide Correction

No one is perfect. We all make mistakes, some accidental, some intentional. Even the best of intentions can lead to mistakes, and frankly, some people make mistakes for selfish reasons or because they don't care. Whatever the reason, a good supervisor will provide appropriate correction at the appropriate time, even if that correction is painful. The writer to the Hebrews reminds us, "No discipline seems pleasant at the time, but painful. Later on, however, it produces a harvest of righteousness and peace for those who have been trained by it" (Heb. 12:11). But, if you are a supervisor who finds yourself needing to provide correction, remember to do so humbly and graciously. After all, who among us has never made a mistake?

Supervisors Provide Evaluation

One of the more difficult tasks of supervision is evaluation. We rarely mind giving positive feedback and kudos for a job well done, but not every job is a job well done. A supervisor who is not honest in his or her evaluation is doomed to perpetuate problems. It neither helps the ministry, nor the staff person or volunteer. Honesty is always the best policy.

Supervisors Provide Care

Those whom God gives you to supervise are people. Don't forget they have hurts, needs, and concerns. Sometimes performance can be impacted negatively by the circumstances of life. Helping to care for the needs of those you work with may not always help you finish a task, but it certainly can help you develop relationships with those who work for and with you. Cared-for people will tend to be hardworking, effective people.

> **"People don't care how much you know, till they know how much you care."**
>
> **—Anonymous**

Supervisors Provide Encouragement

A word of encouragement, a pat on the back, a smile, these are useful tools to a supervisor. When a person is discouraged, it is easy to give up, but an encouraged person is rejuvenated. I'm not sure if anyone has measured productivity as a function of encouragement, but common sense would tell us that encouraged people are more efficient and effective than discouraged ones. If you are a supervisor, add encouragement to your administrative tool bag. You won't regret it.

5. Building Teams

Closely related to the previous element of organizing and supervising people is the idea of team-building. Since groups (not individuals) accomplish ministry, a wise administrator considers how to help people work together effectively. But, effective teams don't just happen. They are built on a foundation of hard work and a commitment to the goals and purposes for which the team exists. Effective teams have members who are committed to five things.

Committed to a Biblical Model of Ministry

As noted earlier in this chapter, the biblical model of ministry was a team model. Christ invested himself in the training of the Twelve. The primary image that Paul uses in the New Testament to describe the church is a body with many parts. As the human body only functions effectively when all the parts work in harmony, so too do teams only function effectively when all the members work in harmony.

Committed to a Shared Philosophy of Ministry

Effective teams are committed to a common purpose reflected in a shared philosophy of ministry. Teams make progress when all the members are moving in the same direction.

Committed to Relationships

Team members must be committed not only to the purpose of the team, but also to each other. To borrow a saying often attributed to families, "teams that play together stay together." I like the way some have adapted it, "teams that pray together stay together." Committed teams value relationships.

Committed to Listening

How well do you listen to others? I mean *truly* listen. We are very good at giving the appearance of listening to someone else when we are really thinking of what we want to say next. If we are more concerned with what we have to say than with listening for understanding, then we are probably part of an ineffective team. Good teams have members committed to listening first and speaking last.

Committed to One Another's Turf

Every member of an effective team has an important role to play. Each brings his or her own experiences, backgrounds, training, and gifting. Effective teams value the contribution of each team member and are committed to ensuring that contribution is guarded and protected.

Characteristics of Effective Teams

- Clear purpose
- Flexible
- Open communication
- Balance group and individual needs
- Cohesive without stifling
- Celebrates diversity
- Members contribute equally
- Objective self-assessment

If you ever played any kind of organized sports, you may have had a coach remind you that "there is no 'I' in 'team'." Sage advice for ministry as well. While teams are made up of individuals, good administrators work to ensure a team functions as a unit with a common agenda, not as a bunch of individuals, each with his or her own agenda.

6. Understanding Organizational Dynamics

During my PhD work, I took courses in organizational theory. Over the years I have come to believe, albeit rather simplistically, that you can distill organizational theory into two main categories—formal organizational dynamics and informal organizational dynamics.

Formal organizational structure is the documented arrangement of an organization, best represented by an organizational chart.[5] Simply stated, formal organizational structure makes clear how the parts of an organization fit together and relate to one another. Knowing this helps members of the organization see how they fit in the organization, specifying to whom they are accountable and who is accountable to them.

But, as important as formal organizational dynamics are, informal organizational dynamics may be more important. I would define informal organizational dynamics as the process an organization follows that is dictated in large measure by its organizational culture.[6] Simply put, informal organizational dynamics identify how things *really* get done in an organization.

Informal structures may not reflect the formal structure of a ministry or organization. A ministry organization may have members who do not have a formal part to play in the organization, a church for example. Yet these individuals can often exert a great deal of influence. Let me illustrate with a scenario I set before my students. You are a new minister of a small country church somewhere in the rural Midwestern United States. This church sits on land given to it by Mr. and Mrs. Smith, long time members of the church and pillars of the community. Mr. and Mrs. Smith held a variety of leadership and ministry positions in the church over many years. Mr. Smith has since passed away, but Mrs. Smith is still a member and attends regularly, though she no longer serves in a formal capacity due to her advanced age.

With that context in mind, who do you think is the most influential person in that church? If you said Mrs. Smith, then you have a good grasp of informal organizational dynamics. As a new pastor, you may have the full support of the formal leadership of the church, but if you don't have Mrs. Smith's support, your tenure may be short-lived! Every ministry around the globe has its Mr. and Mrs. Smith. But even if these individuals are godly, well-loved, and well-meaning people, they will still exert influence that you need to be aware of if you want to have a successful ministry. The problem with informal organizational dynamics is that it takes time to figure them out. It isn't included in the material you initially get from the church or ministry.

The wise ministry leader will allow enough time to get to know and understand the informal culture before he or she begins to make significant changes. In my opinion, getting to know the informal structures of a ministry is a lot like getting to know someone through the dating process before marriage. Just as it takes time to get to know a potential life partner well, it takes time to get to know a ministry well. Give yourself time before you try to change too many things in the ministry. Always remember you may think you have the support of those who have called you to a particular ministry, but at first, you may only have the support of those in formal leadership. What about the informal leaders? You'll need time to discover who they are. You may still be able to accomplish, with God's help and by his grace, all that you believe he has called you to do, but don't rush the process. You will never regret taking more time to understand informal organizational dynamics, which leads me to the next key element of administration.

7. Managing Time

For years as a young administrator at my seminary, I would meet colleagues in the hallway who would ask me how things were going. I would usually respond with, "I just don't have enough time to get everything done!" One day when I said this for the umpteenth time, I remember what I can only describe as a God encounter. The result was that I came to understand that I always have enough time to do the things God wants me to do and if I don't seem to, it's not his fault, it's mine! I realized the reason I never seemed to have enough time was because I wasn't managing my time; I was letting other things and other people manage it for me! Sometimes that may not be our fault alone, but at some point, we have to take responsibility for identifying the things God wants us to do and try not to get sidetracked with all the other things we could

or want to do. In other words, if we try to do more than God has called us to do, we may find ourselves not having enough time. But whose fault is that?

All of us have the same twenty-four hours in a day, so learning a few principles that help maximize the time we have may be helpful. Consider the following principles of wise time management.

Plan Carefully

We have talked about planning. Sometimes even a simple plan can save time. For example, Saturday mornings at home in the spring are a premium for me. A day may start with coffee on the patio with my wife, but before long, I notice something in the yard that needs fixing. So, I head to the garage to get tools to take care of the task. But then, while I am taking care of the first project, I notice something else that needs attention. So off I go for those tools. Then, of course, I will see something else, and then something else, and so on. After a while I've wasted a lot of time making trips into the garage for tools. What if instead, I took a few moments to walk around the yard and make a list of things that need attention, then go to the garage and collect all the tools I need? I may not have saved hours of time, but you see my point. If I had spent a few minutes planning, I might have saved many minutes of wasted activity. Investing a little time in planning is usually a good way to save time.

Anticipate Crises

Crises by their nature are often unanticipated events. You can rarely plan for them because you never know for sure when they will surface. However, good administrators take stock of their ministry environment in order to identify potential crises that may occur on a regular basis. Take for example a nursing home ministry. Residents are usually older and generally in poor health or nearing the end of their lives. What crises might you anticipate will happen more frequently in this environment? It is likely that the death rate will be higher, isn't it? If you know that death is a more frequent crisis, then you know to build this likelihood into your ministry schedule. Without meaning to sound insensitive, you simply cannot put someone's passing on your calendar! You can't tell Mrs. Jones, who may be close to passing into the presence of God, that Tuesday, next week at 3:00 p.m. would be a good time for it to happen! Again, crises do not follow our schedule, but with a little forethought, we can anticipate the types of crises that we may encounter on a more regular basis. Doing so may help us manage our time wisely.

Organize Yourself

Related to good planning on the time-management spectrum is learning to organize yourself well. For example, "to do" lists and daily calendars are great tools for keeping track of our time. Use a filing system instead of a piling system to save time. Ministry is time demanding and it is easy to look at our desks at the end of the day and wonder how they got to be such a mess. That mess can make important things hard to find and cost precious time hunting for them. I have learned over the years that if I take a few moments (I almost always have a few) to at least set aside urgent items that need to be dealt with quickly, I can often reduce

the pile and reduce the time I spend looking for them later. Again, it may not save hours, but even a few minutes add up.

Do you want to save time? Organize yourself in whatever ways work best for you.

Don't Procrastinate

I confess that I struggle with procrastination. I discovered years ago that I could stay busy doing important things while putting off more important things. For example, when I was a student in seminary, my desk was never so clean or organized as it was before I had a big paper due! It was easier to do the less important thing of cleaning my desk, while putting off the more important thing of writing an exegetical paper.

> "Procrastination is my sin.
> It brings me endless sorrow.
> I really must stop doing it.
> I know! I'll start tomorrow!"
> —Author unknown

I know I am not the only person who struggles with this. Some of us think we will have more time tomorrow to do the things that we put off doing today, but we forget that tomorrow will bring its own new tasks. Eventually putting things off catches up with us. Besides, we may not have tomorrow.

Years ago before I began my current role in the academic dean's office at my seminary, my predecessor had left the office one September evening with a desk full of tasks he planned to accomplish the next day. Tragically, he never made it back to the office. The next morning, after his regular exercise, he suffered a massive heart attack while in the shower and never recovered. He was not, by nature, a procrastinator, but regardless the next day never came for him. My point? We can't assume tomorrow. Only God knows our days. And because we can't know tomorrow, it makes sense that we don't needlessly postpone our work.

Conversely, we need to avoid becoming workaholics. Taking time to relax and unwind may make us more efficient in using the time allotted to us. As with all things in life, balance is required.

Manage Phone Calls, Mail, Email, Paperwork

The bane of an administrator's existence can be phone calls, texts, mail and email, and a host of other forms of communication. Ted Engstrom and Alec Mackenzie talk about managing phones and mail (and I would add texts and email) in their insightful book *Managing Your Time: Guidelines on the Effective Use of Your Time*.[7] Even though published in the 1960s, its relevance is timeless. The essence of their concern is that phones, mail (I would add email and text messages), and a host of other means of communication tend to subject us to the time demands of others. Just because someone sends you an email or text message does not mean you are automatically subject to their time schedule. Sometimes urgency and care for others requires prompt action on our part, but matters are not always as crucially important as others may think.

I realize that a new generation has arisen that rarely uses a phone for talking, but many of us in ministry will still have a phone, and, believe it or not, many people still use them to talk with someone on the other end of a call! One way to save time with phone calls is to have an assistant screen those for you. He or she may be able to handle a task that does not require your attention. You don't have an assistant to answer your phones? Do you have voicemail? Voicemail can be your best friend. It allows you to take a call when convenient to you. Even if callers send you a text instead, you are not obligated to respond immediately, if at all. Most cell phones and office phones in today's high-tech world have caller ID. Use it! I usually don't answer calls for which I don't have a contact entered in my phone. If it is important, the caller will leave a message I can check later and make a return call if necessary.

I once attended a lecture by Christian management author, Olan Hendrix. I remember one thing he said that has stuck with me over the years, "Handle it once!" What he meant is that we often will pick up a piece of mail (or in today's world, read an email) look at it, think about what to do with it, then set it aside to get to later. Only to pick it up again later, look at it, think about it some more (or try to remember what we were thinking the first time we picked it up), then set it aside again. His point was that when we do that, we waste time! Better to pick it up once and either deal with it, pass it on to someone else to handle, or throw it away!

Mail and email may require even more careful scrutiny. Just because someone sends you something in the mail or by email, doesn't necessarily obligate you to invest time in opening or reading it. We call this junk mail for a reason. It is designed to grab your attention in the hope that you will read it and act on it. How much time have you spent opening junk mail, just to throw it away or delete it? Don't read it, just delete it! If it turns out that it was really important, you will see it again. If it is important enough to read or handle, read or handle it once. If something needs to be done with it, do it, don't keep setting it aside just to pick it up again later.

Communication is a very important part of administration, and in many ways, today's technology makes it much easier to communicate quickly, inexpensively, and efficiently. At the same time, some people think that if we don't respond immediately, we are being disrespectful. Don't let that attitude enslave you to another's schedule. You want to save valuable time? Learn to manage the different ways people employ to contact you.

Don't Attempt Too Much

As I mentioned at the beginning of this section on controlling our time, one of the biggest time stealers is taking on tasks that others should be doing. This happens because we say "yes" to things for the wrong reasons. These reasons may include not wanting to disappoint the person who asked or thinking we are the best ones for the task. Regardless of our reason for saying yes, the best way to avoid taking on too much is to make sure God is leading us to do it, not someone else. More often than not, the best

way to avoid attempting too much is to simply learn to say "no"!

Do It Right the First Time!

One of the dangers of being too busy and attempting too much is the tendency to rush. When we rush we make mistakes or we don't complete projects appropriately. When this happens, we or others have to redo the work.

> "If you don't have time to do it right the first time, when will you have time to do it over?"
> —Anonymous

Doing things correctly the first time can save time later, and we need to do things carefully. But striving for excellence is not the same as perfectionism. The old saying, "if it's worth doing, it's worth doing right," can create problems if it causes us to put off an important task until we decide we have time to accomplish it perfectly. I wonder if there isn't some grassroots wisdom in rewording that statement by saying "if it's worth doing, it may be worth doing adequately." In other words, "adequate" may not be perfect, but "adequate" works! Administrators will always be faced with what seems like an insurmountable list of tasks for which they are responsible. If a task is important to do, do it well enough the first time so that it doesn't need to be redone, even if it could be better. This will always be a constant struggle for those in leadership and administration. It is a balance between acceptability and perfection, and a balance between efficient use of time and a waste of time.

Lead Effective Meetings

Meetings are inevitable and often necessary. They can be the means by which effective teams accomplish complex and difficult tasks. They take appropriate advantage of the strengths, experience, personality, and knowledge of team members, all of which contribute to better decisions. And yet, most of us have been a part of meetings that have dragged on interminably, were disorganized, and could have taken a fraction of the time that they took to accomplish the agenda. You may not always have the ability to control meetings if you are not the person in charge, but all of us can contribute to a more efficient use of time when meetings are unavoidable.

Again in their book on time management, Engstrom and Mackenzie identify five steps that will help make meetings more effective and waste less time.

1. Make sure that only those people necessary are present. (Don't waste the time of others if they aren't needed.)
2. Be prepared with an agenda and relevant information for the topics to be discussed.
3. If chairing, keep the discussion on track. Strive for consensus on the subject as quickly as is reasonable, while ensuring that everyone has an opportunity to contribute.
4. Make sure all the participants understand the purpose of the meeting.
5. Determine what actions steps will be taken, what decisions will be implemented, and who will be responsible for follow-through.[8]

Following these simple steps will ensure that meetings waste as little time as possible.

Delegate Well

I will spend more time on delegation in the next section, but for now and as it relates to managing time, let me just say that delegation can be a huge time-saver, even if it does not seem so initially. Delegation allows you to pass on to qualified others a task that once delegated, will no longer be required of you. The key here is the word "qualified." As we observed previously, not doing something correctly the first time will require more time to do it correctly the second time, an obvious waste of time. This may also be true of delegation. If we give someone a task to do and don't give them what they need to do it correctly, then any time we might have saved by delegating in the first place will be more than lost when we end up having to help fix a problem because the person to whom the task was delegated was not qualified. Whether you spend time fixing your own mistakes or the mistakes of others, it yields the same result. You still end up spending more time fixing something. Delegation done well can be a great time-saver, but if not done well, it can be a great time-waster.

In summary, the time God has given us is a precious commodity. Each of us has only so many years, months, weeks, days, hours, minutes, and seconds. God has determined the number of our days. He doesn't tell us when our days are up. We rarely have advance warning. It makes sense that we use the time he has given efficiently and effectively so that we may accomplish those things that he has called us to do in ministry and in life. Managing our time is a stewardship, one that we need to take seriously.

8. Delegating Effectively

We have just explored the importance of delegation as it relates to our use of time. We also saw earlier in the chapter in our discussion on sound biblical principles for good administration the importance of delegation, as it protects people and preserves the primary responsibility of leaders. Delegation has also been addressed several times in other chapters of this book. But because delegation is so important to the administrative process, I want to give a little more attention to the topic.

Why Delegate?

Administrators rarely delegate everything they should. This might be for a number of reasons, not the least of which is they don't want to impose on others. Whatever the reason, delegation is essential as illustrated in the figure below. In his book *Management: A Biblical Approach*, Myron Rush explains why delegation is so important, as Figure 19.1 illustrates.[9]

**Figure 19.1 Administrator
Responsibilities versus Efficiency**

Leader's area of responsibility

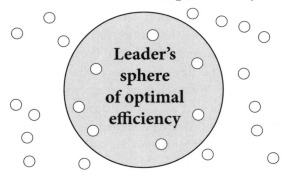

All the small dots in the diagram represent the leader's ultimate areas of responsibility that fall under his or her oversight and direction. The larger shaded circle represents the areas in which the leader is optimally efficient. A quick glance reveals that those who have ultimate responsibility for the tasks and functions of an organization or ministry are not going to be good at all of those tasks and responsibilities. In other words, no leader is going to be good at everything. And yet, all these tasks still need to be accomplished. The principle of delegation suggests if you as a leader can't do everything that needs to be done, it would make sense that you focus on those things which you can do and do well, and find others who can do the other things well, if not better than you.

Don't let pride interfere with delegating. Good delegation requires leaders to admit they aren't good at everything. Admitting this will free you to work toward the success of others in accomplishing a delegated task. Not doing so may result in delegating tasks to unqualified subordinates (a potential time-waster, as noted earlier), which ultimately will require a leader to step in and save the day, but at what cost?

Delegation, however, never allows a leader to blame others if things don't go well. If you are in charge, then you are responsible. The mistakes others make are your mistakes, so it is in your best interest, and the best interest of the organization and others, to learn how to delegate well.

> "Delegation does not abrogate the leader's responsibility!"
> —Kenn Gangel

What to Delegate

Good delegation is complex and requires that leaders know the gifts and abilities of those they lead. Good leaders understand the different levels of delegation. For example, when my children were young, they had certain delegated responsibilities; we called them chores. As they grew older, the complexity of the tasks, the responsibility associated with them, and the consequences for not completing delegated tasks increased. The same is true in any ministry. One can delegate tasks, responsibility, accountability, and authority. Each of these implies a higher level of delegation.

Over the years I have observed in my study of administration and management that not all delegation is equal. I have attempted to summarize those observations into the following four levels:

Level 1—No independent action: Tasks only are delegated. The leader assigns the task (make ten copies of this document for my meeting), and the subordinate performs the task.

Level 2—Recommend and discuss; joint decision: The leader informs subordinate of the task or project and has the subordinate research and present options for completing the task. Leader and subordinate decide together which option is best.

Level 3—Decide and inform: The leader assigns the task. The subordinate determines how best to accomplish the task, carries out the task, and informs the leader of action taken.

Level 4—Independent action: The leader assigns the task or project. The subordinate determines how best to accomplish it and takes care of it.

As you can see, each level of delegation carries with it greater responsibility, authority, and accountability. Consider this real-life example.

When I first began working at the seminary one of my assigned tasks was to assist the associate academic dean with the seminary's commencement. The associate dean would assign tasks for me to complete and I would let him know when the task was finished (Level 1). Then I was given another task. As I grew in my position, the associate dean would give me a task and ask me to research ways that might be more efficient or effective, present those to him, and together, we would make a decision (Level 2). After a few more years, he would simply give me a task and have me decide the best way to proceed with the task (Level 3). I have now been in charge of commencement at Dallas Theological Seminary for over twenty-five years. It is my responsibility now. To be sure, I report directly to the vice-president for academic affairs and the president, especially when a significant change in procedure is pending, but for the most part, I am responsible for the event (Level 4). In fact, I now have a number of people to whom I delegate tasks related to commencement at various levels.

I would make a couple of observations at this point. First, most subordinates don't start off having tasks and responsibilities delegated at the higher levels. It takes time and experience before one can earn the level of trust necessary to be turned loose on a task. Remember, leaders are still ultimately responsible, so it behooves them to make sure the task is done well. Second, levels of delegation are not attached to individuals. While I have a great deal of delegated authority for some tasks as dean of academic administration, I function at a lower level of delegation for others. In other words, a subordinate may function at Level 4 with some tasks and responsibilities, but at a lower level in others. The point of good delegation is to make sure the level of expected action is clear, and the person to whom a responsibility is delegated is qualified to handle that responsibility at that level. Successful delegation hinges on both.

Effective Delegation

Once leaders understand why delegation is important and the various levels of delegation, they still need to know what makes delegation ultimately effective. When delegation is ineffective, it is usually because one or more of the following requirements are overlooked.

Clear Purpose

If the person to whom a task is delegated does not understand the purpose for the task, they may find it difficult to complete the task effectively. Clear purposes enable people to adapt if they run into roadblocks along the way because the ultimate goal is still in view.

Qualified People

As we discussed previously, for delegation to be effective, the individual to whom tasks and responsibilities are delegated must be capable of handling them. It would be a complete disaster, for example, to assign a task to me that requires any artistic ability. No matter how willing I might be, the end result will never be artistic.

Accurate Organizational Structure

Effective delegation results when individuals clearly understand their role and function in the organization. Those parameters protect individuals from exceeding delegated responsibility or inappropriately delegating responsibility to others.

Adequate Resources

Effective delegation requires adequate and appropriate resources for the task—people and finances, for example.

Investment of Time

One of the main reasons leaders don't delegate is the reality that it takes time. It is easier for a leader to handle a task rather than take the time to train others. While it is true that it may take us longer to train someone else to perform a task than it would to perform the task ourselves, it overlooks the fact that delegation is an investment with future returns. Once someone is trained in a task, then the leader is free from that task from that point forward. The saying "it takes money to make money" applies to delegation as well, except I would say with delegation, "it takes time to save time." Supervisors have to view delegation as an investment of time that pays future returns or they will avoid it.

Appropriate Oversight

I have worked at the same institution for more than thirty-three years. I tell people I would have to be "dumb as a rock" not to have learned some things over that time. However, it's easy for me to assume that everyone knows as much as I know after so many years. If I am not careful, I can assign a task with inadequate information and instruction or with inadequate oversight. I simply assume too much. I have learned the best way to avoid this problem is to provide appropriate, but not stifling, oversight. When I assign a task or project to a subordinate, I ask if they understand what I am asking them to do and if they have what they need to accomplish the project. I will regularly check with them to see how the project is going and whether they have any questions. I try not to hover, but I do make sure they know I am available to help and answer questions. This gives them the opportunity to learn while doing. Sometimes people don't know what they don't know or don't know what they need until they encounter a point in the process that requires that knowledge. Good administrators make themselves available as needed.

Trust

Adequate and appropriate oversight helps in delegation, but the emphasis here needs to be on *adequate* and *appropriate*. It is one thing to train someone how to handle a project or task and provide helpful oversight. It is another to expect that others will handle the project or task exactly as you would. While some tasks and projects must follow a tightly prescribed procedure, most do not. Leaders who expect a project to be done exactly as they would do it risk discouraging and frustrating a subordinate who may accomplish the task differently. Constant correction reveals a lack of trust that the person assigned a task is really capable of handling the task. It demotivates and leads to discouragement.

Inevitably those in ministry leadership must delegate; they are neither capable nor qualified by themselves to handle all the demands ministry requires. Since the biblical model is one of shared leadership and ministry, we have little

choice but to learn why to delegate, what to delegate, and the most effective ways to delegate.

9. Motivating People

One of the more difficult tasks administrators face is motivating those whom they lead or manage. Productivity lags when people aren't motivated to excel and, in the absence of motivation, people will easily give up on a task. Motivation can be defined as "any condition in a person that affects that person's readiness to initiate or continue an activity."[10] In other words, motivation is what gets people started and what keeps them going.

Two types of motivation are typically identified in the literature on motivation—external (or extrinsic) and internal (or intrinsic) motivation. Extrinsic motivation comes from an external stimulus. Examples of external motivations would be things like rules and regulations, rewards, praise, punishment (or the threat of), money, and position. Intrinsic motivation comes from inside a person and can include such things as beliefs and convictions, principles, abilities or gifting, passions, and personality. As you look at both lists, you might deduce that internal motivators are better than external ones. And while, external influences can certainly be powerful motivators, internal influences may be more lasting.

> "Motivation is the art of getting people to do what you want them to do because they want to do it."
> —Attributed to Dwight D. Eisenhower

Suppose you are driving on a local highway with a posted speed limit that most people view as a guideline rather than a inviolable rule. You are driving along at an off-peak time of day were there may be less traffic congestion and people can drive at a higher rate of speed, and most are … at speeds significantly higher that the posted limits. All of a sudden you see brake lights from the cars in front of you and everyone is slowing down. Your first thought may be that an accident has occurred up ahead and everyone is slowing down. However, you come around a curve and instead of an accident, you see a policeman who is monitoring the speed of traffic and pulling people over to give them a ticket for driving too fast. All the drivers who were previously speeding are now dutifully driving at the posted speed limit, smiling at the policeman as they drive by. But … as soon as everyone makes it around the next curve in the highway and are out of sight of the policeman, what happens? You guessed it. Everyone speeds up again beyond the posted speed limit. The policeman in this case is an external motivator. Once the motivation is removed, people are no longer motivated to continue their good behavior of driving within the speed limit.

Now let's say that you are a Christian, and your pastor at church just preached a sermon on Romans 13:1–7, a passage in which Paul talks about obeying those in governmental authority over us. Let's say, further, that you are convicted about your driving habits and the fact that you routinely break the speed limit. You then commit yourself to driving at posted speed limits regardless of how fast everyone around you is driving and regardless of whether a policeman is anywhere in sight. You are now internally motivated by your biblical conviction that you should drive at the posted speed, so you do. This kind of motivation can be very long-lasting, because

it is based on your own personal convictions not on an external motivator. As administrators, we should seek to motivate people by helping them to identify their own personal strengths, interests, passions, abilities, and biblical convictions. As we do so, they will be more motivated in their service then they might otherwise be.

We also need to realize that people are motivated by things that challenge and interest them. Figure 19.2 is loosely related to the Yerkes-Dodson Law, which indicates a relationship between performance and readiness to perform.[11] In a similar way, motivation can be shown to relate to the challenge or difficulty of a task. Very simply, as the difficulty of a task increases, so does the motivation to see it through to completion, at least to a point. If a task becomes too difficult, motivation can begin to decline.

As the diagram in Figure 19.2 shows, motivation increases in the face of challenge. Motivation is low when a task is either too easy or impossibly difficult, but there is a point at which we respond to a challenge and are motivated to succeed. For example, I am not motivated to play the simple game Tic-Tac-Toe, because it is a game that can easily result in a draw, neither winning nor losing, if the two players are familiar with the game. I also become demotivated trying to solve a Rubik's Cube, a puzzle that I have never had the time, nor the patience, to figure out how to solve. However, give me a reasonable challenge, something to figure out or do that is neither too easy nor impossibly hard, and I will stick with it until I figure it out and accomplish it. In the same way, administrators need to find ways to assign tasks and responsibilities to others that will challenge but not discourage them. This keeps them engaged and interested in the task or project.

Figure 19.2 Motivation as a Function of Challenge

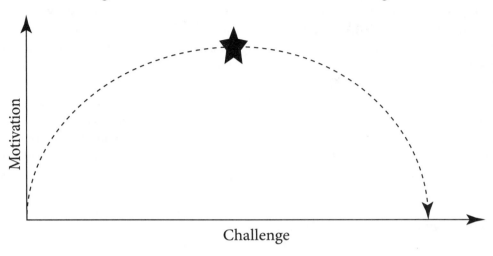

Finding effective ways to motivate our people is an important task of administrators. However, we also need to remember that a fine line exists between motivation and manipulation. While motivation is positive in that it encourages people to begin and continue tasks and responsibilities because they want to, manipulation is negative because it forces people to perform out of fear or guilt. Manipulated people don't serve in ministry because they want to; they serve because they feel that they have been forced or coerced into doing so. Manipulation often results in unproductive personnel, poor quality of service, and burnout. It also may result in people serving in areas of ministry that are not related to their gifting or passion. The end result is poorly run ministries, decreased productivity, and time wasted. Administrators need to guard against manipulation. It can occur easily; and often happens when we, ourselves, are under time and performance pressures. Remember, though, highly motivated people will make the task of administration a blessing. Manipulated people will bring eventual heartache to your administrative efforts.

> Manipulation is the process of, for selfish motives, coercing someone to do something they don't want to do out of a misplaced sense of loyalty or guilt.

10. Allocating and Managing Resources

I have heard it said if it weren't for a lack of people and a lack of money, Christian administration would be easy. I'm not sure it's that simple, but I understand the sentiment. I have yet to encounter a church or ministry organization that appears to have more people than they need or more financial resources than they need. Therefore, good administrators must learn how to manage and allocate ministry resources. It's not as difficult as you might think.

Other chapters in this book give greater attention to this element of administrative process, but you need to see the allocation of resources as a stewardship responsibility.[12] When finances are limited, how do you prioritize expenditures? When staff and volunteers are inadequate, how do you accomplish the work of ministry? These difficult questions can only be answered by thoughtful leadership, prayer, and a commitment to the ministry's sense of calling. That calling is the mission of the ministry and it should drive our resourcing decisions.

11. Communicating Clearly and Often

It is beyond the scope of this text to discuss communication theory in detail. Simply stated, however, communication requires a sender, a message, a receiver, and feedback. The problem is a lot can happen to distort the message. A number of factors can impact good communication—cultural distortions, incongruity between verbal and nonverbal signals, lack of clarity, and a lack of credibility on the part of the sender are just a few. Feedback is important because it allows the receiver and the sender to refine the distortions that impact the intended meaning. However, for this to work, each party to the communication has to be willing to listen with a view toward understanding. Stephen Covey says it well, "Seek first to understand, then to be understood."[13]

> Without credibility, the hearer is likely to presume that what you say is not what you meant!

We live in a complex world, bombarded with messages and sound bites. The days when communication in ministry seemed easy no longer exist. Those in ministry need to understand the challenges to communication. The more complex the issues facing ministries today, the more necessary is good communication, communication delivered in a variety of ways using a variety of mediums—oral, print, and electronic. Ministry leaders need to identify barriers to good communication and how to overcome those barriers, and realize that messages need to be repeated regularly and often. Distractions make it hard to hear what is being communicated. The solution is a broad-based plan for communication that is clear, concise, and meaningful.

Good communication also takes into account that the intended message is not always the message that is heard. Communicating cross-culturally is especially difficult. A message that is clear in one cultural context may not be clear in another—even within the same community!

> "Communication is a meaning exchange, not word exchange."[14]
> —Kenneth O. Gangel and Samuel A. Canine

Effective communication is essential to ministry success. The effective ministry leader understands this and works diligently to communicate clearly.

> "I know that you believe you understand what you think I said, but I'm not sure you realize that what you heard is not what I meant!"[15]
> —Attributed to Robert McCloskey

12. Reproducing Leaders Who Can Lead

As I close this chapter on Christian administration in educational ministry, I would remind the reader of Paul's admonition to Timothy in 2 Timothy 2:1–2:

> You then, my son, be strong in the grace that is in Christ Jesus. And the things you have heard me say in the presence of many witnesses entrust to reliable people who will also be qualified to teach others.

The message of this passage is clear—those in ministry leadership and administration must be willing to invest themselves in the lives of others who will carry the torch of the gospel. This is an ongoing mandate until Christ's return. This form of delegation may have risky consequences. Kenneth Gangel, in his signature work on administration in churches and Christian organizations *Feeding and Leading*, notes that one of the reasons why those in ministry leadership may fail to delegate and reproduce themselves in the lives of others is that "they suspect someone will do the job better than they."[16]

None of us is indispensable. There will always be someone who can do a better job, work better with people, communicate more effectively, or has greater visibility in ministry. But to fear this is to question God's sovereign provision in our lives. If those in ministry truly believe their ministry is a calling from God, then why should they fear someone replacing them? Shouldn't they assume, instead, that as God provided their calling and ministry, he will also sovereignly provide a new place of ministry in the future?

Ultimately it comes down to a question of faithful obedience to the calling and purpose of God in the lives of those who serve him in ministry. When it comes to administration and ministry leadership, obedience requires that we train others in the same way we have been trained for the sake of the ministry and the gospel.

Conclusion

Christian administration is a strategic combination of leadership and management, exercised by gifted and/or trained individuals to assist people, the church, and other Christian organizations in achieving God-given goals for his glory. It requires that we understand the distinctive roles of leadership (vision casting) and management (accomplishing the mission). It is others-focused and God-dependent, otherwise it is no different from administration or leadership in any secular organization.

Christian administration creates order, it delegates to protect leaders and followers as well as to protect the primary calling of those in ministry. It plans, but holds those plans loosely, recognizing that God's plans may be different from our plans. It also seeks to help others identify and employ their unique gifting and calling in ministry. None of these tasks is easy, but the blessing of doing them well for the sake of God and others is worth the effort.

Discussion Questions

1. How would you answer the author's question, "Do you really enjoy administration?" Regardless of your answer, why do you need to learn all you can about effective administration?

2. What is the difference between leadership and management? What different perspective is each likely to bring to the ministry? Why is it important that leaders and managers respect one another and work together?

3. What makes administration Christian? Discuss some of the characteristics of Christian administration that distinguish it from secular administration.

4. What makes administration pastoral? How does good administration protect people?

5. How well do you manage your time? What helpful tips did the author suggest that might help you become more efficient with the time God has given you?

6. Why is delegation important? What keeps administrators from delegating more? Can you identify some of the key elements for making delegation effective?

7. What are some of the reasons the author gives for why leaders fail to invest in reproducing leaders for the next generation?

Resources for Further Study

Berkley, James D., ed. *Leadership Handbook of Management and Administration.* Grand Rapids: Baker Books, 1994.

Covey, Stephen R. *The 7 Habits of Highly Effective People.* New York: Simon & Schuster, 1989.

Covey, Stephen R. *First Things First.* New York: Simon & Schuster, 1994.

Ford, Leighton. *Transforming Leadership.* Downers Grove, IL: InterVarsity Press, 1991.

Gangel, Kenneth O. *Feeding and Leading.* Wheaton, IL: Victor Books, 1989.

Gangel, Kenneth O. *Team Leadership in Christian Ministry.* Chicago: Moody Press, 1997.

Habecker, Eugene B. *Rediscovering the Soul of Leadership.* Wheaton, IL: Victor Books, 1996.

Kouzes, James M. and Barry Z. Posner. *The Leadership Challenge.* 5th ed. San Francisco: Jossey-Bass, 2012.

Lencioni, Patrick. *The Five Dysfunctions of a Team.* San Francisco: Jossey-Bass, 2002.

Mackenzie, Alec. *The Time Trap.* New York: AMACOM, 1997.

Sanders, J. Oswald. *Spiritual Leadership.* Chicago: Moody Press, 1967.

Author Bio

Dr. Jim Thames is the Dean of Academic Administration and Associate Professor of Educational Ministries and Leadership at Dallas Theological Seminary and has been at Dallas for over thirty years. Jim actually enjoys administration and "loves it when a plan comes together!" While a student at the seminary, he worked for and then managed a remodeling and painting company. He has travelled extensively internationally and is actively engaged in educational accreditation for theological schools. He is also active in ministry leadership in his local church. Jim and his wife, Laurie, have two married daughters and look forward to the day when they are blessed with grandchildren.

Endnotes

1. For more information on giftedness, see Bill Hendricks, *The Person Called You: Why You're Here, Why You Matter & What You Should Do With Your Life* (Chicago: Moody, 2014).

2. For more information on mission and vision, see the chapter "Putting It All Together: The Educational Cycle" by George Hillman.

3. Ibid.

4. Ibid.

5. For more information on formal organizational structure and charts, see the chapter "Educational Ministry in the Smaller Church" by Lin McLaughlin. Also see the chapter "Putting It All Together: The Educational Cycle" by George Hillman.

6. For purposes of our discussion, organizational culture can be defined as: "The values and behaviors that contribute to the unique social and psychological environment of an organization. Organizational culture includes an organization's expectations, experiences, philosophy, and values that hold it together, and is expressed in its self-image, inner workings, interactions with the outside world, and future expectations. It is based on shared attitudes, beliefs, customs, and written and unwritten rules that have been developed over time and are considered valid." WebFinance Inc. "Organizational Culture," BusinessDictionary.com, http://www.businessdictionary.com/definition/organizational-culture.html (accessed January 14, 2017).

7. Ted W. Engstrom and R. Alec Mackenzie, *Managing Your Time: Practical Guidelines on the Effective Use of Time* (Grand Rapids: Zondervan, 1967), 178–182.

8. Ibid., 178

9. Myron D. Rush, *Management: A Biblical Approach* (Wheaton, IL: Victor Books, 1983), 138.

10. Thomas Fasokun, Anne Katahoire, and Akpovire Oduaran, *The Psychology of Adult Learning in Africa* (South Africa: Pearson Education, 2005), 83. The authors are referencing the work of Charles Morris and Albert Maisto in *Psychology: An Introduction,* 10th ed. (Upper Saddle River, NJ: Prentice Hall, 1999).

11. Robert M. Yerkes and John D. Dodson, "The Relation of Strength of Stimulus to Rapidity of Habit-Formation," *Journal of Comparative Neurology and Psychology* 18, no. 6 (1908): 527–670.

12. For more information on formal organizational structure and charts, see the chapter "Putting It All Together: The Educational Cycle" by George Hillman.

13. Stephen R. Covey, "Habit Five," in *The 7 Habits of Highly Effective People* (New York: Simon & Schuster, 1989), 235.

14. Kenneth O. Gangel and Samuel A. Canine, *Communication and Conflict Management in Churches and Christian Organizations* (Eugene, OR: Wipf and Stock Publishers, 2002), 16.

15. Attributed to Robert McCloskey during a Pentagon press briefing on the Vietnam War.

16. Kenneth O. Gangel, *Feeding and Leading: A Practical Handbook on Administration in Churches and Christian Organizations* (Grand Rapids: Baker Books, 1996), 177.

Chapter 20
EDUCATIONAL MINISTRY IN THE SMALLER CHURCH

Lin McLaughlin

He is the one we proclaim, admonishing and teaching everyone with all wisdom, so that we may present everyone fully mature in Christ. To this end I strenuously contend with all the energy Christ so powerfully works in me.

—Colossians 1:28–29

I LOVE EDUCATIONAL MINISTRY and have loved it my whole professional life—almost forty years since graduating from college. I have also loved doing educational ministry in the four smaller churches where I have served—the first as an intern overseeing Christian education, the second as the pastor of Christian education, and two others as a volunteer director and leader.

That said, I remember the challenge of working in my first small church. I walked into that wonderful opportunity knowing next to nothing about formal educational ministry programming. I had just left a parachurch college ministry (InterVarsity Christian Fellowship) where I had served for three years in Texas and Kansas. My work with InterVarsity involved doing educational ministry with college students through teaching, discipling, and mentoring. My next career move resulted in me going to work for a church as director of Christian education overseeing all age groups. Consequently I immediately went from working with college students to working with three-year-olds in vacation Bible school in the course of one week. My head was swimming because I was in uncharted waters, a totally alien ministry environment for me in terms of age groups and ministry venue.

I continued to struggle and stumble for some time as I learned the ropes of my new responsibilities. Gradually, I more or less hit my stride as I became familiar with age-group characteristics and church administration. I learned the latter while going to seminary at the same time I worked in the church.

I have felt a connection with educational ministry through all of the ups and downs and in and outs of these ministries. I even changed my degree in seminary to Christian education because of the strength of this connection. This is not to say I haven't had my doubts. At times I've certainly wondered whether I made the right decision. All along the journey, however, God seems to have confirmed my decision.

Definition of Small Church

For the sake of discussion, I define "small church" as being under 150 people including children, youth, and adults. The typical definition puts small churches at a number ranging from 125–150. Though I consider strict limits to be less than helpful, I understand the need to talk in general terms about a numerical range.

> "Jesus calls the church to go and make disciples. This command is given for every church for every individual person. In a small church the same command applies. The only difference is the number of people. In my view if you have one person or 1 million people the functions of the local church in educating people to obey all the Jesus commands are the same. It may look a bit different in how you do it but will basically be the same."[1]
> —Brian Belflower

Educational ministries in small churches present unique opportunities and challenges. Smaller numbers means people of all ages potentially know one another on a deeper and more intimate basis. This builds a solid community experience that many Christians long for in their churches.

The small church environment can also provide a relatively safe place to stretch out one's wings and try new ministries since there can be a greater feeling of safety. Churches of other size categories, particularly large ones, may, however unintentionally, make one feel pressured to perform, even though that is far from anyone person's or group's intentions.

There are also definite challenges to directing an educational ministry in smaller churches and this chapter looks at four of these challenges: age-level grouping; facilities; leadership, management and organizational structure; and recruitment and staffing with volunteers. Most of these areas overlap, so treatment of one set of challenges also relates to others.

> "The greatest spiritual asset to making disciples in the small church is Christian education."[2]
> —Phil Humphries

Age-Level Grouping

Age-level structure is treated first because how age levels are grouped determines, among other things, how many volunteers and how much space you'll need.

Where possible, the small church should combine age groups and grades into the most logical groupings. So combine two- and three-year-olds, four- and five-year-olds, first and second grades, third and fourth grades, and fifth and sixth grades. These combined groups will exhibit some similarities, though admittedly, you'll observe significant differences too. You'll discover curriculum for sale designed for these groupings.[3]

For educational ministry to junior high school students, the most common groupings are sixth through eighth grades or seventh through eighth grades. Make your choice depending on how the local, public, and private schools group their junior high grades in your area. For high school, the most common grouping is ninth through twelfth, with the option of grouping ninth and tenth and then eleventh and twelfth, again depending on numbers.[4]

However, one of the most common challenges facing small churches is how best to group age levels and grades because of uneven distribution of children and teens in any given age group. As a result, you may need to combine more than two age groups. But how do you do that when there may be only three to four children or teens? Again, this is not a problem when you have enough children and/or teens for separate classes or where you combine only two age groups at most.

Another significant challenge involves the lack of volunteers. This scenario also necessitates combining groups together. What if you simply cannot recruit enough volunteers to staff smaller class combinations? Take for example a scenario combining first grade with two other grades. Though not ideal, the first grade could conceivably be combined with either the four- and five-year-olds or, alternatively, the second and third grades. These situations represent the hard reality some small churches face.

In trying to decide which three age groups to combine, I suggest that you group according to maturity and personality. For example, if the question is which age group to put with the first grade, the solution depends on maturity of the first-graders. If they are relatively mature then put them with the second- and third-graders. If they are less mature, then put them with the four- and five-year-olds.

Facilities

Another challenge you'll likely face in a small church is limited availability of facilities. The reality is that many rooms in small churches are multipurpose, for example they may be also used for Sunday school space. Another reason you may be forced to combine age groups is the limited availability of space. Small churches often just don't have enough space for every age group to have their own classroom.

Several options, perhaps obvious ones, to enhance space utilization follow. First, you can divide large spaces using sound absorbing portable dividing walls or partitions. While this is probably the least desirable option, it at least creates a sense of psychological separation and somewhat dampens sounds.

Another option, though somewhat expensive, is to install moveable walls. These walls slide along tracks so that they can be opened up for larger gatherings and sectioned off for smaller ones. This requires some engineering since structural support will be necessary to bear the load of heavy moveable walls. A note of caution: Less expensive and even medium priced walls may be only minimally effective in eliminating or minimizing noise between rooms. Remember, "you get what you pay for." Pleated or accordion-style folding walls often don't provide an effective sound barrier.

A final option is to select curriculum that optimizes both large- and small-space utilization. With large-group–small-group curriculum, multiple age groups meet in the larger space to sing and enjoy a story or drama, perhaps using props and puppets. Then, the large group breaks out into small groups that build on the large group time. These groups could meet in stairwells, large closets, hallways, and even outside locations, spaces that would otherwise be considered unusual or unsuitable for a traditional classroom approach.

Square Footage

However, for optimal learning conditions, consider the space-utilization, square-footage guidelines below:

- Toddlers–Five-Year-Olds
  30 square feet per child
- First–Second Grade
  25 square feet per child
- Third-Fourth Grade
  20 square feet per child
- Fifth Grade–Middle School
  15 square feet per child
- High School
  10–12 square feet per teen[5]

These percentages are based on kinesthetic needs of children. Ironically, the younger the student, the more square feet needed, even though she is physiologically smaller. Kinesthetically speaking, younger age groups are characterized by more frequent and greater range of movement. Young children have a greater need to move, roam, and play. Teens and adults don't have the same needs, or are able to better control themselves physically. Therefore, the spatial needs for teens and adults actually drops with age.

Room Configuration

Room configuration is also important. Chairs and tables should match the physical size of the students. Chairs are available in twelve-, fourteen-, sixteen-, and eighteen-inch heights. Also, tables need to follow suit in terms of height. Thus, tables with adjustable legs are usually preferable. Table shape also needs to be factored in depending on curricular needs and teacher preference. Choose from rectangular, circular, and kidney-shaped tables. As with most topics discussed in this chapter, you'll often find a difference between what is ideal and what is possible in smaller churches. So move as close to the ideal as possible while learning to be content with limitations.

Learning Centers

For younger children and quality educational ministry, you may want to configure rooms that facilitate the creation of learning centers, such as reading, craft and painting, building blocks, audio, puppet and costume, or general play areas. A small church may not have space for all of the learning centers listed above, but use your creativity and innovation to create space for curious learners to thrive.

Moreover, if possible, partition rooms so half is carpeted and the other half-tiled. Locate tables and craft centers on tile surfaces so you can easily clean craft materials (paint, colors, glue, glitter, etc.) off floor and table surfaces. Locate other learning centers such as reading, play, and audio centers on carpeted areas for comfort.

Leadership, Management, and Organizational Structure

Sound leadership and management practices and strong organizational structure are just as important in a small church as in a large one, even if numbers are fewer and the organization is smaller.[6] Organizational quality is always a premium ingredient of effective ministry, which facilitates service, relationships, and community. People tend to thrive or spiritually die, including volunteers, depending on the quality of the organization. Thus, a strong organizational dynamic that encourages participation is a must for churches of all sizes.

> "Each individual needs biblical community with biblical teaching and relationships where the one another's are practiced. They need service inside the church and to the local community. They need to give financially and with their gifts in time. It is exactly the same in a small church of 50 people or in a large church of 50,000 people."[7]
> —Brian Belflower

Leadership

Leadership that casts a vision for ministry excellence will go a long way toward achieving this objective. Ministry excellence involves pursuing the glory of God through quality ministry. However, excellence will look one way in one context and a different way in another. In other words, excellence is relative. The visionary leader will always pursue the glory of God as prescribed in his Word. The challenge lies in working out what excellence purposed in God's glory looks like in any given setting.

Consider the relationship of excellence and faithfulness. Excellence and faithfulness, or stewardship, are virtually synonymous when both relate to doing one's best with what one has been given. God expects no more. Excellence goes awry if you are driven by comparison or infatuated with what money can buy. This is idolatry. We can easily operate in the idolatrous category of excellence, forgetting God only expects us to do our best within the parameters of our resources. When we give in to worldly pressure and compare ourselves with other ministries, we may reap dire consequences for ourselves and those in ministry with us.

What makes for excellence in ministry? In connection with what has been said earlier, excellence begins with the object of one's motivation. The New Testament is clear: God has exalted and will further exalt Christ. Philippians 2:9 states, "Therefore God exalted him to the highest place and gave him the name that is above every name." Obviously, Paul has more than just a mere name in mind. For Paul, one's name was synonymous with the totality of a person. So, we thus understand God has exalted the whole, total being of Christ. Moreover, we would be closer to understanding the superlative "highly exalted" if we thought in infinite or eternal terms. Consequently, we can hardly grasp the full extent of this lofty glorification in our finite minds.

Paul further speaks of Christ's glorification in Colossians 1:15–20, that early hymn to Christ's supremacy, his first rank in creation and the church. It is the riches of this glory God has chosen to make known in Christ (Col. 1:27). This vision of God's, of the New Testament, and of Paul must become our own as the end, for which we pursue ministry excellence, the object of ministry quality.

Having such a vision must be tempered by the fact we pursue such ends within a fallen human condition along with finite skills, abilities, and resources. Therefore, our efforts will not be perfect nor will performance be even across the board. Consequently, we pursue ministry excellence in a relative manner as stated earlier—relative to our resources, skills, and abilities. Otherwise, we may actually unwisely expect too much of ourselves at best, or worship perfection at worst.

Motivating Others through Love

If leadership entails having the right motivation for ourselves, it also requires rightly motivating others. This starts with loving others. Jesus commands his followers to love God and others in citing the greatest of commandments when tested by a scribe in Matthew 22:34–40. There the scribe is only the most recent of religious leaders to test Jesus, perhaps with malevolent motives or through simple curiosity. The latter is harder to believe given the tension between Jesus and the religious-political representatives of various sects—Pharisees, Sadducees, Herodians, and scribes, the equivalent of religious lawyers. The test seems simple enough on the surface to the untrained eye. However, it represented what must have been a fiercely contested debate among Pharisees and scribes. This was made all the more difficult by the fact when interpretive laws—laws created by Pharisees and scribes to demonstrate proper application of the given law—were added to the received law at Mount Sinai, one was left with some 692 laws.

Were they all equal? Were some weightier than others? If so, which ones were the greater and which ones the lesser? If not, how was the average person capable of applying this many laws on a daily basis, much less even be able to remember them?

Into this fray steps Jesus with the incisive clarity and confidence of one taught by the Father. The greatest command was to love God with all of one's heart, soul, and mind, and another commandment was like it, to love others as oneself. And all the other commands were fulfilled in keeping these.

The "One Another" Passages

- Romans 12:10, 16; 13:8; 14:13, 19; 15:5, 7, 14; 16:6
- 1 Corinthians 6:7; 7:5; 11:33; 12:25; 16:20
- 2 Corinthians 13:12
- Galatians 5:15, 17, 26
- Ephesians 4:2, 25, 32; 5:19, 21
- Philippians 2:3
- Colossians 3:9, 13, 16
- 1 Thessalonians 3:12; 4:9, 18; 5:11, 13, 15
- 2 Thessalonians 1:3
- Titus 3:3
- Hebrews 3:13; 10:24–25
- James 4:11; 5:9, 16
- 1 Peter 1:22; 4:8–10; 5:5, 14
- 1 John 1:7; 3:11; 3:23; 4:7, 11–12
- 2 John 1:5
- Revelation 11:10

Thus, the weightier, greater command also falls to the leader who would motivate others—love God, love people. A ministry context pervaded by love lubricates all the necessary machinations, practical activities, and logistics of ministry.

Relational Emphasis

Flowing out of an emphasis on love is a logical emphasis on relationships, also an important aspect of leadership. This is certainly in keeping with the New Testament's emphasis on relationships found in the "one another" passages.

Management

Central to best practices of educational ministry in the small church is the necessity of strong managerial principles.[8] This is a further extension of the discussion about quality and excellence in ministry mentioned earlier. Just because you have smaller numbers does not mean good management is optional. Moreover, most management principles are scalable so that they work equally well with smaller or larger numbers of people, activities, goals, and educational ministries.

1. MBWA Supervision

MBWA is an acronym for "management by walking around," discussed in the book *In Search of Excellence* by Tom Peters and Robert Waterman.[9] The authors relate the principle of walking around the shop floors, warehouse floors, offices, etc., as a means of being accessible to employees as well as spontaneously supervising on an as-needed basis. It also enhances the relational dynamic between supervisors and workers.

I've experienced great success with this in small and medium church settings. This has enabled me to help teachers and other volunteers on countless occasions as they faced small emergencies, curriculum needs, disciplinary issues—you name it. This helped me gain credibility as someone who was in the trenches with my volunteers as opposed to being isolated in an office and removed from the happenings in classrooms. It also afforded me the opportunity to just listen to and encourage others at a timely moment.

2. Ministry Descriptions

Ministry or job descriptions inform a potential volunteer concerning what they can expect of the ministry and what the ministry expects of them.[10] I have found that most volunteers are relieved and even impressed when they see that the job description clearly spells out what they are being asked to do. I developed these with potential volunteers I recruited for staff positions.

Good ministry descriptions contain several key components:

Purpose of the ministry—This ennobles the ministry by declaring why it exists on a spiritual level. Plus, it concisely states what the ministry is about.

Length of service—We should be clear about the length of service we are asking volunteers to commit to, whether it be weeks or months. Moreover, we the recruiters should take that initiative so that the potential volunteer is not placed in the awkward position of asking.

Who the volunteer reports to—Volunteers need to know whom they are accountable to, and the reality that accountability exists speaks well of the ministry.

Who the volunteer works closely with—This component communicates the fact that there is usually a team of people they work alongside, or that there are others in closely associated ministries they can expect to collaborate with on a regular basis. This helps them distinguish between the people they work with from the person they work under. I've experienced a lot of confused volunteers who feel like they have too many bosses giving them conflicting directives. So, it helps to have a document that clears up lines of accountability.

The specific responsibilities of the volunteer— This can include topics like: prepare a weekly lesson, arrive ten minutes before class starts, use the curriculum for lesson preparation, send a birthday card to each child, two adults accompany a child to the bathroom, only women change diapers or accompany a child to the bathroom, pray for each child weekly, etc. This is good delegation.[11] Delegation often fails because it is more work for the delegator than anticipated. However, vague, ambiguous delegation is not delegation at all. Proper delegation requires strong leadership, meaning the leader thinks through the specific tasks this position entails for the volunteer. Otherwise, vague, ambiguous delegation results in confused and discouraged volunteers.

Gifts, skills, and abilities needed for the position— If the volunteer needs specific spiritual gifts for a ministry position, they should be listed. However, not all ministry positions require a spiritual

gift. Perhaps the only thing(s) required for certain positions are skills that can be developed. For example, driving a twenty-passenger bus requires a specific kind of license along with driver training. Working with children does not require the spiritual gift of teaching. Yet, though it does not require a spiritual gift, lesson preparation is both a discipline and a skill that requires cultivating and training.

> "The tragedy of the church today is that the focus is often on talented, rather than the faithful leaders. It is assumed that the church can grow only with exceptionally gifted leaders who have certain personality traits and leadership qualities.... In the early church, what often caught people's attention was the apostles' lack of talent and skill (Acts 4:13; 1 Cor. 2:1–5; 2 Cor. 10:1, 10; 2 Cor. 10:7).... It is not our talents but the power of God that makes us effective."[12]
> —Glenn Daman

Scope of authority—Identify boundaries or parameters that volunteers are to work within. There are three levels of authority. In the first level, you have the authority to make these decisions: E.g., you can depart from the curriculum's lesson plan sequence when something is more pressing; you can utilize a different craft of your choice; supplement the curriculum with learning activities of your choice. Level two involves checking with the leader you report to first. For example, check with your leader before using a different curriculum other than the one you normally use; check with your leader before doing something special on a holiday. The final level involves tasks you should not do: For example, you should not find an unapproved substitute, or completely replace the curriculum with another one.

You may feel this last level is the equivalent of micromanaging or over controlling. If so, feel free to eliminate this step from your ministry description. I include it because over the years I've observed the problems that can arise from issues like those named above. For example, some parents feel strongly about certain holiday observances one way or another. They either want or do not want certain things emphasized. Therefore some care has to be taken to avoid unnecessary offenses and conflicts.

> "[Exemplary] leaders make other people feel strong. They enable others to take ownership of and responsibility for their group's success by enhancing their competence and their confidence in their abilities, by listening to their ideas and acting upon them, by involving them in important decisions, and by acknowledging and giving credit for their contributions.... Leaders accept and act on the paradox of power: we become most powerful when we give our own power away."[13]
> —James Kouzes and Barry Posner

3. Strong Delegation

Most points related to delegation have already been discussed previously under ministry descriptions. But remember these three good delegation practices: responsibility, authority, and accountability.[14] Delegating responsibility simply means that volunteers know what they are being asked to do. Delegating authority means that volunteers understand that they are being given the authority to carry out what is asked of them. Other volunteers who work with them also understand that they have that authority, too. Accountability means that the volunteers' supervisors will occasionally check in with them to see how things are going and discuss their progress. All of these components of delegation have been addressed above under the ministry description section.

4. Corrective Feedback

Sometimes a volunteer needs corrective feedback. This runs the gamut from mannerisms to ethical behavior to teaching style. I have not had to do this often, but I have had to do it because sometimes the welfare of the ministry is at stake.

Obviously, handle this as delicately as possible, but don't avoid it when it is necessary. It's never been easy for me to do, and I have had to bathe it in prayer and summon all my diplomacy and tact. I find the best approach is to be lovingly and tenderly direct. Don't beat around the bush and circle the universe hoping for a soft landing spot. And know that such correction does not always end well. Sometimes a volunteer has chosen to leave a position rather than follow correction and remain in the position.

5. Moving or Removing Volunteers

Even less often than correcting volunteers has been the necessity of removing them. I can count on one hand the number of times I have faced this challenge. If the reason for a problem with a volunteer has to do with ability or skill, then moving them to a different ministry is often a win-win solution. In this scenario, the volunteer is often aware things are not going well and welcomes a change.

Clearly, in worst-case scenarios, these encounters risk a conflict just waiting to happen. Therefore, we have to be as spiritually and relationally ready as possible for tensions and emotions to run high. It has always been uncomfortable for me, but I have recognized that it is just part of leadership to face difficult situations with as much grace and resolve as possible. That said, we have to be prepared to stand our ground.

Books on Dealing with Conflict Issues

Marshall Shelley, *Ministering to Problem People in Your Church: What to Do With Well-Intentioned Dragons*. Minneapolis: Bethany House, 2013.

Ken Sande. *The Peacemaker: A Biblical Guide to Resolving Personal Conflict*. 3rd ed. Grand Rapids: Baker Books, 2004.

Sue Edwards and Kelley Mathews. *Leading Women Who Wound: Strategies for an Effective Women's Ministry*. Chicago: Moody, 2009.

Organizational Structure

The small church, like any church, operates best with structure. The educational ministry benefits from the following structural components.

1. An Organizational Chart

An organization chart, however simple, visualizes the structure of the ministry and identifies who reports to whom.[15] Wes and Sheryl Haystead state,

> A leading supervisor's primary responsibility is to help teachers be successful and feel a sense of satisfaction from their jobs. This kind of support can best happen when the number of people supervised is limited to no more than eight, allowing supervisors to focus on discipling the small group of staff members he or she is responsible for.[16]

The authors go on to provide numerous examples of organizational charts.[17] A simple organizational chart is presented in Figure 20.1. This is just an example. Yours may be different, depending on your form of church government. The top level may just as well be elders or trustees, or even congregation. The second level may be deacons or congregation. The third level may be that of director of educational ministries, followed by teachers at the fourth. In this example, an elder, a volunteer leader, takes on the responsibility of supervising the educational ministry because the only paid staff member in a small church is often the pastor.

Figure 20.1 Simple Church Organization Chart

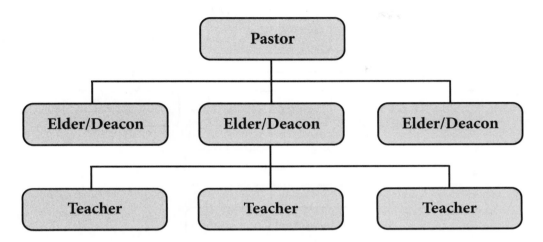

2. Educational Coordinator

In a small church, there may or may not be a full-time or part-time staff person to head up the educational ministry. Most likely it will be a part-time staff member or volunteer. That person could still be called the director or coordinator of the ministry. Ministries must have a clearly designated leader, even in a small church. This person would be under the supervision of a pastor or perhaps head elder, trustee, or head deacon.

3. Age-Level Coordinator

Just below the Educational Coordinator or Director comes the possibility of an age-level coordinator. Such people oversee the major age-level groupings such as early childhood, elementary, and secondary education. This position can potentially provide greater supervision, enhanced relationships, and more immediate resourcing. This position may, however, be a luxury small churches cannot afford because of other volunteer needs and requirements.

"When one thinks of educational ministry in a small church it is only natural to think of the lack of resources necessary to accomplish the task. But contrary to such thinking is the great opportunity to engage each member in his or her responsibility to teach, serve and learn. The '20/80' principle does not exist. The more involved the individual is in educational ministry, the more effective it will be. It's a natural occurrence in the small church."[18]
—Phil Humphries

4. Teachers and Assistant Teachers

Just below the Age-Level Coordinators, or perhaps the Educational Coordinator, are the positions of Teacher and Assistant Teacher, with the latter being below the former on the organizational chart as seen in Figure 20.2.

Figure 20.2 Church Organizational Chart with Educational Coordinator

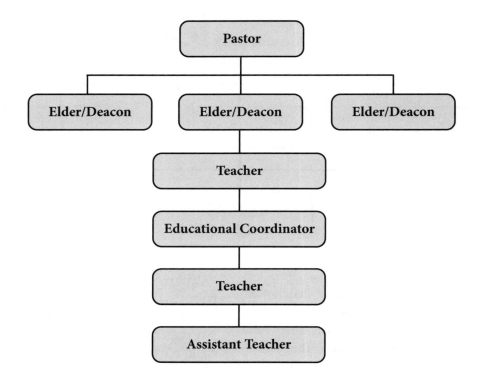

Recruiting and Staffing with Volunteers

A key responsibility of the educational leader is recruiting and staffing. This job is challenging, no matter the size of the church. What follows are several critical components to this all-important task.

1. Create a Culture That Celebrates Volunteers

Few things succeed when it comes to volunteers like regularly celebrating their service. Celebration includes, above all, recognition of volunteers. Be sure it occurs at both individual and group levels. Recognition can be formal as well as informal. You can recognize your volunteers as often as on a weekly basis—powerful because it is so unexpected. And, it's simple, as simple as saying something positive about the quality of their service, or just saying something nice about an admirable approach.

Public celebration occurs when you promote their service or praise them. For example, collect and display pictures of volunteers when they were children or teenagers along with stories about how they were impacted by specific church ministries at a young age. Or create a "volunteer wall" and place their photographs along with descriptions of their ministries. Rotate the photos over a period of weeks if there are a large number of volunteers. This accomplishes several things.

First, it explicitly recognizes the volunteers. Second, it makes a statement about how much the church values the volunteers and their ministry. Third, it informs the church as a whole about its volunteers and varying ministries. Fourth, it helps with recruiting by establishing a positive ministry atmosphere and letting potential volunteers know that they too will be valued for their service.

Also, remember to promote volunteers and their ministries during the main gatherings of the church on Sunday mornings or other times. A final celebratory practice is hosting a lunch or dinner in appreciation and recognition of the volunteer staff of a given area of ministry. The key is regular and pervasive practice of these and other celebratory measures. You shape the culture by volunteer recognition and appreciation. The key is consistency.

2. Ministry Descriptions Clarify Expectations

I've already discussed this topic under the section on management. Suffice it to say that clearly stated and reinforced expectations create an atmosphere of trust. Where trust is high, morale also tends to be high.

3. Careful Supervision Enhances Trust

Careful supervision observes the following maxim: Visibility equals accessibility equals trust. Leaders can be just as invisible and inaccessible in a small church as a large one. All it requires is an office to retreat to away from people. Of course supervision is not just visibility and accessibility. Similar to MBWA, you need to offer help and direction while working alongside your volunteers when you are teaching or working with a class. Also, supervision entails setting clear direction and expectations. This relates to the discussion of ministry descriptions earlier.

Reinforce the volunteer's authority during a timely moment in an encouraging way, or perhaps gently rein in that authority if circumstances warrant it. You hold your volunteers accountable when you apply the MBWA principle. Your seasoned, on-the-spot observations and encouragement go far in recruiting and maintaining a team of inspired volunteers.

4. Regular Encouragement Empowers Others

We should inundate people with encouragement! Many of us tend to under-encourage people, even when we try to be intentional about encouraging them. If I am going to err, I would rather do it on the side of over- rather than under encouragement. I have found that a combination of verbal and written encouragement, along with recognition, works best and provides a variety of different types of encouragement.

Conclusion

In conclusion, educational ministries are important in all sizes of churches, but especially so in the small ones. I wrote this chapter in hopes that it would motivate leaders of small churches to pursue educational ministries with zeal and enthusiasm, even with all of the challenges they face. And as noted, the challenges are numerous. These challenges can be surmounted, however, with attention being given to principles of best practice. May you experience greater success in achieving excellence in your educational ministries, by utilizing the ideas found in this chapter.

Discussion Questions

1. Have you ever belonged to a church of under 150 people, including children, youth, and adults? If so, what did you enjoy about the "small church experience" that might be more difficult to duplicate in a larger church?

2. What are the benefits of ministering in a smaller church?

3. What are the challenges of ministering in a smaller church?

4. What is MBWA (management by walking around), and how can its use enhance a minister's effectiveness?

5. Regardless of the size of the church, what are some of the non-negotiables?

Resources for Further Study

Bierly, Steve R. *Help for the Small-Church Pastor: Unlocking the Potential of Your Congregation.* Grand Rapids: Zondervan, 1995.

Bierly, Steve R. *How to Thrive as a Small-Church Pastor: A Guide to Spiritual and Emotional Well-Being.* Grand Rapids: Zondervan, 1998.

Campbell, Barry. *Smaller Churches Healthy and Growing: Extraordinary Ministry.* Nashville: Lifeway Press, 1998.

Daman, Glenn. *Leading the Small Church: How to Develop a Transformative Ministry.* Grand Rapids: Kregel, 2006.

Haystead, Wes and Sheryl Haystead. *How to Have a Great Sunday School: Ideas, Advice, Forms and Guidelines to Help You Set Up and Run an Effective, Efficient and Exciting Sunday School.* Ventura, CA: Gospel Light, 2000.

Klassen, Ron and John Koessler. *No Little Places: The Untapped Potential of the Small-Town Church.* Grand Rapids: Baker, 1996.

Rush, Myron. *Management: A Biblical Approach*, Wheaton, IL: Victor Books, 1983.

Sande, Ken. *The Peacemaker: A Biblical Guide to Resolving Personal Conflict.* 3rd ed. Grand Rapids: Baker Books, 2004.

Shelley, Marshall. *Ministering to Problem People in Your Church: What to Do with Well-Intentioned Dragons.* Minneapolis: Bethany House, 2013.

Author Bio

Lin McLaughlin is Professor of Educational Ministries and Leadership at Dallas Theological Seminary. Lin has a pastoral heart for education and students. He came to Dallas Theological Seminary with years of experience in parachurch organizations and churches in Texas and Kansas. Lin and his wife have three children and five grandchildren.

Endnotes

1. Brian Belflower, lead pastor, Intersect Church in McKinney, Texas.

2. Phil Humphries, lead pastor, Clearwater Community Church, in Richardson, Texas.

3. For additional information on age-level grouping and curriculum for children's ministry, see the chapter "Formative: Preschoolers and Children" by Jerry Lawrence.

4. For more information on age-level grouping for youth ministries, see the chapter "In Between: Adolescents" by Jay Sedwick.

5. Wes Haystead and Sheryl Haystead, *How to Have a Great Sunday School: Ideas, Advice, Forms and Guidelines to Help You Set Up and Run an Effective, Efficient and Exciting Sunday School* (Ventura, CA: Gospel Light, 2000), 121–124.

6. For more information on leadership, management, and organizational structure; see the chapter "Administering a Healthy Educational Ministry" by Jim Thames. Also see the chapter "Putting It All Together: The Educational Cycle" by George Hillman.

7. Brian Belflower, lead pastor, Intersect Church in McKinney, Texas.

8. For organizational principles, see the chapter "Administering a Healthy Educational Ministry" by Jim Thames.

9. Thomas J. Peters and Robert H. Waterman Jr., *In Search of Excellence: Lessons from America's Best-Run Companies* (New York: Harper Collins, 2006), 289.

10. The following ministry description is based on and adapted from a template produced by Bob Biehl, "Executive Mentoring," http://www.bobbiehl.com.

11. For more on delegation, see the chapter "Administering a Healthy Educational Ministry" by Jim Thames.

12. Glenn Daman, *Leading the Small Church* (Grand Rapids: Kregel, 2006), 45.

13. James Kouzes and Barry Posner, *The Leadership Challenge*, 3rd ed. (San Francisco: Jossey-Bass, 2003), 281, 284.

14. Myron Rush, *Management: A Biblical Approach* (Wheaton, IL: Victor Books, 1983), 144.

15. For more information, see "Putting It All Together: The Educational Cycle" by George Hillman.

16. Haystead and Haystead, *How to Have a Great Sunday School*, 93.

17. Ibid., 93–95.

18. Phil Humphries, lead pastor, Clearwater Community in Richardson, Texas.

Chapter 21
PUTTING IT ALL TOGETHER: THE EDUCATIONAL CYCLE

George M. Hillman, Jr.

Therefore go and make disciples of all nations, baptizing them in the name of the Father and of the Son and of the Holy Spirit, and teaching them to obey everything I have commanded you. And surely I am with you always, to the very end of the age.

—Matthew 28:19–20

AFTER READING ALL OF the great material in this book on educational ministries, you may be thinking: How do you actually implement what you just read? In this chapter, I want to walk you through an educational cycle process that you can use in your ministry setting to either create a new educational ministry or to revitalize an existing one. This educational cycle can be used in any setting: small groups, Sunday school classes, women's ministry, men's ministry, children's ministry, student ministry, evangelism training, leadership training, missions training, discipleship ministry, Bible colleges, etc. Worksheets for each step are provided for you at the end of the chapter.

I recently ran into one of our seminary graduates who pastors a church in the area. He found me at the campus coffee shop one morning and asked me what projects I was working on (I guess he thinks seminary professors are always working on projects). When I told him I was writing a chapter on the educational cycle we teach in one of our core classes for the department, he got excited and said, "That is one of the best things I learned at seminary! I used that educational cycle process to start a ministry at the local prison." It is such a great feeling when you actually see your students using what we teach in the real world.

Most of the thoughts in this chapter are not new or my own creation. Great educators who have gone before helped to guide a previous generation of educational leaders in creating, organizing, and implementing educational ministries. I am personally indebted to Christian educators like Kenneth Gangel, Lois Lebar, and Gene Getz for much of what follows in this chapter.[1] You will see me reference their material extensively. My goal for this chapter is to bring their thoughts on the educational cycle to a new generation of leaders and educators.

As pastors, ministers, and lay leaders, we share a journey to take our people from outside of the faith to mature Christlikeness. The apostle Paul writes,

> So Christ himself gave the apostles, the prophets, the evangelists, the pastors and teachers, to equip his people for works of service, so that the body of Christ may be built up until we all reach unity in the faith and in the knowledge of the Son of God and become mature, attaining to the whole measure of the fullness of Christ.
> —Ephesians 4:11–13

> He is the one we proclaim, admonishing and teaching everyone with all wisdom, so that we may present everyone fully mature in Christ.... So then, just as you received Christ Jesus as Lord, continue to live your lives in him, rooted and built up in him, strengthened in the faith as you were taught, and overflowing with thankfulness.
> —Colossians 1:28; 2:6–7

In many churches and parachurch organizations, the educational programming is routine and in need of reform. Too often the curriculum we offer is out of touch with the real-life needs of our people. Many times our ministry volunteers seem either unmotivated or sometimes missing entirely. Our teaching techniques are antiquated at times—or unfortunately, our people reflect disinterest in the educational programs we offer.[2] The educational cycle described in this chapter represents a way to intentionally educate the people under your care. Even though churches and parachurch organizations come in all shapes and sizes, the basic building blocks for building a vibrant educational ministry remain the same.

> "I believe Christian education is too vital a ministry to let happen by accident or happenstance. We cannot wander from program to program and hope to prepare people for the life of discipleship in today's world."[3]
> —Karen Tye

Holy Spirit and Prayer Foundation

Before you jump into the educational cycle process, I want to stress two things. First, this process must be bathed in prayer. While the following technique could be undertaken in a rote way, the entire process must instead be infused with prayer as you plan and carry out your own educational ministry. The Holy Spirit is the real dynamic in any Christian methodology, because he is active in every learning situation.[4] Anything of lasting value only comes through the power of the Holy Spirit. So make sure you pray through every step. To help you focus on prayer in this process, please see the introduction worksheet at the end of this chapter.

Figure 21.1 The Educational Cycle Process

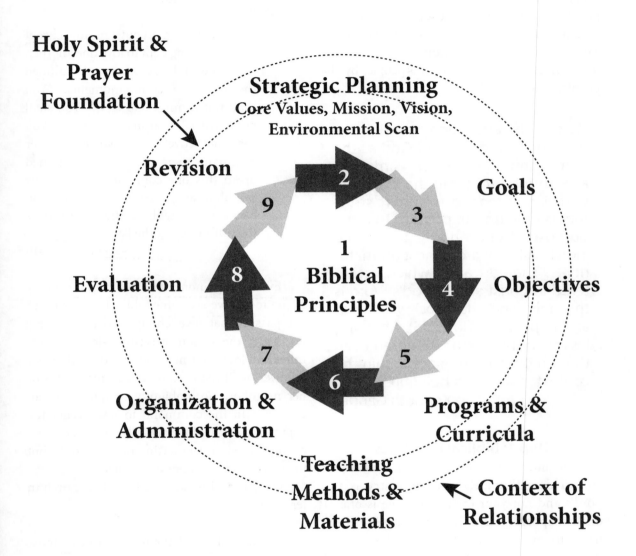

Context of Relationships

2 Second, make sure you include other people in this planning and evaluation process. This process is not some type of "ivory-tower operation" limited to only a few leaders at the top of the organizational chart. Instead, thinking through educational programming requires a cooperative effort involving everyone.

People tend to commit to a program if they have a significant role in its development. The more people you get involved in the process, the more true ownership of the process they will have.[5] Ministry does not just belong to a few at the top. Ministry should be "of the people, by the people, for the people."[6]

> "...church education continually relies upon the Word of God as the sanctifying agent which carries on a cleansing process in the life of the Christian.... Indeed, the entire structure is built on the premise that the purpose of education is to nurture individuals towards Christian maturity.... The education which is centered in Christ and in God's Word is the only kind that God will honor and approve (2 Tim. 2:15). Anything less than this is man-centered even though it may take place within the context of a church building."[7]
> —Kenneth Gangel

Step 1: Biblical Principles

You must first consider what God wants you to do. Ultimately your ministry is the Lord's and not your own. Your role is one of undershepherd, caring for the people he entrusts to you. For Christians, all education in the church must center on the triune Godhead and on his unchanging biblical principles. These biblical principles clearly define the foundation of your ministry. These are timeless principles, applicable to every church in every age, culture, and location.

Consider this example from the apostle Paul to the church in Rome:

> Let no debt remain outstanding, except the continuing debt to love one another, for whoever loves others has fulfilled the law. The commandments, "You shall not commit adultery," "You shall not murder," "You shall not steal," "You shall not covet," and whatever other command there may be, are summed up in this one command: "Love your neighbor as yourself." Love does no harm to a neighbor. Therefore love is the fulfillment of the law.
> —Romans 13:8–10

Even though none of us live in first-century Rome today, we see some biblical principles in this passage that never change and always apply no matter the season or setting—love one another and love your neighbor as yourself. Every follower of Christ is commanded to love his or her neighbor. No ambiguity or qualifiers can be found in the command to love. What the expression of this love actually looks like does change based on the setting or the people, but the command to love never changes.

Or look at this example from the church in Jerusalem:

> They devoted themselves to the apostles' teaching and to fellowship, to the breaking of bread and to prayer.
> —Acts 2:42

While there has existed a wide variety in styles of churches over the past two thousand years, every church has had the marks of teaching, fellowship, breaking of bread, and prayer. These represent some of the things that make a church a functioning church. The form, pattern, structure, organization, method, or even tradition may change based on the needs of our changing culture, but the distinct functions of the church do not change no matter the culture.[8]

These verses from Romans and Acts reflect just two examples. The Bible offers numerous timeless biblical principles that guide every Christian ministry. To start the educational cycle, begin with a prayerful study of the Bible. Look for unchanging biblical principles that uniquely apply to your specific ministry. You may want to review the first couple of chapters of this book to remind yourself of some of these principles. Dozens and dozens of Scripture passages could be considered. However for the purpose of this educational cycle process, only focus on a few (two to four) biblical principles. What are the core biblical principles that drive your ministry, the hallmark Scripture verses you look to constantly? On the worksheet at the end of this chapter, for step 1, record the passage for each biblical principle and then include a short rationale/explanation for each passage.

Step 2: Strategic Planning

The biblical principles you just described in step 1 are timeless, but your ministry seeks to reach twenty-first-century believers and unbelievers in a specific city or a specific people group (children, teenagers, single moms, refugees, senior adults, newlyweds, etc.). The next step involves thinking strategically about how these foundational biblical principles will play out in your own local context with your people. Under this step of strategic planning in the educational cycle, we focus on the areas of core values, mission, environmental scan, and vision.

Step 2a: Core Values

Every organization has a set of core values that describe its identity and culture. Together with the mission and the vision of the organization (which we will explore shortly), the core values represent a part of the organizational DNA. While other things in the organization may change with the seasons, the core values of that organization are foundational beliefs and stay constant.[9]

> "Core values drive and guide the church.... The church's mission determines its port, and the vision is a picture of what it will look like when it arrives at that port. And the church's values, like the engine and rudder of a ship, empower and guide the church towards that destination.... Core values are not something that people simply buy into. They already hold them, and the job of a leader is to help his [or her] people discover or identify what they are. It is a discovery process, not a sell job."[10]
> —Aubrey Malphurs

The core values shape the ministry. My colleague Aubrey Malphurs notes, "Values dictate every decision and influence every action right down to the way we think and the manner in which we execute those actions.... They affect everything about the organization: its decisions, goals, priorities, problems solved, conflicts re-solved, spending, and much more."[11]

Values help to distinguish your church or ministry from other churches or ministries in the same community. Values help to describe those unique elements that attract people to your church or ministry. Different people are drawn to different values. Think about what initially attracted you to your church or ministry. Maybe it was the value of depth in Bible teaching. Maybe it was the value of local outreach in the community. Maybe it was the value of quality and safe children's programming. Maybe it was the value of intergenerational ministry. Maybe it was the value of relationships in small groups. Maybe it was the value of certain social justice issues. Why are you involved with your church or ministry?[12] Why would people drive past other churches to come to your church? Why would people want to join your ministry instead of other ministries?[12]

These core values should come from your study of Scripture. To illustrate, consider the first passage we looked at in step 1 of the educational cycle:

> Let no debt remain outstanding, except the continuing debt to love one another, for whoever loves others has fulfilled the law. The commandments, "You shall not commit adultery," "You shall not murder," "You shall not steal," "You shall not covet," and whatever other command there may be, are summed up in this one command: "Love your neighbor as yourself." Love does no harm to a neighbor. Therefore love is the fulfillment of the law.
>
> —Romans 13:8–10

Coming from this passage, we determined that loving our neighbor represents a timeless biblical principle applicable to all believers everywhere. If we want to translate this idea of love into a core value for our ministry, we might say that we value loving relationships among our members. Or we might say we value loving the local community where we live. Or we might say we value loving those most in need of love. So while the principle of love remains timeless, the expression of love becomes more contextualized to where we find ourselves. Who is my neighbor in need of my love?

While you may be tempted to create a long list of core values, resist that temptation. Research shows people cannot focus on more than three or four values if they really want to impact their behavior.[13] So decide on two to four core values that flow from the biblical principles most important to you and to your ministry. To help you start to think in this direction, these examples exemplify "common" core values churches and ministries hold:

- Family—the relationships between husbands and wives and their children
- Biblical instruction—a familiarity with and desire to know the truths of Scripture
- World missions—spreading the gospel of Christ around the globe
- Encouragement—giving hope to people who at times need some hope
- Giving—providing a portion of one's finances to support the ministry
- Relevance—communicating truth in a way that people can understand
- Prayer—communicating with God

- Evangelism—telling others the good news of Christ
- Team ministry—ministering alongside others
- Creativity—coming up with new ideas and ways of doing ministry
- Worship—attributing worth to God
- Cooperation—working together in the service of the Savior
- Service—mobilizing people to be actively involved in ministry to others
- Diversity—actively engaging people with different heritages and ethnicities, across ages, life stages, and economic means
- Fellowship—spending time with others, encouraging and caring for them[14]

For this step of the educational cycle, describe the constant, passionate, core values that drive your ministry. On the worksheet at the end of this chapter, you will list two to four core values with a one to two sentence rationale/explanation of each core value. These core values should be tightly aligned with biblical principles. How the core values develop out of your biblical principles should be clear. For example if "serving" is a core value for your ministry, the rationale could be, "Every believer volunteers with a servant spirit. As our Lord Jesus Christ served his disciples by washing their feet, so we humble ourselves in service to each other."

Step 2b: Mission Statement

The mission identifies the practical end product of your ministry.[15] The mission for the church is pretty straightforward. Jesus set

the mission of the church two thousand years ago in very concrete terms, and invites us to join him:

> Therefore go and make disciples of all nations, baptizing them in the name of the Father and of the Son and of the Holy Spirit, and teaching them to obey everything I have commanded you. And surely I am with you always, to the very end of the age.
> —Matthew 28:19–20

The mission of the church is to make disciples. Using this command to make disciples as the model, you can adopt this into language that communicates to your people. How would you word this mission to fit your context? Consider some of the following variations on the mission of making disciples:

- For a student ministry—"The student ministry exists to lead students to engage community with one another, engage in relationship with God, and engage the world for Christ."
- For a men's ministry—"Our mission is to make disciples of men who will make disciples."
- For a family ministry—"Our mission is to strengthen marriages and equip parents by honoring God and reflecting Christ in all that we do."
- For a leader training ministry—"It is our mission to train volunteers in basic Bible doctrines and elements of the Christian faith in their preparation for service to the local church."

- For a women's ministry—"Our mission is to craft the inner woman into the image of Christ."
- For a Sunday morning Bible study ministry—"We seek to equip adults to live lives of wisdom by the Spirit, through God's Word, in the context of a supportive Christian community."
- For a young adult ministry—"We are a community of young adults seeking to grow in Christ, live in fellowship, and be a light to the world."
- For a small group ministry—"Our mission is to intimately connect believers through home groups, in order to build one another up into mature followers of Christ and serve together those in need."

The mission helps to set the boundaries of what a ministry should and should not do. If the mission of the church is to make disciples, then serious questions must be asked of every ministry in the church, to determine how each ministry contributes to that overall mission. If we are unclear as to why we do what we do in the church, we end up with blurry outcomes. The mission shapes what we do in all ministry contexts.

> "You will never do ministry that matters until you define what matters…. The most effective organizations know and understand what business they are in or what function they perform. The same holds true for the church that proclaims Jesus Christ."[16]
>
> —Aubrey Malphurs

Figure 21.2 The Mission of the Church

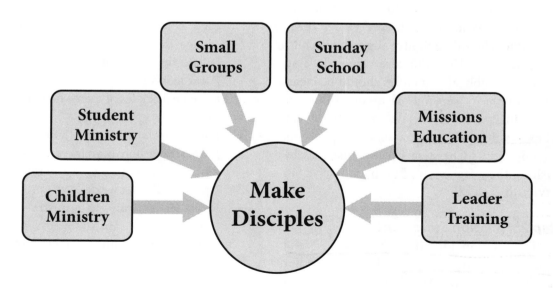

When you know what you are supposed to do, you become more energized toward that effort. When you know what your ministry is supposed to do, you know how to evaluate your progress. The mission gives you a target to aim for.[17]

For this step in the educational cycle, state the mission for your ministry on the worksheet at the end of the chapter. Your mission statement should clearly articulate the focus of the ministry. This should be written as a single, concise sentence. The mission statement must reflect the core values and biblical principles.

Step 2c: Environmental Scan

The temptation is to jump right in and adopt the latest educational ministry from the cutting-edge church with the big national conference. Or the tendency might be to adopt a ministry model from the creative publishing company with slick publicity pieces trying to sell you its curriculum. But before you make any final decision, you must discover the unique needs of your own people in your particular context. It is your responsibility to make the connection between the needs of the particular people God has entrusted to you and solutions for them from God's Word.[18]

> "Whenever we tackle a problem or a new situation, we start with needs. In making changes we start where the change is needed, with people as they are, where they are. A need signifies a lack, a condition requiring supply and relief…. Needs are God's built-in equipment for contacting human nature."[19]
>
> —Lois LeBar

So the question becomes, "Who is your audience and what are their actual needs?" Paying attention to the people represents a fundamental educational task.[20] To do this, you will need to first look inside your church or ministry. Then you will need to identity the specifics of the community outside of your church or ministry. The more information you discover, the better.

Internal Scan: Who Is Coming Already?

To start, take a look at who already actively participates in your ministry. For a church context, here are some things to consider:

- Age—How many people are in the different age groupings (such as preschool, elementary age, junior high and high school age, college age, young adults, median adults, older adults)?
- Education level—What is the average level of education of the people? What is the reading level of adults? What percentage of adults graduated high school? What percentage of adults graduated with a bachelor's degree or higher?
- Marital status—How many people are married and how many are single?
- Gender—How many participants are men and how many are women?
- Ethnicity—What is the predominant ethnic group in your church or ministry? Are there significant numbers of other ethnic groups?
- Income—What is the median household income in your church or ministry? What do your people do to earn a living? Are the people financially giving to the church or ministry?

- Felt needs—What felt needs do the people bring to the church or ministry?[21]

Some of this information can be obtained from membership rosters, but other information will need to be collected through surveys or interviews of your members.

External Scan: Who Is in Your Community?

Beyond the wall of your church or the scope of your ministry, you should also become an expert of the local community.

Where is your community? You need to start with a local description of your community. Ask yourself the following questions to help define the location of your community:

- Distance—On average, what is the travel time for people participating in your church or ministry?
- Boundaries—Are there any natural geographical barriers such as lakes, highways, railroad tracks? Do the people come from within city/county limits or from certain zip codes?
- Location—Are you located in an urban, suburban, rural, or some other kind of community?
- Population—How many people live in the community (total population)? Is this area old and dying, young and growing, or somewhere in between? How many people are unchurched?[22]

Who is in your community? Once you have defined the location of your community, then you need to look at who lives in that community.

You will ask some of the same questions you asked to discover those inside your church or ministry. For example, age, education level, marital status, gender, ethnicity, etc. Then ask these additional questions to learn more about who comprises your community:

- Entertainment—What are the most popular ways to spend free time in the community?
- Felt needs—What are the felt needs of the people in the community and which felt needs would bring them to church and with what expectations? Deep down, what do they really want out of life?
- Perception of Christianity—What are their general preconceptions (or stereotypes) about churches? When and under what circumstances might they visit a church? What feelings might they experience before, during, and after a visit to your church?[23]

In addition to the local community in which you minister, you also want to have a global focus. You do not live in an isolated bubble. Lift your gaze above the horizon of your local community to discover the bigger picture of what is going on in the world and where culture is heading. Good leaders sense what the future holds.[24] What global and national changes currently affect the church? What economic or employment factors exists? What prevailing values and living patterns do you observe?

Putting Both Scans Together

Once you identify your community's demographic information, set it beside the information you gathered from inside your church or ministry and compare the two. Does your church or ministry reflect the local community? What are the similarities and what are the differences? The more the church or ministry is demographically different from its community, the more challenges to reach that community. Not impossible, but challenging.[25]

Now summarize the data you have gathered from your internal and external scans on the worksheet at the end of this chapter. Describe what salient features of your environment you need to know, and factor these into the planning. Also determine what is happening in your changing world that influences the planning and structure of this ministry.

Step 2d: Vision

The final part of the strategic planning step of the educational process is to craft a vivid description of what the actual ministry will look like. Vision flows out of the core values (based on the biblical principles you discovered), the mission (reflective of the commission to make disciples), and the environmental scan (represented by the needs of the people both inside and outside your church or ministry). Vision is "an ideal and unique image of the future for the common good."[26] By image, I mean a compelling visual word image of what your ministry would look like if you accomplished the mission to make disciples. The mission states the direction and the vision paints a word picture of the destination.[27]

A good vision statement is both memorable and invites others to join in. A vision shared only by the leader is not a vision that will last.

The people must share the vision as well. Aubrey Malphurs writes,

> The right vision creates meaning in people's lives, providing them with a cause and giving them a sense of divine purpose. They are a part of something bigger than themselves, something great that God is accomplishing at this time and place in history. They are a part of God's cause. With a shared vision, people see themselves not just as another congregant or a "pew warmer" but as a vital part of a church that is having a powerful impact on a lost and dying world.[28]

> "There is no more powerful engine driving an organization toward excellence and long-range success than an attractive, worthwhile, achievable vision for the future, widely shared."[29]
>
> —Burt Nanus

For the final part of the strategic planning step, vividly describe on the worksheet at the end of this chapter a picture of the future of your ministry you are planning. Verbally describe an ideal future state based on biblical principles, core values, mission, and reflection of your environmental scan. Also discuss what spiritual growth you hope to see happen in the future in the lives of the people involved in and impacted by this ministry. The vision statement should be of sufficient length (at least half a page long) but the vision statement is not the same thing as a longer mission statement.

> "Less than 10% of Protestant pastors can articulate God's vision for their church."[30]
>
> —George Barna

Consider the following example from one of our students at the seminary:

It is the vision of the Eastwood Student Ministry to see class after class of graduating seniors grounded and mature in the faith, going out into their homes, community, and world as influencers for Jesus Christ and his kingdom. We will labor to create an atmosphere of radical, transforming love that prompts students to come inside and belong to a cause greater than the narcissistic idolization of self that the culture offers. We commit to seeing a generation in our church who love the Word of God, who are devoted to its study, who practice it without exception, and who are equipped to show the Word to others according to their various spiritual gifts. We long to see a church that does not set low expectations for students, but rather a church that unleashes students who are equipped and committed to making an impact on the world. We strive alongside families to produce teenagers who are biblically and morally rooted in the Christian faith, even within our present culture of immorality and religious relativity. We will intentionally focus on providing godly and capable men and women to mentor and disciple students in following Jesus Christ, sending them out to reproduce disciples in their own lifetime. We long to see a generation awakened to the glory of God, the supreme value of God above all other loves, and to the desperate pursuit through prayer of revival in our lives, our homes, our communities, our nation, and our world.[31]

Steps 3 and 4: Goals and Objectives

At this point in the educational cycle, you have discovered timeless biblical principles through your study of Scripture, crafted core values which flow out of these timeless biblical principles, adopted a mission statement, conducted an internal and external environmental scan to identify the needs of the people, and painted a vision of what the future will look like when you accomplish the mission. However, at some point you have to move from only dreaming and actually put some action steps together. It is time to set some actual goals and objectives to put a plan in place for the ministry.

Based on what the Bible says, you want to know what you want people to actually do about what the Bible says. To accomplish this, you need to develop goals and objectives related to the here and now.[32] Goals are brief, directional statements about your specific ministry, founded on the biblical principles and core values for the ministry. Objectives then develop the specifics of how to achieve the goals. Objectives break down goals into action steps, such as tasks, roles, positions, responsibilities, dates, etc.[33]

> "Clearly defined mission, goals, objectives, and action steps can do amazing things for ministry organizations. Groups of any size, floundering in a morass of confusion and lacking direction, can immediately begin to move down the field if they understand how to get there…. Goals and objectives provide the wherewithal, the stepping-stones by which we move from where we are now, not to where we would like to be in the future. Without them, we have only dreams."[34]
>
> —Kenneth Gangel

Let me give an illustration of this. From a study of Scripture, we discover a timeless biblical principle of evangelism. God's heart desires for people to experience the grace and love that is only available through Jesus Christ. Every Christian everywhere for all time has been called to share the good news of Jesus Christ to a lost world. Out of this timeless biblical principle, one could then say that a core value of one's ministry might be evangelism. We want God's heart for a lost world to be our heart for a lost world. But how do we put this into action?

Maybe your outreach ministry has become convicted (through your environmental scan) that you need more intentional reach out to your local community with the grace message of Jesus Christ and you want to organize an evangelistic outreach to the community this fall. So what would be the goal and the objectives? Consider the following goal and objectives (see Figure 21.3):

Figure 21.3 Sample Goal and Objectives

Goal
We want to reach our local community with the grace message of Jesus Christ.

↓

Objective #1
Select an outreach director by March 1.

↓

Objective #2
Preach a series on the importance of evangelism and neighborhood outreach during the months of March and April.

↓

Objective #3
Design an evangelistic outreach and training program by July 31.

↓

Objective #4
Conduct the evangelistic outreach by October 31.

As you see, while the goal is more general, the objectives are more targeted. The objectives need to be specific (with dates set and roles identified), measurable (you cannot evaluate what you cannot measure), and realistic (what is reasonable for your church or ministry to accomplish based on size, setting, and resources available), spelling out precisely what you want to do in order to accomplish your goal.[35] As Lois Lebar said, goals and objectives should be "worded concise enough to be kept in focus, specific enough to be achieved, personal enough to change lives."[36]

> "Keep the main thing the main thing. People and organizations have a tendency to stray from priorities. But if we have not prioritized our goals and objectives, we are in danger of achieving the wrong things. We may be efficient (doing things right) without being effective (doing the right things)."[37]
> —Kenneth Gangel

Everything that follows in the educational cycle (programs and curricula, teaching methods and materials, organization and administration, evaluation, revision) can only fall into place once you have clear goals and objectives. Planning becomes impossible without goals and objectives, because you have no target at which to aim. With clear goals and objectives, you do not end up wasting time or effort going in a direction you never intended. With clear goals and objectives, you will be able to select the programs and methods that specifically address the needs of your people. And with clear goals and objectives,

you will evaluate based on the measurable targets you actually set out to accomplish.[38]

For these next two steps in the educational process, you will draft at least one goal related to each core value you developed in your strategic planning step *and* two or more objectives for each goal. Again, see the worksheet at the end of the chapter. The objectives are brief in scope and develop the specifics of how to achieve each of your goals, breaking down the goals into action steps (related to tasks, roles, positions, responsibilities, dates, etc.). The objectives must be specific, clearly measurable, and achievable (realistic but requires you to stretch yourself to attain them).

Step 5: Programs and Curricula *or tools*

In light of the goals and objectives you just developed, your next step involves a description of the actual programs and curricula you plan to use in your ministry to accomplish these goals and objectives and support the mission of the ministry. The various programs and curricula represent tools to help you to create an environment for learning.[39] Much of this book focuses on programs and curricula so I would encourage you to read those chapters that most closely pertain to your own ministry needs and setting. You will also want to become familiar with denominational publishing houses, parachurch curriculum publishers like NavPress or InterVarsity, churches that publish curriculum for others churches to use, or national curriculum publishing companies.

Programs

Suppose from the results of your environmental scan, you discover a need to start a single parent ministry in your church. As you develop your goals and objectives for this ministry, one of your goals would be to equip single parents to meet the unique challenges they face. What program will you use to reach this goal? Will you offer single parenting training as a weekly class on Sunday mornings at the church, or would you offer a Saturday seminar in the community? Or maybe you want to offer training in a family weekend retreat setting, where you can minister to both the single parent and the child? Perhaps you and your team have even brainstormed other ideas. Whatever program you create, describe it in detail in this step of the educational cycle. Again, review the relevant chapters in this book for your own ministry focus. See the worksheets at the end of this chapter, where you can develop your own program for your own ministry.

Curricula

Once you have decided on the program, then your attention turns to the curriculum you will use in the program (see Table 21.1). Continuing with the example of a single parent ministry, will you write your own parenting curriculum? If you are going to write your own, what are the elements you want to make sure you cover in the curriculum? What unique features will you build into your curricula? What pedagogical principles will you follow? How will you package the curriculum?

Or do you want to investigate published curricula others have developed for parenting training focused on single parents? If so, then what should you look for as you review the curricula from other publishers? What age-group provisions do you want the curriculum to reflect? For example, are you only going to focus on the single parents or do you want to also offer a curriculum for the children as well? How should the curriculum be structured, based on the age group?[40] Explain your curriculum choices on the worksheet at the end of this chapter.

Table 21.1 Evaluating Curriculum[41]

Content: What Does It Say?						
Biblical Orientation	**1**	**2**	**3**	**4**	**5**	**N/A**
Does the material exhibit a strong biblical orientation with a high view of Scripture?						
Are proper hermeneutical principles evident in the interpretative process?						
Are the best translations used and is current biblical scholarship employed?						
Comments:						

Content: What Does It Say?						
Christian Values	**1**	**2**	**3**	**4**	**5**	**N/A**
Does the material seek to communicate a value system that is distinctly Christian?						
Are value issues presented and clearly defined, with the various alternatives evident?						
Does the material promote the internalization of the values by the student?						
Comments:						
Life Issues	**1**	**2**	**3**	**4**	**5**	**N/A**
Does the material present and deal with vital issues related to the life of the learner?						
Are contemporary life problems examined with deep insight and sensitivity?						
Are both human and divine perspectives evident?						
Are solutions commensurate with the problems?						
Comments:						
Age-Group Orientation	**1**	**2**	**3**	**4**	**5**	**N/A**
Does the material evidence a clear understanding of developmental task readiness?						
Is the material sufficiently challenging for the age group?						
Does the material show sensitivity to current interests of the age group?						
Is current psychological scholarship evident?						
Comments:						

Philosophy: How Is It Designed?						
Life Orientation	1	2	3	4	5	N/A
Is the ultimate objective of the material related to behavior rather than knowledge?						
Does the material use Scripture as a means to the end of a changed life?						
Does the material spend as much time in application as it does in interpretation?						
Comments:						
Response Orientation	1	2	3	4	5	N/A
Is the material designed to lead the student to an active life-oriented response to the biblical content?						
Does the material allow and encourage individualized student response?						
Do response aims vary in their life orientation?						
Comments:						
Home/Family Orientation	1	2	3	4	5	N/A
Is the material designed to emphasize home and family needs?						
Does the material provide practical suggestions for strengthening the home?						
Is the material relevant to twenty-first-century home situations?						
Comments:						
Organizing Principle	1	2	3	4	5	N/A
Is the organizing principle successfully carried out in all materials?						
Is the organizing principle made clear throughout the materials?						
Comments:						

Methods: How Does It Help?						
Creative Techniques	1	2	3	4	5	N/A
Does material demonstrate a proper understanding of the teaching-learning process?						
Is the teacher encouraged to use a variety of contemporary teaching techniques?						
Comments:						
Teaching Aids	1	2	3	4	5	N/A
Does the material provide sufficient aids for the teacher?						
Are the aids conducive for a variety of situations?						
Is sufficient instruction provided for the use of aids?						
Comments:						
Study Aids	1	2	3	4	5	N/A
Does the material provide additional help for the teacher for preparation for teaching?						
Are suggestions made for additional study on each lesson?						
Are aids provided for both research and teaching techniques?						
Comments:						
Flexibility	1	2	3	4	5	N/A
Will the material fit the situations likely to require it?						
Does the material provide for various levels of competency for both teachers and learners?						
Comments:						

Mechanical Features: How Does It Look?						
Layout	1	2	3	4	5	N/A
Is it easy to look at and read?						
Is it conducive to good study habits?						
Comments:						
Color	1	2	3	4	5	N/A
Does it use color to the best advantage?						
Comments:						
Pictures	1	2	3	4	5	N/A
Are they illustrative and helpful?						
Are they contemporary but not offensive?						
Are they related to student interests?						
Comments:						
Physical Value	1	2	3	4	5	N/A
Are the supplied materials of high quality?						
Are the materials durable and reusable?						
Comments:						

Step 6: Teaching Methods and Materials

Closely associated with your program and curriculum are the teaching methods you will use and the materials you will need for your planned ministry. This step takes you right to your students. This is where the action will take place.[42] How will you implement the program and teach the curriculum? What do you need to accomplish your plans?

Teaching Methods

How we educate should mirror why we educate in the first place. The teaching methods you use should reflect your values, mission, vision, and goals and should help you educate towards them. The teaching methods should also be appropriate for the context and the people in your ministry setting. What works in another church or ministry may not work in your setting for a variety of reasons. And consider those in your ministry. What works with one person with one learning style may not be effective with another person in the same room with a different learning style.

Once you have decided on a program and either found a curriculum or developed your own, what teaching methods will you use to drive the learning so deep that it sticks? In your ministry, different people possess varied educational needs. How will you make sure you connect with them all? Thus, variety becomes essential in your teaching methods. Consider several of the following teaching methods: lecture, discussion groups, role-play, skits, case studies, work groups, creative crafts, songs, "on the job" training, etc.

The temptation is to use methods you grew up with, or teaching methods that are comfortable to you and your learning style. But not everyone is like you. You must always remember the people before you and ask yourself what is the best way to help them learn. The best teaching methods help people achieve your specific learning objectives for them.[43] On the worksheets at the end of this chapter, identify and explain the teaching methods you will use.

Materials

Besides the teaching methods, what materials you will need? Here are some questions to consider:

- Facilities—What are the room/venue needs to run the educational program you have planned? Do you need classroom space at your local facility or will you use some offsite space like homes or retreat centers?
- Equipment—What equipment needs to be in the room when you teach? Is everything already in the room or do you need to buy equipment for the room?
- Curriculum—If you are purchasing the curriculum from an outside vendor, what is the cost for the materials and how many materials do you need to buy? If you write your own curriculum, how will you develop your curriculum and is there any cost involved? Are there additional materials (such as visual aids or teacher training material) that support the curriculum that need to be purchased?
- Supplies—What are the lesson supplies you need for the students (pens, paper,

craft supplies, Bibles, etc.)? Will you provide snacks? What will you need to purchase (paper products, utensils, food, drinks, etc.)? What is your budget for these materials?

This should be a very detailed list. You may want to ask others to help you brainstorm all of the needs to actually implement this ministry. All the required materials/rooms/equipment should be identified along with specific amounts needed and entered on the worksheet for this step.

Step 7: Organization and Administration

getting people! [handwritten]

Ministries do not lead themselves. All the planning and programming become useless unless you have people to carry out the ministry. The paid pastors and ministers do not own the various aspects of a ministry. The ministries in your church or organization should be "of the people, by the people, and for the people."[44] The responsibility of the paid pastors and staff involves the design of a strategy that equips all believers to use their giftings for ministry (Eph. 4:11–13).

You are in the people-development business. This educational cycle process helps to create a ministry but most importantly you want to develop people to serve in various positions of responsibility needed to implement your ministry. Lord willing, both the participants in the ministry and the leaders of the ministry will grow and develop. Leadership empowers your people and creates opportunities for them to discover and use their God-given gifts, abilities, and leadership skills.

> "A properly functioning church educational program does not consist only of a few teachers and many learners but will actually be carried on for mutual edification as God's people help each other to grow in spirituality."[45]
>
> —Kenneth Gangel

Organizational Structure

getting people to do the things. [handwritten]

As soon as you get two people involved in a common project, there comes the next question of who will do what.[46] Chaos and confusion help no one and have no place in Christian leadership. A well-organized ministry structure helps to facilitate all aspects of the ministry.[47] Do not overcomplicate the structure of your ministry. Keep it simple, flexible, and people- (over process-) oriented. Always remember that organizational structure represents a means to the end of helping people.[48] Kenneth Gangel notes, "Since most ministry programs set up just ten years ago will probably not meet the needs of this postmodern world, we must design organizational flexibility that can handle necessary changes to achieve the goals assigned them."[49]

This step in the educational cycle involves designing the organizational architecture of the ministry. It also requires the identification, selection, and recruitment of leaders and workers to staff the ministry. On the worksheet at the end of this chapter, provide a detailed, well-thought-out organizational chart that describes the organizational flow of your ministry. Identify who will lead this ministry, how many assistant leaders and workers will be needed, and to whom the main leader, assistant leaders, and workers will be accountable. Make sure to capture the entire ministry on the chart and include a sufficient number of levels (with appropriate head and subordinate positions).

> "…order and proper function are characteristics of the omnipotent God and therefore ought to mark his church."[50]
> —Kenneth Gangel

what the people do.

Job Descriptions

Leadership is about shared ownership and empowering people. This is not "your" ministry. You want your people to say this is "our" ministry. A key to this ownership involves inviting people to share in the planning as well as determining what each of their roles encompasses in order to accomplish the vision of the ministry. But for people to understand their role, you need to clearly articulate in a tangible way the responsibilities of each role.

(((

Most importantly, you must write job descriptions for every role in your ministry. You need to treat every volunteer as a vital member of your ministry team. Everyone needs to know exactly what they are required to do, what the expectations of their role are, and what they can expect from you as their leader.[51] Job descriptions provide confidence, stability, and accountability for your people.[52] Lois LeBar noted, "Groups need a framework for security, they need to know exactly what their relationship and responsibilities are, they need supervisors who will profitably coordinate their work with that of the other groups."[53]

Give them goals they will achieve.

> "[Exemplary] leaders make other people feel strong. They enable others to take ownership of and responsibility for their group's success by enhancing their competence and their confidence in their abilities, by listening to their ideas and acting upon them, by involving them in important decisions, and by acknowledging and giving credit for their contributions…. Leaders accept and act on the paradox of power: we become most powerful when we give our own power away."[54]
> —James Kouzes and Barry Posner

Remember that in calling people to service, you want to be able to ask specific people to carry out specific ministry tasks for a specific length of time. General open announcements to the crowd during Sunday morning worship, with little specificity, rarely work to mobilize the masses. Instead, you want to have a clear understanding of the leadership needs to put the ministry plan into action and then recruit for those positions.[55]

Step 8 and 9: Evaluation and Revision

The previous steps in the educational cycle seek to answer the question, "What does God want the ministry to accomplish?" These final steps seek to answer the follow-up question, "Has the ministry accomplished what God wanted it to do?" Evaluation involves a planned time of constructive celebration and reflection of what has been accomplished and what needs to change for the future. Evaluation will look at both the process and the product.[56]

Evaluation

The questions asked in evaluation include:

- Does your ministry accomplish what you designed it to do?
- Do you see evidence that people's needs are being met through this ministry?
- Do you see evidence that the ministry outcomes achieve the objectives you set?
- For the next year, what should you keep?
- What should you drop?
- What should you change?[57]

A good leadership team evaluates itself and monitors how it can improve.[58] All of us must be accountable for what we say we will do. Does our ministry serve the mission and the needs of the people? Have we accomplished the goals and objectives we set out? Have we fulfilled the mission of the ministry? Every step in the educational cycle must be considered for evaluation.

> "Evaluation is an essential part of the educational process. We need to be constantly evaluating—every day, week, month, and year; not evaluating primarily what we, the leaders, do but what is happening to our pupils, since all we do is for their benefit.... What kind of product are we turning out?"[59]
>
> —Lois LeBar

Evaluation happens anytime you ask a leader, "How are things going with the ministry?" Evaluation happens anytime you have informal conversations with the leaders or the participants in the program. Evaluation happens anytime you survey your people to find out what they like and don't like about the ministry. Evaluation happens anytime you assess your people to discover what they have learned. Evaluation happens anytime you visit a class and observe what is going on. But the key is to always be asking and watching. If you wait until someone complains or until the people stop coming, then you have waited too long to address the problem.[60]

> "In order to build a strong and faithful educational ministry, we need to be able to see clearly. Seeing clearly calls us to pay attention to what is happening and how it is happening, to discover where growth and change are possible, and to celebrate the gifts we have to offer. We undertake this important process of assessment and evaluation in educational ministry in order to be faithful to our call to 'make disciples.' What we ultimately seek is knowledge that will help us to more faithfully fashion the people of God."[61]
>
> —Karen Tye

On the worksheet at the end of this chapter, describe how you will conduct an evaluation of the ministry you have just planned. When will you first evaluate your ministry? How often will you evaluate your ministry? What evaluation tool(s) will you use to evaluate your ministry (surveys, questionnaires, interviews, focus groups, etc.)? Who will be involved in the evaluation process? Who will know the results of the evaluation? What kind of questions will you ask for evaluative purposes? You need to determine who will administer evaluations, and to whom the results will be reported.

Revision

The educational cycle is not complete until you go through the last step of revision. This step flows out of evaluation and lists specific things that need to be revised, eliminated, or added to strengthen the ministry. Revision provides the bridge from one educational cycle to the next educational cycle. Vague evaluation leads to uncertain planning for the next year, and the clarity gets worse in each new cycle. Evaluation should be specific, with specific recommendations for improvement.[62] What aspects of your ministry need to be revised and updated as a result of your evaluation?

Evaluation should not only discover what is wrong, but also helps you to celebrate what has gone well and where your ministry succeeds in its mission. In those areas where your ministry fulfilled its goals, you can focus your resources and even improve what is good to make it better next time.[63]

> "The effective administrative leader tends to constantly review and revise objectives lest the organization achieve a certain level, plateau there, and fail to move forward."[64]
> —Kenneth Gangel

However, if parts of your ministry have not accomplished your mission, you can use this educational cycle to restructure or repurpose it.

Or you may decide the wisest thing would be to graciously discontinue a part of your ministry that no longer serves its intended function. While the mission never changes, every aspect of a ministry represents a living organism with a life cycle. No form or method is eternal. It comes down to a matter of good stewardship.

Conclusion: Why Plans Fail

As I wrap up this chapter, I would like to address why plans fail. Is it just a matter of working harder to make the plan work or could it be a matter of being wiser on the front end of planning? What do you do if your best laid plans for your ministry fail? Here are some things to consider (much of which represent a review of what I covered in this chapter):

1. No real goals and therefore no real plan—Many goal-setters don't actually know what a real goal is. They may point to some ideal mission such as "improve," "grow," or "increase ministry," but words this vague result in fantasies instead of goals. If your goal statement does not describe a condition or an end-state you want, it is not a goal.

2. No measurable objectives—Objectives are the guides to action. They must contain "action" verbs. Without such action there will be little movement toward goal accomplishment. Objectives must be stated so they are measurable.

3. Failure to anticipate obstacles—Every plan, no matter how carefully prepared, has limitations and built-in conflict over priorities and resources. Effective planners take what at first they perceive to

be large obstacles and break them down into small hurdles. They then develop ways to overcome each one. In short, a plan should be flexible enough to handle obstacles, whether anticipated or not.

4. Lack of milestones for progress review—Plans that fail often have no concrete milestones or dates to review progress, or milestones are allowed to slip by unnoticed. Periodic reviews of progress can alert you to the need to adjust your plans or even your objectives. Milestones reached provide an important sense of accomplishment and desire to succeed further. Effective progress reviews provide a test of direction and pace. They also provide a check on the reality of the plan as you move along.

5. Lack of commitment—Lay leaders may be hindered in long-range planning without a personal commitment from the pastor to support the process; the reverse is also true. Commitment means the willingness to see a plan through to completion. Taking part in the development of goals and objectives stimulates commitment. Involve as many people as possible in the goal-and-objective-writing process.

6. Failure to revise objectives—A sure way to torpedo the best-laid plan involves the failure to restudy and reset objectives when indicated by new facts. Failure results when plans are not flexible enough to respond to changes in circumstances. Rewrite objectives whenever necessary.

7. Failure to learn from experience—Failure to learn from experience arises when planners are unwilling to change their way of doing things. Many take comfort in the thought: "It's worked before; therefore it must be right." This attitude, however, will prevent you from ever finding out if "it is right" for this time until it is too late.[65]

Remember, this ministry belongs to the Lord. You cannot force a ministry to succeed or force people to grow. Your role involves the creation of an environment where the Holy Spirit can do his work in the lives of the people in your care. I pray the process you will undertake will yield much fruit as you serve the Lord alongside your people.

Introduction Worksheet

Choose a <u>specific ministry</u> for your educational cycle ministry plan. It may be within the local church, parachurch, or missions setting.

- *Small Groups*
- *Sunday school*
- *Outreach Ministry*
- *Men's Ministry*
- *Adult Bible Electives*
- *Leadership Training*
- *Women's Ministry*
- *Discipleship Ministry*
- *Children's Ministry, Sunday or Midweek Programs*
- *Other…*

Your Ministry _____

Write a short introduction to explain what ministry you are proposing.

_____

_____

_____

_____

_____

_____

_____

Prayer Worksheet

What value and importance does your ministry place on prayer and dependence on the Holy Spirit as you develop your program? Write a statement in a short paragraph.

_____

_____

_____

_____

_____

_____

_____

_____

_____

_____

_____

_____

_____

_____

Step 1 Worksheet: Biblical Principles

Identify biblical principles for your ministry (two to four principles) with a one- to two-sentence rationale for each.

_____

_____

_____

_____

_____

_____

_____

_____

_____

_____

_____

_____

Step 2a Worksheet: Core Values

What are the constant, passionate, core beliefs that drive your ministry? List them, with an explanation of each one. Show how they relate to your biblical principles.

Value #1

_____

_____

_____

Value #2

_____

_____

_____

Value #3

_____

_____

_____

Value #4

_____

_____

_____

Step 2b Worksheet: Mission Statement

What is your organization supposed to be doing? Write a mission statement. It must be one complete sentence.

_____

_____

_____

_____

_____

_____

_____

_____

_____

_____

_____

_____

Step 2c Worksheet: Environmental Scan

What are the salient features of your environment (internal and external) that you need to know about and factor into your planning? What's happening in your changing world that influences the planning and structure of your ministry?

_____

_____

_____

_____

_____

_____

_____

_____

_____

_____

_____

_____

_____

Step 2d Worksheet: Vision

How do you picture the future of your ministry? What spiritual growth do you hope to see happen in the future, in the lives of the people involved in and impacted by your ministry?

_____

_____

_____

_____

_____

_____

_____

_____

_____

_____

_____

_____

Step 3 and 4 Worksheet: Goals and Objectives

Goals—Establish a direction for your ministry. Write at least one goal for each core value. Include an additional goal related to prayer, with related objectives.

Objectives—Be specific and measurable. Write two or more objectives for each goal. These are action statements which state what you will do to achieve each goal.

Goal #1

_____

_____

Objectives for Goal #1

_____

_____

_____

Goal #2

_____

_____

Objectives for Goal #2

_____

_____

_____

_____

Goal #3

_____

_____

Objectives for Goal #3

_____

_____

Goal #4

_____

_____

Objectives for Goal #4

_____

_____

Prayer Goal

_____

_____

Objectives for Prayer Goal

_____

_____

Step 5 Worksheet: Programs and Curricula

Describe the programs and curricula:

- *Will you write your own curricula? If so, why? What unique features will you build into your curricula? What pedagogical principles will you follow? How will you package it?*
- *Will you use existing curricula? If so, why? What are you looking for in curricula in light of your biblical principles, mission, vision, and goals and objectives?*
- *What age-group provisions do you want each curriculum to reflect? How should the curriculum/program be structured to meet those provisions?*

_____

_____

_____

_____

_____

_____

_____

_____

_____

_____

_____

_____

Step 6 Worksheet: Teaching Methods and Materials

What teaching methods will you use to effectively implement your ministry? For instance, if your ministry is small groups, will your small groups utilize discussion, lecture, Q&A, videos, guest speakers, role-play, etc.? If your ministry is leadership training, will the training only involve content in a lecture or discussion format or will it also require a practicum or OJT (on-the-job training)? You need to list at least three methods.

Teaching methods used and explained:

_____

_____

_____

_____

_____

_____

_____

_____

_____

_____

_____

By way of materials, what facilities and equipment will be required for your ministry? What lesson supplies might be needed, i.e., pens, paper, Bibles, etc.? Snack supplies?

Facilities:

_____

_____

_____

_____

_____

Equipment:

_____

_____

_____

_____

Supplies:

_____

_____

_____

_____

Step 7 Worksheet: Organization and Administration

Design an organizational chart that describes the organizational flow of your ministry. List all positions that are represented on your organizational chart with a brief job description. Use computer software to represent your organizational chart in your final educational cycle proposal.

Step 8 Worksheet: Evaluation

Answer the following questions:

- *When will you first evaluate your ministry?*
- *How often will you evaluate your ministry?*
- *What evaluation tool(s) will you use to evaluate your ministry?*
- *Who will be involved in the evaluation process?*
- *Who will know the results of the evaluation?*
- *What kind of questions will you ask for evaluative purposes?*

_____

_____

_____

_____

_____

_____

_____

_____

_____

_____

_____

Step 9 Worksheet: Revision

What needs to be revised and updated as a result of your evaluation? List at least one hypothetical example.

_____

_____

_____

_____

_____

_____

_____

_____

_____

_____

_____

_____

_____

_____

Discussion Questions

1. What are some of the advantages of using a tool like the educational cycle?

2. What is the difference between a ministry's mission statement and its vision?

3. What kinds of information are you looking for when you do an environmental scan?

4. Why are organizational charts and job descriptions vital to ministries bathed in love?

5. Discuss why our ministry plans sometimes fail. How could using the educational cycle lessen the likelihood that your plans will fail? What is the overall value of such a tool?

Resources for Further Study

Anthony, Michael, ed. *Introducing Christian Education*. Grand Rapids: Baker, 2001.

Gangel, Kenneth. *Feeding and Leading*. Grand Rapids: Baker, 1989.

Gangel, Kenneth. *Team Leadership in Christian Ministry*. Chicago, IL: Moody, 1997.

Getz, Gene. *Sharpening the Focus of the Church*. Rev. ed. Wheaton, IL: Victor, 1984.

Kouzes, James and Barry Posner. *The Leadership Challenge*. 5th ed. San Francisco: Jossey-Bass, 2012.

LeBar, Lois. *Focus on People in Church Education*. Old Tappan, NJ: Revell, 1968.

Malphurs, Aubrey. *Advanced Strategic Planning*. 3rd ed. Grand Rapids: Baker, 2013.

Yount, William, ed. *The Teaching Ministry of the Church*. 2nd ed. Nashville: B&H Academic, 2008.

Author Bio

Dr. George M. Hillman Jr. is Vice President of Student Life, Dean of Students, and Professor of Educational Ministries and Leadership at Dallas Theological Seminary. Dr. Hillman has a passion for education, spiritual formation, and leadership development. He came to Dallas Theological Seminary with years of ministry experience in churches and parachurch organizations in Texas and Georgia. Nationally known in theological field education, he has been active in leadership of both the Association of Theological Field Education and the Evangelical Association of Theological Field Educators. He and his wife have one grown daughter.

CHAPTER 21 APPENDIX: PLANNING: ITS REASONS FOR FAILURE, SYMPTOMS, AND CURES[66]

Reasons for Failure	Symptoms	Cures
No Real Goals	• Do not reflect the church's purpose statement • Talk about program plans • Are vague—sound good; say little • Completely beyond the reach of the church • Not "owned" by membership	• Relate goal to purpose statement • Rewrite goals, so they describe end-states you want to reach or conditions you want to bring about • Involve more persons in goal writing
No Measurable Objectives	• Are not related to a goal • Are not measurable, specific, or time-phased • Do not contain action verbs	• Build each objective from a goal • Answer in objectives such questions as: Who? How many? Where? When? • Identify short-term and long-term objectives • Use action verbs in the statement
Failure to Anticipate Obstacles	• Excessive optimism • Closing your eyes to conflicts • Completion dates not met • "Oops, I forgot!" • Didn't get support when needed • Crises are common	• Take time to list possible obstacles • Be realistic in setting dates • Check program plan details • Talk to program plan manager • Revise program plan or details
Lack of Milestones and Progress Reviews	• Completion dates not set • "It can wait," "I can remember that" • "Let's play this by ear" • Don't really know how you are doing • Everything is short-term; no long-term aspects • Don't remember when the last review took place • No plans revised recently	• Set specific task milestones; stick to them • See that the program plan manager is on the job • Review your progress on the dates set • Ask the question: Are we making enough progress toward the objective?

Reasons for Failure	Symptoms	Cures
Lack of Commitment	• Putting things off • Just doing daily, routine activities • "I don't care what happens" • Have not set priorities • Planners skip meetings • No reports submitted • Pastor or lay members don't "own" the plan	• Involve others in the planning process • Share proposed plans early so new ideas can influence their development • Give the small groups of your church a chance to discuss proposed plans • Talk with each team member to find out the level of his/her commitment • Recruit replacements, as necessary • Celebrate successes you've had
Failure to Revise Objectives	• Plans never change • Being inflexible, refusing to face new facts that call for change • No sense of movement toward objectives • Help not sought when needed • Waste time on programs that don't work • Programs don't fit your priorities	• Deliberately seek feedback • Compare feedback with your standards for achieving the objective • Change emphasis and approach when it is appropriate • Encourage program plan managers to alert planning task force [team or committee] when revision is needed • Review progress more often
Failure to Learn from Experience	• Lose sight of goals • Repeat mistakes • Feedback is ignored • Evaluation standards are not used • Face the same crisis again and again • Unwillingness to change ways of doing things • Never asking, "What did we learn this time?"	• Use milestones to review progress • Have program units, task forces, etc., meet with the planning task force • Keep a record of changes made as a result of evaluation • Concentrate on results, not on giving reports for their own sake

Endnotes

1.   Kenneth Gangel was a prolific author and Christian educator who served as professor and later department chair of Christian Education as well as Academic Dean at Dallas Theological Seminary from 1982 to 1997. His influence at the seminary is still felt to this day, including through the use of his educational cycle process (first developed in his book *Leadership for Church Education* published in 1970). In addition to his years of service at Dallas Theological Seminary, Gangel also served at Calvary Bible College, Trinity Evangelical Divinity School, Miami Christian College, and Toccoa Falls College. In his work on the educational cycle, Gangel was always quick to give credit to Lois LeBar. LeBar was professor of Christian Education at Wheaton College for thirty years (1945–1975) and influenced an entire generation of Christian educators through her teaching and writing. LeBar's thoughts on the educational cycle were first spelled out in her book *Focus on People in Church Education* published in 1968. Gangel also gave credit to Gene Getz for his influence on the further development of the educational cycle, spelled out in Getz's book *Sharpening the Focus of the Church*, first published in 1975.

2.   Peter Benson and Carolyn Eklin, *Effective Christian Education: A National Study of Protestant Congregations—A Summary Report on Faith, Loyalty, and Congregational Life* (Minneapolis: Search Institute, 1990), 58.

3.   Karen Tye, *Basics of Christian Education* (St. Louis: Chalice, 2000), 16.

4.   Kenneth Gangel, *Leadership for Church Education* (Chicago: Moody, 1970), 38.

5.   Kenneth Gangel, *Feeding and Leading* (Grand Rapids, MI: Baker, 1989), 87.

6.   Kenneth Gangel, *Team Leadership in Christian Ministry* (Chicago: Moody, 1997), 111.

7.   Gangel, *Leadership for Church Education*, 34–36.

8.   Gene Getz, *Sharpening the Focus of the Church*, rev ed. (Wheaton, IL: Victor, 1984), 32–46.

9.   Aubrey Malphurs, *Advanced Strategic Planning*, 3rd. ed. (Grand Rapids, MI: Baker, 2013), 146, 150.

10. Ibid., 152, 159.

11. Ibid., 148.

12. Ibid., 162.

13. Ken Blanchard and Phil Hodges, *The Servant Leader* (Nashville: Thomas Nelson, 2003), 50.

14. This list is adapted from the Core Values Audit in Aubrey Malphurs' book *Advanced Strategic Planning*. Malphurs has an entire chapter in the book discovering core values for a ministry that I would highly recommend.

15. Aubrey Malphurs notes, "Purpose is different from mission because it is broader in scope…. [The] purpose of the church is doxological: to honor or glorify God (Rom. 15:6; I Cor. 6:20; 10:31). Thus it is abstract. The mission of the church is practical: to make disciples (Matt. 28:19). It is more concrete. When we make disciples (our mission), we glorify god (our purpose). The focus of purpose and mission is different. The purpose focuses on God. He is the object of our glory, not ourselves or another. The mission focuses on people. We are to disciple people." Malphurs, *Advanced Strategic Planning*, 110.

16. Ibid., 107.

17. Ibid., 106–110.

18. Lois LeBar, *Focus on People in Church Education* (Old Tappan, NJ: Revell, 1968), 38.

19. Ibid., 27.

20. Tye, *Basics of Christian Education*, 69.

21. Malphurs, *Advanced Strategic Planning*, 179–184.

22.   Ibid., 179–181.

23.   Ibid., 181–184.

24.   Ibid., 184.

25.   Ibid., 185.

26.   James Kouzes and Barry Posner, *The Leadership Challenge*, 3rd ed. (San Francisco: Jossey Bass, 2003), 125.

27.   Malphurs, *Advanced Strategic Planning*, 128.

28.   Ibid., 130.

29.   Burt Nanus, *Visionary Leadership* (San Francisco: Jossey-Bass, 1995), 3.

30.   George Barna, *A Fish Out of Water* (Brentwood, TN: Integrity, 2002), 71.

31.   Greg Barnhill, "Educational Plan According to the Ed Cycle: Eastwood Student Ministry" (CE101 Ed Cycle Project, Dallas Theological Seminary, December 2010), 4.

32.   Kenneth Gangel, *Ministering to Today's Adults* (Nashville: Word, 1999), 41.

33.   Education authors differ on the use of the terms "goals," "objectives," and "aims." Even Kenneth Gangel used the terms "objective" and "goal" interchangeably from one book to another (see Gangel, *Leadership for Church Education*, 46; Gangel, *Team Leadership in Christian Ministry*, 279). No matter the terms used, a person constructing an educational cycle will need both general statements and more specific action steps. For the purpose of this chapter, the more general statements will be "goals" and the specific action steps will be "objectives."

34.   Gangel, *Team Leadership in Christian Ministry*, 285.

35.   Gangel, *Feeding and Leading*, 101, 252.

36.   LeBar, *Focus on People in Church Education*, 34.

37.   Gangel, *Team Leadership in Christian Ministry*, 283.

38.   Gangel, *Leadership for Church Education*, 45; Gangel, *Team Leadership in Christian Ministry*, 292; LeBar, *Focus on People in Church Education*, 33.

39.   Tye, *Basics of Christian Education*, 50.

40.   See the various age-level chapters for specific recommendations.

41.   Adapted from material by Dr. Perry Downs, Professor Emeritus of Educational Ministries at Trinity Evangelical Divinity School.

42.   Gangel, *Ministering to Today's Adults*, 42.

43.   Tye, *Basics of Christian Education*, 101–103.

44.   Gangel, *Leadership for Church Education*, 21.

45.   Ibid., 30.

46.   LeBar, *Focus on People in Church Education*, 69.

47.   Gangel, *Team Leadership in Christian Ministry*, 110.

48.   LeBar, *Focus on People in Church Education*, 70–72, 75.

49.   Gangel, *Team Leadership in Christian Ministry*, 111.

50.   Gangel, *Leadership for Church Education*, 55.

51.   Gangel, *Feeding and Leading*, 294–295.

52. Robert Welch, "Job Descriptions That Work," *Your Church* (May/June 1995): 49.

53. LeBar, *Focus on People in Church Education*, 76.

54. Kouzes and Posner, *The Leadership Challenge*, 281, 284.

55. Gangel, *Feeding and Leading*, 144.

56. Gangel, *Team Leadership in Christian Ministry*, 281–282.

57. Gangel, *Ministering to Today's Adults*, 42.

58. Gangel, *Feeding and Leading*, 93.

59. LeBar, *Focus on People in Church Education*, 86–87.

60. Tye, *Basics of Christian Education*, 64–65.

61. Ibid., 113.

62. Gangel, *Feeding and Leading*, 102; Gangel, *Leadership for Church Education*, 77.

63. Tye, *Basics of Christian Education*, 107.

64. Gangel, *Feeding and Leading*, 88.

65. Adapted from Richard Rusbuldt, Richard Gladden, and Norman Green, *Local Church Planning Manual* (Valley Forge, PA: Judson Press, 1977), 231. See an expansion of this material at the end of this chapter.

66. Ibid.

SCRIPTURE INDEX

TOPIC INDEX